New Pseudonyms and Nicknames

OTHER GALE PUBLICATIONS

TRADE NAMES DICTIONARY—Third Edition. 2 volumes. Contains 160,000 alphabetically arranged entries for consumer products and their manufacturers. Product entries give: trade name, brief description, name of manufacturer, and a code identifying the source of the information. Company entries provide company names and addresses. **NEW TRADE NAMES,** 1982 and 1983 supplements. **TRADE NAMES DICTIONARY: COMPANY INDEX.** Rearranges entries from *TND* alphabetically by firm, with separate name and address list of over 33,000 companies.

ENCYCLOPEDIA OF ASSOCIATIONS—Seventeenth Edition. Volume 1, **NATIONAL ORGANIZATIONS OF THE U.S.,** contains over 16,500 entries in 17 categories. With index to organization names and keywords. Volume 2, **GEOGRAPHIC AND EXECUTIVE INDEX.** Volume 3, **NEW ASSOCIATIONS AND PROJECTS,** supplements to Volume 1. With cumulative alphabetical and keyword indexes.

DIRECTORY OF SPECIAL LIBRARIES AND INFORMATION CENTERS—Seventh Edition. Volume 1 contains information on over 16,000 special libraries, information centers, and documentation centers in the U.S. and Canada. Detailed subject index. Volume 2, **GEOGRAPHIC AND PERSONNEL INDEXES.** Volume 3, **NEW SPECIAL LIBRARIES,** a periodical supplement to Volume 1. Cumulatively indexed.

SUBJECT DIRECTORY OF SPECIAL LIBRARIES AND INFORMATION CENTERS—Seventh Edition. A subject arrangement of all entries in *Directory of Special Libraries.* Five volumes covering these major fields: Business and Law, Education and Information Science, Health Sciences, Social Sciences and Humanities, and Science and Technology.

RESEARCH CENTERS DIRECTORY—Seventh Edition. A guide to over 5,500 university-related and other nonprofit research organizations in the U.S. and Canada. With indexes of subjects, institutions, and research centers. **NEW RESEARCH CENTERS,** periodical supplements to RCD. Cumulatively indexed.

STATISTICS SOURCES—Seventh Edition. A subject guide to data on industrial, business, social, educational, financial, and other topics for the U.S. and selected foreign countries. Contains over 23,000 references on about 12,000 subjects.

MANAGEMENT INFORMATION GUIDE SERIES. Authoritative, comprehensive, carefully indexed guides to the literature of such major business and governmental areas as Accounting, Commercial Law, Computers, Insurance, Communications, Transportation, Public Relations, and Economic and Business History.

TRAINING AND DEVELOPMENT ORGANIZATIONS DIRECTORY—Third Edition. Provides detailed profiles of the activities and specialties of hundreds of companies, institutes, and special consulting groups that conduct managerial and supervisory training courses for business firms and governmental agencies. Indexes.

WEATHER ALMANAC—Third Edition. This reference guide to the weather, climate, and air quality of the U.S. and selected key cities provides maps, tables, and charts for those needing precise weather information. Includes a glossary of weather terms and a meteorological primer for amateur weatherpersons.

DIRECTORY OF DIRECTORIES—Second Edition. Contains detailed, up-to-date entries describing nearly 7,000 directories. Adding coverage of foreign directories for this edition, DOD covers business and industrial directories, professional and scientific rosters, and other lists and guides of all kinds. Detailed subject index and title index. **DIRECTORY INFORMATION SERVICE,** interedition supplements.

EPONYMS DICTIONARIES INDEX—First Edition. Cites sources of biographical information on 13,000 eponymous persons, real and imaginary, plus sources of definitions for the 20,000 terms based on their names.

New Pseudonyms and Nicknames

A Guide to New and Newly Noted Epithets, Nicknames, Pen Names, Pseudonyms, Sobriquets, and Stage Names of Contemporary and Historical Persons, Including the Subjects' Real Names, Basic Biographical Information, and Citations for the Sources from Which the Entries Were Compiled

An Interedition Supplement to

Pseudonyms and Nicknames Dictionary
Second Edition

Issue Number 1 ● January 1983

Jennifer Mossman
Editor

Gale Research Company ● Book Tower ● Detroit, Michigan 48226

Senior Editor: Ellen T. Crowley
Editor: Jennifer Mossman
Assistant Editor: Elwanda Houseworth
Production Supervisor: Carol Blanchard
Cover Design: Art Chartow

Computerized photocomposition by Computer Composition Corporation,
Madison Heights, Michigan

Gale's publications in the pseudonyms and nicknames field consist of the following:

Pseudonyms and Nicknames Dictionary

A Guide to Aliases, Appellations, Assumed Names, Code Names, Cognomens, Cover Names, Epithets, Initialisms, Nicknames, Noms de Guerre, Noms de Plume, Pen Names, Pseudonyms, Sobriquets, and Stage Names of Contemporary and Historical Persons, Including the Subjects' Real Names, Basic Biographical Information, and Citations for the Sources from Which the Entries Were Compiled

New Pseudonyms and Nicknames

(An Interedition Supplement to *Pseudonyms and Nicknames Dictionary*)

ISBN 0-8103-0548-8

Printed in the United States of America

Contents

A Word about *New Pseudonyms and Nicknames*

New Pseudonyms and Nicknames (NPN-1) is the first of two supplements to *Pseudonyms and Nicknames Dictionary,* second edition. The second issue of *NPN,* which will appear late in 1983, will cumulate entries in this issue and add thousands of new listings.

The rationale for compiling this supplement and the editorial policies followed in preparing it are essentially the same as those that applied to the second edition, the preface to which is reprinted following this note. A guide to editorial policies and use of the book may be found on page 11.

Expanded Coverage

NPN-1 contains 5,821 original names and 7,790 assumed names of contemporary and historical figures, gathered from over 60 sources. Authors, entertainers, and athletes continue to account for a sizable percentage of the 13,611 entries. Listings can also be found for occupations as diverse as fashion designers, cartoonists, aviators, advertising executives, police chiefs, bank presidents, guerrilla leaders, and FBI undercover agents.

Coverage of American gunfighters who lived during the second half of the nineteenth century has been greatly expanded with the publication of this supplement. Among those listed are: John Barclay Armstrong, who joined the Texas Rangers under the command of L. H. McNelly and was subsequently known as "McNelly's Bulldog," and Thomas J. Smith, called "Bear River Tom" because of his involvement in the Bear River Riot of 1868. Other colorful gunfighter nicknames to be found in this supplement were apparently derived from the individual's physical characteristics or appearance: Red Beard, Longhaired Jim, Three Fingered Jack, Buckskin Frank, and Broken Nose Jack.

The fields of mysticism and parapsychology yielded a large number of cult leaders who adopted religious names or titles as symbols of their newly found faith. This issue of *NPN* contains listings for: British occultist Allan Bennett, who studied Buddhism in Ceylon and returned as "Ananda Metteya"; American yoga authority Pierre Bernard, known to his followers as "Oom the Omnipotent"; and the Hindu monk Narendra Nath Dutt, who assumed the name "Swami Vivekananda."

Names in the News Well Represented

In addition to names from the past that have been newly discovered through research efforts, this supplement also includes listings for individuals who have recently received public attention. Various news magazines, newspapers, and other sources of current information are regularly checked for these new pseudonyms and nicknames. Some of the newsworthy individuals to be found in this issue include the British fleet commander in the Falkland Islands dispute, John "Sandy" Woodward; Salvadoran politician Roberto "Major Bob" d'Aubuisson; Grammy award-winning singer and recording artist Christopher Cross (whose legal name is Christopher Charles Geppert); England's Prince Charles ("The People's Prince") and infant son William ("The Prince of Wails"); mercenary soldier Michael "Mad Mike" Hoare; Guatemalan president Jose Rios Montt (known to his detractors as "Ayatollah" Rios Montt); and Brazilian soccer player Arthur Zico ("The White Pele").

Supplement To Be Used with Base Volume

It should be noted that *New Pseudonyms and Nicknames (NPN)* supplements *Pseudonyms and Nicknames Dictionary (PND).* For this reason, a complete listing of all assumed names attributed to one individual is not repeated in *NPN* if some of these names have already appeared in *PND.* In order to assist users of the supplement, the notation "See also base volume" is added to each entry for which additional pseudonyms or nicknames can be found in the main edition.

Bibliography Included

Entries contain source codes that identify those reference materials used in the compilation of this issue. A key to these symbols and complete bibliographic information can be found in the List of Sources Cited (page 15).

Comments and suggestions are welcome.

Preface to the Second Edition

A variety of circumstances may cause people to adopt or acquire new names. Whether the aim is to protect their privacy, promote a more glamorous image, or conceal a shameful past—inventing another name is often the ideal solution. Thus it is not uncommon to discover authors using pseudonyms or pen names, entertainers with stage names, and criminals taking aliases.

Unlike other types of assumed names, nicknames are usually bestowed by others, and may or may not be complimentary. The popularity enjoyed by a monarch can often be determined merely by examining the types of nicknames that he or she acquired. Alexander "the Great," Richard "the Lion-Hearted," and Ivan "the Terrible" are a few examples that come to mind.

It is the purpose of this publication to identify the original names behind these pseudonyms, stage names, aliases, nicknames, and other types of assumed names selected or acquired by prominent individuals. Basic biographical data, as well as the source(s) from which our information was obtained, are also included.

Expanded Coverage

The first edition of *Pseudonyms and Nicknames Dictionary* (1980) provided a collection of 17,000 original names and 22,000 assumed names, and was limited to those persons who lived into the twentieth century. Two interedition supplements nearly doubled the original collection and included names that had received recent attention through the news media.

With the publication of this second edition, coverage has been expanded to include historical as well as contemporary personalities—a total of 90,000 entries. Listings can now be found for Napoleon Bonaparte, George Washington, Dante, Thomas Aquinas, Plato, William Shakespeare, Johann Sebastian Bach, Julius Caesar, Charlemagne, Confucius, Leonardo da Vinci, Jesus Christ, Michelangelo, Mohammed, and Sir Isaac Newton, as well as Ronald Reagan, Pope John Paul II, "Babe" Ruth, Ernest Hemingway, Elvis Presley, Marilyn Monroe, and Al Capone. Of the nearly 40,000 original names and over 50,000 assumed names to be found in this edition, authors, entertainers, and athletes continue to account for a large percentage of the total collection. The remaining entries cover personalities in a wide variety of fields—politicians, criminals, military leaders, monarchs, popes, clergymen, aristocrats, and business executives, among others.

What's in a Name?

The variety of names collected for *Pseudonyms and Nicknames Dictionary* revealed that the methods of selecting new names are as varied as the reasons for their creation. Some rather unwieldy surnames were simply shortened so that they could be more easily pronounced and remembered (William Claude Dukinfield gained recognition as the talented comic actor W. C. Fields). Anagrams provided convenient disguises for others who wished to conceal their identities (Roger Caras wrote as Roger Sarac). In some instances, a surname was simply dropped, and the middle name used in its place (author Harry Arthur Bates was known as Harry Arthur). Names occasionally lent themselves to obvious punning and word associations. Surely Noel Young could not resist adopting Leon Elder as his pseudonym. Similarly, Robert L. Fish chose to write under the name A. C. Lamprey.

Nicknames, on the other hand, are not necessarily chosen. They may have been acquired because of some unique physical attribute (Big Jim), character trait (Honest Jack), or nationality (The Golden Greek). Professional athletes were frequently given nicknames that reflected their particular skills (Home Run Baker). Surnames have provided the basis for some rather amusing nicknames (Sugar Cain, Soupy Campbell, Boom Boom Cannon, Pickles Dillhoefer, and others). Whether complimentary or insulting, whimsical or pompous, the nicknames collected for this dictionary are usually quite colorful.

Exclusions

Certain types of pseudonyms and nicknames were considered to be very closely related in form to the original names and, therefore, did not warrant inclusion as separate entries. These include common derivatives of given names (Bob for Robert), initials that replace a first or middle name (J. Paul Getty for Jean Paul Getty), and middle names used as pseudonyms (Taylor Caldwell for Janet Taylor Caldwell). Married/maiden name differences are not emphasized unless a woman chose to use her maiden name in some professional capacity.

Acknowledgments

In addition to the reference sources and outside contributors cited in the entries and found in the List of Sources Cited, the editors received many helpful suggestions from a number of individuals and associations. Roger W. Hill, of the North American Radio Archives, Paul Everett, and Andrew C. McKay expanded our coverage of radio and film personalities. John G. Printz, the U.S. Auto Club National Championship Racing Historian, contributed a number of names in the auto racing field. Valuable additions to the sports collection were also provided by the National Basketball Hall of Fame, the National Football League, the Professional Pool Players Association, and the National Jockeys Hall of Fame at Pimlico. David Glagovsky supplied helpful information in a variety of subject areas.

Comments and suggestions for future editions are welcome.

Editorial Policies and Arrangement of Names

Pseudonyms and Nicknames Dictionary (PND) and its supplements, *New Pseudonyms and Nicknames (NPN)*, index original and assumed names in one alphabetic sequence. Both contemporary and historical figures throughout the world are included.

Entries are coded to indicate the sources from which information was gathered. The List of Sources Cited decodes these symbols, and provides complete bibliographic data, where applicable, for users who wish to find additional information about a particular individual. Entries were frequently based on a compilation of information from several sources and do not necessarily represent an exact duplication of material found in any one source. Those entries without source-identification codes were collected through independent research by the editors.

Form of Entries

Within *PND*'s single alphabet, there are two types of entry:

1. The main entry, which consists of six elements:

> Original name
> Dates of birth and (where applicable) death
> Up to three source-identification codes
> Nationality
> Occupation
> Assumed name (or names) by which the individual has become known, highlighted by an asterisk

> **Blair, Eric Arthur** 1903-1950
> [EWL, SF, TCL]
> *British author*
> *Orwell, George

Supplements *(New Pseudonyms and Nicknames)* contain the notation "See also base volume" at the end of each entry for which additional pseudonyms or nicknames can be found in the main edition.

2. The cross reference, which refers the user from the assumed name (pen name, nickname, stage name, etc.) to the original name:

> **Orwell, George**
> *See* Blair, Eric Arthur

Source Conflicts

A variety of sources may have been used to compile an entry, and the editors sometimes found conflicting information. If additional research failed to resolve these discrepancies, various methods were employed to indicate that some uncertainty still exists:

When correct birth dates could not be determined, the earliest date was arbitrarily selected, and a question mark was added to show that some doubt remains. It was particularly necessary to use this procedure with some stage and screen personalities, whose age is traditionally a closely guarded secret.

If differences were found in the form or spelling of a name, both possibilities were incorporated into an entry: Badawi, Mohamed [or Muhammad] Mustafa.

Sources occasionally gave conflicting information in their description of nationalities. For example, one source might determine the nationality based upon place of birth, while a second source might consider length of residence to be of greater importance, and the actual legal status might be difficult to determine in any case. In these instances, *PND* would use a designation such as "British-born" to indicate that, while the place of birth may be known, the actual citizenship is unclear.

Alphabetical Arrangement

All words and letters are considered in alphabetizing except those that are enclosed in brackets. Spacing generally affects alphabetical position, except in the case of surnames compounded of two or more names. These are arranged after the single surname. Particles (De, La, Von, etc.) are considered to be the first element of a surname and will, unless common usage dictates otherwise, be alphabetized as such:

> De Angelis, Alberto
> De Mille, Agnes
> Dean, Mary
> Dean, Robert George
> Dean-Andrews, Simon Paul
> Dean Norwood, Victor
> Deane, Joseph
> Deane, P. Virginia

Articles that begin a nickname, whether in English or other languages, are not considered for alphabetizing purposes. El Gato, for example, will be found in the G's.

Some common abbreviations (Mr., Dr., St., Ste.) are alphabetized as if they were spelled out (Mister, Doctor, Saint, Sainte).

Name Reversals

Most names found in *PND* are alphabetized by surname, followed by the given name(s). There are some entries, however, that do not have the form of first and last names and must, therefore, be handled differently:

> Given names followed by a single initial can be found under the given name:
> *M*alcolm X, *J*ackie O.

> Initials that replace the entire name are alphabetized under the first of the initials:
> *J*.F.K., *L*.B.J.

> When titles are combined with a given name, the entry will be found under the title:
> *U*ncle Miltie, *M*iss Lillian.

Treatment of Nicknames

Some nicknames are quite clearly meant to replace a given name, and thus fit the usual method of handling assumed names: Lefty Aber and Dusty Baker can be found under the surnames (in the A's and B's respectively).

Others cannot logically be made to fit this pattern since they are not commonly used in conjunction with a surname. These nicknames will stand alone: Calamity Jane, [The] Sultan of Swat.

It is not always immediately obvious whether a given nickname is generally used in combination with a surname or whether it should stand alone. In order to ensure that the user is able to locate the nickname, even though the surname may not be known, a double cross reference (by surname and by nickname) is given:

Mehlhorn, Wild Bill
See Mehlhorn, William

Wild Bill Mehlhorn
See Mehlhorn, William

In some cases, the editors had difficulty in deciding when a nickname should be combined with a surname and when it can correctly stand alone. In approaching this and other editorial problems, attempts were made to be as logical as circumstances permitted. Unfortunately, complete consistency was impossible, and the user who is unable to locate a particular name is encouraged to check other possible forms.

List of Sources Cited

AS   Hickok, Ralph. *Who Was Who in American Sports.* New York: Hawthorn Books, Inc., 1971.

BBD   Slonimsky, Nicolas. *Baker's Biographical Dictionary of Musicians.* 5th ed. New York: G. Schirmer, 1971.

BBH   Soderberg, Paul, and Washington, Helen. *The Big Book of Halls of Fame in the United States and Canada.* New York: R. R. Bowker Co., 1977.

BDSA   Knight, Lucian Lamar. *Biographical Dictionary of Southern Authors.* Reprint of the 1929 ed. Detroit: Gale Research Co., 1978.

BL   Wallechinsky, David; Wallace, Irving; and Wallace, Amy. *The People's Almanac Presents the Book of Lists.* New York: William Morrow and Co. Inc., 1977.

BLB   Nash, Jay Robert. *Bloodletters and Badmen.* New York: M. Evans and Co., 1973.

BP   Andersen, Christopher P. *The Book of People.* New York: Perigee Books, 1981.

CA   *Contemporary Authors.* Vols. 103-105. New Revision Series, Vols. 5-6. Detroit: Gale Research Co., 1982.

CD   Smith, Horatio. *Columbia Dictionary of Modern European Literature,* New York: Columbia University Press, 1971 and 1980 eds.

CEC   Scott, Sir Harold. *The Concise Encyclopedia of Crime and Criminals.* New York: Hawthorn Books Inc., 1961.

CLC   *Contemporary Literary Criticism.* Vols. 15-22. Detroit: Gale Research Co., 1981-82.

CMA   Zalkind, Ronald. *Contemporary Music Almanac, 1980/81.* New York: Schirmer Books, 1980.

CR   Blackwell, Earl. *Celebrity Register.* New York: Simon and Schuster, 1973.

DAM   Claghorn, Charles Eugene. *Biographical Dictionary of American Music.* West Nyack, N.Y.: Parker Publishing Co. Inc., 1973.

DBQ   Kenin, Richard, and Wintle, Justin. *The Dictionary of Biographical Quotation.* New York: Alfred A. Knopf, 1978.

DEA   Sharp, R. Farquharson. *A Dictionary of English Authors.* Reprint of the 1904 ed. Detroit: Gale Research Co., 1978.

DI   Green, Jonathon. *The Directory of Infamy.* Toronto: Mills & Boon, 1980.

DIL   Hogan, Robert. *Dictionary of Irish Literature.* Westport, Conn.: Greenwood Press, 1979.

DLE1   Myers, Robin. *A Dictionary of Literature in the English Language from Chaucer to 1940.* New York: Pergamon Press, 1970.

DNA   Wallace, W. Stewart. *A Dictionary of North American Authors Deceased before 1950.* Reprint of the 1951 ed. Detroit: Gale Research Co., 1968.

EC   Golesworthy, Maurice. *Encyclopaedia of Cricket.* 1st and 6th eds. London: Robert Hale, 1962 and 1977.

EE   Seth, Ronald. *Encyclopedia of Espionage.* London: New English Library, 1972.

EF   Treat, Roger. *The Encyclopedia of Football.* 13th ed. New York: A. S. Barnes and Co., 1975.

EMD Steinbrunner, Chris, and Penzler, Otto, eds. *Encyclopedia of Mystery and Detection.* New York: McGraw-Hill Book Co., 1976.

EOP Shepard, Leslie. *Encyclopedia of Occultism & Parapsychology.* 2 vols. and supplement. Detroit: Gale Research Co., 1978-82.

ESF Nicholls, Peter. *The Encyclopedia of Science Fiction.* New York: Granada Publishing Ltd., 1979.

EWG O'Neal, Bill. *Encyclopedia of Western Gunfighters.* Norman, Okla.: University of Oklahoma Press, 1979.

FAA Young, William C. *Famous Actors and Actresses on the American Stage.* New York: R. R. Bowker Co., 1975.

FIR *Films in Review.* New York. National Board of Review of Motion Pictures, Inc., Nov., 1981 - Jun./Jul., 1982.

FR Marcin, Joe, and Byers, Dick. *Football Register.* St. Louis: The Sporting News Publishing Co., 1977.

GF Elliott, Len, and Kelly, Barbara. *Who's Who in Golf.* New Rochelle, N.Y.: Arlington House, 1976.

GS Smith, George B. Taurine Bibliophiles of America. Private communication.

HFF Ashley, Mike. *Who's Who in Horror and Fantasy Fiction.* New York: Taplinger Publishing Co., 1977.

HFN Hamst, Olphar, Esq. *Handbook of Fictitious Names.* Reprint of the 1868 ed. Detroit: Gale Research Co., 1969.

ICB *Illustrators of Children's Books, 1946-56, 1957-66, 1967-76.* Boston: The Horn Book Inc., 1958, 1968, and 1978.

IP Cushing, William. *Initials and Pseudonyms: A Dictionary of Literary Disguises.* Reprint of the 1885 ed. Detroit: Gale Research Co., 1982.

JL Greenberg, Martin H. *The Jewish Lists.* New York: Schocken Books, 1979.

LC Ward, A. C. *Longman Companion to Twentieth Century Literature.* London: Longman Group Ltd., 1970.

LFW Nash, Jay Robert. *Look for the Woman.* New York: M. Evans and Co., 1981.

MA *Michigan Authors.* 2nd ed. Ann Arbor, Mich.: Michigan Association for Media in Education, 1980.

MBF Lofts, W. O. G., and Adley, D. J. *The Men Behind Boys' Fiction.* London: Howard Baker, 1970.

NAD Jack, Alex, ed. *The New Age Dictionary.* Brookline, Mass.: Kanthaka Press, 1976.

NLC *Nineteenth-Century Literature Criticism.* Vols. 1-2. Detroit: Gale Research Co., 1981-82.

NN Noble, Vernon. *Nicknames Past and Present.* London: Hamish Hamilton Ltd., 1976.

NPS Dawson, Lawrence H. *Nicknames and Pseudonyms.* Reprint of the 1908 ed. Detroit: Gale Research Co., 1974.

PAC Ewen, David. *Popular American Composers.* New York: The H. W. Wilson Co., 1962.

PI O'Donoghue, D. J. *The Poets of Ireland.* Reprint of the 1912 ed. Detroit: Gale Research Co., 1968.

PPN Payton, Geoffrey. *Payton's Proper Names.* New York: Frederick Warne, 1969.

RBE Loubet, Nat, and Ort, John. *The Ring Boxing Encyclopedia and Record Book.* 1977 ed. New York: The Ring Book Shop, 1976.

SAT Commire, Anne. *Something about the Author.* Vols. 16-27. Detroit: Gale Research Co., 1979-82.

SFL   Reginald, R. *Science Fiction and Fantasy Literature.* 2 Vols. Detroit: Gale Research Co., 1979.

SG   Gallelo, Al "Scoop." International Veteran Boxers Association. Private communication.

SR   Frommer, Harvey. *Sports Roots.* New York: Atheneum, 1979.

TCCM   Reilly, John M. *Twentieth-Century Crime and Mystery Writers.* New York: St. Martin's Press. 1980.

TLC   *Twentieth-Century Literary Criticism.* Vols. 4-7. Detroit: Gale Research Co., 1981-82.

UH   Gerwig, Henrietta. *University Handbook for Readers and Writers.* New York: Thomas Y. Crowell Co., 1965.

WEC   Horn, Maurice. *The World Encyclopedia of Cartoons.* 2 Vols. New York: Chelsea House Publishers, 1980.

WECO   Horn, Maurice. *The World Encyclopedia of Comics.* 2 Vols. New York: Chelsea House Publishers, 1976.

WFA   Lambert, Eleanor. *World of Fashion.* New York: R. R. Bowker Co., 1976.

WGT   Rock, James A. *Who Goes There.* Bloomington, Ind.: James A. Rock and Co., 1979.

WW   Gribbin, Lenore S. *Who's Whodunit.* University of North Carolina Library Studies, No. 5. Reprint of the 1969 ed. Ann Arbor, Mich.: University Microfilms International, 1978.

YAB   Commire, Anne, ed. *Yesterday's Authors of Books for Children,* Vol. 2. Detroit: Gale Research Co., 1978.

Additional entries were compiled from a variety of newspaper and periodical articles.

A

A.
See Adams, Samuel

A.
See Adams, William Henry Davenport

A.
See Allen, Wilkes

A [Alpha]
See Bowden, John William

A.
See Coxe, Arthur Cleveland

A.
See Southey, Caroline Anne [Bowles]

A.
See Taylor, Ann

A.
See Wilde, Jane Francesca Elgee

A. A.
See Anderson, Adam

A. A.
See Atkins, Anna

A. A. A.
See Adee, Alvey A.

A. Ag.
See Agassiz, Alexander

A. B.
See Adams, Samuel

A. B.
See Beardsley, Aubrey Vincent

A. B.
See Brereton, Austin

A. B. C. D. E.
See Hopkinson, Francis

A. B. M.
See Matthews, Arthur Bache

A. C.
See Carmichael, Andrew Blair

A. C.
See Commins, Andrew

A. C. B.
See Barstow, Amos C.

A. C. C.
See Coxe, Arthur Cleveland

A. C. I. G. [A Cornishman in Gloucestershire]
See White, John

A. D.
See Dawson, A.

A. E. H.
See Hamilton, Anna Elizabeth

A. E. P.
See Polglase, Ann Eaton

A. F. G.
See Gaston, Mrs. A. F.

A. G.
See Gardner, Alexander

A. G.
See Gatty, Alfred

A. G. R.
See Radcliffe, Alida G.

A. H.
See Hamilton, Ann

A. H. A.
See Atteridge, Andrew Hilliard

A. H. G.
See Grant, Alexander Henley

A. H. H.
See Hallam, Arthur Henry

A. H. P.
See Plunkett, Arthur Hume

A. H. R.
See Taylor, Una Ashworth

A. J.
See Jones, Absalom

A. J. K.
See Kemp, A. J.

A. J. M.
See McKenna, Andrew James

A. J. McK.
See McKenna, Andrew James

A. K.
See Kippis, Andrew

A. K.
See Kneeland, Abner

A. L.
See Lee, Abby

A. L. B.
See Barbauld, Anna Letitia

A. L. P. [A London Priest]
See Littledale, Richard

A. M.
See Marvell, Andrew

A. M.
See Miles, Alfred

A. M.
See Munday, Anthony

A. M. B.
See Browne, Montagu

A. M. D.
See Denison, Mary Andrews

A. M., Oxon
See Moses, W. S.

A. M. R.
See Richards, Anna M[atlock], Jr.

A. M. W.?
See Winter, Anna Maria

A. O'L.
See O'Leary, Arthur

A. P.
See Pember, Arthur

A. P.
See Penfield, A.

A. P., M.D.
See Pennecuik, Alexander

A. R.
See Ryan, Arthur

A. S.
See Russell, Thomas

A. S.
See Shackleton, Abraham

A. S. A.
See Atcheson, Alfred S.

A. St. G. S.
See Stopford, A. St. G.

A. T. de V.
See De Vere, Aubrey Thomas

A[rtist] U[nknown]
See Pennell, Joseph

A. W.?
See Winter, Anna Maria

A. W., Mrs.
See Weamys, Anna

Aallyn, Alysse
See Clark, Melissa

Aandy, K. ?-1980   [FIR]
Indian actor
* Jaidev

Aaron, Barney 19th c.   [RBE]
Boxer
* [The] Star of the East

Abarbanell, Jacob Ralph 1852-1922
American author and playwright
* Harrigan and Hart
(See also base volume)

Abauzit, Firmin
See Arouet, Francois Marie

Abbattutis, Giam Alesio
See Basile, Giambattista

Abbey, Margaret
See York, Margaret Elizabeth

Abbot, E. S.   [IP]
British poet
* [An] Amateur

Abbot, Ezra 1819-1884   [IP]
American scholar
* E. A.

Abbot, L. A.   [IP]
British author
* [A] Matrimonial Monomaniac

Abbott, Austin 19th c.   [NPS]
American author
* Benauly [joint pseudonym with Benjamin Abbott and Lyman Abbott]

Abbott, Benjamin 19th c.   [NPS]
American author
* Benauly [joint pseudonym with Austin Abbott and Lyman Abbott]

Abbott, Bud
See Abbott, Burton W.

Abbott, Burton W. ?-1957   [DI]
American murderer
* Abbott, Bud

Abbott, Eleanor Hallowell
See Coburn, Mrs. Fordyce

Abbott, George
See Almy, Frank C.

Abbott, Jacob 1803-1879   [IP]
American author
* J. A.
* One of her Sons
* One of Them
(See also base volume)

Abbott, Joseph 1789-1863   [IP]
Canadian missionary and author
* [An] Emigrant Farmer
* Musgrave, Philip

Abbott, Lyman 1835-1922
[IP, NPS]
American author and clergyman
* Benauly [joint pseudonym with
 Austin Abbott and Benjamin
 Abbott]
* [A] Layman
(See also base volume)

Abbott, Thomas Kingsmill [IP]
British clergyman and author
* Philalethes

Abdallah
See Soromenho, Augusto Pereira

Abdy, Maria Smith 1818-1867 [IP]
British poet
* M. A.

Abeken, Bernhard Rudolf
1780-1866 [IP]
German author
* Andolt, Ernst

Abelard
See Meany, Stephen Joseph

Abeles, Elvin 1907- [CA]
American author and editor
* Bowles, Kerwin

Abell, Bud
See Abell, Harry

Abell, Harry 20th c. [EF]
American football player
* Abell, Bud

Abell, William 17th c. [NPS]
British politician
* Cain's Brother
(See also base volume)

Abercrombie, John 1726-1806 [IP]
Scottish author
* Mawe, Thomas
(See also base volume)

**Abercromby, James [First Baron
Dunfermline]** 1776-1858 [IP]
British author
* [The] Pensioner
(See also base volume)

Aberdeen, E.
See Anderson, James

Abhavananda
See Crowley, Edward Alexander

Abhonmor
See Holland, Denis

Abington, Mrs. 1737-1815 [NPS]
Actress
* Nosegay Nan

Ablett, William [IP]
British author
* Telba

Abos, Geronimo 1715-1760 [BBD]
Maltese composer
* Abos, Girolamo

Abos, Girolamo
See Abos, Geronimo

Abou Ryhan
See Ben-Ahmed, Mohammed

Abraham ben Meir ibn Ezra
1092-1167 [NPS, UH]
*Spanish rabbi, mathematician,
philologist*
* [The] Admirable

Abraham, John 1798- ? [IP]
British poet
* Maharba

Abraham, William 1842- ? [NPS]
Welsh politician
* Mabon

Abrahams, B. [IP]
American physician and author
* [A] Surgeon

Abrams, Abe
See Abrams, Creighton

Abrams, Creighton 1914- [CR]
American army officer
* Abrams, Abe

Abrams, Isaac [IP]
Author
* [The] Wild Methodist

[An] Absent Brother
See Wilson, Daniel

Absinthe, Pere
See Kelly, George C.

Academicas Mentor
See Montagu, Ashley

Achad, Frater
See Jones, Charles Stanfeld

Achenbach, Max 1856-1898 [BBD]
German opera singer
* Alvary, Max

Achui, Sneeze
See Achui, Walter

Achui, Walter 20th c. [EF]
American football player
* Achui, Sneeze

Acland, Henry Wentworth 1815- ?
[IP]
British physician and author
* H. W. A.

Acland, Peter Leopold Dyke 19th
c. [IP]
British author and clergyman
* [A] Clergyman

Acton, Harriet [IP]
British poet
* H. A.

Acton, Martin William 1850- ?
[DNA]
American author
* Nitram, Notca W.

Acton, Mrs. J. A. [NPS]
Author
* Hering, Jeanie

[An] Actor
See Egan, Pierce

[An] Actress
See Ritchie, Anna Cora [Ogden
Mowatt]

Adair, James Makittrick
1728-1802 [IP]
Scottish physician and author
* Goosequil, Benjamin
* Paragraph, Peter

Adam
See Adenet le Roi

Adam de la Halle 1235?-1285
[BBD, NPS]
French musician and playwright
* [Le] Bossu d'Arras [The
 Hunchback of Arras]
(See also base volume)

Adam, William 1751-1839 [IP]
Scottish jurist and author
* Lord Chief Commissioner

Adami, Friedrich 1816- ? [IP]
German author
* Frohberg, Paul

Adamov, Arthur 1908-1970 [CD]
French playwright
* Ern

Adams, Andrew Leith [IP]
Scottish author
* [A] Naturalist

Adams, Angela
See Smith, Catherine R. [Kay]

Adams, Ann [IP]
British author
* [A] Protestant Lady

Adams, Ann Olivia [IP]
American poet
* Astarte

Adams, Arthur [IP]
British author and surgeon
* [A] Naturalist

Adams, Arthur Henry 1872-1936
[DLE1]
*New Zealand-born author,
playwright, poet*
* James, Henry James
(See also base volume)

Adams, Betsy 1942- [MA]
American author, educator, poet
* Jymes, Elisabeth

Adams, Bruin
See Ellis, Edward S[ylvester]

Adams, Charles Francis 1807- ?
[IP]
American statesman
* [A] Whig of the Old School

Adams, Charlotte [IP]
American author
* C. A.

Adams, Cleve F[ranklin]
1895-1949? [TCCM]
American author
* Charles, Franklin [joint
 pseudonym with Robert Leslie
 Bellem]
(See also base volume)

Adams, E. G. 19th c. [IP]
American author
* E. G. A.

Adams, Francis
See Cabet, Etienne

Adams, Francis 1797-1861 [IP]
Scottish physician and scholar
* [A] Scotch Physician

Adams, Francis Colburn 19th c.
[IP]
American author
* Justia, a Know-nothing
* Potter, [Major] Roger Sherman
* [A] Trooper
* Van Truesdale, Pheleg

Adams, Francis William Lauderdale
1862-1893 [DLE1]
Australian author and poet
* Farrell, Agnes

Adams, Frederick W. [IP]
American author
* Shaker

Adams, Henry [Brooks] 1838-1918
[CA, DLE1, TLC]
*American author, philosopher,
historian*
* Amo, Tauraatua i
* Compton, Frances Snow

Adams, Henry Gardiner [IP]
British naturalist
* Nemo

Adams, James 18th c. [IP]
Scottish clergyman
* [A] Lover of Peace and Truth in
 this Church

Adams, James Alonzo 1842-1925
[DNA]
American author and clergyman
* Grapho

Adams, James Fenimore Cooper
See Ellis, Edward S[ylvester]

Adams, John 1735-1826 [IP, NPS]
American president
* [An] American
* [An] American Citizen
* [The] Colossus of the Revolution
* [A] Gentleman
(See also base volume)

Adams, John 19th c. [IP]
Author
* Philo-Ruggles

Adams, John Isaac Ira 1826-1857
[IP]
American educator and journalist
* Izak
* Lightfoot

**Adams, John Michael Geoffrey
Manningham** 20th c.
Barbadian prime minister
* Adams, Tom

Adams, John Quincy 1767-1848
[DBQ, IP]
American president
* [The] Massachusettes Madman
* Sidney, Algernon
(See also base volume)

Adams, Maude
See Kiskadden, Maude

Adams, Mildred
See Kenyon, Mildred Adams

Adams, Nehemiah 1806-1878 [IP]
American clergyman
* Her Father

Adams, Richard Newton 19th c.
[IP]
British clergyman
* Pergamos

Adams, Samuel 1722-1803 [IP]
*American statesman and
revolutionary leader*
* A.
* A. B.
* [An] American
* [A] Bostonian
* Candidus
* [A] Chatterer

Adams, Samuel (Continued)
* [The] Chief Incendiary of the House
* Determinatus
* E. A.
* [An] Elector in 1771
* Father of the American Revolution
* [The] First Politician in the World
* [An] Impartialist
* Instaromnium
* [A] Layman
* Observation
* One of Plutarch's Men
* [The] Palinurus of the Revolution
* Political Parent
* Poplicola, Valerius
* Populus
* Principiis Obsta
* [The] Psalmsinger
* [A] Religious Politician
* Sam the Maltser
* Shippen
* Sincerus
* [A] Son of Liberty
* T. Z.
* Togae, Cedant Arma
* [A] Tory
* Vindex
* [The] Would-be-Cromwell of America
* Z.
(See also base volume)

Adams, Tom
See Adams, John Michael Geoffrey Manningham

Adams, Walter Marsham 1838- ?
[SFL]
Author
* Macaulay, Clarendon

Adams, William Augustus 1865- ?
[PI]
Irish poet
* Smada, Augusto

Adams, William Bridges [IP]
British engineer
* Junius Redivivus

Adams, William Henry Davenport 1828- ? [IP]
British author and journalist
* A.
* Clinton, Walter
* W. H. D. A.

Adams, William Taylor 1822-1897
[DNA]
American author
* Brown, Irving
* Hunter, Clingham
* McCormick, Brooks
* Old Stager
* Winterton, Gayle
(See also base volume)

Adamson, John 1787-1855 [IP]
British antiquary
* J. A.

Adamson, Joy
See Gessner, Friedrike Victoria

Adamson, William Agar 1800- ?
[IP]
Canadian clergyman
* [A] Resident

Adan le Menestrel
See Adenet le Roi

Adastra
See Mirepoix, Camille

Addington, Henry [First Viscount Sidmouth] 1757-1844 [IP]
British statesman
* Lord S.
* [A] Member of Neither Syndicate
(See also base volume)

Addison, Berkeley 19th c. [IP]
British clergyman
* [A] Presbyter

Addison, Henry Robert [IP]
British author and playwright
* [A] Half Pay Officer
* [An] Irish Police Magistrate

Addison, Joseph 1672-1719
[DLE1, IP]
British author, poet, statesman
* Bickerstaff, Isaac, Esq.
* Myrtle, Marmaduke
* [The] Old Whig
* Puzzle, Peter
* [The] Spectator
(See also base volume)

[The] Addison of the United States
See Dennie, Joseph

Adee, Alvey A. [IP]
American scholar
* A. A. A.

Adefumni, King Oba Oseijeman
See King, Walter

Adelaide
See O'Keefe, Adelaide

Adenauer, Konrad 1876-1967
[PPN]
German chancellor
* [Der] Alte [The Old Man]

Adenes
See Adenet le Roi

Adenet le Roi 13th c.
French poet and troubadour
* Adam
* Adan le Menestrel
* Adenes

[An] Adept
See Johnstone, Charles

Adidnac
See Whitaker, Lily

Adina
See Ingraham, Joseph Holt

[The] Adjutant
See Maginn, William

Adler, Pearl 1900-1962 [LFW]
Russian-born American madam
* Adler, Polly

Adler, Polly
See Adler, Pearl

[The] Admirable
See Abraham ben Meir ibn Ezra

[The] Admirable Crichton of Arabia
See Avicenna [or Abou-ibn-Sina]

[The] Admirable Crichton of Germany
See Frederick II

[The] Admirable Crichton of His Day
See Jones, [Sir] William

[The] Admiral
See Howe, Michael

[The] Admiral of the Lake
See Wilson, John

[An] Admirer of the Fine Arts
See Astley, Francis Dukinfield

Adney, Timothy 18th c. [IP]
British poet
* Yenda, Mit

Adonais
See Keats, John

[The] Adonais of the French Revolution
See Chenier, Andre Marie de

Adonis
See O'Dowd, John

Adragool
See Davis, Thomas Osborne

Adriaensen, Emanuel 16th c. [BBD]
Flemish musician
* Hadrianus

Adrian
See Cole, James L.

Adrienne
See Hooper, Susan C.

Adsum
See Donnelly, William M.

[An] Advocate of the Cause of the People
See Hope, John

Ady, John 1744-1812 [IP]
British author
* J. A.

Ady, Mrs. Henry
Author
* Cartwright, Julia

Aedh
See Farrell, Hugh

Aednr-Nos-Seer I'Noh
See Anderson, John

Aelfric ?-1051 [NPS]
Archbishop of York
* Puttock
(See also base volume)

Aeneas 4th c. BC [NPS]
Greek author
* [The] Tactician

Aenid
See O'Reilly, Patrick Thomas

Aeolus
See Canning, George

Aeolus
See Pitt, William [Earl of Chatham]

[The] Aeschylus of France
See Jolyot de Crebillon, Claude Prosper

[Th] Aeschylus of Spain
See Cervantes Saavedra, Miguel de

Aesculapius
See Butler, Dr.

Aesculapius
See Radcliffe, John

Aesop, Abraham
See Newbery, John

[The] Aesop of Arabia
See Lokman

[The] Aesop of Arabia
See Nasser ben Hareth

[The] Aesop of India
See Bidpai [or Pilpay]

Affable Hawk
See Squire, John Collings

Afflis, Dick
See Afflis, William

Afflis, William 20th c. [EF]
American football player
* Afflis, Dick

Afranio de Pavia
See Albonese, Afranio

[The] African
See Alfonso V [or Affonso]

[El] Africano [The African]
See Bellon, Manuel

Afterem, George
See Williams, Harold

Ag-Kaa-Noo-Ma-Gaa-Qua [Friendly Teaching Lady]
See Elliott, Margaret Drake

Agassiz, Alexander [IP]
American naturalist
* A. Ag.

Agassiz, Elizabeth Cary 1822-1907
[IP]
American author and educator
* E. C. A.
(See also base volume)

Agatho ?- 681 [NPS]
Pope
* Thaumaturgus

Agathon [joint pseudonym with Henri Massis]
See De Tarde, Alfred

Agathon [joint pseudonym with Alfred de Tarde]
See Massis, Henri

[An] Aged Minister
See Dickinson, Moses

Agee, Mrs. H. P.
Author
* Lea, Fannie Heaslip

Agent of the American Colonization Society
See Christy, David

Agg, John ?-1813 [IP]
British author and poet
* J. A.

[An] Aghadowey Man
See Orr, Andrew

Agile Penne
See Aiken, Albert W.

Aglaus
See Timrod, Henry

Agnew, David Carnegie A. [IP]
Scottish author
* [A] Free Church Minister

Agnus, Orme
See Higginbotham, John C.

Aguila, Pancho
See Zelaya, Roberto Ignacio

Aguilar, Grace 1816-1847 [IP]
British author
* G. A.

Agujari, Lucrezia 1743-1783
[BBD]
Italian opera singer
* Bastardella
(See also base volume)

Ah-Chin-Le
See Swasey, John B.

**Ahlefeld, Charlotte Sophie Luise
Wilhelmine von** 1781-1849 [NPS]
German author
* Selbig, Elise

Ahlqvist, August Engelbrekt 1826-
? [IP]
Finnish poet and philologist
* Oksanen
* Oksaselta, A.

Ahmed Ibn Hemdem Kiaya 19th c.
[IP]
Turkish author
* Sohailes

[L']Aigle de la France
See Ailly, Pierre d'

Aiken, Albert W. 1846?-1894
[WW]
*American actor, singer, playwright,
author*
* Agile Penne
* Armstrong, [Capt.] Frank P.
* Blake, Redmond?
* Carson, [Major] Lewis W.
* [A] Celebrated Actress
* Davenport, Adelaide
* Davenport, Frances Helen
* Sara, [Col.] Delle
* Thorne, [Lt.] Alfred B.

Aiken, George L. 1830-1876
American actor, playwright, author
* Clyde, Bernard
* Meredith, C. Leon

Aiken, Peter Freeland 19th c. [IP]
British author
* [The] Grandson of R. Aiken

Aikin, John 1747-1822 [IP]
British author and physician
* J. A.
* Uncle John

Aikin, Lucy 1781-1864 [IP]
British author
* Godolphin, Mary

Ailly, Pierre d' 1350-1420 [NPS]
French cardinal and astrologer
* [L']Aigle de la France
(See also base volume)

Aimon, Jacques
See Arouet, Francois Marie

Ained
See Dowling, Richard

Ainslie, George Robert 1776-1839
[IP]
Scottish numismatologist
* [A] Fellow of the Antiquarian
Societies of London and Scotland

Ainslie, Philip Barrington [IP]
British author
* Philo-Scotus

Ainslie, Robert 1766-1838 [IP]
Scottish author
* [A] Father

Ainslie, Whitelaw [IP]
Scottish physician and author
* Caledonicus

Ainsworth, William Harrison
1805-1882 [DLE1, IP, SAT]
British author, playwright, solicitor
* Brown, Will
* Painsworth, W. Harassing
* Ticheburn, Cheviot

Airy, [Sir] George Biddell 1801- ?
[IP]
British astronomer
* [The] Astronomer Royal
* G. B. A.

Airy, Mr.
See Habersham, Robert

Aistis, Jonas
See Aleksandravicius, Jonas

Aitken, Edward Hamilton 1851- ?
[NPS]
Author
* Eha

Aitken, Robert
See Morton, G. A.

Aitken, Robert 1800-1873 [IP]
British clergyman
* [A] Parish Priest

**Aitken, William Maxwell [First
Baron Beaverbrook]** 1879-1964
[CA, PPN]
*Canadian-born author and
newspaper publisher*
* [The] Beaver
* Beaverbrook, William Maxwell
Aitken

Aiton, John [IP]
Scottish clergyman
* [A] Clergyman of the Old School
* [A] Pedestrian

Aix
See Bausman, Frederick

Ajax, Sir
See Harrington, [Sir] John

Akakia, Le Docteur
See Arouet, Francois Marie

Akbar 1542-1605
Emperor of Hindustan
* Guardian of Mankind
(See also base volume)

Akenside, Mark 1721-1770 [IP]
British poet
* [A] Swiss Gentleman
(See also base volume)

Akers, Elizabeth [Chase]
1832-1911 [DNA]
American poet and journalist
* Percy, Florence

Akib, Le rabbin
See Arouet, Francois Marie

Al-So
See Somers, Alexander

Alarcon, Alfonso 19th c. [GS]
Spanish bullfighter
* [El] Pocho [The Rotten One]

Alastor
See Kane, John P.

Alastor
See Saumaise, Claude

Alban 3rd c. [NPS]
Saint
* [The] British Saint Stephen
* [The] Protomartyr of Britain

Alban, Mathias 1621-1712 [BBD]
Italian violin maker
* Albani, Mattia

Albanese, Vannie
See Albanese, Vincent

Albanese, Vincent 20th c. [EF]
American football player
* Albanese, Vannie

Albani, Mattia
See Alban, Mathias

Albano
See Hughes, Terence McMahon

Albee, John 19th c. [IP]
American author
* J. A.

Alberdingk-Thym, Josephus Albertus
1820- ? [IP]
Dutch poet and author
* Forestier, Paul

Albert
See Armstrong, John

Albert, Carl 1908- [CR]
American politician
* [The] Little Giant

Albert Victor 1864-1892 [BL]
Duke of Clarence
* Prince Eddy

Albert III [or Albrecht] 1414-1486
[NPS]
Elector of Brandenburg
* [The] German Achilles
(See also base volume)

Alberti, Sophie [Moedinger] 1826-
? [IP]
German author
* Verena, Sophie

Alberton, Edwin
See Philips, Albert Edwin

Albin, Sebastien
See Cornu, Hortense [Lacroix]

Albonese, Afranio 1480-1560?
[BBD]
*Italian theologian and reputed
inventor of the bassoon*
* Afranio de Pavia

Alboni, Maria Anna 1823-1894
[BBD]
Italian opera singer
* Alboni, Marietta

Alboni, Marietta
See Alboni, Maria Anna

Alby, Ernest Francois Antoine
1809-1868 [IP]
French author
* France, Anatole de

Alcalde, Miguel
See Burgess, Michael Roy

Alcanbara, Osvaldo
See Lopes, Baltasar

Alcantara Herran, Pedro
1800-1872 [NPS]
*Colombian army officer and
statesman*
* Husar de Ayacucho

Alceste
See Assolant, Jean-Baptiste-Alfred

Alceste
See Belmontet, Louis

Alceste
See De Castille, Hippolyte

Alceste
See Laboulaye, Edouard

Alcide, Baron de M.
See Musset, [Louis Charles] Alfred
de

Alcofribas, le Magicien
See Assolant, Jean-Baptiste-Alfred

Alcott, Louisa May 1832-1888
[DLE1, IP]
American author
* Barnard, A. M.
* Periwinkle, Tribulation

Alcott, William Alexander
1798-1859 [IP]
American author and lecturer
* [A] Schoolmaster

Alcuin [or Albinus] 735- 804 [NPS]
British scholar
* [The] Schoolmistress to France
(See also base volume)

Aldam, W. H. [IP]
British author
* [An] Old Man

Alden, Joseph Warren [IP]
American clergyman
* [A] Puritan of the 19th Century

Alden, William L. 1837- ? [IP]
American journalist
* White, Matthew, Jr.
(See also base volume)

Alderson, [Sir] Edward Hall
1787-1857 [IP]
British jurist
* [A] Layman

Alderson, John 1758-1829 [IP]
British physician
* [The] President

Aldred, Ebenezer [IP]
British clergyman
* [A] Unitarian Minister
(See also base volume)

Aldrich, Henry 1647-1710 [DEA]
British author
* Woodhead, A.

Aldrich, Rose [IP]
American author
* Ashleigh, Rose

Aldrich, Thomas Bailey 1836- ?
[DEA, IP]
American author and poet
* T. B. A.

Aleksandravicius, Jonas 1904-1973
[CD]
Lithuanian poet
* Aistis, Jonas
* Kossu-Aleksandravicius, Jonas
* Kuosa-Aleksandriskis, Jonas

Aleria
See Parnell, Frances Isabel

Alethe
See Boland, Eleanor

Alexander 2nd c. [NPS]
Commentator on Aristotle
* [The] Exegete

Alexander, Charles Khalil
1923-1980 [CA]
Egyptian-born actor, playwright, director
* Qadar, Basheer
* Quimber, Mario
(See also base volume)

Alexander, Drawcansir
See Smollett, Tobias George

Alexander, Francesca 19th c. [IP]
American author
* Francesca

Alexander, J. H.
See Japp, Alexander Hay

Alexander, James Lynne [IP]
Author
* [A] Canadian

Alexander, John
See Taylor, Jeremy

Alexander, Josephine 1909- [CA]
American author
* Lora, Josephine

Alexander, Mrs. Cecil Francis 19th c. [IP]
British poet and hymn-writer
* C. F. A.

Alexander, O. C. [IP]
Author
* Rapler, Rob

Alexander, Richard Dykes [IP]
British author
* [A] Layman
* Pacificator

Alexander, [Rev.] Richard W.
See Mercedes, [Sister]

Alexander, Samuel 1749-1824 [IP]
British author
* Aquila
* Verax

Alexander, Samuel Davies 1819- ?
[IP]
American clergyman
* S. D. A.

Alexander, William 1768-1841 [IP]
British author, bookseller, publisher
* Amicus

Alexander I [Aleksandr Pavlovich]
1777-1825 [NPS]
Russian emperor
* Bald Coot Bully
* [The] Coxcomb Czar
* [The] Northern Thor
(See also base volume)

Alexander II 1198-1249 [NPS]
King of Scotland
* [The] Peaceful
(See also base volume)

Alexander III 4th c. BC [NPS]
King of Macedonia
* [The] Bicorned Lord
* [The] Conqueror
* [The] Son of Jupiter Ammon
* That Pellean Conqueror
(See also base volume)

Alexander's Tutor
See Aristotle

Alexis, Katina
See Strauch, Katina [Parthemos]

Alexis, Wilibald
See Haering, Georg Wilhelm Heinrich

Alfarabi
See Ibn-Tarkaw, Abou-Nasr-Mohammed

Alfieri, Vittorio Amadeo
1749-1803 [IP]
Italian poet
* Asmodei, Count

Alfonso V [or Affonso] 1432-1481
[NPS]
King of Portugal
* [The] African
(See also base volume)

Alfonso X [or Alphonso]
1226?-1284 [NPS]
King of Leon and Castile
* [The] Scholar
(See also base volume)

Alford, Fanny [IP]
British author
* [A] Clergyman's Wife

Alford, Henry 1810-1871 [IP]
British clergyman
* [The] Dean of Canterbury
* H. A.

Alfred, H. J. [IP]
Author
* Otter

Alfricobas
See Neuburg, Victor [Benjamin]

Alger, Horatio, Jr. 1832-1899
[SAT]
American author
* Putnam, Arthur Lee

Algie, James 1857-1928 [DNA]
Canadian-born physician and author
* Lloyd, Wallace

Alguno, Senor
See Ames, Nathan

Ali Baba
See Mackay, Aberigh

Ali Bey
See Knapp, Samuel Lorenzo

Ali Mohammed of Shiraz 1819-1850
Founder of Persian religious sect
* Mahdi, Imam
(See also base volume)

Alice
See Condon, Lizzie G.

Alien
See Baker, Mrs. Louis Alien

Aliqua
See Peirson, Eliza O.

[The] Alist
See Barham, Francis Foster

Alister, R.
See Robertson, Alexander

Alkan, Charles-Henri Valentin
See Morhange, Charles-Henri Valentin

Allan, Charles Stuart Hay ?-1880
[IP]
Author
* Stuart, Charles Edward

Allan, J. A. 19th c. [IP]
Canadian poet
* [A] Butterfly

Allan, James MacGrigor [IP]
British author
* [A] Bachelor

Allan, John [IP]
Author
* [A] Special Reporter

Allan, John 19th c. [IP]
Scottish clergyman and author
* Beefeater, Domestic Chaplain to Fill Pots

Allan, John 19th c. [IP]
Scottish clergyman and author
* Kn-Oxonian

Allan, John Hay
See Allen, John Carter

[The] Allan Ramsay of Sicily
See Theocritus

Allan, Thomas 1777-1833 [IP]
Scottish banker and author
* [A] Private Gentleman

Allbeury, Theodore Edward Le Bouthillier [Ted] 1917- [CA]
British author
* Kelly, Patrick
(See also base volume)

Alleber, Henri de
See Di Lappomeraye, Henri

Allegri da Correggio, Antonio
1494-1534 [NPS]
Italian painter
* [The] Ariel of the Italian Renaissance
* [The] Faun of the Italian Renaissance
(See also base volume)

Allen, Benjamin 1789-1829
[DNA, IP]
American author and clergyman
* Osander

Allen, Bill
See Allen, Margaret

Allen, Bill 20th c. [CMA]
American disc jockey
* Allen, Hoss

Allen, Charles [IP]
British author
* One Who has Served Under the Marquis of Dalhousie

Allen, Crash
See Allen, Richard Anthony [Dick]

Allen, Don
See True, Hiram L.

Allen, G. W. [IP]
British poet
* W. G. A.

Allen, George 1792-1883 [IP]
American clergyman and author
* [A] Freeman

Allen, [Charles] Grant [Blairfindie]
1848-1899 [DEA, DLE1, WGT]
British author
* Rayner, Olive Pratt
* Warborough, Martin Leach
(See also base volume)

Allen, Hoss
See Allen, Bill

Allen, Hugh
See Rathborne, St. George

Allen, John
See Clute, Oscar

Allen, John 1760-1830 [IP]
American author
* [A] Citizen of Maryland

Allen, John 1770-1843 [IP]
Scottish philosopher and author
* [A] Necessitarian

Allen, John 1771-1839 [IP]
British educator and author
* [A] Layman

Allen, John 18th c. [IP]
American author and clergyman
* [A] British Bostonian

Allen, John 19th c. [IP]
Author
* Scaevola

Allen, John Carter 1795?-1872 [IP]
Scottish poet
* Allan, John Hay
* Scott, [Sir] Walter, Bart.
* Stuart, John Sobieski Stolberg

Allen, John Mills 1846- ? [BDSA]
American author, attorney, politician
* Private John

Allen, Margaret ?-1949 [DI]
American murderer
* Allen, Bill

Allen, Mary
See Cleveland, Mary

Allen, Phally
See Allen, Verden

Allen, Richard [IP]
British author and printer
* R. A.

Allen, Richard Anthony [Dick]
1942- [CR]
American baseball player
* Allen, Crash

Allen, [Lieut.] Ricky
See Hulten, Gustav Karl

Allen, Robert 19th c. [IP]
British clergyman and author
* [A] Master of Arts of Trinity College, Cambridge

Allen, Stephen Merrill 1819- ? [IP]
American merchant, banker, author
* Alpha
* S. M. A.

Allen, Thomas [IP]
British clergyman and author
* [An] Impartial Hand

Allen, Thomas 1542-1632 [NPS]
British mathematician
* Another Roger Bacon
(See also base volume)

Allen, Verden 1944- [CMA]
Musician
* Allen, Phally

Allen, Wilkes ?-1845 [IP]
American clergyman and author
* A.

Allen, William [IP]
British author
* W. A.

Allendale, Alfred, Esq.
See   Hook, Theodore Edward

Allibone, Samuel Austin 1816-1889
[IP]
American lexicographer and bibliographer
* S. A. A.
(See also base volume)

Allid
See   Lanigan, George Thomas

Allingham, William 1824-1889
[DLE1, IP, PI]
Irish-born poet and author
* Giraldus
* Walker, Patricius

Allinson-James, Mrs. 19th c.   [NPS]
Author
* Triscott, Edith Browning

Allison, George W.
See   Mencken, Henry Louis

Allman, Jonathan
See   Wilson, Robert A.

Alloway, Robert Morellet 1807- ?
[PI]
Irish poet
* Montgomerie, Robert

Allsop, Robert   [IP]
British author
* R. A.

Allua
See   Holland, Denis

Alma
See   Yonge, Charlotte M.

Alma Mater
See   Packford, C. W.

Almon, John 1738-1805   [IP]
British author, editor, bookseller
* [An] Independent Whig

Almore, Caspar
See   Beasley, Frederick Williamson

Almqvist, Karl Jonas Ludvig
1793-1866
Swedish author
* Westermann, Professor

Almy, Frank C. ?-1892   [BLB]
American murderer and burglar
* Abbott, George

Alonso, Manuel 19th c.   [GS]
Spanish bullfighter
* [El] Castellano [The Castillian]

Alouette [Skylark]
See   Richard, Marthe

Aloysius
See   O'Connell, John A.

Alpert, Hollis 1916-   [CA]
American author, film critic, editor
* Carroll, Robert

Alpha
See   Allen, Stephen Merrill

Alpha?
See   Cahill, William

Alpha
See   Lanigan, William

Alsop, Alfred   [IP]
British missionary
* [A] Delver

Alsop, Richard 1761-1815   [IP]
American poet and journalist
* R. A.

Alston, Alfred Henry   [IP]
British naval officer and poet
* [The] Captain of the Cumberland

Alston, Joseph 1778-1816   [IP]
American statesman
* [The] Mountaineer
* [A] Southern Planter

[Der] Alte [The Old Man]
See   Adenauer, Konrad

Altemese, Elethea
See   Thompson, James W.

Alting, Albertus Samuel Carpentier
[IP]
Dutch author
* Philalethes

Alton
See   Taveau, A. L.

Alum, Hardly
See   Sullivan, Edward Dean

Alumni of the University of Edinburgh
See   Lee, John

Alumni of the University of Edinburgh
See   Wilson, George

Alumnus Cantabrigiensis
See   Forster, Thomas

[An] Alumnus of that College
See   Lowell, John

Alvan, [Dr] Sigismund
See   Lassal, Ferdinand

Alvarez, Chanca Diego 15th c.
Spanish scientist and author
* Scribe of the Indies

Alvary, Max
See   Achenbach, Max

Amado, Jorge 1912-   [CR]
Brazilian author
* [The] Brazilian Boccaccio

Amat, Felix 1750-1824   [IP]
Spanish clergyman and author
* Melata, Don Macario Padua

[An] Amateur
See   Abbot, E. S.

[An] Amateur
See   Hooper, George W.

[An] Amateur
See   Wilson, Thomas

[An] Amateur Traveller
See   Webb, James Watson

[The] Ambassador
See   Turner, Samuel

Amber, Miles
See   Sickert, Mrs. Cobden

[The] Ambitious Thane
See   Boswell, James

Ambler, Charles ?-1794   [IP]
British barrister
* [A] Retired Barrister

Ambrose [or Ambrosius] 333?- 397
[BBD]
Saint
* [The] Father of Christian Hymnology

Ambrose, Paul
See   Kennedy, John Pendleton

Ambrosia
See   Berlyn, Mrs. A.

Amelia
See   Welby, Amelia Ball [Coppuck]

Amelia, Annie
See   Garrett, Annie Amelia

Amelia, Carolina Wilhelmina
See   O'Hagan, John

Amelia, Ellen
See   Garrett, Ellen Amelia

Amergin
See   McGee, Thomas D'Arcy

[Un] Americain Citoyen
See   Lee, William

[An] American
See   Adams, John

[An] American
See   Adams, Samuel

[An] American
See   Barton, William

[An] American
See   Beckwith, Julia Catherine
[Hart]

[An] American
See   Child, Lydia Maria [Francis]

[An] American
See   Christy, David

[An] American
See   Church, Benjamin

[An] American
See   De Kay, James E.

[An] American
See   Habich, Edward

[An] American
See   Hopkinson, Joseph

[An] American
See   Inglis, Charles

[An] American
See   Lee, Arthur

[An] American
See   Longfellow, Henry Wadsworth

[An] American
See   Low, Samuel

[An] American
See   Morse, Samuel Finley Breese

[An] American
See   Morse, Sidney Edwards

[An] American
See   Robinson, Alfred

[An] American
See   Wright, Hezekiah Hartley

[The] American Cato
See   White, Hugh Lawson

[The] American Cicero
See   Berrien, John MacPherson

[An] American Citizen
See   Adams, John

[An] American Citizen
See   Brockett, Linus Pierpont

[The] American Consul at London
See   Morse, Freeman H.

[An] American, formerly a Member of Congress
See   Ames, Fisher

[The] American Ice Master
See   Haines, Jackson

[The] American in England
See   Slidell, Alexander

[An] American Indian
See   Horne, Henry, Jr.

[The] American Rabelais
See   Melville, Herman

[The] American Skating King
See   Haines, Jackson

[The] American Tosti
See   Ball, Ernest R.

[The] American Walter Scott
See   Cooper, James Fenimore

[An] American Wanderer
See   Lee, Arthur

Americanus
See   Hamilton, Alexander

[An] Americo-Hibernian Priest
See   Cannon, Francis

Ames, Fisher 1758-1808   [IP]
American statesman and writer
* [An] American, formerly a Member of Congress
* Brutus
* Falkland
(See also base volume)

Ames, Joseph Bushnell 1878-1928
[DNA]
American author
* Gunnison, Lynn

Ames, Nathan 1825-1865   [IP]
American poet
* Alguno, Senor

Ames, Nathaniel ?-1835   [IP]
American author
* N. A.
* [An] Old Sailor

Amfrye, Guillaume 1639-1720
[NPS]
French poet
* [The] Gaul Narquois of Parisian Society
(See also base volume)

Amhergin
See   McGee, Thomas D'Arcy

Amhurst, Nicholas 1697-1742
[IP, NPS]
British editor, poet, politician
* Oldcastle, Humphrey
* [A] Student at Oxford
(See also base volume)

[Un] Ami
See   Hartley, Thomas

Amicus
See   Alexander, William

Amicus
See   Gordon, James

Amicus, C. B. C.   [IP]
British author
* C. B. C. A.

Amner, J. T.   [IP]
British educator
* [A] Head Master under the
London School Board

Amo, Tauraatua i
See   Adams, Henry [Brooks]

Amory, Thomas 1691?-1788   [IP]
British author
* [An] Antiquarian Doctor
* [A] Lady
(See also base volume)

Amos, Winsom 1921-   [MA]
American poet
* Theron, Hilary

Amyand, Arthur
See   Haggard, Edward Arthur

Anacharsis
See   Barthelemy, Jean Jacques

Ananda, Swami Viva
See   Jackson, Editha Salomon

Anastasius
See   Drummond, Henry

Anastasius ?- 886   [NPS]
Librarian of the Vatican
* [The] Librarian
(See also base volume)

Anatol
See   Schnitzler, Arthur

Anber, Paul
See   Baker, Pauline H[alpern]

Anbury, Thomas   [IP]
British author
* [An] Officer

Ancillon, Charles 1656-1715   [IP]
French attorney and jurist
* [A] Person of Honour

Anczyca, Vladislav Ludvig 1823-1883
Polish playwright, author, poet
* Goralczyk, Kasimir

Anderdon, John Lavicount 19th c.
[HFN, IP]
British author
* J. L. A.
* [A] Layman

Anderdon, William Henry   [IP]
British clergyman
* Evans, Owen

Andersdatter, Karla M[argaret]
See   Billings, Karla Margaret
Crosier

Andersen, Hans Christian 1805-1875
Danish author
* [The] Comedy Writer
(See also base volume)

Andersen, Jewell 1923-   [CA]
American author
* Andersen, Juel

Andersen, Juel
See   Andersen, Jewell

Andersen, Mary E.   [IP]
Author
* [A] Looker-On-Here in Vienna

Anderson, Adam ?-1867   [IP]
Irish author
* A. A.

Anderson, Alexander 1845-1909
[IP]
Scottish poet
* [A] Gent
(See also base volume)

Anderson, Andreas   [IP]
Danish author
* [A] Native of Denmark

Anderson, Beverly M.
See   Nemiro, Beverly Anderson

Anderson, Bill
See   Anderson, Walter

Anderson, Bloody Bill
See   Anderson, William

Anderson, C. Farley
See   Mencken, Henry Louis

Anderson, D. L. 1862-1918   [EWG]
American gunfighter
* Wilson, Billy

Anderson, George   [IP]
Scottish author
* Cyclos, a Member of the Glasgow
Skating Club

Anderson, Henry   [IP]
British author
* [A] Gentleman of Lincoln's Inn

Anderson, James   [IP]
Canadian farmer and journalist
* Obiter Dictum

Anderson, James 1739-1808
[IP, NPS]
Scottish editor, author, economist
* Aberdeen, E.
* Aristides
* Candid Enquirer
* Cimon
* [A] Farmer
* Germanicus
* Impartial Hand
* Mercator
* Plain, Henry
* [A] Scot
* Scoto-Britannicus
(See also base volume)

Anderson, John   [IP]
Scottish author
* Aednr-Nos-Seer I'Noh

Anderson, John 18th c.   [IP]
Scottish clergyman and author
* [A] Countreyman

Anderson, John Henry 1815-1874
[BL, NPS]
Scottish magician and actor
* [The] Great Wizard of the North

Anderson, Kristin
See   DuBreuil, Elizabeth Lorinda

Anderson, Linnaeus B.   [IP]
American author
* Elon-Rusticus

Anderson, Ockie
See   Anderson, Oscar

Anderson, Oscar 20th c.   [EF]
American football player
* Anderson, Ockie

Anderson, Patrick   [IP]
Poet and physician
* Whats-You-Call-Him, Clerk to
the Same

Anderson, Ralph
See   Heron, Robert

Anderson, Roberta 20th c.
Author
* Michaels, Fern [joint pseudonym
with Mary Kuczkir]

Anderson, Sonia
See   Daniel, [William] Roland

Anderson, Walter 20th c.   [EF]
American football player
* Anderson, Bill

Anderson, William ?-1864
[BLB, DI]
American gangleader and murderer
* Anderson, Bloody Bill

Anderson, William 20th c.   [PI]
Irish-born poet
* Green, I. V.

Anderton, James 17th c.   [NPS]
Author
* Brereley, John, Priest

Andolt, Ernst
See   Abeken, Bernhard Rudolf

Andrade
See   Corvo de Camoes, Joao de
Andrade

Andre, John 1751-1780   [IP]
British army officer and author
* [A] Dreamer

Andrew, James
See   Mackay, Andrew

Andrew, of Mitchell Street
See   Jones, John Andrew

[The] Andrew Wyeth of Literature
See   Updike, John

Andrews, Addison Fletcher 1857- ?
[IP]
American journalist
* Fledger, Aaron

Andrews, Annulet
See   Ohl, Maude

Andrews, Garnett   [IP]
American author
* [An] Old Georgia Lawyer

Andrews, Gwendolen [Foulke]
1863-1936   [DNA]
American poet
* De Veaux, Richard

Andrews, Henry   [EOP]
British astrologer and author
* Old Moore

Andrews, J. 20th c.   [EF]
American football player
* Andrews, Jabby

Andrews, Jabby
See   Andrews, J.

Andrews, Marian   [ICB]
Author
* Hare, Christopher

Andrews, Miles Peter ?-1814
[IP, NPS]
British playwright
* Arley

Andrews, Sidney 1837-1880   [IP]
American journalist
* Dixon

Andrews, Vickie
See   Smith, Catherine R. [Kay]

Ane of that Ilk
See   Aytoun, William Edmonstoune

Anet, Jean-Baptiste 1661?-1755
[BBD]
French musician
* Baptiste

Angas, George Federick   [IP]
British author
* G. F. A.

Angel Anna
See   Jackson, Editha Salomon

Angelicus, Doctor
See   Aquinas, Thomas [Thomas of
Aquino]

Angelina
See   Levy, Angelina

Angelini, Giovanni Andrea
1624?-1705   [BBD]
Italian composer and author
* Bontempi, Giovanni Andrea

Angell, Hildegarde
See   Smith, Hildegarde Angell

Angelus a Sancto Francisco
See   Mason, Richard

Angers, Felicite 1845-1924   [DNA]
Canadian author
* Conan, Laure

[An] Angler
See   Stoddart, Thomas Tod

Anglus, Phil
See   Penn, William

Angouleme, Duc d'
See   Bourbon, Louis Antoine de

Angove, Emily 1837- ?   [IP]
British author
* Emily

Angove, Grace
See   Michell, Grace [Angove]

[The] Angry
See   Christian II

Angus
See   Forrester, Arthur M.

Angus
See   Williams, Ephie Augustus

Angus, William   [IP]
Scottish author
* Promotion in the Church

Anicetus
See   Clark, William Adolphus

[An] Animal Painter
See   Wilson, James

Anley, Charlotte   [IP]
British author
* C. A.

Ann
See   Thomas, Ann

Ann of Swansea
See   Kemble, Frances Anne
[Fanny]

Anna Maria?
See   Winter, Anna Maria

Annalist
See   Gerard, Frances A.

Anne 1661-1720   [NPS]
Countess of Winchelsea
* [A] Lady

Anne 1665-1714   [NPS]
Queen of England
* Bull, Mrs.
(See also base volume)

Annet, Peter ?-1778   [IP]
British author
* [A] Certain Free Enquirer
* Free Inquirer
* Horologist
* Philalethes, Mencius
* Stilton, W.

Annibale 1527?-1575   [BBD]
Italian musician and composer
* [Il] Padovano

**[The] Annibale Caracci of the Eclectic
School**
See   Campo, Bernardino

Anodos
See   Coleridge, Mary Elizabeth

Anonymous
See   Dawson, Benjamin

Another Barrister
See   Wainwright, Reader

Another Considerable Personage
See   Drummond, [Sir] William

Another Diana
See   Berners, Juliana

Another Gentleman of Lincoln's Inn
See   Edwards, Thomas

Another Joseph
See   Butler, James [Second Duke of
Ormonde]

Another Layman
See   Palfray, Warwick

Another Machiavel
See   Stuart, John [Third Earl of
Bute]

Another Member of Parliament
See   Blackstone, [Sir] William

Another Philip II
See   George III

Another Proteus
See   Sainte Beuve, Charles Auguste

Another Pythagoras
See   Dee, John

Another Reynolds
See   Hoppner, John

Another Roger Bacon
See   Allen, Thomas

Another Roscius
See   Burbage, Richard

Another Tully and Virgil
See   Cartwright, William

Anselm of Laon 1030?-1117   [NPS]
French theologian
* Scholasticus, Doctor
(See also base volume)

Anson, George 1697-1762   [NPS]
British naval officer
* [The] Bulldog of all
   Circumnavigators

Anstey, Christopher 1724-1805
[IP, NPS]
British poet
* Bath Laureat
* C. A., Esq.
* Inkle, Mr.
* Macsaroni, A.
* Twist-Wit, Christopher, Esq.

Anstey, John 1796-1867   [IP]
Irish poet
* J. A.
* [The] Late J. J. S., Esq.
(See also base volume)

Anstruther, Capt.   [IP]
British author
* [The] Man in the Moon

Anthony
See   Taber, Anthony Scott

Anthony, G. W.   [IP]
Author
* Tinto, Gabriel

Anthony, Louisa   [IP]
British author
* L. A.

Anthony, W. B.   [IP]
British author
* W. B. A.

Anthroposophus
See   Vaughan, Thomas

Anthrops
See   Storrs, George

Anti Monopoly
See   Duane, William

Anti Quary
See   Tuthall, William H.

Anti Sejanus
See   Scott, James

Anticant, [Dr.] Pessimist
See   Carlyle, Thomas

[The] Antichrist
See   Gustavus Adolphus

[The] Antichrist of Wit
See   Querno, Camillo

Anticipation
See   Dickinson, John

Antigonus II 1st c. BC   [NPS]
King of Judea
* [The] Hasmonean
(See also base volume)

[An] Antiquarian Doctor
See   Amory, Thomas

[The] Antiquarian Poet
See   Leland, John

Antiquarius
See   Loveday, John

[An] Antiquary
See   Pegge, Samuel

[An] Antiquary
See   Wright, Thomas

Antonio
See   McCarthy, Denis Florence

Antonio degli Organi
See   Squarcialupi, Antonio

Antrobus, Benjamin   [IP]
British author
* B. A.

Anvari 12th c.
Persian poet
* Auhad al-Din Ali
(See also base volume)

Anzelevitz [or Anzelwitz], Benjamin
1891?-1943   [DAM]
*American entertainer and
bandleader*
* [The] Ol' Maestro
(See also base volume)

Apache Bill? Seamans
See   Seamans, William

[The] Apache Kid
See   Has-Kay-bay-nay-ntayl

[An] Ape
See   Pope, Alexander

Ape Gabriel
See   Harvey, Gabriel

[The] Ape of Genius
See   Arouet, Francois Marie

Apes, William   [IP]
American Indian preacher
* [A] Native of the Forest

Aphrodite, J.
See   Livingston, Carole

[The] Apollo of the Fountain of Muses
See   Ronsard, Pierre de

Apollonius of Perga 3rd c. BC
Scholar
* [The] Great Geometer

[The] Apostle of Brabant
See   Livinus

[The] Apostle of Brazil
See   De Nobrega, Manuel

[The] Apostle of Methodism
See   Lee, Jesse

[The] Apostle of Temperance
See   Chiniquy, Charles

[The] Apostle of Wheat
See   Borlaug, Norman

Apperley, Charles James
1777-1843   [NPS]
Welsh author
* [The] Great Historian of the Field
(See also base volume)

Appius
See   Dennis, John

Appledorf, Howard 1941?-1982
American nutrition expert
* [The] Junk Food Professor

Appleton, Jesse 1772-1819   [IP]
American author
* Owen
(See also base volume)

Appleton, John Reed   [IP]
British author and poet
* J. R. A.

Appleton, Nathan 1779-1861   [IP]
American statesman
* [A] Layman of Boston

Appleton, Nathan 1843- ?   [IP]
American author and financier
* N. A.

Applewhite, Marshall Herff 20th c.
[EOP]
American religious cult leader
* Chip

Applewhite, Marshall Herff
(Continued)
* Nincom
* Tiddly
* Winnie
(See also base volume)

Appleyard, Ernest Silvanus   [IP]
British clergyman
* [A] Member of the Church of
England
(See also base volume)

[The] Appollo of the Ring
See   Belcher, James

[An] Apprentice Boy
See   Graham, John

Apraates, Jacob 4th c.   [NPS]
Theologian
* [The] Persian Sage

April, Steve
See   Zinberg, Leonard

Aquila
See   Alexander, Samuel

Aquila Aquilonius
See   Oxenstierna, Axel Gustafsson

Aquilius
See   Wilson, John

Aquinas, Thomas [Thomas of Aquino]
1224-1274   [NPS]
*Italian scholastic philosopher and
saint*
* Angelicus, Doctor
(See also base volume)

Arago, Etienne 1803- ?   [IP]
French poet and journalist
* Ferney, Jules

Araguy, Jean Raymond Eugene d'
1808- ?   [IP]
French author
* Snake, William

Arai Hakuseki
See   Arai Kimiyoshi

Arai Kimiyoshi 1657-1725
Japanese scholar and historian
* Arai Hakuseki

Aramburgo Iznaga, Jaime
1751-1787   [GS]
Spanish bullfighter
* [El] Judio [The Jew]

Arawiyeh, Al-
See   Crellin, Horatio Nelson

Arbeau, Thoinot
See   Tabourot, Jehan

Arbuckle, James 1700?-1746?
[IP, PI]
Irish-born poet
* Hibernicus

Arbuthnot, John 1667-1735
[DEA, IP, NPS]
British author and physician
* Bantley, Doctor
* Eleutherus, Philonomus
* [An] Eminent Lawyer of the
Temple
* J. A.
* [The] King of Inattention
* Sriblerus, Martinus
(See also base volume)

Arcana, Judith
See   Rosenfield, Judith

Archangelo
See Corelli, Angelo

Archbold, John Flather [IP]
British author
* Flather, John

Archer, Edward 1816- ? [IP]
British author
* E. A.

Archer, Frederick [IP]
American author
* F. A.

Archer, George W. [IP]
American author
* Bendbow, Hesper

Archer, Herbert Winslow
See Mencken, Henry Louis

Archer, John Wykeham 1809-1864
[IP]
British artist and antiquary
* Zigzag, Mr., the Elder

Archer-Gilligan, Amy 1869-1928
[LFW]
American murderer
* Sister Amy

Archibald, John Felltan 1856-1919
[DLE1]
Australian journalist and editor
* Archibald, Jules Francois

Archibald, Jules Francois
See Archibald, John Felltan

Archimedes
See Rennie, John

[An] Architect
See Davy, Christopher

[An] Architect
See Hakewill, Arthur William

Ard-na-Erin
See Kelly, John Tarpey

Ardboe
See Millen, F. F.

Arden, Henry T.
See Arnold, Henry Thomas

Arden, Noele
See Dambrauskas, Joan Arden

Aretino, Pietro 1492-1557? [NPS]
Italian author
* Cerberus, A.
* [Le] Voltaire de Son Siecle
(See also base volume)

Argall, Richard 17th c. [NPS]
Poet
* Aylett, Richard

Argonaut
See Hall, Basil

Argus I.
See Knox, W. Mayne

Ariail, David 20th c. [EF]
American football player
* Ariail, Gump

Ariail, Gump
See Ariail, David

Arias, Roberto 20th c. [CR]
Panamanian diplomat
* Arias, Tito

Arias, Tito
See Arias, Roberto

Ariazza, Don Juan Bautista de
1770-1837 [IP]
Spanish poet
* D. J. B. de A.

Aribo Scholasticus
See Aribon

Aribon 1000?-1078? [BBD]
Medieval scholar
* Aribo Scholasticus
* Aribon de Freising
* Aribon de Liege
* Aribon d'Orleans

Aribon de Freising
See Aribon

Aribon de Liege
See Aribon

Aribon d'Orleans
See Aribon

[The] Ariel of the Italian Renaissance
See Allegri da Correggio, Antonio

Arigho, John [EOP]
British astrologer
* Genuine Old Moore

Arigo, Jose
See De Freitas, Jose Pedro

Arion
See Chesterton, George Laval

Ariosto
See Irving, Edward

Ariosto, Lodovico 1474-1533
[NPS]
Italian poet
* [The] Orpheus of His Age
* [The] Walter Scott of Italy
(See also base volume)

[The] Ariosto of Germany
See Goethe, Johann Wolfgang von

Aristarchus 2nd c. BC [NPS]
Greek grammarian and critic
* [The] Prince of Grammarians
(See also base volume)

Aristenete
See Nogaret, Francois Felix

Aristides
See Anderson, James

Aristides
See Hanson, Alexander Contee

Aristides
See McKenney, Thomas Loraine

Aristizabal, Domingo [GS]
Mexican bullfighter
* Castanero Chico [Little Chestnut
  Vendor]

Aristobulus
See Turner, James

Aristocles 4th c. BC [NPS]
Greek philosopher
* [The] Rapt Sage
(See also base volume)

[An] Aristocrat
See Elliot, John Lettsom

Aristotle 4th c. BC [NPS]
Greek philosopher
* Alexander's Tutor
(See also base volume)

Aristus
See Lamoignon, Chretien

Arizona Cy
See Cowdrick, Jesse C.

Arjona Herrera, Francisco
1818-1868 [GS]
Spanish bullfighter
* Cuchares [Large Spoons]

Arkansas Tom Jones
See Daugherty, Roy

Arley
See Andrews, Miles Peter

Armistead, Wilson [IP]
British author
* [A] Friend of the Negro
* Tuvar, Lorenzo

Armitage, Dudley
See Axon, William Edward
Armitage

Armour, Jean ?-1834 [NPS]
Wife of Scottish poet, Robert Burns
* Bonnie Jean

Armroyd, George [IP]
American merchant and author
* [A] Citizen of the United States

Armstrong, Frances Charlotte 19th
c. [IP]
British author
* F. C. A.

Armstrong, [Capt.] Frank P.
See Aiken, Albert W.

Armstrong, [Captain] Jacob D.
See Meeker, Nathan Cook

Armstrong, John 1709-1779 [IP]
Scottish physician and poet
* [A] Free Thinker
(See also base volume)

Armstrong, John 1758-1843 [IP]
American army officer and author
* [An] Old Soldier

Armstrong, John 1771-1797 [IP]
Scottish poet
* Albert

Armstrong, John Barclay
1850-1913 [EWG]
American law officer
* McNelly's Bulldog

Armstrong, Katherine [IP]
American writer
* De Courcy, Kate

Armstrong, Regina
See Niehaus, Mrs. C. H.

Armstrong, Skeffington [IP]
Clergyman and author
* [A] Clergyman

Armstrong, William [IP]
American author
* [A] Reformed Stock Gambler

Armstrong, William 1602?-1658?
[NPS]
Border raider
* Christie's Will

Arnall, William 1715-1741 [IP]
British journalist
* [A] Member of the House of
  Commons
* Walsingham, [Sir] Francis
(See also base volume)

Arnandez, Richard 1912- [CA]
American author and translator
* Edwin, [Brother] B.

Arndt, Ernst Moritz 1769-1860
[IP]
German author and poet
* E. M. A.

Arnee, Frank 1767-1858 [IP]
British clergyman and author
* [A] Member of the Society

Arnold, Alexander S. [IP]
British author
* [A] Sunday School
  Superintendent

Arnold, Augusta [Foote] 1844-1903
[DNA]
American editor
* Ronald, Mary

Arnold de Bruges
See Bruck [or Brouck], Arnold von

Arnold, [Sir] Edwin 1832- ?
[DEA, IP]
British author and poet
* E. A.

Arnold, George W. [IP]
Author
* Strickland, Joe

Arnold, Henry Thomas [IP]
British playwright
* Arden, Henry T.

Arnold, M. E. [IP]
British poet
* M. E. A.

Arnold, Matthew 1822-1888
[IP, NPS]
British poet and critic
* David, the Son of Goliath
* M. A.
(See also base volume)

Arnold, Thomas Kercheter
1800-1853 [IP]
British scholar
* T. K. A.

Arnold, William Delafield
1828-1859 [IP, NPS]
British author
* Punjabee

Arnold, William Thomas [NPS]
Author
* Vigilans sed Aequus

Arnoldo Flamengo
See Bruck [or Brouck], Arnold von

Arnot, Hugo 1749-1786 [IP, NPS]
Scottish historian
* [A] Citizen
* Eugene

Arnot, William [IP]
Scottish clergyman and author
* Bunyan, John, Junior

Arnoux, Charles Albert d' 1820- ?
[IP]
French artist and author
* Bertall

Aronja Reyes, Currito
See Aronja Reyes, Francisco

Aronja Reyes, Francisco
1842-1898 [GS]
Spanish bullfighter
* Aronja Reyes, Currito

Arouet, Francois Marie 1694-1778
[NPS, WGT]
French author and philosopher
* Abauzit, Firmin

Arouet, Francois Marie (Continued)
* Aimon, Jacques
* Akakia, Le Docteur
* Akib, Le rabbin
* [The] Ape of Genius
* Aveline, Le Sieur
* Bigorre, L'Abbe
* [The] Eye of Modern Illumination
* [The] Lord of Irony
* [The] Modern Baillet
* [The] Proteus of Man's Talents
* Ralph, Mr. le Docteur
(See also base volume)

Arran [joint pseudonym with Edith Emma Cooper]
See Bradley, Katharine Harris

Arran [joint pseudonym with Katharine Harris Bradley]
See Cooper, Edith Emma

Arrau, Claudio 1903- [CR]
Chilean musician
* King of the Pianists

Arrigo Tedesco [Henry the German]
See Isaac, Heinrich

Arroway, Francis M.
See Rosmond, Babette

Arrowsmith, Edmund 1585-1628 [NPS]
British clergyman
* Bradshaw
* Rigby

Arrowsmith, R. G. [IP]
British author
* Juvenis

Arsenius 4th c. [NPS]
Egyptian monk
* [The] Great

Artane
See O'Reilly, Thomas F.

Artevelle, Jacques
See Boue de Villiers, Amable Louis

Arthington, Maria ?-1863 [IP]
British author
* [A] Member

Arthur, Timothy Shay 1809-1885 [IP]
American author
* Smith, Mrs. John
(See also base volume)

[An] Artist
See Bengo, John

[An] Artist
See Roberts, Lester A.

Artman, Chang
See Artman, Corwan

Artman, Corwan 20th c. [EF]
American football player
* Artman, Chang

Arundell, Francis Vyvyan Jago 1780-1847 [IP]
British antiquary
* [The] Rector

Arundell, [Sir] John ?-1433? [NPS]
British politician
* [The] Magnificent

Arundell, [Sir] John 1495-1561 [NPS]
British vice-admiral and sheriff
* Jack of Tilbury

Arundell, [Sir] John 1576-1656? [NPS]
British Royalist soldier and politician
* Jack for the King

Arundell, William Arundell Harris 1794-1865 [IP]
British poet
* Harris, Arundell

Asaph
See Dryden, John

Ascher, Carol 1941- [CA]
American author
* Lopate, Carol

Ascher, Isidore G. 1835- ? [IP]
Canadian poet
* Isidore

Ascher, Sheila 1944- [CA]
American author
* Ascher/Straus [joint pseudonym with Dennis Straus]

Ascher/Straus [joint pseudonym with Dennis Straus]
See Ascher, Sheila

Ascher/Straus [joint pseudonym with Sheila Ascher]
See Straus, Dennis

Ash, Edward [IP]
British author and physician
* [A] Member of the Society
* One of its Members
* [A] Protestant Nonconformist

Ash, M. Selby [NPS]
Author
* Jacberus, Raymond

Ashe, Arthur 1943- [BP]
American tennis player
* [The] Shadow

Ashe, Penelope [joint pseudonym with Billie Young]
See Greene, Robert W.

Ashe, Penelope
See Karman, Mal

Ashe, Penelope [joint pseudonym with Robert W. Greene]
See Young, Billie

Ashe, Thomas ?-1835 [IP]
British author
* Captain Light Dragoons
* T. A.

Ashhurst, William Henry ?-1855 [IP]
British author
* Search, John

Ashleigh, Rose
See Aldrich, Rose

Ashley, Florence Emily [IP]
British poet
* F. E. A.

Ashley, George 1724-1808 [IP]
British clergyman and antiquary
* Dr. Taylor's Friend

Ashley, John [IP]
British author
* [A] Wykehamist

Ashley, John [IP]
West Indian author
* [A] Barbadoes Planter

Ashley, John Marks [IP]
British author and clergyman
* J. M. A.

Ashley, Steven
See McCaig, Donald

Ashmont
See Perry, Joseph Franklin

Ashmore, Lewis
See Raborg, Frederick A[shton], Jr.

Ashmore, Ruth
See Mallon, Isabel Allderdice [Sloan]

Ashton, John [IP]
British author
* [A] Man of Business

Ashton [or Assheton], [Sir] Ralph 15th c. [NPS]
British aristocrat
* [The] Black Knight of Ashton

Ashton, Thomas 1716-1775 [IP]
British clergyman and author
* [A] Late Fellow of King's College, Cambridge
(See also base volume)

Ashworth, T. M. [IP]
American author
* Ouno

Asmodei, Count
See Alfieri, Vittorio Amadeo

Asmodeo
See Sheridan, Richard Brinsley

Aspazija
See Rozenberga, Elza

Asper
See Johnson, Samuel

Aspinall, W. B. [IP]
British author
* [An] Invalid

Aspinwall, James [IP]
British author
* [An] Old Stager

Asplin, William [IP]
British clergyman and author
* [A] Master of Arts of the University of Oxford
* Philalethes Rusticus
* [A] Presbyter of the Church of England
* [A] True Son of the Church of England

Assheton-Craven, Charles Audley [IP]
British clergyman and author
* [A] Gentleman

Assolant, Jean-Baptiste-Alfred 1827-1886 [IP, NPS]
French author
* Alceste
* Alcofribas, le Magicien
(See also base volume)

Astarbe
See D'Aubigne, Francoise

Astarte
See Adams, Ann Olivia

Astell, [Hon.] Edward
See Timbury, Jane

Astell, Mary 1668-1731 [IP]
British author
* [A] Daughter of the Church of England
* [A] Lover of her Sex
* Wotton, William, D.D.

Astiz, Alfredo 20th c.
Argentinian naval officer and military enforcer for the junta
* [The] Blond Angel
* [The] Butcher of Cordoba
* [The] Hawk

Astley, Francis Dukinfield [IP]
British poet
* [An] Admirer of the Fine Arts

Astley, John ?-1595 [NPS]
British courtier, politician, author
* [The] English Xenophon

Astley, William 1855-1911 [DLE1]
Australian journalist and author
* Warung, Price

Aston, Anthony 18th c. [IP]
British actor and playwright
* Medley, Matthew
(See also base volume)

Aston, C. Penrhyn [IP]
British author
* One of Themselves

Aston, Helen
See Jordan, Mrs. Arthur

Aston, W. 18th c. [IP]
British scholar
* Touchstone, Timothy

Astor, Adelaide
See Grossmith, Mrs. George, Jr.

Astra
See Elizabeth

Astroea
See Meehan, Alexander S.

[The] Astronomer Royal
See Airy, [Sir] George Biddell

Atcherley, James [IP]
British educator
* [A] Drapier

Atcheson, Alfred S. [IP]
British clergyman and author
* A. S. A.

Atcheson, Thomas [IP]
American author
* Broad Church

[The] Athenian Bee
See Sophocles

[The] Athenian Bee
See Xenophon

[The] Athenian Sage
See Socrates

Athern, Anna
See Pike, Frances West [Atherton]

Atkins, Anna [IP]
British author
* A. A.

Atkins, Chet 1924- [CR]
American country-western performer
* Guitar, Mister

Atkins, [Arthur] Harold 1910- [CA]
British author
* Jackson, J. P.

Atkinson, D. H.   [IP]
British author
* Odman, Jeremiah
* [An] Old Leeds Cropper

Atkinson, Edward   [IP]
American author
* [A] Cotton Manufacturer
* E. A.

Atkinson, Francis Blake   ?-1930
[DNA]
American journalist and naturalist
* Hawksworth, Hallam

Atkinson, G. W.   [IP]
American author
* One of the Raiders

Atkinson, George Francklin   [IP]
British author
* Our Special Correspondent

Atkinson, Jane   [IP]
British author
* Wren, Jenny

Atkinson, [Sir] Jasper 1790-1856
[IP]
British financier
* I. A.

Atkinson, John   [IP]
British financier
* I. A.

Atkinson, William   [IP]
British author
* [The] Enquirer
* [The] Inquirer

Atkinson, William Walker
1862-1932   [EOP]
American author and editor
* Ramachakra, Yogi

[An] Atlas
See   Garrick, David

[An] Atlas
See   Pitt, William

[The] Atlas of Scotch Antiquaries
See   Chalmers, George

Atlee, Philip
See   Phillips, James Atlee

Atom, Ann
See   Walworth, Jeannette R.

Attenborough, Florence G.   [NPS]
Author
* Chrystabel

Atterbury, Francis 1662-1732   [IP]
British clergyman
* [A] Member of the Lower House
   of Convocation

Atteridge, Andrew Hilliard   [IP]
British author
* A. H. A.

Atterley, Joseph
See   Tucker, George

Atthill, Lombe   [IP]
Irish clergyman
* L. A.

[The] Attila of Authors
See   Scioppius, Gaspar

Attwell, Henry   [IP]
British author
* H. A.

Attwood, J. S.   [IP]
British author
* J. S. A.

Atwater, Frederick Mund 1892-1948
American author and columnist
* Atwater, Richard Tupper
* Riq

Atwater, Richard Tupper
See   Atwater, Frederick Mund

Atwood, A. Watson   [IP]
Author
* Rushton, Wattie

Atwood, Mary Ann 1817-1910
[EOP]
Author
* South, M. A.

Aubert, Jacques 1689-1753   [BBD]
French musician
* [Le] Vieux

Aubrey, John 1626-1697   [NPS]
British antiquary
* [The] Wiltshire Antiquary
(See also base volume)

Aubrey, William 1529-1595   [NPS]
British statesman
* [The] Little Doctor

Aubry, Philippe 1744-1812   [IP]
French poet and translator
* P. C. A.

[An] Auctioneer
See   Robins, George

Audin, J. M. V. 1793-1851   [IP]
French author and historian
* Richard

Audran, Prosper Gabriel
1744-1819   [IP]
French attorney
* P. G. A.

Auger, Louis Simon 1772-1827   [IP]
French critic and journalist
* L. S. A.

Augur
See   Blake, William

Augustinus
See   Maginn, William

Augustus
See   Diocletian [Gauis Aurelius
Valerius Diocletianus]

Augustus
See   George II

Augustus
See   Louis XIV

Augustus
See   Maximian [Marcus Aurelius
Valerius Maximianus]

Auhad al-Din Ali
See   Anvari

Auletes, Grazianus Agricola
See   Pfeiffer, Johann Gregor

Aulnay, Louise d'   [IP]
French author
* Gouraud, Julie

Aunt Charlotte
See   Yonge, Charlotte M.

Aunt Elmina
See   Slenker, Elmina [Drake]

Aunt Mary
See   Low, Mary

Aunt Sue
See   Wright, Sarah Anna

Aurelia
See   Mace, Aurelia Gay

Aurelius
See   Chalmers, George

Aurelius
See   Gardner, John

Aureole
See   Berens, Mrs.

Aureolus, Peter 14th c.   [NPS]
Archbishop of Aix
* Facundus, Doctor
(See also base volume)

**Aurevilly, Leon Louis Frederic Jules,
Barbey d'** 1809- ?   [IP]
French author
* Old Noll

Aus Zwei Welten
See   Elizabeth

Aust, Sarah 1741-1811   [NPS]
Author
* Murray, Hon. Mrs.

Austen, Jane 1775-1817   [IP]
British author
* [A] Lady
(See also base volume)

Austin, Alfred 1835-1913
[DLE1, NPS]
British author, poet, barrister
* Lamia

Austin, Arthur
See   Wilson, John

Austin, George Lowell 1849-1893
[DNA, IP]
American author and physician
* Lyndon, Barry

Austin, Harry   [IP]
British author
* [An] Officer

Austin, Ivers James 1808- ?   [IP]
American attorney
* [A] Member of the Boston Bar

Austin, James Trecothick
1784-1870   [IP]
American attorney
* [A] Citizen of Massachusetts

Austin, Lewis   [IP]
British author
* Daly, Frederic
* Lewis, Augustin

Austin, Mary Therese 1849- ?   [IP]
American author
* Betsy B.

Austin, Stephen
See   Stevens, Austin N[eil]

Austin, William   [IP]
British clergyman
* [A] Presbyter of the Church of
   England

Austin, Wiltshire Stanton, Jr.   [IP]
British author and clergyman
* Dayrell, V.

Austin-Ball, Mrs. T.
Author
* Steele, Alice Garland

Australia
See   Heron, Mrs. Hubert

Australie
See   Heron, Emily [Manning]

Australis
See   Moloney, Patrick

[The] Author
See   Axon, William Edward
Armitage

[The] Autocrat of Strawberry Hill
See   Walpole, Horatio [Fourth Earl
of Orford]

Auton, C.
See   Hoppin, Augustus

Autry, Hank
See   Autry, Melvin

Autry, Melvin 20th c.   [EF]
American football player
* Autry, Hank

Auverney, Victor d'
See   Hugo, Victor Marie

Ava, [Madame] Vera P.
See   Salomen, Edith

Avallone, Michael [Angelo], Jr.
1924-   [TCCM]
American author
* Walker, Max
(See also base volume)

Avalon, Arthur
See   Woodroffe, [Sir] John

Avatar of Vishnuland
See   Kipling, Rudyard

Aveline, Le Sieur
See   Arouet, Francois Marie

Aveling, Edward Bibbins
1851-1898   [PI]
British author, poet, playwright
* May, Kenneth
* Nelson, Alec

Avery, Henry M. 1840?- ?
American author
* Martine, [Maj.] Max
* Mohenesto

Avery, Samuel Putnam 1822-1904
[DNA, IP]
American author
* Slick, Sam, Jr.
* Spavery
(See also base volume)

Avi-Yonah, M[ichael]
See   Buchstab, Michael

Avia
See   Way, Arthur S.

Avicebron 1021?-1058
Spanish poet and philosopher
* Ben Judah, Solomon
* Ibn-Gabirol
(See also base volume)

Avicenna [or Abou-ibn-Sina]
980-1037   [NPS]
Arabian physician and philosopher
* [The] Admirable Crichton of
   Arabia
(See also base volume)

Avilez, Frank 20th c.   [CA]
Criminal
* [The] Black Gloved Rapist

Avnery, Uri
See Ostermann, Uri

Avril, [Baron] Adolphe d' [IP]
French author
* Cyrille

Awl, Roby
See Kirkwood, Robert

Axelrad, Sylvia Brody 1914-   [CA]
American author and psychoanalyst
* Brody, Sylvia

Axon, William Edward Armitage
1846- ?   [IP, NPS]
British bibliographer, journalist,
author
* Armitage, Dudley
* [The] Author
* W. E. A. A.

Ayers, Rose
See Greenwood, Lillian Bethel

Aylett, Richard
See Argall, Richard

Aynge, G. A. [IP]
American poet
* G. A. A.

Ayscough, George Edward ?-1779
[IP]
British army officer and author
* [An] Officer in the Guards

Ayscough, Samuel 1745-1804   [IP]
British clergyman and bibliographer
* S. A.
* Vicar of Cudham

Aytoun, William Edmonstoune
1813-1865   [IP]
Scottish author and poet
* Ane of that Ilk
* [A] Layman of the Church
* W. E. A.
(See also base volume)

Ayxela y Torner, Pedro 1824-1892
[GS]
Spanish bullfighter
* Peroy

Azarias, [Brother]
See Mullaney, Patrick Francis

B

B.
See   Barry, Michael Joseph

B.
See   Battier, Henrietta

B.
See   Broderick, A.

B.
See   Littledale, Richard

B.
See   Morse, Samuel Finley Breese

B. A.
See   Antrobus, Benjamin

B. B.
See   Barton, Bernard

B. B.
See   Javal, Camille

B. B.
See   Oliphant, Carolina [Baroness Nairne]

B. F.
See   Herrick, Edward Claudius

B. H. B.
See   Blacker, Beaver Henry

B. K. P.
See   Peirce, Bradford Kinney

B. M. R.
See   Reed, B. Mitchel

B. McG.
See   Magennis, Bernard

B. T.
See   Littledale, Richard

Baba
See   Muktanada, Swami

Babb, Clement Edwin 1821-1906 [DNA]
American author and clergyman
* Uncle Jesse

Babble, Nicholas, Esq.
See   Long, Edward

Babcock, Nicolas
See   Lewis, Tom

Babe of the Abyss
See   Jones, Charles Stanfeld

[The] Baby Farmer
See   Dyer, Amelia Elizabeth

Baby Peggy
See   Cary, Peggy-Jean Montgomery

Bacchus
See   Hunt, [James Henry] Leigh

[A] Bachelor
See   Allan, James MacGrigor

[A] Bachelor of Arts
See   Marshall, A. J. P.

[A] Bachelor of Divinity
See   Irons, William Josiah

[The] Bachelor Painter
See   Reynolds, [Sir] Joshua

Bacon, Dolores Marbourg
See   Bacon, Mary Schell [Hoke]

Bacon, Francis [First Baron Verulam] 1561-1626   [UH]
British philosopher
* [The] Father of Experimental Philosophy
(See also base volume)

Bacon, Mary Schell [Hoke] 1870-1934   [DNA]
American author and playwright
* Bacon, Dolores Marbourg
* Marbourg, Dolores

Bacon, Nathaniel 1647-1676 [BDSA]
American colonial leader
* [The] Jamestown Rebel

Bacon, Roger 1214?-1294   [NPS]
British philosopher
* Hodge, Father
(See also base volume)

Bacon's Alter Ego
See   Matthew, [Sir] Tobias [or Tobie]

Badcock, John 19th c.   [NPS]
Author
* Hinds, John
(See also base volume)

Badger, Joseph E. 1848-1909
American author
* Beau K.
(See also base volume)

Badger, Miss
Author
* Wild Rose

Baer, Mrs.
American author
* Hill, Kate F.

Baeza, Maria Rosario Pilar Martinez Melina 20th c.   [CR]
Spanish-born singer
* Charo

Bagg, Lyman Hotchkiss 1846-1911 [DNA]
American journalist
* Kron, Karl
(See also base volume)

Bailey, Bill
See   Bailey, Edgar

Bailey, Claron 20th c.   [EF]
American football player
* Bailey, Monk

Bailey, Deford 1899-1982
American country-western performer
* [The] Harmonica Wizard

Bailey, Edgar 20th c.   [EF]
American football player
* Bailey, Bill

Bailey, Florence M.
Author
* Merriam, Florence A.

Bailey, Henry 1815- ?   [IP]
British clergyman and author
* H. B.

Bailey, Monk
See   Bailey, Claron

Bailey, Samuel 1791-1870   [IP]
British author and philosopher
* [An] Egyptian Kafir
* [A] Yorkshire Freeholder
* [A] Younger Brother

Bailey, Thomas   [IP]
British author
* [An] Old Tradesman

Bailey, Una Locke   [IP]
American author
* Locke, Una

Bailey, William [Billy]
See   Wilson, William [Bill]

Baillie, E. C. C.   [IP]
British author and poet
* E. C. C. B.

Baillie, Hugh   [IP]
British jurist and author
* [A] Doctor of Laws

Baillie, Joanna 1762-1851 [IP, NPS]
Scottish playwright and poet
* J. B.
* Shakespeare in Petticoats
(See also base volume)

Bailliere, Jean Baptiste Emile 1831- ?   [IP]
French journalist
* J. B. E. B.

Bailly, Emma Berenger   [IP]
French author
* Chandeneux, Claire de

Baines, Minnie Willis
See   Miller, Minnie [Willis]

Baini, Abbate
See   Baini, Giuseppe

Baini, Giuseppe 1775-1844   [BBD]
Italian author and composer
* Baini, Abbate

[The] Baker
See   Martin, Jack

Baker, [Allen] Albert 1910-   [CA]
American author
* Kane, Jack

Baker, Delphine P.   [IP]
American author
* Delphine

Baker, Edna Rose [Ritchings] 20th c.   [EOP]
Wife of American evangelist, George Baker
* Divine, [Mother]

Baker, Frank
See   Burton, [Sir] Richard Francis

Baker, Geoffrey 14th c.   [NPS]
Chronicler
* Walter of Swinbroke

Baker, George 1874?-1965   [EOP]
American evangelist and cult leader
* Divine, [Major] J.
* God in the Sonship Degree
* [The] Messenger
(See also base volume)

Baker, George Melville 1832-1890 [DNA]
American playwright
* Uno

Baker, Harriette Newell 19th c. [IP]
American author
* Leslie, [Mrs.] Madeline
(See also base volume)

Baker, Henry 1703?-1774   [IP]
British poet and naturalist
* Stonecastle, Henry

Baker, Henry 19th c.   [IP]
British author
* [A] Gentleman Late of the Inner
  Temple

Baker, Henry 19th c.
American author
* Rebak, H.

Baker, [Sir] Henry Williams
1821-1877   [IP]
British clergyman and author
* H. W. B.

Baker, [Sir] James
See   Gay, John

Baker, James Loring   [IP]
American author
* Profit and Loss

Baker, Jimmy 20th c.
American boxer
* Baker, School Boy

Baker, Joseph
See   Boulanger, Joseph

Baker, Karle Wilson 1878- ?
[BDSA]
American writer
* Wilson, Charlotte

Baker, Leonard   [IP]
British author
* Drekab, Maistre

Baker, Mrs. Louis Alien 1858- ?
[DNA, NPS]
American author
* Alien

Baker, Pauline H[alpern] 1941-
[CA]
American author
* Anber, Paul

Baker, Rachel 1794- ?   [EOP]
*Delivered religious discourses while
asleep*
* [The] Sleeping Preacher

Baker, Samuel   [IP]
British author
* [A] Seaman's Friend

Baker, School Boy
See   Baker, Jimmy

Baker, Susan [Catherine] 1942-
[CA]
British author and editor
* Richards, Kay

Baker, T. M.   [IP]
American author
* T. M. B.

Baker, Thomas 1656-1740   [IP]
British antiquary
* [A] Gentleman
(See also base volume)

Baker, Tony
See   Baker, Vernon

Baker, Vernon 20th c.   [EF]
American football player
* Baker, Tony

Baker, William Deal 1812-1876
[DNA]
American author
* Hosmat, Hyton

Baker, William Mumford
1825-1883   [DLE1, DNA]
American author and clergyman
* Harrington, George F.

Bald Coot Bully
See   Alexander I [Aleksandr
Pavlovich]

Balduck, Harriet 19th c.   [HFN]
Author
* Harriet

Baldung, Hans 1470-1545   [NPS]
German painter, engraver, designer
* [The] Green
(See also base volume)

Baldwin, Dick
See   Raborg, Frederick A[shton],
Jr.

Baldwin, James 1841-1925   [SAT]
American author, editor, educator
* Dudley, Robert

Baldwin, Rebecca
See   Chappell, Helen

Bale, John 1495-1563   [DEA]
British author and Bishop of Ossory
* Stalbrydge, Henry
(See also base volume)

Balfour, Blasphemous
See   Balfour, [Sir] James

Balfour, Felix
See   Watts, Phillips

Balfour, Jabez 19th c.   [DI]
British swindler
* [The] Napoleon of Finance

Balfour, [Sir] James ?-1583   [NPS]
Scottish jurist and politician
* Balfour, Blasphemous

Balka, Marie
See   Balkany, Marie [Romoka
Zelinger] de

Balkany, Marie [Romoka Zelinger] de
1930-   [CA]
Rumanian-born author
* Balka, Marie

Ball, Ernest R. 1878-1927   [PAC]
American composer
* [The] American Tosti

Ball, Lucille 1911-   [BP]
American comedienne
* Technicolor Tessie

Ball, William 1751?-1824   [PI]
Irish poet
* W. B.

[The] Ballad-Monger
See   Southey, Robert

Balladino, Antonio
See   Munday, Anthony

Ballantyne, James 1772-1833
[NPS]
Scottish printer
* [The] Jenson of the North
(See also base volume)

Ballantyne, Robert Michael
1825-1894   [NPS, SAT]
Scottish-born author, poet, painter
* Comus

Ballard, Guy W. 1878-1939   [EOP]
*American author and leader of
religious cult*
* King, Godfre Ray

Ballinascorney
See   Rooney, William

Ballista, Gigi
See   Ballista, Luigi

Ballista, Luigi   ?-1980   [FIR]
Italian actor
* Ballista, Gigi

Ballou, Maturin Murray
1820-1895   [DNA]
American-born journalist
* Murray, Lieut.

[A] Ball's Bluff Prisoner
See   Harris, W. C.

Ballyhooley
See   Martin, Robert Jasper

Balsamo, Giuseppe 1743-1795
[EOP]
Italian imposter
* [The] Prince of Quacks
(See also base volume)

Baltrasna
See   Rooney, William

Balucki, Michal 1837-1901
Polish playwright and author
* [The] Father of Polish Bourgeois
  Comedy
(See also base volume)

Balzac, Honore de 1799-1850
[NPS]
French author
* Davin, Felix
* R'hoone, Lord
* Saint Aubin, Horace de
(See also base volume)

Balzac, Jean Louis Guez de
1596?-1655?   [NPS]
French author
* Ogier, Le Prieur
(See also base volume)

Bamfylde, Walter
See   Bevan, Tom

Ban, Eoghan
See   Daly, Eugene P.

Banaszek, Cas
See   Banaszek, Casimir Joseph, II

Banaszek, Casimir Joseph, II 1945-
[FR]
American football player
* Banaszek, Cas

[The] Bandit Queen
See   Starr, [Myra] Belle [Shirley]

Banfield, James 20th c.   [EF]
American football player
* Banfield, Tony

Banfield, Tony
See   Banfield, James

Bangs, John Kendrick 1862-1922
[DLE1]
American author
* Drake, Gaston V.
* Gastit, Horace Dodd
* Gray, Blakeney
* Jake, T. C. S.
* Jenkins, Wilberforce
* Kendrick, John
* Mann, A. Sufferan
* Morley, Arthur Spencer
* Podmore, Periwinkle
* Smith, T. Carlyle
(See also base volume)

Banim, John 1798-1842   [DLE1]
Irish poet, playwright, author
* [The] O'Hara Family [joint
  pseudonym with Michael Banim;
  also used alone]
(See also base volume)

Banim, Michael, Jr. 1796-1874
[DLE1]
British author
* [The] O'Hara Family [joint
  pseudonym with John Banim; also
  used alone]
(See also base volume)

Banks, Archibald
See   Crawfurd, Oswald John
Frederick

Banks, [Sir] Joseph 1743-1820
[NPS]
President of the Royal Society
* [The] Knight of Soho Square

Banks, Nancy Huston   [NPS]
Author
* Preston, George

Banks, Sara [Jeanne Gordon Harrell]
1937-   [SAT]
American author
* Harrell, Sara Gordon

Bannville, Fitzstewart
See   Blacker, [Colonel] William

Bantley, Doctor
See   Arbuthnot, John

Bantock, Miles
See   Reddall, Henry Frederick

**Banzu-Mohr-ar-Chat [Great Lady of
the Cat]**
See   Elizabeth

Bapak [Father]
See   Subuh, Muhammad

Baptist
See   O'Brien, Ricard Baptist

Baptist, R. Hernekin
See   Lewis, Ethelreda

Baptiste
See   Anet, Jean-Baptiste

[A] Barbadoes Planter
See   Ashley, John

[Une] Barbare
See   Colban, Marie Sophie
[Schmidt

Barbauld, Anna Letitia 1743-1825
[DEA]
British author
* A. L. B.
* Short, Bob

[A] Barber
See   Moser, Joseph

Barberi, Maria 1855- ?   [LFW]
American murderer
* [The] Tombs Angel

[El] Barbero [The Barber]
See   Pastor, Juan

Barbey d'Aurevilly, Jules Amedee
1808-1889
French author and critic
* [The] High Constable of Letters

Barbour, A. Maynard
See   Barbour, Anna May

Barbour, Anna May ?-1941 [DNA]
American author
* Barbour, A. Maynard

Barclay, John 1582-1621 [DEA]
British author
* Euphormio Lusininus
* Polienus Rhodiensis

[The] Bard of all Time
See Shakespeare, William

[The] Bard of Ballydine
See Larkin, Thomas

[The] Bard of Chivalry
See Tasso, Torquato

[The] Bard of Corsair
See Byron, George Gordon Noel

[The] Bard of Dunclug
See Herbison, David

[The] Bard of Macroom
See Conolly, James

[The] Bard of Night
See Young, Edward

[The] Bard of Penrhyn
See Morris, [Sir] Lewis

[The] Bard of the Bay
See Southey, Robert

[The] Bard of the Dales
See Castillo, John

[The] Bard of the North
See Beattie, James

[The] Bard of Thomond
See Hogan, Michael

[The] Bard of Tyrone
See Devine, James

Bardd Alaw [Master of Song]
See Parry, John

Barebones, Caustic
See Bridges, Thomas

Barendrecht, Cor W. 1934- [MA]
Dutch-born author and poet
* Brecht, William

Barham, Francis Foster 1808-1871
[NPS]
Theologian
* [The] Alist

Barham, Richard Harris
1788-1845 [WGT]
British author and poet
* Scriblerus Oxoniensis
(See also base volume)

Baring, Evelyn [First Earl of Cromer]
1841-1917
British statesman, diplomat, scholar
* [The] Maker of Modern Egypt

Barkley, Clint 19th c. [EWG]
American gunfighter
* Bowen, Bill

Barn Owl
See Howells, Roscoe

Barnard, A. M.
See Alcott, Louisa May

Barnard, Charles 1838-1920
[DNA]
American journalist and playwright
* Gilman, Maria
* Kingsford, Jane

Barnard, Charles 20th c. [EF]
American football player
* Barnard, Hap

Barnard, Hap
See Barnard, Charles

Barnard, Mrs. Charles 1830-1869
[PI]
Irish musician and songwriter
* Claribel?

Barnaval, Louis
See De Kay, Charles

Barnayay, Istvan 20th c. [DI]
Hungarian-born murderer
* Bradley, Stephen

Barnes, Al
See Barnes, Hally

Barnes, Hally 1904- [MA]
American author
* Barnes, Al

Barnes, Jane
See Casey, Jane Barnes

Barnes, Piggy
See Barnes, Walter

Barnes, Seab
See Barnes, Seaborn

Barnes, Seaborn ?-1878 [EWG]
American gunfighter
* Barnes, Seab
* Nubbins Colt

Barnes, Walter 20th c. [EF]
American football player
* Barnes, Piggy

Barnfield, Barney
See Barnfield, Joseph

Barnfield, Joseph 20th c. [DI]
American robber
* Barnfield, Barney

Barnivelt, Esdras
See Pope, Alexander

Baronio, Cesare 1538-1607
Italian historian
* [The] Father of Ecclesiastical
History

Barr, Donald
See Barrett, Charles Leslie

Barra, Gougane
See Ryan, P. J.

Barragan [Coarse Wool Coat]
See Santiago, Isidro

Barreno, Maria Isabel
See Martins, Maria Isabel Barreno
de Faria

Barrer, Gertrude
See Barrer-Russell, Gertrude

Barrer-Russell, Gertrude 1921-
[SAT]
American author and illustrator
* Barrer, Gertrude

Barrett, Aston 20th c. [CMA]
Musician
* Barrett, Family Man

Barrett, Charles Leslie 1879- ?
[DLE1]
Australian author
* Barr, Donald

Barrett, Eaton Stannard
1785-1820 [PI]
Irish poet and playwright
* Hogg, Cervantes
(See also base volume)

Barrett, Family Man
See Barrett, Aston

Barrett, [Rev.] J.
See Maginn, William

[A] Barrister
See Byles, [Sir] John Barnard

[A] Barrister
See Coleridge, [Sir] John Taylor

[A] Barrister
See Dillon, [Sir] John Joseph

[A] Barrister
See Fenton, Richard

[A] Barrister
See Field, Barron

[A] Barrister
See Harris, Richard

[A] Barrister
See Johnson, William

[A] Barrister
See Lawrence, Frederick

[A] Barrister
See Mackintosh, [Sir] James

Barritt, Frances Fuller 1826-1902
American author
* Fane, Florence

Barron, Alfred [IP]
American author and editor
* Q.

Barrow, Albert Stewart [ICB]
Author
* Sabretache

Barrow, Buck
See Barrow, Ivan Marvin

Barrow, Henry ?-1593 [NPS]
Puritan pamphleteer
* Marprelate, Martin

Barrow, Ivan Marvin 20th c. [DI]
American murderer and robber
* Barrow, Buck

Barrow, John 19th c. [IP]
Author
* [A] Private of the 38th Artists'
and Member of the Alpine Club

Barrow, John 19th c. [IP]
British author
* J. B.

Barrow, Rhoda
See Lederer, Rhoda Catharine
[Kitto]

Barry, Eleanor
See Pottasch, Eleanor

Barry, Hangman
See Barry, James

Barry, James [BL]
Author
* Barry, Hangman

Barry, Joseph [IP]
American author
* Josephus, Jr.

Barry, Lod
See Barry, Lodowick

Barry, Lodowick 17th c. [PI]
Irish playwright
* Barry, Lod

Barry, Michael Joseph 1817-1889
[PI]
Irish poet
* B.
* Beta
* Brutus
* De Garcon, Bouillon
* M. J. B.

Barry, Red
See De Acosta, Donald Barry

Barry, Robertine 1866-1910 [DNA]
Canadian-born journalist
* Francaise

Barry, William Whittaker [IP]
British barrister and author
* [An] Englishman

[The] Barrymore of the Bible
See Graham, William Franklin
[Billy]

Barstow, Amos C. [IP]
American manufacturer and author
* A. C. B.

**Barstow, Emma Magdalena Rosalina
Marie Josepha Barbara** 1865-1947
[CA]
Hungarian-born author
* Orczy, Emmuska
(See also base volume)

Bart
See Bartholomew, Charles L.

Barter, Richard 1834-1859 [BLB]
British-born robber
* Rattlesnake Dick

Barth, Alan
See Lauchheimer, Alan

Barth, Karl 1886-1968
Swiss theologian
* [The] Red Pastor

Barthelemy, Jean Jacques
1716-1795 [IP]
French scholar
* Anacharsis

Bartholomew, Charles L.
Author
* Bart

Bartlett, Bailey 1750-1830 [IP]
American patriot and author
* [A] Layman

Bartlett, David W. 1828- ? [IP]
American journalist
* D. W. B.
* Spectator
(See also base volume)

Bartlett, John [IP]
American publisher and bookseller
* J. B.
* Practitioner of More Than Fifty
Years' Experience in the Art of
Angling

Bartlett, M. R. [IP]
American author
* Pippin, Parley

Bartol, Cyrus Augustus 19th c. [IP]
American clergyman and author
* [A] Spectator

Barton, Bernard 1784-1849   [IP]
British poet
* B. B.
(See also base volume)

Barton, Caroline M.
See Brame, Charlotte M.

Barton, Evelyn 19th c.   [IP]
American clergyman and author
* E. B.

Barton, Fanny M.
See Butts, Mrs. M. F.

Barton, Samuel 19th c.   [ESF]
American author and politician
* Roker, A. B.

Barton, William   [IP]
American attorney and author
* [An] American

Barton, William 1603?-1678   [PI]
Irish translator and editor
* W. B.

Barty, James S.   [IP]
Scottish clergyman and author
* Plough, Peter

Barzilauskas, Francis 20th c.   [EF]
American football player
* Barzilauskas, Fritz

Barzilauskas, Fritz
See Barzilauskas, Francis

[A] Base Mechanic Wretch
See Walsh, Michael Paul

Bash, Mrs. Louis H.
Author
* Runkle, Bertha

Basie, William 1904?-   [CR]
American jazz musician
* [The] Jump King
(See also base volume)

Basil
See King, Richard Ashe

Basile, Giambattista 1575-1632
Italian poet
* Abbattutis, Giam Alesio

Basilicus
See Way, Lewis

Baskoff, Ivan
See Meilhac, Henri

Basselin, Olivier ?-1418   [NPS]
French poet
* [The] Father of Bacchanalian
  Poetry in France
* [The] French Drunken Barnaby
* [Le] Pere Joyeux du Vaudeville
(See also base volume)

Basset, Adrien Charles Alexandre
1822-1869   [IP]
French author
* Newil, Charles

Bassett, Charles E.
*American law officer and saloon
operator*
* Bassett, Senator

Bassett, Senator
See Bassett, Charles E.

Bastardella
See Agujari, Lucrezia

Baste, Eugene Pierre 19th c.   [IP]
French playwright
* Grange, Eugene

Bastide, Jenny 1792-1854   [IP]
French author and poet
* Bodin, Camille
(See also base volume)

Bateman, Mary 1768-1809   [LFW]
British murderer
* [The] Yorkshire Witch

[The] Bath Butcher
See Martin, Sam

Bath Laureat
See Anstey, Christopher

Batkins, Jefferson Scattering
See Jones, Joseph Stevens

Battersby, Henry Francis Prevost
1862- ?   [PI]
Irish poet
* Prevost, Francis

Battier, Henrietta ?-1813   [PI]
Irish poet
* B.
* H. B.
* [A] Lady
* Laurel, Countess
* Pindar, Pat

Bauduc, R.
See Segre, Dan V[ittorio]

Bauer, Wright
See Hobart, George Vere

Bauerle, Adolf 1786-1859   [NPS]
Austrian playwright and author
* Horn, Otto

Bausman, Frederick 1861-1931
[DNA]
American author
* Aix

[The] Bavarian Herodotus
See Turmair [or Thurmayr],
Johannes

Bavius
See Martyn, John

Bawel, Bibbles
See Bawel, Edward

Bawel, Edward 20th c.   [EF]
American football player
* Bawel, Bibbles

Bawn, Owen
See Daly, Eugene P.

Baxter, Richard 1615-1691   [NPS]
British author and scholar
* Fullwood, Francis
(See also base volume)

Baxter, W. G.
See Baxter, William Giles

Baxter, William Giles 1856-1888
[WEC]
British cartoonist
* Baxter, W. G.

Bayer, Johann 1572?-1660   [NPS]
German astronomer and clergyman
* [The] Protestant's Mouthpiece

Bayer, Oliver Weld
See Perry, Eleanor

Bayes the Younger
See Rowe, Nicholas

Bayle, Mr.
See Penneck, Henry

Bayle, Monsieur
See Tyssot de Patot, Simon

Baylebridge, William
See Blocksidge, Charles William

Bayley, Alphabet
See Bayley, Frederick W. N.

Bayley, Frederick W. N.
1807?-1852   [PI]
Irish poet
* Bayley, Alphabet

Bayley, [Sir] John 1763-1841
[HFN]
British author
* [A] Layman
* [A] Member of the Established
  Church

Beach, Charles
See Reid, [Thomas] Mayne

Beale, Betty 20th c.   [CR]
American columnist
* [The] High Priestess of
  Washington Society

Bean, Bubba
See Bean, Ernst Ray

Bean, Ernst Ray 1954-   [FR]
American football player
* Bean, Bubba

Beane, Sandy
See Beane, Sawney

Beane, Sawney ?-1435   [DI]
Scottish murderer and bandit
* Beane, Sandy

[The] Bear Leader
See Gifford, William

Bear River Tom
See Smith, Thomas J.

[The] Bearcat
See Starr, Henry

Beard, Edward T. 1828?-1873
[EWG]
American gunfighter
* Beard, Red

Beard, Red
See Beard, Edward T.

Beardie, Earl
See Lindsay, Alexander

Beardsley, Aubrey Vincent
1872-1898   [DLE1]
British artist
* A. B.

Beasley, Frederick Williamson
1808-1878   [DNA]
American author
* Almore, Caspar

[The] Beast of Belsen
See Grese, Irma

[The] Beast of the Black Forest
See Pommerencke, Heinrich

Beatrice
See Manning, Anne

Beattie, James 1735-1803   [NPS]
Scottish author and poet
* [The] Bard of the North

Beau K.
See Badger, Joseph E.

Beauchamp, Philip
See Grote, George

Beaude, Henri 1870-1930   [DNA]
*Canadian-born author and
clergyman*
* D'Arles, Henri

Beaujolais
See Busk, Hans

Beaulieu, Marie-Desire
See Martin-Beaulieu, Marie Desire

Beaumont, Averil
See Hunt, Margaret

Beaumont, Thomas Wentworth 19th
c.   [PI]
Irish poet
* T. W. B.

[The] Beautie of our Tongue
See Chaucer, Geoffrey

[The] Beaver
See Aitken, William Maxwell
[First Baron Beaverbrook]

**Beaverbrook, William Maxwell
Aitken**
See Aitken, William Maxwell
[First Baron Beaverbrook]

Beccaria Anglicus
See Wright, Richard

Bechtol, Hub
See Bechtol, Hubert

Bechtol, Hubert 20th c.   [EF]
American football player
* Bechtol, Hub

Beck, Doc
See Beck, Earl Clifton

Beck, Earl Clifton 1891-1977   [MA]
American author
* Beck, Doc

Beck, Ellen   [PI]
Irish poet
* Rock, Magdalen

Becke, George Lewis 1855-1913
[DLE1]
Australian author
* Becke, Louis

Becke, Louis
See Becke, George Lewis

Becker, Charles ?-1912   [LFW]
American police officer
* [The] Crookedest Cop in New
  York

Beckford, Fonthill
See Beckford, William

Beckford, William 1759-1844
[DLE1, NPS, PPN]
British author
* Beckford, Fonthill
* Jenks, Jacquetta Agneta Mariana
* Marlow, [Lady] Harriet
* Melville, Lewis
* Vathek

Beckwith, Julia Catherine [Hart]
1796-1867   [DLE1]
Canadian author
* [An] American

Becky
See Wells, Mary

[The] Bee of Athens
See Sophocles

[The] Bee of Athens
See Xenophon

Beechcroft, William
See   Hallstead, William F[inn III]

[A] Beef Eater
See   Vasey, George

Beefeater, Domestic Chaplain to Fill Pots
See   Allan, John

Beers, Ethelinda [Elliot] 1827-1897
[DNA]
American author
* Lynn, Ethel
(See also base volume)

Beesley, H. Brent 1946?-
American attorney and businessman
* Doom, Dr.

[The] Beethoven of the Flute
See   Kuhlau, Friedrich D. R.

Begley, W. 20th c.   [NPS]
Author
* [A] Cambridge Graduate

Behman, Bull
See   Behman, Russell

Behman, Russell 20th c.   [EF]
American football player
* Behman, Bull

Beizer, Boris 1934-   [CA]
Belgian-born American author and engineer
* Shedley, Ethan I.

Beland, Lucy 1871-1941   [LFW]
American narcotics peddlar
* Beland, Ma

Beland, Ma
See   Beland, Lucy

Belaney, Archibald Stansfeld 1888-1938   [SAT]
Canadian author and lecturer
* Wa-sha-quon-asin
(See also base volume)

Belaney, George Stansfeld 1888-1938   [DLE1]
Canadian author and naturalist
* Grey Owl

Belani, H. E. R.
See   Haeberlin, Karl Ludwig

Belasco, David 1839-1893   [JL]
British actor
* James, David

Belcher, James 1781-1811   [SG]
British boxer
* [The] Appollo of the Ring
(See also base volume)

Belcher, Supply 1751-1836   [BBD]
American hymn writer
* [The] Handel of Maine

Belden, Bunny
See   Belden, Charles

Belden, Charles 20th c.   [EF]
American football player
* Belden, Bunny

Belden, Gail
See   Belden, Louise Conway

Belden, Louise Conway 1910-   [CA]
American author and historian
* Belden, Gail

Beldham, Billy   [NN]
Cricketer
* Beldham, Silver Billy

Beldham, Silver Billy
See   Beldham, Billy

[The] Belfast Man
See   Davis, Francis

[A] Belfast Student
See   Scott, Thomas Hamilton Maxwell

Belfour, Hugo John 1802-1827
[NPS, WGT]
Clergyman and poet
* Dorset, St. John

Belfour, Mrs.
See   Bradshaigh, Lady

Bell, Ernest
See   Swales, Susan Matilda [Bradshaw]

Bell, J. Cawdor
See   Campbell, John

Bell, J. Freeman
See   Zangwill, Israel

Bell, John Jay 1871-1934   [NPS]
Author
* J. J. B.
(See also base volume)

Bell, Lilian
See   Bogue, Mrs. Arthur Hoyt

Bell, Mrs. Martin
See   Martin, Mrs. Bell

Bell, Nancy R. E. [Meugens] 19th c.
[IP]
British artist and author
* D'Anvers, N.

Bell, Paul
See   Chorley, Henry Fothergill

Bell, Robert Stanley Warren 1871-1921   [SAT]
British author
* Old Fag
(See also base volume)

Bell, Steve
See   Schmock, Helen H.

Bell, Theo
See   Bell, Theopolis

Bell, Theopolis 1953-   [FR]
American football player
* Bell, Theo

Bell, Thomas   [IP]
Scottish poet
* [A] Rhymer

Bell, Tom
See   Hodges, Thomas

Bell, W. L. D.
See   Mencken, Henry Louis

Bell, William 1732-1816   [IP]
British clergyman and author
* Ponder, [Rev.] Peter

Bellak, James Blumtal   [IP]
Composer and author
* Blumtal, James

Bellamy, Atwood C.
See   Mencken, Henry Louis

Bellaw, Americus Wellington 1842- ?
American author and poet
* Jot, Joe, Jr.
* King, Jo
* Nuff, Noah
* Shingle, Solomon?

Bellaw, Americus Wellington
(Continued)
* Whitehorn, Washington

[The] Belle of the Daltons'
See   Ouick, Florence

Bellem, Robert Leslie 1902-1968
[TCCM]
American author
* Charles, Franklin [joint pseudonym with Cleve F(ranklin) Adams]
* Saxon, John A.

Bellemane, Eugene Louis Gabriel de Ferry de 19th c.   [IP]
French author
* Ferry, Gabriel

Bellett, John George   [IP]
Author
* J. G. B.

Belli, Melvin M[ouron] 1907-
[CA, CR]
American attorney
* [The] King of Torts

Bello, Francesco 15th c.   [NPS]
Italian poet
* [The] Blind Poet
(See also base volume)

Belloc, [Joseph] Hilary [Pierre] 1870-1953   [NPS, PPN]
British author
* Chesterbelloc [joint pseudonym with Gilbert Keith Chesterton]
* H. B.
(See also base volume)

Bellon, Manuel 17th c.   [GS]
Spanish bullfighter
* [El] Africano [The African]

Bellows, John 1831- ?   [IP]
British printer and publisher
* J. B.

Belmontet, Louis 1799-1879   [NPS]
French author
* Alceste

Beloe, William 1756-1817   [IP]
British author
* [A] Sexagenarian

Belsham, Thomas 1750-1829   [IP]
British clergyman and author
* T. B.

Beltz, George Frederick ?-1842
[IP]
British author
* L.

Belzebub
See   Bourn, Samuel

Bembury, Henry William 1750-1811   [NPS]
Artist and caricaturist
* Gambado, Geoffrey

Ben-Ahmed, Mohammed   [EOP]
Arabian astrologer
* Abou Ryhan

Ben Judah, Solomon
See   Avicebron

Ben Saddi, Nathan
See   Dodsley, Robert

Ben Sidonia
See   Disraeli, Benjamin

Ben Uzair, Salem
See   Horne, Richard Henry

Benauly [joint pseudonym with Benjamin Abbott and Lyman Abbott]
See   Abbott, Austin

Benauly [joint pseudonym with Austin Abbott and Lyman Abbott]
See   Abbott, Benjamin

Benauly [joint pseudonym with Austin Abbott and Benjamin Abbott]
See   Abbott, Lyman

Benchley, Robert [Charles] 1889-1945   [CA]
American author, actor, humorist
* Fawkes, Guy

Bend Or
See   Westminster, Duke of

Bendbow, Hesper
See   Archer, George W.

Bender, Horace
See   Greenough, Horatio

Bendo, Alexander
See   Carr, Robert

Benedict, David 1778-1874   [IP]
American clergyman and author
* John of Enon

Benedict, Hester A.
See   Dickinson, Mrs. T. P.

Benedict, Ruth 1887-1948
American anthropologist and poet
* Singleton, Anne

Benefice
See   Worley, Frederick U.

Benezet, Anthony 1713-1784   [IP]
American author
* [A] Farmer
* [A] Lover of Mankind

[A] Bengal Civilian
See   Edwards, William

[The] Bengal Shelley
See   Thakura, Ravindranatha

Bengo, John   [IP]
Scottish poet and engraver
* [An] Artist

Bengough, J. D.   [IP]
Canadian author
* Grip

Benham, Daniel   [IP]
British author
* D. B.

Benham, George Chittenden   [IP]
Author
* [A] Victim

Benjamin, Elizabeth Dundas [Bedell] ?-1890   [DNA]
American author
* Ray, Agnes

Benjamin, Park 1809-1864   [IP]
American poet
* Member of the Class of '67
(See also base volume)

Benjamin the Florentine
See   Peirce, Benjamin

Benjie
See   Neuburg, Victor [Benjamin]

Benkert, Heinie
See Benkert, Henry

Benkert, Henry 20th c. [EF]
American football player
* Benkert, Heinie

Benn, Anthony Wedgwood 1925-
[NN]
British government official
* Wedgie

Benn, Mary 19th c. [PI]
Irish poet
* Wilhelm

Bennet, H., M.A.
See Pinkerton, John

Bennet, Philip [IP]
British poet
* [A] Gentleman of Cambridge

Bennet, Theodore 1841-1886
[BBD]
French musician and composer
* Ritter, Theodore

Bennett, [Charles Henry] Allan
1872-1923 [EOP]
British occultist and author
* Bhikku Ananda Metteva [Bliss of
   Loving Kindness]
* Frater Iehi Aour [Let there be
   Light]

Bennett, Charles 1854- ? [IP]
British author
* Daddow, Daniel

Bennett, Charles Henry 19th c. [IP]
British artist
* [The] Owl?

Bennett, J. 19th c. [IP]
British author
* [A] Detective

Bennett, J. W. 19th c. [IP]
British author
* [A] Fellow of the Linnaean and
   Horticultural Societies

Bennett, John [IP, NPS]
British author
* Parley, Peter

Bennett, Lonnie [NN]
Boxer
* [The] Magic Man

Bennett, M., Jr. [IP]
Author
* Persimmons

Bennett, Mary E. 19th c. [IP]
American poet
* Campbell, Mary
* M. E. B.
* Mel, Mary

Bennett, William 19th c. [IP]
British author
* W. B.

Bennett, William James 19th c.
[IP]
British clergyman and author
* [The] Vicar of Frome-Selwood
* W. J. E. B.

Bensen, Donald R. 1927- [CA]
American author and editor
* Flynn, Jackson
* Masters, Zeke
* Thatcher, Julia

Benson, Arthur Christopher
1862-1925 [DEA, DLE1, NPS]
British author
* Carr, Christopher
* H. L. G.
* T. B.
(See also base volume)

Benson, Carl
See Benson, Charles

Benson, Charles 1797-1880 [PI]
Irish poet
* Benson, Carl

Benson, Edgeworth
See Scott, John

Benson, Edward Frederic
1867-1940 [DLE1]
British author
* Dilly, Tante
(See also base volume)

Benson, Eugene 1839-1908 [DNA]
American-born author and painter
* Fleming, George

Benson, Janie [Ollivar] [IP]
American poet
* L'Inconnue

Benson, Rachel
See Jowitt, Deborah

Benson, Robby
See Segal, Robert

Bentham, Edward 1707-1776 [IP]
British clergyman and author
* E. B.
* [A] Tutor and Fellow of a College
   in Oxford

Bentham, Jeremy 1748-1832 [NPS]
British jurist and philosopher
* Jerry the Old Screw
(See also base volume)

Bentkowski, Sophie
See Lavritch, Sophie Bentkowski

Bentkowski-Lavritch, Sonia
See Lavritch, Sophie Bentkowski

Beraud, Marthe 20th c. [EOP]
Claimed to possess psychic powers
* Eva C

Berens, Mrs. [NPS]
Author
* Aureole

Beresford, Hamilton Sydney 19th
c. [PI]
Irish poet
* Beresford, J.
* Ignoto Secondo

Beresford, J.
See Beresford, Hamilton Sydney

Beresford, William 1796?-1876
[PI]
Irish poet
* Magrath, Peter
* O'Sullivan, Denis Barrington

Bereton, Ford
See Crockett, Samuel Rutherford

Berger, Siegfried
See Chelius, Oskar von

Bergerat, Auguste Emile 1845- ?
[NPS]
*French journalist, author,
playwright*
* Caliban

**Berigard [or Beauregard], Claude
Guillermet de** 1578?-1664 [EOP]
French author and alchemist
* Berigard of Pisa

Berigard of Pisa
See Berigard [or Beauregard],
Claude Guillermet de

Berington, Simon 1680-1755
[WGT]
Author
* Di Lucca, [Signor] Gaudentio

Berintho
See Roberthin, Robert

Berkley, [Mrs.] Helen
See Ritchie, Anna Cora [Ogden
Mowatt]

Berlijn, Anton
See Wolf, Aron

Berlyn, Mrs. A. [NPS]
Journalist and author
* Ambrosia

Bernard, Camille
See Rattazzi, [Princess] Marie
Studolmine Bonaparte

Bernard, Jay
See Sawkins, Raymond H[arold]

Bernard, Pierre
See Gonthier, Pierre Theophile

Bernard, Pierre 20th c. [EOP]
American leader of yoga cult
* Oom the Omnipotent
* P. A.

Bernardi, Francesco 1680?-1750?
[BBD]
Italian opera singer
* Senesino, Francesco

Bernardo
See Haslewood, Joseph

Bernardo di Steffanino Murer
See Bernhard der Deutsche

Bernards, Dene
See Sheehan, D. B.

Berners, Juliana 1388?-1486 [NPS]
British writer
* Another Diana

Bernhard der Deutsche ?-1459
[BBD]
*German musician and reputed
inventor of organ pedals*
* Bernardo di Steffanino Murer

Bernhardt, M. A.
See Bernhardt, Marcia A.

Bernhardt, Marcia A. 1926- [MA]
American author
* Bernhardt, M. A.

[Il] Bernia
See Teluccini, Mario

Bernstein, Gerry 1927- [CA]
American author
* Morrison, G. F.

Berquin, Arnaud 1749?-1791
[NPS]
French author
* [The] Friend of Children
(See also base volume)

Berrien, John MacPherson
1781-1856 [BDSA]
American author, statesman, jurist
* [The] American Cicero

**Berry, Charles Edward Anderson
[Chuck]** 1926- [CMA]
*American singer, musician,
songwriter*
* [The] Father of Rock 'n' Roll

Bertall
See Arnoux, Charles Albert d'

Berthome du Lignon 16th c. [EOP]
French sorcerer
* Champagnat

Bertin, Rose
See Laurent, Marie-Jeanne

Bertini, Henri [-Jerome] 1798-1876
[BBD]
British-born musician and composer
* Bertini le Jeune

Bertini le Jeune
See Bertini, Henri [-Jerome]

Bertolotti, Gasparo 1540-1609
[BBD]
Italian musical instrument maker
* Gasparo da Salo

Besant, [Sir] Walter 1836-1901
[DEA, NPS]
British author
* Maurice, Walter
* W. B.

Beschius, C. J. [ICB]
Author
* Goosequill, Grey

Bessiere, Richard [WGT]
French author
* Richard-Bessiere, F. [joint
   pseudonym with Francois
   Richard]

[The] Best of Cut-Throats
See Wellesley, Arthur

[The] Best Vitruvius
See Congreve, William

Beta
See Barry, Michael Joseph

Beta
See Brown, Thomas Edward

Beta
See Hodges, John Frederick

Betsy B.
See Austin, Mary Therese

Betterton, Thomas 1635-1710
[NPS]
British actor
* [The] English Roscius
(See also base volume)

Bevan, Aneurin 1897-1960 [PPN]
British statesman and author
* Celticus
* Nye

Bevan, Tom 1868- ? [YAB]
Welsh author and editor
* Bamfylde, Walter

Bevans, Neile
See Van Slingerland, Nellie
Bingham

Bhikku Ananda Metteva [Bliss of Loving Kindness]
See Bennett, [Charles Henry] Allan

[The] Bibliomaniacal Hercules
See Mordaunt, Clayton

Bibliotheca Ambulans
See Hales, John

Bickerstaff, Isaac
See West, Benjamin

Bickerstaff, Isaac, Esq.
See Addison, Joseph

[The] Bicorned Lord
See Alexander III

Biden, Edmond P. 1898-1959
American writer and director
* [The] Toscanini of the Pratfall
(See also base volume)

Bidpai [or Pilpay] 3rd c. BC [NPS]
Indian author
* [The] Aesop of India
* [The] Indian Aesop

Bidwell, Austin 1847?- ? [DI]
American swindler
* Warren, Frederick Albert

Bierce, Ambrose 1842-1914?
American author
* Bierce, Bitter
(See also base volume)

Bierce, Bitter
See Bierce, Ambrose

Big Ben Brain
See Brain, Benjamin

[The] Big Bomber Boy
See Symington, Stuart

[The] Big Indian
See Olinger, Robert A.

Big O
See O'Connell, Daniel

Big Steve Long
See Long, Steve

Bignon, Jean Paul 1662-1743
[SFL, WGT]
French author
* Hatchett, William
* Sandisson, Mr. de

Bigod, Ralph
See Fenwick, John Ralph

Bigorre, L'Abbe
See Arouet, Francois Marie

Bill the Butcher
See Poole, William

Bill the Jockey
See Morgan, Daniel

Billings, Karla Margaret Crosier
1938- [CA]
American author and poet
* Andersdatter, Karla M[argaret]
* Margaret, Karla

Billion-Dollar Bill
See Proxmire, [Edward] William

Billy Frank
See Graham, William Franklin
[Billy]

Billy the Kid
See Claiborne, William F.

Billy White Shoes
See Johnson, William Arthur

Bingfield, William, Esq.
See Paltock, Robert

Binney, Thomas 1798-1874 [NPS]
Clergyman
* Search, John

Binstead, Arthur M. [NPS]
Author
* Pitcher

Birch, [Rev.] Bushby
See Thornton, Bonnell

[A] Bird at Bromsgrove
See Crane, John

Bird, Frederic Mayer 1838-1908
[DNA]
American author, clergyman, educator
* Timsol, Robert

Bird, Mary Page 1866- ? [BDSA]
American writer and poet
* Christian, Neil

[The] Bishop
See Wilson, Daniel

Bishop, Bertha Thorne
See Rymer, James Malcolm

Bishop, Erwin 20th c. [EF]
American football player
* Bishop, Sonny

Bishop, George Archibald
See Crowley, Edward Alexander

[The] Bishop of Hell
See Gaynham [or Garnham], Dr.

Bishop of Natal
See Colenso, John William

[The] Bishop of Spiritualism
See Morse, J. J.

Bishop, Sonny
See Bishop, Erwin

[The] Bitch of Buchenwald
See Koch, Ilse

Bitter Creek Newcomb
See Newcomb, George

Bitzius, Albert 1797-1854 [SFL]
Author
* Gotthelf, Jeremias

Bixby, John Munson 1800-1876
[DNA]
American author and attorney
* Grayson, E.

[The] Black
See Fulk III

Black
See White, Patrick F.

Black Bart
See Boles, Charles E.

Black Charlie
See Napier, [Sir] Charles

[The] Black Diamond
See Cribb, Tom

[The] Black Diamond
See Ward, Jem

Black Dick Howe
See Howe, Richard

[The] Black Douglas
See Douglas, James

[Th] Black Douglas
See Douglas, William

Black Faced Charlie
See Bryant, Charles

[The] Black Gloved Rapist
See Avilez, Frank

[The] Black Hussar of Literature
See Scott, [Sir] Walter

Black, Ishi
See Gibson, Walter B[rown]

Black, Ivory
See Janvier, Thomas A.

Black Jack
See Kemble, John Philip

Black Jack Christian
See Christian, Will

Black Jack Logan
See Logan, John Alexander

Black, Jonathan
See Von Block, Bela

[The] Black Knight of Ashton
See Ashton [or Assheton], [Sir] Ralph

[The] Black Knight of the Fairways
See Player, Gary

Black Mike Howe
See Howe, Michael

Black, Montgomery
See Holden, [Willis] Sprague

[The] Black Mouthed Zoilus
See Milton, John

[The] Black Napoleon
See Musquito

[The] Black Northern
See Duffy, [Sir] Charles Gavan

[The] Black Panther
See Nappey, Donald

Black, Paul
See Nash, G. Murray

[The] Black Pope
See LaVey, Anton Szandor

Black Tom Fairfax
See Fairfax, Thomas [Third Baron Fairfax]

Black Tom Tyrant
See Wentworth, [Sir] Thomas [First Earl of Stafford]

Black, William
See Longley, William Preston

[The] Black Wonder
See Jones, Charley

[The] Blackbird
See Charles II

[The] Blackbird
See Southey, Robert

[The] Blackbirdy
See Turner, Joseph Mallord William

Blackburn, Douglas 1857-1916
[DLE1]
South African author and journalist
* Sard Erasmus

Blackburn, J. B. [IP]
British author
* J. B.

Blacker, Beaver Henry 19th c. [IP]
British clergyman and author
* B. H. B.

Blacker, [Colonel] William
1777-1855 [PI]
Irish poet
* Bannville, Fitzstewart

Blackham, George E. [IP]
American physician and author
* Cyclos

Blackmar, A. E.
See Blackmar, Armand Edward

Blackmar, Armand Edward
1826-1888 [DAM]
American composer and music publisher
* Blackmar, A. E.
* [The] Voice of the South

Blackmore, [Sir] Richard
1650-1729 [NPS]
British physician and author
* [The] City Bard
* Maurus
(See also base volume)

Blackmore, Richard Doddridge
1825-1900 [DEA, DLE1]
British author and poet
* Melanter

Blackstone, [Sir] William
1723-1780 [IP]
British barrister and legislator
* Another Member of Parliament

Blackton, Peter
See Wilson, Lionel

Blackwell, E. H. [IP]
British barrister
* E. H. B.

Blackwell, Henry [IP]
British fencing instructor
* H. B.

Blackwell, Miss [IP]
British author
* [A] Lady of Fashion

Blackwell, Robert 18th c. [IP]
British author
* R. B.

Blackwood, Thomas [IP]
Author
* [A] Layman of the Church of Scotland

Blades, R. H. [IP]
British author
* R. H. B.

Blades, William 1824- ? [IP]
British author and printer
* W. B.

Blair, Andrew 19th c. [WGT]
Author
* Tenth President of the World Republic

Blair, David [IP]
Australian critic
* Robinson, Jack, Jr.

Blair, Linda 1959- [BP]
American actress and horsewoman
* McDonald, Martha

Blair, Mary E.   [IP]
American educator and author
* St. Ursula

Blair, Patrick   [IP]
Scottish physician
* Servetus, Michael, M.D.

Blair, T. C.
See   Blair, Thomas

Blair, Thomas 20th c.   [EF]
American football player
* Blair, T. C.

Blake, Dionysius
See   Scanlan, Michael

Blake, E. A.
See   Gowing, Emilia Aylmer

Blake, Henry A. 1840- ?   [IP, NPS]
Irish author
* McGrath, Terence

Blake, Jack ?-1895   [BLB, EWG]
American gunfighter
* Blake, Tulsa Jack

Blake, James Vila 1842- ?   [IP]
American clergyman and author
* J. V. B.

Blake, Margaret
See   Schem, Lida Clara

Blake, Mary Elizabeth 1849- ?   [PI]
Irish-born poet
* Marie

[The] Blake of the Twentieth Century
See   Gibran, Kahlil

Blake, Patrick
See   Egleton, Clive [Frederick]

Blake, Redmond?
See   Aiken, Albert W.

Blake, Robert
See   Thompson, Robert Hely

Blake, Rodney
See   Clemens, William
Montgomery

Blake, Tulsa Jack
See   Blake, Jack

Blake, William 1757-1827
[IP, NPS]
British poet, painter, engraver
* Augur
* Pictor Ignotus [Painter Unknown]
* W. B.

Blake, William 19th c.   [RBE]
Boxer
* Dublin Tricks

Blake, William O. 19th c.   [DNA]
American editor
* Prescott, Thomas H.

Blakey, Robert 1795-1878   [IP]
British author
* Hackle, Palmer
* Oliver, Nathan, Esq.
* Verax

Blakie, Alexander 19th c.   [IP]
American clergyman and author
* [A] Presbyterian

Blakie, G. W.   [IP]
Scottish poet and artist
* Plain, Timothy

Blanckenmueller, Johann
1496-1570   [BBD]
German composer
* Walter [or Walther], Johann

Blanco White, Amber 1887-1981
[CA]
Author
* Reeves, Amber

Bland, Dorothea 1762-1816   [NPS]
Irish actress
* Romp, Miss
(See also base volume)

Bland, E. A.   [WW]
Author
* E. A. B. D.

Bland, James A. 1854-1911   [PAC]
American composer
* [The] Prince of Negro
Songwriters

Bland, Richard 1710-1776   [BDSA]
American author and patriot
* [The] Virginia Antiquary

Blane, Gertrude
See   Blumenthal, Gertrude

Blasius, Docteur
See   Grousset, Paschal

[The] Blasphemer
See   Cromwell, Oliver

[The] Blasphemer
See   Lucian

[The] Blaspheming Doctor
See   Johnson, Samuel

Blatchford, Montague   [NPS]
Author
* Blong, Mont

Blatchford, Robert 1851- ?   [NPS]
Editor
* Nunquam

Blayds, Charles Stuart 1831-1884
[DEA, DLE1]
British author, poet, barrister
* C. S. C.
* Calverley, Charles Stuart

Blaze, Ange Henri 1813-1888
[NPS]
German poet, critic, translator
* Lagenevais, F. de
* Werner, Hans
(See also base volume)

Blazer, J. S.
See   Scott, Justin

Blear-Eye
See   Robert II

[The] Blear-Eyed
See   Brandolini, Aurelius

Blest Swan
See   Crashaw, Richard

Blevins, Andy ?-1887   [EWG]
American gunfighter
* Cooper, Andy

[The] Blind Harper
See   Parry, John

[The] Blind Mechanician
See   Strong, John

[The] Blind Naturalist
See   Huber, Francois

[The] Blind Poet
See   Bello, Francesco

[The] Blind Poet
See   Groto, Luigi

[The] Blind Poet
See   Milton, John

[The] Blind Poetess of Donegal
See   Browne, Frances

Block, Lawrence 1938-   [TCCM]
American author
* Harrison, Chip
* Kavanagh, Paul

[A] Blockaded British Subject
See   Hopley, Catherine C.

[The] Blockhead
See   Wordsworth, William

Blocksidge, Charles William
1883-1942   [DLE1]
Australian poet
* Baylebridge, William

[The] Blond Angel
See   Astiz, Alfredo

Blong, Mont
See   Blatchford, Montague

Bloodgood, Bert
See   Bloodgood, Elbert

Bloodgood, Elbert 20th c.   [EF]
American football player
* Bloodgood, Bert

Bloody Bill Anderson
See   Anderson, William

Bloomfield-Moore, Clara Sophia
[Jessup] 1824-1899   [DNA]
American author and poet
* Moreton, Clara
* Ward, H. O.

Bloomingdale, Alfred 1916-   [CR]
American business executive
* [The] Father of the Credit Card

Bloomsbury Dick
See   Rigby, Richard

Blount, Annie R. 1839- ?   [BDSA]
American poet and editor
* Woodbine, Jennie

Blue, Martha Ward
See   Ward, Martha Craft

Bluebeard
See   Landru, Henri

Bluebell
See   Browne, Hester G.

Bluemantle, [Mrs.] Bridget
See   Thomas, Elizabeth

[A] Bluenose
See   Fenety, George E.

Blueskin Dick
See   Culmer, Richard

Bluestring, Robin
See   Walpole, [Sir] Robert [First
Earl of Orford]

Bluff Harry
See   Henry VIII

Bluffstein, Sophie 1854-1891
[LFW]
Russian swindler
* [The] Golden Hand

Blumberg, Rhoda L[ois Goldstein]
1926-   [CA]
American sociologist and author
* Goldstein, Rhoda L.

Blumenthal, Gertrude 1907-1971
[CA, SAT]
American author, editor, publisher
* Blane, Gertrude

Blumtal, James
See   Bellak, James Blumtal

Blunt, Joseph 1792-1860   [DNA]
American author and attorney
* Marcus

Bluster, Lord
See   Fox, Henry Richard Vassall
[Third Baron Holland]

Boaistual de Launay, Pierre
?-1556   [WGT]
French author
* Chelidonius Tigurinus

Boake, Capel
See   Kerr, Doris Boake

Boanerges
See   Irving, Edward

[The] Boar of the Forest
See   Hogg, James

[The] Boaster of Crimes
See   Orleans, Philippe II d'

Boate, Henrietta 19th c.   [PI]
Irish poet
* O'Neill, Henrietta Bruce

Boateng, Yaw Maurice
See   Brunner, Maurice Yaw

[The] Bobbed-Haired Bandit
See   Cooney, Cecelia [Roth]

Bocanegra [Black Mouth]
See   Fuentes, Manuel

Bocquillon, Guillaume-Louis
1781-1842   [BBD]
French music educator
* Wilhem, Guillaume-Louis

Bodin, Camille
See   Bastide, Jenny

Boerhaave, Hermann 1668-1738
[NPS]
Dutch physician and philosopher
* [The] Hippocrates of Our Age
(See also base volume)

Boethius, Anicius Manlius Severinus
470?- 524   [NPS]
Roman philosopher
* [The] Captain in Music
(See also base volume)

Bogan of Bogan, Mrs.
See   Oliphant, Carolina [Baroness
Nairne]

Bogart, Neil 1943?-1982
*American record producer and
entertainment mogul*
* Disco, Mr.

Bogue, Mrs. Arthur Hoyt
Author
* Bell, Lilian

Bohun, Hugh
See   Cronin, Bernard [Charles]

Boileau-Despreaux, Nicolas
1636-1711 [NPS]
French critic and poet
* [The] Poet of Reason
(See also base volume)

Boland, Eleanor 19th c. [PI]
Irish poet
* Alethe

Bold Jack Donahoe
See Donahoe, Jack

[El] Bolero [The Bolero Dancer]
See Hernandez, Francisco

Boles, Charles E. 1820- ? [DI]
American stagecoach robber
* Black Bart
* Bolton, Charles E.

Boleskine, Lord
See Crowley, Edward Alexander

Bolin, Bookie
See Bolin, Treva

Bolin, Treva 20th c. [EF]
American football player
* Bolin, Bookie

Bolina, Jack la
See Vecchi, Augustus Victor

Bolte, John Willard 1884-1942
[DNA]
American author
* Willard, John

Bolton, Charles E.
See Boles, Charles E.

Bonaparte, Joseph 1768-1844
King of Naples and Spain
* Survilliers, Comte de

Bonaparte, Louis 1778-1846 [NPS]
King of Holland
* St. Lue, Comte de

Bonaparte, Napoleon 1769-1821
[NPS]
Emperor of France
* [The] Contractor General
* [The] Corsican Fiend
* [The] Eagle
* [A] French Coxcomb
* God Hanuman
* [The] New Sesostris
* That God of Clay
(See also base volume)

Bonaventura, Father
See Stuart, Charles Edward Louis
Philip Casimir

Boncoeur, L.
See Urbino, Levina [Buoncuore]

Bones, Brudder
See Scott, John F.

Bonis, Melanie 1858-1937 [BBD]
French composer
* Mel-Bonis

Bonner, Antoinette 1892-1920
[LFW]
American jewel thief
* [The] Queen of Diamonds

Bonner, Edmund 1500-1569 [NPS]
Bishop of London
* London Little-Grace
(See also base volume)

Bonnerive, Capt. [NPS]
French author
* De Lys, Georges

Bonnie Jean
See Armour, Jean

Bontempi, Giovanni Andrea
See Angelini, Giovanni Andrea

Booker, Anton S.
See Randolph, Vance

Bookhouse, Louis 1897-1944
[BLB, DI]
American underworld figure
* Buchalter, Lepke
* Judge Louis
* Little Lepke

Boon-Jones, Margaret
See Zarif, Margaret Min'imah

Boone, Henry L.
See St. John, Percy Bollingbroke

Boone, John 18th c. [RBE]
Boxer
* [The] Fighting Grenadier

Booth, Geoffrey
See Tann, Jennifer

Boquillon, Onesime
See Humbert, Albert

Border Boss
See Hughes, John Reynolds

Borderer Between Two Ages
See Scott, [Sir] Walter

Borel, Pierre Bord d'Hautoine
1809-1859 [NPS]
French journalist and author
* [The] Lycanthrope
(See also base volume)

[The] Borgia of America
See Wise, Martha Hasel

Boris the Gypsy
See Buriatov, Boris

Borlaug, Norman 1914- [CR]
American agricultural scientist
* [The] Apostle of Wheat

Borth, Christian Carl 1896-1976
[MA]
American author
* Borth, Christy

Borth, Christy
See Borth, Christian Carl

[The] Boss of Chinatown
See Gee, Charlie

**[Le] Bossu d'Arras [The Hunchback
of Arras]**
See Adam de la Halle

[The] Bossuet of the Protestant Pulpit
See Saurin, Jacques

[A] Bostonian
See Adams, Samuel

Boswell
See Johnson, W. B.

Boswell, [Sir] Alexander 1775-1822
[NPS]
British antiquary and poet
* Gray, Simon

Boswell, James 1740-1795 [NPS]
Scottish attorney and author
* [The] Ambitious Thane
* [The] Curious Scrap-Monger
* Dapper Jemmy
* Laelius
* Thou Jackall

Boswell, James (Continued)
* Will o' the Wisp
(See also base volume)

Boswell Redivivus
See Hazlitt, William

Bottle, Joshua T. 19th c. [PI]
Playwright
* J. T. B.

Bottled Beer
See Nowell, Alexander

Bottomless Pit
See Pitt, William

Bottomley, Horatio Williams
1860-1933 [DI]
British swindler
* [The] Friend of the Poor

[La] Bouche de Ciceron
See Pot, Philippe

Boucher de, Crevecoeur de Perthes
1788-1868 [IP]
French archaeologist and author
* Christophe, M., Vigneron

**[Le] Boucher Royaliste [The Royalist
Butcher]**
See Lasseran-Massencome
[Seigneur de Montluc]

Bouchery, Madame
See Weber, Jeanne

Boucicault, D. L.
See Boucicault, Dionysius Lardner

Boucicault, Dionysius Lardner
1822-1890 [PI]
Irish-born actor and playwright
* Boucicault, D. L.

Boudreaux, F. J. [IP]
American author
* [A] Father of the Society of Jesus

Boue de Villiers, Amable Louis 1834-
? [IP]
French journalist and author
* Artevelle, Jacques
* [Le] Capitaine Lancelot
* De Ferrieres, Raymond
* De Vernon, Guy
* [Le] Docteur Rouge
* Mirliter

Boulanger, Joseph ?-1800 [BLB]
Canadian-born murderer and pirate
* Baker, Joseph

Boulay-Paty, Evariste Cyprien
1804-1864 [IP]
French poet
* Mariaker, Elie

Bouligny, Mrs. M. E. Parker [IP]
American author
* [A] Lady

Bounce, Benjamin
See Carey, Henry

Bourbon, Louis Antoine de
1775-1844 [NPS]
Last dauphin of France
* Angouleme, Duc d'
* Hilt, Prince

**Bourbon, Louis II de [Prince de
Conde]** 1621-1686 [NPS]
French army officer
* [Le] Heros de l'Histoire
(See also base volume)

Bourdaloue, Louis 1632-1704
[NPS]
French clergyman
* [The] Demosthenes of French
Divines
(See also base volume)

Bourdillon, Francis 19th c. [IP]
British clergyman and author
* F. B.

Bourke, Hannah Maria 19th c. [PI]
Irish poet
* H. M. B.

Bourke, James J. 1837-1894 [PI]
Irish poet
* Tiria

Bourn, Samuel [IP]
British clergyman and author
* Belzebub

Bourne, George [IP]
American author and clergyman
* [A] Citizen of Virginia
* [A] Virginian Presbyter

Bourne, Henry Richard Fox [IP]
British author
* H. R. F. B.

Bourne, Stephen [IP]
Author
* [A] Late Stipendiary Magistrate
in Jamaica

Bousell, John [IP]
British author
* Shoe, Aminidab

Boutell, Clarence Burley
1908-1981 [CA]
American author and columnist
* Boutell, Clip

Boutell, Clip
See Boutell, Clarence Burley

Bouton, Henri 1885-1965 [BL]
American magician
* Frederick the Great
(See also base volume)

Bouvier, Blackjack
See Bouvier, John Vernou, III

Bouvier, John Vernou, III 1891-1957
American broker
* Bouvier, Blackjack

Bovery, Jules
See Bovy, Antoine-Nicolas-Joseph

Bovy, Antoine-Nicolas-Joseph
1808-1868 [BBD]
Belgian musician and conductor
* Bovery, Jules

Bovy-Lysberg, Charles-Samuel
1821-1873 [BBD]
Swiss musician and composer
* Lysberg, Charles-Samuel

Bowden, James [IP]
British author
* [A] Member of the Society of
Friends

Bowden, John 1751-1817 [IP]
American clergyman and author
* [A] Churchman

Bowden, John William 1798-1844
[IP]
British author and poet
* A [Alpha]

Bowdler, Henrietta 1743-1784 [IP]
British author and poet
* [A] Lady Lately Deceased

Bowdler, Thomas 1754-1825 [IP]
British author
* [A] Friend to Both
* T. B.

Bowdoin, James 1727-1790 [IP]
American statesman and author
* [A] Citizen of Massachusetts

Bowen, B. M.
See Muzzy, Bertha

Bowen, Bill
See Barkley, Clint

Bowen, C. E. [IP]
British author
* C. E. B.

Bowen, C. J. [IP]
British clergyman and author
* C. J. B.

Bowen, Francis 1811- ? [IP]
American philosopher and author
* F. B.

Bowen, [Sir] George Ferguson
1821-1899 [IP]
British colonial administrator
* G. F. B.
(See also base volume)

Bowen, [Ivor] Ian 1908- [CA]
Welsh-born author and economist
* Hogarth, Charles [joint
  pseudonym with John Creasey]

Bowles, Kerwin
See Abeles, Elvin

[A] Boy
See Nordhoff, Charles

[The] Boy Baccaleur
See Wolsey, Thomas

[The] Boy Bachelor
See Wotton, William

[The] Boy Bishop
See Nicholas of Bari

[The] Boy Chief of the Pawnees
See Burgess, Ed A.

[The] Boy on the Psychiatrist's Couch
See Reed, B. Mitchel

[The] Boy with the Golden Arm
See Bradshaw, Terry

Boyce, Neith
See Hapgood, Mrs. Hutchins

Boyd, Carse
See Stacton, David [Derek]

Boyd, Mary Stuart 20th c. [NPS]
Author
* Dacre, J. Colne

Boyd, Oliver H. K.
Author
* O. H. K. B.

Boyle, John 1822?-1885 [PI]
Irish-born poet
* Green, Jasper
* J. B.
* Milo
* Mylo
* O'Donnell, Roderick
* Pontiac

Boyle, [Capt.] Robert
See Chetwood, William Rufus

Boylston, Peter
See Curtis, George Ticknor

Boz
See Walsh, John

Brab
See Moore-Brabazon, J. T. C.

Brace, Benjamin
See McCutcheon, Ben Frederick

Brackenridge, Hugh Henry
1748-1816 [DLE1]
Scottish-born poet and playwright
* Democritus

Bradey, Barney
See Parkes, William Theodore

Bradley, Edward 1827-1889
[DLE1]
*British author, clergyman,
illustrator*
* Funnyman, A.
(See also base volume)

Bradley, Katharine Harris
1846-1914 [DLE1]
British author and poet
* Arran [joint pseudonym with
  Edith Emma Cooper]
(See also base volume)

Bradley, Stephen
See Barnayay, Istvan

Bradman, [Sir] Donald George
[NN]
Australian cricketer
* [The] Don

Bradshaigh, Lady 18th c. [NPS]
*Friend of British author, Samuel
Richardson*
* Belfour, Mrs.

Bradshaw
See Arrowsmith, Edmund

Bradshaw, Terry 1948- [CR]
American football player
* [The] Boy with the Golden Arm

Bradstreet, Anne 1612-1672 [NPS]
American poet
* [The] Glory of Her Sex
* [The] Mirror of Her Age
(See also base volume)

Brady, Gentleman Matt
See Brady, Matthew

Brady, Matthew 19th c. [DI]
Australian bushranger
* Brady, Gentleman Matt

Brae, Andrew Edmund 19th c.
[HFN]
British author
* [A] Detective

Bragg, Mabel Caroline 1870-1945
[SAT]
American author
* Piper, Watty

[The] Brahan Seer
See Odhar, Coinneach [Kenneth
Ore]

Brahe, Tycho 1546-1601 [NPS]
Danish astronomer
* Praestantissimus Mathematicus
(See also base volume)

**[The] Brain and the Buddha of
American Zen**
See Watts, Alan [Wilson]

Brain, Benjamin 1753-1794 [RBE]
British boxer
* Brain, Big Ben

Brain, Big Ben
See Brain, Benjamin

Braithwaite, Richard 1588?-1673
[WGT]
British poet
* Corymboeus
* Hesychius Pamphilus
* Musaeus Palatinus
* Philogenes Panedonius
* Pomerano, Castalio
(See also base volume)

Braman, Karen Jill 1943- [MA]
American author
* Braman, Kitte

Braman, Kitte
See Braman, Karen Jill

Brame, Charlotte M. 1836-1884
British author
* Barton, Caroline M.
* C. M. B.
* Norton, Mrs. Florice
* Thorne, Dora

Bramin
See Sterne, Laurence

Bramine
See Draper, Elizabeth

Brandolini, Aurelius 1440?-1497
[NPS]
Italian poet
* [The] Blear-Eyed
(See also base volume)

Brandon, Johnny 20th c. [CA]
*British-born American composer,
songwriter, dancer*
* Edwards, Francis
* Franks, Ed
* Martinelli, Ricardo
* Rich, Gerry

Brandon, Robert Joseph 1918-
[CA]
British-born author
* Brandon, Robin

Brandon, Robin
See Brandon, Robert Joseph

Brandt, Keith
See Sabin, Louis

Brandt, Michael 1814-1870 [BBD]
Hungarian composer
* Mosonyi, Mihaly

Brandy, Jonas
See Moore, John

Brannagan, Patrick 19th c. [RBE]
American boxer
* Brannagan, Scotty

Brannagan, Scotty
See Brannagan, Patrick

Brannan, William Penn 1825-1866
[PI]
American poet
* Brown, Vandyke?

Brannigan, Dr.
See Carroll, John

Bras de Fer
See William

Braschi, Giovanni Angelo
1717-1799 [NPS]
Pope
* [The] Great Harlot
(See also base volume)

Brasco, Don
See Pistone, Joseph D.

Brass Pen
See Lestrange, Joseph

Bratny, Roman
See Mularczyk, Roman

[The] Brave Jersey Muse
See Prynne, William

Brayman, James O. 1815-1887
American editor
* Thorne, Harley?

[The] Brazen Bully
See Lowther, [Sir] James

[The] Brazen Defender of Corruption
See Canning, George

[A] Brazen Wall Against Popery
See Taylor, Thomas

[The] Brazilian Boccaccio
See Amado, Jorge

[The] Breaker
See Morant, Harry H.

Breaux, Daisy
See Calhoun, Cornelia Donovan
[O'Donovan]

Brecht, William
See Barendrecht, Cor W.

Brenan, John 1768?-1830 [PI]
Irish poet
* J. B.

Brenan, Joseph 1828-1857 [PI]
Irish-born poet
* J. B., Cork

Brennan, Edward John 1845- ? [PI]
Irish poet
* Brenon, E. St. John

Brennan, Peter J. 1918- [CR]
*American labor leader and
government official*
* Hardhat, Mr.

Brenon, E. St. John
See Brennan, Edward John

Brent, Carl
See Willett, Edward

Brent of Bin Bin
See Franklin, [Stella Maria Sarah]
Miles

Brereley, John, Priest
See Anderton, James

Brereton, Austin [NPS]
Journalist and critic
* A. B.

Breuer, Hans
See Breuer, Johann Peter Joseph

Breuer, Johann Peter Joseph
1868-1929 [BBD]
German opera singer
* Breuer, Hans

[The] Brewer
See Cromwell, Oliver

Briand, Aristide 1862-1932 [CD]
French statesman
* [The] Great Peacemaker

Briareus of the King's Bench
See Scarlett, [Sir] James [First Baron Abinger]

Bride, Louisa
See Culhane, Kate

Bridges, Alfred Bryant Renton 1901- [CR]
Australian-born American labor leader
* Bridges, Harry

Bridges, Beau
See Bridges, Lloyd Vernet, III

Bridges, Harry
See Bridges, Alfred Bryant Renton

Bridges, Lloyd Vernet, III 1941-
[BP, CR]
American actor
* Bridges, Beau

Bridges, Madeline S.
See De Vere, Mary Ainge

Bridges, Mrs. [NPS]
Author
* Forrester, Mrs.

Bridges, Thomas 18th c.
[NPS, WGT]
Playwright and author
* Barebones, Caustic
* Cotton, Junior

Bridget
See Coen, John

Briggs, Jimuel
See Thompson, Thomas Phillips

Brighouse, Harold 1882-1958
[DLE1]
British author and playwright
* Conway, Olive [joint pseudonym with John Walton]

Bright Eyes
See Inshtatheamba

Bright, John 1811-1889 [NPS]
British orator and statesman
* [The] Quaker Solon of Rochdale
(See also base volume)

Bright, Mary Chavelita [Dunne]
1860-1945 [NPS]
British author, playwright, translator
* Chavelita, Mary
(See also base volume)

Brigid
See Murphy, Katharine Mary

[The] Brilliant
See Rupert

Brinckman, Karl G. 1764-1847
[NPS]
Swedish diplomat and poet
* Selmar

Brioni
See Savini-Brioni, Gaetano

[The] Bristol Junius
See Gutch, John Mathew

[The] Bristol Unknown
See Burrows, Bill

Britain's Josiah
See Charles I

Britannico, Mercurio
See Hall, Joseph

Britannicus
See Needham, Marchamont

Britannicus
See Ramsay, Allan, Jr.

Britannicus, Mela
See Kelsall, Charles

[A] British Bostonian
See Allen, John

[The] British Cassius
See Sidney [or Sydney?], Algernon

[The] British Juvenal
See Churchill, Charles

[The] British Lion
See Richard I

[The] British Orson Welles
See Russell, Ken

[The] British Pallas
See Churchill, John [First Duke of Marlborough]

[The] British Pliny
See Camden, William

[The] British Saint Stephen
See Alban

[The] British Solomon
See James I

[A] British Subject
See Head, [Sir] Francis Bond

[The] British Timon
See Gosling, Charles

Britten, Emma Hardinge
1823-1899 [EOP]
Author, composer, songwriter, who claimed to possess psychic powers
* Reinhold, Ernest

Brlic-Mazuranic, Ivana 1874-1938
[CD]
Croatian author
* [The] Croatian Andersen

Broad Church
See Atcheson, Thomas

Broadaxe
See Knapp, Martin

Broadhead, Helen Cross 1913-
[CA, SAT]
American author
* Cross, Helen Reeder

Broadhead, James [IP]
British author
* [A] Citizen of the World

Brocius, Curly Bill
See Graham, William B.

Brocius, William
See Graham, William B.

Brock, Ben
See Howells, Roscoe

Brock, Leonard 19th c. [BLB]
American trainrobber
* Waldrip

Brockett, John Trotter 1788-1842
[IP]
British antiquary
* J. T. B.

Brockett, Linus Pierpont 1820- ?
[IP]
American author
* [An] American Citizen
* Philobiblius

Brockway, Thomas 1744-1807 [IP]
American clergyman and author
* [The] European Traveller

Brocky Jack Norton
See Norton, J. S.

Broderick, A. [IP]
British poet
* B.

Broderip, William John 1787-1859
[IP]
British barrister and author
* [A] Naturalist

Brodribb, John Henry 1838-1905
[IP]
British actor
* Irving, [Sir] Henry

Brody, Sylvia
See Axelrad, Sylvia Brody

Broekel, Johanne Antonie 1819- ?
[IP]
Danish educator and author
* Brook, A.

Broken Nose Jack
See McCall, John

Bromet, William ?-1850 [IP]
British surgeon and antiquary
* [A] Lounger
* Plantagenet

Bromfield, William 1712-1792 [IP]
British author and surgeon
* W. B.

Bromley, Henry
See Wilson, Anthony

Bromley, M. I. [IP]
British poet
* M. I. B.

Bromley, William [IP]
British statesman and author
* [A] Gentleman

Bronson, Wolfe
See Raborg, Frederick A[shton], Jr.

Bronte, Charlotte 1816-1855 [NPS]
British author
* Townshend, Charles
(See also base volume)

Brook, A.
See Broekel, Johanne Antonie

Brook, Mary 1726?-1782 [IP]
British author
* M. B.

Brooke, E. [IP]
British author
* E. B.

Brooke, Frances [Moore]
1745-1789 [IP]
British author and playwright
* Spinster

Brooke, Henry 1706-1783 [IP]
Irish poet
* Farmer
* Oxoniensis

Brooke, John Charles 1748-1794
[IP]
British antiquary
* J. B.

Brooke, Miss 19th c. [PI]
Irish author and poet
* Byrrne, E. Fairfax

Brooke, Robert [BBH]
American fox hunter
* [The] Father of American Fox Hunting

Brookens, Brookie
See Brookens, Thomas Dale [Tom]

Brookens, Thomas Dale [Tom] 1953-
American baseball player
* Brookens, Brookie

Brooks, Buffalo Bill
See Brooks, William L.

Brooks, Bully
See Brooks, William L.

Brooks, Edwy Searles 1889-1965
[TCCM]
British author
* Ross, Carlton
(See also base volume)

Brooks, William L. ?-1874 [EWG]
American gunfighter
* Brooks, Buffalo Bill
* Brooks, Bully

[A] Brother Methodist
See Gough, Benjamin

Brougham, Henry Peter 1778-1868
[NPS]
Scottish statesman and jurist
* Dominie Hairy
* [The] God of Whiggish Idolatry
* Jupiter Placens [The Pleasant Jupiter]
* Lord B.
* Tomkins, Isaac
(See also base volume)

Broughton, H., B.C.S.
See Trevelyan, [Sir] George Otto

Broughton, Jack 1704-1789
[BBH, RBE]
British boxer
* [The] Father of Boxing

[The] Brown
See Mackay, Robert

Brown, David
See Myller, Rolf

Brown, Douglas
See Gibson, Walter B[rown]

Brown, George Douglas 1869-1902
[DLE1]
Scottish author and educator
* King, Kennedy
(See also base volume)

Brown, Irving
See Adams, William Taylor

Brown, Isaac
See Motherwell, William

Brown, James
See Robertson, Joseph

Brown, James 1928?- [CMA]
American singer and songwriter
* [The] Original Disco Man
(See also base volume)

Brown, James Baldwin 1785-1843
[NPS]
British author and barrister
* Epsilon

Brown, John 1800-1859   [NPS]
American abolitionist
* Brown, Ossawatomie
(See also base volume)

Brown, Jones
See Munby, Arthur Joseph

Brown, Lee Patrick 1938?-
American police chief
* No Rap
* [The] Sphinx

Brown, Mahlon A.?
See Ellis, Edward S[ylvester]

Brown, Marilyn McMeen Miller
1938-   [CA]
American author and poet
* Miller, Marilyn McMeen

Brown, Ossawatomie
See Brown, John

Brown, Thomas Edward 1830-1897
[DLE1, NPS]
British poet and author
* Beta
* [The] Manx Poet

Brown, Thomas, Redivivus
See Cornwallis, Caroline Frances

Brown, Vandyke?
See Brannan, William Penn

Brown, Will
See Ainsworth, William Harrison

Brown, William Linn 19th c.   [HFN]
American author
* [A] Fisher in Small Streams

Browne, Frances 1816-1879   [DIL]
Irish poet and author
* [The] Blind Poetess of Donegal

Browne, Gordon Frederick
1858-1932   [ICB]
British illustrator
* Nobody, A.

Browne, Henriette
See De Boutellier, Sophie

Browne, Hester G. 19th c.   [HFN]
Author
* Bluebell

Browne, Lewis Allen 1876-1937
[DNA]
American playwright
* Dash, Paul R.

Browne, Maurice   [PI]
Irish poet
* Maggie

Browne, Montagu 19th c.   [NPS]
Author
* A. M. B.

Browne, Thomas 1787?- ?   [PI]
Irish-born journalist and poet
* Buckthorn, Jonathan
* Foudriangle?
* J. G.

Brownell, Charles F.
See Mencken, Henry Louis

Brownell, John F.
See Mencken, Henry Louis

Browning, Henry C.
See Ritchie, Anna Cora [Ogden Mowatt]

Broyle, M.
See Neuburg, Victor [Benjamin]

[The] Bruce of the Fourteenth Century
See Mandeville, [Sir] John

Bruce, Thomas 1766-1831   [NPS]
Seventh Earl of Elgin
* [The] Modern Pict

Bruck [or Brouck], Arnold von
1470?-1554   [BBD]
Flemish composer
* Arnold de Bruges
* Arnoldo Flamengo

Brummagem Joe
See Chamberlain, Joseph

Brummel, Buck
See Brummel, George Bryan

Brummel, George Bryan 1778-1840
[NPS]
British leader of fashionable society
* Brummel, Buck
(See also base volume)

Brumore
See Guyton de Morveau, N.

Brunefille, G. E.
See Campbell, Lady Colin

Brunner, Maurice Yaw 1950-   [CA]
Ghanaian-born author
* Boateng, Yaw Maurice

Brunold, Friedrich
See Meyer, August Friedrich

Brunswick
See Gilder, Jeannette

Brutus
See Ames, Fisher

Brutus
See Barry, Michael Joseph

Brutus
See Coram, Robert

Brutus
See Felton, John

Brutus
See Mackenzie, Henry

Brutus
See Morse, Samuel Finley Breese

[The] Brutus of Our Republic
See Haselrig, [Sir] Arthur

Bryan, Ella Howard   [BDSA]
American author and poet
* Dangerfield, Clinton

Bryant, Black Face
See Bryant, Charles

Bryant, Charles ?-1891
[BLB, EWG]
American gunfighter
* Black Faced Charlie
* Bryant, Black Face

Bryant, Mrs.
See Ouick, Florence

Bryant, Samuel Drake 1768-1854
[FAA]
British-born American actor
* Drake, Samuel, Sr.

Bryce, James 19th c.   [PI]
Irish poet
* Dunwoodie, Dominick

Bubier, Edward Trevert 1858-1904
[DNA]
American author and engineer
* Trevert, Edward

Buchalter, Lepke
See Bookhouse, Louis

Buchan, Anna ?-1948   [DLE1]
Scottish author
* Douglas, Olive

Buchan, John 1875-1940   [YAB]
Scottish-born author
* Tweedsmuir, Baron
(See also base volume)

Buchanan, George 1506-1582
[DEA, NPS]
Scottish historian and author
* M. G. B.
* [The] Sage

Buchanan, W. B. 19th c.   [IP]
American poet
* W. B. B.

Buchinsky, Charles 1922-   [BP]
American actor
* [Le] Sacre Monstre [The Sacred Monster]
(See also base volume)

Buchstab, Michael 1904-1974   [CA]
Austrian-born Israeli author, editor, archaeologist
* Avi-Yonah, M[ichael]

Buck, James Smith 1812-1892
[IP, SFL, WGT]
American author
* Ichabod
* [The] Prophet James

Buck, Spencer
See Woodham, Mrs.

Bucke, Charles 1781-1847   [IP]
British author
* C. B.

Buckfield, Reginald Sidney 20th c.
[DI]
Murderer
* Buckfield, Smiler

Buckfield, Smiler
See Buckfield, Reginald Sidney

Buckingham, James Silk
1786-1855   [IP]
British author
* [A] Proprietor of India Stock

Buckingham, Joseph H.   [IP]
American journalist
* J. H. B.

Buckingham, Joseph Tinker
1779-1861   [IP]
American journalist
* Cobweb
* J. T. B.
* Moth
* Period, Pertinax and Co.

Buckingham, Leicester Silk
1825-1867   [IP]
British playwright
* Matthews and Co.

[The] Buckinghamshire Dragon
See Grenville, George Nugent

Buckland, Francis Trevelyan
1826-1880   [IP]
British naturalist and author
* [A] Fisherman and Zoologist
(See also base volume)

Buckland, Raymond 1934-   [EOP]
British-born author and illustrator
* Robat [Cult name]
(See also base volume)

Buckland, Rosemary 20th c.   [EOP]
British-born American occultist
* Rowen, Lady [Cult name]

Buckley, Doris Heather
See Buckley Neville, Heather

Buckley, Michael Bernard
1831-1872   [PI]
Irish author and poet
* L. D. Y.
* Y., Cork

Buckley, Theodore William Alois
1825-1856   [IP]
British author
* Fitzjersey, Horace
(See also base volume)

Buckley Neville, Heather 1910-
[CA]
American author
* Buckley, Doris Heather

Buckmaster, Henrietta
See Stephens, Henrietta Henkle

Buckskin Frank Leslie
See Leslie, Nashville Franklin

Buckskin Sam
See Hall, Samuel Stone

Buckthorn, Jonathan
See Browne, Thomas

Budd, G. H.   [IP]
British author
* G. H. B.

Budd, James   [IP]
British clergyman and author
* J. B.

[The] Buddha of the West
See Emerson, Ralph Waldo

Bude, John
See Elmore, Ernest Carpenter

Budge, Edward 1800-1865   [IP]
British clergyman and author
* E. B.

Budge, Jane 1832- ?   [IP]
British author
* [A] Lady

Budge, John 1787-1864   [IP]
British clergyman and author
* J. B.

Budworth, Joseph   [IP]
British poet and officer
* [A] Rambler

Buffalo Bill Brooks
See Brooks, William L.

Buffett, Edward Payson 1833-1904
[DNA]
American author and physician
* Van Arkel, Garret

[Le] Buffon Odieux
See Sully, Jean Baptiste

Buford, Harry T.
See Velasquez, Loretta Janeta

Bull, Mrs.
See Anne

[The] Bulldog of all Circumnavigators
See Anson, George

Bullen, A. H. 20th c.   [NPS]
Editor
* Urban, Sylvanus

Buller, Bob
See Maginn, William

[The] Bulwark of the State
See Pelham, [Sir] Henry

Bulwer-Lytton, Edward George Earle Lytton 1803-1873   [DEA, NPS]
British author and playwright
* Bulwig
* E. B. L.
* E. L. B.
(See also base volume)

Bulwig
See Bulwer-Lytton, Edward George Earle Lytton

Bunbury, [Sir] H. E. 1778-1860 [NPS]
British soldier, historian, politician
* Soame, [Sir] Henry F. R.

Bunch, Eugene ?-1889   [BLB, DI]
American train robber
* Gerald, Captain

Bundy, Mac
See Bundy, McGeorge

Bundy, McGeorge 1919-   [CR]
American presidential advisor
* Bundy, Mac

Bunn, Alfred 1796?-1860   [NPS]
British theatrical manager and playwright
* Good Friday
(See also base volume)

Bunny, Benjamin
See Housman, Laurence

Bunyan, John, Junior
See Arnot, William

Bunyanus
See Weeks, William Raymond

Buor, Joy Olney 1918-   [MA]
American author
* Lytle, Joy Oleny Mann

Burbage, Richard 1566-1619?
[NPS, UH]
British actor
* Another Roscius
(See also base volume)

Burch, Monte G. 1943-   [CA]
American author
* Gregory, Mark

Burchard, Franz 1799-1835   [WEC]
German cartoonist and printmaker
* Doerbeck

Burdick, Austin C.
See Cobb, Sylvanus, Jr.

Burgess, Ed A. 19th c.
American entertainer
* [The] Boy Chief of the Pawnees

Burgess, Michael Roy 1948-   [CA]
American publisher and author
* Alcalde, Miguel
* Clarke, Boden
* Demotes, Michael
* Durand, G. Forbes

Burgess, Michael Roy (Continued)
* Grazhdanin, Misha
* Harding, Peter
* Kapel, Andrew
* Lawson, Jacob
* Miletus, Rex
* Mobley, Walt
* Nimble, Jack B.
* Painter, Daniel
* Rale, Nero
* Reginald
* Sharpe, Lucretia
* Spartacus, Tertius
(See also base volume)

Burgh, James 1714-1775   [WGT]
Author
* Vander Neck, J.

Burghley, Feltham
See Ward, C. A.

Burgin, George Brown 1856-1944 [NPS]
British author
* Smee, Wentworth
(See also base volume)

Burgoyne, John 1722?-1792
[NN, NPS]
British army officer and playwright
* Gentleman Johnny
* Swagger, General
* That Martial Macaroni
(See also base volume)

Buriatov, Boris 20th c.
Russian singer, allegedly involved in diamond theft ring
* Boris the Gypsy

Burke, Deaf
See Burke, James

Burke, Edmund 1729-1797
[DIL, HFN]
British statesman, orator, author
* [The] Father of Modern Conservatism
* [A] Late Noble Writer
(See also base volume)

Burke, James 1809-1845
[BBH, RBE]
British boxer
* Burke, Deaf
* [The] Deaf Un

Burke, John ?-1873   [DNA]
American poet
* Rubek, Sennoia

Burke, John [Frederick] 1922-
[TCCM]
British author
* Burke, Owen
(See also base volume)

Burke, [Sir] John Bernard 19th c.
[PI]
Irish poet
* J. B. B.

Burke, Martha Jane [Canary] 1848?-1903   [NPS]
American frontier figure
* Cherokee Sal
(See also base volume)

[The] Burke of Our Age
See Macaulay, Thomas Babington [First Baron Macaulay]

Burke, Owen
See Burke, John [Frederick]

Burkett, Jackie
See Burkett, Walter Jackson

Burkett, Walter Jackson 20th c.
[EF]
American football player
* Burkett, Jackie

Burlington Harry
See Flitcroft, Henry

Burman, Alice Caddy 1896?-1977
[SAT]
Canadian-born illustrator
* Caddy, Alice

Burnell, Herman 20th c.   [EF]
American football player
* Burnell, Max

Burnell, Max
See Burnell, Herman

Burnet, [Sir] Thomas 1694-1753
[NPS]
British author
* Doggrel, [Sir] Iliad [joint pseudonym with George Ducket]

Burnett, William Riley 1899-
[TCCM]
American author
* Monahan, John
(See also base volume)

Burns, Robert 1759-1796   [NPS]
Scottish poet
* [The] Heaven-Taught Ploughman
(See also base volume)

Burr, William Henry 1819-1908
[DNA]
American journalist
* Historicus

Burris, Bo
See Burris, James

Burris, James 20th c.   [EF]
American football player
* Burris, Bo

Burroughs, Lewis ?-1786   [PI]
Irish poet
* Wagstaffe, Jeffrey

Burrow, Reuben Houston ?-1890
[BLB]
American trainrobber
* Burrow, Rube

Burrow, Rube
See Burrow, Reuben Houston

Burrowes, Robert 1756?-1841   [PI]
Irish songwriter
* R. B.?

Burrows, Bill 19th c.   [RBE]
Boxer
* [The] Bristol Unknown

Burstein, Rona 1934-   [BP]
American columnist
* Rona Rat
(See also base volume)

Burt, Olive Woolley 1894-   [CA]
American author
* Oliver, Burton

Burton, Ben F.
See Robertson, Ben F.

Burton, Jennie Davis 19th c.
American author
* Glenn, Gipsy

Burton Junior
See Lamb, Charles

Burton, [Sir] Richard Francis 1821-1890   [DEA, PI]
British explorer and author
* Baker, Frank
* F. R. G. S.
(See also base volume)

Burtt, Thomas   [IP]
British poet
* T. B.

Burwell, Adam Hood   [IP]
Canadian poet
* Erie-us

Burwell, Lettie M.   [IP]
American author
* Thacker, Page

Bury, Charlotte Susan Maria [Campbell] 1775-1861   [IP]
British author
* [A] Flirt
* [A] Lady of Rank

Bury, James   [IP]
British author
* [An] Englishman
* One Who Respects Them

Busby, Mabel Janice 1903-1982
[CA]
American politician and former madam
* Gump, Sally
(See also base volume)

Bush, William   [IP]
American author
* Pickle, Prometheus

Bushby, Henry Jeffreys 1820- ?
[IP]
British author
* [A] Non Combatant

Bushnell, Mrs. William H. 19th c.
American author
* Luqueer, Helen

Bushnell, William H. 1823- ?
American author, poet, editor
* Webber, Frank

Busk, Hans 1815- ?   [IP]
British author
* Beaujolais

Buskin, [Captain] Sock
See Sorel, W. J.

Busnois, Antoine
See De Busne, Antoine

Bussy, George [Fourth Earl of Jersey] 1735-1805   [NN]
British courtier
* [The] Prince of Macaronies

Busterkeys, Walter
See Liberace, Wladziu Valentino

[The] Busybody
See Franklin, Benjamin

[The] Butcher
See Shehu, Mehmet

[The] Butcher of Cordoba
See Astiz, Alfredo

[The] Butcher's Dog
See Wolsey, Thomas

Butler, Charles 1750-1832   [IP]
British author and jurist
* C. B.

Butler, Dr. ?-1617 [NPS]
Physician to King James I
* Aesculapius

Butler, Dr. 1774-1853 [NPS]
Educator
* Pomposus

Butler, Edward 20th c. [EF]
American football player
* Butler, Sol

Butler, Eleanor ?-1829 [IP]
Irish author
* Eleonora

Butler, James 1610-1688 [NN]
British royalist leader
* James the White
(See also base volume)

Butler, James [Second Duke of Ormonde] 1665-1745 [NPS]
Lord Lieutenant of Ireland
* Another Joseph

Butler, John 1717-1802 [IP]
British clergyman
* [A] Country Clergyman
* Vindex
* [A] Whig

Butler, John 19th c. [IP]
British author
* [An] Officer in the Hon. E. I. Co's
  Bengal Native Infantry

Butler, Joseph 1692-1752 [IP]
British theologian and author
* [A] Young Clergyman
(See also base volume)

Butler, Rab
See Butler, Richard Austen

Butler, Richard Austen 1902-1982
[PPN]
British politician
* Butler, Rab

Butler, Robert [IP]
Scottish barrister
* Sergeant B

Butler, S. [IP]
Author
* [A] Gentleman of Bristol

Butler, Samuel 1612-1680
[DEA, DLE1, NPS]
British author and poet
* Canne, John
* [The] Glory and Scandal of His
  Age
* Prynne, William

Butler, Skip
See Butler, William Foster

Butler, Sol
See Butler, Edward

Butler, Thomas Ambrose
1837-1897 [PI]
Irish-born poet
* Eblana

Butler, William Archer
1814?-1848 [PI]
Irish poet
* W. A. B.

Butler, William Foster 1947-
[EF, FR]
American football player
* Butler, Skip

Butler, William John 19th c. [IP]
British clergyman and author
* W. J. B.

Butt, Beatrice Mary
See Hutt, Mrs. W.

Butt, Boswell, Esq.
See Ross, Charles Henry

Butt, Mrs. E. O. [IP]
British author
* E. O. B.

[A] Butterfly
See Allan, J. A.

Butterworth, William
See Schroeder, Henry

Butts, Mrs. M. F. [IP]
Author
* Barton, Fanny M.

Buzz
See Walsh, Michael Paul

Bye, Deodatus 1745-1826 [IP]
British printer and author
* D. B.

Byerley, Thomas 1788-1826 [IP]
British editor
* Percy, Sholto
(See also base volume)

Byles, [Sir] John Barnard
1801-1884 [IP]
British barrister and author
* [A] Barrister

Byng, Frederick [NPS]
* Poodle
* Pry, Paul

Byrd, Harry Flood 1887-1966
American politician
* Economy, Mr.

Byrde, Richard
See Neuburg, Victor [Benjamin]

Byrne, Hannah 19th c. [PI]
Irish poet
* H. B.
* H. B-y-e
* Zelia

Byrne, Julia C. 1819-1894 [NPS]
Author
* Matilda, Julia

Byrne, William A. 20th c. [PI]
Irish poet
* Dara, William

Byron, George Gordon Noel
1788-1824 [NPS]
British poet
* [The] Bard of Corsair
* Glenravon, Lord
* [A] Literary Vassal
* [The] Mocking Bird of Our
  Parnassian Ornithology
* Quevedo Redivivus
* [A] Tempest Cleaving Swan
(See also base volume)

Byron, Lord
See Polidori, Louis Eustache

Byrrne, E. Fairfax
See Brooke, Miss

C

* Indicates Assumed Name

C.
See Child, Maria [Little]

C.
See Curran, Henry Grattan

C.
See Cuthbertson, James Lister

C.
See Kickham, Charles Joseph

C.
See O'Donnell, John Francis

C.
See Southey, Caroline Anne
[Bowles]

C. A.
See Adams, Charlotte

C. A.
See Anley, Charlotte

C. A. D.
See De Wint, Mrs. C. A.

C. A. D. A.
See Cordell, Charles

C. A., Esq.
See Anstey, Christopher

C. A. J.
See Jones, Charles Alfred

C. B.
See Bucke, Charles

C. B.
See Butler, Charles

C. B. C. A.
See Amicus, C. B. C.

C. B. M.
See Martin, Clara [Barnes]

C. C.
See Casey, Charles

C. C.
See Chorley, Charles

C. C.
See Clark, Charles

C. C.
See Coghlan, Charles

C. C.
See Cordell, Charles

C. C. D.
See Dawson, Charles Carroll

C. C. V. G.
See Wetherell, Dawson

C. E.
See Elliott, Charlotte

C. E. B.
See Bowen, C. E.

C. E. M.
See Mudie, Charles Edward

C. E. S., Sir
See Scott, [Sir] Claude Edward

C. F.
See Foster, Catharine

C. F. A.
See Alexander, Mrs. Cecil Francis

C. F. G.
See Gore, Catherine Grace Frances
[Moody]

C. F. M.
See Cusack, Mary Frances

C. G. D.
See Duffy, [Sir] Charles Gavan

C. H.
See Hoey, John Cashel

C. I.
See Innes, Cosmo

C. J. B.
See Bowen, C. J.

C. J. D.
See Dunphie, Charles James

C. J. K.
See Kickham, Charles Joseph

C. J. M.
See Coyne, Joseph

C. J. M., Mr.
See Mickle, Charles Julius

C. K. P.
See Paul, Charles Kegan

C. L. M.
See McIlvaine, Clara

C. M.
See Mackinnon, Campbell

C. M.
See MacLaughlin, Charles

C. M. B.
See Brame, Charlotte M.

C. M. C.
See Caddell, Cecilia Mary

C. M. H.
See Hewins, C. M.

C. M., Vicar of Brixworth
See Marshall, Charles

C. N.
See Wilson, John

C. O. F.
See O'Flaherty, Charles

C. P.
See Howard, [Lady] Catherine

C. P. M.
See Male, Christopher Parr

C. P. M.
See Meehan, Charles Patrick

C. P. M., Sch.
See Mulvany, Charles Pelham

C. R.
See Reeve, Clara

C. S.
See Sackville, Charles [Second
Duke of Dorset]

C. S. C.
See Blayds, Charles Stuart

C. S. W., Captain the Honble.
See Wortley, Charles Stuart

C. 3. 3.
See Wilde, Oscar Fingal
O'Flahertie Wills

C. W.
See White, Charlotte

C. W.
See Wolfe, Charles

C. W. S.
See Smith, Charles William

Cabet, Etienne 1788-1856   [WGT]
French author
* Adams, Francis

Cable, George Washington
1844-1925   [CA, TLC]
American author
* Lazarus, Felix
(See also base volume)

Cabot, Sabby
See Cabot, Sebastian

Cabot, Sebastian 1918-   [CR]
British-born actor
* Cabot, Sabby

Caccini, Francesca 1588-1640?
[BBD]
Italian composer
* [La] Cecchina

Cacus
See Dennis, John

Caddell, Cecilia Mary 1814-1877
[PI]
Irish author and poet
* C. M. C.

Caddy, Alice
See Burman, Alice Caddy

Cadwalader, George, Gent.
See Dodington, George Bubb

Caecilius
See Cecil, Robert Arthur Talbot
[Third Marquis of Salisbury]

Caen, Herb 1916-   [CR]
American columnist
* San Francisco, Mr.

Caesar, [Gaius] Julius 1st c. BC
[NPS]
Roman general and statesman
* Daphnis
* [The] Flower of All the
  Aristocrats
(See also base volume)

[The] Caesar of Style
See Savini-Brioni, Gaetano

Caffyn, William 19th c.   [EC]
British cricketer
* [The] Surrey Pet

Cahill, William 19th c.   [PI]
Irish poet
* Alpha?

Caillou, Alan
See Lyle-Smythe, Alan

Cain, J. V.
See Cain, James

Cain, James 20th c.   [EF]
American football player
* Cain, J. V.

Caine, Geff?
See Rohr, Wolf Detlef

Caine, Hall
See Hall, Thomas H.

Cain's Brother
See Abell, William

Caird, Mona   [NPS]
Author
* Hutton, G. M.

Caius
See Currie, James

Cajetan
See Elfinger, Anton

Calchas
See Garvin, James Louis

Calcraft, John William
See Cole, John William

Calderone, Mary S[teichen] 1904-
[CA]
American author and physician
* Martin, Mary Steichen

[The] Caledonian Comet
See Scott, [Sir] Walter

Caledonicus
See Ainslie, Whitelaw

Calhoun, Cornelia Donovan
[O'Donovan] 1864-1949 [DNA]
American author
* Breaux, Daisy

Caliban
See Bergerat, Auguste Emile

California Bill Hodges
See Hodges, William

Calisthenes
See Quincy, Josiah

Calkins, Rodello 1920- [CA]
American author
* Hunter, Rodello

Callanan, Jeremiah Joseph
1795-1829 [PI]
Irish poet
* Hidalla

Callaway, Hugh G. 1885-1949
[EOP]
British occultist and author
* Fox, Oliver

Callenbach, Franz 1663-1743
[WGT]
Author
* Wurmsaam, Vermelio

Calloway, Cabell 1907- [CR]
American bandleader and singer
* [The] King of Hi-De-Ho
(See also base volume)

Callum Beg
See Mack, J. G. O.

Calverley, Charles Stuart
See Blayds, Charles Stuart

Calvert, Patricia 1931- [CA]
American author
* Freeman, Peter J.

Calvi, Roberto 1920?-1982
Italian bank president
* God's Banker

[The] Calvinistical Pope
See Knox, John

Camanche Bill Porter
See Porter, William

Camara
See Luque y Gonzalez, Antonio

[The] Cambrian Shakespeare
See Williams, Edward

Cambridge, Ada
See Cross, Mrs. G. F.

[A] Cambridge Graduate
See Begley, W.

[A] Cambridge M. A.
See Knott, Robert Rowe

[The] Cambridge Rapist
See Cook, Peter

Camden, William 1551-1623
[DEA, NPS]
British historian
* [The] British Pliny
* M. N.
(See also base volume)

Cameron, [Sir] Evan 1629-1719
[NPS]
Scottish chieftain
* Lochiel
(See also base volume)

Camillus
See Duane, William

Campana
See Chichester, Frederick Richard

Campbell, Archibald 1598-1661
[NPS]
Scottish aristocrat
* Gillespie, Grumach
(See also base volume)

Campbell, Bartley T. 1843-1888
American author, journalist, poet
* South, Edwin

Campbell, Erving
See Pratt, Jacob Loring

Campbell, Helen [Stuart]
1839-1918 [DNA]
American author
* Wheaton, Campbell

Campbell, John 1708-1775 [NPS]
Scottish author
* Claridge, John, Shepherd
(See also base volume)

Campbell, John 1810-1874 [DNA]
Irish-born author and publisher
* Bell, J. Cawdor

Campbell, Lachlan
See Campbell, Minnie Spence
[Eakin]

Campbell, Lady Colin [ICB, NPS]
British author and art critic
* Brunefille, G. E.
* Vera

Campbell, Mary
See Bennett, Mary E.

Campbell, Minnie Spence [Eakin]
?-1940 [DNA]
American poet
* Campbell, Lachlan

Campbell, Raymond 20th c. [EF]
American football player
* Campbell, Soup

Campbell, Soup
See Campbell, Raymond

Campbell, Thomas 1777-1844
[NPS]
British poet
* [The] Dromedary
* Tam
(See also base volume)

Campbell, Thomas 19th c. [PI]
Irish poet
* M'Blashmole, Pat

Campbell, Woodrow 20th c. [EF]
American football player
* Campbell, Woody

Campbell, Woody
See Campbell, Woodrow

Campion, John Thomas 1814- ?
[PI]
Irish poet
* Carolan
* J. T. C.
* [The] Kilkenny Man
* S. F. C.
* Spes
* Urbs Marmoris

Campion, Rosamond
See Rosmond, Babette

Campo, Bernardino 1522-1584
[NPS]
Italian painter
* [The] Annibale Caracci of the
Eclectic School

Canada Bill Jones
See Jones, William

[A] Canadian
See Alexander, James Lynne

[The] Canadian Keats
See Lampman, Archibald

[The] Canadian Kipling
See Service, Robert William

Canale, John 20th c. [EF]
American football player
* Canale, Whit

Canale, Whit
See Canale, John

Canavarro, M. A. de S.
Author
* Sanghamita, [Sister]

Candid Enquirer
See Anderson, James

Candidus
See Adams, Samuel

Candidus
See Inglis, Charles

Canham, Erwin Dain 1904-1982
[CR]
American journalist
* Canham, Spike

Canham, Spike
See Canham, Erwin Dain

Canne, John
See Butler, Samuel

Canning, George 1770-1827 [NPS]
British prime minister
* Aeolus
* [The] Brazen Defender of
Corruption
* Jocular Samson
(See also base volume)

Cannon, Alexander 1896-1963?
[EOP]
*British psychiatrist, hypnotist,
author*
* Kushog Yogi of Northern Thibet
* Master-The-Fifth of the Great
White Lodge of the Himalayas

Cannon, Francis 19th c. [PI]
Irish-born clergyman and poet
* [An] Americo-Hibernian Priest

Cannon, Ravenna
See Mayhar, Ardath F[rances]

Cannon, Tom 1790-1858 [RBE]
Boxer
* [The] Great Gun of Windsor

[El] Cano [The Grey-Haired One]
See Jimenez y Melendez, Manuel

Canova, Leon 1902?-1980 [FIR]
Comedian and musician
* Canova, Zeke

Canova, Zeke
See Canova, Leon

Cantabar
See Harris, Josiah

Canton, Frank
See Horner, Joe

[Le] Capitaine Lancelot
See Boue de Villiers, Amable Louis

[A] Capitalist
See Van Deusen, Alonzo

[A] Cappoquin Girl
See Walsh, John

Capsadell, Louisa
See Hammond, Henrietta [Hardy]

[The] Captain in Music
See Boethius, Anicius Manlius
Severinus

Captain Light Dragoons
See Ashe, Thomas

[The] Captain of the Cumberland
See Alston, Alfred Henry

Carberiensis
See Davis, Eugene

Carbery, Ethna
See MacManus, Anna

Carew, Will
See Milligan, Ernest

Carey, Ernestine Gilbreth 1908-
[CLC]
American author
* Gilbreth, Ernestine

Carey, George Seville 1743-1807
[NPS]
British poet
* Telltruth, Paul

Carey, Henry ?-1743 [NPS]
British poet and musician
* Bounce, Benjamin
(See also base volume)

Carey, Thomas Joseph 1853- ?
[DNA]
American author and publisher
* Payne, F. M.
* See, T. J.

Carey, William Paulet 1759-1839
[PI]
Irish poet
* O'Pindar, Scriblerus Murtough
* W. P. C.
* W. P. C-y

Carington, W[alter] Whateley
See Smith, Walter Whateley

Carleton, Carrie
See Wright, Mary [Booth]

Carleton, George
See Holland, Denis

Carleton, William 1794-1869 [PI]
Irish author
* W. C.
(See also base volume)

Carleton, William, Jr. 1829-1897
[PI]
Irish poet
* W. C., Jun.

Carli, Audrey 1932- [MA]
American author
* Craig, Beth
* Patyn, Ann

Carlisle, D. M.
See Cook, Dorothy Mary

Carlo, Tyran
See Davis, Billy

Carlson, Henry 20th c. [EF]
American football player
* Carlson, Red

Carlson, Judith Lee 1952- [CA]
American author
* Lee, Judy

Carlson, Red
See Carlson, Henry

Carlton, Robert
See Hall, Baynard Rush

Carlyle, Alexander 1722-1805
[NPS]
Scottish clergyman
* [A] Freeholder
(See also base volume)

Carlyle, Thomas 1795-1881 [NPS]
Scottish author and historian
* Anticant, [Dr.] Pessimist
(See also base volume)

Carlyon, Edward Augustus 19th c.
[HFN]
Author
* Coelebs

Carman, [William] Bliss 1861-1929
[DLE1]
Canadian-born poet
* Norman, Louis

Carmarthen, K.
See Leeds, Duchess of

Carmichael, Andrew Blair
1780-1854 [PI]
Irish poet
* A. C.

Carmona y Luque, Jose 1825-1881
[GS]
Spanish bullfighter
* [El] Panadero [The Baker]

Carnes, Capt.
See Cummings, M. J.

Carolan
See Campion, John Thomas

Carolan
See O'Callaghan, John Cornelius

Carolan, R.
See Sedley, Arthur Osborne Lionel

Caroline Matilda 1751-1775 [NPS]
Queen of Denmark
* [The] Queen of Tears

Caroliniensis
See Holmes, Isaac Edward

Caroll, Nonie
See Murphy, Nonie Carol

Carpenter, Anna May ?-1900
[DNA]
American poet
* Grey, Jane
* Morrow, May

Carpenter, Duffy
See Hurley, John J[erome]

Carpenter, Philip Pearsall
1819-1877 [IP]
British naturalist and author
* P. P. C.

Carpenter, Russell Lant 19th c. [IP]
British clergyman and author
* R. L. C.

[The] Carpenter's Son
See Hall, Ellis

Carpio, Salvador Cayetano 1920?-
Salvadoran guerrilla leader
* Marcial

Carr, Christopher
See Benson, Arthur Christopher

Carr, Dabney 1743-1773 [IP]
American statesman and author
* Cecil, Dr.

Carr, Frank [IP]
British author and merchant
* Crosse, Launcelot
* [A] Merchant

Carr, H. D.
See Crowley, Edward Alexander

Carr, Margaret 1935- [CA, TCCM]
British author
* Kerr, Carole
(See also base volume)

Carr, Robert ?-1645 [NPS]
British politician
* Bendo, Alexander

Carr, William 19th c. [HFN, IP]
British clergyman and author
* [A] Native of Craven

Carra, Emma
See Stibbes, Agnes Jean

Carrat de Vaux, Alexandre [IP]
French author
* Rieux, A. de

Carrick, John [IP]
Author
* J. C.

Carrick-on-Suir, L.?
See Leyne, Maurice Richard

Carrington, E. [IP]
British author
* [An] Old Bachelor

Carrington, George 19th c. [IP]
British naval officer and author
* [An] University Man

Carrington, Margaret Jirvin [IP]
American author
* M. J. C.
* [An] Officer's Wife

Carrion, Manuel 1842-1883 [GS]
Spanish bullfighter
* [El] Coracero [The Cuirassier]

Carrodus, John Tiplady
See Carruthers, John Tiplady

Carrol, S.
See Centlivre, Susannah

Carroll, Charles 1737-1832 [IP]
American patriot and author
* [The] First Citizen

Carroll, Dixie
See Cook, Carroll Blaine

Carroll, John [PI]
Irish songwriter
* Brannigan, Dr.

Carroll, John 1735-1815 [IP]
American author and clergyman
* [A] Catholic Clergyman

Carroll, John 19th c. [IP]
Canadian clergyman and author
* [A] Spectator of the Scenes

Carroll, Robert
See Alpert, Hollis

Carroll, T. G. [IP]
Irish author
* T. G. C.

Carrotty Nell Coles
See Coles, Frances

Carruthers, John Tiplady
1836-1895 [BBD]
British musician
* Carrodus, John Tiplady

Carruthers, William A.
1818-1850? [IP]
American author
* [A] Virginian

Carson, John William [Johnny]
1925- [CR]
American comedian
* [The] Great Carsoni

Carson, [Major] Lewis W.
See Aiken, Albert W.

Carteaux, Felix [IP]
Author
* F. C.

Carter, Abby [Allin] [IP]
American author
* Nilla

Carter, Ashley
See Whittington, Harry
[Benjamin]

Carter, Elizabeth 1717-1806 [IP]
British poet
* Chariessa
* E. C., Mrs.
(See also base volume)

Carter, Hi C
See Carter, Howard

Carter, Howard 20th c.
American basketball player
* Carter, Hi C

Carter, John 18th c. [CEC]
British smuggler
* [The] King of Prussia

Carter, Lorene
See Jones, Lillie Mae

Carter, Nick
See Doughty, Francis W.

Carter, Nick
See Lynds, Dennis

Carter, Nick
See Smith, Martin William

Carter, Russell Kelso 1849-1928
[DNA]
American author and educator
* Kenyon, Orr

Carter, Ruth
See Robertson, Sarah Franklin
[Davis]

Carter-Smith, Grace [NPS]
Author
* Cusack, George

[A] Carthusian
See Ryder, W. J. D.

Cartwright, Julia
See Ady, Mrs. Henry

Cartwright, N.
See Scofield, Norma Margaret
Cartwright

Cartwright, William 1611-1643
[NPS]
British poet and playwright
* Another Tully and Virgil
* Drusus
(See also base volume)

Carver, John
See Dodge, Nathaniel Shatswell

Cary, Peggy-Jean Montgomery 1918-
*American writer and former child
film star*
* Baby Peggy
(See also base volume)

Casas, Julian 1816-1882 [GS]
Spanish bullfighter
* [El] Salamanquino [The Man
from Salamanca]

Casaubon, Isaac 1559-1614 [NPS]
Swiss scholar and critic
* Hortibonus [or Hortusbonus], Is.

Casca
See Chamberlain, Joseph

Case, Pete
See Case, Ronald

Case, Ronald 20th c. [EF]
American football player
* Case, Pete

Casey, Charles 19th c. [PI]
Irish poet
* C. C.

Casey, James 1824-1909 [PI]
Irish poet
* [A] Catholic Priest
* J. K. C.
* Sedulius, Caius

Casey, Jane Barnes 1942- [CA]
American author
* Barnes, Jane

Casey, John Keegan 1846-1870
[PI]
Irish author and poet
* Kilkeevan
(See also base volume)

Casey, Patrick
See Thurman, Wallace

[A] Cashel Girl
See Walsh, Michael Paul

Caspipina, Tamoc
See Duche, Jacob

Cassidy, Patrick Sarsfield 1852- ?
[PI]
Irish-born poet
* Diarmuid

Cassidy, William L[awrence Robert]
20th c. [CA]
American author
* Schwabe, William

Cassio
See Gould, Edward S.

Castanero Chico [Little Chestnut Vendor]
See Aristizabal, Domingo

[El] Castellano [The Castillian]
See Alonso, Manuel

Castelmary
See De Castan, [Count] Armand

Castelot, Andre
See Storms, Andre

Castelot, Jacques
See Storms, Jacques

Castillo, John 1792-1845 [PI]
Irish poet
* [The] Bard of the Dales

Castleton, Charles
See Cobb, Sylvanus, Jr.

[The] Cat
See Catesby, [Sir] William

[The] Cat
See Timotheus

Catesby, [Sir] William ?-1485
[NN, NPS]
British politician
* [The] Cat

[A] Catholic and a Burkist
See MacKenna, Theobald

[The] Catholic Bishop of Bantry
See Dicker, Thomas

[A] Catholic Clergyman
See Carroll, John

[A] Catholic Priest
See Casey, James

[A] Catholick
See Nokes, William

Catholicus
See Cotton, Henry

Catholicus, Johannes
See Rutty, John

Catinat, Nicholas 1637-1712
[NPS]
French army officer
* [The] Father of Thought
(See also base volume)

Cato
See Gordon, Thomas

Cattle Kate Watson
See Watson, Ella

Catto, Max[well Jeffrey] 1909-
[CA]
British author and playwright
* Finkell, Max
(See also base volume)

Cave, Edward 1691-1754 [NPS]
Author
* Newton, R.
(See also base volume)

Cavellus
See McCall, Patrick Joseph

Cavendish, William Spencer
1790-1858 [NPS]
Sixth Duke of Devonshire
* [The] Maecenas and Lucullus of His Island

Caviare
See Keats, John

Caviare
See O'Donnell, John Francis

Cayce, Edgar 1877-1945 [EOP]
American psychic healer
* [The] Sleeping Prophet

Cayzer, Charles William 1869- ?
[NPS]
Poet
* Wynne, Charles Whitworth

[La] Cecchina
See Caccini, Francesca

Cecil
See Fisher, Sidney George

Cecil, Dr.
See Carr, Dabney

Cecil, Robert Arthur Talbot [Third Marquis of Salisbury] 1830-1903
[NPS]
British statesman
* Caecilius
(See also base volume)

Celano
See Corsi [or Corso], Giuseppe

Celatus
See Owen, Robert

[A] Celebrated Actress
See Aiken, Albert W.

Celler, Ludovic
See Leclerc, Louis

Cellier, Elizabeth 17th c. [NPS]
British midwife
* [The] Popish Midwife

Celticus
See Bevan, Aneurin

Celticus
See McMahon, Heber

Cement Head
See Semenko, Dave

[The] Censor General of Literature
See Nichols, John

[The] Censor of the Age
See Gifford, William

[El] Centauro Torero [The Centaur Bullfighter]
See Diaz Salinas, Ponciano

Centlivre, Susannah 1667-1722
[NPS]
Playwright
* Carrol, S.

Centz, P. C.
See Sage, Bernard Janin

Cerberus, A.
See Aretino, Pietro

[A] Certain Free Enquirer
See Annet, Peter

Cervantes Saavedra, Miguel de
1547-1616 [NPS]
Spanish author
* [Th] Aeschylus of Spain
(See also base volume)

Cesti, Marc' Antonio
See Cesti, Pietro

Cesti, Pietro 1623-1669 [BBD]
Italian composer
* Cesti, Marc' Antonio

Cetina, Gutierre de 1518?-1572?
Spanish poet and soldier
* Vandalio

Chadwick, Elizabeth [Bigley]
1859-1907 [LFW]
American swindler
* De Vere, Lydia
* [The] Queen of Ohio
(See also base volume)

Chalmers, George 1742-1825
[NPS]
Scottish author
* [The] Atlas of Scotch Antiquaries
* Aurelius
(See also base volume)

Chamberlain, Joseph 1836-1914
[NPS]
British statesman
* Brummagem Joe
* Casca
* Moatlodi
(See also base volume)

Chambers, Rusty
See Russell, Francis Chambers

Chambers, [Sir] William
1726-1796 [NPS]
Architect
* [The] Lime and Mortar Knight
(See also base volume)

Champagnat
See Berthome du Lignon

Champagne Charlie
See Thorpe, Charles

[The] Champion of Human Law
See Selden, John

Champlain, Samuel de 1567?-1635
[BBH]
French explorer
* [The] Father of New France

Champlin, Edwin Ross 1854- ?
Author
* Fairfield, Clarence

Champseix, Mme. [NPS]
Author
* Leo, Andre

[The] Chancellor of Human Nature
See Hyde, Edward [First Earl of Clarendon]

Chandeneux, Claire de
See Bailly, Emma Berenger

Chang Hor-gee 1897-1978 [LFW]
Chinese-born American embezzler
* Gee, Dolly

Chang Tso-lin ?-1928 [PPN]
Governor of Manchuria
* [The] Old Marshal

Chang Yong Ja 20th c.
South Korean swindler
* Curb Money Queen

Channing, C. G. Fairfax
See Gross, Christian Channing

Channing, Carol 1921- [CR]
American actress and singer
* [The] Little Girl from Little Rock

[The] Chanticleere
See Taylor, John

Chap., Geor.
See Chapman, George

Chapeau, Ellen Chazel 1844- ?
[BDSA]
American author and playwright
* Esperance

[The] Chaplain
See Peirce, Bradford Kinney

[A] Chaplain in H. M. Indian Service
See Mackay, James

[The] Chaplain to the Mayoralty
See Dillon, Robert Crawford

Chapman, George 1559?-1634
[DEA]
British poet and playwright
* Chap., Geor.
* G. C.
* G. W., Gent.
(See also base volume)

Chapman, John Stanton Higham
1891-1972 [SAT]
British-born American author
* Connell, Kirk [joint pseudonym with Mary Hamilton (Ilsley) Chapman]
* Ilsley, Dent [joint pseudonym with Mary Hamilton (Ilsley) Chapman]
* Selkirk, Jane [joint pseudonym with Mary Hamilton (Ilsley) Chapman]
(See also base volume)

Chapman, Mary Hamilton [Ilsley]
1895- [SAT]
American author
* Connell, Kirk [joint pseudonym with John Stanton Higham Chapman]
* Ilsley, Dent [joint pseudonym with John Stanton Higham Chapman]
* Selkirk, Jane [joint pseudonym with John Stanton Higham Chapman]
(See also base volume)

Chappell, Helen 1947- [CA]
American author
* Baldwin, Rebecca

Char, Friedrich Ernst 1865-1932
[BBD]
German composer and conductor
* Char, Fritz

Char, Fritz
See Char, Friedrich Ernst

Charbon
See Coke, Desmond

Charfy, Guiniad
See Smeeton, George

Chariessa
See Carter, Elizabeth

[A] Charity Organizationist
See Wright, J. Hornsby

Charles 1083?-1127 [NN]
Count of Flanders
* [The] Dane
(See also base volume)

Charles 1948-
Prince of Wales
* [The] People's Prince

Charles, Franklin [joint pseudonym with Robert Leslie Bellem]
See Adams, Cleve F[ranklin]

Charles, Franklin [joint pseudonym with Cleve F(ranklin) Adams]
See Bellem, Robert Leslie

Charles, Gordon H[ull] 1920- [CA]
American author
* Hull, Charles

Charles I [or Karl] 742- 814 [NPS]
King of the Franks and Emperor of the West
* David
(See also base volume)

Charles I 1600-1649 [NPS]
King of England
* Britain's Josiah
(See also base volume)

Charles II 1630-1685 [NPS]
King of England
* [The] Blackbird
* Fabius
* [The] Great Physician
* Our Setting Sun
* [The] Royal Wanderer
(See also base volume)

Charles II 1661-1700 [NN]
King of Spain
* [The] Desired
(See also base volume)

[The] Charmer of the World
See Scott, [Sir] Walter

Charo
See Baeza, Maria Rosario Pilar Martinez Melina

Charruthers, Robert 1799-1878 [IP]
Scottish journalist, publisher, author
* R. C.

Chartrand, Joseph Demers 1852-1905 [DNA]
Canadian author
* Des Ecorres, Charles

Chase, Frank Eugene 1857-1920 [DNA]
Playwright
* Seaman, Abel

Chase, Naomi Feigelson 1932- [CA]
American author and poet
* Feigelson, Naomi

Chasuble, Archdeacon
See Marshall, Thomas William

[A] Chatterer
See Adams, Samuel

Chatto, William Andrew 1805- ? [HFN]
British author
* W. A. C.
(See also base volume)

Chaucer, Geoffrey 1340-1400 [NPS, UH]
British poet
* [The] Beautie of our Tongue
* [The] English Ennius
* [The] God of English Poets
* Our English Homer
(See also base volume)

Chauncey, Shelton
See Nicholls, Charles Wilbur de Lyon

Chauvin [or Caulvin?], Jean 1509-1564 [NPS]
French theologian and religious reformer
* [The] Demon of Geneva
(See also base volume)

Chavelita, Mary
See Bright, Mary Chavelita [Dunne]

Chaviaras, Strates 1935- [CA]
Greek-born American poet and author
* Haviaras, Stratis

Cheke, [Sir] John 1514-1557 [NPS]
Greek scholar and statesman
* [The] Exchequer of Eloquence

Chelidonius Tigurinus
See Boaistual de Launay, Pierre

Chelius, Oskar von 1859-1923 [BBD]
German composer
* Berger, Siegfried

Chelleri, Fortunato
See Keller, Fortunato

Chelson, Tom
See Hill, Tom

Cheng, F. T.
See Cheng, Tien-hsi

Cheng, Tien-hsi 1884-1970 [CA]
Chinese diplomat and author
* Cheng, F. T.

Chenier, Andre Marie de 1762-1794 [NPS]
French poet
* [The] Adonais of the French Revolution
(See also base volume)

Chenoweth, George 20th c. [EF]
American football player
* Chenoweth, Red

Chenoweth, Mrs.
See Soule, Minnie Meserve

Chenoweth, Red
See Chenoweth, George

Cherne, Leo
See Chernetsy, Leo

Chernetsy, Leo 1912- [CR]
American economist, sculptor, author
* Cherne, Leo

Cherokee Sal
See Burke, Martha Jane [Canary]

Cherub Dicky
See Suett, Richard

Chesbro, Marcel 20th c. [EF]
American football player
* Chesbro, Red

Chesbro, Red
See Chesbro, Marcel

[The] Cheshire Cat
See Cheshire, Maxine

Cheshire, Maxine 1930- [CR]
American columnist
* [The] Cheshire Cat

Chesney, Esther
See Dargan, Clara V.

Chester, Harriet Mary 1830- ? [PI]
Irish poet
* H. M. C.

Chester, Norley
See Underdown, Emily

Chesterbelloc [joint pseudonym with Gilbert Keith Chesterton]
See Belloc, [Joseph] Hilary [Pierre]

Chesterbelloc [joint pseudonym with (Joseph) Hilary (Pierre) Belloc]
See Chesterton, Gilbert Keith

Chesterton, George Laval 1856- ? [NPS]
Journalist and author
* Arion

Chesterton, Gilbert Keith 1874-1936 [PPN]
British author
* Chesterbelloc [joint pseudonym with (Joseph) Hilary (Pierre) Belloc]
(See also base volume)

Chetwood, William Rufus ?-1766 [WGT]
British author
* Boyle, [Capt.] Robert

Chevalier, Guillaume-Sulpice 1804-1866 [WEC]
French cartoonist
* Gavarni, Paul

Chevalier, H. E.
See Sears, Edward Isidore

[The] Chian Father
See Homer

Chibborn, E. [IP]
Irish journalist
* H.

Chicago May
See Lambert, May

Chichester, Frederick Richard 1827-1853 [PI]
Irish poet
* Campana
(See also base volume)

[El] Chiclanero [The Man from Chiclana]
See Redondo y Dominguez, Jose

Chicot
See Sargent, Epes Winthrop

Chidananda, Swami
See Rao, Sridhar

[The] Chief
See De Valera, Eamon

[The] Chief Incendiary of the House
See Adams, Samuel

[The] Chiel
See Cox, Erle

Chierico, Dedimo
See Foscolo, Niccolo

Child, David Lee 1794-1874 [IP]
American attorney and editor
* Probus

Child, Lydia Maria [Francis] 1802-1880 [IP]
American author
* [An] American
* [A] Lady of Massachusetts

Child, Maria [Little] 1797-1877 [IP]
American writer
* C.
* Delafield

Child, Mrs. Harris Robbins
Author
* Stuart, Eleanor

Child, Mrs. Richard Washburn
Author
* Parker, Maude

[A] Child of Hell
See Ezzelino IV

[The] Child of Luebeck
See Heinecken, Christian Heinrich

[A] Child of Nature
See Sheehan, Michael Francis

Child, Theodore [IP]
American journalist
* Th. C.

Childe, Edward Vernon 1804-1861 [IP]
American journalist
* E. V. C.
* [A] "States"-man

Childs, George Borlase 1816- ? [IP]
British surgeon and author
* Cirujano, M. M. C.

[The] Child's Poet
See Field, Eugene

Chilly Charley
See Clark, Charles

Chiniquy, Charles 19th c. [NPS]
* [The] Apostle of Temperance

[Il] Chiozzotto
See Croce, Giovanni

Chip
See Applewhite, Marshall Herff

[A] Chip of the Young Block
See Stewart, Maria Stewart

Chip, Will
See More, Hannah

Chitov, Panajot, 1830- ? [IP]
Bulgarian author
* Panajot, H.

Chittenden, Hiram Martin 1858-1917 [DNA]
American author and historian
* Phucher, Itothe

Chittenden, Newton H. [IP]
American author
* [A] Resident

Ch'o, Chou
See Shu-Jen, Chou

Chor-Episcopus
See Waugh, John

Chorley, Charles 1810-1874 [IP]
British journalist
* C. C.
* Tugmutton, Timothy, Esq.

Chorley, Henry Fothergill
1808-1872 [IP, NPS]
British author, art critic, journalist
* Bell, Paul
* H. F. C.

[El] Chorro [The Fountain]
See Moreno, Anthony

Christabel
See Downing, Mary

Christen, Ada
See Christine, Friderik

[A] Christian
See Hewetson, William

Christian, Black Jack
See Christian, Will

Christian, Charles [IP]
American author
* [A] Citizen

Christian, Neil
See Bird, Mary Page

Christian, Paul
See Pitois, J. B.

Christian, Sydney [NPS]
Author
* Lord, M. L.

Christian, Theophilus, Esq.
See Owen, John

[A] Christian Whig
See Watson, Richard

Christian, Will ?-1897 [EWG]
American gunfighter
* Christian, Black Jack
* 202
* Williams, Ed

Christian II 1480?-1559 [NPS]
King of Denmark, Norway, and Sweden
* [The] Angry
(See also base volume)

Christianson, Oliver 20th c.
Author and cartoonist
* Revilo

Christianson, Willard Erastus
1864-1938 [EWG]
American gunfighter
* [The] Mormon Kid
(See also base volume)

Christie, Agatha [Mary Clarissa]
1891-1976 [CR]
British author and playwright
* [The] Mistress of Misdirection
(See also base volume)

Christie, William 1750-1823 [IP]
Scottish-American clergyman and author
* [A] Protestant Dissenter

Christie's Will
See Armstrong, William

Christina-Marie
See Umscheid, Christina Marie

Christine, Friderik 1844- ? [IP]
Austrian poet
* Christen, Ada

Christison, Robert [IP]
British clergyman and author
* [A] Dissenting Minister
* [An] Ex Dissenting Minister

Christophe, M., Vigneron
See Boucher de, Crevecoeur de Perthes

Christophers, Samuel Woolcock
1810- ? [IP]
British clergyman and author
* [An] Old Cornish Boy

Christy, David 1802- ? [IP]
Author
* Agent of the American Colonization Society
* [An] American

Christy, Edwin Byron 1838-1866
[IP]
American singer
* E. C. B.
* Fox, Charley

Chroniqueuse
See Sikes, Olive [Logan]

Chrysal
See Scott, [Sir] William [Lord Stowell]

Chrystabel
See Attenborough, Florence G.

Chrystal, Thomas B. [IP]
American journalist
* Krys
(See also base volume)

Chu, Vincent
See Zhu Hongshen

Chuikov, Vasily I. 1900?-1982
Russian military leader
* Stubbornness, General

Church, Benjamin 1734-1776 [IP]
American scholar, physician, poet
* [An] American
* Elizaphan of Parnach
* [A] Son of Liberty
* [A] Young Gentleman
(See also base volume)

Church, Edward, Jr. 1779-1845
[IP]
American author and businessman
* [A] Gentleman Formerly of Boston

Church, Thomas 18th c. [IP]
American author
* T. C.

Churchill, Charles 1731-1764
[NPS]
British author and poet
* [The] British Juvenal
(See also base volume)

Churchill, John [First Duke of Marlborough] 1650-1722 [NPS]
British army officer
* [The] British Pallas
* Hocus, Humphrey
(See also base volume)

Churchill, May Vivienne
See Lambert, May

[A] Churchman
See Bowden, John

[A] Churchman
See Lorimer, John Gordon

[A] Churchman
See Smedley, Edward

Churchman, Theophilus
See Heylyn, Peter

Cibber, Colley 1671-1757 [NPS]
British actor and playwright
* [The] Spagnolet of the Theatre
(See also base volume)

Ciccio di Majo
See Majo, Giovanni

Cicero, Marcus Tullius
See Melmoth, William

[The] Cicero of Portugal
See Osorio, Jeronymo

Cienfuegos, Ferman
See Sancho Castaneda, Eduardo

Cieppe, G.
See Pelly, Gerald Conn

Cilffriw, Gwynfor
See Griffith, Thomas Gwynfor

Cimon
See Anderson, James

Cineo, Jose 1841-1899 [GS]
Spanish bullfighter
* [El] Cirineo [The Assistant]

[El] Cirineo [The Assistant]
See Cineo, Jose

Cirujano, M. M. C.
See Childs, George Borlase

Cisternes de Coutiras, Gabrielle Anne de 1805- ? [IP]
French author
* Dash, La Comtesse
* Reynaud, Jacques

[A] Citizen
See Arnot, Hugo

[A] Citizen
See Christian, Charles

[A] Citizen
See Hack, James

[A] Citizen of Aberdeen
See Gordon, William

[A] Citizen of Baltimore
See Tyson, John S.

[A] Citizen of Maryland
See Allen, John

[A] Citizen of Massachusetts
See Austin, James Trecothick

[A] Citizen of Massachusetts
See Bowdoin, James

[A] Citizen of Massachusetts
See Curtis, George Ticknor

[A] Citizen of New England
See Hooke, Josiah

[A] Citizen of Pennsylvania
See Ingersoll, Charles

[A] Citizen of Pennsylvania
See Packard, Frederick Adolphus

[A] Citizen of the United States
See Armroyd, George

[A] Citizen of the United States
See Poinsett, Joel Roberts

[A] Citizen of the West
See Mackay, Robert

[A] Citizen of the West
See Owen, Robert Dale

[A] Citizen of the World
See Broadhead, James

[A] Citizen of Virginia
See Bourne, George

[The] City Bard
See Blackmore, [Sir] Richard

[The] City Items Scribe
See Cowdrick, Jesse C.

[A] Civil War Captain
See Rolfe, Maro Orlando

Civis
See Hoey, Christopher Clinton

Civis
See Russell, [Sir] Henry

Civis
See Scott, [Sir] William [Lord Stowell]

Claiborne, William F. 1860-1882
[EWG]
American gunfighter
* Billy the Kid

Claire, Amelie [NPS]
Author
* Stuart, Esme

Clan-na-Rory
See Roddy, John Gerald

Clanton, Ike
See Clanton, Joseph Isaac

Clanton, Joseph Isaac ?-1887
[EWG]
American gunfighter
* Clanton, Ike

Clanton, N. H. 19th c.
[CEC, EWG]
American gunfighter
* Clanton, Old Man

Clanton, Old Man
See Clanton, N. H.

Clara Augusta
See Jones, Clara Augusta

Clare, Bertie
See Vizetelly, Edmund

Clare, George
See Klaar, George

Clare, Gilbert de 1243-1295 [NPS]
Eighth Earl of Gloucester
* [The] Red
(See also base volume)

Clarence
See Mangan, James Clarence

Claribel?
See Barnard, Mrs. Charles

Claridge, John, Shepherd
See Campbell, John

Clark, Capt.
See Clark, Charles Dunning

Clark, Charles 1806-1880 [NPS]
Author
* C. C.
* Chilly Charley

Clark, Charles Dunning 1843-1892
American author and journalist
* Clark, Capt.
* DeForrest, Barry

Clark, Charles Dunning (Continued)
* Hamilton, Wm. J.

Clark, Fuss
See Clark, Harold

Clark, Harold 20th c. [EF]
American football player
* Clark, Fuss

Clark, James Alfred 1886- [WEC]
American cartoonist and illustrator
* Clark, Rene

Clark, Joseph ?-1696? [NPS]
British posture-master
* Clark, Proteus

Clark, Kenneth Sherman
1882-1945 [DNA]
American author and musician
* Leach, Clifford

Clark, Lydia Benson
See Meaker, Eloise

Clark, Melissa 1949- [CA]
American author and playwright
* Aallyn, Alysse

Clark, Nobby
See Clark, William

Clark, Proteus
See Clark, Joseph

Clark, Rene
See Clark, James Alfred

Clark, Robert 1928- [CR]
American painter
* Indiana, Robert

Clark, Sabina
See Willman, Marianne

Clark, William 1840-1887 [RBE]
British-born boxer
* Clark, Nobby

Clark, William Adolphus
1825-1906 [DNA]
American poet
* Anicetus

Clarke, Boden
See Burgess, Michael Roy

Clarke, J. Clayton 1840-1871
[ICB]
British illustrator
* Kyd

Clarke, Jean
See Tuttle, Charles Richard

Clarke, Marion 19th c. [PI]
Irish poet
* Drake, Miriam

Clarke, Mrs. [NPS]
Author
* Lindsay, Mayne

Clarke, Old
See Clarke, William

Clarke, Owen
See Martin, James

Clarke, Samuel 1675-1729 [NPS]
British philosopher and clergyman
* [A] Reasoning Engine
(See also base volume)

Clarke, Sarah J. 1840-1929 [DNA]
American author
* Shirley, Penn

Clarke, William 1798-1856 [EC]
British cricketer
* Clarke, Old

[The] Classic Rambler
See Johnson, Samuel

Claudero, Son of Nimrod
See Wilson, James

Claudia
See Hack, Mary P.

Clauren, H.
See Heun, Karl Gottlob Samuel

Clay, Henry 1777-1852 [NPS]
American statesman
* Gallant Harry of the West
* Grand Old Man
* [The] Savior of His Country
(See also base volume)

Clay Pipe Alice
See Mackenzie, Alice

Cleary, Thomas Stanislaus
1851-1898 [PI]
Irish poet
* Free Lance
* O'Dunn, Denis
* Telephone, Tom

Cleaveland, Mrs. Willis M. 20th c.
[EOP]
Claimed to possess psychic powers
* Smead, Mrs.

Cleeve, Lucas
See Kingscote, Mrs. Howard

Clelland, Catherine
See Townsend, Doris McFerran

Clemens Anglicanus
See Turton, Thomas

Clemens, Rodgers
See Lovin, Roger Robert

Clemens, Samuel Langhorne
1835-1910 [CA, TLC]
American author
* Grumbler
* Josh
* Muggins
* Snodgrass, Thomas Jefferson
(See also base volume)

Clemens, William Montgomery
1860-1931 [DNA]
American author and genealogist
* Blake, Rodney

Clements, Emmanuel ?-1887
[EWG]
American gunfighter
* Clements, Mannen

Clements, Emmanuel, Jr. ?-1908
[EWG]
American gunfighter
* Clements, Mannie

Clements, Gyp
See Clements, John Gipson

Clements, John Gipson 19th c.
[BLB]
American gunfighter
* Clements, Gyp

Clements, Mannen
See Clements, Emmanuel

Clements, Mannie
See Clements, Emmanuel, Jr.

Clemo, Ebenezer 1831?-1860
[DNA]
British-born author
* Maple Knot

Cleon
See Long, Edward

[A] Clergyman
See Acland, Peter Leopold Dyke

[A] Clergyman
See Armstrong, Skeffington

[A] Clergyman
See Horne, George

[A] Clergyman
See Morrison, John

[A] Clergyman
See Tyrwhitt, Richard

[A] Clergyman in the Country
See Horbery, Matthew

**[A] Clergyman of the Church of
England**
See Dawson, Benjamin

**[A] Clergyman of the Church of
England**
See Margoliouth, Moses

**[A] Clergyman of the Church of
England**
See Pace, William

**[A] Clergyman of the Church of
England**
See Plumptre, John

**[A] Clergyman of the Church of
England**
See Richmond, Legh

**[A] Clergyman of the Episcopal
Church, in England**
See Heygate, William Edward

[A] Clergyman of the Old School
See Aiton, John

[A] Clergyman's Daughter
See Gaye, Selina

[A] Clergyman's Daughter
See Lloyd, Emma F.

[A] Clergyman's Wife
See Alford, Fanny

[A] Clergyman's Wife
See Hart, Fanny [Wheeler]

Clericus
See Meehan, Charles Patrick

Clericus
See Tormey, Michael

Cleveland, Mary 1917- [CA]
American author and horse-trainer
* Allen, Mary
* Twelveponies, Mary

Cliffe, Leigh
See Jones, George

Clifford, Ella
See Paull, Minnie E. [Kenney]

Clifton, Bud
See Stacton, David [Derek]

Clifton, Dan ?-1896 [BLB, EWG]
American gunfighter
* Dynamite Dick

Clifton, Tom
See Robbins, Alfred Farthing

Clinche, Hugh ?-1847 [PI]
Irish poet
* H. C.

Clinton, De Witt 1769-1828 [DNA]
American statesman and author
* Grotius
(See also base volume)

Clinton, Walter
See Adams, William Henry
Davenport

Clio
See Gough, Richard

Clio
See O'Reilly, Edward James

Clio
See Rickman, Thomas

Cliodhna
See O'Donovan Rossa, Mary Jane

Clissmann, Anne 1945- [CA]
Irish author
* Clune, Anne

Clogheen, H.
See Heffernan, Michael J.

Clonmeliensis
See Hickie, Daniel B.

Clontarf
See O'Brien, Thomas

Close, John 1816-1891 [NPS]
Author
* Close, Poet
* Veritas
(See also base volume)

Close, John George 19th c. [PI]
Irish poet
* J. G. C.

Close, Poet
See Close, John

Cloutier, Helen H.
See Schmock, Helen H.

[The] Clown Prince of Comedy
See Leopold, Isaiah Edwin

[The] Clownish Sycophant
See Wordsworth, William

Clune, Anne
See Clissmann, Anne

Clute, Oscar 1873-1902 [DNA]
Author
* Allen, John

Clyde, Bernard
See Aiken, George L.

[The] Coal Master
See Lambton, John George [First
Earl of Durham]

Coates, Joseph Hornor 1849-1930
[DNA]
American journalist
* Cotes, Hornor

Cobb, Clayton W.
See Patten, J. Alexander

Cobb, Sylvanus, Jr. 1823-1887
[DNA, WW]
American author and clergyman
* Burdick, Austin C.
* Castleton, Charles
* Dunlap, Walter B.
* Fitzwhistler, Enoch
* Symus, the Pilgrim

Cobb, Sylvanus, Jr. (Continued)
* Winslow, Amos, Jr.

Cobb, Weldon J. 19th c.   [WW]
American author and journalist
* Ulmar, Genevieve

Cobbett, William 1762-1835   [NPS]
British author, journalist, politician
* [The] Hampshire Farmer
* Trumpeter of Pitt
(See also base volume)

[The] Cobbling Wonder of Ashburton
See Gifford, William

Coburn, Louis
See Cohen, Louis

Coburn, Mrs. Fordyce
Author
* Abbott, Eleanor Hallowell

Cobweb
See Buckingham, Joseph Tinker

Cochet, Georges 1872- ?   [EOP]
French author, musician, poet, who claimed to possess psychic powers
* Forthuny, Pascal

Cochrane, Gordon Stanley 1903-1962
American baseball player
* Cochrane, Iron Mike
(See also base volume)

Cochrane, Iron Mike
See Cochrane, Gordon Stanley

Cockburn, Catherine 1679-1749
[NPS]
Scottish playwright
* [The] Female Philosopher of the North
(See also base volume)

Cockburn, [Francis] Claud
1904-1981   [CA]
Scottish journalist and author
* Cork, Patrick
* Drew, Kenneth
(See also base volume)

Cockeyed Frank Loving
See Loving, Frank

Cocking, George [Little]
See Onslow, George

Code, Henry Brereton
See Cody, Henry Brereton

Codrus
See Settle, Elkanah

Cody, Henry Brereton ?-1830?
[PI]
Irish author and poet
* Code, Henry Brereton
* Greendrake, Gregory
* H. B. C.

Coelebs
See Carlyon, Edward Augustus

Coelebs in Search of a Wife
See Martley, John

Coen, John 19th c.   [PI]
Irish poet
* Bridget
* Patricius

Coffee, James 20th c.   [EF]
American football player
* Coffee, Pat

Coffee, Pat
See Coffee, James

Coggins, Paschal Heston
1852-1917   [DNA]
American author and attorney
* Marlow, Sidney

[La] Coghetta [Little Cook]
See Gabrielli, Caterina

Coghlan, Charles   [IP]
British playwright
* C. C.

Cohen, Alexander 1920-   [CR]
American producer
* [The] Millionaire Boy Angel

Cohen, D. S.   [IP]
American author
* Shortcut, Daisy

Cohen, Francis 1788-1861
[DEA, JL]
British author and historian
* Palgrave, [Sir] Francis

Cohen, Louis 1915-   [CA]
American author and editor
* Coburn, Louis

Cohn, Martin 1829- ?   [IP]
German author
* Mels, August
* Spavento, Don

Coigney, Virginia 1917-   [CA]
American author
* Travers, Virginia

Coilus
See Flecher, Henry McDonald

Coke, Desmond 1879- ?   [NPS]
British author
* Charbon

Coke, Edward Thomas 19th c.   [IP]
British army officer and author
* [A] Subaltern

Colange, Auguste Leo de 1819- ?
[IP]
French poet and journalist
* Dr. Leo

Colban, Marie Sophie [Schmidt 1814-
?   [IP]
Norwegian author
* [Une] Barbare

Colbatch, John 18th c.   [IP]
British author
* J. C., M.D.
* [A] Person Concer'n'd

Colburn
See James, Franklin

Colcroft, James
See Cole, John Webb

Coldstreamer
See Graham, Harry

Cole, Francis Edward Baston 1813-
?   [IP]
British clergyman and author
* [A] Cornish Curate

Cole, Francis Sewell   [IP]
British author
* Effessea
* F. S. C.

Cole, Harriet Adelia Ann [Burleigh]
1836-1865   [IP]
American author
* Guare, June

Cole, [Sir] Henry 1808-1882   [IP]
British author
* Denarius
* F. S.
(See also base volume)

Cole, James L. 1799-1823   [IP]
American poet
* Adrian

Cole, John Webb ?-1872   [IP]
British translator
* Colcroft, James

Cole, John William 1793?-1870
[PI]
Irish author, actor, stage-manager
* Calcraft, John William

Cole, L. M.   [IP]
British author
* L. M. C.

Cole, Lois Dwight 1903-1979   [CA]
American author
* Lattin, Ann
* Taylor, Lois Dwight Cole
(See also base volume)

Cole, Owen Blayney 1808-1886
[PI]
Irish poet
* O. B. C.

Cole, William   [IP]
British clergyman and poet
* W. C., Rev.

Colebrooke, [Sir] George   [IP]
British author and politician
* [A] Layman

Coleman, Lyman 1796-1881   [IP]
American educator and clergyman
* L. C.

Coleman, Patrick James 1867- ?
[PI]
Irish poet
* Nemo

Coleman, William   [IP]
American author
* [A] Voice from Kentucky

Colenso, John William 1814-1883
[IP]
British clergyman and author
* Bishop of Natal

Coleridge, [Sir] John Taylor
1790-1876   [HFN, IP]
British jurist, poet, author
* [A] Barrister

Coleridge, Mary Elizabeth ?-1907
[NPS]
Poet
* Anodos

Coleridge, Samuel Taylor
1772-1834   [DLE1, NPS]
British poet, philosopher, critic
* Comberback, Silas Tomkyn
* Higginbottom, Nehemiah
* [The] High Priest of Romanticism
* Porson, Professor [joint pseudonym with Robert Southey]
* [A] Second Johnson
(See also base volume)

Coles, Carrotty Nell
See Coles, Frances

Coles, Charles Barwell 19th c.
[HFN]
Author
* Major A.

Coles, Frances 1866?-1891   [BL]
Prostitute and murder victim
* Coles, Carrotty Nell

Coles, Miriam
See Harris, Mrs. Sydney S.

Colette, Sidonie Gabrielle
1873-1954   [CA]
French author
* Willy
(See also base volume)

Colin
See Cunningham, William

Colleen
See Pender, Margaret T.

[A] Collegian
See Simms, William Gilmore

Colleton, John
See Marks, Robert Walter

Collier, Hiram Price 1860-1913
[DNA]
American author
* Collins, Percy

Collin, Jacques Albin Simon
1794-1881   [WGT]
French author
* Collin de Plancy, J. A. S.
* Homidas-Peath, Sir
* J. A. S. C. de P.
* Loyseau, Jacques
(See also base volume)

Collin de Plancy, J. A. S.
See Collin, Jacques Albin Simon

Collins, Al 20th c.   [CMA]
American disc jockey
* Collins, Jazzbo

Collins, Cuthbert Dale 1897-1956
[DLE1]
Australian author
* Fennimore, Stephen

Collins, Edward James Mortimer
1827-1876   [DEA, WGT]
British author
* Cotton, Robert Turner

Collins, Jazzbo
See Collins, Al

Collins, John Norman 1947?-   [DI]
American murderer
* [The] Ypsilanti Ripper

Collins, Percy
See Collier, Hiram Price

Collins, Tom
See Furphy, Joseph

Collins, [William] Wilkie
1824-1889   [NLC]
British author and playwright
* [The] Father of the English Detective Novel

Collins, William 1721-1759   [NPS]
Poet
* [The] Mad Poet

Collopy, William 19th c.   [PI]
Irish poet
* Desmond

Colman, George 1762-1836
[HFN, NPS]
Author, playwright, poet
* George the Grinner
* Griffinhoof, Arthur
* [The] Temple Leech

Colmont, Marie
See Delavaud, Marie Collin

Colon
See Dennie, Joseph

Colon and Spondee
See Tyler, Royall

[The] Colonel
See Kray, Ronald [Ronnie]

Colosimo, Diamond Jim
See Colosimo, James

Colosimo, James 1877-1920 [DI]
American underworld figure
* Colosimo, Diamond Jim
(See also base volume)

[A] Colossus
See Rhodes, Cecil

[The] Colossus of the Revolution
See Adams, John

Colquitt, Alfred Holt 1824- ?
[BDSA]
American author, statesman, army officer
* [The] Hero of Olustee

Colson, Sylvester
See Curtis, Winslow

Columella
See Moore, Clement Clarke

Colzie, Cornelius Connie 1954-
[FR]
American football player
* Colzie, Neal

Colzie, Neal
See Colzie, Cornelius Connie

Coman
See Kelly, James J.

Comanche Jack Stilwell
See Stilwell, Simpson E.

Combe, T.
See Huguenin, Adele

Comberbach
See Orr, Andrew

Comberback, Silas Tomkyn
See Coleridge, Samuel Taylor

[The] Comedy Writer
See Andersen, Hans Christian

Comer, Jack 1912- ? [DI]
American underworld figure
* Comer, Spot

Comer, Spot
See Comer, Jack

Comfort, Mrs. J. A. [NPS]
Author
* Marchant, Bessie

Commins, Andrew 1832- ? [PI]
Irish poet
* A. C.
* Dawe, John, jun.
* [The] Gael
* O'Toole, Phelim

[A] Committee Man
See Nightingale, Joseph

Common Sense
See Goldsmith, Oliver

Common Sense
See Phillips, [Sir] Richard

Commoner
See Gould, William

Commoner, Barry 1917- [CR]
American biologist
* [The] Paul Revere of Ecology

Commonwealth Didapper
See Needham, Marchamont

[A] Comprehensionist
See Wilson, Frederick J.

Compton, Frances Snow
See Adams, Henry [Brooks]

Compton, Henry 1632-1713 [NPS]
British clergyman
* Jack Boots

Compton, Margaret
See Harrison, Amelia [Williams]

Computer Bob McNamara
See McNamara, Robert Strange

Comstock, Augustus 1837- ?
American author
* Starbuck, Roger

Comus
See Ballantyne, Robert Michael

Conaciensis
See Hughes, Matthew F.

Conan, Laure
See Angers, Felicite

Concobar, Clann
See O'Mulrenin, Richard Joseph

Condon, Lizzie G. 1857- ? [PI]
Irish poet
* Alice
* L. G. C.
* Lizzie

Condon, Thomas 1834?-1864 [PI]
Irish poet
* Maelmuire

Confuter, Captain
See Nash [or Nashe?], Thomas

Congdon, Charles Taber
1821-1891 [DNA]
American journalist and poet
* Potter, Paul

Congreve, William 1670-1729
[NPS]
British playwright
* [The] Best Vitruvius
(See also base volume)

Coningsby, Christopher
See Harris, Samuel Smith

Conkling, Margaret Cockburn
1814-1890 [DNA]
American author
* Lunettes, Henry

Conn, George 20th c. [EF]
American football player
* Conn, Tuffy

Conn, Tuffy
See Conn, George

Connell, Kirk [joint pseudonym with Mary Hamilton (Ilsley) Chapman]
See Chapman, John Stanton Higham

Connell, Kirk [joint pseudonym with John Stanton Higham Chapman]
See Chapman, Mary Hamilton [Ilsley]

Connelly, Celia [Logan Kellogg]
1837-1904 [DNA]
American journalist
* Fairfax, L.

Connolly, Charlotte 1836-1899
[EOP]
Claimed to possess psychic powers
* Fowler, Lottie

Connor, Kitty
See McKowen, James

Conolly, James ?-1791 [PI]
Irish poet
* [The] Bard of Macroom

[The] Conqueror
See Alexander III

[The] Conqueror
See Matthias Corvinus

[The] Conqueror
See Maximilian I

Conrad, Bobby Joe
See Conrad, Robert

Conrad, Robert 20th c. [EF]
American football player
* Conrad, Bobby Joe

Conroy, J. D.
See Rymer, James Malcolm

Conselheiro, Antonio
See Medes Macial, Antonio
Vicente

[A] Conservative
See Elliot, John Lettsom

Conservative, Mr.
See Goldwater, Barry [Morris]

[A] Consistent Protestant
See Watson, Richard

Constable, Archibald 1775-1821
[NPS]
Publisher
* [The] Czar of Muscovy

Constable, Michael 19th c. [PI]
Irish poet
* M. C.

Constant, Alphonse Louis
1810?-1875 [EOP]
French author and occultist
* [The] Last of the Magi
(See also base volume)

Constantin, L. A.
See Hesse, Lepold Auguste
Constantin

Constantius I [Flavius Valerius Constantius] 250?- 306 [NPS]
Roman emperor
* [The] Pale
(See also base volume)

Constellano, Juan
See Lewis, John Woodruff

Constellano, Mrs. Illion
See Lewis, Harriet Newell

[A] Constitutional Reformer
See Rutter, John

[The] Contractor General
See Bonaparte, Napoleon

Converse, Harriet [Maxwell]
1836-1903 [DNA]
American author
* Musidora

Converse, Harriet [Maxwell]
(Continued)
* Salome

[The] Converted Jacobin
See Wordsworth, William

Conway, H. B.
See Coulson, H. B.

Conway, Olive [joint pseudonym with John Walton]
See Brighouse, Harold

Conway, Olive [joint pseudonym with Harold Brighouse]
See Walton, John

Cook, Carroll Blaine 1883-1922
[DNA]
American author
* Carroll, Dixie

Cook, Dorothy Mary 1907- [CA]
British author
* Carlisle, D. M.
(See also base volume)

Cook, Linen
See Cook, Robert

Cook, Mrs. George Cram
Author
* Glaspell, Susan

Cook, Peter 1928- [DI]
British rapist
* [The] Cambridge Rapist

Cook, Robert 1646?-1728? [NPS]
British eccentric
* Cook, Linen

Cook, William Wallace 1867-1933
[DNA, MA]
American author
* Edwards, John Milton
* Standish, Burt
(See also base volume)

Cooke, [Sir] George 1768-1837
[NPS]
British army officer
* Kangaroo

Cooke, John Esten 1830-1886
[DNA]
American author
* Todkill, Anas
(See also base volume)

Cooke, M. E.
See Creasey, John

Coombe-Tennant, Winifred Margaret Serocold 1874-1956 [EOP]
Claimed to possess psychic powers
* Willett, Mrs.

Coomes, Oliver [Oll] 1845-1921
American author
* Dexter, Will

Coon, Edward 20th c. [EF]
American football player
* Coon, Ty

Coon, Ty
See Coon, Edward

Cooney, Cecelia [Roth] 1904- ?
[LFW]
American bandit
* [The] Bobbed-Haired Bandit

Cooper, A. N. 1850- ? [NPS]
Clergyman and author
* [The] Walking Parson

Cooper, Andy
See Blevins, Andy

Cooper, Anthony Ashley
1621-1683 [NPS]
British statesman
* Little Machiavel
* Old Tony
* Shaftesbury, First Earl of
* Shiftesbury
* Tapsky

Cooper, Cecil Celester 1949-
American baseball player
* Cooper, Coop
(See also base volume)

Cooper, Coop
See Cooper, Cecil Celester

Cooper, Edith Emma 1862-1913
[DLE1]
British author and poet
* Arran [joint pseudonym with
   Katharine Harris Bradley]
(See also base volume)

Cooper, James Fenimore
1789-1851 [DNA, MBF, NPS]
American author
* [The] American Walter Scott
* Littlepage, Cornelius
* Morgan, Jane
(See also base volume)

Cooper, John 1575?-1626 [BBD]
British musician
* Coperario

Cooper, Lynna
See Fox, Gardner Francis

Cooper, Samuel 1609-1672 [NPS]
British painter
* Vandyck in Little
(See also base volume)

Cootehill, M.
See Sadleir, Mary Anne

Coover, Wayne?
See Rohr, Wolf Detlef

Copeland, James ?-1857 [BLB]
American murderer
* [The] Great Southern Land Pirate

Coperario
See Cooper, John

Copleston, John Gay 19th c. [IP]
British clergyman and author
* [A] Sojourner

Copper, Basil 1924- [TCCM]
British author
* Falk, Lee

Copper Face
See Cromwell, Oliver

Copper, Frederic Taber
Author
* Winter, Calvin

Copper Nose
See Cromwell, Oliver

Coppernosed Saint
See Cromwell, Oliver

Coppinger, Cruel
See Coppinger, Daniel

Coppinger, Daniel 18th c. [CEC]
Danish smuggler
* Coppinger, Cruel

Coppinger, Matthew
See Dryden, John

Coppola, Frank 1900?-1982
Sicilian-born underworld figure
* Coppola, Three Fingers

Coppola, Three Fingers
See Coppola, Frank

Copywell, James
See Woty, William

Cor-de-Chasse
See Stockton, William T.

[El] Coracero [The Cuirassier]
See Carrion, Manuel

Coram, Robert [IP]
American politician and author
* Brutus

Corannus
See Henry VIII

Corbet, William John 1824-1909
[PI]
Irish poet
* Wildair, Harry

Corbett, Thomas 18th c. [IP]
British author
* T. C.

Corcoran, Peter
See Reynolds, John Hamilton

Cordell, Charles [IP]
British clergyman and author
* C. A. D. A.
* C. C.

Corder, Susanna 1788-1864 [IP]
British author
* [A] Total Abstainer

Corelli, Angelo 1653-1713 [NPS]
Italian musician
* Archangelo

Corey, John ?-1721? [IP]
British playwright
* J. C.

Corfield, Frederick [IP]
British author
* F. C.

Corinne
See Dahlgren, Sarah Madeleine
[Vinton]

Cork, Patrick
See Cockburn, [Francis] Claud

Corkling, Mary Anne [Yates] 19th
c. [IP]
British author
* Yates, M.

Corlett, John 1841- ? [NPS]
British writer
* [The] Master
(See also base volume)

Corley, Daryll 20th c.
American basketball player
* Corley, Rhino

Corley, Rhino
See Corley, Daryll

Cormack, John Rose [IP]
Scottish physician and author
* J. R. C.

Cornelius, Siegfried 1911- [WEC]
Danish cartoonist
* Moco [Joint signature with Jorgen
   Mogensen]
(See also base volume)

Cornell, Bo
See Cornell, Robert Paul

Cornell, J. H. [IP]
American clergyman and author
* [A] Priest of the Congregation of
   the Holy Redeemer

Cornell, Robert Paul 1949-
[EF, FR]
American football player
* Cornell, Bo

Corner, George Richard 1801-1863
[IP]
British barrister and antiquary
* G. R. C.

[El] Corneta [The Bugle]
See Martin Sevilla, Francisco

Corney the Rhymer
See Hughes, Terence McMahon

[A] Cornish Curate
See Cole, Francis Edward Baston

Cornish, Kate 20th c. [BDSA]
American poet
* Courtland, Kil

[The] Cornish Poet
See Michael, Blaunpayn

Cornu, Hortense [Lacroix] 19th c.
[IP]
French author
* Albin, Sebastien

Cornwall, Baby
See Proctor, Bryan Waller

Cornwall, Ebenezer [IP]
British author
* E. C.

Cornwallis, Caroline Frances
1786-1858 [IP]
British author
* Brown, Thomas, Redivivus
* [A] Pariah

Corporal
See Haines, Zenas T.

Corry, Thomas H. ?-1887 [PI]
Irish poet and botanist
* T. H. C.

Corsi [or Corso], Giuseppe 17th c.
[BBD]
Italian composer
* Celano

[The] Corsican Fiend
See Bonaparte, Napoleon

Cortissoz, Ellen M. H.
Author
* Hutchinson, Ellen M.

Corvinus
See Twiss, [Sir] Travers

Corvo de Camoes, Joao de Andrade
1824- ? [IP]
Poet and educator
* Andrade

Cory, Charles Barney 1857-1921
[DNA, IP]
American author
* Nox, Owen

Coryell, John Russell 1848-1924
[DNA]
American author
* Russell, Lucy May
(See also base volume)

Corymboeus
See Braithwaite, Richard

Cosel, Charlotte von 1818- ? [IP]
German poet
* Von Adelheid, Auer

Cosmo
See Gutch, John Mathew

[A] Cosmopolitan
See Dix, John

[A] Cosmopolite
See Martin, Alfred Tobias John

Costan, James ?-1973 [LFW]
American political activist
* Shakur, Zayd Malik

Costello, Mrs. Vincent
Author
* Johnson, Fanny Kemble

Costillares [Big Ribs]
See Rodriguez, Joaquin

Cosway, Richard 1740-1821 [NPS]
Painter
* [The] Macaroni Painter

Cotes, Hornor
See Coates, Joseph Hornor

Cotes, Humphrey 18th c. [IP]
British author
* N. C. M. S. C.

Cotes, Mrs. E. 20th c. [NPS]
Canadian journalist and author
* Duncan, Sara Jeanette

Cotton, Henry 1790-1879 [IP]
British clergyman and author
* Catholicus

Cotton, Junior
See Bridges, Thomas

[A] Cotton Manufacturer
See Atkinson, Edward

Cotton, Mr.
See Perreau, Henri

Cotton, Robert Turner
See Collins, Edward James
Mortimer

Cotton, William Charles 19th c.
[IP]
British translator
* W. C. C.

Couch, Jonathan 1789-1870 [IP]
British naturalist and author
* Ipolperroc
* Video

Coues, Samuel Elliott ?-1867 [IP]
American author
* Elliott

Coulson, H. B. 1850- ? [IP]
British actor
* Conway, H. B.

Coulter, DeWitt 20th c. [EF]
American football player
* Coulter, Tex

Coulter, Tex
See Coulter, DeWitt

[The] Count
See Morris, John Scott [Jack]

[A] Countreyman
See Anderson, John

[A] **Country Clergyman**
See Butler, John

[A] **Country Clergyman**
See Ingram, Robert

[A] **Country Clergyman**
See Sikes, Thomas

[A] **Country Clergyman**
See Wake, William

[A] **Country Clergyman**
See Wilson, Plumpton

[A] **Country Curate**
See McHale, M. J.

[A] **Country Curate**
See Tayler, Charles Benjamin

[A] **Country Curate**
See White, James

[A] **Country Editor**
See Hooper, Johnson J.

[A] **Country Gentleman**
See Polwhele, Richard

[A] **Country Gentleman**
See Turton, [Sir] Thomas

[A] **Country Minister**
See Wroe, Caleb

[A] **Country Parson?**
See Hayman, Samuel

[A] **Country Schoolmaster**
See Leggett, William

Court Evil
See Courteville, Raphael

Court, Wesli
See Turco, Lewis

Courtenay, John, Jr. ?-1794   [PI]
Irish poet
* J. C., jun.

Courteville, Raphael ?-1772   [NPS]
British musician and author
* Court Evil

Courthope, William James
1842-1917   [NPS]
British author
* Homo Novus
(See also base volume)

Courtland, Kil
See Cornish, Kate

Courtright, Longhaired Jim
See Courtright, Timothy Isaiah

Courtright, Timothy Isaiah
1848-1887   [EWG]
American law officer and gunfighter
* Courtright, Longhaired Jim

Cousin Alice
See Tabor, E.

Cousin Bridget
See Lamb, Mary

Coutts, Tristram   [NPS]
Author
* Smiff, Sam

Couvreur, Jessie Catherine [Huybers]
1848?-1897   [DLE1, NPS]
Australian author and journalist
* Tasma

Coveney, [Sister] Mary 19th c.   [PI]
Irish poet
* Moi-Meme

Coventry, John
See Palmer, John Williamson

Covertside, Naunton
See Davies, Naunton

[The] **Covington Poet**
See O'Connor, Paul

Cowan, C.
See Jobling, Charlotte

Cowdrick, Jesse C. 1859-1899
[WW]
American author and poet
* Arizona Cy
* [The] City Items Scribe

Cowell, Joe
See Witchett, Joseph Leatherley

Cowles, Gardner 1901-   [CR]
American publisher
* Cowles, Mike

Cowles, Mike
See Cowles, Gardner

Cowley, Abraham 1618-1667
[NPS]
British poet
* Our English Virgil
* Our Pindar
(See also base volume)

Cowslip
See Wells, Mary

Cox, Erle 1873-1950   [DLE1]
Australian author and journalist
* [The] Chiel

Cox, Henry Hamilton 1769?-1821
[DNA]
Irish poet
* Hamilton, Henry

Cox, James Anthony 1926-   [CA]
American author and editor
* Porter, Mark

Cox, M. B.
See West, Noel

Cox, Marie-Therese Henriette
1925-   [CA]
Turkish-born author, scriptwriter, producer
* Cox, Molly

Cox, Molly
See Cox, Marie-Therese Henriette

[The] **Coxcomb Bookseller**
See Murray, John

[The] **Coxcomb Czar**
See Alexander I [Aleksandr Pavlovich]

Coxe, Arthur Cleveland 1818- ?
[HFN]
Author
* A.
* A. C. C.
(See also base volume)

Coxe, Edward D. 19th c.
[SFL, WGT]
Author
* [A] Fugitive

Coxe, Henry, Esq.
See Millard, John

Coxe, Tench 1755-1824   [DNA]
American author and economist
* Juriscola

Coyle, Matthew 1862- ?   [PI]
Irish-born poet
* [The] Smiddy Muse

Coyne, Joseph 1839-1891   [PI]
Irish writer and poet
* C. J. M.

Cozens, Alexander ?-1786   [NPS]
British painter
* [The] Father of English
    Water-Colour Painting

Crabbe, George 1754-1832   [NPS]
British clergyman and poet
* Nature's Sternest Painter
(See also base volume)

Crafts, Wilbur Fisk 1850-1922
[DNA]
American author and clergyman
* Fisk, Callene
(See also base volume)

[The] **Craggy-Faced Inquisitor**
See McClellan, John

Craig, Beth
See Carli, Audrey

Craig, Cornelius, Jr. 1948-
[EF, FR]
American football player
* Craig, Neal

Craig, Evelyn Quita 1917-   [CA]
Barbadian-born American author
* Langdale, Eve

Craig, J. H.
See Hogg, James

Craig, Nancy
See Maslin, Alice

Craig, Neal
See Craig, Cornelius, Jr.

Crane, Ichabod
See Thomas, John Daniel

Crane, John 19th c.   [HFN]
Author
* [A] Bird at Bromsgrove

Crane, Stephen [Townley]
1871-1900   [DNA, YAB]
American-born author and poet
* Smith, Johnston

Cranston, Charles
See Judson, Edward Zane Carroll

Crashaw, Richard 1605-1650
[NPS]
Poet
* Blest Swan

Crates 4th c. BC   [NPS]
Athenian philosopher
* [The] Door-Opener

Craven, Charles 18th c.   [UH]
Governor of the Carolinas
* Harrison, Gabriel

Craven, Mary
See Ffoulkes, Mrs.

Crawfie
See Crawford, Marion

Crawford, Marion 20th c.   [PPN]
British royal governess and author
* Crawfie

Crawford, Oswald
See Harris, William Richard

Crawfurd, Oswald John Frederick
1834-1909   [NPS]
British author and poet
* Banks, Archibald
* Turner, Alexander Freke
(See also base volume)

Crawley, Councillor
See Croker, John Wilson

Crayne, Christopher
See Neuburg, Victor [Benjamin]

Crayon, Christopher
See Ritchie, James Ewing

Crayon, Geoffrey, Jr.
See Darley, George

[The] **Crazy Cajun**
See Meaux, Huey

Creasey, John 1908-1973
[CA, TCCM]
British author
* Cooke, M. E.
* Hogarth, Charles [joint
    pseudonym with (Ivor) Ian
    Bowen]
(See also base volume)

[The] **Crediton Poet**
See Jones, C.

Creed, Mrs. J. P.   [NPS]
Author
* Mack, Louise

Creffeld, Edmund Franz 1868-1906
[DI]
German-born American imposter
* Creffield, Joshua Elijah

Creffield, Joshua Elijah
See Creffeld, Edmund Franz

Cregan, Con
See Dowe, William

Crellin, H. N.
See Crellin, Horatio Nelson

Crellin, Horatio Nelson 19th c.
[SFL, WGT]
British author
* Arawiyeh, Al-
* Crellin, H. N.

Cremazie, Octave 1827-1879
Canadian poet
* [The] Father of French Canadian
    Poetry

Crescendo
See Kalisch, A.

Crescentini, Girolamo 1762-1846
[BBD]
Italian singer
* Orfeo Italiano

Cresswell, Frank
See Murphy, Francis Stack

Creutzbergs, Amadei
See Sinhold Von Schutz, Philipp
Balthasar

Cribb, Tom 1781-1848   [NN, NPS]
British boxer
* [The] Black Diamond

Crichton, Harry
See Weir, Henry Crichton

Crichton, John
See Guthrie, Norman Gregor

Crilly, Daniel 1857- ?   [PI]
Irish poet, journalist, politician
* Curry, Owen
* Leinad
* Trevor, Ross E.

[A] **Crimean Chaplain**
See Wright, Henry Press

Cringle, Tom
See Scott, Michael

Cringle, Tom
See Walker, William

Crino
See Tilden, Samuel Jones

Crispin
See Wagstaffe, William

Critchley, Lynne
See Radford, Richard F[rancis], Jr.

Critic and Censor General
See Thornton, Bonnell

Crito
See Millar, John

[The] **Croatian Andersen**
See Brlic-Mazuranic, Ivana

Croce, Giovanni 1560?-1609   [BBD]
Venetian composer
* [Il] Chiozzotto

Crockett, Samuel Rutherford
1860-1914   [DEA, DLE1]
British author
* Bereton, Ford
(See also base volume)

Croft, Milburn 20th c.   [EF]
American football player
* Croft, Tiny

Croft, Tiny
See Croft, Milburn

Croft, Windy
See Croft, Winfield

Croft, Winfield 20th c.   [EF]
American football player
* Croft, Windy

Croke, J. Greenbag
See Hasbrouck, Joseph

Croker, John Wilson 1780-1857
[NPS]
British author
* Crawley, Councillor
(See also base volume)

Croker, Thomas Crofton
1798-1854   [PI]
Irish author
* T. C. C.
(See also base volume)

Croly, Catiline
See Croly, George

Croly, George 1780-1860   [NPS]
Irish author and clergyman
* Croly, Catiline
(See also base volume)

Cromarty, Deas
See Watson, Mrs. Robert A.

Crome, John 1768-1821   [PPN]
British painter
* Old Crome

Cromwell, Oliver 1599-1658
[NN, NPS, PPN]
Lord Protector of England
* [The] Blasphemer
* [The] Brewer
* Copper Face
* Copper Nose
* Coppernosed Saint
* Crumhell
* Fountain, Brother
* [A] Glorious Villain
* [The] Great Independent
* [The] Great Leviathan of Men
* His Noseship
* Immortal Rebel
* [The] Impious
* Megaletor
* Noll
* Nosey
* Ruby Nose
* [The] Sagest of Usurpers
* [The] Town Bull of Ely
(See also base volume)

Cromwell, Richard 1626-1712
[NN]
Lord Protector of England
* King Dick
(See also base volume)

Cronin, Bernard [Charles] 1884- ?
[DLE1]
Australian author
* Bohun, Hugh
(See also base volume)

[The] **Crookedest Cop in New York**
See Becker, Charles

Crop, Lord
See Gordon, George

Crosby, Nellie 1829-1915   [LFW]
American swindler
* Peck, Ellen
* [The] Queen of Confidence Women

Cross, Christopher
See Geppert, Christopher Charles

Cross, Gilbert B. 20th c.   [CA]
American author and editor
* Winters, Jon

Cross, Helen Reeder
See Broadhead, Helen Cross

Cross, Mrs. G. F. 1844- ?   [NPS]
Author
* Cambridge, Ada

Cross, Robert C. 1850-1923   [EOP]
Astrologer
* Raphael VI

Crosse, Launcelot
See Carr, Frank

Crossman, C. O.
See Maginn, William

Crossman, P. J.
See Maginn, William

Crossman, P. P.
See Maginn, William

Crouch, Nathaniel 1681-1736
[NPS]
British author
* R. B.
(See also base volume)

Crowe, John O'Beirne 1825-1878
[PI]
Irish poet
* J. O. B. C.

Crowell, Mary Reed 1847-1934
American author
* Emerce

Crowley, Denis O. 1852- ?   [PI]
Irish author
* Dunboy

Crowley, Edward Alexander
1875-1947   [CA, EOP, TLC]
British author, mystic, cult figure
* Abhavananda
* Bishop, George Archibald
* Boleskine, Lord
* Carr, H. D.
* [A] Gentleman of the University of Cambridge
* Khan, [Prince] Chioa
* Perdurabo, Frater [I Will Endure to the End]
* St. E. A. of M. and S.
* Svareff, [Count] Vladimir
* Therion, Master
* Verey, [Rev.] C.
(See also base volume)

Crowquill, Alfred
See Forrester, Charles Robert

Crowther, Brian
See Grierson, Edward

Croxall, Samuel ?-1752   [NPS]
British author, translator, clergyman
* [A] Gentleman Commoner of Oxford
* Ironside, Nestor

Crucelli, F.
See Sidey, James A.

Cruck-a-leaghan
See Macfadyen, Dugald

[The] **Cruel Judge**
See Tiptoft, John

Cruger, Julia Grinnell [Storrow]
?-1920   [DNA]
French-born author and poet
* Gordon, Julien

Cruikshank, George 1792-1878
[NPS]
* [The] Prince of Caricaturists

Crumhell
See Cromwell, Oliver

Cruz, Florentino 19th c.   [BLB]
American gunfighter
* Cruz, Indian Charlie

Cruz, Indian Charlie
See Cruz, Florentino

Cu-Ulad
See Hoey, John Cashel

Cuan
See McGrath, John

Cuchares [Large Spoons]
See Arjona Herrera, Francisco

Cuchares de Cordoba
See Luque, Antonio

Cuchullin
See Dillon, Thomas

Cudgel, Cuthbert
See Houston, Thomas

Cugat, Xavier 1900-   [CR]
Spanish-born bandleader
* [The] Rhumba King

Cuillinn, Sliabh
See O'Hagan, John

Culhane, Kate 19th c.   [PI]
Irish poet
* Bride, Louisa

Cullen, Countee
See Porter, Countee Leroy

Cullen, John 1837- ?   [PI]
Irish poet
* Llucen

Cullen, P. J. 1856- ?   [PI]
Irish poet
* P. C.

Culmer, Richard 17th c.   [NPS]
British clergyman
* Blueskin Dick
(See also base volume)

Culotta, Nino
See O'Grady, John [Patrick]

Culpepper, Edward 20th c.   [CR]
Entertainer
* Pepper, Jack

[A] **Cumberland Land-Owner**
See Graham, [Sir] James Robert George

Cumberland, Stuart
See Garner, Charles

Cummings, Doc
See Cummings, Samuel M.

Cummings, Elizabeth 19th c.   [IP]
American author
* E. C.

Cummings, Floyd 1951?-
Boxer
* Cummings, Jumbo

Cummings, Jumbo
See Cummings, Floyd

Cummings, M. J. 19th c.   [IP]
American author
* Carnes, Capt.

Cummings, Samuel M. ?-1882
[EWG]
American gunfighter
* Cummings, Doc

Cummins, Alexandrine [Macomb]
[IP]
American author
* His Wife

Cunliffe-Owen, Frederick
Author
* Fontenoy, Marquis de

Cunningham, Bob
See Dikty, Julian May

Cunningham, H. S. 19th c.   [IP]
British author
* H. S. C.

Cunningham, John William
1780-1861   [IP]
British author, poet, clergyman
* Sancho
(See also base volume)

Cunningham, Timothy 18th c.   [IP]
British barrister
* [A] Gentleman of the Middle Temple

Cunningham, Virginia
See Holmgren, Virginia C[unningham]

Cunningham, William 1781-1804
[PI]
Irish poet
* Colin

Cuoq, Jean Andre 19th c.   [IP]
Canadian clergyman and philologist
* N. O., Ancien Missionaire

Cuore, L. B.
See Urbino, Levina [Buoncuore]

Curb Money Queen
See Chang Yong Ja

[Le] Cure de Meudon
See Rabelais, Francois

Curgenoen, John Brendon 19th c.
[IP]
British physician
* Tretane

[The] Curious Scrap-Monger
See Boswell, James

Curlew
See McKowen, James

Curlewis, Ethel S. [Turner] 1872- ?
[NPS]
Author
* Turner, Ethel

Curley, Dorothy Nyren 1927-   [CA]
American writer, editor, poet
* St. Pierre, Dorothy
(See also base volume)

Curly Bill Brocius
See Graham, William B.

Curran, Henry Grattan 1800-1876
[IP, PI]
Irish barrister, poet, translator
* C.
* H. G. C., Esq.

Currens, Jane 1915-   [CA]
American author
* Fitz-Randolph, Jane [Currens]

Currie, E.   [IP]
Scottish clergyman and author
* One Who has a Tear for Others as
    Well as Himself

Currie, James 1756-1805   [IP]
Scottish physician and author
* Caius
* Philo Musa
* Wilson, Jasper

Currie, John 18th c.   [IP]
Scottish clergyman and author
* [A] Minister of the Church of
    Scotland

Curro Guillen
See Herrera Rodriguez, Francisco

Curry, Owen
See Crilly, Daniel

Cursham, Mary Ann   [IP]
British author and poet
* [A] Lady
* M. A. C.

Curties, T. J. Horsley 19th c.
[SFL, WGT]
Author
* Horsley, T. J.

Curtin, Philip
See Lowndes, Marie [Adelaide]
Belloc

Curtis, Caroline G. 1827- ?   [IP]
American author
* Winchester, Arnold
(See also base volume)

Curtis, Dick 19th c.   [RBE]
British boxer
* [The] Pet of the Fancy

Curtis, E. J.   [IP]
Author
* Smith, Shirley

Curtis, George Ticknor 1812-1894
[DNA, IP]
American author, attorney, historian
* Boylston, Peter
* [A] Citizen of Massachusetts
* G. T. C.
* Phocion

Curtis, George William 1824-1892
[IP]
American author
* [A] Traveller
(See also base volume)

Curtis, Ike
See Curtis, Isaac

Curtis, Isaac 20th c.   [EF]
American football player
* Curtis, Ike

Curtis, Winslow ?-1826   [BLB]
American murderer and pirate
* Colson, Sylvester

Curtius
See Taylor, John

Curtius
See Thompson, John

Cusack, George
See Carter-Smith, Grace

Cusack, Mary Frances 1829?-1899
[IP, PI]
Irish author and poet
* C. F. M.
* [The] Nun of Kenmare
(See also base volume)

Cushing, Paul
See Wood-Seys, Roland Alexander

Cushman, Corinne
See Victor, Metta Victoria Fuller

[A] Custom-House Officer
See Russell, William

Cuthbertson, James Lister
1851-1910   [DLE1]
Australian poet
* C.

Cuyler, Duke
See Meserve, Arthur Livermore

Cycling's Elder Statesman
See Pratt, Charles E.

Cyclos
See Blackham, George E.

**Cyclos, a Member of the Glasgow
Skating Club**
See Anderson, George

[The] Cyprian Queen
See Fairfax, Mary

Cyrilla
See Tautphoeus, Jemima
[Montgomery]

Cyrille
See Avril, [Baron] Adolphe d'

Cyrus 6th c. BC   [NPS]
King of Persia
* [The] Great Founder of the
    Persian Name
(See also base volume)

[The] Czar of Muscovy
See Constable, Archibald

D

D.
See Dewey, Orville

D.
See Dickinson, John

D.
See Duffy, [Sir] Charles Gavan

D.
See McCarthy, Denis Florence

D. A. Y.
See Davy, David Elisha

D. B.
See Benham, Daniel

D. B.
See Bye, Deodatus

D. C. L.
See Dodgson, Charles Lutwidge

D. D., Cantab
See Wilson, Richard

D. F. B.
See Hoey, John Cashel

D. F. C.
See Flanagan, Charles

D. F. McC.
See McCarthy, Denis Florence

D. G.
See Garrick, David

D. G. M.
See McDermott, George

D. G. M.
See Mitchell, Donald Grant

D. H.
See Gough, Richard

D. H.
See Holland, Denis

D. I.
See Innes, Duncan

D. J.
See Jones, David

D. J. B. de A.
See Ariazza, Don Juan Bautista de

D. L.?
See Lane, Denny

D. L.
See Littledale, Richard

D. M. L.
See Lenihan, D. M.

D. M'L.
See Meehan, Charles Patrick

D. N. S.
See Williams, Richard Dalton

D. P.
See Moultrie, Gerard

D. S.
See Steuart, Daniel

D. W.
See Wilson, Daniel

D. W. B.
See Bartlett, David W.

Dabney, Virginius 1835-1894
[DNA]
American author
* Whacker, John Bouche

Dacre, J. Colne
See Boyd, Mary Stuart

Dacus
See Daniel, Samuel

Daddow, Daniel
See Bennett, Charles

Daddy O, Doctor
See Winslow, Vernon

Daft Jamie
See Wilson, James

Daft Pate Macmillan
See Macmillan, Kirkpatrick

Daft, Tennyson J.
See Morgan, Thomas P. [Tom]

Dahlgren, Sarah Madeleine [Vinton]
1825-1898   [DNA]
American author and poet
* Corinne

D'Albeno, Vicomte
See Rattazzi, [Princess] Marie
Studolmine Bonaparte

Dalcassian
See Fenelon, Timothy Brendan

Dale
See Nettles, Bonnie Lu

Dale, Annan
See Johnston, James Wesley

Dale, Thomas F.   [NPS]
Author
* Stoneclink

Dali, Salvador 1904-   [CR]
Spanish painter
* Dollars, Avida

Dallas, John
See Duncan, W[illiam] Murdoch

Dallas, Richard
See Williams, Nathan Winslow

Dally the Tall
See Eliot, Grace Dalrymple

Dalriada
See Knox, David B.

Dalton, Grat
See Dalton, Grattan

Dalton, Grattan 1865-1892
[BLB, EWG]
American gunfighter
* Dalton, Grat

Daly, Eugene P. 1860- ?   [PI]
Irish poet
* Ban, Eoghan
* Bawn, Owen
* Mor, Eoghan
* Old Carroll the Bard

Daly, Frederic
See Austin, Lewis

Daly, Rann
See Palmer, Edward Vance

Daly, T. A. 1871- ?   [UH]
American poet
* [The] Laureate of the Dago

Dambrauskas, Joan Arden 1933-
[CA]
British author
* Arden, Noele

Damer, Anne Seymour 1749-1828
[NPS]
British sculptor
* Our Female Phidias

Danberry, Mr.
See Disraeli, Benjamin

Dance, James ?-1774   [IP]
British actor and playwright
* Love, James
* Scriblerus Maximus

[The] Dancing Madonna
See Mondrian, Piet[er Cornelis]

[The] Dandy Bishop
See Pelham, George

[The] Dane
See Charles

Dane, Hal
See M'Fall, Haldane

Dangerfield, Clinton
See Bryan, Ella Howard

Danhaki, Harold 1947-   [CR]
*Puerto Rican-born actor and
comedian*
* Woodlawn, Holly

Daniel
See Garcia, Eduarda

Daniel, Bp. of Calcutta
See Wilson, Daniel

Daniel, George 1790-1864   [HFN]
Author
* P. P.
(See also base volume)

Daniel, John
See Morris, Ralph

Daniel, [William] Roland
1880-1969   [TCCM]
British author
* Anderson, Sonia

Daniel, Rosa   [UH]
*Friend of British poet, Edmund
Spencer*
* Rosalind

Daniel, Samuel 1562-1619   [NPS]
British poet
* Dacus
(See also base volume)

Daniell, J.   [EC]
British cricketer
* Daniell, Prophet

Daniell, Prophet
See Daniell, J.

Danielovitch, Issur 1916-   [CR]
American actor
* Demsky, Isidore
* Douglas, Kirk

Danks, H. P.
See Danks, Hart Pease

Danks, Hart Pease 1834-1903
[PAC]
American composer
* Danks, H. P.

D'Anvers, N.
See Bell, Nancy R. E. [Meugens]

Daphnis
See Caesar, [Gaius] Julius

[The] Dapper
See Vaughan, Thomas

Dapper Jemmy
See Boswell, James

Dara, William
See Byrne, William A.

Darby, John Nelson 19th c. [HFN]
Author
* J. N. D.

Darby, Mary
See Robinson, Mary Darby

Dare, Ishmael
See Jose, Arthur Wilberforce

Dargan, Clara V. 19th c. [PI]
American writer and poet
* Chesney, Esther
(See also base volume)

[The] Dark Lady of American Letters
See Sontag, Susan

Dark Musgrave
See Lewis, Matthew Gregory

D'Arles, Henri
See Beaude, Henri

Darley, George 1795-1846
[DEA, NLC, PI]
Irish-born poet, playwright, author
* Crayon, Geoffrey, Jr.
* G. D.
* Lacy, John
* Penseval, Guy

Darley, William ?-1840 [PI]
Irish poet and artist
* W. D.

Darling, John A.
Author
* Mignon, August

Dartigue, Laure
See Lebrun, Pauline Guyot

D'Arvie, Claudia
See Jackson, Editha Salomon

Darwin, Erasmus 1731-1802 [NPS]
British physician, poet, naturalist
* That Bright Luminary

Dash, La Comtesse
See Cisternes de Coutiras,
Gabrielle Anne de

Dash, Paul R.
See Browne, Lewis Allen

D'Aubigne, Francoise 1635-1719
[NPS]
Wife of King Louis XIV of France
* Astarbe
(See also base volume)

D'Aubigy, Pierre
See Mencken, Henry Louis

D'Aubuisson, Roberto 20th c.
Salvadoran politician
* Major Bob

Daudet, Alphonse 1840-1897
[NPS]
French author
* L'Isle, Jean de
(See also base volume)

Dauge, Henri
See Hammond, Henrietta [Hardy]

Daugherty, Roy 1870-1924
[BLB, EWG]
American gunfighter
* Jones, Arkansas Tom

[A] Daughter of the Church of England
See Astell, Mary

Davenport, Adelaide
See Aiken, Albert W.

Davenport, Frances Helen
See Aiken, Albert W.

Davey, Mad Tom
See Davey, Thomas

Davey, Thomas 19th c. [DI]
British politician
* Davey, Mad Tom

David
See Charles I [or Karl]

David [UH]
King of Judah and Israel
* Sweet Singer of Israel

David, Ben
See Jones, John

David, Henry Winter 1817-1865
[DNA]
American author
* Huetten, Ulric von

David, Leon
See Jacob, [Cyprien] Max

David, the Son of Goliath
See Arnold, Matthew

Davidhof, Karl 1838-1889 [JL]
Russian musician
* Davydov, Karl

Davidson, Bogumil 1818-1872 [JL]
German actor
* Dawison, Bogumil

Davidson, Cotton
See Davidson, Frank

Davidson, Frank 20th c. [EF]
American football player
* Davidson, Cotton

Davidson, John 1857-1906 [UH]
Scottish poet
* [The] Poet of Armageddon

Davies, Clara 1861-1943 [BBD]
Welsh singer and choral conductor
* Novello-Davies, Clara

Davies, John Evan Weston 20th c.
[TCCM]
British author
* Mather, Berkely

Davies, Mrs. David
Author
* Kennedy, Margaret

Davies, Naunton 19th c. [NPS]
Author
* Covertside, Naunton

Davies, Robert 1770-1836 [NPS]
Welsh author
* Ddu o'r Glyn, Robin
(See also base volume)

D'Avigdor, Elim Henry 1841-1895
[SFL]
Author
* Wanderer

Davin, Felix
See Balzac, Honore de

Davis, Arthur Hoey 1868-1935
[DLE1, NPS]
Australian author
* Rudd, Steele

Davis, Billy 20th c. [CMA]
American songwriter and record producer
* Carlo, Tyran

Davis, Butch
See Davis, John

Davis, Corbett 20th c. [EF]
American football player
* Davis, Corby

Davis, Corby
See Davis, Corbett

Davis, Edward 1816-1841 [DI, JL]
British-born gangleader
* [The] Jewboy
* Teddy the Jewboy

Davis, Elaine
See Mahnken, Elaine

Davis, Eugene 1857-1897 [PI]
Irish poet and author
* Carberiensis
* E. D.
* Fontenoy
* Roe, Owen
* Sivad
* Tuathal, Cairn

Davis, Francis 1810-1885 [PI]
Irish poet
* [The] Belfast Man

Davis, Hope 19th c. [PI]
Irish composer
* Temple, Hope

Davis, J. P. ?-1862 [NPS]
Painter
* Davis, Pope

Davis, John 20th c. [EF]
American football player
* Davis, Butch

Davis, Mollie E. [Moore] [IP]
American poet
* Moore, Mollie E.

Davis, Pope
See Davis, J. P.

Davis, Richard 20th c. [EF]
American football player
* Davis, Ted

Davis, Roosevelt 20th c. [EF]
American football player
* Davis, Rosey

Davis, Rosalind [IP]
British playwright and composer
* Rosalind

Davis, Rosey
See Davis, Roosevelt

Davis, Sarah Matilda [IP]
American author
* S. M. D.

Davis, Ted
See Davis, Richard

Davis, Thomas Osborne 1814-1845
[PI]
Irish poet
* Adragool
* R. L.

Davis, Thomas Osborne (Continued)
* T. D.
* [A] True Celt
* Vacuus
* [A] Young Squire
(See also base volume)

Davis, Varina Anne Jefferson
1864-1898 [DNA]
American author
* Davis, Winnie
(See also base volume)

Davis, Wendell 1776-1830 [IP]
American author
* [A] Member of the Humane Society

Davis, William 1627-1690 [DI]
Welsh highwayman
* [The] Golden Farmer

Davis, William Augustus [IP]
American physician and author
* W. A. D.

Davis, Winnie
See Davis, Varina Anne Jefferson

Davison, Edward 19th c. [IP]
British clergyman and author
* E. D.

Davitt, Michael 1846-1906 [PI]
Irish poet
* M. D., Heslingden

Davus
See Tattersall, John Cecil

Davy, Christopher [IP]
British architect and author
* [An] Architect

Davy, David Elisha 1769-1851 [IP]
British antiquary
* D. A. Y.

Davy, John 1790-1868 [IP]
British physician and author
* J. D.

Davydov, Karl
See Davidhof, Karl

Dawe, John, jun.
See Commins, Andrew

Dawes, Matthew [IP]
British barrister and author
* [A] Gentleman of the Inner Temple
* M. D.

Dawes, Rufus 1803-1859 [IP]
American poet and journalist
* Smythe, Samuel

Dawes, Thomas 1757-1825 [IP]
American poet
* Trowell, Adjutant
* [A] Young Gentleman

Dawes, William [IP]
British architect and author
* Goff, Elijer

Dawison, Bogumil
See Davidson, Bogumil

Dawson, A. [IP]
British author and music teacher
* A. D.
* [An] Old Lady

Dawson, Benjamin 1729-1814 [IP]
British clergyman and author
* Anonymous

Dawson, Benjamin (Continued)
* [A] Clergyman of the Church of
   England

Dawson, Charles Carroll 1833- ?
[IP]
American author
* C. C. D.

Dawson, Erasmus
See Devon, Paul

Dawson, Henry Barton 1821- ? [IP]
British-born historian and journalist
* H. B. D.

Dawson, John 20th c.   [CMA]
Musician and singer
* Dawson, Marmeduke

Dawson, John William 1820- ? [IP]
British geologist, naturalist, author
* J. W. D.

Dawson, Marmeduke
See Dawson, John

Day, Benjamin Henry 1810-1889
[DNA]
American author and journalist
* Richardson, Jabez

Day, J. Fitzgerald 19th c.   [PI]
Irish poet
* FitzErin

Day, Mrs. S. A. 1858- ? [BDSA]
American author
* Gardener, Helen Hamilton

Dayan, Moshe 1915-1981   [CA]
*Israeli army officer, diplomat,
author*
* [The] Mysterious Cyclops of
   Israeli Politics

Dayrell, V.
See Austin, Wiltshire Stanton, Jr.

Ddu o'r Glyn, Robin
See Davies, Robert

De Acosta, Donald Barry
1912-1980   [FIR]
American actor
* Barry, Red
(See also base volume)

De Acton, Eugenia
See Lewis, Alethea [Brereton]

De Bookworms, Baron
See Lucy, [Sir] Henry William

De Boscosel de Chastelard, Pierre
See Ireland, William Henry

De Boutellier, Sophie 1829-1901
[NPS]
French painter and etcher
* Browne, Henriette

De Brath, Stanley 1854-1937
[EOP]
*British psychic researcher, author,
translator*
* Desertis, V. C.

De Brehat, Alfred
See Guezenec, Alfred

De Busne, Antoine ?-1492 [BBD]
French-born composer
* Busnois, Antoine

De Castan, [Count] Armand
1834-1897   [BBD]
French opera singer
* Castelmary

De Castille, Hippolyte   [NPS]
French author
* Alceste

De Chambure, Auguste L.
1789-1832   [NPS]
French army officer
* [Le] Diable

De Courcy, Kate
See Armstrong, Katherine

De Courcy, Richard 1743-1803
[PI]
Irish clergyman, author, poet
* [The] Good Vicar
* R. D.

De Eranso, Catalina 17th c.   [BL]
*Spanish male impersonator and
soldier*
* Diaz Ramirez de Guzman, Alonso

De Ferrieres, Raymond
See Boue de Villiers, Amable Louis

De Freitas, Jose Pedro 1918-1971
[EOP]
Claimed to possess psychic powers
* Arigo, Jose

De Garcon, Bouillon
See Barry, Michael Joseph

De Girardin, Delphine 1804-1855
[NPS]
Author
* Delaunay, [Le Vicomte] Charles
   de

De Gleva, Mary
See Roberts, Mary

De Grimston, Mary Ann 20th c.
[EOP]
Founder of religious cult
* [The] Goddess
* [The] Oracle of God

De Grimston, Robert Moor Sylvester
See Moor, Robert

De Hautecloque, Vicomte 20th c.
[PPN]
French army officer
* Leclerc

De Herlagnez, Pablo
See Verlaine, Paul [Marie]

De Jean, J.
See Frazer, John de Jean

De Kay, Charles   [NPS]
Author
* Barnaval, Louis

De Kay, James E. 19th c.   [HFN]
Author
* [An] American
(See also base volume)

De Kelmar, Louis
See Rattazzi, [Princess] Marie
Studolmine Bonaparte

De La Cruz, Pedro 17th c.   [GS]
Spanish bullfighter
* [El] Mamon [The Nursling]

**De la Haye, Louis Marie [Vicomte de
Cormenin]** 1788-1868   [IP]
French author
* Timon

De Lancy, FitzHugh
See Wilde, Richard Henry

De Linska, [The] Count
See Prado

De Listonai, Mr.
See Villeneuve

De Lys, Georges
See Bonnerive, Capt.

De Mattos, Mrs.   [NPS]
Author
* Herz-Garten, Theodor

**De Mesange, [Reverend] Pierre
Cordelier Pierre**
See Tyssot de Patot, Simon

De Mille, James 1837-1880   [WGT]
Author
* Gaul, Gilbert

De Moe, Gus
See De Moe, William

De Moe, William 20th c.   [EF]
American football player
* De Moe, Gus

De Morgan, William 1839-1917
[UH]
British author
* [The] Modern Dickens

De Nobrega, Manuel 1517-1570
[NPS]
Jesuit missionary
* [The] Apostle of Brazil

De Pontaumont
See Lechanteur, M. E.

De Ponty, Marguerite
See Mallarme, Stephane

De Quille, Dan
See Wright, William

**[The] De Quincey of Danish
Literature**
See Jacobsen, J. P.

De Quincey, Thomas 1785-1859
[NN, NPS]
British author
* My Admirable Crichton
* [The] Opium Eater
(See also base volume)

De Roovroy, Claude Henri
1760-1825   [NAD]
French philosopher
* Saint Simon

De Rougemont, Louis 19th c.   [DI]
Leader of Australian aborigines
* King of the Cannibal Isles

De Rupe
See Roche, Frances Maria

De Salluste [or Salustius?], Guillaume
1544-1590   [NPS]
French poet
* [The] French Solomon
(See also base volume)

De Tarde, Alfred 20th c.   [CD]
Author
* Agathon [joint pseudonym with
   Henri Massis]

De Tourville, Henri
See Perreau, Henri

De Trabeck, Sophie
See Lavritch, Sophie Bentkowski

De Valera, Eamon 1883-1975
[NN]
Irish statesman and military leader
* [The] Chief
(See also base volume)

De Veaux, Richard
See Andrews, Gwendolen [Foulke]

De Verdi, Marie
See Mencken, Henry Louis

De Verdon, T. K.
See Verdon, Thomas Kirwan

De Vere, [Sir] Aubrey
See Hunt, Aubrey

De Vere, Aubrey Thomas
1814-1902   [PI]
Irish poet
* A. T. de V.

De Vere, Lydia
See Chadwick, Elizabeth [Bigley]

De Vere, Mary ?-1830   [PI]
Irish poet
* M. de V.

De Vere, Mary Ainge 19th c.   [PI]
American poet
* Bridges, Madeline S.

De Vernon, Guy
See Boue de Villiers, Amable Louis

De Voraggio, Giacomo 1230-1298
[NPS]
Author
* James of the Sink-Hole
(See also base volume)

De Waltram, Lanner
See Wood, John

De Weese, Ebby
See De Weese, Everett

De Weese, Everett 20th c.   [EF]
American football player
* De Weese, Ebby

De Weindeck, Winteler 19th c.
[WGT]
Author
* Fighton, [Capt.] George Z.

De Wint, Mrs. C. A.   [IP]
American poet
* C. A. D.

De Wolf, Michael 1500?-1567
[BBD]
Flemish composer
* Lupus, Michael

Deacon, Leslie 20th c.   [EOP]
*British nurse who claimed to possess
psychic powers*
* Stella C.

Deacon, William Frederick 19th c.
[HFN]
Author
* [The] Editor of a Quarterly
   Review

Deadman, Emmett 1918-   [CA]
American author
* Dedmon, Emmett

Deadwood Dick
See Love, Nat

Deady, John Christmas 1849-1884
[PI]
Irish poet
* [The] Poet of Duhallow

[The] Deaf Un
See Burke, James

Dean, Frances
See Grasle, Elizabeth

Dean Harry
See Wilkinson, Henry

Dean, Mrs. Andrew
See Sidgwick, Cecily

[The] Dean of Canterbury
See Alford, Henry

Deane, D. C.
See Tucker, Eleonora C.

Deane, Martha
See Taylor, Marian Young

Dearborn, Andrew
See Gardner, Lewis J.

Debar, Mrs. Diss
See Jackson, Editha Salomon

[The] Deck Hand Champion of America
See McCoole, Mike

Dedmon, Emmett
See Deadman, Emmett

Dee, John 1527-1608 [NPS]
Welsh astrologer and mathematician
* Another Pythagoras
(See also base volume)

Deeming, Frederick Bayley 1854-1892 [DI]
British-born murderer
* Swanston, Baron
* Williams, Albert O.

[The] Defender of the People
See Milton, John

DeFluent, Amelie
See Gallup, Lucy

[The] Deformed
See Laar [or Laer], Pieter van

DeForrest, Barry
See Clark, Charles Dunning

Dekker, Carl
See Lynds, Dennis

Delafield
See Child, Maria [Little]

Delaney, Art[hur]
See McCluskie, Mike

Delany, William J. 1844- ? [PI]
Irish author and poet
* Zingaro

Delaunay, [Le Vicomte] Charles de
See De Girardin, Delphine

Delavaud, Marie Collin [ICB]
Author
* Colmont, Marie

Delgado y Guerra, Jose 1754-1801 [GS]
Spanish bullfighter
* Pepe-Illo [Little Joey]

Delius, Nikolaus 19th c. [HFN]
Author
* Dr. D.
(See also base volume)

[The] Deliverer of God's People
See Elizabeth I

Della Arpa
See Michi, Orazio

Della Casa, Giovanni 1503-1556 [NPS]
Italian prelate, poet, orator
* [The] Lord Chesterfield of Italy

Della Torre, Raoul
See Mencken, Henry Louis

Delorme, Andre
See Julien, Charles-Andre

Delorme, Charles
See Rumball, Charles

Delorme, Joseph
See Sainte Beuve, Charles Auguste

[The] Delphic Oracle
See Wagner, Cosima

Delphine
See Baker, Delphine P.

Delta
See Dorrian, Patrick

Delupis, Ingrid 1939- [CA]
Swedish-born author and barrister
* Detter, Ingrid
* Doimi di Delupis, Ingrid

[A] Delver
See Alsop, Alfred

[A] Delver into Antiquity
See Turnbull, William Barclay David Donald

DeMille, Alexandria
See DuBreuil, Elizabeth Lorinda

DeMille, Nelson 1943- [CA]
American author
* Kay, Ellen
* Ladner, Kurt
* Matthews, Brad

Deming, Richard 1915- [SAT]
American author
* Moor, Emily
(See also base volume)

Democritus
See Brackenridge, Hugh Henry

[The] Demon of Darkness
See Gifford, William

[The] Demon of Geneva
See Chauvin [or Caulvin?], Jean

Demos
See Woods, James

[The] Demosthenes of French Divines
See Bourdaloue, Louis

[The] Demosthenes of Southern Methodism
See Pierce, George Foster

Demotes, Michael
See Burgess, Michael Roy

Dempsey, William Harrison 1895- [CR]
American boxer
* Jack the Giant Killer
(See also base volume)

Dempster, C. L. H. 19th c. [NPS]
Author
* Vera

Demsky, Isidore
See Danielovitch, Issur

Denarius
See Cole, [Sir] Henry

Denham, Avery Strakosch ?-1970 [CA]
American author and journalist
* Strakosch, Avery

Denis, Charlotte [joint pseudonym with Denis Plimmer]
See Plimmer, Charlotte

Denis, Charlotte [joint pseudonym with Charlotte Plimmer]
See Plimmer, Denis

Denison, Mary Andrews 1826-1911
American author
* A. M. D.
* Edson, N. I.
(See also base volume)

Denney, Diana 1910- [CA, SAT]
British author and illustrator
* Gri
* Ross, Diana

Dennie, Joseph 1768-1812 [DLE1]
American author
* [The] Addison of the United States
* Colon
* Saunter, Samuel
(See also base volume)

Dennis, John 1657-1734 [NPS]
British critic and playwright
* Appius
* Cacus
(See also base volume)

Dennis, Mike
See Dennis, Walter

Dennis, Walter 20th c. [EF]
American football player
* Dennis, Mike

Densyli
See Sidney, L.

Denton, H. B.
See Taylor, Edgar

Dentry, Robert
See White, Osmar Egmont Dorkin

[A] Deputy
See Thornton, Bonnell

Dereksen, David
See Stacton, David [Derek]

Dermody, Thomas 1775-1802 [PI]
Irish poet
* Myrtle, Marmaduke

Derrick, Frances
See Notley, Frances Eliza Millett

Derrick, Graham
See Raby, Derek Graham

Derry Boy
See Roddy, William

Derry Down Derry
See Lear, Edward

Derzhavin, Gavril 1743-1816
Russian poet and statesman
* [The] Singer of Catherine

Des Ecorres, Charles
See Chartrand, Joseph Demers

Des Voignes, Jules Verne 1886-1911 [DNA]
American author
* Olney, Oliver

DeSalvo, Albert 1932-1973 [DI]
American murderer
* [The] Measuring Man
(See also base volume)

Desennuyee, A.
See Gore, Catherine Grace Frances [Moody]

Desertis, V. C.
See De Brath, Stanley

Deshayes, Catherine ?-1680 [LFW]
French murderer
* [La] Voisin

Desiderius Pastor
See Moultrie, Gerard

[The] Desired
See Charles II

Desmond
See Collopy, William

Desmond
See McCarthy, Denis Florence

D'Esperance, Elizabeth
See Hope, Elizabeth

Desperdicios [Leftovers]
See Dominguez y Campos, Manuel

Dessauer, Leopold 1810-1874 [JL]
Actor
* Dessoir, Ludwig

Dessoir, Ludwig
See Dessauer, Leopold

D'Este, Ippolito 1479-1520 [NPS]
Clergyman
* Good Seed of Hercules

[A] Detective
See Bennett, J.

[A] Detective
See Brae, Andrew Edmund

[A] Detective
See Russell, William

[A] Detective Police Officer
See Russell, William

Detector
See Drury, Henry Joseph Thomas

Detector
See Gauntlett, Henry

Determinatus
See Adams, Samuel

Detter, Ingrid
See Delupis, Ingrid

Detzer, Karl 1891- [MA]
American author
* Henderson, William
* Woods, Leland
(See also base volume)

[The] Devil of Dewsbury
See Oldroyd, Richard

[The] Devil's Prophet
See Steinschneider, Hermann [or Heinrich?]

Devine, James ?-1890 [PI]
Irish poet
* [The] Bard of Tyrone

Devlin, Joseph 1869- ? [PI]
Irish poet
* Northern Gael
* O'Brien, Jennie

Devon, Paul 19th c. [SFL]
Author
* Dawson, Erasmus

Devoniensis
See Jones, J. P.

Dewey, Orville 1794-1882 [IP]
American clergyman and author
* D.
* [A] English Traveller

Dewhurst, Jane [IP]
British poet
* J. D.

Dexter, Franklin 1793-1857 [IP]
American attorney and author
* Hancock

Dexter, John Haven 1791-1876
[IP]
American merchant and author
* Philagathus

Dexter, Samuel, Sr. 1761-1816 [IP]
American jurist and statesman
* [A] Junior Sophister

Dexter, Will
See Coomes, Oliver [Oll]

Dey, Haryot Holt
See Dey, Hattie [Hamblin] Cahoon

Dey, Hattie [Hamblin] Cahoon 19th c.
American author
* Dey, Haryot Holt

Dey, Marmaduke
See Van Rensselar, Frederick

D'Hardelot, Guy
See Rhodes, Helen

Dharma, Buck
See Roeser, Donald

Dhearg, Lamh
See McCall, William

Dhuy, Suil
See Graves, Alfred Perceval

Di Giovanni, Stefano 1392-1450
[NAD]
Sienese artist
* Sassetta

Di Lappomeraye, Henri 1839-1891
[NPS]
French critic and lecturer
* Alleber, Henri de

Di Lucca, [Signor] Gaudentio
See Berington, Simon

[Le] Diable
See De Chambure, Auguste L.

Dial, Buddy
See Dial, Gilbert

Dial, Gilbert 20th c. [EF]
American football player
* Dial, Buddy

Diamond Dick
See St. Leon, Ernest

Diamond Jim Colosimo
See Colosimo, James

Diarmuid
See Cassidy, Patrick Sarsfield

Diarr, H. C.
See Dowling, Richard

Diaz Cantoral, Manuel 1811-1858
[GS]
Spanish bullfighter
* Lavi

Diaz Ramirez de Guzman, Alonso
See De Eranso, Catalina

Diaz Salinas, Ponciano 1858-1897
[GS]
Mexican bullfighter
* [El] Centauro Torero [The
Centaur Bullfighter]

Dibble, Nancy Ann 1942- [CA]
American author
* Dibell, Ansen

Dibdin, Charles 1745-1814 [NPS]
British playwright, actor, composer
* [The] True Laureate of England
(See also base volume)

Dibdin, Thomas Frognall
1776-1847 [IP, NPS]
British bibliographer
* Lysander
* [A] Member of the Roxburghe
Club
* [The] Modern Indagator
Invictissimus
* Rosicrucius
* T. F. D.
(See also base volume)

Dibdin, Thomas John 1771-1841
[IP, NPS]
British playwright, songwriter, actor
* Merchant, T.

Dibell, Ansen
See Dibble, Nancy Ann

Dicaiophilus Cantabrigiensis
See Long, Roger

Dick, Dr.
See Downing, Denis J.

Dick, John [IP]
Scottish author
* [A] Fellow of the Society of
Antiquaries of Scotland

Dick, William Brisbane 1828- ?
[IP]
American author and publisher
* Mayne, Leger D.
(See also base volume)

Dickens, Charles 1812-1870
[IP, NPS]
British author
* Sparks, Godfrey
* [A] Subscriber
* Tibbs
* W. P.
* Your Constant Reader
(See also base volume)

Dicker, Thomas [IP]
British author
* [The] Catholic Bishop of Bantry
* [A] Man of Business

Dickinson, Emily Elizabeth
1830-1886 [DLE1]
American poet
* [A] Feminine Blake
* [The] New England Mystic

Dickinson, John 1732-1808
[DLE1, IP]
American statesman and author
* Anticipation
* D.
* [A] Gentleman in Philadelphia
* [A] North American
* [The] Penman of the Revolution
(See also base volume)

Dickinson, Moses 1696-1778 [IP]
American clergyman and author
* [An] Aged Minister

Dickinson, Mrs. T. P. [IP]
American author
* Benedict, Hester A.

Dickinson, W. L. 19th c. [IP]
British author
* W. L. D.

Dickson, Samuel Henry 1798-1872
[IP]
British author and physician
* [A] London Physician
(See also base volume)

Didier, Eugene Lemoine [IP]
American author
* Lemoine

Didwin, Isaac
See Sturdy, William Allen

Diego, Juan 16th c. [NAD]
*Mexican Indian who claimed to
possess psychic powers*
* Singing Eagle

Diekenga, I. E. [IP]
American author
* Don

Digges, Leonard 1588-1635 [IP]
British poet
* L. D.

**[A] Dignify'd Clergy-man of the
Church of England**
See Hickes, George

Digress, Deloraine
See Habersham, Robert

Dikty, Julian May 1931- [CA]
American author
* Cunningham, Bob
* Falconer, Lee N.
* Feilen, John
* Grant, Matthew G.
* Thorne, Ian
* Thorne, Jean Wright
* Zanderbergen, George
(See also base volume)

[A] Dilettante
See Gardiner, William

Dilg, William [IP]
American poet
* See, Henricus von

Dillinger, John Herbert 1903- ?
[DI]
American bank robber
* Lawrence, James
(See also base volume)

Dillon, Emile Joseph [NPS]
Journalist and author
* Lanin, E. B.
* Voces Catholicae

Dillon, [Sir] John Joseph ?-1837
[IP]
British barrister and author
* [A] Barrister
* Hiberno-Anglus
* Publicus Severus

Dillon, John Talbot [IP]
British author
* [An] English Traveller in Spain

Dillon, Robert Crawford
1795-1848 [IP]
British clergyman and author
* [The] Chaplain to the Mayoralty

Dillon, Thomas ?-1852 [PI]
Irish poet
* Cuchullin
* Logan
* O'Donnell, Mary

Dilly, Tante
See Benson, Edward Frederic

Dinerstein, Michael 1916- [CA]
British author and playwright
* Dines, Michael

Dines, Michael
See Dinerstein, Michael

**Diocletian [Gauis Aurelius Valerius
Diocletianus]** 245- 313 [NPS]
Roman emperor
* Augustus
(See also base volume)

Dion
See Sheares, John

Dioscorides, Dr.
See Harting, Pieter

Diplomaticus
See Guerra y Sanchez, Ramiro

Dirk
See Gringhuis, Richard H.

Dirks, Marion 20th c. [EF]
American football player
* Dirks, Mike

Dirks, Mike
See Dirks, Marion

Dirrill, Charles
See Sill, Richard

Disco, Mr.
See Bogart, Neil

Disraeli, Benjamin 1804-1881
[NPS]
British prime minister and author
* Ben Sidonia
* Danberry, Mr.
* [The] Gay Lothario of Politics
(See also base volume)

[A] Dissenter in the Country
See Peirce, James

[A] Dissenting Minister
See Christison, Robert

[A] Dissenting Minister
See Leask, William

[The] Distiller of Syllables
See Mossop, Henry

[A] Distinguished Southern Journalist
See Pollard, Edward Alfred

Disturnell, John 19th c. [HFN]
Author
* J. D.

Diver, Jenny
See Jones, Mary

Diversity
See Scott, William B.

Divine, [Mother]
See Baker, Edna Rose [Ritchings]

[The] Divine
See Shakespeare, William

Divine, [Major] J.
See Baker, George

[The] Divine Novelist
See Shiga, Naoya

Dix, John 1798-1880 [HFN]
Author
* [A] Cosmopolitan
(See also base volume)

Dix Quaevidi
See North, Edward

Dixon
See Andrews, Sidney

Dixon, Ella Hepworth [NPS]
Author and journalist
* Wynman, Margaret

Dixon, Granby
See Kingsley, Henry

Dixon, Jeanne 1936- [CA]
American author
* Harper, Mary Wood
* Stone, Josephine Rector

Dixon, Margaret 1670-1753
[LFW]
Scottish murderer
* Half Hanged Maggie

Dixon, Medina 20th c.
American basketball player
* Ice Woman

Dixon, Sydenham [NPS]
Author
* Vigilant

Dixon, W. W. [NPS]
Author
* Thormanby

Dobbs, Johnny
See Kerrigan, Michael

Dobbs, [Rev.] Philetus
See Wayland, Heman Lincoln

Dobson, Austin
See Dobson, Henry A.

Dobson, Henry A.
Author
* Dobson, Austin

[Le] Docteur Rouge
See Boue de Villiers, Amable Louis

[The] Doctor
See Southey, Robert

Dr. D.
See Delius, Nikolaus

Dr. Leo
See Colange, Auguste Leo de

Dr. McK.
See McKenna, Theobald

[A] Doctor of Divinity, But Not of Oxford
See Raffles, Thomas

[A] Doctor of Hypocrisie
See Perne, Andrew

[A] Doctor of Laws
See Baillie, Hugh

Dr. Taylor's Friend
See Ashley, George

Dodd, William 1729-1777 [NPS]
Clergyman
* [The] Macaroni Parson

Dodge, Daniel
See DuBreuil, Elizabeth Lorinda

Dodge, Gil
See Hano, Arnold

Dodge, Nathaniel Shatswell
1810-1874 [DNA]
American author and journalist
* Carver, John

Dodgson, Charles Lutwidge
1832-1898 [DEA]
British author
* D. C. L.
(See also base volume)

Dodington, George Bubb
1691-1762 [NPS]
British author, politician, poet
* Cadwalader, George, Gent.

Dods, [Mistress] Margaret, of Cleikum Inn, St. Ronan's
See Johnstone, Christina Jane

Dodsley, Robert 1703-1764 [DEA]
British author, editor, publisher
* Ben Saddi, Nathan
(See also base volume)

Doerbeck
See Burchard, Franz

[The] Dog
See Lovell, Francis

Doggrel, [Sir] Iliad [joint pseudonym with George Ducket]
See Burnet, [Sir] Thomas

Doggrel, [Sir] Iliad [joint pseudonym with (Sir) Thomas Burnet]
See Ducket, George

Doheny, Michael 1805-1863 [PI]
Irish poet
* Eiranach
* M. D.
* [A] Tipperary Man?

Doherty, John 19th c. [PI]
Irish poet
* Laracy, Larry
* Policeman X
* Z

Doimi di Delupis, Ingrid
See Delupis, Ingrid

Doinel, Jules [EOP]
Author who claimed to possess psychic powers
* Kostka, Jean

Doinnall-na-glanna
See Lane, Denny

Doire
See Ward, Patrick J.

Dolan, John T. 20th c.
American political fund-raiser
* Dolan, Terry

Dolan, Terry
See Dolan, John T.

Dollard, James Benjamin 1872- ?
[PI]
Irish-born writer and poet
* Slievenamon

Dollard, William 1861- ? [PI]
Irish clergyman and poet
* Exul

Dollars, Avida
See Dali, Salvador

Dollfuss, Engelbert 20th c. [NN]
Chancellor of Austria
* [The] Pocket Dictator

Dollinger, Johann Joseph Ignaz
1799-1890 [NPS]
German theologian and author
* Quirinus
(See also base volume)

Domal, C.
See Simmons, William Hammatt

Domela, Harry 1904- ? [DI]
Russian imposter
* Korff, Baron
* Lieven, Prince

[Il] Domenichino
See Sarti, Giuseppe

Dominguez, Juan de Dios
1825-1881 [GS]
Spanish bullfighter
* Isleno [Islander]

Dominguez y Campos, Manuel
1816-1886 [GS]
Spanish bullfighter
* Desperdicios [Leftovers]

Dominie Hairy
See Brougham, Henry Peter

Dominie Legacy Picken
See Picken, Andrew

Domville, [Sir] William 19th c.
[HFN]
British author
* [A] Layman

[The] Don
See Bradman, [Sir] Donald George

Don
See Diekenga, I. E.

Don Juan
See Slaughter, John Horton

[The] Don Juan of Literature
See Sainte Beuve, Charles Auguste

Donahoe, Bold Jack
See Donahoe, Jack

Donahoe, Jack ?-1830 [DI]
Australian bushranger
* Donahoe, Bold Jack
* [The] Wild Colonial Boy

Donaldson, Margaret 1926- [CA]
Scottish author and psychologist
* Salter, Margaret Lennox

Donall-na-Glanna
See Lane, Denny

Donard, Slieve
See McManus, Patrick

Doncourt, Chevalier A. de
See Drohojowska, Antoinette Josephine Francoise Anne

Donnell, Gerry
See Donnell, John

Donnell, John 20th c. [EF]
American football player
* Donnell, Gerry

Donnelly, James 1824-1868 [PI]
Irish poet
* Lanty the Flint
* Maglone, Barney
* M'Keown, Darby
* O'Hare, Roger

Donnelly, William M. 1856?-1885
[PI]
Irish-born writer and poet
* Adsum

Donnigan, Dregs
See Weirich, Bob

Donoho, Thomas Seton 19th c. [PI]
Poet
* [The] Poet of Ivy Wall

Donzel Dick
See Harvey, Richard

Doodle
See Ryan, Thomas

Dooley, Martin
See Dunne, Finley Peter

Doom, Dr.
See Beesley, H. Brent

[The] Door-Opener
See Crates

Doran, Charles Guilfoyle
1835?-1909 [PI]
Irish poet
* [The] Galley Head Poet

Dorcastriensis
See Harris, Thaddeus Mason

Dore, [Louis Christophe Paul] Gustave
See Dorer, Louis Christophe Paul Gustave

Dorer, Louis Christophe Paul Gustave
1832-1883 [SAT]
French painter, sculptor, illustrator
* Dore, [Louis Christophe Paul] Gustave

Doris, Charles 19th c. [HFN]
French author
* One Who has Never Quitted Him for Fifteen Years

Dorrian, Patrick ?-1891 [PI]
Irish poet
* Delta

Dorrington, Edward?
See Longueville, Peter

Dorset, St. George
See Stephens, George

Dorset, St. John
See Belfour, Hugo John

Double, Luke
See Hyde, Thomas Alexander

Doublefee, [Sir] Bullface
See Norton, Fletcher [First Baron Grantley]

Doudeney, D. A. 1811-1894 [NPS]
Clergyman and author
* Old Jonathan

Douds, Forrest 20th c. [EF]
American football player
* Douds, Jap

Douds, Jap
See Douds, Forrest

Doughsmell, Pete
See Rozelle, Alvin Ray

Doughty, Francis W. 20th c.
American author
* Carter, Nick
(See also base volume)

Douglas
See Reed, Andrew

Douglas, Elsa Fitzgibbon 20th c.
[DLE1]
Author
* Normyx [joint pseudonym with Norman Douglas]

Douglas, George 1412?-1462
[NPS]
Fourth Earl of Angus
* [The] Red Douglas

Douglas, James 1426-1488 [NPS]
Ninth Earl of Douglas
* [The] Black Douglas

Douglas, Kirk
See Danielovitch, Issur

Douglas, Norman 1868-1952
[DLE1]
Author
* Normyx [joint pseudonym with Elsa Fitzgibbon Douglas]

Douglas, Olive
See Buchan, Anna

Douglas, William ?-1390 [NPS]
Lord of Nithsdale
* [Th] Black Douglas

Douglas, William 1724-1810 [NPS]
Earl of March and Duke of Queensberry
* Old Tick
* Piccadilly, Lord
(See also base volume)

Doull, Bruce 20th c.
Australian football player
* [The] Flying Doormat

Dousterswivel
See Spuzheim, John Gaspar

Dow, Ethel
See Kohon, Ethel [Chadowski]

Dowdell, Dorothy [Florence] Karns
1910- [CA]
American author
* McAllister, Amanda

Dowden, Richard
See Maginn, William

Dowe, William 1815-1891 [PI]
Irish poet and journalist
* Cregan, Con
* Muskerry, Major

Dowell, Gwyn 20th c. [EF]
American football player
* Dowell, Mule

Dowell, Mule
See Dowell, Gwyn

Dowling, Bartholomew 1823-1863
[PI]
Irish poet and author
* Hard Knocks
* Masque
* [The] Southern

Dowling, James D. ?-1837 [PI]
Irish painter and actor
* Herbert, James D.

Dowling, Richard 1846-1898
[NPS, PI]
Irish author and poet
* Ained
* Diarr, H. C.
* Fall, Marcus
* Kink, Emmanuel
* Wildon, R. G.

Down the Hill Jack
See Morgan, Daniel

Downey, Joseph 1846?-1870 [PI]
Irish poet
* Shamrock

Downey, Richard 1859-1898 [PI]
Irish poet
* Muscadel

Downing, Denis J. 1871?-1909 [PI]
Irish journalist and songwriter
* Dick, Dr.

Downing, Ellen Mary Patrick
1828-1869 [PI]
Irish poet
* E. M. P. D.
* Mary

Downing, Mary 1815-1881 [PI]
Irish poet
* Christabel
* M. F. D.
* Myrrha

Downs, Sarah Elizabeth [Forbush]
1843- ? [DNA]
American author
* Sheldon, Georgie

Doyle, [Sir] Arthur Conan
1858-1930 [EOP]
British physician and author
* [The] St. Paul of Spiritualism

Doyle, James Warren 1786-1861
[PI]
Irish clergyman and poet
* J. K. L. [James of Kildare and Leighlin]

Doyle, John 19th c. [WEC]
British artist and cartoonist
* H. B.

Doyle, Martin
See Hickey, Ross

Doyle, Mina
See Young, Mrs. C. W.

Doyle, Mrs. James R.
Author
* James, Martha

[The] Dragon Lady
See Knight, Frances

Drake, [Sir] Francis 1540?-1596
[NPS]
British naval officer and navigator
* England's Neptune

Drake, Gaston V.
See Bangs, John Kendrick

Drake, Miriam
See Clarke, Marion

Drake, Peter
See Green, Matthew

Drake, Samuel, Sr.
See Bryant, Samuel Drake

[A] Drangan Boy
See Ryan, Thomas

Draper, Elizabeth 18th c. [UH]
Friend of British author, Laurence Sterne
* Bramine

[A] Drapier
See Atcherley, James

Drayham, William
See Mencken, Henry Louis

Drea, E. V. 19th c. [PI]
Irish poet
* Ned of the Hills

[A] Dreamer
See Andre, John

Drekab, Maistre
See Baker, Leonard

Drella
See Warhola, Andrew

Dreoilin
See Fahy, Francis Arthur

Drew, D'Arcy
See Mivart, St. George Jackson

Drew, Kenneth
See Cockburn, [Francis] Claud

Drew, Pierce William 19th c.
[HFN, IP]
Irish clergyman and author
* P. W.

Drewe, Edward [IP]
British author and army officer
* [An] Officer of the British Army

Drewe, Patrick [IP]
Author
* [A] Lover of the Church of England

Drial, J. E.
See Laird, Jean E[louise]

Driberg, Thomas Edward Neil [Tom]
1905-1976 [CA]
British author, journalist, politician
* Hickey, William

Driggs, George W. [IP]
American army officer and author
* G. W. D.
* [A] Non Commissioned Officer

Drinker, John [IP]
British author
* [A] Tradesman

Driscoll, Terry
See Jackson, John

Driver, Thomas [IP]
American author
* Uncle Tom's Nephew

**Drohojowska, Antoinette Josephine
Francoise Anne** 1822- ? [IP]
French author
* Doncourt, Chevalier A. de

[The] Dromedary
See Campbell, Thomas

Drummond, Henry 1786-1860 [IP]
British politician and author
* H. D.
* One of his Constituents

Drummond, Henry 1851-1897
[NPS]
Writer
* Anastasius

Drummond, Robert Hay
1711-1776 [IP]
British prelate and author
* Robert, Lord Bishop of Sarum

Drummond, Spencer Rodney 19th
c. [IP]
British clergyman and author
* S. R. D.

Drummond, [Sir] William ?-1828
[IP]
Scottish author
* Another Considerable Personage

Drummond, William Abernethy
[IP]
Scottish clergyman and author
* W. A. D.

Drury, Dr. 1750-1834 [NPS]
British educator
* Probus

Drury, Henry Joseph Thomas
1778?-1841 [IP, NPS]
British educator, clergyman, author
* Detector
* Menalcas

Drury, Karl
See Fawcett, Edgar

Drusus
See Cartwright, William

Drusus
See Shakespeare, William

Dryden, John 1631-1700? [NPS]
British poet
* Asaph
* Coppinger, Matthew
* Ignoramus
* Old Squab
(See also base volume)

Dryham, James
See Mencken, Henry Louis

Drysdale, William [IP]
American journalist
* W. D.

Du Baudrier, Sieur
See Swift, Jonathan

Du Bois, Edward 1775?-1850
[IP, WGT]
British barrister and author
* [A] Knight Errant
* Old Knick
* St. Leon, [Count] Reginald de

Du Camp, Jules
See Lecomte, Jules

Du Hault, Jean
See Grindel, Eugene

Du Tremblay, Joseph 17th c. [EE]
French intelligence agent
* [Son] Eminence Grise [The Gray Cardinal]

Duane, William 1760-1835 [IP]
American politician and journalist
* Anti Monopoly
* Camillus
* Dwight, Jasper

Duane, William 1808- ? [IP]
American attorney and author
* W. D.

Dublin Tricks
See Blake, William

Dubourg, Felix [IP]
French actor
* Neuville, Auguste

DuBreuil, Elizabeth Lorinda
1924-1980 [CA]
American author
* Anderson, Kristin
* DeMille, Alexandria
* Dodge, Daniel
* Griffen, Edmund

DuBreuil, Elizabeth Lorinda
(Continued)
* Hagen, Lorinda
* Hanley, Elizabeth
* Maitland, Margaret
* Mark, Jon
* Power, Catherine
* Summer, Brian
* Vaughn, Toni
(See also base volume)

Duche, Jacob 1739-1798 [IP]
American clergyman and author
* Caspipina, Tamoc
* [A] Gentleman of Foreign Extraction
* [A] Gentleman Who Resided Some Time in Philadelphia

[The] Duchess
See Spinelli, Evelita Juanita

[The] Duchess of Park Avenue
See Hampton, Hope

Ducket, George ?-1732 [NPS]
British author and politician
* Doggrel, [Sir] Iliad [joint pseudonym with (Sir) Thomas Burnet]

Duclaux, Agnes Mary Frances [Robinson] 1857- ?
Author
* Robinson, Agnes Mary F.

Ducote, Moon
See Ducote, Richard

Ducote, Richard 20th c. [EF]
American football player
* Ducote, Moon

Dudley, Robert
See Baldwin, James

Duff, James 1776-1857 [NPS]
Fourth Earl of Fife
* [The] Spanish Grandee

Duffy, [Sir] Charles Gavan 1816-1903 [PI]
Irish poet and editor
* [The] Black Northern
* C. G. D.
* D.
* Heder, Ben
* [The] O'Donnell
* [An] Operative
* [A] Town Councillor

Duffy, Paddy
See Duffy, Patrick

Duffy, Patrick 1864-1890 [AS]
American boxer
* Duffy, Paddy

Dufrechou, Carole
See Monroe, Carole

Dugall, George ?-1850? [PI]
Irish poet
* [The] Schoolmaster at Home

Duganne, Augustine Joseph Hickey 1823-1884
American author and poet
* Manners, Motley
* Townley, Arthur?

Duggan, Dionysius
See Maginn, William

Dukaine, Paul
See Dukes, [Sir] Paul

Duke, Angie
See Duke, Angier Biddle

Duke, Angier Biddle 1915- [CR]
American government official
* Duke, Angie

Dukes, [Sir] Paul 1889-1967 [EOP]
British author and Yoga authority
* Dukaine, Paul

[A] Dumpling-Eater
See Stona, Thomas

Dun, Mao
See Yen Ping, Shen

Dunajew, Wanda von
See Sacher-Masoch, Aurora von

Dunbar, Edward
See Smith, David MacLeod

Dunboy
See Crowley, Denis O.

Duncan, Julia Coley
See Sather, Julia Coley Duncan

Duncan, Sara Jeanette
See Cotes, Mrs. E.

Duncan, W[illiam] Murdoch 1909-1976 [CA, TCCM]
Scottish author
* Dallas, John
(See also base volume)

Duncathail
See Varian, Ralph

Dunkin, Robert 19th c. [NPS]
Author
* Snaffle

Dunlap, Jack 20th c. [EWG]
American gunfighter
* Three Fingered Jack

Dunlap, Walter B.
See Cobb, Sylvanus, Jr.

Dunlap, William 1766-1839 [NLC]
American theatre manager and playwright
* [The] Father of American Drama
(See also base volume)

Dunlop, John Colin 1842- ? [NPS]
Author
* [The] Teeger

Dunlop, Tiger
See Dunlop, William

Dunlop, William 1792-1848 [DLE1]
Scottish-Canadian author and physician
* Dunlop, Tiger
(See also base volume)

Dunne, Finley Peter 1867-1936 [DLE1]
American satirist
* Dooley, Martin
(See also base volume)

Dunne, J. T. 1837- ? [NPS]
Soldier, journalist, author
* H. R. N.
* Hi Regan

Dunphie, Charles James 1820?-1908 [PI]
Irish author and poet
* C. J. D.
* T. C. D.

Dunsmuir, Amy
See Oliphant, Mrs.

Dunwoodie, Dominick
See Bryce, James

Duprey, Richard A[llen] 1929- [CA]
American author
* Fields, Alan

Durand, G. Forbes
See Burgess, Michael Roy

Durand, [Sir] H. Mortimer 1850- ? [NPS]
Diplomat and author
* Roy, John

Durand, Mrs. Albert C.
Author
* Sawyer, Ruth

Durandus, Gulielmus 1237-1296 [NPS]
French prelate and jurist
* [The] Speculator

Duringer, Fats
See Duringer, Rudolph

Duringer, Rudolph ?-1931 [DI]
American murderer
* Duringer, Fats

Durkan, Patrick Francis ?-1910 [PI]
Irish-born poet
* Swinford Boy

Durrant, Theo
See Durrant, William Henry Theodore

Durrant, William Henry Theodore 1874-1898 [BLB]
American murderer
* Durrant, Theo

Durst, Lavada 20th c. [CMA]
American disc jockey
* Hepcat, Dr.

[The] Dusseldorf Vampire
See Kurten, Peter

Dustwich, Jonathan
See Smollett, Tobias George

[The] Dutch Shakespeare
See Van der Vondel, Joost

Dutch William
See William III

Dutens, Louis 1730-1812 [NPS]
Diplomat and writer
* [The] Literary Sir Plume

Dutt, Narendra Nath 1862-1902 [EOP]
Founder of Indian religious cult
* Vivekananda, Swami

Duvall, Claude 1643-1670 [DI]
French highwayman
* [The] Rembrandt or Raphael of the Profession

[The] Dwarf of Blood
See Newnham-Davis, Col.

Dwiggins, W. A.
Type designer and puppeteer
* W. A. D.

Dwight, Jasper
See Duane, William

Dwight, Olivia
See Hazzard, Mary

Dwight, Tilton
See Quint, Wilder Dwight

Dyer, Amelia Elizabeth 1839-1896 [DI, LFW]
British murderer
* [The] Baby Farmer
* [The] Reading Baby Farmer

[The] Dying Titan
See Greene, Robert

Dynamite Dick
See Clifton, Dan

Dyson, Jeremiah 1722-1776 [NPS]
Politician
* Mungo

E

E. A.
See Abbot, Ezra

E. A.
See Adams, Samuel

E. A.
See Archer, Edward

E. A.
See Arnold, [Sir] Edwin

E. A.
See Atkinson, Edward

E. A. B. D.
See Bland, E. A.

E. B.
See Barton, Evelyn

E. B.
See Bentham, Edward

E. B.
See Brooke, E.

E. B.
See Budge, Edward

E. B. L.
See Bulwer-Lytton, Edward George Earle Lytton

E. C.
See Cornwall, Ebenezer

E. C.
See Cummings, Elizabeth

E. C. A.
See Agassiz, Elizabeth Cary

E. C. B.
See Christy, Edwin Byron

E. C. C. B.
See Baillie, E. C. C.

E. C. M.
See Tucker, Eleonora C.

E. C., Mrs.
See Carter, Elizabeth

E. D.
See Davis, Eugene

E. D.
See Davison, Edward

E. D. K.
See Keeling, Elsa D'Esterre

E. E. M.
See Millard, E. E.

E. F.
See Fawcett, Edgar

E. F.
See Forsyth, Ebenezer

E. F., Jr.
See Fell, Edward, Jr.

E. F. L.
See Lloyd, Emma F.

E. G. A.
See Adams, E. G.

E. H.
See Hayes, Edward

E. H.
See Holmes, Emra

E. H. B.
See Blackwell, E. H.

E. J.
See Jolly, Emily

E. L.
See Simons, Lydia Lillybridge

E. L. B.
See Bulwer-Lytton, Edward George Earle Lytton

E. M.
See Mangin, Edward

E. M. A.
See Arndt, Ernst Moritz

E. M. F.
See Foster, E. M.

E. M. P. D.
See Downing, Ellen Mary Patrick

E. O. B.
See Butt, Mrs. E. O.

E. P. H.
See Hollister, Edward Payson

E. S.
See Stewart, Mrs. W.

E. S.
See Sweetman, Elinor Mary

E. S. M.
See Martin, Edward Sanford

E. S., Miss
See Shackleton, Elizabeth

E. T.
See Tasker, E.

E. V. C.
See Childe, Edward Vernon

E. W.
See Waller, Edmund

E. W.
See Ward, Edward

[The] Eagle
See Bonaparte, Napoleon

[The] Earl
See Herbert, George Robert Charles

Eastern Jewel 1906-1948 [LFW]
Japanese spy
* Kawashima, Yoshiko

Easy, [Sir] Charles
See Johnson, Samuel

Easy, James
See Heywood, James

Eaton, Cyrus 1883- ? [CR]
American business executive
* [The] Last of the Tycoons

Eaton, Edith 1867-1914 [DNA]
Author
* Siu Sin Far

Eaton-Back, Mrs. B. 20th c. [NPS]
Author
* Vane, Derek

Ebenstein, William 1910-1976 [CA]
Austrian-born American author and political scientist
* Elwin, William

Eberts, Beanie
See Eberts, Bernard

Eberts, Bernard 20th c. [EF]
American football player
* Eberts, Beanie

Eblana
See Butler, Thomas Ambrose

Echard, L.
See Pegge, Samuel

Echegaray y Eizaguirre, Jose [Maria Waldo] 1832-1916 [CA, TLC]
Spanish playwright
* Hayaseca y Eizaguirre, Jorge

[El] Ecijano [The Man from Ecija]
See Jimenez Ripoll, Juan

Eckberg, Gus
See Eckberg, Gustavus

Eckberg, Gustavus 20th c. [EF]
American football player
* Eckberg, Gus

Eclipse, Count
See O'Kelly, Dennis

Economy, Mr.
See Byrd, Harry Flood

Eddison, Mrs. Octavius [NPS]
Journalist and author
* Frost, George

Eden, Edna 20th c. [CR]
American fashion model
* Hartford, Eden

Edgefield, John
See Iliff, John Edgar

[The] Editor of a Quarterly Review
See Deacon, William Frederick

Edmonds, George
See Meriwether, Elizabeth [Avery]

Edmonson, Ice
See Edmonson, Keith

Edmonson, Keith 20th c.
American basketball player
* Edmonson, Ice

Edouart, Alexander 1895?-1980 [FIR]
Special effects expert and photographer
* Edouart, Farciot

Edouart, Farciot
See Edouart, Alexander

Edson, N. I.
See Denison, Mary Andrews

Educated Edward
See Edward

Edward 1330-1376 [NPS]
Prince of Wales
* [The] Invincible Soldier
(See also base volume)

Edward 1964?-
Youngest son of Queen Elizabeth of England
* Educated Edward

Edward VII 1841-1910 [NPS, PPN]
King of England
* [The] Squire of Sandringham
* Tum-Tum
(See also base volume)

Edwardes, Lawrence
See Neuburg, Victor [Benjamin]

Edwards, Alfred S.
Author
* Sevenoaks

Edwards, Cid
See Edwards, Cleophus

Edwards, Cleophus 20th c. [EF]
American football player
* Edwards, Cid

Edwards, Eleanor Lee
See Victor, Metta Victoria Fuller

Edwards, Eli
See McKay, Claude

Edwards, Francis
See Brandon, Johnny

Edward's French Lady
See St. Laurent, Julie de

Edwards, John Milton
See Cook, William Wallace

Edwards, Jules
See Judson, Edward Zane Carroll

Edwards, Oliver
See Haley, [Sir] William

Edwards, Thomas 1696-1757 [IP]
British critic, poet, scholar
* Another Gentleman of Lincoln's
   Inn
* [The] Other Gentleman of
   Lincoln's Inn
* T. E.

Edwards, Thomas A. [IP]
Australian journalist
* Ollapod

Edwards, William [IP]
British author
* [A] Bengal Civilian

Edwin, [Brother] B.
See Arnandez, Richard

Efferidi, Aziz Mehmed
See Zevi, Sabbatai

Effessea
See Cole, Francis Sewell

Eflor, Oram
See Rolfe, Maro Orlando

Egan, Dad
See Egan, William

Egan, John [IP]
Irish journalist
* Junius Hibernicus

Egan, John 20th c. [EF]
American football player
* Egan, Red

Egan, Pierce 1772-1849 [IP]
British sportswriter
* [An] Actor
(See also base volume)

Egan, Red
See Egan, John

Egan, William 19th c. [DI]
American law officer
* Egan, Dad

Egar, John H. 19th c. [IP]
American clergyman and author
* [The] Rector

Egelshem, Wells ?-1786 [IP]
British printer and poet
* Winkey

Egerton, Francis Charles Granville
[Third Earl of Ellesmere]
1515-1547 [NPS]
British poet
* Granville, Charles

Egerton, Mary Margaret ?-1858
[IP]
Author
* [A] Lady of Rank

Egerton-Warburton, Rowland Eyles
1804-1891 [DLE1]
British poet
* Rambling Richard

Egghard, Julius
See Hardegen, Count

Eggleston, Edward 1837-1902 [IP]
American author
* Higgins, Zoraster
* Leisurely Saunterer
(See also base volume)

Eginardus
See Manley, Mary de la Riviere

Egleton, Clive [Frederick] 1927-
[CA, TCCM]
British author
* Blake, Patrick
* Tarrant, John

[An] Egyptian Kafir
See Bailey, Samuel

Eha
See Aitken, Edward Hamilton

Ehrenkron, Irenico
See Sinhold Von Schutz, Philipp
Balthasar

Eily
See O'Leary, Ellen

Einhorn, Virginia Hilu
See Hilu, Virginia

Eiranach
See Doheny, Michael

Eithne
See Ryan, Michael

Ekberg, Gus
See Ekberg, Gustav

Ekberg, Gustav 20th c. [EF]
American football player
* Ekberg, Gus

Flagnitin, J.
See Nightingale, Joseph

Elaine
See Kaufman, Elaine

[The] Elder Wallack
See Wallack, James William

Eleanor ?-1241 [NPS]
Niece of King John of England
* [The] Fair Maid of Brittany
(See also base volume)

[An] Elector in 1771
See Adams, Samuel

Eleonora
See Butler, Eleanor

Elethea, Abba
See Thompson, James W.

Eleutherus, Philonomus
See Arbuthnot, John

Elfinger, Anton 1821-1864 [WEC]
Austrian cartoonist
* Cajetan

Elfrida
See Inchbald, Elizabeth [Simpson]

Elgin, Mary
See Stewart, Dorothy Mary

Elhegos
See Goss, Elbridge Henry

Elias, Samuel 1808-1843 [RBE]
British boxer
* Young Dutch Sam

Eliot, Annie
See Trumbull, Annie Eliot

Eliot, [Sir] Charles 20th c. [NPS]
Author
* Odysseus

Eliot, Francis Perceval 1755-1818
[IP]
British author
* Falkland

Eliot, Grace Dalrymple
1758?-1823 [NPS]
Friend of King George IV of England
* Dally the Tall

Eliot, Samuel Atkins 1798-1862
[IP]
American merchant and author
* [A] Member of the Corporation

Elizabeth 1765-1839 [NPS]
Countess of Sutherland
* Banzu-Mohr-ar-Chat [Great
   Lady of the Cat]

Elizabeth 1843-1916 [NPS]
Queen of Rumania and author
* Astra
* Aus Zwei Welten
(See also base volume)

Elizabeth I 1533-1603 [NPS, UH]
Queen of England
* [The] Deliverer of God's People
* [The] Fair Vestal
* [The] Glory of her Sex
* [The] Miracle of Time
* Tanaquill
* [The] True Diana
* [The] Untamed Heifer
(See also base volume)

Elizaphan of Parnach
See Church, Benjamin

Elkins, Chief
See Elkins, Fait

Elkins, Fait 20th c. [EF]
American football player
* Elkins, Chief

Ellem, Mr.
See Hennessy, William Charles

Ellemjay, Louise 19th c. [BDSA]
American author
* L. M. J.

Ellen of Exeter
See Mackenzie, Anne Maria

Ellenborough, Jane Elizabeth [Digby]
1807-1882 [IP]
British author
* Ianthe

Ellenwood, Henry S. 19th c. [IP]
American author
* Pindar, Peter, Jr.

Ellenwood, Henry S. (Continued)
* X.
(See also base volume)

Ellerton, John Lodge
See Lodge, John

Ellice, Edward 1786?-1863 [IP]
British politician
* Mercator
(See also base volume)

Elliot, Frances [Minto] [IP]
British author
* [An] Idle Woman

Elliot, John Lettsom [IP]
Author
* [An] Aristocrat
* [A] Conservative
* [A] Protectionist

Elliott
See Coues, Samuel Elliott

Elliott, Babs
See Walters, Barbara

Elliott, Charles Wyllys 1817-1883
[IP]
American author
* White, [Mr.] Thom

Elliott, Charlotte 1789-1871 [IP]
British hymn-writer
* C. E.
* [A] Lady

Elliott, Emilia
See Jacobs, Caroline Emilia

Elliott, Margaret Drake 1904-
[MA]
American author and poet
* Ag-Kaa-Noo-Ma-Gaa-Qua
   [Friendly Teaching Lady]

Ellis, Alexander John
See Sharpe, Alexander John

Ellis, Edward S[ylvester] 1840-1916
American author
* Adams, Bruin
* Adams, James Fenimore Cooper
* Brown, Mahlon A.?
* Faulkner, Frank
* Gwynne, Oscar A.
* Gwynne, Oswald A.
* Hunter, [Lieut.] Ned
* Lasalle, George E.
* Millbank, [Capt.] H. R.
* Randolph, Geoffrey
* Robins, Rollo
* St. Mox, E. S.
* Thoman, Egbert S.
* [A] U. S. Detective
(See also base volume)

Ellis, Herbert
See Wilson, Lionel

Ellis, John Fanshawe
See Wilde, Jane Francesca Elgee

Ellis, Speed
See Ellis, Walter

Ellis, Walter 20th c. [EF]
American football player
* Ellis, Speed

Ellison, Henry Leopold
See Zeckhausen, Henry Leopold

Elliston, Robert William
1774-1831 [NPS]
British actor
* [The] Napoleon of Drury Lane
(See also base volume)

Elloie
See Stith, Zoda

Ellora
See Jackson, Editha Salomon

Elmore, Belle
See Mackamotzki, Kunigunde

Elmore, Ernest Carpenter 1901-
[TCCM]
British author
* Bude, John

Elmwood
See Lowell, James Russell

Elon-Rusticus
See Anderson, Linnaeus B.

Elphinstone, Leslie
See Ollif, S. L. E.

Elrington, Stephen Nolan
See Nolan, Stephen

Elwes, A. W. 19th c.   [BDSA]
American poet
* [A] Lady of Virginia?

Elwin, William
See Ebenstein, William

Elyot, [Sir] Thomas 1499?-1546
[NPS]
Author
* [The] Learned Knight

Elzevir
See Murdoch, [Sir] Walter Logie
Forbes

Emendator
See Whitefoord, Caleb

Emerald Isle
See Hepburn, Duncan D.

Emerce
See Crowell, Mary Reed

Emerson, Banjo
See Emerson, Pete

Emerson, Grover 20th c.   [EF]
American football player
* Emerson, Ox

Emerson, Ox
See Emerson, Grover

Emerson, Pete 19th c.   [CEC]
American thief
* Emerson, Banjo

Emerson, Ralph Waldo 1803-1882
[NPS]
American author and poet
* [The] Buddha of the West
* [A] Winged Franklin
(See also base volume)

Emigrant
See Sidney, Samuel

[An] Emigrant Farmer
See Abbott, Joseph

Emiliane, Gabriel d'
See Gavin, Antoine

Emily
See Angove, Emily

**[Son] Eminence Grise [The Gray
Cardinal]**
See Du Tremblay, Joseph

[An] Eminent English Counsel
See Longley, John

[An] Eminent Lawyer of Connecticut
See Hooker, John

[An] Eminent Lawyer of the Temple
See Arbuthnot, John

Eminescu, Mihail
See Iminovici, Mihail

Emmet, Robert 1778-1803   [PI]
Irish patriot and poet
* Trebor

Emptor Caveat
See Stephen, [Sir] George

Endfield, Mercedes
See Von Block, Bela

Endore, [Samuel] Guy 1900-1970
[CA]
American author and screenwriter
* Relis, Harry

Endymion
See Nash, William

Engebretsen, Paul 20th c.   [EF]
American football player
* Engebretsen, Tiny

Engebretsen, Tiny
See Engebretsen, Paul

Engel, George 19th c.   [DI]
American forger
* [The] Terror of Wall Street

Engelhardt, Charles Anthony
See Engelhardt, Zephyrin

Engelhardt, Zephyrin 1851-1934
[DNA]
*German-born author, historian,
clergyman*
* Engelhardt, Charles Anthony

Engelmann, J. C. 1754-1815   [BBD]
German composer
* Kaffka, Johann Christoph

England, S.
See Porson, Richard

England's Neptune
See Drake, [Sir] Francis

England's Nestor
See Hawkins, [Sir] John

Englebrecht, John 17th c.   [EOP]
Claimed to possess psychic powers
* [The] George Fox of Germany

[The] English Aretine
See Nash [or Nashe?], Thomas

[The] English Bayard
See Gordon, Charles George

[An] English Detective
See Russell, William

[The] English Ennius
See Chaucer, Geoffrey

[The] English Juvenal
See Wither, George

[The] English Mastiff
See Milton, John

[An] English Mercury
See Hall, Joseph

[The] English Milo
See Raleigh, [Sir] Walter

[The] English Moliere
See O'Keefe, John

[The] English Roscius
See Betterton, Thomas

[The] English Terence
See Shakespeare, William

English, Thomas Dunn 1819-1902
[DLE1]
American author and poet
* Ogden, Christol
* Payne, F. M.
* Quickens, Quarles
(See also base volume)

[A] English Traveller
See Dewey, Orville

[An] English Traveller in Spain
See Dillon, John Talbot

[The] English Xenophon
See Astley, John

[An] Englishman
See Barry, William Whittaker

[An] Englishman
See Bury, James

[An] Englishman
See Gordon, Thomas

[An] Englishman
See Paine, Thomas

[An] Englishwoman
See Waldie, Charlotte Anne

Eno, William Phelps 1858-1945
*American writer and traffic safety
consultant*
* [The] Father of Traffic Safety

Enos
See Stone, Cecil Percival

[The] Enquirer
See Atkinson, William

[The] Ensign
See Maginn, William

Enton, Harry 1854-1927
American writer
* Free, [Maj.] Mickey
* Gilman, Wenona
* Harrison, Harry
* Ironclad
(See also base volume)

Entwistle, Florence Vivienne
1889?-1982   [CA]
Artist and photographer
* Vivienne

Eos
See Leamy, Edmund

[The] Epic Renegade
See Southey, Robert

Epsilon
See Brown, James Baldwin

Erasmus, W. J.
See Wilson, Erasmus

Ercole, Velia 20th c.   [DLE1]
Australian author
* Gregory, Margaret

Eremus
See Wilson, John

Eric 10th c.   [NPS]
Norwegian navigator
* [The] Red

Erickson, Michael 20th c.   [EF]
American football player
* Erickson, Mickey

Erickson, Mickey
See Erickson, Michael

Ericsson, Leif   [BBH]
Norwegian explorer
* [The] Lucky

Erie-us
See Burwell, Adam Hood

Erionnach
See O'Mulrenin, Richard Joseph

Erionnach
See Sigerson, George

Ern
See Adamov, Arthur

Errym, Malcolm J.
See Rymer, James Malcolm

Erskine, Thomas 1750-1823   [NPS]
British barrister and politician
* Jupiter Tonans [The Thundering
Jupiter]

Erto, Pasquale 1895-   [EOP]
*Italian chemist who claimed to
possess psychic powers*
* [The] Human Rainbow

Erz-Philosopher
See Nicolai, Christopher Friedrich

Eschmeyer, Reinhart Ernst 1898-
[CA]
American author and clergyman
* Eshmeyer, R. E.

Escobar, Marisol 1930-   [CR]
French-born sculptor
* Marisol

Eshmeyer, R. E.
See Eschmeyer, Reinhart Ernst

Esmonde, Alice
See Ryan, Margaret Mary

Esop, Master
See Gifford, William

[El] Espartero
See Garcia y Cuesta, Manuel

Esperance
See Chapeau, Ellen Chazel

Espos, Carolino
See Mina, Lino Amalia Espos Y

[An] Essayist on the Passions
See Michell, Nicholas

Esse, James
See Stephens, James

Essenus
See Jones, John

[An] Essex Justice
See Johnston, Andrew

Estcourt, Richard 1668-1712
[NPS]
Actor and playwright
* Mirror, Tom

Este, Charles 18th c.   [NPS]
British poet
* Este, Morosoph

Este, Morosoph
See Este, Charles

Estebanez, Joaquin
See Tamayo y Baus, Manuel

Estienne, Robert
See Le Bonnieres, Robert

Etherege, [Sir] George
1635?-1691?   [NPS]
British playwright
* Gentle George
(See also base volume)

Ethna
See MacManus, Anna

Ethne
See Thompson, Marie M.

Ettingsall, Thomas ?-1850?   [PI]
Irish poet and writer
* Greydrake, Geoffrey

Etumos
See Hamilton, May Charlotte

Eugene
See Arnot, Hugo

Eulalie
See Russell, Matthew

Euphormio Lusininus
See Barclay, John

Eureka
See Ralston, Thomas N.

Eureka
See Sheridan, John

Europaeus, Lucius Cornelius
See Scotti, Giulio Clemente

[The] European Traveller
See Brockway, Thomas

Eusebius
See Nickolls, Robert Boucher

Eusebius
See Rack, Edmund

Eusebius Exoniensis
See Polwhele, Richard

Eustace
See Read, William

Eustace 13th c.   [NPS]
French freebooter
* [The] Monk

Euwe, Machgielis 1901-1981   [CA]
Dutch chess player and author
* Euwe, Max

Euwe, Max
See Euwe, Machgielis

Eva C
See Beraud, Marthe

Evans, Dale
See Smith, Frances Octavia

**Evans, [Sir] Edward Ratcliffe Garth
Russell** 1881-1957   [PPN]
*British explorer, naval officer,
author*
* Evans of the Broke

Evans, Gwynne
See Welby, John Robson

Evans, Harold 20th c.   [PPN]
*Public relations adviser to British
prime minister, Harold Macmillan*
* Evans the Leak

Evans, Marian 1819-1880   [NPS]
British author
* Lewes, Marian
(See also base volume)

Evans of the Broke
See Evans, [Sir] Edward Ratcliffe
Garth Russell

Evans, Owen
See Anderdon, William Henry

Evans the Leak
See Evans, Harold

Evelyn, Chetwood, Esq.
See Pell, Robert Conger

Evelyn, John 1620-1706   [DEA]
British author
* J. E.
(See also base volume)

Evergreen, Anthony
See O'Rourke, John

Every, Henry 17th c.   [DI]
Pirate
* Every, Long Ben

Every, Long Ben
See Every, Henry

Ewart, Charles
See Lyte, Charles

Ewing, Juliana [Horatia Gatty]
1841-1885   [SAT]
British author
* Gatty, Juliana Horatia
(See also base volume)

[An] Ex Dissenting Minister
See Christison, Robert

[An] Ex Hussar
See Heron, A.

[The] Exchequer of Eloquence
See Cheke, [Sir] John

[The] Exegete
See Alexander

[An] Experienced Carver
See Foster, George G.

[An] Experienced Teacher
See Wrifford, Anson

Exploralibus
See Haywood, Eliza [Fowler]

Exul
See Dollard, William

[The] Eye of Modern Illumination
See Arouet, Francois Marie

[An] Eye Witness
See Lamb, Charles

[An] Eye Witness
See Stock, Joseph

[An] Eye Witness
See Tanner, Henry

Ezzelino IV 1194-1259   [NPS]
*Chief of the Ghibellines and
Governor of Vicenza*
* [A] Child of Hell
(See also base volume)

F

* Indicates Assumed Name

F.
See Forster, Thomas

F.
See Frazer, John de Jean

F.
See Littledale, Richard

F. A.
See Archer, Frederick

F. B.
See Bourdillon, Francis

F. B.
See Bowen, Francis

F. B.
See Rogers, Henry

F. C.
See Carteaux, Felix

F. C.
See Corfield, Frederick

F. C. A.
See Armstrong, Frances Charlotte

F. E.
See Smith, Frederick Edwin [First Earl of Birkenhead]

F. E. A.
See Ashley, Florence Emily

F. G.
See Godwin, Francis

F. G. L.
See Lee, Frederick George

F. G. W.
See Waldron, Francis Godolphin

F. J. F.
See Fox, Francis J.

F. J. P.
See Pakenham, F. J.

F. L. M.
See Morse, F. L.

F. M.
See Martin, Frederick

F. R.
See Littledale, Richard

F. R. G. S.
See Burton, [Sir] Richard Francis

F. R., of Barrie
See Rye, Francis

F. S.
See Cole, [Sir] Henry

F. S. A.
See Wainwright, Latham

F. S. C.
See Cole, Francis Sewell

F. T.
See Trollope, Frances

F. W.
See Wilson, Francis

F. W
See Wrangham, Francis

Fabbri, Nancy Rash 1940-   [CA]
American author
* Harrison, Mary

Fabell, Peter 15th c.   [NPS]
Magician
* [The] Merry Devil of Edmonton

Fabius
See Charles II

Fabricius, Johan [Johannes] 1899-[CA]
Indonesian-born author and playwright
* Wigmore

[The] Fabulous
See Osorio, Manuel Luiz

Facchiano, Albert 20th c.
American underworld figure
* Facchiano, Chink

Facchiano, Chink
See Facchiano, Albert

Facundus, Doctor
See Aureolus, Peter

Fadiman, Clifton 1904-   [CR]
American author and radio personality
* Fadiman, Kip

Fadiman, Kip
See Fadiman, Clifton

Fago, Nicola 1677-1745   [BBD]
Italian composer
* [Il] Tarantino

Fahey, Pooch
See Fahey, William Roger [Bill]

Fahey, William Roger [Bill] 1950-
American baseball player
* Fahey, Pooch

Fahrney, Madcap
See Fahrney, Merry

Fahrney, Merry 20th c.   [CR]
American heiress
* Fahrney, Madcap

Fahy, Francis Arthur 1854- ?   [PI]
Irish-born poet, author, songwriter
* Dreoilin

Fail, Lia
See Fenelon, Timothy Brendan

Fair, Frank
See Winn, Jane Frances

[The] Fair Maid of Brittany
See Eleanor

[The] Fair Vestal
See Elizabeth I

Fairburn, Edwin 19th c.   [WGT]
British author
* Mohoao

Fairfax, Black Tom
See Fairfax, Thomas [Third Baron Fairfax]

Fairfax, L.
See Connelly, Celia [Logan Kellogg]

Fairfax, Mary   [NPS]
Duchess of Buckingham
* [The] Cyprian Queen

Fairfax, Thomas [Third Baron Fairfax] 1612-1671   [NPS]
Commander of the Parliamentary Army
* Fairfax, Black Tom
* Great Croysado
(See also base volume)

Fairfield, Clarence
See Champlin, Edwin Ross

Fairholt, F. W. 1814-1866   [NPS]
Engraver and author
* London Antiquary
(See also base volume)

Fairlamb, Sampson
See Paulding, James Kirke

[The] Fairy Singer
See Spenser, Edmund

Falconer, Lee N.
See Dikty, Julian May

Falconer, William 1730-1769 [NPS]
Author
* [A] Sailor
(See also base volume)

Falk, Lee
See Copper, Basil

Falkland
See Ames, Fisher

Falkland
See Eliot, Francis Perceval

Falkland
See Scott, John Robert

Fall, Marcus
See Dowling, Richard

Falstaff, Jake
See Fetzer, Herman

Family Man Barrett
See Barrett, Aston

Fancy's Child
See Shakespeare, William

Fancy's Favourite
See Goldsmith, Oliver

Fane, Florence
See Barritt, Frances Fuller

Farigoule, Louis 1885-1972   [CD]
French author, playwright, poet
* Hicks, John H.
(See also base volume)

Farina, Brick
See Farina, Ralph

Farina, Ralph 20th c.   [EF]
American football player
* Farina, Brick

[A] Farmer
See Anderson, James

[A] Farmer
See Benezet, Anthony

Farmer
See Brooke, Henry

Farmer, A. W.
See Seabury, Samuel

[A] Farmer in Cheshire
See Stillingfleet, Benjamin

Farmer, May
See Wilson, Mrs. E. V.

Farquharson, Charlie
See Harron, Don[ald]

Farrar, Venice 20th c.   [EF]
American football player
* Farrar, Vinney

Farrar, Vinney
See Farrar, Venice

Farrell, Agnes
See Adams, Francis William
Lauderdale

Farrell, Hugh 19th c. [PI]
Irish poet
* Aedh

Farrell, Joseph 1841-1885 [PI]
Irish author and poet
* H. L.
* J. F.

Farren, Elizabeth 1759?-1829
[NPS]
*Countess of Derby and former
actress*
* [The] Maid of the Oaks

[The] Fastest Tongue in the West
See Reed, B. Mitchel

[A] Father
See Ainslie, Robert

[A] Father
See Tighe, William

Father Charles
See Meehan, Charles Patrick

[The] Father of Aikido
See Uyeshiba, Morihei

[The] Father of American Drama
See Dunlap, William

**[The] Father of American Fox
Hunting**
See Brooke, Robert

[The] Father of American Golf
See Reid, John

**[The] Father of American
Universalism**
See Murray, John

**[The] Father of Bacchanalian Poetry
in France**
See Basselin, Olivier

[The] Father of Basketball
See Naismith, James

[The] Father of Boxing
See Broughton, Jack

[The] Father of British Lyceums
See Kitson, Alfred

[The] Father of Christian Hymnology
See Ambrose [or Ambrosius]

[The] Father of Comedy
See Homer

[The] Father of Communism
See Marx, Karl

[The] Father of Ecclesiastical History
See Baronio, Cesare

[The] Father of Ecology
See Leopold, Aldo

[The] Father of English Hexameter
See Harvey, Gabriel

[The] Father of English Music
See Tallis, Thomas

**[The] Father of English Periodical
Literature**
See Steele, [Sir] Richard

**[The] Father of English Water-Colour
Painting**
See Cozens, Alexander

[The] Father of Existentialism
See Sartre, Jean-Paul

**[The] Father of Experimental
Philosophy**
See Bacon, Francis [First Baron
Verulam]

[The] Father of Fivepin Bowling
See Ryan, Thomas J.

**[The] Father of French Canadian
Poetry**
See Cremazie, Octave

[The] Father of Geology
See Steno, Nicolas

**[The] Father of Hungarian Literary
Criticism**
See Kazinczy, Ferenc

[The] Father of Italian History
See Muratori, Ludovico Antonio

[The] Father of Judo
See Kamo, Jigoro

[The] Father of Karate
See Funakoshi, Gichin

[The] Father of Line Engraving
See Heath, James

[The] Father of Modern Canada
See Macdonald, [Sir] John
Alexander

[The] Father of Modern Conservatism
See Burke, Edmund

[The] Father of Modern Geology
See Lyell, [Sir] Charles

**[The] Father of Modern Greyhound
Racing**
See Smith, Owen P.

[The] Father of Modern Miscellanies
See Montaigne, Michel Eyquem de

[The] Father of Musical Comedy
See Tanner, James T.

[The] Father of Neo-Plasticism
See Mondrian, Piet[er Cornelis]

[The] Father of New France
See Champlain, Samuel de

[The] Father of Pastoral Poetry
See Theocritus

[The] Father of Photography
See Niepce, Joseph Nicephore

[The] Father of Poets
See Johnson, Ben[jamin]

**[The] Father of Polish Bourgeois
Comedy**
See Balucki, Michal

[The] Father of Rock 'n' Roll
See Berry, Charles Edward
Anderson [Chuck]

**[The] Father of Ski Jumping and
Slalom**
See Nordheim, Sondre

[The] Father of Skiing
See Nordheim, Sondre

[The] Father of Television
See Zworykin, Vladimir Kosma

Father of the American Revolution
See Adams, Samuel

**[The] Father of the American School
of New Economics**
See Heller, Walter

**[The] Father of the Chinese
Renaissance**
See Hu Shih

[The] Father of the Credit Card
See Bloomingdale, Alfred

[The] Father of the Danish Drama
See Holberg, Louis [or Ludvig]

**[The] Father of the English Detective
Novel**
See Collins, [William] Wilkie

[The] Father of the English Turf
See Frampton, Tregonwell

**[The] Father of the Modern Realist
Novel**
See Verga, Giovanni

**[The] Father of the Nashville
Racecourse**
See Jackson, Andrew

[The] Father of the Pole Vault
See Goldie, George

**[The] Father of the Racing Pigeon
Sport in America**
See Goldman, Fred

[A] Father of the Society of Jesus
See Boudreaux, F. J.

[The] Father of the Waltz
See Strauss, Johann, Sr.

[The] Father of the Western
See Grey, Pearl

[The] Father of Thought
See Catinat, Nicholas

[The] Father of Traffic Safety
See Eno, William Phelps

Faulkner, Frank
See Ellis, Edward S[ylvester]

[The] Faun of the Italian Renaissance
See Allegri da Correggio, Antonio

Faustina, Madame
See Perriman, Florence

Favato, Carino 20th c. [DI]
American murderer and robber
* [The] Philadelphia Witch

[The] Favorite of the Nation
See Talbot, Charles

Fawcett, Edgar 19th c. [IP]
American author and poet
* Drury, Karl
* E. F.

Fawcett, Joseph ?-1804 [IP]
British clergyman and author
* Swan, [Sir] Simon, Bart.

Fawkes, Francis 1721-1777 [IP]
British clergyman, poet, scholar
* [A] Gentleman of Cambridge

Fawkes, Guy
See Benchley, Robert [Charles]

Fay
See Snead, Fayette

Fay, Joseph Dewey 1780-1825 [IP]
American attorney and author
* Howard

Fay, Theodore Sedgwick 1807- ?
[IP]
American author and journalist
* [A] Quiet Man
* Sedley, F.

Feardana
See Joyce, Robert Dwyer

Feargail
See McGee, Thomas D'Arcy

Feather, Chief
See Feather, Elvin

Feather, Elvin 20th c. [EF]
American football player
* Feather, Chief
* Feather, Tiny

Feather, Tiny
See Feather, Elvin

[The] Federal Farmer
See Lee, Richard Henry

Feigelson, Naomi
See Chase, Naomi Feigelson

Feigner, Eddie [BBH]
Athlete
* [The] King

Feilding, Dorothy 1884- [TCCM]
British author
* Fielding, A. E.
(See also base volume)

Feilen, John
See Dikty, Julian May

Feldmann, Susan Judith 1928-1969
[CA]
American author and educator
* Taubes, Susan

Felix, Pastor
See Lockhart, Arthur John

Fell, Edward, Jr. 1804-1835 [IP]
British author
* E. F., Jr.

Fell, John 1735-1797 [IP]
British clergyman and author
* Phileleutheros

**[A] Fellow of the Antiquarian
Societies of London and Scotland**
See Ainslie, George Robert

[A] Fellow of the Antiquarian Society
See Gower, Foote

**[A] Fellow of the Linnaean and
Horticultural Societies**
See Bennett, J. W.

**[A] Fellow of the Royal and
Antiquarian Societies**
See Forshall, Josiah

**[A] Fellow of the Society of
Antiquaries of Scotland**
See Dick, John

Fellowes, Robert 1770-1847 [IP]
British author
* Philalethes, M.A., Oxon
(See also base volume)

Fellows, John ?-1770? [IP]
Poet and hymn-writer
* Philanthropos

Fels, Joachim
See Hagen, Theodor

Felton, John 1595?-1628   [NPS]
*British army officer who
assassinated the Duke of
Buckingham*
* Brutus
(See also base volume)

Feltrim
See Rooney, William

[The] Female Forger
See Rudd, Mrs.

**[The] Female Philosopher of the
North**
See .Cockburn, Catherine

[A] Feminine Blake
See Dickinson, Emily Elizabeth

Fenelon, Timothy Brendan   [PI]
Irish poet
* Dalcassian
* Fail, Lia
* Rochefort, Harold

Fenety, George E. 19th c.   [IP]
Canadian journalist
* [A] Bluenose

Feng, Chin
See Liu, Sydney [Chieh]

Fenn, Eleanor 1744-1813   [ICB, IP]
British author
* Lovechild, Laurence
* Lovechild, Solomon
(See also base volume)

Fennell, Greville   [IP]
British author
* Greville F., of Barnes

Fennell, James   [IP]
American author
* Nobody, Nemo

Fennell, Patrick 1842- ?   [PI]
Irish-born poet and engineer
* Maguire, Shandy
* [The] Poet Laureate of the
Railroad

Fennimore, Stephen
See Collins, Cuthbert Dale

Fenton, Richard ?-1821   [IP]
Welsh barrister and author
* [A] Barrister

Fenwick, E. P.
See Way, Elizabeth Fenwick

Fenwick, Elizabeth
See Way, Elizabeth Fenwick

Fenwick, John Ralph   [IP]
British physician and author
* Bigod, Ralph

Ferdinand I ?-1065   [NPS]
King of Castile and Leon
* [The] Happy
(See also base volume)

Ferguson, Adam 1724-1816   [IP]
Scottish historian and author
* [A] Gentleman in the Country

Ferguson, Charles   [IP]
Scottish barrister and author
* Member of the Faculty of
Advocates

Ferguson, John Clark   [IP]
British poet
* Lee, Alfred

Ferguson, Peter K.   [IP]
American author
* Wonder, Jak

Ferguson, Robert ?-1714   [NPS]
*Scottish conspirator and political
pamphleteer*
* Judas
(See also base volume)

Ferguson, Samuel 1815- ?   [IP]
Irish barrister and poet
* Hefferman, [Mr.] Michael

[The] Fermanagh True Blue
See Young, Robert

Fermin, Philippe 18th c.   [IP]
British author
* [A] Person Who Lived There Ten
Years

Fermoy
See Pigot, John Edward

Fernandez, Manny
See Fernandez, Manuel Jose

Fernandez, Manuel Jose 1951-
[FR]
American football player
* Fernandez, Manny

Fernandez, Raymond ?-1951   [DI]
American murderer
* [The] Lonely Hearts Killer
* Martin, Charles

Fernandez Navarette, Juan
1526-1575   [NPS]
Spanish painter
* [The] Mute
(See also base volume)

Ferney, Jules
See Arago, Etienne

Fernihough, John C.   [IP]
British artist and author
* [A] Local Artist

Ferris, J. J.   [NN]
Australian cricketer
* [The] Fiend

Ferry, Gabriel
See Bellemane, Eugene Louis
Gabriel de Ferry de

Fest, Ernst
See Mayer, Eduard Heinrich

Fetz, Gus
See Fetz, Gustave

Fetz, Gustave 20th c.   [EF]
American football player
* Fetz, Gus

Fetzer, Herman 1899-1935   [DNA]
American author and columnist
* Falstaff, Jake

Ffoulkes, Mrs. 20th c.   [NPS]
Author
* Craven, Mary

Fiachra, Hi
See Rooney, William

[Il] Fiammingo
See John of Bologna

Fibbleton, George
See Green, Asa

Fiddling Conyers
See Middleton, Conyers

[The] Fiddling Knight
See Hawkins, [Sir] John

Fidelis
See Machar, Agnes Maule

Field, Barron 19th c.   [HFN]
Author
* [A] Barrister

Field, Eugene 1850-1895
American poet and journalist
* [The] Child's Poet

Field, Martyn
See Horner, Frederick William

Field, Nathaniel 1587-1633   [DEA]
British author
* N. F.

Field, Peter [joint pseudonym with
Thayer Hobson]
See Hobson, Laura Z.

Field, Peter [joint pseudonym with
Laura Z. Hobson]
See Hobson, Thayer

Fielding, A. E.
See Feilding, Dorothy

Fielding, H.
See Hall, H. Fielding

Fielding, Henry
See Ireland, William Henry

Fielding, Henry 1707-1754
[DLE1, NPS]
British author and playwright
* Gulliver, Lemuel
* Keyber, [Mr.] Conny
* Orlando the Fair
* Scriblerus Secundus, H.
* [The] Shakespeare of Novelists
* Trott-Plaid, John, Esq.
* Vinegar, [Capt.] Hercules
(See also base volume)

Fielding, Sarah 1710-1768   [NPS]
Author
* [A] Lady

Fields, Alan
See Duprey, Richard A[llen]

[The] Fiend
See Ferris, J. J.

**Fiennes, William [First Viscount Saye
and Sele]** 1582-1662   [DBQ]
British politician
* [The] Godfather
(See also base volume)

Fiery Fred Trueman
See Trueman, Fred

Figaro in Dublin
See Ronayne, Dominick

[The] Fighting Grenadier
See Boone, John

[The] Fighting Little Judge
See Wallace, George Corley

Fighton, [Capt.] George Z.
See De Weindeck, Winteler

Figulus, Wolfgang
See Toepfer, Wolfgang

Figwood, John, Barrister-at-Law
See Le Fanu, J[oseph] Sheridan

Filicchia, Ralph 1935-   [CA]
American author
* Michaels, Ralph

Filumena   [UH]
Saint
* [The] Thaumaturgus of the
Nineteenth Century

Finder, Martin
See Salzmann, Siegmund

Findley, W.   [NPS]
Author
* Umber, George

Fingerling, Winged Eel
See Ingber, Elliot

Fink, William
See Mencken, Henry Louis

Finkell, Max
See Catto, Max[well Jeffrey]

Finn, Charles 1878?-1982
American clergyman
* Finn, Zip

Finn, Edmund 1819-1898   [DLE1]
Irish author and journalist
* Garryowen

Finn, Frank Stanislaus 19th c.
American actor and author
* Lawless, Eve?

Finn, [Sister] Mary Paulina
1842-1935   [DNA]
American poet
* Pine, M. S.

Finn, Mickey
See Jarrold, Ernest

Finn, Zip
See Finn, Charles

Finola
See Varian, Elizabeth Willoughby

Fion
See O'Connell, Maurice

Fionbarr
See Varian, Ralph

Fionbarra
See Murphy, James J.

Fionn, Paistin
See Keegan, James

Fionn, Pastheen
See Keegan, James

Fionna, Flann
See Stritch, Andrew F. Russell

Fionnuala
See Kelly, Mary Anne

[The] Firebrand of His Country
See Knox, John

Firinne
See Pigot, John Edward

Firmiani, Petri
See Zacharie de Lisieux, Pere

[The] First Citizen
See Carroll, Charles

[The] First Lady of Disco
See Gaines, La Donna Andrea

[The] First Lyrist of France
See Ronsard, Pierre de

[The] First Man of Letters in Europe
See Southey, Robert

[The] First of Existing Writers
See Goethe, Johann Wolfgang von

[The] First Politician in the World
See Adams, Samuel

[The] First Tycoon of Teen
See Spector, Phil

Fischer, Albert Dietrich 1925-   [CR]
German opera singer
* [The] Thinking Man's Baritone
(See also base volume)

Fisguill, Richard
See Wilson, Richard Henry

Fish, Mr.
See Rabito, Anthony

Fish, Robert L. 1912-1981   [TCCM]
American author
* Roberts, Lawrence
(See also base volume)

Fisher, Barbara 1940-   [CA]
American author and playwright
* Perry, Barbara Fisher

[A] Fisher in Small Streams
See Brown, William Linn

Fisher, John 19th c.   [BLB]
American gunfighter
* Fisher, King

Fisher, King
See Fisher, John

Fisher, Sidney George 1809-1871
[DNA]
American author, poet, attorney
* Cecil

[A] Fisherman and Zoologist
See Buckland, Francis Trevelyan

Fisk, Callene
See Crafts, Wilbur Fisk

Fitz A.
See Fitzachary, John Christopher

Fitz Mac
See McCarthy, Fitzjames

Fitz-Randolph, Jane [Currens]
See Currens, Jane

Fitzachary, John Christopher
1840-1902   [PI]
Irish poet and author
* Fitz A.
* Geraldine
* Sexton, Annie

FitzAdam, Adam
See Stanhope, Philip Dormer

Fitzadam, Ismael
See Macken, John

FitzErin
See Day, J. Fitzgerald

Fitzgerald, Anna A. 1842-1865   [PI]
Canadian-born poet
* Raphael, [Sister] Anna

Fitzgerald, Francis Alexander
1805-1897   [PI]
Irish poet
* I. H.

Fitzgerald, George Robert
1748?-1786   [PI]
Irish-born duellist and poet
* G. R. F.
(See also base volume)

Fitzgerald, Gerald ?-1583   [EOP]
16th Earl of Desmond
* [The] Great Earl

Fitzgerald, Joseph 1793-1856   [PI]
Irish poet
* J. F.

Fitzgerald, Percy Hetherington
1834-1925   [NPS]
Author
* One of the Boys
(See also base volume)

FitzGerald, Shafto Justin Adair 1859-
?   [NPS]
Author and playwright
* Hannaford, Justin
* O'Neil, Carolan

Fitzgerald, William Thomas
1759-1829   [PI]
British poet
* [The] Loyal Poet
(See also base volume)

Fitzgibbon, Edmund 1552?- 1608
[NPS]
Irish soldier
* [The] White Knight

Fitzhugh, Francis
See Mackay, Francis Alexander

Fitzjersey, Horace
See Buckley, Theodore William
Alois

Fitzmonkey, Edward Borrowlaski
See Fitzsimons, Edward John

Fitzpatrick, James ?-1787   [BLB]
American robber
* Flash, Sandy

Fitzpatrick, John 1859- ?   [PI]
Irish author and poet
* [A] Priestman
* Smaragdus

Fitzpatrick, Patrick Vincent
1792-1865   [PI]
Irish poet and humorist
* Padraig, Padraic Giolla

Fitzsimmons, Fitz
See Fitzsimmons, Frank

Fitzsimmons, Frank 1908-   [CR]
American labor leader
* Fitzsimmons, Fitz

Fitzsimon, Ellen 1805-1883   [PI]
Irish author and poet
* L. N. F.

Fitzsimons, Edward John
1771-1824   [PI]
Irish poet
* Fitzmonkey, Edward Borrowlaski

Fitztravesty, Blaize, Esq.
See Maginn, William

FitzVictor, John
See Shelley, Percy Bysshe

Fitzwhistler, Enoch
See Cobb, Sylvanus, Jr.

Five Per Cent, Mr.
See Gulbenkian, Calouste

Flaccus Horatius
See Wright, Robert William

Flammenberg, Lawrence
See Kahlert, Karl F[riedrich]

Flanagan, Charles 1830-1856   [PI]
Irish clergyman and poet
* D. F. C.

Flanagan, Dorothy Belle
See Hughes, Dorothy B[elle]

Flanagan, Edward 19th c.   [PI]
Irish poet
* [The] Poet of the Moy

Flanagan, Hoot
See Flanagan, William

Flanagan, William 20th c.   [EF]
American football player
* Flanagan, Hoot

Flanders, Henry 1824-1911   [DNA]
American author and attorney
* Thurston, Oliver

Flash, Sandy
See Fitzpatrick, James

Flather, John
See Archbold, John Flather

Flecher, Henry McDonald 1840- ?
[PI]
Irish-born author and poet
* Coilus

Flecker, Herman Elroy 1884-1915
[UH]
British poet
* [The] Last of the Parnassians
(See also base volume)

Fledger, Aaron
See Andrews, Addison Fletcher

Fleming, Alice Kipling 1868-1948
[EOP]
British poet who claimed to possess
psychic powers
* Holland, Mrs.

Fleming, George
See Benson, Eugene

Fleming, Margaret 1803-1811
[DLE1]
Scottish writer and poet
* Margerie, Pet

[The] Flemish Blacksmith
See Matsys, Quentin

Flemming, Harford
See McClellan, Harriet [Hare]

Fletcher, John 1579-1625   [NPS]
Playwright
* [A] Limb of Shakespeare
* [The] Muses' Darling

Fletcher, Phineas 1582-1650   [NPS]
Poet
* [The] Spenser of His Age

Fleurange
See Lefevre, Lily Alice

[A] Flirt
See Bury, Charlotte Susan Maria
[Campbell]

Flitcroft, Henry 1697-1769   [NN]
British architect
* Burlington Harry

[The] Flogster
See William IV

Florence Marion K.
See Kaye, John William

[The] Flower of All the Aristocrats
See Caesar, [Gaius] Julius

Fludd, Robert 1574-1637   [NPS]
British physician and philosopher
* Frizius, Joachim

Fludd, Robert (Continued)
* Otreb, Rudolf
(See also base volume)

[The] Flying Doormat
See Doull, Bruce

[The] Flying Flapper of Freeport
See Smith, Elinor

Flynn, Jackson
See Bensen, Donald R.

Fodhla, Ollamh
See Mullen [or Mullins?], Michael

Foe, Daniel 1663?-1731   [EE, NPS]
British author
* Goldsmith, Alexander
* Guilot, Claude
* [A] Ministering Friend
(See also base volume)

Fogel, Helen 1917-
American singer
* Forrest, Helen

Fogie, Francis
See Payson, George

Foley, Thomas David 1948-
[EF, FR]
American football player
* Foley, Tim

Foley, Tim
See Foley, Thomas David

Folio, Felix
See Page, John

Fontaines, Louis
See Zacharie de Lisieux, Pere

Fontenoy
See Davis, Eugene

Fontenoy, Marquis de
See Cunliffe-Owen, Frederick

Foote, Samuel 1722-1777   [NPS]
British comedian and playwright
* [The] Proteus
(See also base volume)

Foote, Samuel, Jr.
See Wrangham, Francis

Forager, Philip
See Maginn, William

Forbes, Colin
See Sawkins, Raymond H[arold]

Forbes-Robertson, Frances   [NPS]
Author
* Harrod, Frances

Ford, Harry
See Moskowitz, Harry

Ford, Mrs. Gerard
See Stockley, Mrs. Vesey

Ford, William 1821- ?   [NPS]
Author
* St. Clair, William

[A] Foreigner
See Watterston, George

[A] Foremast Man
See Rose, Edward Hampden

Forester, Bill
See Forester, George

Forester, George 20th c.   [EF]
American football player
* Forester, Bill

Forestier, Auber
See Moore, Annie Aubertine [Woodward]

Forestier, Paul
See Alberdingk-Thym, Josephus Albertus

Forgione, Francesco 1887-1968 [EOP]
Italian friar who claimed to possess psychic powers
* Pio. Padre [da Pietralcini]

Forhan, Marcel Louis 1884-1917 [EOP]
French author who claimed to possess psychic powers
* Yram

Forrest, Helen
See Fogel, Helen

Forrest, John Lawrence 1815-1858 [PI]
Irish-born poet
* One of Ireland's Ballad Poets

Forrest, Julian
See Wagenknecht, Edward [Charles]

Forrest, Mary
See Freeman, Julia Deane

Forrester, Arthur M. 1850-1895 [PI]
Irish poet and author
* Angus
* Tell, William

Forrester, Charles Robert 1803-1850 [IP, NPS]
British author and poet
* Crowquill, Alfred
* Willis, Hal, Student-at-Law

Forrester, Dexter J.
See Goldfrap, John Henry

Forrester, Izola
See Merrifield, Mrs. Reuben

Forrester, Mrs.
See Bridges, Mrs.

Forshall, Josiah 1797-1863 [IP]
British scholar
* [A] Fellow of the Royal and Antiquarian Societies

Forster, Johann Georg Adams 1754-1792 [IP]
German naturalist and author
* J. G. A. F.

Forster, John [IP]
British author
* Philanthropos

Forster, John 1812-1876 [IP]
British barrister, author, journalist
* J. F.

Forster, Josiah 1726-1790 [IP]
British author
* [A] Quaker

Forster, Samuel 18th c. [IP]
British author
* [A] Gent

Forster, Thomas 1789-1860 [IP]
British astronomer, naturalist, author
* Alumnus Cantabrigiensis
* F.

Forster, Thomas (Continued)
* [The] Honorary Foreign Secretary to the Annual Friends' Society
* Philochelidon
* [A] Physician
* [Un] Physicien Voyageur
* Verax

Forsyth, Ebenezer 19th c. [IP]
Scottish author
* E. F.
* [A] Student

Forsyth, Jean
See McIlwraith, Jean Newton

Fortescue
See Sampson, William

Forth, George
See Frederic, Harold

Forthuny, Pascal
See Cochet, Georges

Fosberry, Thomas Vincent 19th c. [IP]
British clergyman and author
* T. V. F.

Foscolo, Niccolo 1778-1827 [IP, NPS]
Italian author and poet
* Chierico, Dedimo
* Fudgiolo
* Ortis, Jacopo
(See also base volume)

Fossil Willy
See Simpson, Edward

Foster, Arnold [IP]
British author
* One Who Knows

Foster, Catharine [IP]
British poet and hymn-writer
* C. F.

Foster, Clement le Neve 1841- ? [IP]
British geologist and author
* Ossola

Foster, E. M. 18th c. [SFL]
Author
* E. M. F.

Foster, George G. [IP]
American author and publisher
* [An] Experienced Carver

Foster, Hannah [Webster] [IP]
American author
* [A] Lady of Massachusetts

Foster, James 19th c. [IP]
American soldier and author
* [An] Ohio Volunteer

Foster, John 1770-1843 [IP]
British author
* [A] Quiet Looker-on.

Foster, Olive [Leonard] 1819-1881 [IP]
American poet and hymn-writer
* O. L. F.

Foster, Theodosia Maria [Toll] 1838-1923 [DNA]
American author
* Huntington, Faye

Foster, Thomas [IP]
British author
* Juniper, Julius
* Philostratus

Foudriangle?
See Browne, Thomas

Fouleweather, Adam
See Nash [or Nashe?], Thomas

Foulis, Hugh
See Meldrum, David S.

Foulis, Oliver
See Lloyd, David

[The] Founder of English Commercial Law
See Murray, William [First Earl of Mansfield]

[The] Founder of Modern Danish Literature
See Holberg, Louis [or Ludvig]

[The] Founder of Modern Opera
See Scarlatti, Alessandro

Fountain, Brother
See Cromwell, Oliver

Fowler, Lottie
See Connolly, Charlotte

Fox, Charles James 1749-1806 [NPS, UH]
British statesman
* [A] Hercules
* Ultimus Romanorum
(See also base volume)

Fox, Charley
See Christy, Edwin Byron

Fox, Connie
See Fox, Hugh [Bernard, Jr.]

Fox, Francis J. 1847- ? [PI]
Irish-born poet
* F. J. F.

Fox, Gardner Francis 1911- [CA]
American author
* Cooper, Lynna
(See also base volume)

Fox, Henry Richard Vassall [Third Baron Holland] 1773-1840 [NPS]
British politician and author
* Bluster, Lord

Fox, Hugh [Bernard, Jr.] 1932- [MA]
American educator and author
* Fox, Connie
* Poitiers, Angele
* Tallafierro, Gabriel
(See also base volume)

[The] Fox of the Everglades
See Gonzalez, Jorge

Fox, Oliver
See Callaway, Hugh G.

Fox, Patrick J. 1844- ? [PI]
Irish-born poet
* O'Dowd, Phelim

[El] Fraile [The Friar]
See Mulas, Pedro

Frampton, Tregonwell 1641-1727 [BBH]
British horse trainer
* [The] Father of the English Turf

Francaise
See Barry, Robertine

France, Anatole de
See Alby, Ernest Francois Antoine

Frances, Margaret
See Milne, Frances Margaret

Francesca
See Alexander, Francesca

Franchi, Eda
See Vickers, Antoinette L.

Francis 1454-1487? [NPS]
First Viscount Lovell
* Lovell, Our Dogge

Francis, Charles
See Holme, Bryan

Francisco
See Hughes, Matthew F.

Frank, Dr.
See Perry, Joseph Franklin

Franklin, Benjamin
See Hasek, Jaroslav [Matej Frantisek]

Franklin, Benjamin 1706-1790 [NPS]
American statesman, philosopher, diplomat
* [The] Busybody
(See also base volume)

Franklin, Edward Zeus
See Wickes, Edward Zeus Franklin

Franklin, [Stella Maria Sarah] Miles 1879-1954 [DLE1, TLC]
Australian author
* Brent of Bin Bin

Franks, Ed
See Brandon, Johnny

Franzero, Carlo Maria 1892- [CA]
Italian-born author
* Franzero, Charles Marie

Franzero, Charles Marie
See Franzero, Carlo Maria

Frascone, Sally Blind
See Frascone, Salvatore

Frascone, Salvatore ?-1978
American underworld figure
* Frascone, Sally Blind

Frater Iehi Aour [Let there be Light]
See Bennett, [Charles Henry] Allan

Frazer, Bud
See Frazer, G. A.

Frazer, G. A. 1864-1896 [EWG]
American law officer
* Frazer, Bud

Frazer, John de Jean 1810?-1852 [DIL, PI]
Irish poet
* De Jean, J.
* F.
* J.
* Maria
* [The] Poet of the Workshop
* Robertson, J.
* Y.
* Z.

Frederic, Harold 1856-1898 [DEA]
American author and journalist
* Forth, George

Frederick the Great
See Bouton, Henri

Frederick the Noble
See Frederick II

Frederick I 1372-1440 [NPS]
Elector of Brandenburg
* [The] Penniless

Frederick II 1194-1250 [NPS]
Emperor of Germany
* [The] Admirable Crichton of Germany
(See also base volume)

Frederick II 1413-1471 [NPS]
Elector of Brandenburg
* [Le] Pieux
(See also base volume)

Frederick II 1712-1786 [NPS]
King of Prussia
* Frederick the Noble
* [The] Glorious Protestant
* [The] Happy
* That Metromaniac Prince
(See also base volume)

[A] Free Church Minister
See Agnew, David Carnegie A.

Free Inquirer
See Annet, Peter

Free Lance
See Cleary, Thomas Stanislaus

[A] Free Man
See Snelling, William Joseph

Free, [Maj.] Mickey
See Enton, Harry

[A] Free Thinker
See Armstrong, John

Freed, Alan 20th c. [CMA]
American disc jockey
* [The] Moondog
* [The] Pied Piper of Rock 'n' Roll

Freedgood, Morton 1912?-
[TCCM]
American author
* Morton, Stanley
(See also base volume)

[A] Freeholder
See Carlyle, Alexander

[A] Freeman
See Allen, George

Freeman, James Midwinter
1827-1900 [DNA]
American author and clergyman
* Ranger, Roger

Freeman, Julia Deane 19th c.
[DNA]
Author
* Forrest, Mary

Freeman, Kathleen 1897-1959
[TCCM]
British author
* Wick, Stuart Mary
(See also base volume)

Freeman, Peter J.
See Calvert, Patricia

Freemantle, Brian [Harry] 1936-
[TCCM]
British author
* Maxwell, John

Frehley, Ace
See Frehley, Paul

Frehley, Paul 1951- [CMA]
American singer and musician
* Frehley, Ace

Frelon [The Wasp]
See Freron, Elie-Catherine

French, Arthur
See Neuburg, Victor [Benjamin]

[A] French Coxcomb
See Bonaparte, Napoleon

[A] French Detective
See Russell, William

[The] French Drunken Barnaby
See Basselin, Olivier

French, Emily
See O'Donnell, John Francis

[The] French James Fenimore Cooper
See Sue, Marie Joseph

[The] French Marston
See Mairet, Jean

[The] French Michelangelo
See Puget, Pierre

[The] French Solomon
See De Salluste [or Salustius?], Guillaume

[The] French Tartini
See Gavinies, Pierre

[A] French Traveller
See Simond, Louis

[The] Frenchified Coxcomb
See Walpole, Horatio [Fourth Earl of Orford]

Freron, Elie-Catherine 1719-1776
[NPS]
French journalist
* Frelon [The Wasp]
(See also base volume)

Friedrich, Johan [NPS]
Author
* Janus

[A] Friend
See Lee, Mary Elizabeth

[The] Friend of Children
See Berquin, Arnaud

[The] Friend of Good Sense
See Homer

[A] Friend of Religious Liberty
See Paley, William

[The] Friend of Sinners
See Hawthorne, Nathaniel

[A] Friend of the Negro
See Armistead, Wilson

[The] Friend of the Poor
See Bottomley, Horatio Williams

[A] Friend of the Road
See Wright, Elizur

[A] Friend of Truth
See Scott, George

[A] Friend to American Enterprise
See Simmons, George W.

[A] Friend to Both
See Bowdler, Thomas

[A] Friend to Education
See Pole, Thomas

[A] Friend to Humanity
See Robinson, Mary Darby

[A] Friend to the Church of England
See Maseres, Francis

[A] Friend to the Natural and Religious Rights of Mankind
See Graham, William

[A] Friend to True Liberty
See Rack, Edmund

Frith, Mary 1589?-1664? [LFW]
British pickpocket
* Markham, Mary
(See also base volume)

Frizius, Joachim
See Fludd, Robert

[The] Frog
See Roberts, Gene

Frog, M.
See Labat, Jean-Yves

Frohberg, Paul
See Adami, Friedrich

From Beyond the Seas
See Louis IV

Frost, George
See Eddison, Mrs. Octavius

Frost, Jack
See Rosenberg, John Paul [Jack]

Frost, John 1800-1859 [DNA]
American author
* Ramble, Robert

Frump, Babe
See Frump, Milton

Frump, Milton 20th c. [EF]
American football player
* Frump, Babe

Fry, E. N. Leigh
See Lefroy, E. N.

Fry, Mrs. T. P.
Author
* Kaye-Smith, Sheila

Fuchs, Melchior 1560?-1615
[BBD]
German composer
* Vulpius, Melchior

Fudgiolo
See Foscolo, Niccolo

Fuentes, Manuel 1837-1889 [GS]
Spanish bullfighter
* Bocanegra [Black Mouth]

Fuerst, Milan 1888-1967 [CD]
Hungarian poet and author
* Fuest, Milan

Fuest, Milan
See Fuerst, Milan

[A] Fugitive
See Coxe, Edward D.

Fulk III 972-1040 [NPS]
Count of Anjou
* [The] Black

Fuller, Bucky
See Fuller, R. Buckminster

Fuller, Earl 20th c.
American basketball player
* Fuller, World

Fuller, R. Buckminster 1895- [CR]
American architect, inventor, philosopher, author
* Fuller, Bucky

Fuller, Thomas 1606-1661 [DEA]
British author and editor
* T. F.

Fuller, World
See Fuller, Earl

Fullwood, Francis
See Baxter, Richard

Funakoshi, Gichin [BBH]
Karate expert
* [The] Father of Karate

Funnyman, A.
See Bradley, Edward

Furlong, Patrick M. [PI]
Irish clergyman and poet
* Murphy, Thomas James
* T. J. M.

Furlong, Thomas 1794-1827 [PI]
Irish poet
* [The] Hermit in Ireland
* W.

Furman, Garrit 1782-1848 [DNA]
Author and poet
* Rusticus, Gent.

Furphy, Joseph 1841-1912 [DLE1]
Australian author
* Collins, Tom

Fury, Bridget
See Swift, Delia

Fuss and Feathers
See Scott, Winfield

Futabatei Shimei
See Hasegawa, Tatsunosuke

Fyffe, R. E.
See Sutherland, Duchess of

G

G.
See Gilborne, John

G.
See Pegge, Samuel

G. A.
See Aguilar, Grace

G. A. A.
See Aynge, G. A.

G. B. A.
See Airy, [Sir] George Biddell

G. C.
See Chapman, George

G. D.
See Darley, George

G. F. A.
See Angas, George Federick

G. F. B.
See Bowen, [Sir] George Ferguson

G. G.
See Grossmith, George, Jr.

G. G.
See Harper, H. G.

G. H. B.
See Budd, G. H.

G. H. M.
See Moore, George Henry

G. H. S.
See Supple, Gerald Henry

G. I.
See Iliff, George

G. M. D.
See McDermott, George

G. M., Esq.
See Matthews, George

G. P.
See Peele, George

G. R.
See Ripley, George

G. R. C.
See Corner, George Richard

G. R. F.
See Fitzgerald, George Robert

G. T. C.
See Curtis, George Ticknor

G. T. L.
See Lanigan, George Thomas

G. W. D.
See Driggs, George W.

G. W., Gent.
See Chapman, George

G. W. M.
See Marshall, George W.

Gabriel in Gabardine
See Graham, William Franklin [Billy]

Gabriel, Manny
See Gabriel, Martin Manuel

Gabriel, Martin Manuel ?-1982
American jazz musician
* Gabriel, Manny

Gabrielli, Caterina 1730-1796
[BBD]
Italian opera singer
* [La] Coghetta [Little Cook]

Gabrini, Niccolo 1313-1354
[NPS, UH]
Italian patriot
* Liberator of Rome
* Ultimus Romanorum
(See also base volume)

Gadadhar 1836-1886   [EOP]
Indian mystic
* Ramakrishna, Sri

Gadd, Paul 1944-   [CMA]
British singer
* Raven, Paul
(See also base volume)

[The] Gael
See Commins, Andrew

Gaelique, Morven le
See Jacob, [Cyprien] Max

Gaetano [or Caetani], Benedetto
1235?-1303   [NPS]
Pope
* [The] Leader of the Modern
   Pharisees
* Misleader of the Papacy
(See also base volume)

Gaillard
See Lacenaire, Pierre-Francois

Gaines, Albert Cecil
See Grissom, Arthur Colfax

Gaines, Garry
See Patterson, Virginia [Sharpe]

Gaines, La Donna Andrea 1948-
[BP]
American singer
* [The] First Lady of Disco
* [The] Queen of Disco
* Summer, Donna
(See also base volume)

Gainsborough, Thomas 1727-1788
[NPS]
British painter
* [The] Painter Patriot
(See also base volume)

Galitzin, Vasili 1633?-1713?   [NPS]
Russian army officer and politician
* [The] Happy
(See also base volume)

Gall
See Pigot, John Edward

Gallagher, Bridget ?-1894   [PI]
Irish poet
* McGinley, Bridget

Gallant Harry of the West
See Clay, Henry

Gallant Young Juvenal
See Meres, Francis

[The] Galley Head Poet
See Doran, Charles Guilfoyle

[The] Gallic Pharaoh
See Louis XIV

Gallichan, Mrs. Walter 1866- ?
[NPS]
British author
* Hartley, C. Gasquoine

Gallichan, Walter M. 1861- ?
[NPS]
British author
* Mortimer, Geoffrey
(See also base volume)

Gallius [or Gaelus]
See Mackenzie, Andrew

[El] Gallo [The Rooster]
See Gomez y Garcia, Fernando

Gallup, Lucy 1911-   [MA]
American author
* DeFluent, Amelie

Gallus, Johannes ?-1543?   [BBD]
Flemish composer
* Jean le Cocq
* Maitre Jean
* Mestre Jhan

Galt, John 1779-1839
[DEA, DLE1, NPS]
British author
* Great Gander of Glasgow
* Jobbry, Archibald
* Mailings, Malachi
* Picken, Andrew
(See also base volume)

Galway, Robert Conington
See McCutchan, Philip [Donald]

[The] Gam Girl
See Grasle, Elizabeth

Gambado, Geoffrey
See Bembury, Henry William

[The] Game Chicken
See Pearce, Henry

Ganconagh
See Yeats, William Butler

Gandee, Sherwin 20th c.   [EF]
American football player
* Gandee, Sonny

Gandee, Sonny
See Gandee, Sherwin

[The] Gangster's Nightmare
See McClellan, John

Gant, Matthew
See Hano, Arnold

Garcia 958-1001   [NPS]
King of Navarre
* [The] Trembler

Garcia, Eduarda   [IP]
South American author
* Daniel

Garcia, Francisco Javier
1731-1809   [BBD]
Spanish composer
* Garcia, Padre
* [Lo] Spagnoletto

Garcia, Jose 19th c.   [GS]
Spanish bullfighter
* [El] Platero [The Silversmith]

Garcia, Padre
See Garcia, Francisco Javier

Garcia y Cuesta, Manuel
1866-1894   [GS]
Spanish bullfighter
* [El] Espartero

Garden, George   [IP]
Scottish clergyman and author
* [An] Unknown Friend

Gardener, Helen Hamilton
See   Day, Mrs. S. A.

Gardener, Sylvan 19th c.   [IP]
American author
* [The] Rain Water Doctor

Gardiner, Darkie
See   Gardiner, Frank

Gardiner, Frank 1830- ?   [DI]
Australian bushranger
* Gardiner, Darkie
* [The] Prince of High Tobymen

Gardiner, John Sylvester John
1765-1830   [IP]
American clergyman and author
* X. Z.

Gardiner, Mrs. William   [IP]
American author
* Her Mother

Gardiner, R.   [IP]
British barrister and author
* R. G., a Clerk of the Court of
   Common Pleas

Gardiner, Richard   [IP]
British author
* Honeycomb, William, Esq.

Gardiner, W.   [IP]
British translator
* [A] Gentleman of the Inner
   Temple

Gardiner, William 1770-1853   [IP]
British author
* [A] Dilettante

Gardner, Alexander   [IP]
Scottish author
* A. G.

Gardner, George H.   [IP]
British naval officer and author
* [A] Retired Captain, R.N.

Gardner, John   [IP]
American author
* Aurelius

Gardner, John Lane 1793-1869   [IP]
American army officer and author
* [An] Officer of the Line

Gardner, Lewis J. 1836-1909
American author
* Dearborn, Andrew
* Swift, Lewis J.

Gardner, Margery Aimee
1914?-1946   [DI]
American murder victim
* Gardner, Ocelot Margie

Gardner, Milton 20th c.   [EF]
American football player
* Gardner, Moose

Gardner, Moose
See   Gardner, Milton

Gardner, Ocelot Margie
See   Gardner, Margery Aimee

Gardner, William   [IP]
British author
* W. G.

Garfield, Brian [Francis] Wynne
1939-   [TCCM]
American author
* Ives, John
* Mallory, Drew
(See also base volume)

Garland, Luke
See   Whitson, John H.

Garner, Charles 19th c.   [SFL]
Author
* Cumberland, Stuart

Garner, Robert 19th c.   [IP]
British naturalist and author
* [A] Naturalist

Garnet, Clew
See   Judson, Edward Zane Carroll

Garnham, Robert Edward
1753-1802   [IP]
British clergyman and author
* Terrae Filius

Garrard, George 1760-1826   [NPS]
Painter and sculptor
* Thou Myron of the Age

Garrard, Kenner
See   Nolan, Louis Edward

Garrett, Annie Amelia 19th c.
[NPS]
Author
* Amelia, Annie

Garrett, Ellen Amelia 19th c.   [NPS]
Author
* Amelia, Ellen

Garrick, David 1716-1779
[IP, NPS]
British actor
* [An] Atlas
* D. G.
* Little Davy
* Lyddal
* Nipclose, [Sir] Nicholas, Bart.
* Oakly
* [The] Proteus of the Stage
(See also base volume)

Garrick, Marion Eva 1725-1822
[IP]
German author
* Violette

Garryowen
See   Finn, Edmund

Garvie, William   [IP]
Canadian journalist
* Rooney, Barney

Garvin, James Louis 1868-1947
[NPS]
British journalist and author
* Calchas
(See also base volume)

Garvin, Paul L[ucian]
See   Goldberger, Paul L[ucian]

Gaskell, Elizabeth Cleghorn
1810-1865   [DLE1]
British author
* Mills, Cotton Mather, Esq.
(See also base volume)

[The] Gaslight Man
See   Hickman, Tom

[The] Gasman
See   Hickman, Tom

Gasparo da Salo
See   Bertolotti, Gasparo

Gaspey, Thomas 19th c.   [IP]
British author and journalist
* Godfrey, George

Gassett, Henry 1813- ?   [IP]
American author
* [A] Member of the Suffolk
   Committee

Gastit, Horace Dodd
See   Bangs, John Kendrick

Gaston, Mrs. A. F. 19th c.
[HFN, IP]
British author
* A. F. G.

Gatchell, Charles 1851-1910
[DNA]
American author and physician
* King, Thorold

Gates, Eleanor
See   Tully, Mrs. Richard Walton

Gathercole, Michael Augustus 19th
c.   [IP]
British clergyman and author
* L. S. E.

Gatty, Alfred 1813- ?   [IP]
British clergyman and author
* A. G.

Gatty, Juliana Horatia
See   Ewing, Juliana [Horatia
Gatty]

Gaul, Gilbert
See   De Mille, James

**[The] Gaul Narquois of Parisian
Society**
See   Amfrye, Guillaume

[The] Gaulonite
See   Judas

Gauntlett, Henry   [IP]
British clergyman and author
* Detector

Gauntley, William 1775-1860   [IP]
British author
* [A] Temperate Drinker
* W. G.

Gautier, Alain
See   Sobhraj, Gurmukh

[The] Gavarni of Berlin
See   Hosemann, Theodor

Gavarni, Paul
See   Chevalier, Guillaume-Sulpice

Gavin, Amanda
See   Gibson-Jarvie, Clodagh

Gavin, Antoine 1680- ?   [IP]
French clergyman and author
* Emiliane, Gabriel d'

Gavin, Buck
See   Gavin, Patrick

Gavin, Patrick 20th c.   [EF]
American football player
* Gavin, Buck

Gavinies, Pierre ?-1800   [NPS]
Musician
* [The] French Tartini

Gay, A. Nolder
See   Koelsch, William Alvin

Gay, John 1685-1732   [DEA]
British poet and playwright
* Baker, [Sir] James
(See also base volume)

[The] Gay Lothario of Politics
See   Disraeli, Benjamin

Gaye, Selina   [IP]
British author
* [A] Clergyman's Daughter

Gayer, Chet
See   Gayer, Walter

Gayer, Walter 20th c.   [EF]
American football player
* Gayer, Chet

Gayet, Sebastien 1815- ?   [IP]
French author and actor
* Rheal, Sebastien

Gayles, Joseph 1844-1873   [BLB]
American gangleader
* Socco the Bracer

Gaynham [or Garnham], Dr. 18th c.
[NPS]
Clergyman
* [The] Bishop of Hell

Gebel, Guenther 1937-   [CR]
German circus performer
* Gebel-Williams, Guenther

Gebel-Williams, Guenther
See   Gebel, Guenther

Geber 9th c.   [EOP]
Arab scholar
* Sofi, Abou Moussah Djafar al-
(See also base volume)

Gee, Charlie 20th c.   [LFW]
Chinese-born embezzler
* [The] Boss of Chinatown

Gee, Dolly
See   Chang Hor-gee

Geisel, Helen 1898-1967   [SAT]
American author
* Palmer, Helen Marion

Geller, Evelyn
See   Gottesfeld, Evelyn

[The] Gem of Asia
See   Irenaeus

Gemsege, Paul
See   Pegge, Samuel

Generali, Mercandetti 1773-1832
[BBD]
Italian composer
* Generali, Pietro

Generali, Pietro
See   Generali, Mercandetti

[The] Generous
See   Khosru I [or Chosroes]

Geniaccio [Little Genius]
See   Giugiaro, Giorgetto

Genovese, Vince 20th c.   [CA]
Author
* Thisby [joint pseudonym with
   Dona M. Turner]

[A] Gent
See   Anderson, Alexander

[A] Gent
See   Forster, Samuel

Gent
See   Lovecraft, Howard Phillips

Gent, George 20th c.   [EF]
American football player
* Gent, Pete

Gent, Pete
See   Gent, George

Gentil, Spirito
See Hanna, George W.

Gentle George
See Etherege, [Sir] George

[The] Gentle Giant
See Johnson, Rafer

[A] Gentleman
See Adams, John

[A] Gentleman
See Assheton-Craven, Charles
Audley

[A] Gentleman
See Baker, Thomas

[A] Gentleman
See Bromley, William

[A] Gentleman
See Mottley, John

[A] Gentleman
See Ramsay, James

[A] Gentleman
See Wakefield, Priscilla [Bell]

[A] Gentleman
See White, John

[A] Gentleman, a Descendant of Dame Quickly
See White, James

[A] Gentleman Commoner of Oxford
See Croxall, Samuel

[The] Gentleman Fighter
See Humphries, Richard

[A] Gentleman Formerly of Boston
See Church, Edward, Jr.

Gentleman, Francis 1728-1784
[SFL, WGT]
Irish author
* Lunatic, [Sir] Humphrey, Bart.

[The] Gentleman Highwayman
See Maclaine, James

[A] Gentleman in Boston
See Tappan, Lewis

[A] Gentleman in London
See Paching, Resta

[A] Gentleman in Philadelphia
See Dickinson, John

[A] Gentleman in the Country
See Ferguson, Adam

[A] Gentleman in the Service of the East India Company
See Robertson, Henry D.

Gentleman Johnny
See Burgoyne, John

[A] Gentleman Late of the Inner Temple
See Baker, Henry

Gentleman Matt Brady
See Brady, Matthew

[A] Gentleman of Bristol
See Butler, S.

[A] Gentleman of Cambridge
See Bennet, Philip

[A] Gentleman of Cambridge
See Fawkes, Francis

[A] Gentleman of Foreign Extraction
See Duche, Jacob

[A] Gentleman of Gloucestershire
See Shuckburgh, Charles

[A] Gentleman of Lincoln's Inn
See Anderson, Henry

[A] Gentleman of Middlesex
See Johnston, James

[A] Gentleman of the Army
See Steele, [Sir] Richard

[A] Gentleman of the Inner Temple
See Dawes, Matthew

[A] Gentleman of the Inner Temple
See Gardiner, W.

[A] Gentleman of the Middle Temple
See Cunningham, Timothy

[A] Gentleman of the Middle Temple
See Ralph, James

[A] Gentleman of the University of Cambridge
See Crowley, Edward Alexander

[A] Gentleman of the University of Oxford
See Shelley, Percy Bysshe

[A] Gentleman on his Travels
See Scott, Sarah

[A] Gentleman Resident in the Neighborhood
See Snart, Charles

[A] Gentleman Who Resided Some Time in Philadelphia
See Duche, Jacob

[A] Gentleman Who Was a Swede
See Sthalberg, George

[A] Gentleman Who Was In the Town
See Michelborne, John

Genuine Old Moore
See Arigho, John

Genzale, Johnny 20th c.   [CMA]
Musician
* Thunders, Johnny

[A] Geologist
See Pengelly, William

[The] George Fox of Germany
See Englebrecht, John

George, Miss
See Oldmixon, Georgina Sidus

George the Greater
See George IV

George the Grinner
See Colman, George

George II 1683-1760   [NPS]
King of England
* Augustus
* [The] Great Patron of Mankind
(See also base volume)

George III 1738-1820   [NN, NPS]
King of England
* Another Philip II
* Robinson, Ralph
(See also base volume)

George IV 1762-1830   [NN, NPS]
King of England
* George the Greater
* [The] Prince of Princes
* Prinny
(See also base volume)

Geppert, Christopher Charles 1952?-
American singer
* Cross, Christopher

Gerald
See Pelly, Gerald Conn

Gerald, Captain
See Bunch, Eugene

Geraldine
See Fitzachary, John Christopher

Gerard, Frances A.   [NPS]
Author
* Annalist

Gerard, James Watson 1823-1900
[DNA]
American author and attorney
* Pelican, A.
* Shelley, A. Fishe
* Sombre, Samuel

Gerden, Friedrich Carl
See Greve, Felix Paul

Gerhards, Gerhard [or Geert]
1466?-1536   [NPS]
Dutch scholar
* [The] Glory of Netherland
* [The] Glory of the Priesthood
(See also base volume)

[The] German Achilles
See Albert III [or Albrecht]

[A] German Countess
See Hahn-Hahn, Ida Maria Louisa
Frederika Gustava

[The] German Dominie Sampson
See Jung, Heinrich

[The] German Hector
See Joachim II

[The] German Pascal
See Hardenberg, Friedrich von

[The] German Princess
See Moders [or Meders?], Mary

[The] German Siddons
See Schroeder, Sophie [Buerger]

Germanicus
See Anderson, James

Gessner, Friedrike Victoria
1910-1980   [CLC]
Austrian author and ethologist
* Adamson, Joy

Geyl, Pieter [Catharinus Arie]
1887-1966   [CA]
Dutch author, poet, historian
* Merwe, A. v.d.

Ghosh, Mukunda Lal 1893-1952
[EOP]
Indian-born leader of religious cult
* Yogananda, Paramahansa

[The] Ghost of Vandegrab
See Mackintosh, [Sir] James

Giancanelli, Harold 20th c.   [EF]
American football player
* Giancanelli, Skippy

Giancanelli, Skippy
See Giancanelli, Harold

[A] Giantess of Genius
See More, Hannah

Giaver, Bill
See Giaver, Einar

Giaver, Einar 20th c.   [EF]
American football player
* Giaver, Bill

Gibb, Barry
See Gibb, Douglas

Gibb, Douglas 1947-   [BP]
British-born singer
* Gibb, Barry

Gibbon, Edwarda
See Stone, C. J.

Gibbons, James Sloan 1810-1892
[DNA]
American author
* Morris, Robert

Gibbons, Lucy
See Morse, Lucy G.

Gibbons, William 1649-1728   [NPS]
Physician
* Mirmillo

Gibbs, George 1815-1873   [DNA]
American author and historian
* Morrow, Gilbert

Gibbs, Guy 20th c.   [EF]
American football player
* Gibbs, Sonny

Gibbs, [Cecilia] May 1877-1969
[CA]
British-born author, artist, illustrator
* Kelly, C. M. O.

Gibbs, Sonny
See Gibbs, Guy

Gibran, Kahlil 1883-1931   [CA]
Lebanese-born American author and poet
* [The] Blake of the Twentieth Century

Gibson, Alfred   [NPS]
Author
* Rover

Gibson, George Herbert 1881-1932
[DNA]
Scottish author and physician
* Rae, Herbert

Gibson, Walter B[rown] 1897-
[TCCM]
American magician and author
* Black, Ishi
* Brown, Douglas
* Kineji, Maborushi
(See also base volume)

Gibson-Jarvie, Clodagh 1923-   [CA]
British author
* Gavin, Amanda

Gifford, Franklin Kent 1861-1948
[DNA]
American author and clergyman
* Newman, Richard Brinsley

Gifford, William 1756-1826   [NPS]
British critic and poet
* [The] Bear Leader
* [The] Censor of the Age
* [The] Cobbling Wonder of Ashburton
* [The] Demon of Darkness
* Esop, Master
* Grosvenor's Cobbler
(See also base volume)

Gil y Peire, Joaquin 1825-1862
[GS]
Spanish bullfighter
* [El] Huevatero [The Egg Seller]

Gilbert, Anne Jane [Hartley]
1821-1904   [FAA]
British-born actress
* Gilbert, Grandma

Gilbert, Grandma
See   Gilbert, Anne Jane [Hartley]

Gilbert, Sam 20th c.
*American industrialist and
basketball team supporter*
* Papa G.

Gilbert, Zelia 1838-1892   [BBD]
French opera singer
* Trebelli, Zelia

Gilborne, John 18th c.   [PI]
Irish physician and poet
* G.

Gilbreth, Ernestine
See   Carey, Ernestine Gilbreth

Gildas [or Gildus] 516- 570   [NPS]
British author
* [The] Wisest of the Bretons
(See also base volume)

Gilder, Jeannette 1849-1916
American journalist
* Brunswick
(See also base volume)

Gilla-Erin
See   McGee, Thomas D'Arcy

Gilla-Patrick
See   McGee, Thomas D'Arcy

Gilland, James ?-1811   [PI]
Irish poet and author
* Z. X.

Gillelan, G[eorge] Howard 1917-
[CA]
American author
* Purdy, [Captain] Jim

Gillespie, Grumach
See   Campbell, Archibald

Gillmore, Rufus Hamilton
1879-1935   [DNA]
American author
* Hamilton, Rufus

Gillooly, Edna Rae 1932-   [BP]
American actress
* Rae, Edna
(See also base volume)

Gillray, Junior
See   Hess, David

Gillray, Paris
See   Schadow, Gottfried

[The] Gillyflower of Liverpool
See   Roscoe, William

Gilman, Bradley 1857-1932   [DNA]
American author and clergyman
* Wentworth, Walter

Gilman, Caroline [Howard]
1794-1888   [DNA]
American author and poet
* Packard, Clarissa

Gilman, Maria
See   Barnard, Charles

Gilman, Wenona
See   Enton, Harry

Gilman, Wenona
See   Schoeffel, Florence Blackburn
[White]

Gilray, J. D.
See   Mencken, Henry Louis

Gilson, Barbara
See   Gilson, Charles James Louis

Gilson, Charles James Louis
1878-1943   [YAB]
British author and army officer
* Gilson, Barbara

Gimbel, Sophie 1898?-1981
American fashion designer
* Sophie of Saks Fifth Avenue
(See also base volume)

Ginez de Sepulveda, Juan
1490-1572   [NPS]
Spanish theologian and historian
* [The] Spanish Livy
(See also base volume)

Gingold, Hermoine 1897-   [CR]
British comedienne
* Phillips, Rosina

Ginsberg, Arnie 20th c.   [CMA]
American disc jockey
* Ginsberg, Woo Woo

Ginsberg, Woo Woo
See   Ginsberg, Arnie

Giordanello
See   Giordani, Giuseppe

Giordani, Giuseppe 1753?-1798
[BBD]
Italian composer
* Giordanello

Giraldus
See   Allingham, William

Giugiaro, Giorgetto 1939?-
Italian industrial designer
* Geniaccio [Little Genius]

Giuliano, Salvatore 1922- ?   [DI]
Sicilian bandit and murderer
* Giuliano, Turi

Giuliano, Turi
See   Giuliano, Salvatore

Giuseppe del Gesu
See   Guarneri, Giuseppe
Bartolomeo

Givins, Robert Cartwright
1845-1915   [DNA]
Canadian-born author
* Trebor, Snivig C.

Glacken, Edward Scott 20th c.   [EF]
American football player
* Glacken, Scotty

Glacken, Scotty
See   Glacken, Edward Scott

Gladstone, William Ewart
1809-1898   [NN]
British statesman
* H. O. M.
* [The] Heartless Old Man
* Old Glad-Eye
(See also base volume)

Gladwin, William Zachary
See   Zollinger, Gulielma

Glaspell, Susan
See   Cook, Mrs. George Cram

Glass, Charles 20th c.   [EF]
American football player
* Glass, Chip

Glass, Chip
See   Glass, Charles

Glauer, Adam 1875-1945   [EOP]
Founder of German occult society
* Sebottendorf, Rudolf Freiherr von

[The] Gleaner
See   McQuin, [Abbe] Ange Denis

Glenn, Gipsy
See   Burton, Jennie Davis

Glenn, William 19th c.   [PI]
Irish clergyman and poet
* [A] Village Curate

Glenravon, Lord
See   Byron, George Gordon Noel

Glockenhammer, Walter
See   Wells, Herbert George

[The] Glorious Protestant
See   Frederick II

[A] Glorious Villain
See   Cromwell, Oliver

[The] Glory and Scandal of His Age
See   Butler, Samuel

[The] Glory of Her Sex
See   Bradstreet, Anne

[The] Glory of her Sex
See   Elizabeth I

[The] Glory of Netherland
See   Gerhards, Gerhard [or Geert]

[The] Glory of Scotland
See   Ossian

[The] Glory of the English Stage
See   Shakespeare, William

[The] Glory of the Human Intellect
See   Shakespeare, William

[The] Glory of the Muses
See   Smith, [Sir] Thomas

[The] Glory of the Priesthood
See   Gerhards, Gerhard [or Geert]

Glubb, John Bagot 1897-   [CA]
British author
* Glubb Pasha

Glubb Pasha
See   Glubb, John Bagot

Glubbins, Mrs.
See   Robinson, Clara I. N.

Gluss, Brian 1930-   [CA]
*British-born American playwright
and educator*
* Gluzman, Brian

[The] Glutton of Literature
See   Magliabecchi, Antonio [or
Anthony]

Gluzman, Brian
See   Gluss, Brian

Gnagy, Jon
See   Gnagy, Michael Jacques

Gnagy, Michael Jacques
1907?-1981   [CA]
*American author, artist, television
performer*
* Gnagy, Jon

God Hanuman
See   Bonaparte, Napoleon

God in the Sonship Degree
See   Baker, George

[The] God of English Poets
See   Chaucer, Geoffrey

[The] God of Our Idolatry
See   Shakespeare, William

[The] God of Whiggish Idolatry
See   Brougham, Henry Peter

[The] Goddess
See   De Grimston, Mary Ann

Godebrie, Jacques 1445?-1529
[BBD]
Flemish composer
* Jacotin

[The] Godfather
See   Fiennes, William [First
Viscount Saye and Sele]

Godfrey
See   Gould, Sylvester C.

Godfrey, George
See   Gaspey, Thomas

[A] Godless Regent
See   Orleans, Philippe II d'

[The] Godmother
See   Luisi, Marie

[The] Godmother of the Abbey
Theatre
See   Gregory, [Lady] Isabella
Augusta Persse

Godolphin, Mary
See   Aikin, Lucy

God's Banker
See   Calvi, Roberto

Godwin, Francis 1562-1633   [WGT]
British author, historian, clergyman
* F. G.
* Gonsales, Domingo

Godwin, Mary 1759-1797   [NPS]
British author
* Marguerite
(See also base volume)

Goethe, Johann Wolfgang von
1749-1832   [NPS]
German poet and philosopher
* [The] Ariosto of Germany
* [The] First of Existing Writers
* [The] Illustrious
(See also base volume)

Goetz, Dana 1964?-
American actress
* Hill, Dana

Goff, Elijer
See   Dawes, William

Going, Ellen Maud 1859-1925
[DNA]
American-born author
* Hardinge, E. M.

Goldberg, Hyman 1908?-1970
[CA]
American author and columnist
* Penny, Prudence

Goldberger, Paul L[ucian] 1919-
[CA]
Austrian-born linguist and author
* Garvin, Paul L[ucian]

[The] Golden Farmer
See Davis, William

[The] Golden Hand
See Bluffstein, Sophie

Goldfrap, John Henry 1879-1917
[DNA]
American author
* Forrester, Dexter J.
* Payson, [Lieut.] Howard
* West, Marvin
(See also base volume)

Goldie, George [BBH]
Track and field athlete
* [The] Father of the Pole Vault

Goldman, Fred [BBH]
American pigeon racer
* [The] Father of the Racing Pigeon
 Sport in America

Goldsmith, Alexander
See Foe, Daniel

Goldsmith, Oliver 1728-1774
[DEA, NN, NPS]
British author, poet, playwright
* Common Sense
* Fancy's Favourite
* Noll
* Willington, James
(See also base volume)

Goldstein, Arthur D[avid] 1937-
[TCCM]
American author
* Ross, Albert

Goldstein, Rhoda L.
See Blumberg, Rhoda L[ois
Goldstein]

Goldwater, Barry [Morris] 1909-
[CR]
American politician
* Conservative, Mr.
(See also base volume)

[The] Goliath of the Philistines
See Needham, Marchamont

Golma
See Ryan, James

Gomez y Garcia, Fernando
1847-1897 [GS]
Spanish bullfighter
* [El] Gallo [The Rooster]

Gongora y Argote, Luis de
1561-1627 [NPS]
Spanish poet
* [The] Prince of Lyric Poets
(See also base volume)

Gonsales, Domingo
See Godwin, Francis

Gonthier, Pierre Theophile
1853-1917 [DNA]
Canadian author and clergyman
* Bernard, Pierre

Gonzaga, Ludovico di III
1414-1478 [NPS]
Marquis of Mantua
* [The] Turk

Gonzalez, Bombillo
See Gonzalez, Jorge

Gonzalez, Francisco 1784-1843
[GS]
Spanish bullfighter
* Panchon [Big Belly]

Gonzalez, Jorge 1932?-
Cuban-born guerrilla leader
* [The] Fox of the Everglades
* Gonzalez, Bombillo

Good Friday
See Bunn, Alfred

Good Seed of Hercules
See D'Este, Ippolito

[The] Good Vicar
See De Courcy, Richard

Goode, John 1829-1909 [BDSA]
American author and politician
* [The] Grand Old Man of Virginia

Goodman, Maude
See Scanes, Mrs. A. E.

Goodwin, Charles 20th c. [EF]
American football player
* Goodwin, Ted

Goodwin, Ted
See Goodwin, Charles

Goosequil, Benjamin
See Adair, James Makittrick

Goosequill, Grey
See Beschius, C. J.

Goppagh, Coul
See Gordon, Robert Hunter

Goralczyk, Kasimir
See Anczyca, Vladislav Ludvig

Gordon, Ad
See Hano, Arnold

Gordon, Charles George 1833-1885
[NPS]
British army officer
* [The] English Bayard
(See also base volume)

Gordon, Clarence [ICB]
Author
* Vieux Moustache

Gordon, Francis S. ?-1882 [PI]
Irish poet
* Nemo

Gordon, George 1751-1793 [NPS]
British politician
* Crop, Lord

Gordon, James 19th c. [IP]
Scottish advocate and author
* Amicus

Gordon, John M. [IP]
American author
* Vindex

Gordon, Julien
See Cruger, Julia Grinnell
[Storrow]

Gordon, Robert Hunter 1815-1857
[PI]
Irish poet and physician
* Goppagh, Coul

Gordon, Thomas 1684?-1750 [IP]
Scottish author
* Cato
* [An] Englishman
* [A] Layman

Gordon, Walter
See Gowing, William

Gordon, William 18th c. [IP]
Author
* [A] Citizen of Aberdeen

Gordon, William (Continued)
* Parenthenopeus Hereticus

Gordy, Robert 20th c. [CMA]
American songwriter
* Kayli, Bob

Gore, Catherine Grace Frances
[Moody] 1799-1861
[DEA, HFN, IP]
British author
* C. F. G.
* Desennuyee, A.

Gore, Christopher 1758-1827 [IP]
American statesman and author
* Manlius

Gore, John [Baron Annaly] [IP]
British jurist and author
* [A] Noble Lord and Eminent
 Lawyer

[The] Gorilla Murderer
See Nelson, Earle Leonard

Gorman, Charles O. [IP]
American politician and author
* [An] Irish Catholic Whig

Gorman, Thomas Murray 19th c.
[IP]
British clergyman and author
* T. M. G.

Goslin, S. B. 19th c. [IP]
British author
* S. B. G.

Gosling, Charles 1657?-1747? [IP]
British author
* [The] British Timon

Gosman, Klaus 1941- [DI]
German murderer
* [The] Midday Murderer

Gosnell, Samuel 19th c. [PI]
Irish poet and surgeon
* O'Fogarty, Fogarty

Goss, Elbridge Henry 1830- ? [IP]
American author
* Elhegos

Goss, Warren Le 19th c. [IP]
American soldier and author
* [A] Soldier

Gosset, Isaac 1735?-1812 [NPS]
Bibliographer
* Gosset, Milk-White
* Lepidus

Gosset, Milk-White
See Gosset, Isaac

[The] Gossip
See L'Ermite, Tristan

Gottesfeld, Evelyn 1948- [CA]
American author and editor
* Geller, Evelyn

Gotthelf, Jeremias
See Bitzius, Albert

Gough, Benjamin [IP]
British clergyman and author
* [A] Brother Methodist

Gough, Catherine 1931- [SAT]
British author
* Mulgan, Catherine

Gough, John [IP]
British clergyman and author
* Philalethes

Gough, Richard 1735-1809
[IP, NPS]
British historian
* Clio
* D. H.
* [A] Layman
* R. G.
* R. G., Junior
(See also base volume)

Gould, Edward S. 1808-1885 [IP]
American merchant and author
* Cassio
* [The] Man in the Claret Colored
 Coat

Gould, James L. [IP]
American author
* Hunter, Harry

Gould, Sylvester C. 1840- ? [IP]
American journalist
* Godfrey

Gould, William 18th c. [IP]
British clergyman and author
* Commoner

Gouraud, Julie
See Aulnay, Louise d'

Governor of the Ranges
See Howe, Michael

Gowan, William [IP]
American author and bookseller
* Western Memorabilia

Gower, Erskine
See Sutherland, Duchess of

Gower, Foote [IP]
British physician and author
* [A] Fellow of the Antiquarian
 Society

Gowing, Emilia Aylmer 1846-1905
[PI]
British poet, author, playwright
* Blake, E. A.

Gowing, William 19th c. [PI]
Actor
* Gordon, Walter

Gracchus
See O'Callaghan, John Cornelius

[The] Grace of Courts
See Sackville, Charles [Sixth Earl
of Dorset]

Grace, William Gilbert 1848-1915
[NN, NPS, PPN]
British cricketer
* W. G.
(See also base volume)

Grady, Spectacle
See Grady, Thomas

Grady, Thomas ?-1820? [PI]
Irish poet
* Grady, Spectacle
* Power, David?
* [A] Young Gentleman

Grafe, Felix
See Greve, Felix Paul

Grafton-Smith, Adele [NPS]
Author
* Nomad

Graham, Elizabeth Susanna
[Davenport] 1763-1844 [IP]
British author
* Tidy, Theresa

Graham, Esther ?-1859   [IP]
Scottish author
* Wildfire, Madge

Graham, H. 19th c.   [EC]
Australian cricketer
* [The] Little Dasher

Graham, Harry   [NPS]
Author
* Coldstreamer
* Streamer, Col. D.

Graham, James 20th c.   [EF]
American football player
* Graham, Kenny

Graham, [Sir] James Robert George
1792-1861   [IP]
British statesman and author
* [A] Cumberland Land-Owner

Graham, John
See   Phillips, David Graham

Graham, John 1774-1844   [PI]
Irish clergyman and poet
* [An] Apprentice Boy

Graham, John 18th c.   [IP]
Scottish clergyman and author
* [A] Member of the Synod of
   United Original Seceders

Graham, Kenny
See   Graham, James

Graham, Robert 1786-1845   [IP]
Scottish physician, botanist, author
* R. G.

Graham, Sheilah
See   Shiel, Lily

Graham, William   [IP]
British clergyman and author
* [A] Friend to the Natural and
   Religious Rights of Mankind

Graham, William B. 1857-1882
[BLB, EWG]
*American cattle rustler and
gunfighter*
* Brocius, Curly Bill
* Brocius, William

Graham, William Franklin [Billy]
1918-   [BP, CR]
American evangelist
* [The] Barrymore of the Bible
* Billy Frank
* Gabriel in Gabardine
* [The] President's Preacher

Grahame, James 1765-1811   [NPS]
Scottish poet
* [The] Sabbath Bard
(See also base volume)

[Le] Grand
See   Louis XIV

Grand Old Man
See   Clay, Henry

Grand Old Man
See   Stevens, Thaddeus

[The] Grand Old Man of Virginia
See   Goode, John

[La] Grande Therese
See   Humbert, Therese

Grandelius, Everett 20th c.   [EF]
American football player
* Grandelius, Sonny

Grandelius, Sonny
See   Grandelius, Everett

[The] Grandfather of Russian Song
See   Titov, Nikolay Alexeyevitch

[The] Grandson of R. Aiken
See   Aiken, Peter Freeland

Granella, Victor
See   Tangermann, Friedrich
Wilhelm

Grange, Eugene
See   Baste, Eugene Pierre

Grannell, Robert J. 19th c.   [PI]
Irish poet
* Rannaill, Clan

Grant, Alexander Henley 19th c.
[HFN]
British author and journalist
* A. H. G.

Grant, Allan
See   Wilson, James Grant

Grant, Matthew G.
See   Dikty, Julian May

Granville, Charles
See   Egerton, Francis Charles
Granville [Third Earl of Ellesmere]

Granville of a Former Age
See   Howard, Henry

Grapho
See   Adams, James Alonzo

Grasle, Elizabeth 1916-1973   [DBQ]
American actress
* Dean, Frances
* [The] Gam Girl
(See also base volume)

Grattan, H. P.
See   Plunkett, Henry Willoughby
Grattan

Grave-digger, Gabriel
See   Harvey, Gabriel

Gravenites, Nick 20th c.   [CMA]
American singer and songwriter
* [The] Greek

Graves, Alfred Perceval 1846-1931
[PI]
Irish music publisher and poet
* Dhuy, Suil
(See also base volume)

Grawoig, Sheila
See   Miller, Sheila

Gray, Betsy
See   Poole, Gray Johnson

Gray, Blakeney
See   Bangs, John Kendrick

Gray, Carl
See   Park, Charles Carroll

Gray, Dorothy
See   Guck, Dorothy [Gray]

Gray, E. Conder
See   Japp, Alexander Hay

Gray, Louisa
See   Walsh, Michael Paul

Gray, Rosalie
See   Mann, Delos H.

Gray, Simon
See   Boswell, [Sir] Alexander

Gray, Walter T.
See   Victor, Metta Victoria Fuller

Grayson, E.
See   Bixby, John Munson

Grayson, Georgina
See   Jones, Elizabeth Marina

Grazhdanin, Misha
See   Burgess, Michael Roy

[The] Great
See   Arsenius

[The] Great
See   Kamehameha I

[The] Great
See   Kurigalzu I

[The] Great
See   Mendoza, Pedro Gonzalez de

[The] Great
See   Sancho IV

[The] Great American Faro Banker
See   Parsons, Reuben

[The] Great Auruncian
See   Lucilius, Caius

Great Caliban
See   Johnson, Samuel

[The] Great Carsoni
See   Carson, John William
[Johnny]

Great Croysado
See   Fairfax, Thomas [Third Baron
Fairfax]

[The] Great Earl
See   Fitzgerald, Gerald

[The] Great Epigrammatist
See   Heywood, John

**[The] Great Founder of the Persian
Name**
See   Cyrus

Great Gander of Glasgow
See   Galt, John

[The] Great Geometer
See   Apollonius of Perga

[The] Great God Pan
See   Wordsworth, William

[The] Great Gospel Gun
See   Milton, John

[The] Great Gun of Windsor
See   Cannon, Tom

[The] Great Harlot
See   Braschi, Giovanni Angelo

Great Heir of Fame
See   Shakespeare, William

[The] Great Historian of the Field
See   Apperley, Charles James

[The] Great Independent
See   Cromwell, Oliver

[The] Great Kill-Cow of Christendom
See   Saumaise, Claude

[The] Great Laker
See   Wordsworth, William

[The] Great Leviathan of Men
See   Cromwell, Oliver

**[The] Great Master in the Science of
Grimace**
See   Woodward, Henry

[The] Great Pan
See   Saumaise, Claude

[The] Great Patron of Mankind
See   George II

[The] Great Peacemaker
See   Briand, Aristide

[The] Great Physician
See   Charles II

[The] Great Ponzi
See   Ponzi, Carlo

**[The] Great Preserver of Pope and
Shakespeare**
See   Warburton, William

[The] Great Rabbi of Jazz
See   Hampton, Lionel Leo

**[The] Great Shepherd of the Mantuan
Plains**
See   Vergilius Maro, Publius

[The] Great Soul of Numbers
See   Johnson, Ben[jamin]

[The] Great Southern Land Pirate
See   Copeland, James

[The] Great Stone Face
See   Heifetz, Jascha

[The] Great Stone Face
See   Sullivan, Ed

[The] Great Theban
See   Pindar

[The] Great Western Land Pirate
See   Murrel, John A.

[The] Great Wizard of the North
See   Anderson, John Henry

Greathead, Bertie 1759-1826
[NPS]
Author
* That Deep-Mouthed Theban

[The] Greek
See   Gravenites, Nick

[The] Green
See   Baldung, Hans

Green, Asa 1789-1837?   [DNA]
American author
* Fibbleton, George
(See also base volume)

Green, Bobby Joe
See   Green, Robert

Green, Christopher
See   Smyth, Patrick G.

Green, Deborah 1948-   [CA]
American author
* Zook, Deborah

Green, I. V.
See   Anderson, William

Green, Jasper
See   Boyle, John

Green, Matthew 1696-1737   [DLE1]
British poet
* Drake, Peter

Green, Olive
See   Reed, Myrtle

Green, Robert 20th c.   [EF]
American football player
* Green, Bobby Joe

Greenberg, Jan 1953?-
American author
* Gregory, Jill

Greenburger, Ingrid Elisabeth
1913-   [CA]
German-born author
* Rainer, George

Greendrake, Gregory
See Cody, Henry Brereton

Greene, Robert 1560?-1592
[DEA, NPS]
British author, playwright, poet
* [The] Dying Titan
* [The] Homer of Women
* Norfolciensis
* R. G.
* [A] Second Ovid
* Shakespeare's Predecessor
(See also base volume)

Greene, Robert W. 1929-   [CA]
American author
* Ashe, Penelope [joint pseudonym
   with Billie Young]

Greenough, Horatio 1805-1852
[DNA]
American author and sculptor
* Bender, Horace

Greenwood, Lillian Bethel 1932-
[CA]
Canadian author
* Ayers, Rose

Gregg, Trashy
See Gregg, Tresham Dames

Gregg, Tresham Dames
1799?-1881   [PI]
Irish playwright, poet, author
* Gregg, Trashy

Gregory, Earl 20th c.   [EF]
American football player
* Gregory, Jack

**Gregory, [Lady] Isabella Augusta
Persse** 1852-1932   [CA, DLE1]
Irish playwright, producer, poet
* [The] Godmother of the Abbey
   Theatre
(See also base volume)

Gregory, J. Dennis
See Williams, John A[lfred]

Gregory, Jack
See Gregory, Earl

Gregory, Jill
See Greenberg, Jan

Gregory, Margaret
See Ercole, Velia

Gregory, Mark
See Burch, Monte G.

Grennan, Jean Marie 1926-   [CR]
American college administrator
* Jacqueline, [Sister]

Grenville, George Nugent
1788-1850   [NPS]
British author and statesman
* [The] Buckinghamshire Dragon
(See also base volume)

Grenville, John Ashley Soames
See Guhrauer, John Ashley Soames

Grenville, Mrs. Arthur   [NPS]
Author
* Oram, Mona K.

Grese, Irma 1923-1945   [LFW]
German murderer
* [The] Beast of Belsen

Greve, Elsa
See Greve, Felix Paul

Greve, Felix Paul 1879-1948   [CA]
German-born Canadian author
* Gerden, Friedrich Carl
* Grafe, Felix
* Greve, Elsa
* Thorer, Konrad
* Thorne, Edouard
(See also base volume)

Greville F., of Barnes
See Fennell, Greville

Greville Minor
See Spender, John Alfred

Grey, Jane
See Carpenter, Anna May

Grey, Katharine
See Smith, Katharine Grey [Hogg]

Grey Owl
See Belaney, George Stansfeld

Grey, Pearl 1872-1939
American author
* [The] Father of the Western
* Grey, Zane

Grey, Zane
See Grey, Pearl

Greydrake, Geoffrey
See Ettingsall, Thomas

Gri
See Denney, Diana

Griego, Francisco ?-1875
[BLB, EWG]
American gunfighter
* Griego, Pancho

Griego, Pancho
See Griego, Francisco

Grierson, Edward 1914-1975
[TCCM]
British author
* Crowther, Brian
(See also base volume)

Grievous, Peter, Esq.
See Hopkinson, Francis

Griffen, Edmund
See DuBreuil, Elizabeth Lorinda

Griffin, Buffin
See Griffin, Dale

Griffin, Dale 20th c.   [CMA]
Musician
* Griffin, Buffin

Griffin, Gerald 1803-1840   [PI]
Irish poet and playwright
* Joseph, G.
* Oscar

Griffinhoof, Arthur
See Colman, George

Griffith, A[rthur] Leonard
See Griffiths, Arthur Leonard

Griffith, Thomas Gwynfor 1926-
[CA]
Welsh-born author and translator
* Cilffriw, Gwynfor

Griffiths, Arthur Leonard 1920-
[CA]
British-born clergyman and author
* Griffith, A[rthur] Leonard

Griffiths, Kitty Anna 20th c.   [CA]
British-born author and broadcaster
* Mrs. G.

Grimbosh, Herman
See Mackay, Charles

Grindel, Eugene 1895-1952
[CA, TLC]
French poet
* Du Hault, Jean
* Hervent, Maurice
(See also base volume)

Gringhuis, Richard H. 1918-1974
[CA]
American author and illustrator
* Dirk
(See also base volume)

Grip
See Bengough, J. D.

Grissom, Arthur Colfax 1869-1901
American author
* Gaines, Albert Cecil

Gristy, Bill 19th c.   [EWG]
American gunfighter and bandit
* White, Bill

Griswold, Alphonso Miner 1834-1891
American author
* Griswold, Sandy
(See also base volume)

Griswold, Frances Irene [Burge]
1826-1900   [DNA]
American author
* Phelps, S. B.

Griswold, Sandy
See Griswold, Alphonso Miner

Gross, Christian Channing
1895-1933   [DNA]
American author and diplomat
* Channing, C. G. Fairfax

Grossetete, Robert 1174-1253
[EOP]
British theologian and scholar
* Robert of Lincoln
(See also base volume)

Grossmith, George, Jr. 1847- ?
[NN, NPS]
British actor
* G. G.
* [The] Society Clown

Grossmith, Mrs. George, Jr.   [NPS]
Author
* Astor, Adelaide

Grosvenor, Melville Bell 1902?-1982
*American editor and president of the
National Geographic Society*
* M. B. G.

Grosvenor, Robert 1767-1845
[NPS]
First Marquis of Westminster
* Poluflosboio, Lord

Grosvenor's Cobbler
See Gifford, William

Grote, George 1794-1871
[DEA, NPS]
British author, editor, historian
* Beauchamp, Philip

Grotius
See Clinton, De Witt

Groto, Luigi 1541-1585   [NPS]
Italian poet
* [The] Blind Poet
(See also base volume)

Grousset, Paschal 1845?-1909
[NPS]
French politician and author
* Blasius, Docteur
* Moray, Tiburce
* Virey, Leopold
(See also base volume)

Gruda [A Clod of Earth]
See Wojtyla, Karol

Grumbler
See Clemens, Samuel Langhorne

Grumbler, Anthony
See Hoffman, David

Grundy, Miss
See Sneed, M. A.

Guardian of Mankind
See Akbar

Guare, June
See Cole, Harriet Adelia Ann
[Burleigh]

Guarneri, Giuseppe Bartolomeo
1698-1744   [BBD]
Italian violin maker
* Giuseppe del Gesu

Guarneri, Pietro 1695-1762   [BBD]
Italian violin maker
* Peter of Venice

Guarneri, Pietro Giovanni
1655-1720   [BBD]
Italian violin maker
* Peter of Mantua

Guck, Dorothy [Gray] 1913-   [MA]
American author
* Gray, Dorothy

Guerra y Sanchez, Ramiro
1880-1970   [CA]
Cuban-born author and educator
* Diplomaticus

Gueulette, Thomas Simon
1683-1766   [SFL]
Author
* T. S. G.

Guezenec, Alfred 1823-1866
[WGT]
French author
* De Brehat, Alfred

Guggenheim, William 1868-1941
[DNA]
American author
* Williams, Gatenby

Guhion
See Young, Robert

Guhrauer, John Ashley Soames
1928-   [CA]
British historian and author
* Grenville, John Ashley Soames

Guilot, Claude
See Foe, Daniel

Guiney, Louise Imogen 1861- ?   [PI]
American author and poet
* P. O. L.

Guinness, Alec 1914- [CR]
British actor
* [The] Man of a Thousand Faces

Guitar, Mister
See Atkins, Chet

Gulbenkian, Calouste [PPN]
Armenian financier
* Five Per Cent, Mr.

Gulliver, Lemuel
See Fielding, Henry

Gulliver, Lemuel, Junior
See Whitmore, H.

Gump, Sally
See Busby, Mabel Janice

Gune, Jagannath Ganesh 1883- ?
[EOP]
Indian educator, author, leader of religious sect
* Kuvalayananda, Swami

Gunn, Harriet 19th c. [HFN]
Author
* [A] Lady

Gunn, Henry Mayo 19th c. [HFN]
Author
* H. M. G.

[The] Gunner
See Skeffington, [Sir] William

Gunnison, Lynn
See Ames, Joseph Bushnell

Gunpowder Percy
See Pope, Alexander

Gushington, Angelina
See Radcliffe-Cooke, Charles Wallwyn

Gustavus Adolphus 1594-1632
[NPS]
King of Sweden
* [The] Antichrist
* Sweden's Glory
(See also base volume)

Gutch, John Mathew 1777-1861
[IP]
British journalist
* [The] Bristol Junius
* Cosmo
* [An] Octogenarian

Guthrie, Norman Gregor
1877-1929 [DNA]
Canadian author and poet
* Crichton, John

Gutowsky, Ace
See Gutowsky, Leroy

Gutowsky, Leroy 20th c. [EF]
American football player
* Gutowsky, Ace

Guyton de Morveau, N. [IP]
French author
* Brumore

Gwilliam, John [IP]
British poet
* [A] Professor

Gwin, Thomas 1656-1720 [IP]
British author
* T. G.

Gwinnett, Richard ?-1717 [IP]
British author
* Pylades

Gwynn, Albinia [IP]
Author
* [A] Lady

Gwynne, Oscar A.
See Ellis, Edward S[ylvester]

Gwynne, Oswald A.
See Ellis, Edward S[ylvester]

Gyllenstierna, Erik
See Swansson, Lars

[The] Gypsy
See Mace, Jem

[The] Gypsy
See Smith, Arthur

H

H.
See Chibborn, E.

H.
See Harkin, Hugh

H.
See Hoey, Christopher Clinton

H.
See Holland, Denis

H.
See Hughes, Thomas

H.
See Sigerson, Hester

H. A.
See Acton, Harriet

H. A.
See Alford, Henry

H. A.
See Attwell, Henry

H. B.
See Bailey, Henry

H. B.
See Battier, Henrietta

H. B.
See Belloc, [Joseph] Hilary [Pierre]

H. B.
See Blackwell, Henry

H. B.
See Byrne, Hannah

H. B.
See Doyle, John

H. B. C.
See Cody, Henry Brereton

H. B. D.
See Dawson, Henry Barton

H. B. G.
See Talcott, Mrs. Hersey Bradford [Goodwin]

H. B-y-e
See Byrne, Hannah

H. C.
See Clinche, Hugh

H. C. M. W.
See Watson, Henry Crocker Marriott

H. D.
See Drummond, Henry

H. E. S. L.
See Leech, H. E. S.

H. F. C.
See Chorley, Henry Fothergill

H. G. C., Esq.
See Curran, Henry Grattan

H. H.
See Haines, Herbert

H. H.
See Hutton, Hugh

H. J. B. N.
See Nicholson, Henry Joseph Boone

H. K.
See Kierman, Harriet

H. K.
See Kirchhoffer, Henry

H. L.
See Farrell, Joseph

H. L. G.
See Benson, Arthur Christopher

H. M. B.
See Bourke, Hannah Maria

H. M. C.
See Chester, Harriet Mary

H. M. G.
See Gunn, Henry Mayo

H. N.
See Nelson, Henry

H. N.
See Norris, Henry

H. O. M.
See Gladstone, William Ewart

H. R. F. B.
See Bourne, Henry Richard Fox

H. R. N.
See Dunne, J. T.

H. S.
See Thomas, Ralph

H. S. C.
See Cunningham, H. S.

H. S. M.
See Maine, Henry James Stuart

H. S. S.
See Stokes, Henry Sewell

H. St. A. K.
See Kitching, Mrs. H. St. A.

H. W.
See Walpole, Horatio [Fourth Earl of Orford]

H. W. A.
See Acland, Henry Wentworth

H. W. B.
See Baker, [Sir] Henry Williams

H. W. L.
See Lucy, [Sir] Henry William

H-y
See Hoey, Christopher Clinton

Haarmann, Fritz 1879-1924   [DI]
German murderer
* [The] Hanover Vampire

Habberton, John 1842- ?   [IP, NPS]
American author, journalist, soldier
* Their Latest Victim
* Uncle Harry
(See also base volume)

Habersham, Robert ?-1832   [IP]
American author
* Airy, Mr.
* Digress, Deloraine

Habich, Edward   [IP]
American author
* [An] American

Hack, James 1758-1829   [IP]
British author
* [A] Citizen

Hack, Maria 1778-1844   [IP]
British author
* M. H.

Hack, Mary P. 19th c.   [IP]
British author
* Claudia

Hacker, Franz 1836- ?   [IP]
German author
* Seeburg, Franz von

Hackett, Jan Michele 1952-   [CA]
American author
* Kerouac, Jan

Hackle, Palmer
See Blakey, Robert

Haddad, Legs
See Haddad, Sharyn

Haddad, Sharyn 20th c.   [BP]
American singer
* Haddad, Legs

Hadfield, John ?-1803   [DI]
British imposter
* Hope, Colonel

Hadrianus
See Adriaensen, Emanuel

Haeberlin, Karl Ludwig 1784- ?   [IP]
German author
* Belani, H. E. R.

Haering, Georg Wilhelm Heinrich 1798-1871   [IP]
German author
* Alexis, Wilibald

Hagarty, [Sir] John Hawkins 1816-1900   [IP, PI]
Irish-born poet, jurist, author
* Zadig

Hagen, Benediel 1844-1906   [RBE]
German-born American boxer
* Hogan, Ben

Hagen, Lorinda
See DuBreuil, Elizabeth Lorinda

Hagen, Theodor 1823-1871   [BBD]
German-born author and editor
* Fels, Joachim

Haggard, Edward Arthur 1860-1925   [NPS]
British author, historian, poet
* Amyand, Arthur

Hagglund, Joel 1879-1915   [DBQ]
American labor leader
* Hill, Joe

Hahn-Hahn, Ida Maria Louisa Frederika Gustava 1805-1879   [IP]
German author
* [A] German Countess

Haight, Sarah [Rogers]   [IP]
American author
* [A] Lady of New York

Haines, Harry 20th c.   [EF]
American football player
* Haines, Hoot

Haines, Herbert 19th c.   [IP]
British author
* H. H.

Haines, Hoot
See Haines, Harry

Haines, Jackson ?-1875   [SR]
American ice skating promoter
* [The] American Ice Master
* [The] American Skating King

Haines, Zenas T. 19th c.   [IP]
American soldier and author
* Corporal

Hakewell, James Ridgway 19th c.
[IP]
British author
* J. R. H.

Hakewill, Arthur William
1808-1856   [IP]
British architect and author
* [An] Architect

Hakim, Bukhtyar Rustomji Ratanji
1898-1936   [DI]
Indian-born murderer
* Ruxton, Buck

Hakluyt, Richard 1552?-1616
[DEA]
British author and translator
* R. H.

Haldane, Harry
See Heslop, R. O.

Hales, John 1584-1656   [NPS]
British clergyman
* Bibliotheca Ambulans
(See also base volume)

Haley, [Sir] William 20th c.   [PPN]
British journalist
* Edwards, Oliver

Half Hanged Maggie
See Dixon, Margaret

[A] Half Pay Officer
See Addison, Henry Robert

Hall, Basil 1788-1844   [NPS]
British naval officer and author
* Argonaut
(See also base volume)

Hall, Baynard Rush 1798-1863
[DLE1]
*American clergyman, educator,
author*
* Carlton, Robert

Hall, Charles Val 20th c.   [EF]
American football player
* Hall, Tim

Hall, E. B.   [NPS]
Author
* Tallentyre, S. G.

Hall, Eliza Calvert
See Obenchain, Eliza Caroline
[Calvert]

Hall, Ellis 16th c.   [NPS]
Considered himself to be a prophet
* [The] Carpenter's Son
(See also base volume)

Hall, H. Fielding   [NPS]
Author
* Fielding, H.

Hall, Joseph 1574-1656   [WGT]
British prelate
* Britannico, Mercurio
* [An] English Mercury
(See also base volume)

Hall, [Jesse] Lee 1849-1911   [EWG]
American law officer
* Hall, Red

Hall, Red
See Hall, [Jesse] Lee

Hall, Robert
See Heylyn, Peter

Hall, Samuel Carter 1800-1889
[PI]
Irish author and poet
* S. C. H.

Hall, Samuel Stone 1838-1886
American author
* Buckskin Sam

Hall, Thomas H.
Author
* Caine, Hall

Hall, Tim
See Hall, Charles Val

Hallam, Arthur Henry 1811-1833
[DEA]
British author
* A. H. H.
* T. H. E. A.

Hallam, Classic
See Hallam, Henry

Hallam, Henry 1777-1859   [NPS]
British historian, critic, author
* Hallam, Classic

Halliwell, James Orchard
1820-1889   [HFN]
British librarian and scholar
* J. O. H.
(See also base volume)

Halloran, Clarence 20th c.   [EF]
American football player
* Halloran, Dimp

Halloran, Dimp
See Halloran, Clarence

Halloran, Laurence Hynes
1766-1831   [PI]
Irish-born clergyman and poet
* O'Halloran, Laurence
* Philo-Nauticus

Halls, Geraldine [Mary] 1919-   [CA]
Australian author
* Jay, Charlotte
* Jay, G. S.

Hallstead, William F[inn III] 1924-
[CA]
American author
* Beechcroft, William

Halpin, William 1825-1852   [PI]
Irish-born American poet and author
* T. H.

Halpine, Charles Graham
1829-1868   [DLE1]
American author and poet
* [The] Letter H.
(See also base volume)

Halsey, Harlan Page 1837-1898
[WGT, WW]
American author
* O'Neil, Wolf
* Taylor, Judson R.
(See also base volume)

Halstead, Ada L.
See Newhall, Laura Eugenia

Hametovich, Rudolf 1938-   [CR]
Russian-born dancer
* Nureyev, Rudolf

Hamilton, Alexander 1757-1804
[DLE1]
American statesman
* Americanus
(See also base volume)

Hamilton, Ann 19th c.   [PI]
Irish poet
* A. H.

Hamilton, Anna Elizabeth 19th c.
[PI]
Irish poet
* A. E. H.

Hamilton, Betsy
See Moore, Idora [McClellan]

Hamilton, Henry
See Cox, Henry Hamilton

Hamilton, Henry
See Spalding, John Lancaster

Hamilton, May Charlotte 19th c.
[PI]
Irish poet
* Etumos

Hamilton, Ralph
See Stratemeyer, Edward L.

Hamilton, Rufus
See Gillmore, Rufus Hamilton

Hamilton, Thomas 1680-1735
[NPS]
Sixth Earl of Haddington
* Simon the Skipper

Hamilton, William
See Head, Richard

Hamilton, Wm. J.
See Clark, Charles Dunning

Hammer, Jacob
See Oppenheimer, Joel [Lester]

Hammett, Samuel Adams
1816-1865   [DNA]
American author and journalist
* Paxton, Philip

Hammond, Henrietta [Hardy]
1854-1883   [DNA]
American author
* Capsadell, Louisa
* Dauge, Henri

[The] Hampshire Farmer
See Cobbett, William

Hampton, Hope 1898?-1982
American actress and opera singer
* [The] Duchess of Park Avenue

Hampton, Lionel Leo 1913-   [CR]
American jazz musician
* [The] Great Rabbi of Jazz

Hancock
See Dexter, Franklin

Hancock, Carol Helen Brooks
See Hancock, Morgan

Hancock, Morgan 1941-   [CA]
American author
* Hancock, Carol Helen Brooks

Hand, Dora 19th c.   [BLB]
American showgirl
* Keenan, Fannie

[The] Handel of Maine
See Belcher, Supply

Hands, Bull
See Hands, Thomas

Hands, Thomas 19th c.   [RBE]
Boxer
* Hands, Bull

Hanley, Elizabeth
See DuBreuil, Elizabeth Lorinda

Hanna, David 1917-   [CA]
American author and journalist
* James, Anthony
* Laine, Gloria

Hanna, George W. 19th c.   [SFL]
Author
* Gentil, Spirito

Hannaford, Justin
See FitzGerald, Shafto Justin
Adair

Hanner, Dave
See Hanner, Joel

Hanner, Joel 20th c.   [EF]
American football player
* Hanner, Dave

Hano, Arnold 1922-   [CA]
American author
* Dodge, Gil
* Gant, Matthew
* Gordon, Ad
* Heller, Mike

[The] Hanover Vampire
See Haarmann, Fritz

Hanratty, James ?-1962   [DI]
American murderer
* Ryan, J.

Hanson, Alexander Contee
1749-1806   [DNA]
American author and jurist
* Aristides

[A] Haole
See Liholiho, A.

Hapgood, Mrs. Hutchins
Author
* Boyce, Neith

[The] Happy
See Ferdinand I

[The] Happy
See Frederick II

[The] Happy
See Galitzin, Vasili

[The] Happy Highbrow
See Ludden, Allen [Ellsworth]

Happy Jack Morco
See Morco, John

Happy Jack Ulyett
See Ulyett, George

Harbaugh, Thomas Chalmers
1849-1924
American author and poet
* Old Sleuth
(See also base volume)

Harcourt, Helen
See Warner, Helen Garnie

Hard Knocks
See Dowling, Bartholomew

Hardegen, Count 1834-1867   [BBD]
Austrian musician
* Egghard, Julius

Hardenberg, Friedrich von 1772-1801
German poet
* [The] German Pascal
(See also base volume)

Hardhat, Mr.
See Brennan, Peter J.

Hardin, John Wesley 1853-1895
[BLB, EWG]
American gunfighter
* Hardin, Wes
* Little Arkansas
* Swain, J. H., Jr.

Hardin, Wes
See Hardin, John Wesley

Harding, Peter
See Burgess, Michael Roy

Hardinge, E. M.
See Going, Ellen Maud

Hardinge, George 1744-1816
[NPS]
Author
* [The] Waggish Welsh Judge
(See also base volume)

Hardkoppig Piet
See Stuyvesant, Petrus

Hardman, Frederick
See Postl, Karl Anton

Hardy, Thomas 1840-1928
[CA, UH]
British author, poet, playwright
* [The] Millet of Literature
* [The] Millet without the Angelus
* [The] Novelist of Wessex
* [The] Wessex Novelist

Hare, Augustus William 19th c.
[NPS]
British poet
* Two Brothers [joint pseudonym
with Julius Charles Hare]

Hare, Christopher
See Andrews, Marian

Hare, Emily
See Johnson, Laura [Winthrop]

Hare, Francis 1671-1740   [NPS]
Bishop of Chichester
* Philo Criticus

Hare, Julius Charles 19th c.   [NPS]
Author
* Two Brothers [joint pseudonym
with Augustus William Hare]

Harkin, Hugh 1791-1854   [PI]
Irish poet
* H.
* Heber?
* Picken, Henry

Harlan, James Jefferson 19th c.
American gunfighter
* [The] Off Wheeler

Harley, Steve
See Nice, Steven

Harmon, Ham
See Harmon, Hamilton

Harmon, Hamilton 20th c.   [EF]
American football player
* Harmon, Ham

[The] Harmonica Wizard
See Bailey, Deford

Harness, William 19th c.   [HFN]
Author
* Presbyter Catholicus

Harpe, Big
See Harpe, William Micajah

Harpe, Little
See Harpe, Wiley

Harpe, Wiley 1770- ?   [BLB, DI]
American murderer and robber
* Harpe, Little
* Roberts

Harpe, William Micajah
1768-1799   [BLB]
American murderer and robber
* Harpe, Big

Harper
See Washington, George

Harper, H. G. 1851- ?   [NPS]
Journalist and author
* G. G.

Harper, Mary Wood
See Dixon, Jeanne

Harrell, Sara Gordon
See Banks, Sara [Jeanne Gordon
Harrell]

Harriet
See Balduck, Harriet

Harriet
See White, Harriet

Harrigan and Hart
See Abarbanell, Jacob Ralph

Harriman, Edward Henry
1848-1909   [CR]
*American financier and railroad
executive*
* [The] Little Giant of Wall Street

Harrington, George F.
See Baker, William Mumford

Harrington, Grace D.
See Lewis, Harriet Newell

Harrington, James 1611-1677
[DEA]
British author and translator
* J. H.

Harrington, [Sir] John 1561-1612
[NPS]
Courtier
* Ajax, Sir

Harris, Andrea
See Walker, Irma Ruth [Roden]

Harris, Arundell
See Arundell, William Arundell
Harris

Harris, Bo
See Harris, Clint Lee

Harris, Clint Lee 1953-   [FR]
American football player
* Harris, Bo

Harris, Corra White 1869- ?
[BDSA]
American author and columnist
* Harris, Mrs. Lundy H.

Harris, Joel Chandler 1848-1908
[DNA]
American author and editor
* Skinflint, Obediah
(See also base volume)

Harris, John 1784-1858   [IP]
British author
* Q. in the Corner

Harris, Joseph Hemington 19th c.
[HFN, IP]
British clergyman and author
* Presbyter Anglicanus

Harris, Josiah 1821- ?   [IP]
British author and journalist
* Cantabar
* Ishmael
* [A] Philanthropist
* Saint Meva

Harris, Karol 1899?-1982
American cartoonist
* Harris, Ken

Harris, Ken
See Harris, Karol

Harris, Lavinia
See Johnston, Norma

Harris, Mrs. Lundy H.
See Harris, Corra White

Harris, Mrs. Sydney S. 1834- ?
[IP]
American author
* Coles, Miriam

Harris, N. Sayre 19th c.   [IP]
American clergyman and author
* Secretary and General Agent

Harris, Richard   [IP]
British barrister and author
* [A] Barrister

Harris, Samuel Smith 1841-1888
[DNA]
*American-born author and
clergyman*
* Coningsby, Christopher

Harris, Thaddeus Mason
1768-1842   [IP]
American clergyman and author
* Dorcastriensis
* [A] Student of Harvard
University

Harris, W. C.   [IP]
American soldier and author
* [A] Ball's Bluff Prisoner

Harris, William Richard
1847-1923   [DNA]
*Irish-born author, historian,
clergyman*
* Crawford, Oswald

Harrison, Amelia [Williams]
1852-1903   [DNA]
Author
* Compton, Margaret

Harrison, Chip
See Block, Lawrence

Harrison, Gabriel
See Craven, Charles

Harrison, George 19th c.   [IP]
British author
* His Grandson

Harrison, Harry
See Enton, Harry

Harrison, Jennie
See Tomkins, Jane Harrison

Harrison, John 1796-1852   [IP]
British author
* J. H.

Harrison, Mary
See Fabbri, Nancy Rash

Harrison, Susannah 18th c.   [IP]
British poet
* [A] Young Woman

Harrison, Susie Frances [Riley]
1859-1935   [DLE1, PI]
Canadian author and poet
* Seranus

Harriss, Julia Mildred   [IP]
American poet
* [The] Minstrel Maiden of Mobile

Harrod, Frances
See Forbes-Robertson, Frances

Harron, Don[ald] 1924-   [CA]
Canadian actor, author, playwright
* Farquharson, Charlie
* Rosedale, Valerie

Harrowe, Fiona
See Hurd, Florence

Harry, Deborah 1944-   [BP]
American singer
* [The] Monroe of Punk

Harry the Kid
See Head, Harry

Harsch, Hilya
See Jelly, George Oliver

Harsha, David Addison 1827- ?
[IP]
American author
* [A] Pilgrim

Hart, Adolphus M. 1834- ?   [IP]
Canadian author and attorney
* [A] Hoosier

Hart, Alexandra 1939-   [CA]
American author and artist
* Jacopetti, Alexandra

Hart, C. W.   [IP]
American attorney and author
* [A] Member of the Bar

Hart, Charles
See Quantrill, William Clarke

Hart, Dee 20th c.   [EF]
American football player
* Hart, Pete

Hart, Fanny [Wheeler]   [IP]
British author
* [A] Clergyman's Wife

Hart, Kate
See Kramer, Roberta

Hart, Pete
See Hart, Dee

Harte, Jerome Alfred 1854- ?   [IP]
American author
* Zulano

Hartford, Eden
See Eden, Edna

Harting, Pieter 1812-1885
[SFL, WGT]
Author
* Dioscorides, Dr.

Hartley, C. Gasquoine
See Gallichan, Mrs. Walter

Hartley, May Laffan 19th c.   [IP]
Irish author
* [The] Irish Charles Dickens

Hartley, Thomas 1707-1784   [IP]
British clergyman and author
* [Un] Ami

Hartley, Thomas 1748-1809   [IP]
American soldier, statesman, author
* Phocion

Hartmann, Agnes [Taubert] von 19th c. [IP]
German author
* Taubert, A.

Hartmann, Eduard von 1842- ? [IP]
German philosopher and author
* Robert, Karl

Hartmann, Moritz 1821-1872 [IP]
German poet
* Mauritius, Pfaffe

Hartshorne, Henry 1823-1897 [DNA]
American-born author and physician
* L'Estrange, Corinne

Hartstonge, Matthew Weld
See Weld, Matthew

Harvard, Senior
See Ward, Henry Dana

Harvey, Alex 1935- [CMA]
Scottish musician
* [The] Tommy Steele of Scotland

Harvey, Annie Jane [Tennant]
?-1898 [WW]
Author
* Hope, Andree

Harvey, Gabriel 1545?-1630?
[NPS]
British poet
* Ape Gabriel
* [The] Father of English
  Hexameter
* Grave-digger, Gabriel
* [The] Homer of this Age
* Lipsian Dick
(See also base volume)

Harvey, James 20th c. [EF]
American football player
* Harvey, Waddy

Harvey, Richard [NPS]
British astronomer and astrologer
* Donzel Dick
(See also base volume)

Harvey, Richard 19th c. [HFN]
Author
* R. H.

Harvey, Waddy
See Harvey, James

Has-Kay-bay-nay-ntayl 19th c.
[DI]
American Indian bandit and outlaw
* [The] Apache Kid

Hasbrouck, Joseph 1840- ? [DNA]
Author and attorney
* Croke, J. Greenbag

Hasegawa, Tatsunosuke 1864-1909
Japanese author and translator
* Futabatei Shimei

Hasek, Jaroslav [Matej Frantisek]
1883-1923 [CA, TLC]
Czech author and poet
* Franklin, Benjamin
* Hellenhofferu, Vojtech Kapristian
  z
* Ruffian, M.

Haselrig, [Sir] Arthur ?-1661
[NPS]
British politician
* [The] Brutus of Our Republic

Haslewood, Joseph 1769-1833
[NPS]
British bibliographer
* Bernardo
(See also base volume)

[The] Hasmonean
See Antigonus II

[The] Hat
See McVitie, Jack

Hatchett, William
See Bignon, Jean Paul

Hatfield, S. E.
See Miles, Sibella [Hatfield]

Hathaway, Anne
See Ingham, Mrs. W. A.

Hatteras, Amelia
See Mencken, Henry Louis

Hauck, Louise [Platt] 1883-1943
[DNA]
American author
* Randall, Jean
(See also base volume)

Hauffe, Frederica 1801-1829
[EOP]
Claimed to possess psychic powers
* [The] Seeress of Prevorst

[The] Haunted Man
See Williams, Richard Dalton

Hauser, Gayelord
See Hauser, Helmut Eugene
Benjamin Gellert

**Hauser, Helmut Eugene Benjamin
Gellert** 1895- [CR]
German-born nutritionist and author
* Hauser, Gayelord

Havemeyer, Theodore A.
1834-1897 [GF]
*American business executive and
author*
* [The] Sugar King

Havens, Cordelia
See Walcott, Josephine

Haviaras, Stratis
See Chaviaras, Strates

[The] Hawk
See Astiz, Alfredo

Hawker, Robert Stephen
1803-1875 [DLE1]
British poet and antiquary
* Reuben

Hawkins, [Sir] John 1532-1595
[NPS]
British naval officer
* England's Nestor

Hawkins, [Sir] John 1719-1789
[NPS]
British author
* [The] Fiddling Knight

Hawkins, Nehemiah 1833-1928
[DNA]
Author
* Rogers, William

Hawkins, Rip
See Hawkins, Ross

Hawkins, Ross 20th c. [EF]
American football player
* Hawkins, Rip

Hawksworth, Hallam
See Atkinson, Francis Blake

Hawthorne, Nathaniel 1804-1864
[NPS]
American author
* [The] Friend of Sinners

Hawtrey, Dr. 1789-1862 [NPS]
British educator
* Priscian

Hay, Timothy
See Rollins, Montgomery

Hayaseca y Eizaguirre, Jorge
See Echegaray y Eizaguirre, Jose
[Maria Waldo]

Hayes, Edward 19th c. [PI]
Irish-born poet and barrister
* E. H.

Hayes, John 1775-1838 [NPS]
Naval officer
* Hayes, Magnificent

Hayes, Magnificent
See Hayes, John

Hayes, S.
See O'Grady, Standish Hayes

Hayley, William 1745-1820 [NPS]
British poet
* [The] King of the English Poets
(See also base volume)

Hayman, Samuel 1818- ? [PI]
Irish author and poet
* [A] Country Parson?

Hays, Jacob 1772-1850 [CEC]
American detective
* Hays, Old

Hays, Old
See Hays, Jacob

Haywood, Eliza [Fowler]
1693?-1756 [DEA, SFL]
British author and translator
* Exploralibus
* [The] Son of a Mandarin

Hazelton, Harry
See McNamara, William Franklin

Hazlitt, William 1778-1830 [NPS]
British author
* Boswell Redivivus
(See also base volume)

Hazzard, Mary 1928- [CA]
American author and playwright
* Dwight, Olivia

Head, [Sir] Francis Bond
1793-1875 [HFN]
British traveller and author
* [A] British Subject
(See also base volume)

Head, Harry ?-1881 [EWG]
American gunfighter
* Harry the Kid

**[A] Head Master under the London
School Board**
See Amner, J. T.

Head, Richard 1637?-1678?
[WGT]
Irish playwright
* Hamilton, William
* Latroon, M.
(See also base volume)

Healy, Chip
See Healy, William

Healy, William 20th c. [EF]
American football player
* Healy, Chip

[The] Heartless Old Man
See Gladstone, William Ewart

Heath, James 1756-1834 [NPS]
British engraver
* [The] Father of Line Engraving

Heathorne, Caroline 1784?-1888
[NPS]
Lived to the age of 104
* [The] Maid of Kent

Heaton, Augustus Goodyear
1844-1930 [DNA]
American author and artist
* Shuffle, Rube

[The] Heaven-Taught Ploughman
See Burns, Robert

[The] Heavy Horseman
See Quillinan, Edward

Heber?
See Harkin, Hugh

Heder, Ben
See Duffy, [Sir] Charles Gavan

Hedgeland, Isabella Kelly 19th c.
[WGT]
British author
* Kelly, Isabella

Hefferman, [Mr.] Michael
See Ferguson, Samuel

Heffernan, Michael J. ?-1885 [PI]
Irish author and playwright
* Clogheen, H.
* Josephine
* M. H.
* Mullinahone, Eileen
* Romeo

Hefner, Paul
See Tabori, Paul

Hegan, Alice Caldwell
See Rice, Mrs. Cale Young

Hegmun, Ira
See Maguire, H. N.

Hegyesi, Louis
See Spitzer, Louis

Heifetz, Jascha 1901- [CR]
Russian-born violinist
* [The] Great Stone Face

Heilly, Georges d'
See Poinsot, Antoine Edmond

Heinecken, Christian Heinrich
1721-1725 [NPS]
German child prodigy
* [The] Child of Luebeck
(See also base volume)

Heinfetter, Herman
See Parker, Frederick

Heinrick, Hugh 1831-1877 [PI]
Irish author and editor
* McErin, Hugh

Heinz, H. J., II
See Heinz, Henry James, II

Heinz, Henry James, II 1908- [CR]
American business executive
* Heinz, H. J., II

Heister, Amalie
See Sachsen, Amalie Frederike
Auguste Herzogin von

Heiter, Ernst
See Sechter, Simon

Held, Peter
See Vance, John Holbrook [Jack]

Heldau
See Lubanski, Jules Clement
Ladislas

Helfenstein, Ernest
See Smith, Elizabeth Oakes

Hellenhofferu, Vojtech Kapristian z
See Hasek, Jaroslav [Matej
Frantisek]

Heller, Mike
See Hano, Arnold

Heller, Walter 1915-   [CR]
American economist
* [The] Father of the American
  School of New Economics

Hellman, Sylvia 20th c.   [EOP]
German-born leader of religious cult
* Radha, [Swami] Sivananda

Helluin, Francis 20th c.   [EF]
American football player
* Helluin, Jerry

Helluin, Jerry
See Helluin, Francis

Helvetius
See Schweitzer, Johann-Friedrich

Helvidius
See Madison, James

Hely, John 1724-1794   [PI]
Irish politician and poet
* Hutchinson, John Hely
* J. H. H.

Hemingway, Margaux
See Hemingway, Margot

Hemingway, Margot 1955-   [BP]
American actress and model
* Hemingway, Margaux

Hempel, George 1859-1921
American philologist
* Rheinhardt, Rudolph H.
(See also base volume)

Henderson, F. C.
See Mencken, Henry Louis

Henderson, J. Stanley
See Willett, Edward

Henderson, Jimmie 1954-   [CMA]
American musician
* Henderson, Little Jimmie

Henderson, Little Jimmie
See Henderson, Jimmie

Henderson, William
See Detzer, Karl

Hendrian, Dutch
See Hendrian, Oscar

Hendrian, Oscar 20th c.   [EF]
American football player
* Hendrian, Dutch

Henke, Bob 20th c.   [CMA]
Musician
* Henke, Willard

Henke, Willard
See Henke, Bob

Henley, John 1692-1756   [NPS]
British clergyman
* Orator Bronze
* Quir, Dr.
(See also base volume)

Henley, Robert 1708-1772   [NPS]
First Earl of Northington
* Tilbury, Tom

Hennessey, Caroline [joint
pseudonym with Sylvia Von Block]
See Von Block, Bela

Hennessey, Caroline [joint
pseudonym with Bela Von Block]
See Von Block, Sylvia

Hennessy, William Charles
1860?-1898   [PI]
Irish poet
* Ellem, Mr.
* Herbert, Charles
* Seehaitch
* Truthful James
* W. H.

Henrietta
See Nethercott, Henrietta

Henry de Loundres ?-1228   [NPS]
Archbishop of Dublin
* Scorchvillein

Henry Frederick 1745-1790   [NPS]
Duke of Cumberland
* Morgan, Squire

Henry of Lausanne 12th c.   [NPS]
French leader of religious sect
* [The] Hermit
(See also base volume)

Henry, Pat
See Scarnato, Patrick Henry

Henry, Patrick
See Sigerson, George

Henry, Raymond Varo 19th c.   [PI]
Irish poet
* Heudro, Raymond

Henry V 1387-1422   [UH]
King of England
* Prince Hal
(See also base volume)

Henry VI 1421-1471   [NPS]
King of England
* Ill-Fated Henry
* [The] Royal Saint
(See also base volume)

Henry VIII 1491-1547   [NPS, UH]
King of England
* Bluff Harry
* Corannus
(See also base volume)

Hensel, Octavia
See Seymour, Mary Alice [Ives]

Hepburn, David 1857- ?   [PI]
Irish-born poet
* Slievegallion

Hepburn, Duncan D. 19th c.   [PI]
Scottish poet
* Emerald Isle

Hepcat, Dr.
See Durst, Lavada

Her Father
See Adams, Nehemiah

Her Father
See Hooker, Edward William

Her Mother
See Gardiner, Mrs. William

Herbert, Charles
See Hennessy, William Charles

Herbert, George Robert Charles
1850- ?   [IP]
13th Earl of Pembroke
* [The] Earl

Herbert, James D.
See Dowling, James D.

Herbison, David 1800-1880   [PI]
Irish poet
* [The] Bard of Dunclug

[A] Hercules
See Fox, Charles James

Heremon
See Mulchinock, William
Pembroke

Hering, Jeanie
See Acton, Mrs. J. A.

Herman, Victor 20th c.
Russian-born aviator and author
* [The] Lindbergh of Russia

Hermes
See Miles, Henry, Jr.

[The] Hermit
See Henry of Lausanne

[The] Hermit in Ireland
See Furlong, Thomas

[The] Hermit in Oscott
See Moore, John

[The] Hermit of Marlow
See Shelley, Percy Bysshe

Hernandez, Francisco 19th c.   [GS]
Spanish bullfighter
* [El] Bolero [The Bolero Dancer]

Herne, Thomas 1722- ?   [IP]
British author
* Phileleutherus Cantabrigiensis
* Philonagnostes Criticus

[The] Hero of Olustee
See Colquitt, Alfred Holt

[The] Herodotus of Arabian History
See Masudi, al

Heron, A.   [IP]
Author
* [An] Ex Hussar

Heron, Agnes 19th c.   [IP]
American singer
* Natali, Agnes

Heron, Brother
See Vane, [Sir] Henry [Harry]

Heron, Emily [Manning]   [IP]
British poet
* Australie

Heron, Fanny 19th c.   [IP]
American singer
* Natali, Fanny

Heron, Mrs. Hubert 19th c.   [PI]
Australian poet
* Australia

Heron, Robert 1764-1807   [IP]
Scottish author
* Anderson, Ralph

[Le] Heros de l'Histoire
See Bourbon, Louis II de [Prince de
Conde]

Herrera Rodriguez, Francisco
1783-1820   [GS]
Spanish bullfighter
* Curro Guillen

Herrick, Edward Claudius
1811-1862   [IP]
American scholar
* B. F.

Herrick, Huldah
See Ober, Sarah Endicott

Herrick, N. 18th c.   [IP]
British author
* N. H.

Herron, James 20th c.   [EF]
American football player
* Herron, Pat

Herron, Pat
See Herron, James

Herschel, [Sir] John
See Locke, Richard Adams

Hershman, Morris 1926-   [CA]
American author
* Roffman, Sara
* Templeton, Janet
* Victor, Sam
(See also base volume)

Hervent, Maurice
See Grindel, Eugene

Hervey, Eleonora Louisa 1811- ?
[IP]
British author
* Russell, Margaret

**Hervey, John [Baron Hervey of
Ickworth]** 1696-1743   [IP]
British author and politician
* [A] Member of the House of
  Commons
* [A] Nobleman
(See also base volume)

Herz-Garten, Theodor
See De Mattos, Mrs.

Heslop, R. O.   [IP]
British author
* Haldane, Harry

Hess, David 1770-1843   [WEC]
Swiss cartoonist
* Gillray, Junior
* Hildebrandt, Daniel

Hesse, Lepold Auguste Constantin
?-1844   [IP]
Dutch bookseller and author
* Constantin, L. A.

Hesychius Pamphilus
See Braithwaite, Richard

Heudro, Raymond
See Henry, Raymond Varo

Heun, Karl Gottlob Samuel
1771-1854   [IP]
German author
* Clauren, H.

Hewerdine, Thomas   [IP]
British clergyman and author
* T. H.

Hewetson, William   [IP]
British author
* [A] Christian

Hewins, C. M.   [IP]
American author
* C. M. H.

Hewitt, John   [IP]
British antiquary
* I. H.

Hewitt, Mary Elizabeth   [IP]
American poet
* Jane
(See also base volume)

Hewson, Hugh 1724-1809   [IP]
British hairdresser and author
* Strap, Hugh

Heygate, William Edward 1816- ?
[IP]
British clergyman and author
* [A] Clergyman of the Episcopal
   Church, in England
* W. E. H.

Heylyn, Peter 1600-1662   [DLE1]
British author, theologian, historian
* Churchman, Theophilus
* Hall, Robert

Heywood, James   [IP]
British author
* Easy, James

Heywood, John 1497?-1580?
[NPS]
Playwright
* [The] Great Epigrammatist
* [The] Old English Epigrammatist

Heywood, Samuel   [IP]
British barrister and author
* [A] Layman

Heywood, Thomas 1575?-1650?
[DEA]
British author and translator
* T. H.

Hi C Carter
See   Carter, Howard

Hi Many
See   Kelly, John Tarpey

Hi Regan
See   Dunne, J. T.

Hibbert, Frederick 20th c.   [CMA]
Jamaican musician
* Hibbert, Toots

Hibbert, Toots
See   Hibbert, Frederick

Hibernicus
See   Arbuckle, James

Hibernicus
See   Lecky, William Edward
Hartpole

Hibernicus
See   Lonergan, Thomas S.

Hiberno-Anglus
See   Dillon, [Sir] John Joseph

Hiccoeus
See   Hickie, Daniel B.

Hickes, George 1642-1715   [IP]
British clergyman and author
* [A] Dignify'd Clergy-man of the
   Church of England

Hickes, T.   [IP]
British pharmacist and author
* T. H., Pharmacop, Rustican

Hickey, James Harden   [IP]
Author
* Saint Patrice

Hickey, Michael Patrick 1861- ?
[PI]
Irish clergyman and poet
* [An] Irish Priest
* L. K. Y.
* M. P. H.
* Seamrog
* Viator

Hickey, Ross 1790- ?   [IP]
Irish clergyman and author
* Doyle, Martin

Hickey, William
See   Driberg, Thomas Edward Neil
[Tom]

Hickie, Daniel B. 19th c.   [PI]
Irish poet and editor
* Clonmeliensis
* Hiccoeus
* Tipperariensis

Hickling, George 19th c.   [IP]
British poet
* Rusticus

Hickman, Tom 1785- ?   [NN]
British boxer
* [The] Gaslight Man
* [The] Gasman

Hicks, Emilie Earle [Steele] 1820-
? [IP]
British author
* [A] Lady

Hicks, John H.
See   Farigoule, Louis

Hicks, Tyler Gregory 1921-   [CA]
American author and engineer
* Murphy, Louis J.

Hicks, William Watkin
1837-1915?   [DNA]
Author and publisher
* Light, Golden

Hickson, Mrs. Murray
See   Kitcat, Mrs. S. A. P.

Hidalla
See   Callanan, Jeremiah Joseph

Higginbotham, John C.   [NPS]
Author
* Agnus, Orme

Higginbottom, Nehemiah
See   Coleridge, Samuel Taylor

Higgins, John Calhoun Pinckney
1848-1914   [EWG]
American gunfighter
* Higgins, Pink

Higgins, Matthew James
1815-1868   [DLE1]
British author
* Paterfamilias
(See also base volume)

Higgins, Pink
See   Higgins, John Calhoun
Pinckney

Higgins, William 18th c.   [PI]
Irish poet and playwright
* W. H.

Higgins, Zoraster
See   Eggleston, Edward

[The] High Church Trumpet
See   Sacheverell, Henry

[The] High Constable
See   Lee, William

[The] High Constable of Letters
See   Barbey d'Aurevilly, Jules
Amedee

[The] High Priest of LSD
See   Leary, Timothy

[The] High Priest of Romanticism
See   Coleridge, Samuel Taylor

**[The] High Priestess of Washington
Society**
See   Beale, Betty

[A] High Private
See   Quincy, Samuel Miller

Hightower, Jim 1943?-
American editor and politician
* Hightower, Whole Hog

Hightower, Whole Hog
See   Hightower, Jim

Hildebrandt, Daniel
See   Hess, David

Hildesheim, Ferdinand 1811-1885
[JL]
German composer and conductor
* Hiller, Ferdinand

Hill, Agnes [Leonard] 1842-1917
[DNA]
American author and journalist
* Myrtle, Molly

Hill, Dana
See   Goetz, Dana

Hill, Flamingo
See   Hill, Virginia

Hill, George Canning 1835-1898
[DNA]
American author and journalist
* Myrtle, Lewis
(See also base volume)

Hill, Ike
See   Hill, Talmadge

Hill, Joe
See   Hagglund, Joel

Hill, [Sir] John 1716-1775   [NPS]
British author
* [The] Universal Butt of all
   Mankind
(See also base volume)

Hill, John 20th c.   [EF]
American football player
* Hill, Kid

Hill, John Stark 1950-   [FR]
American football player
* Hill, Otto

Hill, Kate F.
See   Baer, Mrs.

Hill, Kid
See   Hill, John

Hill, Otto
See   Hill, John Stark

Hill, Rowland   [NPS]
Journalist
* Rip

Hill, Talmadge 20th c.   [EF]
American football player
* Hill, Ike

Hill, Tom ?-1878   [EWG]
American gunfighter
* Chelson, Tom

Hill, Virginia 1916-1966   [LFW]
American narcotics peddlar
* Hill, Flamingo

Hiller, Ferdinand
See   Hildesheim, Ferdinand

Hiller, Flora
See   Hurd, Florence

Hilt, Prince
See   Bourbon, Louis Antoine de

Hilton, David
See   Wheeler, David Hilton

Hilton, Maud?
See   Howard, Adah M.

Hilu, Virginia 1929?-1976   [CA]
American editor
* Einhorn, Virginia Hilu

Hinchman, Hub
See   Hinchman, Hubert

Hinchman, Hubert 20th c.   [EF]
American football player
* Hinchman, Hub

Hincks, [Rev.] E.
See   Maginn, William

Hinds, John
See   Badcock, John

Hinton, Grassy
See   Hinton, J. W.

Hinton, Howard 1834-1920   [DNA]
American author
* Morley, Ralph

Hinton, J. W. 20th c.   [EF]
American football player
* Hinton, Grassy

Hippisley Coxe, Antony D[acres]
1912-   [CA]
British author
* Lacy, Charles

[The] Hippocrates of Our Age
See   Boerhaave, Hermann

His Father
See   Thurber, Charles

His Grandson
See   Harrison, George

His Intimate Friend
See   Lowell, John

His Mother
See   Johnston, Marianne C. [Howe]

His Noseship
See   Cromwell, Oliver

His Sister
See   Wilson, Jessie Aitken

His Wife
See   Cummins, Alexandrine
[Macomb]

His Wife
See   Lowe, Martha A. [Perry]

Historicus
See   Burr, William Henry

Hite, Robert Woodson ?-1882
[EWG]
American gunfighter
* Hite, Wood

Hite, Wood
See Hite, Robert Woodson

Ho Chi Minh [He Who Enlightens]
See Nguyen That Thanh

Hoare, Mad Mike
See Hoare, Michael

Hoare, Michael 1919?-
Mercenary leader
* Hoare, Mad Mike

Hoare, Robert J[ohn] 1921-1975
[CA]
British author
* King, Adam

Hobart, George Vere 1867-1926
[DNA]
Canadian-born author and playwright
* Bauer, Wright
* Lott, Noah
* McHugh, Hugh

Hobart, Robertson
See Lee, Norman

Hobbes, Thomas 1588-1679
[DEA, NPS]
British philosopher
* Our Malmesbury Philosopher
* R. R.
* T. H.
(See also base volume)

Hobbs, Aspasia
See Hubbard, Elbert

Hobson, Laura Z. 20th c.
American author
* Field, Peter [joint pseudonym with Thayer Hobson]

Hobson, Thayer 20th c.
American author
* Field, Peter [joint pseudonym with Laura Z. Hobson]

Hoch, Johann 1860-1906 [DI]
German-born American murderer and robber
* [The] Stockyard Bluebeard

Hocus, Humphrey
See Churchill, John [First Duke of Marlborough]

Hodge, Father
See Bacon, Roger

Hodges, California Bill
See Hodges, William

Hodges, John Frederick 1815-1899
[PI]
Irish poet and chemist
* Beta
* J. F.

Hodges, Thomas ?-1856 [EWG]
American gunfighter
* Bell, Tom

Hodges, William
American frontiersman
* Hodges, California Bill

Hodgkinson, John
See Meadowcroft, John

Hoey, Christopher Clinton
1831?-1885 [PI]
Irish poet and author
* Civis
* H.
* H-y

Hoey, John Cashel 1828-1892 [PI]
Irish journalist and poet
* C. H.
* Cu-Ulad
* D. F. B.

Hofer
See Magennis, Bernard

Hoffman, Arnold 20th c. [EF]
American football player
* Hoffman, Jake

Hoffman, David 1784-1854 [DNA]
American author and attorney
* Grumbler, Anthony

Hoffman, Jake
See Hoffman, Arnold

Hoffmann, E. T. A.
See Hoffmann, Ernst Theodor Wilhelm

Hoffmann, Ernst Theodor Wilhelm
1776-1822 [SFL]
Author
* Hoffmann, E. T. A.

Hogan, Ben
See Hagen, Benediel

Hogan, Michael 1832-1899
[DIL, PI]
Irish poet
* [The] Bard of Thomond
* M. H., Thomond
* Thomond

Hogarth, Charles [joint pseudonym with John Creasey]
See Bowen, [Ivor] Ian

Hogarth, Charles [joint pseudonym with (Ivor) Ian Bowen]
See Creasey, John

[The] Hogarth of Bavaria
See Pocci, Franz Von

Hogg, Cervantes
See Barrett, Eaton Stannard

Hogg, James 1770-1835
[DEA, NPS]
British author and poet
* [The] Boar of the Forest
* Craig, J. H.
(See also base volume)

Holbach, [Baron] Paul Henri Dietrich d' 1723-1789 [NPS]
French philosopher
* [Le] Premier Maitre d'Hotel de la Philosophie

Holberg, Louis [or Ludvig]
1684?-1754 [NPS, WGT]
Danish author
* [The] Father of the Danish Drama
* [The] Founder of Modern Danish Literature
* Klimius, Nicolas
* Mikkelsen, Hans
(See also base volume)

Holcroft, Thomas 1745-1809
[DLE1, NPS]
British author and playwright
* Vincent, William

Holden, [Willis] Sprague
1909-1973 [MA]
American author, journalist, educator
* Black, Montgomery

Holland, Denis 1826-1872 [PI]
Irish journalist and poet
* Abhonmor
* Allua
* Carleton, George
* D. H.
* H.
* Lamhdearg
* Le Reveur
* O'Callanan, David
* Otho

Holland, Mrs.
See Fleming, Alice Kipling

Holleman, Bo
See Holleman, Harlan

Holleman, Harlan 1927?-1982
Chairman of state Republican Party
* Holleman, Bo

Hollins, Dorothea [NPS]
Author
* North, Theophila

Hollister, Cash
See Hollister, Cassius M.

Hollister, Cassius M. 1845-1884
[EWG]
American law officer
* Hollister, Cash

Hollister, Edward Payson 1839-1877
American author and attorney
* E. P. H.

Holm, Bernard 20th c. [EF]
American football player
* Holm, Tony

Holm, Tony
See Holm, Bernard

Holme, Bryan 1913- [CA, SAT]
British-born American editor, publisher, author
* Francis, Charles

Holmes, Emra 1839- ? [PI]
Irish author and poet
* E. H.

Holmes, H. H.
See Mudgett, Herman Webster

Holmes, Harry Howard
See Mudgett, Herman Webster

Holmes, Isaac Edward 1796-1867
[BDSA]
American author and politician
* Caroliniensis

Holmes, James 20th c. [EF]
American football player
* Holmes, Pat

Holmes, Pat
See Holmes, James

Holmgren, Virginia C[unningham]
1909- [SAT]
American author
* Cunningham, Virginia

Holt, Harry
See Le Clerc, Clara

Holt, John Saunders 1826-1886
[BDSA, DNA]
American author and attorney
* Page, Abraham

Holt, Polly
See Le Clerc, Clara

Holt, William
See Maginn, William

Home, Cecil
See Webster, Julia Augusta

Homer [NPS]
Greek poet
* [The] Chian Father
* [The] Father of Comedy
* [The] Friend of Good Sense
* [The] Prince of Poets
(See also base volume)

[A] Homer of a Poet
See Scott, [Sir] Walter

[The] Homer of this Age
See Harvey, Gabriel

[The] Homer of Women
See Greene, Robert

Homer's Fastest Friend
See Perrault, Charles

Homidas-Peath, Sir
See Collin, Jacques Albin Simon

Homo Novus
See Courthope, William James

Honeycomb, Henry
See Hunt, [James Henry] Leigh

Honeycomb, William, Esq.
See Gardiner, Richard

Honie-Tongued
See Shakespeare, William

[The] Honorary Foreign Secretary to the Annual Friends' Society
See Forster, Thomas

[The] Honorary Secretary
See Hopkinson, J.

Honos Alit Artes
See Munday, Anthony

[The] Hook
See Hookstratten, E. Gregory

Hook, Theodore Edward
1788-1841 [DLE1, IP, NPS]
British author
* Allendale, Alfred, Esq.
* Tekeli
(See also base volume)

Hooke, Josiah [IP]
American educator and author
* [A] Citizen of New England

Hooker, Edward William 1794- ?
[IP]
American clergyman and author
* Her Father

Hooker, John [IP]
American attorney and author
* [An] Eminent Lawyer of Connecticut

Hookstratten, E. Gregory 20th c.
American attorney and television agent
* [The] Hook

Hooper, George W. [IP]
American author
* [An] Amateur

Hooper, Johnson J. ?-1863 [IP]
American attorney and journalist
* [A] Country Editor
(See also base volume)

Hooper, Samuel 1808-1875 [IP]
American merchant, statesman, author
* [A] Merchant of Boston

Hooper, Susan C. 19th c.   [IP]
American author
* Adrienne

[A] Hoosier
See   Hart, Adolphus M.

Hooten, Charles   [IP]
British author
* Thurland, Bilberry

Hope, Andree
See   Harvey, Annie Jane [Tennant]

Hope, Colonel
See   Hadfield, John

Hope, Elizabeth 1855-1919   [EOP]
Claimed to possess psychic powers
* D'Esperance, Elizabeth

Hope, [Lady] Esther
See   St. John, Percy Bollingbroke

Hope, Graham
See   Hope, Jessie

Hope, Grandmother
See   Knight, Mrs. Henry Gally

Hope, Jessie 20th c.   [NPS]
Author
* Hope, Graham

Hope, John 18th c.   [IP]
Scottish politician and author
* [An] Advocate of the Cause of the
  People

Hopkins, David ?-1814   [IP]
British author
* [A] Late Resident at Bhagulpore

Hopkins, Jeune
See   Hopkins, Squire D.

Hopkins, Samuel Miles 1772-1837
[IP]
American attorney and author
* [A] House Holder

Hopkins, Squire D. 19th c.   [SFL]
Author
* Hopkins, Jeune
* St. L., Vic

Hopkins, William 1706-1786   [IP]
British clergyman and author
* [A] Member of the Church of
  England

Hopkins-Jones, Lewis Brian
1942-1969   [CMA]
British musician
* Jones, Brian

Hopkinson, Francis 1737-1791
[DLE1, IP]
American jurist, author, statesman
* A. B. C. D. E.
* Grievous, Peter, Esq.

Hopkinson, J.   [IP]
British naturalist and author
* [The] Honorary Secretary

Hopkinson, Joseph 1770-1842   [IP]
American poet and jurist
* [An] American

Hopley, Catherine C.   [IP]
British author
* [A] Blockaded British Subject

Hopper, Clarence   [IP]
British author
* Ithuriel

Hopper, Claude
See   O'Carroll, Louis Ely

Hoppin, Augustus 1828-1896
[DNA, IP]
American author and artist
* Auton, C.

Hoppner, John 1759-1810   [NPS]
Painter
* Another Reynolds

Horace 1st c. BC   [NPS]
Roman poet
* [The] Prince of Lyrical Roman
  Poets

Horam, the Son of Asmar
See   Ridley, James

Horatius
See   Twiss, Horace

Horbery, Matthew 1707-1773   [IP]
British clergyman and author
* [A] Clergyman in the Country

Horlock, K. W.   [IP]
British author
* Scrutator

Horn, Otto
See   Bauerle, Adolf

Horn, Peter [Rudolf Gisela] 1934-
[CA]
Czech-born poet
* Skelton, Roger

Hornbook, Doctor
See   Wilson, John

Hornby, A. N. 19th c.   [EC]
British cricketer
* Hornby, Monkey

Hornby, Monkey
See   Hornby, A. N.

Horne, George 1730-1792   [IP]
British clergyman and author
* [A] Clergyman
* One of the People Called
  Christians
* [An] Undergraduate
* Z.

Horne, Henry, Jr.   [IP]
Author
* [An] American Indian

Horne, John 1736-1812   [NPS]
British politician and philologist
* [The] Macaroni Parson
(See also base volume)

Horne, Richard Henry 1803-1884
[DEA, IP]
British author, editor, poet
* Ben Uzair, Salem
* M. I. D.
* Watts, Ephraim
(See also base volume)

Horner, Frederick William 1854- ?
[NPS]
British author and politician
* Field, Martyn

Horner, J. C.
See   Horner, John Curwen

Horner, Joe 1849-1927   [EWG]
American gunfighter
* Canton, Frank

Horner, John Curwen 1922-   [CA]
Australian author
* Horner, J. C.

Horner, Mrs. Frederick   [NPS]
Author
* Teerius, Miss

Horning, Clarence 20th c.   [EF]
American football player
* Horning, Steamer

Horning, Steamer
See   Horning, Clarence

Horologist
See   Annet, Peter

Horos, Laura
See   Jackson, Editha Salomon

Horos, Theodore
See   Jackson, Frank Dutton

Horsley, T. J.
See   Curties, T. J. Horsley

Hortensius
See   Ramsay, D.

Hortibonus [or Hortusbonus], Is.
See   Casaubon, Isaac

Horton, Charles Johnson
See   Noyes, Edwin

Hosemann, Theodor 1807-1875
[WEC]
*German cartoonist, illustrator,
painter*
* [The] Gavarni of Berlin

Hoskins, Cyril Henry 1911?-
[EOP]
British author
* Kuan-suo, Dr.
(See also base volume)

Hoskyns, John 19th c.   [HFN]
Author
* [A] Physician

Hosmat, Hyton
See   Baker, William Deal

[The] Hot Headed Monk
See   Luther, Martin

Hot Sauce Saucier
See   Saucier, Kevin Andrew

Hotman, Francis   [UH]
Court jester
* Triboulet

Hotteterre, Jacques ?-1760?
[BBD]
French musician
* [Le] Romain

Houblon, James 1592?-1682   [NPS]
British merchant
* Pater Bursae Londoniensis

Houghton, Michael 20th c.   [EOP]
British poet and occultist
* Juste, Michael

Hound Dog Kelly
See   Kelly, James

[A] House Holder
See   Hopkins, Samuel Miles

Housman, Laurence 1865-1959
[DLE1]
British author, poet, playwright
* Bunny, Benjamin

Houston, Thomas 1777?-1803   [PI]
Irish poet
* Cudgel, Cuthbert

Houston, W. M. Chapman 20th c.
[PI]
Irish poet
* Mountjoy, Desmond

Hovey, Wayne
See   Johnston, William

Howard
See   Fay, Joseph Dewey

Howard, Adah M. 20th c.
Author
* Hilton, Maud?

Howard, Alfred 19th c.   [PI]
Irish author and poet
* Kelly, Paddy

Howard, [Lady] Catherine
1831-1882   [PI]
Irish poet
* C. P.

Howard, Charles 1746-1815   [NPS]
11th Duke of Norfolk
* [The] Jockey

Howard, Dosie
See   Howard, Robert

Howard, George
See   Leslie, George Leonidas

Howard, H. M.
See   Mudgett, Herman Webster

Howard, Henry 1515-1547   [NPS]
British poet
* Granville of a Former Age

Howard, Leigh
See   Lee Howard, Leon Alexander

Howard, Robert 20th c.   [EF]
American football player
* Howard, Dosie

Howe, Black Dick
See   Howe, Richard

Howe, Black Mike
See   Howe, Michael

Howe, Michael ?-1818   [DI]
British-born Australian bushranger
* [The] Admiral
* Governor of the Ranges
* Howe, Black Mike

Howe, Richard 1726-1799   [NPS]
British naval officer
* Howe, Black Dick

Howells, Roscoe 1919-   [CA]
Welsh author
* Barn Owl
* Brock, Ben

Howie the Horse
See   Samuels, Howard

Hsiang, Yeh
See   Liu, Sydney [Chieh]

Hsun K'uang 3rd c. BC
Chinese philosopher
* Hsun-tzu [Master Hsun]

Hsun, Lu
See   Shu-Jen, Chou

Hsun-tzu [Master Hsun]
See   Hsun K'uang

Hu Shih 1891-1962
*Chinese philosopher, statesman,
author*
* [The] Father of the Chinese
  Renaissance

Huang Ti [BBH]
Emperor of China
* [The] Yellow Emperor

Hubbard, Elbert 1856-1915 [DNA]
American author, editor, printer
* Hobbs, Aspasia
(See also base volume)

Hubburd, Oliver
See Middleton, Thomas

Huber, Francois 1750-1831 [NPS]
Swiss naturalist
* [The] Blind Naturalist

Hudon, Maxime 1841-1914 [DNA]
Canadian author, poet, clergyman
* Paris, Firmin

Hudson, Edward 1743-1821 [PI]
Irish poet
* [A] Patrician

Hudson, Robert 20th c. [DI]
British business executive
* [The] Soap King

Huetten, Ulric von
See David, Henry Winter

[El] Huevatero [The Egg Seller]
See Gil y Peire, Joaquin

Huff, Jacob K. 1851-1910 [DNA]
Poet and journalist
* Moses, Faraway

Hughes, Adelaide Manola [Mould]
1884-1923 [DNA]
Poet
* Monola, Adelaide

Hughes, Dorothy B[elle] 1904-
[CA]
American author
* Flanagan, Dorothy Belle

Hughes, John 1797-1864 [PI]
Irish-born clergyman, poet, author
* Leander

Hughes, John Reynolds 1857-1946
[EWG]
American law officer
* Border Boss

Hughes, Matthew F. 1834-1895
[PI]
Irish poet
* Conaciensis
* Francisco

Hughes, Terence McMahon
1812-1849 [PI]
Irish author and poet
* Albano
* Corney the Rhymer
* O'Niall
* [The] Red Hand
* Theta
* Turlough

Hughes, Thomas 1822-1896 [DEA]
British author and editor
* H.
(See also base volume)

Hughitt, Ernest 20th c. [EF]
American football player
* Hughitt, Tommy

Hughitt, Tommy
See Hughitt, Ernest

Hugo, Victor Marie 1802-1885
[NPS]
French author
* Auverney, Victor d'
(See also base volume)

Hugoni
See Young, Robert

Huguenin, Adele [NPS]
Author
* Combe, T.

Hull, Charles
See Charles, Gordon H[ull]

Hulten, Gustav Karl ?-1945 [DI]
British murderer
* Allen, [Lieut.] Ricky

[The] Human Bloodhound
See Kraus, Josef

[The] Human Rainbow
See Erto, Pasquale

[The] Human Wildcat
See Soto, Juan

Humbert, Albert 1835-1886 [WEC]
French cartoonist and illustrator
* Boquillon, Onesime

Humbert, Therese 1860-1916 [DI]
French imposter
* [La] Grande Therese

Humboldt, Gay
See Naramore, Gay Humboldt

Hume, David 1711-1776 [NPS]
Scottish philosopher and historian
* [The] Prince of Sceptics
(See also base volume)

Hume, John Ferguson 1830- ?
[DNA]
Author
* Niles, Willys

Hume, Ruth [Fox] 1922-1980
[SAT]
American author
* Irving, Alexander

**Humphrey [Duke of Gloucester and
Earl of Pembroke]** 1391-1447
[NPS]
Lord Protector of England
* [The] Protector
(See also base volume)

Humphrey, Buddy
See Humphrey, Loyie

Humphrey, Loyie 20th c. [EF]
American football player
* Humphrey, Buddy

Humphries, Richard 18th c. [RBE]
Boxer
* [The] Gentleman Fighter

Humphry, Mrs. C. E. [NPS]
Journalist and author
* Madge

Hunt, Aubrey 1788-1846 [PI]
Irish poet and playwright
* De Vere, [Sir] Aubrey

Hunt, H. L.
See Hunt, Haroldson Lafayette

Hunt, Haroldson Lafayette 1889-
[CR]
American industrialist
* Hunt, H. L.

Hunt, Isaac 1742?-1809 [DNA]
*Barbadian-born author, attorney,
clergyman*
* Retort, Jack

Hunt, Isaac 20th c. [EF]
American football player
* Hunt, Zeke

Hunt, John [NPS]
* Prince John

Hunt, [James Henry] Leigh
1784-1859 [NPS, SFL]
British author and poet
* Bacchus
* Honeycomb, Henry
* King Leigh
* Sprat, James
(See also base volume)

Hunt, Margaret 19th c. [NPS]
Author
* Beaumont, Averil

Hunt, Zeke
See Hunt, Isaac

Hunter, Bill
See Hunter, George

Hunter, Clingham
See Adams, William Taylor

Hunter, George 20th c. [EF]
American football player
* Hunter, Bill

Hunter, Harry
See Gould, James L.

Hunter, Joan
See Yarde, Jeanne Betty Frances
Treasure

Hunter, [Lieut.] Ned
See Ellis, Edward S[ylvester]

Hunter, Rodello
See Calkins, Rodello

Hunter, Valancy
See Meaker, Eloise

Huntington, Edward Stanton 19th
c. [SFL, WGT]
Author
* Stanton, Edward

Huntington, Faye
See Foster, Theodosia Maria [Toll]

Hurd, Florence 1918- [CA]
American author
* Harrowe, Fiona
* Hiller, Flora

Hurley, John J[erome] 1930-
[CA, TCCM]
American author
* Carpenter, Duffy
* Rafferty, S. S.

Hurlothrumbo
See Simpson, Thomas

Husar de Ayacucho
See Alcantara Herran, Pedro

Huss, John 1369?-1415 [NPS]
Bohemian religious reformer
* [The] Morning Star of the
Reformation

Hussein 1675?-1729 [NPS]
Shah of Persia
* [The] Nutmeg of Delight

[The] Hustler
See Liquori, Marty

Hutchinson, Ellen M.
See Cortissoz, Ellen M. H.

Hutchinson, John Hely
See Hely, John

Hutt, Mrs. W. [NPS]
Author
* Butt, Beatrice Mary

Hutton, G. M.
See Caird, Mona

Hutton, Hugh 1795-1871 [PI]
Irish clergyman, poet, author
* H. H.

**Hyde, Edward [First Earl of
Clarendon]** 1609?-1674 [NPS]
British statesman and historian
* [The] Chancellor of Human
Nature

Hyde, Ned
See Kenealy, Edward Vaughan
Hyde

Hyde, Thomas Alexander
1859?-1925 [DNA]
Scottish-born author and clergyman
* Double, Luke

Hynes, Alfred D. ?-1871
Author
* Ringwood, Ralph

I

I. A.
See   Atkinson, [Sir] Jasper

I. A.
See   Atkinson, John

I am Tear 'Em
See   Roebuck, John Arthur

I. H.
See   Fitzgerald, Francis Alexander

I. H.
See   Hewitt, John

Iago, William 1836- ?   [IP]
British clergyman and author
* W. I.

Ianthe
See   Ellenborough, Jane Elizabeth [Digby]

Ibn-Gabirol
See   Avicebron

Ibn-Tarkaw, Abou-Nasr-Mohammed ?- 954   [EOP]
Turkish scholar and musician
* Alfarabi

Ice Woman
See   Dixon, Medina

Ichabod
See   Buck, James Smith

Ida
See   White, Ida L.

Ide, Francis Otis [Ogden] 1853-1927   [DNA]
American author
* Ogden, Ruth

Ide, Simeon   [IP]
American author
* Their Wellwisher

[An] Idle Woman
See   Elliot, Frances [Minto]

[The] Idol of the Age
See   Rabelais, Francois

Idris Vychan
See   Jones, John

Ierne
See   Madden, Richard Robert

Ignatius of Loyola
See   Loyola y Balda, Ingio de

Ignoramus
See   Dryden, John

Ignoto Secondo
See   Beresford, Hamilton Sydney

Iliff, George   [IP]
British educator and author
* G. I.

Iliff, John Edgar 1852-1917
American author
* Edgefield, John

Ilin, M.
See   Marshak, Il'ia Iakovlevich

Ill-Fated Henry
See   Henry VI

[The] Illuminated Doctor
See   Taylor, Thomas

Illuminatus, Doctor
See   Taylor, Thomas

[The] Illustrious
See   Goethe, Johann Wolfgang von

Illustrious Conqueror of Common-Sense
See   Southey, Robert

[The] Illustrious Doctor
See   Marsh [or de Marisco], Adam

Illustrious Philip
See   Sidney, [Sir] Philip

Ilsley, Dent [joint pseudonym with Mary Hamilton (Ilsley) Chapman]
See   Chapman, John Stanton Higham

Ilsley, Dent [joint pseudonym with John Stanton Higham Chapman]
See   Chapman, Mary Hamilton [Ilsley]

Iminovici, Mihail 1850-1889   [CD]
Rumanian poet
* Eminescu, Mihail

Imlay, Talma 20th c.   [EF]
American football player
* Imlay, Tut

Imlay, Tut
See   Imlay, Talma

Immerito
See   Spenser, Edmund

Immortal Rebel
See   Cromwell, Oliver

[The] Impaler
See   Vlad V

[An] Impartial Hand
See   Allen, Thomas

Impartial Hand
See   Anderson, James

[An] Impartial Hand
See   Turner, Daniel

[An] Impartial Inquirer
See   Ralph, James

[An] Impartialist
See   Adams, Samuel

[The] Impious
See   Cromwell, Oliver

Imrie, Richard
See   Pressburger, Emeric

Inca-Pablo-Ozollo
See   Sears, Alfred Francis

Inchbald, Elizabeth [Simpson] 1756-1821   [IP]
British actress, playwright, author
* Elfrida

Inchiquin
See   Ingersoll, Charles Jared

Inchiquin
See   Southey, Robert

[The] Incomparable
See   Shakespeare, William

[An] Independent Whig
See   Almon, John

[The] Indian Aesop
See   Bidpai [or Pilpay]

Indian Charlie Cruz
See   Cruz, Florentino

[An] Indian Journalist
See   Knighton, William

Indiana, Robert
See   Clark, Robert

Indra Devi
See   Petersen, Eugenie

Induna
See   Townshend, Horace

Ingber, Elliot 20th c.   [CMA]
Musician
* Fingerling, Winged Eel

Ingersleben, Emilie von   [IP]
German author
* Rothenfels, Emmy von

Ingersoll, Charles 1805- ?   [IP]
American author
* [A] Citizen of Pennsylvania

Ingersoll, Charles Jared 1782-1862 [IP]
American statesman and author
* Inchiquin

Ingersoll, Joseph Reed 1786-1868 [IP]
American attorney, statesman, author
* [A] Northern Man

Ingham, Harvey A.   [IP]
American clergyman and author
* [A] Lover of the World

Ingham, Mrs. W. A.   [IP]
American author
* Hathaway, Anne

Ingleby, Clement Mansfield 1823-?   [IP]
British critic and philosopher
* Jabez

Inglis, Charles 1734-1816   [IP]
American clergyman and author
* [An] American
* Candidus
* Papinian
* [A] Son of Truth and Decency

Inglis, John ?-1850   [IP]
British author
* One of the Alumni

Inglis, John 1763-1834   [IP]
Scottish clergyman and author
* One of the Ministers of Edinburgh

Inglis, W.   [IP]
British author
* J. B.

Ingraham, Joseph Holt 1809-1860 [IP]
American clergyman and author
* Adina
(See also base volume)

Ingraham, Prentiss 1843-1904
American author
* King, [Midshipman] Tom W.
(See also base volume)

Ingram, James 1774-1850   [IP]
British clergyman and author
* J. I.

Ingram, John Kells 1823-1907   [PI]
Irish poet
* S. T. C. D.?

Ingram, Robert 1727-1804   [IP]
British clergyman and author
* [A] Country Clergyman

[An] Inhabitant
See Pownall, Henry

[An] Inhabitant of New England
See Morse, Jedediah

[The] Inimitable
See Waller, Edmund

Inkle, Mr.
See Anstey, Christopher

Inmerito
See Javitch, Daniel Gilbert

Innes, Cosmo [IP]
Scottish author
* C. I.

Innes, Duncan [IP]
Scottish author
* D. I.
* [A] Layman

Innes, William [IP]
British author
* [A] West India Merchant

Innsley, Owen
See Jennison, Lucy White

[The] Inquirer
See Atkinson, William

Insanguine, Giacomo [Antonio Francesco Paolo Michele] 1728-1795 [BBD]
Italian composer
* Monopoli

Inshtatheamba [IP]
Indian author
* Bright Eyes

Instaromnium
See Adams, Samuel

[The] Intellectual Eunuch
See Stewart, Robert [Viscount Castlereagh]

[An] Invalid
See Aspinall, W. B.

[The] Invincible Soldier
See Edward

Invisible Sam
See Vose, Reuben

Ionesco, Eugene 1912- [CR]
Rumanian-born playwright
* [The] Picasso of the Contemporary Drama

Ipolperroc
See Couch, Jonathan

Ireland, Alexander 19th c. [IP]
British author
* Philobiblos

Ireland, Joseph N. [IP]
American author
* [A] Play-Goer

Ireland, Patrick
See O'Doherty, Brian

Ireland, Shakespeare
See Ireland, William Henry

Ireland, William Henry 1777-1835 [HFN, IP]
British author
* De Boscosel de Chastelard, Pierre
* Fielding, Henry
* Ireland, Shakespeare
* Pen Dragon, Anser, Esq.

Ireland, William Henry (Continued)
* Sculptor, Satiricus, Esq.
(See also base volume)

Ireland, William W. [IP]
Author
* [An] Officer who Served There

Irenaeus 130?- 208? [NPS]
Saint
* [The] Gem of Asia
(See also base volume)

Ireton, Rollo
See Shirley, Ralph

[An] Irish Catholic Whig
See Gorman, Charles O.

[The] Irish Champion
See Langan, Jack

[The] Irish Charles Dickens
See Hartley, May Laffan

[An] Irish Exile
See McGee, Thomas D'Arcy

[An] Irish Gentleman
See Walford, Thomas

[An] Irish Gentleman Lately Deceased
See Maginn, William

[The] Irish Girl
See Parker, Sarah

[The] Irish Heiress
See Martin, Mrs. Bell

[An] Irish Helot
See Madden, Bernard Joseph

[An] Irish Land Owner
See Martin, Thomas

[An] Irish Missionary Priest
See O'Hanlon, John

Irish Molly
See Jobling, Charlotte

[An] Irish Police Magistrate
See Addison, Henry Robert

[An] Irish Priest
See Hickey, Michael Patrick

[An] Irish Traveller
See Twiss, Richard

[The] Iron Butterfly
See Reynolds, Mary Frances

Iron Irene
See Schroeder, Irene

Iron Mike Cochrane
See Cochrane, Gordon Stanley

Iron, Mrs. N. C. [IP]
American author
* Stella

Ironclad
See Enton, Harry

Irons, Lettie Artley ?-1875
American author and poet
* Prescott, Paul J.

Irons, William Josiah 1812-1883 [IP]
British clergyman and author
* [A] Bachelor of Divinity

Ironside, Nestor
See Croxall, Samuel

Irvin, Cecil 20th c. [EF]
American football player
* Irvin, Tex

Irvin, Tex
See Irvin, Cecil

Irvine, Alexander [IP]
Scottish clergyman and author
* [A] Minister of the Church of Scotland

Irving, Albert 20th c.
American basketball player
* Irving, Silk

Irving, Alexander
See Hume, Ruth [Fox]

Irving, Edward 1792-1834 [NPS]
Scottish clergyman
* Ariosto
* Boanerges
(See also base volume)

Irving, [Sir] Henry
See Brodribb, John Henry

Irving, Minna
See Odell, Minna

Irving, Silk
See Irving, Albert

Irwin, Thomas Caulfield 1823-1892 [PI]
Irish poet
* T. C. I.
* T. I.

Isaac, Heinrich 1450?-1517 [BBD]
Dutch composer
* Arrigo Tedesco [Henry the German]

Isabel
See Ritchie, Anna Cora [Ogden Mowatt]

Ishizuka, Sagen 19th c. [NAD]
Japanese physician
* Vegetable, Dr.

Ishmael
See Harris, Josiah

Isidore
See Ascher, Isidore G.

Isleno [Islander]
See Dominguez, Juan de Dios

[The] Italian Gluck
See Jommelli, Niccolo

[The] Italian Marryat
See Vecchi, Augustus Victor

Ith
See O'Connell, Maurice

Ithuriel
See Hopper, Clarence

Ivanhoe
See McCombe, W. J.

Iveagh
See Magennis, Bernard

Ivers, Hardinge Furenzo 19th c. [HFN]
Author
* [A] Roman Catholic
(See also base volume)

Iverson, Christopher 20th c. [EF]
American football player
* Iverson, Duke

Iverson, Duke
See Iverson, Christopher

Ives, John
See Garfield, Brian [Francis] Wynne

Ivy
See Stewart, Mrs. Dugald

Iyer, Kuppuswami 1887-1963 [EOP]
Indian leader of religious sect
* Sivananda, Swami

Izak
See Adams, John Isaac Ira

J

* Indicates Assumed Name

J.
See Frazer, John de Jean

J.
See Kickham, Charles Joseph

J. A.
See Abbott, Jacob

J. A.
See Adamson, John

J. A.
See Ady, John

J. A.
See Agg, John

J. A.
See Aikin, John

J. A.
See Albee, John

J. A.
See Anstey, John

J. A.
See Arbuthnot, John

J. A. S. C. de P.
See Collin, Jacques Albin Simon

J. B.
See Baillie, Joanna

J. B.
See Barrow, John

J. B.
See Bartlett, John

J. B.
See Bellows, John

J. B.
See Blackburn, J. B.

J. B.
See Boyle, John

J. B.
See Brenan, John

J. B.
See Brooke, John Charles

J. B.
See Budd, James

J. B.
See Budge, John

J. B.
See Inglis, W.

J. B. B.
See Burke, [Sir] John Bernard

J. B., Cork
See Brenan, Joseph

J. B. E. B.
See Bailliere, Jean Baptiste Emile

J. B. P.
See Payne, J. Bertrand

J. C.
See Carrick, John

J. C.
See Corey, John

J. C., jun.
See Courtenay, John, Jr.

J. C. M.
See Mangan, James Clarence

J. C., M.D.
See Colbatch, John

J. D.
See Davy, John

J. D.
See Dewhurst, Jane

J. D.
See Disturnell, John

J. E.
See Evelyn, John

J. F.
See Farrell, Joseph

J. F.
See Fitzgerald, Joseph

J. F.
See Forster, John

J. F.
See Hodges, John Frederick

J. F. M.
See Murray, John Fisher

J. F. O'D.
See O'Donnell, John Francis

J. F. T.
See Tuttle, Joseph Farrand

J. G.
See Browne, Thomas

J. G.?
See Sheehan, John

J. G. A. F.
See Forster, Johann Georg Adams

J. G. B.
See Bellett, John George

J. G. C.
See Close, John George

J. G. L.
See Lockhart, John Gibson

J. H.
See Harrington, James

J. H.
See Harrison, John

J. H. B.
See Buckingham, Joseph H.

J. H. B. M.
See Mountain, Jacob Henry Brooke

J. H. H.
See Hely, John

J. H. M.
See Monk, James Henry

J. I.
See Ingram, James

J. I. W.
See Wilson, John Iliffe

J. J. B.
See Bell, John Jay

J. J. T.
See Tayler, John James

J. J. W.
See Walsh, John

J. K.
See Jones, Walter

J. K.
See Keats, John

J. K.
See Keble, John

J. K. C.
See Casey, James

J. K. L. [James of Kildare and Leighlin]
See Doyle, James Warren

J. L.
See Leadbetter, J.

J. L.
See Love, John, Jr.

J. L. A.
See Anderdon, John Lavicount

J. L. M.
See Martin, J. L.

J. L. W.
See Watson, Jean L.

J. L'E
See Lestrange, Joseph

J. M.?
See Magin, Joseph

J. M.
See Marston, John

J. M.
See Martin, Josiah

J. M.
See Milton, John

J. M.
See Montgomery, James

J. M.
See Morgan, James

J. M.
See Murphy, James

J. M. A.
See Ashley, John Marks

J. M., Esq., F.R.S.
See Mortimer, John

J. M. R.?
See O'Ryan, Julia M.

J. McD.
See McDonald, James

J. McD.
See McDonald, John

J. N. D.
See Darby, John Nelson

J. N. McK.
See McKane, James Niall

J. O. B. C.
See Crowe, John O'Beirne

J. O. H.
See Halliwell, James Orchard

J. O'C.
See O'Callaghan, John Cornelius

J. O'H.
See O'Hagan, John

J. O'N.?
See O'Neill, John

J. P.
See Pedder, James

J. R.
See Ritson, Joseph

J. R.
See Ruskin, John

J. R.
See Ryan, James

J. R. A.
See Appleton, John Reed

J. R. C.
See Cormack, John Rose

J. R. H.
See Hakewell, James Ridgway

J. R., Jun.
See Ryland, John

J. R. L.
See Lowell, James Russell

J. S.
See Sheares, John

J. S.
See Shirley, James

J. S.
See Stewart, Jessie

J. S. A.
See Attwood, J. S.

J. S. D. S. P.
See Swift, Jonathan

J. T.
See Thomas, James, Jr.

J. T. B.
See Bottle, Joshua T.

J. T. B.
See Brockett, John Trotter

J. T. B.
See Buckingham, Joseph Tinker

J. T. C.
See Campion, John Thomas

J. T., D.D.
See Taylor, Jeremy

J. T., de Saint-Germain
See Tardieu, Jules Romain

J. T. K.
See Kelly, John Tarpey

J. T--n
See Maginn, William

J. U. U.
See Wills, James

J. V. B.
See Blake, James Vila

J. W.
See Walsh, John

J. W.
See Wauchope, John

J. W.
See White, James

J. W.
See Wilson, John

J. W.
See Wright, John

J. W. D.
See Dawson, John William

J. W., Deceased, in Usum Amicorum
See Wilson, John

J. W. L.?
See Lanktree, J. W.

J. W. L.
See Laughlin, John William

Jabez
See Ingleby, Clement Mansfield

Jacberus, Raymond
See Ash, M. Selby

Jack Boots
See Compton, Henry

Jack for the King
See Arundell, [Sir] John

Jack of Tilbury
See Arundell, [Sir] John

Jack the Dripper
See Pollock, [Paul] Jackson

Jack the Giant Killer
See Dempsey, William Harrison

Jackanapes
See Pole, William de la

Jackey Jackey
See Westwood, William John

Jackling, Thomas 1750-1791
[RBE]
British boxer
* Johnson, Tom

Jackson, Andrew 1767-1845 [BBH]
American president
* [The] Father of the Nashville
  Racecourse
(See also base volume)

Jackson, Barbara [Ward]
1914-1981 [CA]
British author, economist, political adviser
* Ward, Barbara

Jackson, Blockey
See Jackson, Frank

Jackson, Bricktop
See Jackson, Mary Jane

Jackson, Dalton Sharman 1950-
[FR]
American football player
* Jackson, Rusty

Jackson, Editha Salomon 1849- ?
[EOP]
American occult swindler
* Ananda, Swami Viva
* Angel Anna
* D'Arvie, Claudia
* Debar, Mrs. Diss
* Ellora
* Horos, Laura
* Madame Helena
* Montez, Editha Gilbert
* Solomons, Blanche

Jackson, Frank 1856- ? [EWG]
American gunfighter
* Jackson, Blockey

Jackson, Frank Dutton 20th c.
[EOP]
American occult swindler
* Horos, Theodore

Jackson, Gentleman
See Jackson, John

Jackson, J. P.
See Atkins, [Arthur] Harold

Jackson, John ?-1857 [PI]
Irish author
* Driscoll, Terry

Jackson, John 1769-1845
[NN, NPS, RBE]
British boxer
* Jackson, Gentleman

Jackson, Mary Jane 1836- ? [LFW]
American murderer and prostitute
* Jackson, Bricktop

Jackson, Rusty
See Jackson, Dalton Sharman

Jackson, Stephanie
See Werner, Vivian

[A] Jacksonian Democrat
See Sennott, George

Jacob, Eugene 1847-1942 [EOP]
French astrologer
* Star, Ely

Jacob, [Cyprien] Max 1876-1944
[TLC]
French author, poet, librettist
* David, Leon
* Gaelique, Morven le

[The] Jacobite Robber
See Whitney, James

Jacobs, Caroline Emilia 1872-1909
[DNA]
Author
* Elliott, Emilia

Jacobs, Susan
See Quinn, Susan

Jacobsen, J. P. 1847-1885 [NPS]
Danish naturalist
* [The] De Quincey of Danish
  Literature

Jacopetti, Alexandra
See Hart, Alexandra

Jacopo [or Giacomo] da Lentini
1180?-1240?
Italian poet
* [Il] Notaro

Jacotin
See Godebrie, Jacques

Jacqueline, [Sister]
See Grennan, Jean Marie

Jacques, Marie-Louise Victorine
[Grones] 1868- ? [LFW]
French murderer
* Myrtel, Hera

Jade, [Sir] John [NPS]
* Jehu

Jahn, Joseph Michael 1943- [CA]
American author
* Marshall, H. H.

Jahnsenykes, William
See Jenks, William

Jaidev
See Aandy, K.

Jake, T. C. S.
See Bangs, John Kendrick

Jakeman, Andrew 20th c. [CMA]
Musicians' business manager
* Riviera, Jake

James, Anthony
See Hanna, David

James, Buck
See James, Franklin

James, Croak
See Paterson, James

James, David
See Belasco, David

James, Franklin 1843-1915
[BLB, EWG]
American bank and trainrobber
* Colburn
* James, Buck
* Woodson, B. J.

James, G. P. R.
See James, George Payne
Rainsford

James, George Payne Rainsford
1799-1860 [WGT]
British author
* James, G. P. R.
(See also base volume)

James, Henry James
See Adams, Arthur Henry

James, Jesse Woodson 1847-1882
[BLB]
American bank and trainrobber
* Woodson
(See also base volume)

James, Martha
See Doyle, Mrs. James R.

James of the Sink-Hole
See De Voraggio, Giacomo

James, Police Captain
See Van Orden, William H.

James, Rick
See Johnson, James

James the White
See Butler, James

James I 1566-1625 [NN, NPS]
*King of England and Scotland [as
James VI]*
* [The] British Solomon
* [A] Prentise in the Divine Art of
  Poesy
(See also base volume)

James II 1633-1701 [NPS]
King of England
* [A] Second Constantine
(See also base volume)

James IV 1473-1513 [NPS]
King of Scotland
* [The] Star of the Stuart Line
(See also base volume)

Jameson, Judith
See Neyland, James [Elwyn]

[The] Jamestown Rebel
See Bacon, Nathaniel

Jane
See Hewitt, Mary Elizabeth

Jane, Paul
See Soust de Borkenfeldt, Adolphe
van

Janeczko, Paul B[ryan] 1945- [CA]
American author, poet, educator
* Wolny, P.

Janus
See Friedrich, Johan

Janus
See Le Bonnieres, Robert

Janvier, Thomas A. [NPS]
Author
* Black, Ivory

Japp, Alexander Hay 1839-1905
[DEA, NPS]
British author and editor
* Alexander, J. H.
* Gray, E. Conder
* Orme, Benjamin
* Page, H. A.
* Rose, A. N. Mount
* Scot, A. F.

Japrisot, Sebastien
See Rossi, Jean Baptiste

Jaquess, Lindel 20th c. [EF]
American football player
* Jaquess, Pete

Jaquess, Pete
See Jaquess, Lindel

Jarrold, Ernest
Author
* Finn, Mickey

Javal, Camille 1934- [CR]
French actress
* B. B.
(See also base volume)

Javitch, Daniel Gilbert 1941- [CA]
French-born author
* Inmerito

Jay, Charlotte
See Halls, Geraldine [Mary]

Jay, Edith K. Spicer [NPS]
Author
* Prescott, E. Livingston

Jay, G. S.
See Halls, Geraldine [Mary]

[The] Jealous Stoneybatter Man
See Williams, Richard Dalton

Jean Jacques
See Rousseau, Jean-Jacques

Jean le Cocq
See Gallus, Johannes

Jefferson, Janet
See Mencken, Henry Louis

Jeffrey, William
See Pronzini, Bill

Jeffries 19th c. [DI]
Scottish-born Australian murderer
* [The] Monster

Jehu
See Jade, [Sir] John

Jehu Junior
See Pellegrini, Carlo

Jelly, George Oliver 1909- [CA]
British author and poet
* Harsch, Hilya
(See also base volume)

Jemison, Louisa 19th c. [BDSA]
American writer
* Sinclair, Ellery

Jenkins, Wilberforce
See Bangs, John Kendrick

Jenks, Jacquetta Agneta Mariana
See Beckford, William

Jenks, William 1778-1866 [DNA]
American author and clergyman
* Jahnsenykes, William

Jennings, Patrick
See Mayer, Sydney Louis

Jennings, Thomas
See Maginn, William

Jennings, Wild Bill
See Jennings, William P.

Jennings, William P. 20th c.
American banker
* Jennings, Wild Bill

Jennison, Lucy White 1850- ?
[DNA]
Poet
* Innsley, Owen

Jenny
See Peel, [Sir] Robert

[The] Jenson of the North
See Ballantyne, James

Jephson, D. L. A. [EC]
British cricketer
* Jephson, Lobster

Jephson, Lobster
See Jephson, D. L. A.

Jer
See O'Donovan Rossa, Jeremiah

Jerrold, Douglas William
1803-1857 [NLC, NPS]
British author and playwright
* Punch, Mr.
* Q.
(See also base volume)

Jerry Sneak Russell
See Russell, Samuel

Jerry the Old Screw
See Bentham, Jeremy

Jesus Christ ?- 29? [PPN, UH]
Founder of Christianity
* [The] New Adam
* Prince of Peace
* [The] Second Adam
* [The] Sun of Righteousness
(See also base volume)

[The] Jewboy
See Davis, Edward

Jewett, John Howard [ICB]
Author
* Warner, Hannah

Jezreel, James Jershom
See White, James

Jimenez, Francisco ?-1891 [GS]
Spanish bullfighter
* Rebujina [Rumpus]

Jimenez, Juan 1783-1866 [GS]
Spanish bullfighter
* [El] Morenillo [Little Swarthy
One]

Jimenez Ripoll, Juan 1858-1899
[GS]
Spanish bullfighter
* [El] Ecijano [The Man from
Ecija]

Jimenez y Melendez, Manuel
1814-1852 [GS]
Spanish bullfighter
* [El] Cano [The Grey-Haired
One]

Jo
See Roddy, John Gerald

Joachim II 1505-1571 [NPS]
Elector of Brandenburg
* [The] German Hector
(See also base volume)

[The] Joan of Arc of Tennis
See Margot of Hainault

Jobbry, Archibald
See Galt, John

Jobling, Charlotte ?-1902 [PI]
Irish poet
* Cowan, C.
* Irish Molly

[The] Jockey
See Howard, Charles

Jocular Samson
See Canning, George

Jogand-Pages, Gabriel Antoine
1854-1907 [EOP, NPS]
French journalist
* Taxil, Leo

John 1167?-1216 [NPS]
King of England
* Sans Terre
(See also base volume)

John of Bologna 1530-1608 [NPS]
Italian sculptor
* [Il] Fiammingo

John of Enon
See Benedict, David

John R
See Richbourg, John

Johnny Behind-the-Deuce
See O'Rourke, John

Johnny the Mick
See Walsh, Johnny

Johnson, Ben[jamin] 1574?-1637
[NPS]
British playwright and poet
* [The] Father of Poets
* [The] Great Soul of Numbers
(See also base volume)

Johnson, Bud
See Johnson, Howard B.

Johnson, Dictionary
See Johnson, Samuel

Johnson, Donald Bruce 1909- [CA]
American author
* Johnstone, D[onald] Bruce

Johnson, Effie
See Richmond, Euphemia Johnson
[Guernsey]

Johnson, Emily Pauline 1860-1913
[DLE1]
Canadian poet
* Tekahionwake

Johnson, Evelyn 20th c.
American basketball player
* Sweet E's

Johnson, Fanny Kemble
See Costello, Mrs. Vincent

Johnson, Howard B. 1932- [CR]
American business executive
* Johnson, Bud

Johnson, Hugh 20th c.
*American army officer and
government official*
* Johnson, Ironpants

Johnson, Irish
See Johnson, John Henry

Johnson, Ironpants
See Johnson, Hugh

Johnson, Jack 20th c. [EWG]
American law officer
* Johnson, Turkey Creek

Johnson, James 1954?-
American musician
* James, Rick

Johnson, Jay
See Johnson, Oliver

Johnson, John Henry ?-1826
[NPS]
Impersonator
* Johnson, Irish

Johnson, Laura [Winthrop]
1825-1889 [DNA]
American poet
* Hare, Emily

Johnson, Magic
See Johnson, Richie

Johnson, Oliver 20th c. [EF]
American football player
* Johnson, Jay

Johnson, Rafer 1935- [CR]
*American track and field athlete,
sportscaster, actor*
* [The] Gentle Giant

Johnson, Richie 20th c.
American basketball player
* Johnson, Magic

Johnson, Samuel 1709-1784
[NN, NPS]
British lexicographer
* Asper
* [The] Blaspheming Doctor
* [The] Classic Rambler
* Easy, [Sir] Charles
* Great Caliban
* Johnson, Dictionary
* [The] Last of the Tories
* [A] Learned Attila
* Our Letter'd Polypheme
* Our Literary Whale
* [The] Respectable Hottentot
* Surly Sam
(See also base volume)

Johnson, Tom
See Jackling, Thomas

Johnson, Turkey Creek
See Johnson, Jack

Johnson, Van 1916- [CR]
American actor
* [The] Voiceless Sinatra

Johnson, W. B. [IP]
American author
* Boswell

Johnson, William 18th c. [IP]
British barrister and author
* [A] Barrister

Johnson, William 1823-1892
[DLE1]
British poet
* W. J.
(See also base volume)

Johnson, William Arthur 1952-
[FR]
American football player
* Billy White Shoes
(See also base volume)

Johnston, Andrew 19th c. [IP]
British author
* [An] Essex Justice

Johnston, Henry Erskine
1777-1830? [NPS]
Scottish-born actor
* [The] Scottish Roscius

Johnston, James 18th c.   [IP]
British author
* [A] Gentleman of Middlesex

Johnston, James Wesley
1847-1936 [DNA]
Irish-born author and clergyman
* Dale, Annan

Johnston, Keith 19th c.   [IP]
British author
* Keith, Leslie

Johnston, Mabel A. [Stevenson]
?-1945 [DNA]
Author and artist
* Marney, Suzanne

Johnston, Marianne C. [Howe] 19th
c. [IP]
American author
* His Mother

Johnston, Norma 20th c.   [CA]
American author and editor
* Harris, Lavinia
* St. John, Nicole

Johnston, Richard Malcolm
1822-1898 [IP]
American author
* [An] Old Man
(See also base volume)

Johnston, W. F. [IP]
American journalist
* Malakoff

Johnston, William 1829- ? [IP]
Irish author and politician
* Hovey, Wayne

Johnstone, Charles 1719?-1800
[IP, SFL, WGT]
Irish-born author and journalist
* [An] Adept
* Oneiropolos

Johnstone, Christina Jane [IP]
Scottish author
* Dods, [Mistress] Margaret, of
  Cleikum Inn, St. Ronan's

Johnstone, D[onald] Bruce
See Johnson, Donald Bruce

Johnstone, Edith
See Ruding, Mrs. Walter

Johnstone, George 18th c.   [IP]
British author
* Philorthos

Joilet, Charles 1832- ? [NPS]
French author
* Telio, J.

**Joinville, Francois Ferdinand Philippe
Louis Marie d'Orleans** 1818- ? [IP]
French author
* Trognon, A.

Jolly, Emily 19th c.   [IP]
British author
* E. J.
* Lady Who Prefers to be
  Anonymous

Jolyot de Crebillon, Claude Prosper
1707-1777 [NPS]
French author
* [The] Aeschylus of France

Jommelli, Niccolo 1714-1774
[BBD]
Italian composer
* [The] Italian Gluck

Joncieres, Victorin de
See Rossignol, Felix Ludger

Jones, A. J. 20th c.
American football player
* Jones, Jam

Jones, Absalom [IP]
American author
* A. J.

Jones, Arkansas Tom
See Daugherty, Roy

Jones, Brian
See Hopkins-Jones, Lewis Brian

Jones, Bullet
See Jones, Johnny

Jones, C. ?-1792 [IP]
British poet
* [The] Crediton Poet

Jones, Canada Bill
See Jones, William

Jones, Casey
See Jones, James

Jones, Charles A. 1815?-1851   [IP]
American poet and attorney
* Tinto, Dick

Jones, Charles Alfred 19th c.   [IP]
British educator and author
* C. A. J.

Jones, Charles Stanfeld 1886-1950
[EOP]
British occultist and author
* Achad, Frater
* Babe of the Abyss

Jones, Charley 1831- ?   [RBE]
Boxer
* [The] Black Wonder
* Travers, Bob

Jones, Clara Augusta 1839-1905
[DNA, WGT]
American author and poet
* Clara Augusta
* Strong, Hero
* Thorn, Kate
(See also base volume)

Jones, Cornelia [IP]
American author
* Sommers, Jane R.

Jones, David 18th c.   [IP]
British author
* D. J.

Jones, David 18th c.   [IP]
Clergyman and author
* [A] Welch Freeholder

Jones, Elizabeth Marina 20th c.
[DI]
British murderer
* Grayson, Georgina

Jones, Emma Garrison 1833-1898
American author
* Walraven, E. G.

Jones, Gentleman
See Jones, Richard

Jones, George [IP]
British author
* Cliffe, Leigh

Jones, Gertrude Warden 20th c.
[NPS]
Author
* Warden, Gertrude

Jones, Griffith Robert ?-1867   [IP]
Welsh author
* Lleyon, Gutto

Jones, Ignatius
See Worth, Gorham A.

Jones, Inigo 1573-1653   [NPS]
British architect
* Master Surveyor
(See also base volume)

Jones, J. P. [IP]
British clergyman and author
* Devoniensis

Jones, Jam
See Jones, A. J.

Jones, James 20th c.   [EF]
American football player
* Jones, Casey

Jones, James Athearn 1791-1854
[IP]
American author
* [An] Officer in the Army of
  Wolfe

Jones, James Thomas
See Leslie, Mary

Jones, John 1765-1827   [IP]
Welsh clergyman and author
* David, Ben
* Essenus
* Philalethes

Jones, John 1774- ?   [IP]
British poet
* [An] Upper Servant

Jones, John 1804-1887
Welsh biblical commentator
* Idris Vychan

Jones, John 1821?-1878   [NPS]
Welsh author
* Mathetes

Jones, John Andrew   [IP]
British author
* Andrew, of Mitchell Street

Jones, John Beauchamp 1810-1866
[DNA, IP]
American author and journalist
* [A] Rebel War Clerk
* [A] Roving Printer
* Shortfield, Luke
* [A] Squatter

Jones, John Matthew 19th c.   [IP]
British author
* [The] Naturalist

Jones, Johnny 20th c.
American basketball player
* Jones, Bullet

Jones, Joseph Stevens 1809-1877
[IP]
American actor and playwright
* Batkins, Jefferson Scattering

Jones, Lillie Mae 1930-
American singer
* Carter, Lorene
(See also base volume)

Jones, Mary 1700-1740 [LFW]
British pickpocket
* Diver, Jenny

Jones of Nayland
See Jones, William

Jones, [Dr.] Pleasant
See Starnes, Ebenezer

Jones, Richard 1779-1851   [NPS]
Actor and playwright
* Jones, Gentleman

Jones, Robert Baker 19th c.   [HFN]
British barrister and poet
* R. B. J.

Jones, Thomas 1530-1620?   [NPS]
Welsh poet and genealogist
* Moethu
* Twm Shon Catti

Jones, Walter 1722-1756   [PI]
Irish poet
* J. K.
* W. M.

Jones, William ?-1877   [BLB, DI]
British-born gambler and swindler
* Jones, Canada Bill
* [The] King of the Three Card
  Monte Players

Jones, William 1726-1800   [BBD]
British clergyman and musician
* Jones of Nayland

Jones, [Sir] William 1746-1794
[NPS]
British linguist
* [The] Admirable Crichton of His
  Day
(See also base volume)

Jonson, Ben[jamin] 1574?-1637
[NPS]
British playwright and poet
* [A] Rival to the God of Harmonie
* Torquatus
(See also base volume)

Jonsson, Olaf 20th c.   [EOP]
*Swedish engineer who claimed to
possess psychic powers*
* [The] Psychic Engineer

Jordan, Mrs. 1762-1816   [NPS]
*Actress and mistress of King
William IV*
* Little Pickle

Jordan, Mrs. Arthur
Author
* Aston, Helen

Jordan, Robert Furneaux
1905-1978 [TCCM]
British author
* Player, Robert

Jordon, Mildred Arlene 1918-
[MA]
American author
* Millicent

Jorrocks, John
See Surtees, Robert Smith

Jose, Arthur Wilberforce
1863-1934 [DLE1]
British-born Australian author
* Dare, Ishmael

Josef
See Sullivan, James Frank

Joseph, G.
See Griffin, Gerald

Josephine
See Heffernan, Michael J.

Josephus, Jr.
See Barry, Joseph

Josh
See Clemens, Samuel Langhorne

Jot, Joe, Jr.
See Bellaw, Americus Wellington

Jove's Poet
See Lover, Samuel

Jovial Bob Stine
See Stine, Robert Lawrence

Jowitt, Deborah 1934-   [CA]
American dancer, choreographer, translator
* Benson, Rachel

Joyce, Robert Dwyer 1830-1883
[PI]
Irish poet
* Feardana
* Merulan

[The] Joyous
See Van Aeken [or Van Aken], Hieronymus

Judas
See Ferguson, Robert

Judas
See Peel, [Sir] Robert

Judas 1st c.   [NPS]
Leader of Jewish uprising
* [The] Gaulonite
(See also base volume)

Judd, Winnie Ruth 1909-
[DI, LFW]
American murderer
* [The] Tiger Woman
* [The] Trunk Murderer

Judge Louis
See Bookhouse, Louis

[El] Judio [The Jew]
See Aramburgo Iznaga, Jaime

Judson, Edward Zane Carroll
1822?-1886
American author
* Cranston, Charles
* Edwards, Jules
* Garnet, Clew
* Manners, Julia
* Minturn, Edward
(See also base volume)

Julien, Charles-Andre 1891-   [CA]
French author and historian
* Delorme, Andre

[The] Jump King
See Basie, William

Jumpin' George Oxford
See Oxford, George

June, Caroline Silver
See Smith, Laura Rountree

June, Harold   [WGT]
Author
* Kateley, Walter?

Jung, Heinrich 1740-1817   [NPS]
German author and mystic
* [The] German Dominie Sampson
(See also base volume)

Junia
See Whitefoord, Caleb

[A] Junior Sophister
See Dexter, Samuel, Sr.

Juniper, Julius
See Foster, Thomas

Junius Americanus
See Lee, Charles

Junius Hibernicus
See Egan, John

Junius Redivivus
See Adams, William Bridges

Junius Secundus
See Kelsall, Charles

[The] Junk Food Professor
See Appledorf, Howard

Jupiter Placens [The Pleasant Jupiter]
See Brougham, Henry Peter

Jupiter Tonans [The Thundering Jupiter]
See Erskine, Thomas

Juriscola
See Coxe, Tench

Jurnak, Sheila
See Miller, Sheila

Juste, Michael
See Houghton, Michael

Justia, a Know-nothing
See Adams, Francis Colburn

Juvenis
See Arrowsmith, R. G.

Jymes, Elisabeth
See Adams, Betsy

K

K.
See Kearney, Patrick

K. of K.
See Kitchener, Horatio Herbert
[First Earl Kitchener of Khartoum]

Kadmus, G.
See Rawson, Albert Leighton

Kaffka, Johann Christoph
See Engelmann, J. C.

Kafu, Nagai
See Sokichi, Nagai

Kahl, Cy
See Kahl, Cyrus

Kahl, Cyrus 20th c.   [EF]
American football player
* Kahl, Cy

Kahlert, Karl F[riedrich]
1765-1813   [SFL, WGT]
Author
* Flammenberg, Lawrence
* Stein, Bernard

Kain, Saul
See Sassoon, Siegfried [Lorraine]

Kalisch, A. 1863- ?   [NPS]
British music critic
* Crescendo
* Staccato

Kamchi, David 12th c.   [NPS]
Jewish grammarian and clergyman
* Radak

Kamehameha I 1758?-1819   [NPS]
King of the Hawaiian Islands
* [The] Great
(See also base volume)

Kamien, Marcia 1933-   [CA]
American author
* Rose, Marcia [joint pseudonym
   with Rose Novak]

**Kaminsky [or Kominski?], David
Daniel** 1913-   [CR]
American entertainer
* Royalty's Favorite Entertainer
(See also base volume)

Kamo, Jigoro   [BBH]
Judo expert
* [The] Father of Judo

Kampov, Boris Nikolayevich
1908-1981   [CA]
Russian journalist and author
* Polevoi, Boris

Kane, Edward
See Knox, Kathleen

Kane, Henry 1918-   [TCCM]
American author
* McCall, Anthony

Kane, Jack
See Baker, [Allen] Albert

Kane, John P. 1860- ?   [PI]
Irish poet
* Alastor

Kane, Paul
See Simon, Paul Frederick

Kangaroo
See Cooke, [Sir] George

Kapel, Andrew
See Burgess, Michael Roy

Karman, Mal 1944-   [CA]
American author and screenwriter
* Ashe, Penelope

Karpinski, Stanislaw 1892?-1982
Polish aviator
* Poland's Billy Mitchell

Karu, Baruch 1899-1972   [CA]
Russian-born author and translator
* Krupnik, Baruch

Kateley, Walter?
See June, Harold

Katharine
See Stephens, Louise G.

Kati
See Rekai, Kati

Katz, Marjorie P.
See Weiser, Marjorie P[hillis]
K[atz]

Kaufman, Elaine 20th c.   [CR]
American restaurateur
* Elaine

Kaumeyer, Dorothy 1914-   [CA]
American actress and author
* Stanton, Dorothy

Kavanagh, Paul
See Block, Lawrence

Kavanagh, Rose 1859-1891   [PI]
Irish poet and author
* Ruby
* Uncle Remus

Kawashima, Yoshiko
See Eastern Jewel

Kay, Ellen
See DeMille, Nelson

Kaye, Barbara
See Muir, Marie Agnes

Kaye, Eff
See Konstam, F.

Kaye, John William 1840-1895   [PI]
British clergyman and poet
* Florence Marion K.

Kaye, Lorin [joint pseudonym with
Lorin Andrews Lathrop]
See Konstam, F.

Kaye, Lorin [joint pseudonym with F.
Konstam]
See Lathrop, Lorin Andrews

Kaye-Smith, Sheila
See Fry, Mrs. T. P.

Kayli, Bob
See Gordy, Robert

Kazan, Lainie
See Levine, Lainie

Kazinczy, Ferenc 1759-1831
Hungarian author and translator
* [The] Father of Hungarian
   Literary Criticism

Kearney, Patrick ?-1900?   [PI]
Irish poet
* K.

Keary, C. F. 19th c.   [NPS]
Author
* Matrice, H. Ogram

Keats, John 1795-1821
[DLE1, NPS, UH]
British poet
* Adonais
* Caviare
* J. K.
* Pestleman Jack

Keble, John 1792-1866   [DEA]
British author and translator
* J. K.

Keegan, James 1860-1894   [PI]
Irish-born writer and poet
* Fionn, Paistin
* Fionn, Pastheen
* Macaedhagain
* Orion

Keegan, John 1809-1849   [PI]
Irish poet
* [A] Man of 25

Keeling, Elsa D'Esterre 1860?- ?
[PI]
Irish writer and poet
* E. D. K.

Keelivine, Christopher
See Picken, Andrew

Keen, Allen 20th c.   [EF]
American football player
* Keen, Rabbit

Keen, Rabbit
See Keen, Allen

Keenan, Fannie
See Hand, Dora

Keene, Lieut.
See Rathborne, St. George

Keith, Alyn Yates
See Morris, Eugenia Laura
[Tuttle]

Keith, Leslie
See Johnston, Keith

Kelleher, Killer
See Kelleher, Michael Dennis
[Mick]

Kelleher, Michael Dennis [Mick]
1947-
American baseball player
* Kelleher, Killer

Keller, Fortunato 1686-1757   [BBD]
Italian composer and choral director
* Chelleri, Fortunato

Keller, Godfrey
See Keller, Gottfried

Keller, Gottfried 17th c.   [BBD]
German-born harpsichord teacher
* Keller, Godfrey

Kelley, Arthur Gordon 1912-   [CR]
*American radio and television
personality*
* Linkletter, Art

Kelley, Dwight 20th c.   [EF]
American football player
* Kelley, Ike

Kelley, Ike
See Kelley, Dwight

Kelley, Nora 1854-1938   [LFW]
American murderer
* Toppan, Jane

Kelly, Australian
See Kelly, James

Kelly, C. M. O.
See Gibbs, [Cecilia] May

Kelly, Clancy
See Kelly, Clarence

Kelly, Clarence 20th c.   [EF]
American football player
* Kelly, Clancy

Kelly, Denis 1841-1870?   [PI]
Irish poet
* Pendennis
* Sined

Kelly, Ed O. ?-1904   [EWG]
American gunfighter
* Kelly, Red

Kelly, Edward [Ned] 1854-1880
[CEC]
Australian gangleader
* [The] Last of the Bushrangers

Kelly, George C. 1849?-1895
[DNA]
American author
* Absinthe, Pere
* Payne, Harold

Kelly, George R. 1897-1954   [LFW]
American bootlegger and kidnapper
* Kelly, Pop Gun
(See also base volume)

Kelly, Hound Dog
See Kelly, James

Kelly, Isabella
See Hedgeland, Isabella Kelly

Kelly, James   [BBH]
American army officer and dog racing enthusiast
* Kelly, Hound Dog

Kelly, James 19th c.   [RBE]
Boxer
* Kelly, Australian

Kelly, James J. 1845?- ?   [PI]
Irish clergyman and poet
* Coman

Kelly, Jeanette
See Kelly, Mary Jane

Kelly, John Simms 20th c.   [EF]
American football player
* Kelly, Shipwreck

Kelly, John Tarpey 1864-1899   [PI]
Irish poet
* Ard-na-Erin
* Hi Many
* J. T. K.
* Slieve-Bloom

Kelly, Mary Anne 1825?-1910   [PI]
Irish poet
* Fionnuala
(See also base volume)

Kelly, Mary I. 1856-1884   [PI]
Irish-born poet
* O'Hanlon, Mary I.

Kelly, Mary Jane 1864?-1888   [BL]
Prostitute and murder victim
* Kelly, Jeanette

Kelly, Paddy
See Howard, Alfred

Kelly, Patrick
See Allbeury, Theodore Edward Le Bouthillier [Ted]

Kelly, Peter Burrowes 1811-1883
[PI]
Irish author
* [A] Member of the Irish Bar

Kelly, Pop Gun
See Kelly, George R.

Kelly, Red
See Kelly, Ed O.

Kelly, Shipwreck
See Kelly, John Simms

Kelsall, Charles 19th c.   [WGT]
Author
* Britannicus, Mela
* Junius Secundus
(See also base volume)

Kelsey, Jeannette Garr [Washburn]
1850- ?   [DNA]
Author
* Warren, Patience

Kelty, Mary Ann 19th c.   [HFN]
Author
* M. A. K.

Kemble, Frances Anne [Fanny]
1809-1893   [NPS]
Actress
* Ann of Swansea

Kemble, John Philip 1757-1823
[NN]
British actor
* Black Jack

Kemp, A. J. 19th c.   [HFN]
Author
* A. J. K.

Kemp, Bishop
See Kemp, M. C.

Kemp, Father
See Kemp, Robert

Kemp, M. C.   [EC]
British cricketer
* Kemp, Bishop

Kemp, Robert 1820-1897   [BBD]
American conductor
* Kemp, Father

Ken, Thomas 1637-1711   [DEA]
British author and clergyman
* T. K.

Kendal?
See Rolleston, Thomas William Hazen

Kendrick, John
See Bangs, John Kendrick

Kenealy, Edward Vaughan Hyde
1819-1880   [PI]
Irish writer and poet
* Hyde, Ned

Kenealy, William 1828-1876   [PI]
Irish poet
* William of Munster

Kennan, George Frost 1904-   [CR]
American diplomat and author
* Mr. X

Kennecott, G. J.
See Viksnins, George J[uris]

Kennedy, James 1855- ?   [BLB]
American murderer
* Kennedy, Spike

Kennedy, John Pendleton
1795-1870   [DLE1, DNA]
American politician and author
* Ambrose, Paul
(See also base volume)

Kennedy, Margaret
See Davies, Mrs. David

Kennedy, Patrick 1801-1873   [NPS]
Irish author
* Whitney, Harry

Kennedy, Rose
See Victor, Metta Victoria Fuller

Kennedy, Spike
See Kennedy, James

Kennedy, Studdart 20th c.   [PPN]
Clergyman
* Woodbine Willie

Kennedy, Thomas 1803?-1842   [PI]
Irish poet and barrister
* O'More

Kenny, Annie M. 19th c.   [PI]
Irish poet
* Stormy Petrel

Kenny, P. D. 20th c.   [NPS]
Author
* Pat

Kent, Constance 1844- ?   [CEC]
British murderer
* King, Emilie

Kent, Karlene
See Norton, Edith Eliza [Ames]

Kenyon, John 1812-1869   [PI]
Irish poet
* N. N.

Kenyon, Mildred Adams
1894-1980   [CA]
American author, journalist, translator
* Adams, Mildred

Kenyon, Orr
See Carter, Russell Kelso

Kern, Canyon
See Raborg, Frederick A[shton], Jr.

Kernan, Will Hubbard 1845-1905
[BDSA]
American poet and journalist
* Lamar, Kenneth

Kernighan, Robert Kirkland 1857-
?   [PI]
Canadian poet
* [The] Khan

Kerouac, Jan
See Hackett, Jan Michele

Kerr
See Pinnix, Hannah Courtney [Baxter]

Kerr, Carole
See Carr, Margaret

Kerr, Doris Boake 1895-1945
[DLE1]
Australian author
* Boake, Capel

Kerr, Sophie
See Underwood, Mrs. S. K.

Kerrigan, Michael ?-1895   [BLB]
American bankrobber
* Dobbs, Johnny

Kertland, William 19th c.   [PI]
Irish author and poet
* W. K.

Kessler, Joseph Christoph
See Koetzler, Joseph Christoph

Kettell, Samuel 1800-1885   [DNA]
American author and editor
* Short and Fat, Sampson
(See also base volume)

Kewen, Edward John Cage
1825-1879   [DNA]
American poet and politician
* Quillem, Harry

Keyber, [Mr.] Conny
See Fielding, Henry

[The] Khan
See Kernighan, Robert Kirkland

Khan, [Prince] Chioa
See Crowley, Edward Alexander

Khosru I [or Chosroes] 531- 579
[NPS]
King of Persia
* [The] Generous
(See also base volume)

Kickham, Charles Joseph
1828-1882   [PI]
Irish author and poet
* C.
* C. J. K.
* J.
* Momonia
* Mullinahone, K.
* Slievenamon

Kierman, Harriet 19th c.   [PI]
Irish author
* H. K.

Kiki of Montparnasse
See Prin, Marie

Kilgallen, Mary 19th c.   [PI]
Irish poet
* Merva

Kilkeevan
See Casey, John Keegan

[The] Kilkenny Man
See Campion, John Thomas

Killeen
See Plunkett, George Noble

Killen, James Bryce 1845- ?   [PI]
Irish author and poet
* Le Nord
* [A] Mere Irishman

Killester
See Rooney, William

Killin' Jim Miller
See Miller, James B.

Kilmartin
See Walsh, John

Kimmins, G. T.   [NPS]
Author
* Sister Grace

Kinder, Kathleen
See Potter, Kathleen Jill

Kineji, Maborushi
See Gibson, Walter B[rown]

[The] King
See Feigner, Eddie

King, Adam
See Hoare, Robert J[ohn]

King, Basil
See King, William Benjamin

King Dick
See Cromwell, Richard

King, Edward 1612-1637 [NPS]
Friend of British poet, John Milton
* Lycidas

King, Emilie
See Kent, Constance

King, Fay
See King, H. Lafayette

King, Godfre Ray
See Ballard, Guy W.

King, H. Lafayette 20th c. [EF]
American football player
* King, Fay

King, Jo
See Bellaw, Americus Wellington

King, Kennedy
See Brown, George Douglas

King Leigh
See Hunt, [James Henry] Leigh

[The] King of Dramatists
See Poquelin, Jean Baptiste

[The] King of Fire
See Thompson, Benjamin

[The] King of Folly
See Mortimer, Roger

[The] King of Hi-De-Ho
See Calloway, Cabell

[The] King of Inattention
See Arbuthnot, John

[The] King of Phrases
See Leclerc, Georges Louis [Comte de Buffon]

[The] King of Poets
See Spenser, Edmund

[The] King of Prussia
See Carter, John

King of the Arabesque
See Schroedter, Adolf

[The] King of the Badgers
See Shinborn, Max

[The] King of the Bankrobbers
See Leslie, George Leonidas

King of the Cannibal Isles
See De Rougemont, Louis

[The] King of the Commons
See Litster, John

[The] King of the English Poets
See Hayley, William

King of the Pianists
See Arrau, Claudio

[The] King of the Seaside Postcard
See McGill, Donald Fraser Gould

[The] King of the Three Card Monte Players
See Jones, William

King of the Witches
See Sanders, Alex

[The] King of Thrillers
See Wallace, Walter

[The] King of Torts
See Belli, Melvin M[ouron]

King, Richard Ashe [NPS]
Journalist and author
* Basil
* O'Brien, Desmond

King, Samuel
See Webb, John Joshua

King, Thorold
See Gatchell, Charles

King, Tom
See Ouick, Florence

King, [Midshipman] Tom W.
See Ingraham, Prentiss

King Tut
See Tutankhamun

King, Walter 20th c.
American leader of tribal village
* Adefumni, King Oba Oseijeman

King, William 1663-1712 [WGT]
British author
* Sorbiere, Monsieur

King, William Benjamin 1859-1928
[DLE1]
Canadian author
* King, Basil

Kingman, Dong
See Kingman, Tsang

Kingman, Tsang 1911- [CR]
American painter
* Kingman, Dong

Kingscote, Mrs. Howard [NPS]
Author and linguist
* Cleeve, Lucas

Kingsford, Jane
See Barnard, Charles

Kingsley, Henry 1830-1876
[DEA, DLE1]
British author
* Dixon, Granby

Kink, Emmanuel
See Dowling, Richard

Kinney, Elizabeth C. [Dodge] [IP]
American author and poet
* Stedman

Kip, Leonard [IP]
American attorney and author
* [A] Member of the Bar

Kip, William Ingraham 1811- ?
[IP]
American clergyman and author
* [A] Member of the N.Y. Geneal. and Biog. Society

[The] Kipling of Canada
See Service, Robert William

Kipling, Rudyard 1865-1936 [UH]
British author
* Avatar of Vishnuland

Kippis, Andrew 1725-1795 [IP]
British clergyman and author
* A. K.

Kirchhoffer, Henry 19th c. [PI]
Irish poet
* H. K.

Kirchmann, Jacob 1710-1792
[BBD]
German-born British harpsichord maker
* Kirkman, Jacob

Kirkland, Charles Pinckney 19th c.
[IP]
American attorney and author
* [An] Officer in the Field

Kirkman, Jacob
See Kirchmann, Jacob

Kirkwood, Robert [IP]
Scottish author
* Awl, Roby

Kirschner, L. 19th c. [IP]
American author
* Schubin, Ossip

Kirwan, Rose 19th c. [PI]
Irish poet
* Rose

Kiskadden, Maude 1872-1953
[FAA]
American actress
* Adams, Maude

Kissinger, Henry Alfred 1923- [CR]
American scholar and diplomat
* [The] Playboy of the Western Wing
(See also base volume)

Kister, W. H. [IP]
American journalist
* Raleigh, Richard

Kit
See Wilson, John

Kitcat, Mrs. S. A. P. [NPS]
Author
* Hickson, Mrs. Murray

Kitchener, Horatio Herbert [First Earl Kitchener of Khartoum]
1850-1916 [PPN]
British army officer
* K. of K.

Kitching, Mrs. H. St. A. [IP]
British author
* H. St. A. K.
* [A] Lady

Kitson, Alfred 1855-1934 [EOP]
British educator and leader of religious sect
* [The] Father of British Lyceums

Klaar, George 20th c.
Austrian-born advertising executive and author
* Clare, George

Kleiner, Rheinhart [WGT]
Author
* St. John, Randolph

Kleinschmidt, Black
See Kleinschmidt, Lena

Kleinschmidt, Lena 19th c. [CEC]
American thief
* Kleinschmidt, Black

Klencke, Hermann 1813-1881 [IP]
German physician and author
* Maltitz, Hermann von

Klenovsky, Paul
See Wood, [Sir] Henry J.

Klikspaan
See Kneppelhout, Jan

Klimius, Nicolas
See Holberg, Louis [or Ludvig]

Kn-Oxonian
See Allan, John

Knapp, Henry Ryder ?-1817 [IP]
British clergyman and author
* Peeping Tom

Knapp, John Leonard 1767-1845
[IP]
British naturalist and author
* [A] Naturalist

Knapp, Martin [IP]
American author
* Broadaxe

Knapp, Samuel Lorenzo
1784?-1838 [IP]
American author
* Ali Bey
* Robertson, Ignatius Loyola
* Shahcolen, a Hindu Philosopher Residing in Philadelphia

Kneeland, Abner 1774-1844 [IP]
American journalist
* A. K.

Kneppelhout, Jan 1814- ? [IP]
Dutch author
* Klikspaan

Knickerbocker, Jr.
See Suydam, John Howard

Knight, Ashton [IP]
Author
* Sarti, Signor

Knight, Charles 1791-1873 [IP]
British author and publisher
* S. T.
* Smith, Grandfather
* Von Bluggen, Vander
(See also base volume)

[A] Knight Errant
See Du Bois, Edward

Knight, Frances 1905- [CR]
American immigration officer
* [The] Dragon Lady

Knight, Frederick 1791-1849 [IP]
American poet
* [A] Student at Law

Knight, Henry Cogswell 1788-1835
[DNA, IP]
American poet
* Singleton, Arthur, Esq.

Knight, Mrs. Henry Gally 19th c.
[IP]
British author
* Hope, Grandmother

[The] Knight of Soho Square
See Banks, [Sir] Joseph

Knight, Olivia 1830- ? [PI]
Irish poet, author, translator
* Thomasine

Knight, Russ 20th c. [CMA]
American disc jockey
* Knight, Weird Beard

Knight, T. [IP]
British author
* T. K.

Knight, Ted
See Konopka, Tadeus Wladyslaw

Knight, Weird Beard
See Knight, Russ

Knighton, William   [IP]
British author
* [An] Indian Journalist

Knocksedan
See Rooney, William

Knott, Robert Rowe 19th c.   [IP]
British clergyman and author
* [A] Cambridge M. A.

Knowles, Frederic Lawrence
1869-1905   [DNA]
American author and editor
* Paget, R. L.

Knowles, James Sheridan
1784-1862   [DEA, PI]
Irish playwright
* Selim

Knox, David B.   [PI]
Irish poet
* Dalriada

Knox, John 1505-1572   [NPS]
*Scottish religious reformer and
author*
* [The] Calvinistical Pope
* [The] Firebrand of His Country
* That Religious Machiavel
(See also base volume)

Knox, Kathleen 19th c.   [PI]
Irish poet
* Kane, Edward

Knox, W. Mayne 20th c.   [PI]
Irish poet
* Argus I.

Koch, Ilse 1917-1971   [LFW]
German murderer
* [The] Bitch of Buchenwald
* [The] Red Witch

Koelsch, William Alvin 1933-   [CA]
American author
* Gay, A. Nolder

Koetzler, Joseph Christoph
1800-1872   [BBD]
German musician
* Kessler, Joseph Christoph

Kohon, Ethel [Chadowski]
1890-1946   [DNA]
British-born author
* Dow, Ethel

Koltzoff, Alexei Vasilievitch
1809-1842   [NPS]
Russian poet
* [The] Russian Burns

Konarsky, Matt
Miner
* Tchaikovsky, Telephones

Konopka, Tadeus Wladyslaw 1923-
[BP]
American actor and comedian
* Knight, Ted

Konovalov, Vassily
See Pedachenko, Alexander

Konstam, F. 19th c.   [NPS]
Author
* Kaye, Eff
* Kaye, Lorin [joint pseudonym
   with Lorin Andrews Lathrop]

Korff, Baron
See Domela, Harry

Korn, Friedrich 1803-1850   [WGT]
Author
* Nork, F.

Kornbluth, Cyril M. 1923-1958
[CA]
American author
* Towers, Ivar
(See also base volume)

Kossu-Aleksandravicius, Jonas
See Aleksandravicius, Jonas

Kostka, Jean
See Doinel, Jules

Koy, James Theo 20th c.   [EF]
American football player
* Koy, Ted

Koy, Ted
See Koy, James Theo

Krag, Mary Miller
See Wight, Emily [Carter]

Kramer, Roberta 1935-   [CA]
American author and poet
* Hart, Kate

Krantz, Philip
See Rombro, Jacob

Kraus, Josef 1892-   [EOP]
*Czech performer who claimed to
possess psychic powers*
* [The] Human Bloodhound
* [The] Man with Six Senses
* Marion, Frederick
* [The] Telepathic Phenomenon

Krause, Henry 20th c.   [EF]
American football player
* Krause, Red

Krause, Lyda Farrington
1864-1939   [DNA]
West Indian-born author
* Yechton, Barbara

Krause, Red
See Krause, Henry

Kray, Reginald [Reggie] 1933- ?
[DI]
British underworld figure
* [The] Quiet One

Kray, Ronald [Ronnie] 1933- ?   [DI]
British underworld figure
* [The] Colonel

Krebs, Karl August
See Miedcke, Karl August

Krishna Venta
See Pencovic, Francis Heindswater

Krislov, Alexander
See Lee Howard, Leon Alexander

Kroge, Suds
See Wardrop, David

Kron, Karl
See Bagg, Lyman Hotchkiss

Krupnik, Baruch
See Karu, Baruch

Krys
See Chrystal, Thomas B.

Kuan-suo, Dr.
See Hoskins, Cyril Henry

Kuczkir, Mary 20th c.
Author
* Michaels, Fern [joint pseudonym
   with Roberta Anderson]

Kuhlau, Friedrich D. R. 1786-1832
[NPS]
German composer and musician
* [The] Beethoven of the Flute

Kuhn, Charles Harris 1892-   [WEC]
American cartoonist
* Kuhn, Doc

Kuhn, Doc
See Kuhn, Charles Harris

Kuosa-Aleksandriskis, Jonas
See Aleksandravicius, Jonas

Kup
See Kupcinet, Irv

Kupcinet, Irv 1912-   [CR]
American columnist
* Kup

Kurigalzu I   [NPS]
King of Babylonia
* [The] Great

Kurten, Peter 1883-1930   [DI]
British murderer
* [The] Dusseldorf Vampire

Kushog Yogi of Northern Thibet
See Cannon, Alexander

Kuvalayananda, Swami
See Gune, Jagannath Ganesh

Kyd
See Clarke, J. Clayton

Kyd, Thomas 1557?-1595?   [DEA]
*British author, playwright,
translator*
* T. K.

L

L.
See Beltz, George Frederick

L.
See Littledale, Richard

L.
See O'Neill, John

L. A.
See Anthony, Louisa

L. A.
See Atthill, Lombe

L. C.
See Coleman, Lyman

L. D.
See Digges, Leonard

L. D. Y.
See Buckley, Michael Bernard

L. E.
See Pegge, Samuel

L. F. F. M.
See Miller, Lydia Falconer

L. G. C.
See Condon, Lizzie G.

L. K. Y.
See Hickey, Michael Patrick

L. M.
See Tucker, Eleonora C.

L. M. C.
See Cole, L. M.

L. M. J.
See Ellemjay, Louise

L. M. W. M., Rt. Hon.
See Montagu, Mary Wortley

L. N. F.
See Fitzsimon, Ellen

L. P.
See Munday, Anthony

L. P. W.
See Wright, Lucy Pauline

L. S.
See Stephen, [Sir] Leslie

L. S. A.
See Auger, Louis Simon

L. S. E.
See Gathercole, Michael Augustus

L. T.
See Twining, Louisa

L. W.
See Waldo, Leonard

L. W. J. S.
See Thisted, V[aldemar] Adolph

La Barr, Creighton
See Von Block, Bela

La Touche, Geoffry
See Snow, Theodore William

Laar [or Laer], Pieter van
1613?-1674?   [NPS]
Dutch painter
* [The] Deformed
(See also base volume)

Labat, Jean-Yves 20th c.   [CMA]
Musician
* Frog, M.

L'Abbe, Joseph Barnabe Saint-Sevin
See Saint Sevin, Joseph Barnabe

Laboulaye, Edouard 1811-1883
[NPS]
French author
* Alceste

Lacenaire, Pierre-Francois
1800-1836   [CEC]
French assassin, thief, forger
* Gaillard

[The] Lackey
See Leclerc du Tremblay, Francois

Lacy, Charles
See Hippisley Coxe, Antony
D[acres]

Lacy, John
See Darley, George

Lacy, Willoughby 18th c.   [PI]
Irish poet
* One Formerly Possessed of the
  Place

Ladner, Kurt
See DeMille, Nelson

[A] Lady
See Amory, Thomas

[A] Lady
See Anne

[A] Lady
See Austen, Jane

[A] Lady
See Battier, Henrietta

[A] Lady
See Bouligny, Mrs. M. E. Parker

[A] Lady
See Budge, Jane

[A] Lady
See Cursham, Mary Ann

[A] Lady
See Elliott, Charlotte

[A] Lady
See Fielding, Sarah

[A] Lady
See Gunn, Harriet

[A] Lady
See Gwynn, Albinia

[A] Lady
See Hicks, Emilie Earle [Steele]

[A] Lady
See Kitching, Mrs. H. St. A.

[A] Lady
See Mackenzie, Mary Jane

[A] Lady
See Martin, Mrs. E. Throop

[A] Lady
See Nicol, Martha

[A] Lady
See O'Brien, Mary

[A] Lady
See Plumptre, Annabella

[A] Lady
See Ritchie, Anna Cora [Ogden
Mowatt]

[A] Lady
See Wray, Mary

[A] Lady in England
See Tickell, Thomas

[A] Lady Lately Deceased
See Bowdler, Henrietta

[A] Lady of Boston
See Nickerson, Susan D.

[A] Lady of Fashion
See Blackwell, Miss

[A] Lady of Massachusetts
See Child, Lydia Maria [Francis]

[A] Lady of Massachusetts
See Foster, Hannah [Webster]

[A] Lady of New York
See Haight, Sarah [Rogers]

[A] Lady of Rank
See Bury, Charlotte Susan Maria
[Campbell]

[A] Lady of Rank
See Egerton, Mary Margaret

[A] Lady of Virginia?
See Elwes, A. W.

Lady Who Prefers to be Anonymous
See Jolly, Emily

Laelius
See Boswell, James

Laelius, Gaius 2nd c. BC   [NPS]
Roman general and statesman
* [The] Wise
(See also base volume)

Lagenevais, F. de
See Blaze, Ange Henri

Lageniensis
See Mangan, James Clarence

Laine, Gloria
See Hanna, David

Laird, Jean E[louise] 1930-   [CA]
American writer
* Drial, J. E.
(See also base volume)

Laire, Criad
See Rooney, William

Lake, Kenneth R[obert] 1931-   [CA]
British writer
* Market Man
* Mentor
* Roberts, K.
* Xeno
(See also base volume)

Lakeman, Stephen 1812-1897   [JL]
British army officer
* Mazar Pasha

Lalitananda, Swami
See Rego, Leonora

Lamar, Kenneth
See Kernan, Will Hubbard

Lamb, Charles 1775-1834   [NPS]
British author and poet
* Burton Junior
* [An] Eye Witness
* Old Honesty
(See also base volume)

Lamb, Mary 1765-1847   [NPS]
British author
* Cousin Bridget
(See also base volume)

Lambert, May 1876-1929   [LFW]
*Irish-born American bank robber
and swindler*
* Chicago May
* Churchill, May Vivienne
* Latimer, May
* [The] Queen of the Badgers

**Lambton, John George [First Earl of
Durham]** 1792-1840   [NPS]
British politician
* [The] Coal Master

Lamech
See Lynch, Michael

Lamhdearg
See Holland, Denis

Lamia
See Austin, Alfred

Lamme, Buck
See Lamme, Emerald

Lamme, Emerald 20th c.   [EF]
American football player
* Lamme, Buck

Lamoignon, Chretien 1644-1709
[NPS]
French politician
* Aristus

[The] Lamp of India
See Pandit, Vijaya Lakshmi

Lampman, Archibald 1861-1899
[DLE1]
Canadian poet
* [The] Canadian Keats

Lancaster, Lydia
See Meaker, Eloise

Lancaster, William P.
See Leicester-Warren, John Byrne
[Baron de Tabley]

Lancet
See McSwiney, Stephen Myles

Landor, Charles
See Stickney, Caroline

Landor, Walter Savage 1775-1864
[NPS]
British author and poet
* That Deep-Mouthed Boeotian
(See also base volume)

Landru, Henri ?-1922   [PPN]
French murderer
* Bluebeard

Landsfeldt, Countess
See Salomen, Edith

Lane, Chancery, Esq.
See Wilson, James Edwin

Lane, Denny 1818-1895   [PI]
Irish poet
* D. L.?
* Doinnall-na-glanna
* Donall-na-Glanna

Lane, Mary E. Bradley 19th c.
[SFL, WGT]
Author
* Zarovitch, [Princess] Vera

Lane, Plonk
See Lane, Ronnie

Lane, Ronnie 1948-   [CMA]
Musician
* Lane, Plonk

Lang, S.
See Stoddard, Richard Henry

Langan, Jack 1799?-1846   [RBE]
Irish boxer
* [The] Irish Champion

Langdale, Eve
See Craig, Evelyn Quita

Langey, Guillaume du Bellay
1491-1553   [NPS]
*French army officer, diplomat,
author*
* Ogdoades

Lanigan, George Thomas
1845-1886   [DLE1, PI]
Canadian journalist and poet
* Allid
* G. T. L.
* Toxopholite
(See also base volume)

Lanigan, William 1820?- ?   [PI]
Irish clergyman and poet
* Alpha

Lanihan, Peter 19th c.
American frontiersman
* Lanihan, Rattlesnake Pete

Lanihan, Rattlesnake Pete
See Lanihan, Peter

Lanin, E. B.
See Dillon, Emile Joseph

Lanktree, J. W. 19th c.   [PI]
Irish author and poet
* J. W. L.?

Lansford, Alex 20th c.   [EF]
American football player
* Lansford, Buck

Lansford, Buck
See Lansford, Alex

Lantern
See Marquis, Donald Robert Perry

Lanty the Flint
See Donnelly, James

Laracy, Larry
See Doherty, John

Larkin, Peter O'Neill 19th c.   [PI]
Irish poet
* P. L.

Larkin, Thomas 1795?-1850?   [PI]
Irish poet
* [The] Bard of Ballydine

Larkin, William
See Stiles, William Larkin [Billy]

Larrette, C. H. 1846- ?   [NPS]
Journalist and author
* Old Athlete

Larrowe, Marcus Dwight 1832- ?
[DNA]
Author
* Loisette, Alphonso

Larson, Frederic 20th c.   [EF]
American football player
* Larson, Ojay

Larson, Harry 20th c.   [EF]
American football player
* Larson, Pete

Larson, Ojay
See Larson, Frederic

Larson, Pete
See Larson, Harry

Larteguy, Jean
See Osty, Lucien Pierre Jean

Larwood, Joshua 19th c.   [HFN]
British author and clergyman
* [A] Sailor

Lary, Frank Strong 1931-
American baseball player
* Lary, Taters
(See also base volume)

Lary, Taters
See Lary, Frank Strong

Lasalle, George E.
See Ellis, Edward S[ylvester]

Lascelles, Robert   [NPS]
Author
* Piscator

Lassal, Ferdinand 1825-1864
[JL, UH]
*German political organizer and
theorist*
* Alvan, [Dr] Sigismund
* Lassalle, Ferdinand

Lassalle, Ferdinand
See Lassal, Ferdinand

**Lasseran-Massencome [Seigneur de
Montluc]** 1501-1577   [NPS]
French marshal
* [Le] Boucher Royaliste [The
Royalist Butcher]

[The] Last Gleeman
See Moran, Michael

[The] Last of the Bushrangers
See Kelly, Edward [Ned]

[The] Last of the Great Bohemians
See Rexroth, Kenneth

[The] Last of the Magi
See Constant, Alphonse Louis

[The] Last of the Parnassians
See Flecker, Herman Elroy

[The] Last of the Tories
See Johnson, Samuel

[The] Last of the Tycoons
See Eaton, Cyrus

**[A] Late Fellow of King's College,
Cambridge**
See Ashton, Thomas

[A] Late Graduate of Oxford
See Naghten, Frederick

[The] Late J. J. S., Esq.
See Anstey, John

[A] Late Noble Writer
See Burke, Edmund

[A] Late Resident at Bhagulpore
See Hopkins, David

**[A] Late Stipendiary Magistrate in
Jamaica**
See Bourne, Stephen

**[A] Late Very Learned and Reverend
Divine**
See Pegge, Samuel

Lathrop, Annie Wakeman 20th c.
[NPS]
Author
* Wakeman, Annie

Lathrop, Lorin Andrews 1858- ?
[NPS]
Author
* Kaye, Lorin [joint pseudonym
with F. Konstam]
(See also base volume)

Latimer, May
See Lambert, May

Latroon, M.
See Head, Richard

Lattin, Ann
See Cole, Lois Dwight

Lauchheimer, Alan 1906-1979
[CA]
American journalist and author
* Barth, Alan
* [The] Liberal Conscience of
Washington

Laughlin, John William 19th c.   [PI]
Irish clergyman and author
* J. W. L.

Laura Maria
See Robinson, Mary Darby

[The] Laureate of the Dago
See Daly, T. A.

[The] Laureate of the Nursery
See Rands, William Brighty

Laurel, Countess
See Battier, Henrietta

Laurent, Jacques
See Laurent-Cely, Jacques

Laurent, Marie-Jeanne
1744-1812?   [WFA]
French fashion designer
* Bertin, Rose
* [The] Minister of Fashion

Laurent-Cely, Jacques 1919-   [CD]
French author
* Laurent, Jacques
* Varenne, Alberic
(See also base volume)

Laurier, Silver Tongued
See Laurier, [Sir] Wilfrid

Laurier, [Sir] Wilfrid 1841-1919
Canadian statesman
* Laurier, Silver Tongued

Laurin, Anne
See McLaurin, Anne

Lavedan, Henri L. E. 1859- ?
[NPS]
French author
* Manchecourt

Laver, Rocket
See Laver, Rod

Laver, Rod 1938-   [CR]
Australian tennis player
* Laver, Rocket

LaVey, Anton Szandor 1930-
[EOP]
Leader of American religious cult
* [The] Black Pope

Lavi
See Diaz Cantoral, Manuel

Lavritch, Sophie Bentkowski 1905-
[EOP]
Russian-born editor and writer
* Bentkowski, Sophie
* Bentkowski-Lavritch, Sonia
* De Trabeck, Sophie

[A] Law Clerk
See Russell, William

Lawless, Eve?
See Finn, Frank Stanislaus

Lawlor, Denis Shine 1808-1887
[PI]
Irish poet
* Oscotian
* Oscotiensis

Lawrence, Frederick 1821?-1867
[HFN]
British author and barrister
* [A] Barrister

Lawrence, James
See Dillinger, John Herbert

Lawrence, Stacy 1928?-1982
American entertainer
* Stormy

Lawrence, Steven C.
See Murphy, Lawrence A[ugustus]

Lawrence, Thomas Edward
1888-1935   [DLE1, PPN]
British author, soldier, adventurer
* Ross, J. H.
(See also base volume)

[The] Lawrence Welk of American
Painting
See Rockwell, Norman Percival

[The] Law's Expounder
See Romilly, [Sir] Samuel

Lawson, Jacob
See Burgess, Michael Roy

Lawton, Ethel Chapin 1903-   [MA]
American author and poet
* [The] Poetry Lady

[A] Lawyer
See Stewart, [Sir] James

[A] Lay Baronet
See Martin, [Sir] Henry

Lay, Elzy
See Lay, William Ellsworth

[A] Lay Gentleman
See Lee, Francis

Lay Member of the British and
Foreign Bible Society
See Stokes, George

[A] Lay Member of the Committee
See Rivington, William

Lay, William Ellsworth 1862-1934
[EWG]
American gunfighter
* Lay, Elzy
* McGinnis, William

[A] Layman
See Abbott, Lyman

[A] Layman
See Adams, Samuel

[A] Layman
See Alderson, [Sir] Edward Hall

[A] Layman
See Alexander, Richard Dykes

[A] Layman
See Allen, John

[A] Layman
See Anderdon, John Lavicount

[A] Layman
See Bartlett, Bailey

[A] Layman
See Bayley, [Sir] John

[A] Layman
See Colebrooke, [Sir] George

[A] Layman
See Domville, [Sir] William

[A] Layman
See Gordon, Thomas

[A] Layman
See Gough, Richard

[A] Layman
See Heywood, Samuel

[A] Layman
See Innes, Duncan

[A] Layman
See Lowe, Solomon

[A] Layman
See Ribbans, Frederick
Bolingbroke

[A] Layman
See Stock, John Edmonds

[A] Layman
See Talbot, George Foster

[A] Layman
See Turner, Sharon

[A] Layman
See Waldo, Peter

[A] Layman
See Witherby, William

[A] Layman
See Wornum, Ralph Nicholson

[A] Layman of Boston
See Appleton, Nathan

[A] Layman of the Church
See Aytoun, William Edmonstoune

[A] Layman of the Church of England
See Watson, John

[A] Layman of the Church of Scotland
See Blackwood, Thomas

Layne, Pyngle
See Turner, J. Fox

Lazarro, Sofia
See Scicolone, Sofia Villani

Lazarus, Felix
See Cable, George Washington

Lazetich, Mike
See Lazetich, Milan

Lazetich, Milan 20th c.   [EF]
American football player
* Lazetich, Mike

Le Baron, Grace
See Upham, Grace Le Baron
[Locke]

Le Baron, Marie
See Urie, Mary Le Baron
[Andrews]

Le Bonnieres, Robert 1850-1895
[NPS]
French journalist and author
* Estienne, Robert
* Janus

Le Breton, Anna Letitia [Aikin] 19th
c.   [IP]
British author
* One of a Literary Family

Le Breton, Mrs. John
See Murray-Ford, Alice May
[Harte-Potts]

Le Breton, Thomas
See Murray-Ford, Thomas

Le Clerc, Clara 19th c.   [IP]
American author
* Holt, Harry
* Holt, Polly

Le Fanu, J[oseph] Sheridan
1814-1873   [WGT]
Irish author
* Figwood, John, Barrister-at-Law

Le Nord
See Killen, James Bryce

Le Normand, Marie 1772-1843
[EOP]
French occultist
* [The] Sybil of the Faubourg Saint
Germain

Le Reveur
See Holland, Denis

Lea, Fannie Heaslip
See Agee, Mrs. H. P.

Lea, Henry Charles 1825- ?   [IP]
American author and publisher
* Mizpah

Leach, Bone
See Leach, Richard Max [Rick]

Leach, Clifford
See Clark, Kenneth Sherman

Leach, Richard Max [Rick] 1957-
American baseball player
* Leach, Bone

Leadbetter, J. 19th c.   [IP]
British author
* J. L.

[The] Leader of the Modern Pharisees
See Gaetano [or Caetani],
Benedetto

Leamy, Edmund 1848-1904   [PI]
Irish poet
* Eos

Leander
See Hughes, John

Lear, Edward 1812-1888   [SAT]
British author and illustrator
* Derry Down Derry

[A] Learned Attila
See Johnson, Samuel

[A] Learned Gorilla
See White, Richard Grant

[The] Learned Knight
See Elyot, [Sir] Thomas

Leary, John 19th c.   [LFW]
American gang member
* Leary, Red

Leary, Red
See Leary, John

Leary, Timothy 1920-
American psychologist and author
* [The] High Priest of LSD

Leask, William   [IP]
British clergyman and author
* [A] Dissenting Minister

Leather Apron
See Pizer [or Kosminski?]

Leathes, Mrs. Stanley 19th c.   [IP]
British author
* M. G.

Leavitt, Ruby R.
See Rohrlich, Ruby

Lebeau, Eugene   [IP]
French poet
* Ruy-Blas, Eugene

Lebengood, Fungy
See Lebengood, Howard

Lebengood, Howard 20th c.   [EF]
American football player
* Lebengood, Fungy

Leberecht, Peter
See Tieck, Johann Ludwig

Lebert, Siegmund
See Levy, Siegmund

Lebrun, Camille
See Lebrun, Pauline Guyot

Lebrun, Pauline Guyot 1805- ?   [IP]
French author
* Dartigue, Laure
* Lebrun, Camille
* Saint Leger, Fabien de
(See also base volume)

Lechanteur, M. E.   [IP]
French author
* De Pontaumont

Lechmere, E.   [IP]
Author
* Stratford, Edmund

Lecky, Walter
See McDermott, William

Lecky, William Edward Hartpole
1838-1903   [DLE1]
Irish historian and author
* Hibernicus

L'Eclair
See Odum, Mary Hunt McCaleb

Leclerc
See De Hautecloque, Vicomte

Leclerc, Georges Louis [Comte de
Buffon] 1707-1788   [NPS]
French scientist, naturalist, author
* [The] King of Phrases

Leclerc, Louis 1799-1854   [IP]
French economist and author
* Celler, Ludovic

Leclerc, Victor
See Parry, Albert

Leclerc du Tremblay, Francois
1577-1638   [NPS]
French monk and diplomat
* [The] Lackey
(See also base volume)

Lecomte, Jules 1814-1864   [IP]
French journalist
* Du Camp, Jules
* Van Engelyom

Lederer, Rhoda Catharine [Kitto]
1910-   [CA]
British author
* Barrow, Rhoda

Lee, Abby [IP]
American author
* A. L.

Lee, Alfred
See Ferguson, John Clark

Lee, Ann 1736-1784 [NAD]
British-born religious leader
* Wisdom, Mother
(See also base volume)

Lee, Arthur 1740-1792 [IP, NPS]
American diplomat and author
* [An] American
* [An] American Wanderer
* Monitor
* [An] Old Member of Parliament
(See also base volume)

Lee, Charles 1731-1782 [IP]
British-born army officer and author
* Junius Americanus

Lee, Charles C.
See Rose, Martha Emily
[Parmelee]

Lee, Francis 17th c. [IP]
British author
* [A] Lay Gentleman

Lee, Frederick George 19th c. [IP]
British clergyman and poet
* F. G. L.

Lee, Henry Boyle 19th c.
[SFL, WGT]
Author
* M'Crib, Theophilus

Lee, Jesse 1758-1816 [BDSA]
American author and clergyman
* [The] Apostle of Methodism

Lee, John 1780-1859 [IP]
Scottish clergyman and author
* Alumni of the University of
   Edinburgh

Lee, Judy
See Carlson, Judith Lee

Lee, Mary Elizabeth 1813-1849
[IP]
American author and poet
* [A] Friend
(See also base volume)

Lee, Norman 1905-1962 [TCCM]
British author
* Hobart, Robertson
(See also base volume)

**Lee, Rachel Frances Antonina
Dashwood** 1770?-1829 [IP]
British author
* Philopatria
* R. F. A.

Lee, Richard Henry 1732-1794 [IP]
American statesman and author
* [The] Federal Farmer

Lee, Sarah [Willis Bowdich]
1791-1856 [IP]
British author
* [A] Traveller

Lee, Stannie
See Webb, Laura S.

Lee, Susan Richmond 20th c. [NPS]
Author
* Yorke, Curtis

Lee, William ?-1840 [IP]
American author
* [Un] Americain Citoyen

Lee, William (Continued)
* [The] High Constable

Lee Howard, Leon Alexander
1914-1979? [CA]
British author, editor, journalist
* Howard, Leigh
* Krislov, Alexander

Leech, H. E. S. [IP]
British author
* H. E. S. L.

Leech, John 1817-1864 [NPS]
Caricaturist
* Pen, A., Esq.

Leeds, Duchess of [NPS]
Author
* Carmarthen, K.

Leeds, William Henry [IP]
British architect and author
* W. H. L.

Lees, James Cameron [IP]
Scottish clergyman and author
* M'Rory, [Rev] Rory
* Rag, Tag, and Bobtail
(See also base volume)

Lee's Old War Horse
See Longstreet, James

Leese, George 19th c. [BLB]
American gangleader
* Leese, Snatchem

Leese, Snatchem
See Leese, George

Leeson, R. A.
See Leeson, Robert [Arthur]

Leeson, Robert [Arthur] 1928- [CA]
British author and journalist
* Leeson, R. A.

Lefevre, [Sir] George William
1797-1846 [IP]
British physician and author
* [A] Travelling Physician

Lefevre, Lily Alice 19th c. [PI]
Irish poet
* Fleurange

Lefroy, E. N. [NPS]
Author
* Fry, E. N. Leigh

Legge, Alfred Owen [IP]
British author
* One of her Sons
(See also base volume)

Leggett, William 1802-1839 [IP]
American journalist
* [A] Country Schoolmaster
* [A] Midshipman of the U.S. Navy

Legion
See Sullivan, Robert Baldwin

Legrand, Louis, M.D.? [joint
pseudonym with Orville J. Victor]
See Victor, Metta Victoria Fuller

Legrand, Louis, M.D.? [joint
pseudonym with Metta Victoria
Fuller Victor]
See Victor, Orville J.

Legurregui, Jose 17th c. [GS]
Spanish bullfighter
* [El] Pamplones [Man from
   Pamplona]

Lehmann, Rudolf Chambers
1856-1929 [NPS]
British author
* Vagrant
(See also base volume)

**Leicester-Warren, John Byrne [Baron
de Tabley]** 1835-1895 [DEA]
British author and poet
* Lancaster, William P.

**Leina, Wil. D', Esq., of the Outer
Temple**
See Wilson, Daniel

Leinad
See Crilly, Daniel

Leird, Henry J. 20th c.
Author
* Palmer, Tom

Leisurely Saunterer
See Eggleston, Edward

Lejeune, Anthony
See Thompson, Edward Anthony

Leland, John 1506-1552 [NPS]
British scholar and antiquary
* [The] Antiquarian Poet

Lemoine
See Didier, Eugene Lemoine

Lenard, Darryl 20th c.
American basketball player
* Lenard, Pee Wee

Lenard, Pee Wee
See Lenard, Darryl

Lenel
See O'Leary, Ellen

Lenihan, D. M. [PI]
Irish poet
* D. M. L.

[The] Lenny of the Seventies
See Thomas, Michael Tilson

Lentz, Harry 20th c. [EF]
American football player
* Lentz, Jack

Lentz, Jack
See Lentz, Harry

Leo, Andre
See Champseix, Mme.

Leon y Lopez, Juan 1788-1854
[GS]
Spanish bullfighter
* Leoncillo [Little Lion]

Leonard
See Perrugia, Vincenzo

Leonard, Ray 1956-
American boxer
* [The] Sugar Man
(See also base volume)

Leoncillo [Little Lion]
See Leon y Lopez, Juan

Leopold, Aldo 20th c. [BBH]
Hunter and educator
* [The] Father of Ecology

Leopold, Isaiah Edwin 1886-1966
[FAA]
American entertainer
* [The] Clown Prince of Comedy
* [The] Perfect Fool
(See also base volume)

Lepidus
See Gosset, Isaac

L'Ermite, Tristan 1405-1493
[NPS]
Servant of King Louis XI of France
* [The] Gossip

Lermontoff, Mikhail Yurievitch
1814-1841 [NPS]
Russian poet and author
* [The] Poet of the Caucasus

Leroy
See Roy, Hippolyte

Leskov, Nikolai Semenovich
1831-1895
Russian author
* Stebnitski

Leslie, Buckskin Frank
See Leslie, Nashville Franklin

Leslie, George Leonidas 1842-1884
[BLB]
American bankrobber
* Howard, George
* [The] King of the Bankrobbers
* Western George

Leslie, [Mrs.] Madeline
See Baker, Harriette Newell

Leslie, Mary 1842-1920 [DNA]
Canadian author and poet
* Jones, James Thomas

Leslie, Nashville Franklin ?-1925?
[EWG]
American gunfighter
* Leslie, Buckskin Frank

Lesser, Milton 1928- [CA]
American author
* Wilder, Stephen
(See also base volume)

Lester, John
See Werner, Vivian

L'Estrange, Corinne
See Hartshorne, Henry

Lestrange, Joseph 1775?- ? [PI]
Irish poet
* Brass Pen
* J. L'E

Leto, Pomponio
See Vitelleschi, Marchese

Lett, William Pittman 1810?- ?
[PI]
Irish-born journalist and poet
* Ryan, Sweeney

[The] Letter H.
See Halpine, Charles Graham

Levasseur, Marie Claude Josephe
1749-1826 [BBD]
French singer
* Levasseur, Rosalie
* Mlle. Rosalie

Levasseur, Rosalie
See Levasseur, Marie Claude
Josephe

[The] Leveller in Poetry
See Quarles, Francis

Lever, Charles James 1806-1872
[DEA, NPS]
Irish author
* Templeton, Horace
* Tramp, Tilbury
(See also base volume)

Levine, Lainie 1940-   [CR]
American singer
* Kazan, Lainie

Levy, Angelina 19th c.   [HFN]
Songwriter
* Angelina

Levy, Siegmund 1822-1884   [BBD]
German musician
* Lebert, Siegmund

Lewars, Mrs. Harold
Author
* Singmaster, Elsie

Lewes, Marian
See   Evans, Marian

Lewis, Alethea [Brereton]
1749-1827   [WGT]
British author
* De Acton, Eugenia
* [A] Person Without A Name

Lewis, Augustin
See   Austin, Lewis

Lewis, Caleb
See   Lewis, Edwin Herbert

Lewis, Charles 20th c.   [EF]
American football player
* Lewis, Mac

Lewis, Edwin Herbert 1866-1938
[DNA]
American author and educator
* Lewis, Caleb

Lewis, Ethelreda ?-1946   [DLE1]
South African author
* Baptist, R. Hernekin

Lewis, Frank 20th c.   [LFW]
American gangleader
* Lewis, Jumbo

Lewis, Harriet Newell 1841-1878
American author
* Constellano, Mrs. Illion
* Harrington, Grace D.
* Old Contributor [joint pseudonym
   with Julius Warren Lewis]

Lewis, John Frederick 1805-1876
[NPS]
British painter and etcher
* Lewis, Spanish

Lewis, John Woodruff 1835-1919
American author and poet
* Constellano, Juan
* Lewis, Juan

Lewis, Juan
See   Lewis, John Woodruff

Lewis, Julius Warren 1833-1920
American author
* Old Contributor [joint pseudonym
   with Harriet Newell Lewis]
* Piper, A. G.
(See also base volume)

Lewis, Jumbo
See   Lewis, Frank

Lewis, M. G.
See   Lewis, Matthew Gregory

Lewis, Mac
See   Lewis, Charles

Lewis, Matthew Gregory
1775-1818   [NPS, WGT]
British poet, playwright, author
* Dark Musgrave
* Lewis, M. G.

Lewis, Matthew Gregory
(Continued)
* [The] Monk
* [The] Prince of Dandies
(See also base volume)

Lewis, Spanish
See   Lewis, John Frederick

Lewis, Stuart 1756?-1818   [NPS]
Scottish poet
* [The] Mendicant Bard

Lewis, Tom 1940-   [CA]
American author, poet, editor
* Babcock, Nicolas

Leyne, Maurice Richard
1820-1854   [PI]
Irish journalist and poet
* Carrick-on-Suir, L.?
* M. R. L.
* Zozimus

Li Fei-kan 1904-   [CA, CLC]
Chinese author
* Pa Chin

Liberace, Wladziu Valentino 1919-
[BP]
American pianist
* Busterkeys, Walter
(See also base volume)

**[The] Liberal Conscience of
Washington**
See   Lauchheimer, Alan

Liberator of Rome
See   Gabrini, Niccolo

Libertas
See   O'Callaghan, Thomas
O'Donnell

[The] Librarian
See   Anastasius

Lichtveld, Lodewijk Alphonsus Maria
1906?-   [BBD]
*Surinamese author, poet,
playwright, composer*
* Lichtveld, Lou

Lichtveld, Lou
See   Lichtveld, Lodewijk Alphonsus
Maria

Licks, H. E.
See   Merriman, Mansfield

**Liddle, Christina Catherine Fraser
Tytler** 19th c.   [NPS]
Author
* Tytler, C. C. Fraser

Lien, Edirb Cam
See   McBride, Neil

Lieven, Prince
See   Domela, Harry

Light, Golden
See   Hicks, William Watkin

Lightfoot
See   Adams, John Isaac Ira

Lightfoot, Captain
See   Martin, Michael

Liholiho, A. 19th c.   [HFN]
Author
* [A] Haole

Lilburne
See   Ralph, James

Lilburne, John 1613-1657   [NPS]
British political agitator
* Sturdy John
(See also base volume)

Liles, Elvin 20th c.   [EF]
American football player
* Liles, Sonny

Liles, Sonny
See   Liles, Elvin

[A] Limb of Shakespeare
See   Fletcher, John

[The] Lime and Mortar Knight
See   Chambers, [Sir] William

Limey Stomper
See   Washington, George

Lincoln, Victoria 1904-1981   [CA]
American author
* Lowe, Victoria Lincoln

L'Inconnue
See   Benson, Janie [Ollivar]

Lind, Harry 20th c.   [EF]
American football player
* Lind, Mike

Lind, Mike
See   Lind, Harry

[The] Lindbergh of Russia
See   Herman, Victor

Lindsay, Alexander ?-1454   [NPS]
Fourth Earl of Crawford
* Beardie, Earl
* [The] Tiger Earl

Lindsay, Mayne
See   Clarke, Mrs.

Linkletter, Art
See   Kelley, Arthur Gordon

Linn, Buck
See   Linn, Charlie

Linn, Charlie 19th c.   [BLB]
American gunfighter
* Linn, Buck

Linskill, Mary 1840-1891   [NPS]
Author
* Yorke, Stephen

[The] Lion of Kent
See   Mynn, Alfred

[The] Lion of the North
See   Parr, George

Lipsian Dick
See   Harvey, Gabriel

Liquori, Marty 20th c.   [CR]
American track and field athlete
* [The] Hustler

L'Isle, Jean de
See   Daudet, Alphonse

Lismore
See   Walsh, John

[The] Listener
See   Wilson, Caroline [Fry]

[A] Literary Revolutionist
See   Warburton, William

[The] Literary Sir Plume
See   Dutens, Louis

[A] Literary Vassal
See   Byron, George Gordon Noel

Litster, John ?-1381   [NPS]
Leader of British peasants' revolt
* [The] King of the Commons

Little Arkansas
See   Hardin, John Wesley

Little Bill Raidler
See   Raidler, Bill

[The] Little Boatman
See   Wordsworth, William

[The] Little Dasher
See   Graham, H.

Little Davy
See   Garrick, David

Little Dick
See   West, Dick

[The] Little Doctor
See   Aubrey, William

[A] Little Druid-Wight
See   Pope, Alexander

[The] Little Giant
See   Albert, Carl

[The] Little Giant of Wall Street
See   Harriman, Edward Henry

[The] Little Girl from Little Rock
See   Channing, Carol

Little Jimmie Henderson
See   Henderson, Jimmie

Little Lepke
See   Bookhouse, Louis

Little Machiavel
See   Cooper, Anthony Ashley

[The] Little Man of Twickenham
See   Pope, Alexander

Little Michael Lord
See   Lord, Michael

Little Moses
See   Olajuwon, Akeem Abdul

Little Pickle
See   Jordan, Mrs.

Little Red Starkweather
See   Starkweather, Charles

[The] Little Sculptor
See   Roubillac, Louis Francois

[The] Little Wonder
See   Sayers, Tom

[The] Little Wonder
See   Wisden, John

Littledale, Richard 1833-1890   [PI]
Irish clergyman and author
* A. L. P. [A London Priest]
* B.
* B. T.
* D. L.
* F.
* F. R.
* L.
* P. C. E.
* P. P. B. K.

Littlepage, Cornelius
See   Cooper, James Fenimore

[The] Littlest Defector
See   Polovchak, Walter

Liu, Sydney [Chieh] 1920-   [CA]
Chinese author
* Feng, Chin

Liu, Sydney [Chieh] (Continued)
* Hsiang, Yeh

Live Again, Dr.
See   Rusk, Howard

Livingston, Carole 1941-   [CA]
American author
* Aphrodite, J.

Livingston, M. Jay
See   Livingston, Myran Jabez, Jr.

Livingston, Myran Jabez, Jr. 1934-
[CA]
American author, director, producer
* Livingston, M. Jay

Livingston, Patrick 1945?-
American FBI undercover agent
* Salamone, Pat

Livinus 7th c.   [NPS]
Saint
* [The] Apostle of Brabant

Lizzie
See   Condon, Lizzie G.

Ll. G.
See   Lloyd George, David

[A] Llanbrynmair Farmer
See   Roberts, S.

Llenodo
See   O'Donnell, Francis Hugh

Llewellyn, Edward
See   Llewellyn-Thomas, Edward

Llewellyn-Thomas, Edward 1917-
[CA]
British-born author
* Llewellyn, Edward

Lleyon, Gutto
See   Jones, Griffith Robert

Lloyd, David 1635-1692   [NPS]
Author
* Foulis, Oliver

Lloyd, Emma F. 19th c.   [HFN]
Author
* [A] Clergyman's Daughter
* E. F. L.

Lloyd, Flossie
See   Lloyd, John

Lloyd, Francis Bartow 19th c.
[BDSA]
American author, attorney, journalist
* Saunders, Rufus, The Sage of Rocky Creek

Lloyd, John 20th c.   [BP]
British tennis player
* Lloyd, Flossie

Lloyd, Wallace
See   Algie, James

Lloyd George, David 1863-1945
[PPN]
British prime minister
* Ll. G.
(See also base volume)

Llucen
See   Cullen, John

[A] Local Artist
See   Fernihough, John C.

Lochiel
See   Cameron, [Sir] Evan

Locke, John 1632-1704   [DEA]
British author and philosopher
* Philanthropus

Locke, Richard Adams 1800-1871
[WGT]
British-born American author
* Herschel, [Sir] John

Locke, Una
See   Bailey, Una Locke

Lockfast
See   Simmons, William Hammatt

Lockhart, Arthur John 1850-1926
[DNA]
Canadian-born author and clergyman
* Felix, Pastor

Lockhart, John Gibson 1794-1854
[DEA, DLE1]
Scottish author and critic
* J. G. L.
* [The] Scorpion
(See also base volume)

Lockwood, Ingersoll 1841-1918
[DNA]
American author, attorney, editor
* Longman, Irwin

Lodge, John 1801-1873   [BBD]
British poet and composer
* Ellerton, John Lodge

Loewe, Frederick 1904-   [PAC]
American composer
* Loewe, Fritz

Loewe, Fritz
See   Loewe, Frederick

Logan
See   Dillon, Thomas

Logan
See   Thorpe, Thomas Bangs

Logan, Black Jack
See   Logan, John Alexander

Logan, Jake
See   Smith, Martin William

Logan, John Alexander 1826-1886
[NPS, UH]
American army officer and statesman
* Logan, Black Jack
(See also base volume)

Logan, John Daniel 1869-1929
[DLE1]
Canadian poet, author, scholar
* Novicius, Aloysius

Logan, Olive
See   Sikes, Olive [Logan]

Loges, Francois de
See   Villon, Francois

[The] Loggerhead of London
See   Pitt, William [Earl of Chatham]

Loisette, Alphonso
See   Larrowe, Marcus Dwight

Lokman 5th c.   [NPS]
Arabic philosopher
* [The] Aesop of Arabia

[Il] Londinese
See   Sammartini [or San Martini], Giuseppe

London Antiquary
See   Fairholt, F. W.

London, Babe
See   London, Jean

London, Jean 1901?-1980   [FIR]
Entertainer
* London, Babe

London Little-Grace
See   Bonner, Edmund

[A] London Merchant
See   Stokes, C. W.

[A] London Physician
See   Dickson, Samuel Henry

[A] Londoner
See   White, Walter

[The] Lonely Hearts Killer
See   Fernandez, Raymond

Lonergan, Thomas S. 1861- ?   [PI]
Irish-born poet and journalist
* Hibernicus

Long Ben Every
See   Every, Henry

Long, Big Steve
See   Long, Steve

Long, Edward ?-1809   [IP]
British author
* Cleon

Long, Edward 1734-1813   [IP]
British author
* Babble, Nicholas, Esq.
* [A] Planter

Long, George 1800- ?   [IP]
British scholar
* [A] Member of the University of Cambridge

Long, Isaac 1899?-
American banker
* Long, Zack

Long John
See   Long, John [Jack]

Long, John [Jack] 19th c.   [EWG]
American law officer
* Long John

Long Liz Stride
See   Stride, Elizabeth

Long, Roger 1680-1770   [IP]
British clergyman, astronomer, author
* Dicaiophilus Cantabrigiensis

Long, Silent
See   Lynch, Thomas Took

Long, Steve ?-1868   [EWG]
American gunfighter
* Long, Big Steve

Long, Zack
See   Long, Isaac

Longfellow, Henry Wadsworth
1807-1882   [IP]
American poet
* [An] American
* Strongfellow, Professor
(See also base volume)

Longhaired Jim Courtright
See   Courtright, Timothy Isaiah

Longley, John   [IP]
British barrister and author
* [An] Eminent English Counsel

Longley, Wild Bill
See   Longley, William Preston

Longley, William Preston
1850?-1878   [DI, EWG]
American murderer and bandit
* Black, William
* Longley, Wild Bill
* Patterson, Jim

Longman, Irwin
See   Lockwood, Ingersoll

Longstreet, James 1821-1904
[BDSA]
American army officer and author
* Lee's Old War Horse
(See also base volume)

Longueville, Peter 18th c.   [WGT]
Author
* Dorrington, Edward?

Longueville, T.   [NPS]
Author
* [The] Prig

Longworth, Alice Roosevelt
1884?-1980   [CR]
Daughter of American president, Theodore Roosevelt
* Mrs. L.
(See also base volume)

Looker, O. N.
See   Urner, Nathan D.

Looker-On
See   Meldrum, David S.

Looker-On
See   Stainton, J.

[A] Looker-On-Here in Vienna
See   Andersen, Mary E.

Loomis, George Washington, Jr.
1813-1865   [BLB]
American murderer and robber
* Loomis, Wash

Loomis, Wash
See   Loomis, George Washington, Jr.

Lopate, Carol
See   Ascher, Carol

Lopes, Baltasar 1907-   [CD]
Portuguese author and poet
* Alcanbara, Osvaldo

Lopez, Angel 1825-1898   [GS]
Spanish bullfighter
* [El] Regatero [The Haggler]

Lopez, Aurelio Alejandro 1948-
Mexican-born baseball player
* Lopez, Lopey
(See also base volume)

Lopez, Lopey
See   Lopez, Aurelio Alejandro

Lora, Josephine
See   Alexander, Josephine

Lord B.
See   Brougham, Henry Peter

[The] Lord Chesterfield of Italy
See   Della Casa, Giovanni

Lord Chief Commissioner
See   Adam, William

Lord, John Keast 19th c.   [IP]
British author
* [The] Wanderer

Lord, Little Michael
See Lord, Michael

Lord M.
See Morres, Hervey Redmond

Lord, M. L.
See Christian, Sydney

Lord, Michael 1973?-
American child evangelist and faith healer
* Lord, Little Michael

Lord, Nathan 1793-1870   [IP]
American clergyman and author
* [A] Northern Presbyter

[The] Lord of Irony
See Arouet, Francois Marie

Lord, Phillips H.
See Yolen, Will [Hyatt]

Lord S.
See Addington, Henry [First Viscount Sidmouth]

Lord, W. B. 19th c.   [IP]
British artist
* W. B. L.

Lorimer, John Gordon   [IP]
Scottish clergyman and author
* [A] Churchman

[The] Lost Leader
See Wordsworth, William

Lothian, Maurice   [IP]
Scottish barrister and author
* [A] Sincere Friend of the People

Lotinga, W.   [NPS]
Author
* Lynx, Larry
* Magpie

Lott, Noah
See Hobart, George Vere

Lou
See Van Voorthuizen [or Voorthuyzen], Louwrens

Loudon, John Claudius 1783-1843
[IP]
Scottish author
* [A] Scottish Farmer and Land Agent

Louis IV 921- 954   [NPS]
King of France
* From Beyond the Seas
(See also base volume)

Louis XIV 1638-1715   [NPS]
King of France
* Augustus
* [The] Gallic Pharaoh
* [Le] Grand
(See also base volume)

Louis XV 1710-1774   [IP]
King of France
* Zeokinizul
(See also base volume)

[A] Lounger
See Bromet, William

Lourdoneix, Paul de   [IP]
French author
* Pierre et Paul

Love, James
See Dance, James

Love, John, Jr. 18th c.   [IP]
British author
* J. L.

Love, Nat 19th c.
American cowboy and gunfighter
* Deadwood Dick

Lovechild, Laurence
See Fenn, Eleanor

Lovechild, Solomon
See Fenn, Eleanor

Lovecraft, Howard Phillips
1890-1937   [CA, TLC]
American author
* Gent
* Softly, Edgar
* Willie, Frederick
(See also base volume)

Loveday, John 1742-1809   [IP]
British author
* Antiquarius
* Vindex
(See also base volume)

Lovejoy, Mary Evelyn [Wood]
1847-1928   [DNA]
American author and historian
* Traine, Gypsey

Lovel, Robert   [IP]
British poet
* Moschus

Lovell, Francis 1454-1487   [NN]
Lord Chamberlain to King Richard III of England
* [The] Dog

Lovell, John 1835- ?   [IP]
British journalist
* Zeta

Lovell, Our Dogge
See Francis

Lovemore, [Sir] Charles
See Manley, Mary de la Riviere

[A] Lover of Christ
See Ryland, John Collett

[A] Lover of her Sex
See Astell, Mary

[A] Lover of his Country
See Macintosh, William

[A] Lover of Mankind
See Benezet, Anthony

[A] Lover of Peace and Truth in this Church
See Adams, James

[A] Lover of the Church of England
See Drewe, Patrick

[A] Lover of the Protestant Religion
See Wright, William

[A] Lover of the World
See Ingham, Harvey A.

[A] Lover of Truth
See Wilson, David

[A] Lover of Truth and Liberty
See Ralph, James

Lover, Samuel 1797-1868
[DEA, NPS, PI]
Irish musician, painter, songwriter, author
* Jove's Poet
* Trovato, Ben

Lovering, John 1788- ?   [IP]
American author
* Notional, Nehemiah

Lovett, John 1765-1818   [IP]
American poet
* [A] Washingtonian

Lovin, Roger Robert 1941-   [CA]
American writer
* Clemens, Rodgers
(See also base volume)

Loving, Cockeyed Frank
See Loving, Frank

Loving, Frank 1854?-1882   [EWG]
American gunfighter
* Loving, Cockeyed Frank

Low, Mary   [IP]
British author
* Aunt Mary

Low, Samuel 1765- ?   [IP]
American poet and playwright
* [An] American

Lowe, Bull
See Lowe, George

Lowe, George 20th c.   [EF]
American football player
* Lowe, Bull

Lowe, [Sir] Hudson 1769-1844
[NPS]
Governor of St. Helena
* Turnkey

Lowe, Joseph 1845?-1899?
[BLB, EWG]
American gunfighter
* Lowe, Rowdy Joe

Lowe, Martha A. [Perry]   [IP]
American poet
* His Wife

Lowe, Rowdy Joe
See Lowe, Joseph

Lowe, Solomon 18th c.   [IP]
British author
* [A] Layman

Lowe, Victoria Lincoln
See Lincoln, Victoria

Lowell, Francis Cabot 1855-1911
[DNA]
American author and jurist
* Orne, Philip

Lowell, James Russell 1819-1891
[HFN, IP]
American author, poet, diplomat
* Elmwood
* J. R. L.
* Nye, Columbus
(See also base volume)

Lowell, John 1769-1840   [IP]
American attorney and author
* [An] Alumnus of that College
* His Intimate Friend
(See also base volume)

Lowndes, Marie [Adelaide] Belloc
1868-1947   [TCCM]
British author
* Curtin, Philip

Lowther, [Sir] James 1736-1802
[NPS]
British politician
* [The] Brazen Bully
* Seventy Four, Lord
(See also base volume)

[The] Loyal Poet
See Fitzgerald, William Thomas

Loyes, Charles Auguste 1841- ?
[NPS]
French artist, journalist, author
* Montbard, Georges

Loyola y Balda, Ingio de 1491-1556
Saint
* Ignatius of Loyola

Loyseau, Jacques
See Collin, Jacques Albin Simon

Lubanski, Jules Clement Ladislas
?-1907   [NPS]
Author
* Heldau
* Star, Jean

Lubin
See Perrault, Claude

Lucas, Edward Verrall 1868-1938
[DLE1]
British author
* Ward, E. D.
(See also base volume)

Lucas Garcia, Benedicto 20th c.
Guatemalan army officer
* Lucas Garcia, Benny

Lucas Garcia, Benny
See Lucas Garcia, Benedicto

Lucasta
See Sacheverell, Lucy

Lucasta
See Waite, Ada Lakeman

Lucchesi, Aldo
See Von Block, Bela

Lucey, Thomas Elmore 1874- ?
[BDSA]
American poet
* [The] Poet Entertainer of the Ozarks

Lucian 120- 180   [NPS]
Greek author
* [The] Blasphemer
(See also base volume)

Lucilius, Caius 2nd c. BC   [NPS]
Roman poet
* [The] Great Auruncian
(See also base volume)

[The] Lucky
See Ericsson, Leif

Lucy, [Sir] Henry William
1845-1924   [NPS]
British author
* De Bookworms, Baron
* H. W. L.
(See also base volume)

Ludden, Allen [Ellsworth]
1918?-1981   [CA, SAT]
American television and radio producer, game show host, author
* [The] Happy Highbrow

Ludlow, Johnny
See Wood, Mrs. Henry

Ludlum, Robert 1927-
[CLC, TCCM]
American author
* Shepherd, Michael
(See also base volume)

Luigi
See Pelletier, Alexis

Luisi, Marie 1936?-
American advertising executive
* [The] Godmother

Luiskovo, Andrey
See Pedachenko, Alexander

Luke, Thomas
See Masterton, Graham

Lumpkin, Father
See Lumpkin, Roy

Lumpkin, Roy 20th c.   [EF]
American football player
* Lumpkin, Father

Lunatic, [Sir] Humphrey, Bart.
See Gentleman, Francis

Lunettes, Henry
See Conkling, Margaret Cockburn

Lupus, Michael
See De Wolf, Michael

Luque, Antonio 1838-1887   [GS]
Spanish bullfighter
* Cuchares de Cordoba

Luque y Gonzalez, Antonio
1814-1859   [GS]
Spanish bullfighter
* Camara

Luqueer, Helen
See Bushnell, Mrs. William H.

Lusian's Luckless Queen
See Maria I

Lusus, Larry, Esq.
See O'Brien, William

Luther, Martin 1483-1546   [NPS]
German religious reformer
* [The] Hot Headed Monk
* Martin, [Brother]
(See also base volume)

[The] Lycanthrope
See Borel, Pierre Bord d'Hautoine

Lycidas
See King, Edward

Lyddal
See Garrick, David

Lyell, [Sir] Charles 1797-1875
British geologist
* [The] Father of Modern Geology

Lyfick, Warren
See Reeves, Lawrence F.

Lying Old Fox
See Walpole, Horatio [Fourth Earl of Orford]

[The] Lying Traveller
See Mandeville, [Sir] John

Lyle-Smythe, Alan 1914-
[CA, TCCM]
*British-born American author,
screenwriter, playwright*
* Caillou, Alan

Lyly, John 1554-1606   [NPS]
British author
* Tullius Anglorum
(See also base volume)

Lynch, Edward
See Sutton, William Francis
[Willie]

Lynch, Michael 1852- ?   [PI]
American poet
* Lamech

Lynch, Mrs. Henry 19th c.   [PI]
Irish poet
* Personne

Lynch, Thomas Took 1818-1871
[PI]
British author and hymn writer
* Long, Silent

Lyndon, Amy
See Radford, Richard F[rancis],
Jr.

Lyndon, Barry
See Austin, George Lowell

Lynds, Dennis 1924-   [CA]
American author
* Carter, Nick
* Dekker, Carl
* Sadler, Mark
(See also base volume)

Lynn, Ethel
See Beers, Ethelinda [Elliot]

Lynx, Larry
See Lotinga, W.

Lyon, Babe
See Lyon, George

Lyon, George 20th c.   [EF]
American football player
* Lyon, Babe

Lyons, Leonard
See Sucher, Leonard

Lyons, Sophie 1848-1924   [LFW]
American swindler
* Owens, Fannie
* [The] Queen of Crime
* Wilson, Kate
* Wilson, Mary

Lyre, Pinchbeck
See Sassoon, Siegfried [Lorraine]

Lysander
See Dibdin, Thomas Frognall

Lysberg, Charles-Samuel
See Bovy-Lysberg, Charles-Samuel

Lyte, Charles 1935-   [CA]
British author
* Ewart, Charles

Lytle, Joy Oleny Mann
See Buor, Joy Olny

Lyttle, Wesley Guard 1844-1896
[PI]
Irish writer and poet
* Robin

Lytton, Edward
See Wheeler, Edward Lytton

M

* Indicates Assumed Name

M.
See Malone, Michael

M.
See McCarthy, Denis Florence

M.
See McGee, Thomas D'Arcy

M.
See Monckton, Rose C.

M.
See Moore, George Henry

M.
See Moultrie, Gerard

M.
See Mulchinock, William Pembroke

M.
See Murphy, James

M.
See Pender, Margaret T.

M. A.
See Abdy, Maria Smith

M. A.
See Arnold, Matthew

M. A. C.
See Cursham, Mary Ann

M. A. K.
See Kelty, Mary Ann

M. B.
See Brook, Mary

M. B. G.
See Grosvenor, Melville Bell

M. C.
See Constable, Michael

M. C.
See Mullen [or Mullins?], Michael

M. D.
See Dawes, Matthew

M. D.
See Doheny, Michael

M. D.
See McAleese, Daniel

M. D., Heslingden
See Davitt, Michael

M. de V.
See De Vere, Mary

M. E. A.
See Arnold, M. E.

M. E. B.
See Bennett, Mary E.

M. E. C. W.
See Walcott, Mackenzie Edward Clarke

M. E. M.
See Martin, M. E.

M. F. D.
See Downing, Mary

M. G.
See Leathes, Mrs. Stanley

M. G. B.
See Buchanan, George

M. H.
See Hack, Maria

M. H.
See Heffernan, Michael J.

M. H., Thomond
See Hogan, Michael

M. I. B.
See Bromley, M. I.

M. I. D.
See Horne, Richard Henry

M. J. B.
See Barry, Michael Joseph

M. J. C.
See Carrington, Margaret Jirvin

M. J. I.
See O'Donovan Rossa, Mary Jane

M. J. R.
See Ryan, Michael

M. J. S.
See O'Sullivan, Michael John

M J. W.
See Whitty, Michael James

M. K.?
See McKenna, Andrew James

M. M. D.
See Pearle, Mary

M. M. P.
See Manning, Patrick M.

M. McD.
See McDermott, Martin

M. McD.
See McDermott, Mary

M. My. R.
See Ryan, Margaret Mary

M. N.
See Camden, William

M. N.
See Wotton, William

M. N-g-t
See Nugent, Michael

M. O'C.
See O'Connell, Maurice

M. O'D.
See Maginn, William

M. P.
See O'Connell, John

M. P. H.
See Hickey, Michael Patrick

M. R.
See Russell, Matthew

M. R.
See Ryan, Margaret Mary

M. R. L.
See Leyne, Maurice Richard

M. S.
See Stokes, Margaret MacNair

M. T. P.
See Pender, Margaret T.

M. U.
See Uniacke, Mary

M. W.
See Wilson, Miles

M. W. R.
See Rooney, M. W.

M. W. S.
See Savage, Marmion Wilmo

Mabon
See Abraham, William

Mac
See McGinley, Peter Toner

Mac
See McMahon, George Yielding

Mac Erin
See McHenry, James

Mac the Knife
See McNamara, Robert Strange

Macaedhagain
See Keegan, James

[The] Macaroni Painter
See Cosway, Richard

[The] Macaroni Parson
See Dodd, William

[The] Macaroni Parson
See Horne, John

Macaulay, Clarendon
See Adams, Walter Marsham

Macaulay, Thomas Babington [First Baron Macaulay] 1800-1859 [NPS]
British statesman and author
* [The] Burke of Our Age
* Quongti, Richard
* [The] Son of the Saint
(See also base volume)

MacBrady, Thady
See O'Flanagan, Theophilus

Maccheta, Blanche Roosevelt [Tucker] 1853-1898 [DNA]
American-born author and opera singer
* Roosevelt, Blanche

Macdonald, [Sir] John Alexander 1815-1891 [BBH]
Canadian prime minister
* [The] Father of Modern Canada
(See also base volume)

MacDowell, Edward Alexander 1861-1908 [BBD]
American composer
* Thorn, Edgar

Mace, Aurelia Gay 1835-1910 [DNA]
Author
* Aurelia

Mace, Jem 1831-1910 [RBE]
British boxer
* [The] Gypsy

Macer
See Philips, Ambrose

Macfadyen, Dugald 19th c. [PI]
Scottish poet and composer
* Cruck-a-leaghan

MacFlecknoe
See Shadwell, Thomas

Macgowan
See Smyth, John

Machado e Silva, Andrada 1773-1845 [NPS]
Brazilian statesman
* [The] Mirabeau of Brazil

Machar, Agnes Maule 1837-1917
[DLE1]
Canadian poet and author
* Fidelis

Macintosh, William 18th c.   [IP]
Scottish author
* [A] Lover of his Country

Mack, J. G. O. 1872- ?   [NPS]
Author
* Callum Beg

Mack, Louise
See Creed, Mrs. J. P.

Mack, Red
See Mack, William

Mack, William 20th c.   [EF]
American football player
* Mack, Red

Mackamotzki, Kunigunde ?-1910
[DI]
Entertainer and murder victim
* Elmore, Belle
* Turner, Cora

Mackarness, John Fielder 19th c.
[IP]
British clergyman and author
* One of Themselves

Mackarness, Matilda Anne   [IP]
British author
* Sunbeam, Susie
(See also base volume)

Mackay, Aberigh 1849-1881   [IP]
Indian author
* Ali Baba

Mackay, Andrew 1759-1809   [IP]
Scottish mathematician and author
* Andrew, James

Mackay, Charles 1814- ?   [IP]
Scottish poet and journalist
* Grimbosh, Herman
* Wagstaffe, John, Esq., of Wilbye
  Grange
(See also base volume)

Mackay, Francis Alexander 19th c.
[IP]
Scottish poet
* Fitzhugh, Francis

Mackay, James   [IP]
British clergyman and author
* [A] Chaplain in H. M. Indian
  Service

Mackay, K. 20th c.   [EC]
Australian cricketer
* Mackay, Slasher

Mackay, Robert 1714-1771   [NPS]
Gaelic poet
* [The] Brown

Mackay, Robert 19th c.   [HFN]
American author
* [A] Citizen of the West

Mackay, Slasher
See Mackay, K.

Macken, John 1784-1823   [PI]
Irish poet
* Fitzadam, Ismael

MacKenna, Theobald ?-1809   [IP]
Irish barrister and author
* [A] Catholic and a Burkist

Mackenzie, Alice 1842?-1889   [BL]
Prostitute and murder victim
* Clay Pipe Alice

Mackenzie, Andrew 1780-1839
[PI]
Irish poet
* Gallius [or Gaelus]

Mackenzie, Anne Maria   [IP]
British author
* Ellen of Exeter

Mackenzie, C. F. 19th c.   [IP]
British author
* [Il] Musannif

Mackenzie, Henry 1745-1831
[IP, NPS]
Scottish author
* Brutus
* [The] Northern Addison
(See also base volume)

Mackenzie, James ?-1761   [IP]
Scottish physician and author
* [A] Physician

Mackenzie, Mary Jane   [IP]
British author
* [A] Lady

Mackenzie, Peter   [IP]
Scottish author
* [The] Odd Fellow
* [A] Ten Pounder

Mackenzie, Robert Shelton
1809-1880?   [IP, PI]
Irish-born author and poet
* R. S. M.
* Sholto

Mackenzie, William 19th c.   [IP]
Scottish clergyman and author
* W. M.

Mackenzie, William Henry
1862-1883   [PI]
Irish author and poet
* Skez

Mackenzie, William Lyon
1795-1861   [IP]
Canadian journalist
* Swift, Patrick

Mackinnon, Campbell 19th c.   [IP]
British poet
* C. M.

Mackintosh, [Sir] James
1765-1832   [IP]
Scottish philosopher and historian
* [A] Barrister
* [The] Ghost of Vandegrab
(See also base volume)

MacL.
See McLaughlin, Patrick O'Conor

Maclaine, James 18th c.   [DI]
Irish-born British highwayman
* [The] Gentleman Highwayman

MacLaughlin, Charles 1690-1797
[DEA]
British actor and author
* C. M.
(See also base volume)

Maclean, John 1851-1928   [DNA]
Scottish-born author
* Rustler, Robin

MacLean, Sallie 20th c.   [CR]
Dancer
* [La] Trianita

MacManus, Anna 1866-1902   [PI]
Irish poet
* Carbery, Ethna
* Ethna

Macmillan, Daft Pate
See Macmillan, Kirkpatrick

Macmillan, Kirkpatrick 19th c.
[BBH]
Scottish inventor
* Macmillan, Daft Pate

MacOwen, Arthur H.   [DNA]
Author
* Wheeler, Chris

MacOwen, Robert 1744?-1812   [PI]
Irish poet and actor
* Owenson, Robert
* R. N. O.

Macsaroni, A.
See Anstey, Christopher

Macshimi, Gillespie
See Simson, Archibald

Mad Dan the Murrimbidgee Terror
See Morgan, Daniel

Mad Mike Hoare
See Hoare, Michael

[The] Mad Monk in the Monastery
See Reed, B. Mitchel

[The] Mad Poet
See Collins, William

Mad Tom Davey
See Davey, Thomas

Madame Helena
See Jackson, Editha Salomon

Madcap Betsy
See Von Furstenberg-Hedringen,
Elizabeth Caroline Maria Agatha
Felicitas

Madden, Bernard Joseph 19th c.
[PI]
Irish poet
* [An] Irish Helot

Madden, Richard Robert
1798-1886   [PI]
Irish poet
* Ierne
* R. R. M.

Maddox, No Name 1934-   [BP]
American murderer
* Manson, Charles

Madge
See Humphry, Mrs. C. E.

Madison, James 1751-1836   [NPS]
American president
* Helvidius
(See also base volume)

Madison, Virginia
See Putnam, Sarah

**[The] Maecenas and Lucullus of His
Island**
See Cavendish, William Spencer

Maelmuire
See Condon, Thomas

Maery, Helen
See Mug, [Sister] Mary Theodosia

Maevius
See Russell, Richard

Maffie, Jazz
See Maffie, John

Maffie, John 20th c.   [DI]
American robber
* Maffie, Jazz

Magellan, Fernando de 1470-1521
[NPS]
Portuguese navigator and explorer
* Mighty Eagle

Magennis, Bernard 1833-1911   [PI]
Irish poet
* B. McG.
* Hofer
* Iveagh

Maggie
See Browne, Maurice

Maggiolo, Achille 20th c.   [EF]
American football player
* Maggiolo, Chick

Maggiolo, Chick
See Maggiolo, Achille

[The] Magic Man
See Bennett, Lonnie

Magin, Joseph 19th c.   [PI]
Irish poet
* J. M.?

Maginn, William 1793-1842
[NPS, PI]
Irish author and journalist
* [The] Adjutant
* Augustinus
* Barrett, [Rev.] J.
* Buller, Bob
* Crossman, C. O.
* Crossman, P. J.
* Crossman, P. P.
* Dowden, Richard
* Duggan, Dionysius
* [The] Ensign
* Fitztravesty, Blaize, Esq.
* Forager, Philip
* Hincks, [Rev.] E.
* Holt, William
* [An] Irish Gentleman Lately
  Deceased
* J. T--n
* Jennings, Thomas
* M. O'D.
* Middlestitch, Giles
* Mulligan, Morty Macnamara
* P. P. P.
* P. T. T.
* Petre, Olinthus
* R. F. P.
* R. T. S.
* Scott, Ralph Tuckett
* Seward, W.
* [The] Standard Bearer
(See also base volume)

Magliabecchi, Antonio [or Anthony]
1633-1714   [NPS]
Florentine bibliophile
* [The] Glutton of Literature
(See also base volume)

Maglone, Barney
See Donnelly, James

[The] Magnificent
See Arundell, [Sir] John

[Le] Magnifique
See Roux, Paul Pierre

Magpie
See Lotinga, W.

Magrath, Peter
See Beresford, William

Maguire, H. N.
Author
* Hegmun, Ira

Maguire, Shandy
See Fennell, Patrick

[The] Magus of the Times
See Sterling, Edward

Mahan, Red
See Mahan, Walter

Mahan, Walter 20th c.   [EF]
American football player
* Mahan, Red

Maharba
See Abraham, John

Mahdi, Imam
See Ali Mohammed of Shiraz

Mahn, Mack
See McMahon, Patrick James

Mahnken, Elaine 20th c.   [FIR]
Fashion model
* Davis, Elaine

Mahoney, Frank 20th c.   [EF]
American football player
* Mahoney, Ike

Mahoney, Ike
See Mahoney, Frank

Mahony, Francis Sylvester
1804-1866   [PI]
Irish-born journalist
* O'Dryskull, Teddy
(See also base volume)

[The] Maid of Kent
See Heathorne, Caroline

[The] Maid of the Oaks
See Farren, Elizabeth

Mailings, Malachi
See Galt, John

Maimonides [or Moses ben Maimon]
1135-1204
Spanish scholar, philosopher, author
* [The] Second Moses
(See also base volume)

Main, John
See Parsons, Elsie Worthington
[Clews]

Maine, Henry James Stuart
1822-1888   [DEA]
British author
* H. S. M.

Maire
See Murray, John Fisher

Mairet, Jean 1604-1686   [NPS]
Playwright
* [The] French Marston

Maitland, John Wilson
See Watson, William

Maitland, Margaret
See DuBreuil, Elizabeth Lorinda

Maitland, Thomas
See Swinburne, Algernon Charles

Maitre Jean
See Gallus, Johannes

Majo, Giovanni 1732-1770   [BBD]
Italian composer
* Ciccio di Majo

Major A.
See Coles, Charles Barwell

Major Bob
See D'Aubuisson, Roberto

Makepeace, Joanna
See York, Margaret Elizabeth

[The] Maker of Modern Egypt
See Baring, Evelyn [First Earl of
Cromer]

Malack, Muly
See Noah, Mordecai Manuel

Malakoff
See Johnston, W. F.

Maldclewith, Ronsby
See Smith, Byron Caldwell

Male, Christopher Parr 19th c.
[HFN]
Author
* C. P. M.

Malesevich, Bronislaw 20th c.   [EF]
American football player
* Malesevich, Bronko

Malesevich, Bronko
See Malesevich, Bronislaw

Malherbe, Francois de 1555-1628
[NPS]
French poet
* [The] Tyrant of Words and
Syllables
(See also base volume)

Mallarme, Stephane 1842-1898
[CD]
French poet
* De Ponty, Marguerite
* Satin, Miss

Mallock, William Hurrell
1849-1923   [NPS]
British author
* Moore, Wentworth
(See also base volume)

Mallon, Isabel Allderdice [Sloan]
1857-1898   [DNA]
American author and journalist
* Ashmore, Ruth

Mallory, Drew
See Garfield, Brian [Francis]
Wynne

Malone, Carroll
See McBurney, William B.

Malone, Edmund 1741-1812   [NPS]
Critic and author
* Marcellus

Malone, Michael ?-1891?   [PI]
Irish writer and poet
* M.

Malpass, Barbara Ann 20th c.   [BL]
*American runaway who
masqueraded as a male*
* Williams, Charles Richard

Maltitz, Hermann von
See Klencke, Hermann

Mamin, Dmitrii Narkisovich   [ICB]
Author
* Mamin-Siberiak

Mamin-Siberiak
See Mamin, Dmitrii Narkisovich

[El] Mamon [The Nursling]
See De La Cruz, Pedro

[The] Man Behind the Frown
See McClellan, John

[The] Man in the Claret Colored Coat
See Gould, Edward S.

[The] Man in the Cloak
See Mangan, James Clarence

[The] Man in the Iron Mask
See Sullivan, Ed

[The] Man in the Moon
See Anstruther, Capt.

[The] Man in the Moon
See Thomson, William

[The] Man Mouse
See More, Henry

[The] Man of a Thousand Faces
See Guinness, Alec

[The] Man of Black Renown
See Wilberforce, William

[A] Man of Business
See Ashton, John

[A] Man of Business
See Dicker, Thomas

Man of Kent
See Nicoll, [Sir] William
Robertson

[The] Man of Steel
See Origen

[The] Man of the People
See Thomson, William

[A] Man of 25
See Keegan, John

[The] Man with a Wig
See Parr, Samuel

[The] Man with Six Senses
See Kraus, Josef

Manchecourt
See Lavedan, Henri L. E.

**[The] Manchester Prison
Philanthropist**
See Wright, Thomas

Mandelbaum, Fredericka
1818?-1889?   [BLB, CEC]
American criminal
* Mandelbaum, Marm
* Mandelbaum, Mother

Mandelbaum, Marm
See Mandelbaum, Fredericka

Mandelbaum, Mother
See Mandelbaum, Fredericka

Manders, Clarence 20th c.   [EF]
American football player
* Manders, Pug

Manders, Pug
See Manders, Clarence

Mandeville, Bernard de
1670?-1733   [DEA]
British author
* Phil-Porney

Mandeville, [Sir] John 1300-1372
[NPS, UH]
British author and explorer
* [The] Bruce of the Fourteenth
Century
* [The] Lying Traveller

Mandrake, Ethel Belle
See Thurman, Wallace

Mangan, James Clarence
1803-1849   [PI]
Irish poet
* Clarence
* J. C. M.
* Lageniensis
* [The] Man in the Cloak
* Monos
* [The] Mourner
* Terrae Filius
* Vacuus
* [A] Yankee

Mangin, Edward ?-1852   [PI]
Irish poet
* E. M.

Manley, Jack
See Webb, Charles Hull

Manley, Mary de la Riviere
1663?-1724   [SFL, WGT]
British playwright
* Eginardus
* Lovemore, [Sir] Charles
(See also base volume)

Manlius
See Gore, Christopher

Mann, A. Chester
See Roberts, Philip Ilott

Mann, A. Sufferan
See Bangs, John Kendrick

Mann, Delos H. 1824-1906   [DNA]
American author and physician
* Gray, Rosalie

Manners, Julia
See Judson, Edward Zane Carroll

Manners, Motley
See Duganne, Augustine Joseph
Hickey

Manning, Anne 1807-1879   [NPS]
Author
* Beatrice
(See also base volume)

Manning, Doc
See Manning, George Felix

Manning, George Felix 19th c.
[BLB]
American cattle rancher
* Manning, Doc

Manning, Patrick M. 19th c.   [PI]
Irish poet
* M. M. P.

Manning, Roosevelt 20th c.   [EF]
American football player
* Manning, Rosie

Manning, Rosie
See Manning, Roosevelt

Manotoc, Tomas 1950?-
*Son-in-law of Philippine president,
Ferdinand Marcos*
* Manotoc, Tommy

Manotoc, Tommy
See Manotoc, Tomas

Mansfield, Mrs. M. F.
Author
* McManus, Blanche

Manske, Edgar 20th c.   [EF]
American football player
* Manske, Eggs

Manske, Eggs
See Manske, Edgar

Manson, Charles
See Maddox, No Name

Mantequilla
See Soto, Fernando

Mantovano, Alberto
See Ripa, Alberto da

[The] Manx Poet
See Brown, Thomas Edward

Manzano y Pelayo, Jose
1828-1869   [GS]
Spanish bullfighter
* [El] Nili

Maple Knot
See Clemo, Ebenezer

Mapleton, Mark
See Wilson, Robert

Maps
See Nicholson, John

Marais, Jaap
See Marais, Jacob

Marais, Jacob 20th c.
South African politician
* Marais, Jaap

Marble, Dan
See Marble, Danforth

Marble, Danforth 1810-1849
[FAA]
American actor
* Marble, Dan

Marbourg, Dolores
See Bacon, Mary Schell [Hoke]

Marcellus
See Malone, Edmund

Marcellus
See Marteau, Amedee

Marcellus
See Ramsay, Allan, Jr.

[The] Marcellus of Our Tongue
See Oldham, John

[The] Marcellus of the English Nation
See Sidney, [Sir] Philip

March Pane
See Perugini, Mark

Marchant, Bessie
See Comfort, Mrs. J. A.

Marchant, Charles
See White, John Duncan

Marchesi, Luigi 1754-1829   [BBD]
Italian singer
* Marchesini

Marchesini
See Marchesi, Luigi

Marcial
See Carpio, Salvador Cayetano

Marcos, Imee
See Marcos, Maria Imelda

Marcos, Maria Imelda 1956?-
*Daughter of Philippine president,
Ferdinand Marcos*
* Marcos, Imee

Marcus
See Blunt, Joseph

Marcus
See Swift, Deane

Margaret, Karla
See Billings, Karla Margaret
Crosier

Margerie, Pet
See Fleming, Margaret

Margites [The Booby]
See Theobald, Lewis

Margoliouth, Moses 19th c.   [HFN]
Author
* [A] Clergyman of the Church of
England

Margot of Hainault 15th c.   [BBH]
French tennis player
* [The] Joan of Arc of Tennis

Marguerite
See Godwin, Mary

Marguerite
See Pender, Margaret T.

Maria
See Frazer, John de Jean

Maria I 1734-1816   [NPS]
Queen of Portugal
* Lusian's Luckless Queen

Mariaker, Elie
See Boulay-Paty, Evariste Cyprien

Marie
See Blake, Mary Elizabeth

Mario S.
See Scopoli-Biasi, Isabella

Marion, Frederick
See Kraus, Josef

Marisol
See Escobar, Marisol

Marius, Caius 2nd c. BC   [UH]
Roman general
* [The] Third Romulus
(See also base volume)

Marjoram, J.
See Mottram, Ralph Hale

Mark, Jon
See DuBreuil, Elizabeth Lorinda

Market Man
See Lake, Kenneth R[obert]

Markham, Mary
See Frith, Mary

Markov, Georgi 1929?-1978   [CA]
Bulgarian author and playwright
* St. George, David [joint
pseudonym with David Atlee
Phillips]

Marks, Mrs. L. S.
Author
* Peabody, Josephine Preston

Marks, Richard 19th c.   [HFN]
British author and clergyman
* One Who Loves the Souls of the
Lambs
(See also base volume)

Marks, Robert Walter 20th c.
Author
* Colleton, John

Marley
See Marlowe, Christopher

Marlin, Hilda
See Van Stockum, Hilda

Marling, Matt
See Webb, Charles Hull

Marlow, [Lady] Harriet
See Beckford, William

Marlow, Sidney
See Coggins, Paschal Heston

Marlowe, Christopher 1564-1593
[NPS]
British playwright
* Marley
* [A] Second Shakespeare
(See also base volume)

Marney, Suzanne
See Johnston, Mabel A.
[Stevenson]

**Marnix, Philip Van [Baron Sainte
Aldegonde]** 1538-1598   [NPS]
Dutch statesman
* Rabbotenus, Isaac

Maronic, Duke
See Maronic, Dusan

Maronic, Dusan 20th c.   [EF]
American football player
* Maronic, Duke

Marprelate, Martin
See Barrow, Henry

Marprelate, Martin
See Throckmorton, Job

Marprelate, Martin
See Udall, John

Marquis, Donald Robert Perry
1878-1937   [DLE1]
American author, poet, journalist
* Lantern

Marryatt, Frederick 1792-1848
[NPS]
Author
* [A] Sea Fielding
(See also base volume)

Marsh [or de Marisco], Adam 13th
c.   [NPS]
British monk
* [The] Illustrious Doctor

Marshak, Il'ia Iakovlevich   [ICB]
Author
* Ilin, M.

Marshall, A. J. P. 19th c.   [IP]
British author
* [A] Bachelor of Arts

Marshall, Charles   [IP]
British clergyman and author
* C. M., Vicar of Brixworth

Marshall, Frances 20th c.   [NPS]
Author
* St. Aubyn, Alan

Marshall, George W. 19th c.   [IP]
British author
* G. W. M.

Marshall, H. H.
See Jahn, Joseph Michael

Marshall, Robert 20th c.   [EF]
American football player
* Marshall, Rube

Marshall, Rube
See Marshall, Robert

Marshall, Thomas William
1815-1877   [IP]
British clergyman and author
* Chasuble, Archdeacon

Marston, Edward 1825-1914   [IP]
British author and publisher
* [A] Publisher
(See also base volume)

Marston, John 1575-1634
[DEA, NPS]
British playwright
* J. M.
* Millidus
* W. K.
(See also base volume)

Marston, Mildred
See Scott, Anna [Kay]

Marteau, Amedee   [IP]
Author
* Marcellus

Martin, [Brother]
See Luther, Martin

Martin, Alfred Tobias John
1802-1850   [IP]
British poet
* [A] Cosmopolite

Martin, Charles
See Fernandez, Raymond

Martin, Clara [Barnes] 19th c.   [IP]
American author
* C. B. M.

Martin, Edward Sanford 1856- ?
[IP]
American poet
* E. S. M.

Martin, Edward Winslow
See McCabe, James Dabney

Martin, Ellis
See Ryan, Marah Ellis

Martin, Frederick ?-1864   [IP]
British clergyman and author
* F. M.

Martin, George Madden
See Martin, Mrs. Atwood R.

Martin, [Sir] Henry 1801-1863   [IP]
British author
* [A] Lay Baronet
(See also base volume)

Martin, J. L. ?-1848   [IP]
American poet
* J. L. M.

Martin, Jack   [NN]
Boxer
* [The] Baker
* Master of the Rolls

Martin, James 1783-1860   [PI]
Irish poet
* Clarke, Owen
* McBlab, Thady
* O'Connell, Philip

Martin, James Sullivan   [IP]
American author
* [A] Revolutionary Soldier

Martin, Josiah 18th c.   [IP]
British author
* J. M.

Martin, M. E. 19th c.   [PI]
Irish poet
* M. E. M.

Martin, Mary Steichen
See Calderone, Mary S[teichen]

Martin, Michael 1775-1822
[BLB, DI, IP]
Irish-born highwayman
* Lightfoot, Captain

Martin, Mrs. Atwood R.
Author
* Martin, George Madden

Martin, Mrs. Bell 1815-1850
[IP, NPS]
Irish author
* Bell, Mrs. Martin
* [The] Irish Heiress
* [The] Princess of Connemara

Martin, Mrs. E. Throop   [IP]
American author
* [A] Lady

Martin, Plugger Bill
See Martin, William

Martin, Robert Jasper ?-1905   [PI]
Irish poet
* Ballyhooley
* R. J. M.

Martin, Sam 18th c.   [RBE]
Boxer
* [The] Bath Butcher

Martin, Selina   [IP]
British author
* S. M.

Martin, Shel
See Rooney, William

Martin, [Sir] Theodore 1816-1909
[DEA]
Scottish-born British author
* T. M.
(See also base volume)

Martin, Thomas   [IP]
Irish barrister and author
* [An] Irish Land Owner

Martin, William ?-1867   [IP]
British author and publisher
* Old Chatty Cheerful
(See also base volume)

Martin, William 19th c.   [BBH]
American bicycle racer
* Martin, Plugger Bill

Martin-Beaulieu, Marie Desire
1791-1863   [BBD]
French composer and author
* Beaulieu, Marie-Desire

Martin Sevilla, Francisco
1857-1888   [GS]
Spanish bullfighter
* [El] Corneta [The Bugle]

Martine, [Maj.] Max
See Avery, Henry M.

Martinelli, Ricardo
See Brandon, Johnny

Martinez, Lorencillo
See Martinez, Lorenzo Manuel

Martinez, Lorenzo Manuel 17th c.
[GS]
Spanish bullfighter
* Martinez, Lorencillo

Martini, Giambattista 1706-1784
[BBD]
Italian composer
* Martini, Padre

Martini, Padre
See Martini, Giambattista

**Martins, Maria Isabel Barreno de
Faria** 1939-   [CA]
Portuguese author
* Barreno, Maria Isabel

Martley, John 1844-1882   [PI]
Irish poet
* Coelebs in Search of a Wife

Martyn, John 1699-1768   [IP]
British author and botanist
* Bavius

[The] Martyr of the Solway
See Wilson, Margaret

Marvell, Andrew 1621-1678   [DEA]
British poet and satirist
* A. M.
* Rivetus, Andreas, Junior
(See also base volume)

Marx, Karl 1818-1883   [JL]
German political theorist
* [The] Father of Communism

Mary
See Downing, Ellen Mary Patrick

Mary
See St. John, Mary

Mary   [PPN]
Mother of Jesus
* Mater Dolorosa
* [The] Mother of God
(See also base volume)

Mary of Buttermere
See Robinson, Mary

Maseres, Francis 1731-1824   [IP]
British barrister and author
* [A] Friend to the Church of
England

Maskell, William 1814- ?   [IP]
British clergyman and author
* W. M., A Beneficed Priest

Maslin, Alice 1914?-1981   [CA]
American broadcaster and editor
* Craig, Nancy

Mason, Richard 1601-1678   [NPS]
British clergyman
* Angelus a Sancto Francisco

Masque
See Dowling, Bartholomew

[The] Massachusettes Madman
See Adams, John Quincy

Masse, James
See Tyssot de Patot, Simon

Massens, Jakob
See Tyssot de Patot, Simon

Massey, James
See Tyssot de Patot, Simon

Massinger, Philip 1583-1640
[DEA, NPS]
British playwright
* Our Mercurie

Massinger, Philip (Continued)
* P. M.
(See also base volume)

Massis, Henri 1886-1970   [CD]
French author
* Agathon [joint pseudonym with
Alfred de Tarde]

[The] Master
See Corlett, John

**[A] Master of Arts of the University
of Oxford**
See Asplin, William

**[A] Master of Arts of Trinity College,
Cambridge**
See Allen, Robert

Master of the Rolls
See Martin, Jack

Master Surveyor
See Jones, Inigo

**Master-The-Fifth of the Great White
Lodge of the Himalayas**
See Cannon, Alexander

Masters, Zeke
See Bensen, Donald R.

Masterson, Whit [joint pseudonym]
See McIlwain, David

Masterton, Graham 1946-   [CA]
British author
* Luke, Thomas

Mastiff Cur
See Wolsey, Thomas

Mastrogany, August 20th c.   [EF]
American football player
* Mastrogany, Gus

Mastrogany, Gus
See Mastrogany, August

Masudi, al ?- 957   [NPS]
Arabic historian
* [The] Herodotus of Arabian
History

Mater Dolorosa
See Mary

Mather, Berkely
See Davies, John Evan Weston

Mather [or Mathers], David 1844?-
?   [BLB, EWG]
American murderer and robber
* Mather, Mysterious Dave

Mather, Mysterious Dave
See Mather [or Mathers], David

Mathetes
See Jones, John

Mathetes
See Wilson, John

Mathews, Louise
See Tooke, Louise Mathews

Matilda, Julia
See Byrne, Julia C.

Matrice, H. Ogram
See Keary, C. F.

[A] Matrimonial Monomaniac
See Abbot, L. A.

Matson, Oliver 20th c.   [EF]
American football player
* Matson, Ollie

Matson, Ollie
See Matson, Oliver

Matsys, Quentin 1460-1529   [NPS]
Flemish painter
* [The] Flemish Blacksmith
(See also base volume)

Matthew, [Sir] Tobias [or Tobie]
1577-1655   [NPS]
British courtier, diplomat, author
* Bacon's Alter Ego

Matthews and Co.
See Buckingham, Leicester Silk

Matthews, Arthur Bache 19th c.
[HFN]
Author
* A. B. M.

Matthews, Brad
See DeMille, Nelson

Matthews, George 1818?-1847   [PI]
Irish poet
* G. M., Esq.

Matthews, James Brander
1852-1929   [DNA]
American author and educator
* Penn, Arthur

Matthews, Stanley 1915?-   [NN]
British soccer player
* [The] Wizard Dribbler
(See also base volume)

Matthias Corvinus 1442?-1490
[NPS]
King of Hungary
* [The] Conqueror
(See also base volume)

Mauder, Dutch
See Mauder, Louis

Mauder, Louis 20th c.   [EF]
American football player
* Mauder, Dutch

M'Aulay, Allan
See Stewart, Charlotte

Maurice, Walter
See Besant, [Sir] Walter

Mauritius, Pfaffe
See Hartmann, Moritz

Maurus
See Blackmore, [Sir] Richard

Maury, J. C. F.
See Tillet, Auguste

Mawe, Thomas
See Abercrombie, John

Max, Edwin 1909?-1980   [FIR]
Actor
* Miller, Edwin

Max-Muller, Friedrich
See Muller, Friedrich

**Maximian [Marcus Aurelius Valerius
Maximianus]** ?- 310   [NPS]
Roman emperor
* Augustus
(See also base volume)

Maximilian I 1573-1651   [NPS]
Duke of Bavaria
* [The] Conqueror
(See also base volume)

Maximov, Leon Samsonov 1930-
[CA]
Russian-born author and playwright
* Maximov, Vladimir
  [Yemelyanovich]

Maximov, Vladimir [Yemelyanovich]
See Maximov, Leon Samsonov

Maxwell, A. E. [joint pseudonym
with Evan Maxwell]
See Maxwell, Ann [Elizabeth]

Maxwell, A. E. [joint pseudonym
with Ann (Elizabeth) Maxwell]
See Maxwell, Evan

Maxwell, Ann [Elizabeth] 1944-
[CA]
American author
* Maxwell, A. E. [joint pseudonym
  with Evan Maxwell]

Maxwell, C. L. 19th c. [EWG]
American gunfighter
* Maxwell, Gunplay

Maxwell, Evan 20th c. [CA]
American author
* Maxwell, A. E. [joint pseudonym
  with Ann (Elizabeth) Maxwell]

Maxwell, Gunplay
See Maxwell, C. L.

Maxwell, John
See Freemantle, Brian [Harry]

May Fly
See Somerset, Wellington

May, Kenneth
See Aveling, Edward Bibbins

May, Reginald
See Stokes, J. Lemacks

May, Thomas 1595-1650 [DEA]
British poet and historian
* T. M.
(See also base volume)

Mayer, Eduard Heinrich
1821-1907 [NPS]
German poet
* Fest, Ernst

Mayer, Sydney Louis 1937- [CA]
American-born author and editor
* Jennings, Patrick

Mayer, Wilhelm 1831-1898 [BBD]
Czech musician
* Remy, W. A.

Mayfair, Bertha
See Raborg, Frederick A[shton],
Jr.

Mayhar, Ardath F[rances] 1930-
[CA]
American poet and author
* Cannon, Ravenna
(See also base volume)

Mayne, Leger D.
See Dick, William Brisbane

Mayo, Herbert 1796-1852 [NPS]
British physiologist and surgeon
* [The] Middlesex Owl

Mazar Pasha
See Lakeman, Stephen

M'Blashmole, Pat
See Campbell, Thomas

McAleese, Daniel 1833?-1900 [PI]
Irish journalist and poet
* M. D.
* Ossian
* Ruadh

McAllister, Amanda
See Dowdell, Dorothy [Florence]
Karns

McAllister, Amanda
See Meaker, Eloise

McBlab, Thady
See Martin, James

McBride, Neil 20th c. [PI]
Irish-born poet
* Lien, Edirb Cam

McBurney, William B. ?-1892 [PI]
Irish poet
* Malone, Carroll

McC.
See McCausland, Dominick

McCabe, James Dabney
1842-1883 [DNA]
American author and historian
* Martin, Edward Winslow

McCabe, William Bernard
1801-1891 [PI]
Irish poet
* W. B. M.

McCaig, Donald 20th c. [CA]
American author and poet
* Ashley, Steven

McCall, Anthony
See Kane, Henry

McCall, John 1820-1902 [PI]
Irish author and poet
* Scrutator

McCall, John 1850?-1877 [EWG]
American gunfighter
* Broken Nose Jack
* Sutherland, Bill

McCall, Patrick Joseph 1861- ?
[PI]
Irish poet and translator
* Cavellus

McCall, William 1821-1881 [PI]
Irish poet
* Dhearg, Lamh

McCallum, Francis McNeill
1824-1857 [DI]
Scottish-born Australian bushranger
* Melville, Captain

McCarthy, Cal
See McCarthy, Charles, Jr.

McCarthy, Charles, Jr. 1869-1895
[AS, RBE]
American boxer
* McCarthy, Cal

McCarthy, Denis Florence
1817-1882 [PI]
Irish poet and playwright
* Antonio
* D.
* D. F. McC.
* Desmond
* M.
* S. E. Y.
* Trifolium
* Vig
(See also base volume)

McCarthy, Fitzjames 19th c. [PI]
American journalist and poet
* Fitz Mac

McCarthy, Mary Stanislaus
1850?-1897 [PI]
Irish poet
* S. M. S.

McCarty, Bones
See McCarty, James

McCarty, James 19th c.
American gunfighter
* McCarty, Bones

McCausland, Dominick 1806-1873
[PI]
Irish author and attorney
* McC.

McChester, George 19th c. [RBE]
Boxer
* McCloskey, Country

McClellan, George Brinton
1826-1885 [NPS]
American army officer
* [The] Modern Belisarius
(See also base volume)

McClellan, Harriet [Hare] 19th c.
[DNA]
Author
* Flemming, Harford

McClellan, John 1896- [CR]
American politician
* [The] Craggy-Faced Inquisitor
* [The] Gangster's Nightmare
* [The] Man Behind the Frown

McClelland, Diane Margaret 1931-
[CA]
British author
* Pearson, Diane

McClelland, M. G.
See McClelland, Mary Greenway

McClelland, Mary Greenway
1853-1895 [WGT]
American author
* McClelland, M. G.

McCloskey, Country
See McChester, George

McCloskey, Henry 1829?-1869
[PI]
Irish-born journalist and poet
* Paddy

McCluskie, Mike ?-1871
[BLB, EWG]
American gunfighter
* Delaney, Art[hur]

McCombe, W. J. 1871- ? [PI]
Irish poet
* Ivanhoe

McCoole, Mike 1837-1886 [RBE]
Irish-born American boxer
* [The] Deck Hand Champion of
  America

McCormick, Brooks
See Adams, William Taylor

McCormick, Philip
See Wilson, Edwin P.

McCorry, Peter 19th c. [PI]
Irish-born journalist and poet
* McSherry, Shandy

McCoy, M. C.
See McCoy, Michael Charles

McCoy, Michael Charles 1953-
[FR]
American football player
* McCoy, M. C.

McCutchan, Philip [Donald] 1920-
[TCCM]
British author
* Galway, Robert Conington
* Wigg, T. I. G.
(See also base volume)

McCutcheon, Ben Frederick
1875-1934 [DNA]
American author and journalist
* Brace, Benjamin

McDermott, George 19th c. [PI]
Irish poet and barrister
* D. G. M.
* G. M. D.

McDermott, Martin 1823-1905
[PI]
Irish poet
* M. McD.

McDermott, Mary 19th c. [PI]
Irish poet
* M. McD.

McDermott, William 1863-1913
[DNA, PI]
Irish poet, author, clergyman
* Lecky, Walter

McDevitt, Neil 19th c. [PI]
Irish poet
* N. M.?
* Naas, N.

McDonald, James 19th c. [PI]
Irish poet
* J. McD.

McDonald, John 1846- ? [PI]
Irish poet
* J. McD.

McDonald, Martha
See Blair, Linda

McDonald, Peter 1836?-1890 [PI]
Irish poet
* P. McD.?
* Roc Noir

McDonnell, John 20th c. [EF]
American football player
* McDonnell, Mickey

McDonnell, Mickey
See McDonnell, John

McElroy, Bucky
See McElroy, William

McElroy, William 20th c. [EF]
American football player
* McElroy, Bucky

McEntee, P. 19th c. [PI]
Irish poet
* P. McG.

McErin, Hugh
See Heinrick, Hugh

McEwen, William Dalzell
1787-1828 [PI]
Irish poet and clergyman
* Walsingham

McFarlan, James 1832-1862 [PI]
Scottish poet
* [The] Pedlar Poet

McFerran, Ann
See Townsend, Doris McFerran

McFerran, Doris
See Townsend, Doris McFerran

McFinn, Denis
See O'Connell, Maurice

McGaura, Conner
See Ryan, James

McGee, Darky
See McGee, Thomas D'Arcy

McGee, Molly
See McGee, Sylvester

McGee, Sylvester 20th c. [EF]
American football player
* McGee, Molly

McGee, Thomas D'Arcy
1825-1868 [PI]
Irish-born Canadian author, poet, statesman
* Amergin
* Amhergin
* Feargail
* Gilla-Erin
* Gilla-Patrick
* [An] Irish Exile
* M.
* McGee, Darky
* Montanus
* Sarsfield
* T. D. M.
(See also base volume)

McGeoghegan, Thomas J. 1836- ?
[PI]
Irish-born poet
* Mel

McGill, Donald Fraser Gould
1875-1962 [WEC]
British cartoonist
* [The] King of the Seaside
  Postcard

McGill, Patrick 1891- ? [PI]
Irish poet
* [The] Navvy Poet

McGinley, Bridget
See Gallagher, Bridget

McGinley, Peter Toner 1857- ?
[PI]
Irish poet
* Mac

McGinnis, William
See Lay, William Ellsworth

McGrady, James ?-1855 [PI]
Irish poet
* Shemus of Ullinagh
* [The] Talking Man

McGrath, John 1864- ? [PI]
Irish poet and journalist
* Cuan

McGrath, Terence
See Blake, Henry A.

McGregor, Gregor 1786-1845 [DI]
British swindler
* [The] Prince of Poyais

McHale, M. J. 1845?-1887 [PI]
Irish clergyman and poet
* [A] Country Curate

McHale, Richard 1862- ? [PI]
Irish poet
* Ricardo

McHenry, James 1785?-1845
[DNA, PI, WGT]
Irish author and poet
* Mac Erin
* Secondsight, Solomon

McHenry, [Col.] Oram R.
See Rolfe, Maro Orlando

McHugh, Hugh
See Hobart, George Vere

McHugh, Pat
See McHugh, William

McHugh, William 20th c. [EF]
American football player
* McHugh, Pat

McIlvaine, Clara ?-1890? [PI]
Irish poet
* C. L. M.

McIlwain, David 1921- [CA]
British author
* Masterson, Whit [joint
  pseudonym]
(See also base volume)

McIlwraith, Jean Newton
1859-1938 [DLE1]
Canadian author
* Forsyth, Jean

McIvor, Ivor Ben
See Welsh, Charles

McKane, James Niall 1849-1878
[PI]
Irish-born poet
* J. N. McK.

McKay, Claude 1890-1948 [CA]
Jamaican-born author and poet
* Edwards, Eli

McKay, J. K.
See McKay, John Kenneth

McKay, John Kenneth 1953- [FR]
American football player
* McKay, J. K.

McKenna, Andrew James
1833-1872 [PI]
Irish poet and journalist
* A. J. M.
* A. J. McK.
* M. K.?

McKenna, Theobald ?-1808 [PI]
Irish poet and physician
* Dr. McK.

McKenney, Thomas Loraine
1785-1859 [DNA]
American author
* Aristides

McKinney, Thomas L. 19th c.
[EWG]
American law officer
* McKinney, Tip

McKinney, Tip
See McKinney, Thomas L.

McKowen, James 1814-1889 [PI]
Irish poet
* Connor, Kitty
* Curlew

McLaren, Moray [David Shaw]
1901-1971 [CA]
Scottish author and playwright
* Murray, Michael

McLaughlin, Patrick O'Conor 1851-
? [PI]
Irish author and poet
* MacL.

McLaurin, Anne 1953- [SAT]
American author
* Laurin, Anne

McLoughlin, R. B.
See Mencken, Henry Louis

McMahon, George Yielding
?-1886 [PI]
Irish poet and barrister
* Mac

McMahon, Heber 1851-1880 [PI]
Irish poet
* Celticus
* Noham, Cam
* Skian

McMahon, Patrick James 1860- ?
[PI]
Scottish poet
* Mahn, Mack

McManus, Blanche
See Mansfield, Mrs. M. F.

McManus, Patrick 1863-1886 [PI]
Irish poet
* Donard, Slieve
* Sunbeam

McMullan, William John
1813-1863 [PI]
Irish poet
* Oge, Hector
* Paddy, Scot, the Piper

McNally, Leonard 1752-1820 [PI]
Irish playwright, author, poet
* Plunder

McNamara, Computer Bob
See McNamara, Robert Strange

McNamara, Robert Strange 1916-
[CR]
*American business executive and
government official*
* Mac the Knife
* McNamara, Computer Bob

McNamara, William Franklin 1855-
? [PI]
American poet
* Hazelton, Harry

McNelly's Bulldog
See Armstrong, John Barclay

McPhail, Buck
See McPhail, Howard

McPhail, Howard 20th c. [EF]
American football player
* McPhail, Buck

McPherson, Amy
See McPherson, Forrest

McPherson, Forrest 20th c. [EF]
American football player
* McPherson, Amy

McPherson, Mrs. H. M.
Author
* West, Jessamyn

McQuin, [Abbe] Ange Denis
1756-1823 [PI]
French-born poet and author
* [The] Gleaner

M'Crib, Theophilus
See Lee, Henry Boyle

McSherry, Shandy
See McCorry, Peter

McSwiney, Stephen Myles ?-1890
[PI]
Irish physician and poet
* Lancet

McVitie, Jack ?-1967 [DI]
British underworld figure
* [The] Hat

Me Too
See Platt, Thomas Collier

Meadowcroft, John 1767-1805
[FAA]
British-born actor
* Hodgkinson, John

Meagher, John Francis 1848- ?
[PI]
Irish poet and author
* Slievenamon

Meagher, Patrick J. 1810-1880
[PI]
Irish-born journalist
* O'Meagher, Patrick J.

Meagher, Thomas Francis
1823-1867 [PI]
*Irish-born American politician and
army officer*
* O'Keeffe, Cornelius
(See also base volume)

Meaker, Eloise 1915- [CA]
American author and columnist
* Clark, Lydia Benson
* Hunter, Valancy
* Lancaster, Lydia
* McAllister, Amanda

Meany, Stephen Joseph 1825-1888
[PI]
Irish poet and journalist
* Abelard
* Werner

[The] Measuring Man
See DeSalvo, Albert

Meat Cleaver Weaver
See Weaver, Eddie

Meaux, Huey 20th c. [CMA]
American disc jockey
* [The] Crazy Cajun

Medes Macial, Antonio Vicente
1835-1897 [EOP]
Brazilian cult leader
* Conselheiro, Antonio

Medhurst, Mr. 19th c. [EOP]
Astrologer and author
* Raphael III

[A] Medical Man
See Watson, Forbes

Medicus
See Slade, Daniel Denison

Medicus
See Watson, George Bott Churchill

Medley, Matthew
See Aston, Anthony

Meehan, Alexander S. ?-1852 [PI]
Irish poet
* Astroea
* [The] Spirit of the Nation

Meehan, Charles Patrick
1812-1890 [PI]
Irish author and poet
* C. P. M.
* Clericus
* D. M'L.
* Father Charles
* Sister Mary

Meehan, Thomas 18th c. [PI]
Irish poet
* T. M.

Meek, Margaret
See Spencer Meek, Margaret
[Diston]

Meek, Matthew
See Ramsay, Richard

Meeker, N. C.
See Meeker, Nathan Cook

Meeker, Nathan Cook 1817-1879
[WGT]
American author
* Armstrong, [Captain] Jacob D.
* Meeker, N. C.

Meeker, Nellie J. 19th c. [DNA]
Author
* Valentine, Jane

Megaletor
See Cromwell, Oliver

Meilach, Dona Z[weigoron] 1926-
[CA]
American author
* Stanli, Sue

Meilhac, Henri 1832-1897 [NPS]
French playwright and author
* Baskoff, Ivan

Meinhold, Johann Wilhelm
1797-1851 [WGT]
German author
* Schweidler, Abraham

Meirion
See Owen, William

Mel
See McGeoghegan, Thomas J.

Mel, Mary
See Bennett, Mary E.

Mel-Bonis
See Bonis, Melanie

Melanter
See Blackmore, Richard Doddridge

Melata, Don Macario Padua
See Amat, Felix

Meldrum, David S. 1865- ? [NPS]
Author and journalist
* Foulis, Hugh
* Looker-On

Melmoth, William 1666-1743
[NPS]
Author and attorney
* Cicero, Marcus Tullius

Mels, August
See Cohn, Martin

Melville, Captain
See McCallum, Francis McNeill

Melville, Herman 1819-1891 [UH]
American author
* [The] American Rabelais

Melville, Lewis
See Beckford, William

Melville, Lewis
See Thackeray, William
Makepeace

[A] Member
See Arthington, Maria

[A] Member
See Wakefield, Edward Gibbon

[A] Member of Lincoln's Inn
See Raithby, John

[A] Member of Neither Syndicate
See Addington, Henry [First
Viscount Sidmouth]

[A] Member of the Bar
See Hart, C. W.

[A] Member of the Bar
See Kip, Leonard

[A] Member of the Boston Bar
See Austin, Ivers James

[A] Member of the Church of England
See Appleyard, Ernest Silvanus

[A] Member of the Church of England
See Hopkins, William

[A] Member of the Church of England
See Thornthwaite, J. A.

[A] Member of the Church of Scotland
See Pollock, John

Member of the Class of '67
See Benjamin, Park

[A] Member of the College of Justice
See Watson, James

[A] Member of the College of Physicians
See Wainewright, Jeremiah

[A] Member of the Congregation
See Moule, Joseph

[A] Member of the Convention of Royal Burghs of Scotland
See Scott, David Dundas

[A] Member of the Corporation
See Eliot, Samuel Atkins

[A] Member of the Established Church
See Bayley, [Sir] John

[A] Member of the Executive Committee
See Mott, Jordan L.

Member of the Faculty of Advocates
See Ferguson, Charles

[A] Member of the H. of A. of Newfoundland
See Morris, Patrick

[A] Member of the House of Commons
See Arnall, William

[A] Member of the House of Commons
See Hervey, John [Baron Hervey of
Ickworth]

[A] Member of the Humane Society
See Davis, Wendell

[A] Member of the Irish Bar
See Kelly, Peter Burrowes

[A] Member of the Lower House of Convocation
See Atterbury, Francis

[A] Member of the N.Y. Geneal. and Biog. Society
See Kip, William Ingraham

[A] Member of the Roxburghe Club
See Dibdin, Thomas Frognall

[A] Member of the Society
See Arnee, Frank

[A] Member of the Society
See Ash, Edward

[A] Member of the Society of Friends
See Bowden, James

[A] Member of the Suffolk Committee
See Gassett, Henry

[A] Member of the Synod of United Original Seceders
See Graham, John

[A] Member of the Univ. of Camb.
See Nixon, Edward John

[A] Member of the University of Cambridge
See Long, George

[A] Member of the Vermont Bar
See Thompson, Daniel P.

Memoriter
See Pae, David

Menalcas
See Drury, Henry Joseph Thomas

Menander
See Paine, Robert Treat, Jr.

Menander
See Warton, Thomas

Mencken, Henry Louis 1880-1956
American author and editor
* Allison, George W.
* Anderson, C. Farley
* Archer, Herbert Winslow
* Bell, W. L. D.
* Bellamy, Atwood C.
* Brownell, Charles F.
* Brownell, John F.
* D'Aubigy, Pierre
* De Verdi, Marie
* Della Torre, Raoul
* Drayham, William
* Dryham, James
* Fink, William
* Gilray, J. D.
* Hatteras, Amelia
* Henderson, F. C.
* Jefferson, Janet
* McLoughlin, R. B.
* Morgan, Harriet
* Peregoy, George Weems
* Ratcliffe, James P.
* [The] Ringmaster
* Thompson, Francis Clegg
* Trimball, W. H.
* W. G. L.
* Watson, Irving S.
* Wharton, James
* Woodruff, Robert W.
(See also base volume)

[The] Mendicant Bard
See Lewis, Stuart

Mendoza, Pedro Gonzalez de
1428-1495 [UH]
Spanish prelate, statesman, soldier
* [The] Great

Menenius
See Starkey, Digby Pilot

Menippus
See Sealy, Robert

[The] Men's Dior
See Savini-Brioni, Gaetano

Mentor
See Lake, Kenneth R[obert]

Mentor
See Urner, Nathan D.

Menzies, Sutherland
See Stone, Elizabeth

Mercator
See Anderson, James

Mercator
See Ellice, Edward

Mercedes, [Sister] 1846- ? [DNA]
American poet
* Alexander, [Rev.] Richard W.

[A] Merchant
See Carr, Frank

[A] Merchant of Boston
See Hooper, Samuel

Merchant, T.
See Dibdin, Thomas John

Mercouri, Maria Amalia 1925-
[BP]
Greek actress
* Mercouri, Melina

Mercouri, Melina
See Mercouri, Maria Amalia

[A] Mere Irishman
See Killen, James Bryce

Meredith, C. Leon
See Aiken, George L.

Meres, Francis 1565-1647 [NPS]
Clergyman and author
* Gallant Young Juvenal

Meriwether, Elizabeth [Avery]
1832-1917 [DNA]
American author and playwright
* Edmonds, George

Merlin
See Murray, David Christie

Merlin, [Brother]
See Reuss, Theodor

Merriam, Florence A.
See Bailey, Florence M.

Merrifield, Mrs. Reuben
Author
* Forrester, Izola

Merrill, James Milford 1847-1936
American author
* Old Timer
* Parrish, Wendal
* Redwing, Morris

Merriman, Mansfield 1848-1925
[DNA]
American author and engineer
* Licks, H. E.

Merriwell, Frank
See Whitson, John H.

[The] Merry Devil of Edmonton
See Fabell, Peter

Merry, Malcolm J.
See Rymer, James Malcolm

Merry, Robert 1755-1798 [NPS]
British poet and playwright
* Oziosi [The Lazybones]
(See also base volume)

Merton, Ambrose, Gent.
See Thoms, William John

Merulan
See Joyce, Robert Dwyer

Merva
See Kilgallen, Mary

Merwe, A. v.d.
See Geyl, Pieter [Catharinus Arie]

Mesec, Iggy
See Mesec, Ignatius

Mesec, Ignatius 20th c. [EF]
American football player
* Mesec, Iggy

Meserve, Arthur Livermore
1838-1896
American author
* Cuyler, Duke
* Saco

[The] Messenger
See Baker, George

Mestre Jhan
See Gallus, Johannes

Metcalfe, Frederick 1817?- ? [IP]
British clergyman and author
* [The] Oxonian

Metress, James F[rancis]
See Metress, Seamus P.

Metress, Seamus P. 1933- [CA]
American author and anthropologist
* Metress, James F[rancis]

Meurice, Blanca
See Von Block, Bela

Meusnier, Georges [IP]
Author
* Robert, Karl

Meyer, August Friedrich 1811- ?
[IP]
German poet
* Brunold, Friedrich

Meyer, Siegbert 1841- ? [IP]
German author
* Siegmey

Meyler, Walter Thomas 19th c.
[PI]
Irish poet
* W. T. M.

**Meynell, Alice [Christiana Gertrude
Thompson]** 1847-1922 [TLC]
British author, editor, poet
* Oldcastle, Alice
* Phillimore, Francis
* Thompson, A. C.

M'Fall, Haldane 1860- ? [NPS]
Soldier, author, art critic
* Dane, Hal

Michael, Blaunpayn 13th c. [NPS]
British poet
* [The] Cornish Poet

Michaels, Fern [joint pseudonym
with Mary Kuczkir]
See Anderson, Roberta

Michaels, Fern [joint pseudonym
with Roberta Anderson]
See Kuczkir, Mary

Michaels, Ralph
See Filicchia, Ralph

Michel de Notredame 1503-1566
French astrologer
* Nostradamus

Michel, F. Fernand 19th c. [IP]
French author
* Real, Anthony

Michel, Tom
See Michel, William

Michel, William 20th c. [EF]
American football player
* Michel, Tom

Michelborne, John 18th c. [IP]
Irish historian and author
* [A] Gentleman Who Was In the
  Town

Michell, Grace [Angove] 1839- ?
[IP]
British author
* Angove, Grace

Michell, Nicholas 1807-1880 [IP]
British author and poet
* [An] Essayist on the Passions

Michi, Orazio 1595?-1641 [BBD]
Italian composer
* Della Arpa

Michie, Archibald [IP]
British critic
* Robinson, Jack

[The] Mick
See Yule, Joe, Jr.

Mickle, Charles Julius [IP]
British author
* C. J. M., Mr.

[The] Microphone of God
See Sheen, Peter

[The] Midday Murderer
See Gosman, Klaus

[A] Middle Aged Citizen
See Russell, R.

Middlemass, Hume 19th c. [IP]
British author
* Mignionette
* Thistle

[The] Middlesex Owl
See Mayo, Herbert

Middlestitch, Giles
See Maginn, William

Middleton, Conyers 1683-1750
[NPS]
Theologian and scholar
* Fiddling Conyers

Middleton, Henry 1771-1846 [IP]
American statesman and author
* [A] South Carolinian

Middleton, Patrick 18th c. [IP]
British clergyman and author
* P. M.

Middleton, Thomas 1570?-1627
[DEA]
British author and playwright
* Hubburd, Oliver
* T. M.

Middling, Theophilus
See Snider, Denton Jacques

[The] Midget King of Swing
See Short, Robert Waltrip [Bobby]

[A] Midshipman of the U.S. Navy
See Leggett, William

Miedcke, Karl August 1804-1880
[BBD]
German composer
* Krebs, Karl August

Mighty Eagle
See Magellan, Fernando de

[The] Mighty Minstrel
See Scott, [Sir] Walter

[The] Mighty Minstrel of Old Mole
See Spenser, Edmund

Mignionette
See Middlemass, Hume

Mignon, August
See Darling, John A.

Mikkelsen, Hans
See Holberg, Louis [or Ludvig]

[Il] Milanese
See Sammartini [or San Martini],
Giovanni Battista

Milbourne, Luke ?-1720 [IP]
British author
* Tom of Bedlam

Miles, Alfred 1796-1851 [IP]
British author
* A. M.

Miles, Henry, Jr. [IP]
American author
* Hermes

Miles, Richard
See Perreau-Saussine, Gerald

Miles, Sibella [Hatfield] 1800- ?
[IP]
British poet
* Hatfield, S. E.

Miletus, Rex
See Burgess, Michael Roy

**Milkomane, George Alexis
Milkomanovich** 1903- [CA]
*Russian-born British physician and
author*
* Redwood, Alec
(See also base volume)

Mill, John Stuart 1806-1873
[IP, NPS]
British philosopher and author
* [The] Saint of Rationalism
* Wickliffe

Millais, Ruth
See Mulholland, Rosa

Millar, John 1735-1801 [IP]
Scottish jurist and author
* Crito

Millard, E. E. 19th c. [IP]
American author
* E. E. M.
(See also base volume)

Millard, John [IP]
British author and librarian
* Coxe, Henry, Esq.

Millbank, [Capt.] H. R.
See Ellis, Edward S[ylvester]

Millen, F. F. [IP]
American journalist
* Ardboe
* Trefoil
* Verdad

Miller, Cincinnatus Heine
1848-1913 [UH]
American poet and playwright
* [The] Oregon Byron
(See also base volume)

Miller, Deacon
See Miller, James B.

Miller, Edward 20th c. [EF]
American football player
* Miller, Shorty

Miller, Edwin
See Max, Edwin

Miller, Emily [Huntington] [IP]
American author
* Purdy

Miller, Heinie
See Miller, Henry

Miller, Henry 20th c. [EF]
American football player
* Miller, Heinie

Miller, James B. 1866-1909 [EWG]
American gunfighter
* Miller, Deacon
* Miller, Killer
* Miller, Killin' Jim

Miller, Killer
See Miller, James B.

Miller, Killin' Jim
See Miller, James B.

Miller, Leonard 1864-1939 [UH]
British author
* [The] Novelist's Novelist
(See also base volume)

Miller, Lydia Falconer 1805- ?
[HFN]
Author
* L. F. F. M.
(See also base volume)

Miller, Marilyn McMeen
See Brown, Marilyn McMeen
Miller

Miller, Minnie [Willis] 1845- ?
[DNA]
American author
* Baines, Minnie Willis

Miller, Poi
See Miller, Robert

Miller, Robert 20th c. [EF]
American football player
* Miller, Poi

Miller, Sheila 1936- [CA]
American author and poet
* Grawoig, Sheila
* Jurnak, Sheila
* Raeschild, Sheila

Miller, Shorty
See Miller, Edward

[The] Millet of Literature
See Hardy, Thomas

[The] Millet without the Angelus
See Hardy, Thomas

Millicent
See Jordon, Mildred Arlene

Millidus
See Marston, John

Milligan, Alice L. 20th c. [PI]
Irish poet
* Olkyrn, Iris

Milligan, Ernest 20th c. [PI]
Irish poet
* Carew, Will

[The] Millionaire Boy Angel
See Cohen, Alexander

Mills, Cotton Mather, Esq.
See Gaskell, Elizabeth Cleghorn

Mills, Faith
See Payne, Odessa Strickland

Milman, Henry Hart 1791-1868
[NPS]
Clergyman
* [The] Poet Priest

Milne, Frances Margaret 1846- ?
[PI]
Irish-born poet
* Frances, Margaret

Milner, Bill
See Milner, Charles

Milner, Charles 20th c. [EF]
American football player
* Milner, Bill

Milo
See Boyle, John

Milonas, Rolf
See Myller, Rolf

Milton, John 1608-1674
[DEA, NPS]
British poet
* [The] Black Mouthed Zoilus
* [The] Blind Poet
* [The] Defender of the People
* [The] English Mastiff
* [The] Great Gospel Gun
* J. M.
* [The] Rival of Homer
(See also base volume)

Mina, Lino Amalia Espos Y
1809-1832 [BLB]
Spanish-born murderer and thief
* Espos, Carolino

Minehaha, Cornelius
See Wedekind, Benjamin Franklin

Miner, Enoch Newton ?-1923
[DNA]
Author
* Typist, Topsy

Ming the Merciless
See Sigoloff, Sanford C.

[The] Minister
See Peel, [Sir] Robert

[The] Minister of Fashion
See Laurent, Marie-Jeanne

[A] Minister of the Church of England
See Webster, George Edis

[A] Minister of the Church of Scotland
See Currie, John

[A] Minister of the Church of Scotland
See Irvine, Alexander

[A] Minister of the Gospel
See Wilson, Joseph

[A] Minister of the Interior
See Whiting, Sydney

[A] Ministering Friend
See Foe, Daniel

Minor, Dryden
See O'Donnell, Francis Hugh

Minority of One
See Stanhope, Charles [Third Earl of Stanhope]

[The] Minstrel Maiden of Mobile
See Harriss, Julia Mildred

Mintun, Jake
See Mintun, John

Mintun, John 20th c. [EF]
American football player
* Mintun, Jake

Minturn, Edward
See Judson, Edward Zane Carroll

[The] Mirabeau of Brazil
See Machado e Silva, Andrada

[The] Miracle of Time
See Elizabeth I

Miranda, Roque 1799-1843 [GS]
Spanish bullfighter
* Rigores [Precise One]

Mirepoix, Camille 1926- [CA]
British author and journalist
* Adastra

Mirliter
See Boue de Villiers, Amable Louis

Mirmillo
See Gibbons, William

[The] Mirror of Her Age
See Bradstreet, Anne

Mirror, Tom
See Estcourt, Richard

[The] Mirror-Upholder of His Age
See Shakespeare, William

Misleader of the Papacy
See Gaetano [or Caetani], Benedetto

Misosarum, Gregory
See Swift, Jonathan

Miss P.
See Plumptre, Anne

Mr. X
See Kennan, George Frost

[The] Mistress of Misdirection
See Christie, Agatha [Mary Clarissa]

Mitchell, Donald Grant 1822- ?
[HFN]
American author
* D. G. M.
(See also base volume)

[The] Mitred Layman
See O'Beirne, Thomas Lewis

Mivart, St. George Jackson
1827-1900 [DEA]
British author
* Drew, D'Arcy

Mizpah
See Lea, Henry Charles

M'Keown, Darby
See Donnelly, James

Mlle. Rosalie
See Levasseur, Marie Claude Josephe

Moan, Emmett 20th c. [EF]
American football player
* Moan, Kelly

Moan, Kelly
See Moan, Emmett

Moatlodi
See Chamberlain, Joseph

Mobley, Walt
See Burgess, Michael Roy

[The] Mock Preacher
See Whitefield, George

[The] Mocking Bird of Our Parnassian Ornithology
See Byron, George Gordon Noel

Moco [Joint signature with Jorgen Mogensen]
See Cornelius, Siegfried

Moco [Joint signature with Siegfried Cornelius]
See Mogensen, Jorgen

[The] Modern Baillet
See Arouet, Francois Marie

[The] Modern Belisarius
See McClellan, George Brinton

[The] Modern Dickens
See De Morgan, William

[The] Modern Indagator Invictissimus
See Dibdin, Thomas Frognall

[The] Modern Pict
See Bruce, Thomas

[The] Modern Stagirite
See Warburton, William

[A] Modern Troubadour
See O'Carroll, Patrick

[The] Modern Zoilus
See Perrault, Charles

Moders [or Meders?], Mary
1643-1673 [LFW]
British swindler
* [The] German Princess

[A] Modus
See Swift, Jonathan

Moethu
See Jones, Thomas

Mogensen, Jorgen 1922- [WEC]
Danish cartoonist and sculptor
* Moco [Joint signature with Siegfried Cornelius]

Mohenesto
See Avery, Henry M.

Mohoao
See Fairburn, Edwin

Moi-Meme
See Coveney, [Sister] Mary

Molenda, Bo
See Molenda, John

Molenda, John 20th c. [EF]
American football player
* Molenda, Bo

Molloy, Joseph Fitzgerald
1859-1908 [PI]
Irish author
* Wilding, Ernest

Moloney, Patrick 19th c. [PI]
Irish physician and poet
* Australis

Moltke, Hellmuth Karl Bernhard von
1800-1891 [NPS]
Prussian army officer
* [The] Taciturn
(See also base volume)

Momonia
See Kickham, Charles Joseph

Mona
See O'Mahony, Timothy J.

[Il] Monaco [The Monk]
See Morandi, Giorgio

Monahan, John
See Burnett, William Riley

Monck, Mary C. F.
See Munster, Mary C. F.

Monckton, Rose C. 19th c. [HFN]
Author
* M.

Mondrian, Piet[er Cornelis]
1872-1944
Dutch painter
* [The] Dancing Madonna
* [The] Father of Neo-Plasticism

Monitor
See Lee, Arthur

[The] Monk
See Eustace

[The] Monk
See Lewis, Matthew Gregory

Monk, James Henry 19th c. [HFN]
Author
* J. H. M.

Monks, P.
See O'Donnell, John Francis

Monola, Adelaide
See Hughes, Adelaide Manola [Mould]

Monopoli
See Insanguine, Giacomo [Antonio Francesco Paolo Michele]

Monos
See Mangan, James Clarence

Monroe, Carole 1944- [CA]
American author
* Dufrechou, Carole

[The] Monroe of Punk
See Harry, Deborah

[The] Monster
See Jeffries

Montagu, Ashley 1905- [CA]
British-born anthropologist and author
* Academicas Mentor

Montagu, Mary Wortley
1689-1762 [DEA, NPS, UH]
British author and poet
* L. M. W. M., Rt. Hon.
* Sappho
(See also base volume)

Montague, Jeanne
See Yarde, Jeanne Betty Frances Treasure

Montaigne, Michel Eyquem de
1533-1592 [NPS]
French philosopher and author
* [The] Father of Modern Miscellanies

Montanus
See McGee, Thomas D'Arcy

Montbard, Georges
See Loyes, Charles Auguste

Montclair, J. W.
See Weidemeyer, John William

Montcorbier, Francois de
See Villon, Francois

Montero, Antonio Maria 1818- ?
[GS]
Spanish bullfighter
* [El] Zurdo [Lefthanded One]

Montes, Francisco 1805-1851   [GS]
Spanish bullfighter
* Montes, Paquiro

Montes, Paquiro
See Montes, Francisco

Montez, Editha Gilbert
See Jackson, Editha Salomon

Montgomerie, Robert
See Alloway, Robert Morellet

Montgomery, James 1771-1854
[DEA, DLE1, NPS]
Scottish poet
* J. M.
* Positive, Paul
* Sheffield, Classic
* Silvertongue, Gabriel
(See also base volume)

Montgomery, John Wilson
1835?-1911 [PI]
Irish author
* Sweet Bard of Bailieborough

Montgomery, Robert 1807-1855
[NPS]
Poet
* Montgomery, Satan

Montgomery, Satan
See Montgomery, Robert

Moody, D. L.
See Moody, Dwight Lyman

Moody, Dwight Lyman 1837-1899
[LC]
American evangelist and author
* Moody, D. L.

[The] Moondog
See Freed, Alan

Moone, Kid
See Moone, Nick

Moone, Nick 20th c.   [RBE]
Boxer
* Moone, Kid

Mooney, Tex
See Schupbach, O. T.

Moonlight, Captain
See Scott, Andrew George

Moor, Emily
See Deming, Richard

Moor, Robert 20th c.   [EOP]
Founder of religious cult
* De Grimston, Robert Moor Sylvester

Moore, Annie Aubertine [Woodward]
1841-1929 [DNA]
American author and musician
* Forestier, Auber

Moore, Bucky
See Moore, William

Moore, Chuck
Author
* Stone, Willie

Moore, Clement Clarke 1779-1863
[DLE1, SAT]
American author, theologian, poet
* Columella

Moore, Eugenia
See Ouick, Florence

Moore, Ezekiel, Jr. 1943-   [EF, FR]
American football player
* Moore, Zeke

Moore, Francis 1657-1715?
[EOP, NPS]
British physician, astrologer, educator
* Moore, Old

Moore, George Henry 1811-1870
[PI]
Irish poet
* G. H. M.
* M.

Moore, Hannah [Hudson]
1857-1927 [DNA]
American author and journalist
* Moore, N. Hudson

Moore, Idora [McClellan]
1843-1929 [DNA]
American author
* Hamilton, Betsy

Moore, John 1807-1856   [PI]
British poet
* Brandy, Jonas
* [The] Hermit in Oscott
* Pleon
* Romeo

Moore, Justina 19th c.   [NPS]
Author
* Pritchard, Martin J.

Moore, M. Louise 19th c.   [SFL]
Author
* [An] Untrammeled Free-Thinker

Moore, Marna
See Reynolds, [Marjorie] Moira Davison

Moore, Mollie E.
See Davis, Mollie E. [Moore]

Moore, N. Hudson
See Moore, Hannah [Hudson]

Moore, Old
See Moore, Francis

Moore, Thomas 1779-1852
[NPS, PI]
Irish poet
* [The] Pander of Venus
* Rustifucius, Trismegistus
* T. M.
* [The] Young Catullus of His Day
(See also base volume)

Moore, Wentworth
See Mallock, William Hurrell

Moore, William 20th c.   [EF]
American football player
* Moore, Bucky

Moore, Zeke
See Moore, Ezekiel, Jr.

Moore-Brabazon, J. T. C. 20th c.
[PPN]
British pioneer motorist and aviator
* Brab

Moorman, Maurice 20th c.   [EF]
American football player
* Moorman, Mo

Moorman, Mo
See Moorman, Maurice

Mor, Cahal
See O'Conor, Charles Patrick

Mor, Eoghan
See Daly, Eugene P.

Mor, McCarthaigh
See Varian, Ralph

Moran, Michael 1794?-1846
[DIL, PI]
Irish composer, singer, poet
* [The] Last Gleeman
* Zozimus

Morandi, Giorgio 1891?-1964
Italian painter
* [Il] Monaco [The Monk]

Morant, Breaker
See Morant, Harry H.

Morant, Harry H. ?-1899   [DLE1]
Australian army officer and poet
* [The] Breaker
* Morant, Breaker

Morata, Jaido
See Vickers, John

Moravia, Alberto
See Pincherle, Alberto

Moray, Tiburce
See Grousset, Paschal

Morco, Happy Jack
See Morco, John

Morco, John ?-1873   [BLB, EWG]
American gunfighter
* Morco, Happy Jack

Mordaunt, Clayton 1730-1799
[NPS]
British author
* [The] Bibliomaniacal Hercules

More, Hannah 1745-1833
[DEA, DLE1, NPS]
British author, poet, playwright
* Chip, Will
* [A] Giantess of Genius
* Our Little David
* [The] Tenth Muse

More, Henry 1614-1687   [NPS]
British clergyman and philosopher
* [The] Man Mouse
* Philalethes, Alazonomastix
(See also base volume)

Moreau, Hegesippe 1810-1838
[NPS]
French poet
* Myosotis

Morel-Retz, Louis-Pierre
1825-1899 [WEC]
French painter and cartoonist
* Stop

[El] Morenillo [Little Swarthy One]
See Jimenez, Juan

Moreno, Anthony 20th c.   [DI]
French swindler
* [El] Chorro [The Fountain]

Moreton, Clara
See Bloomfield-Moore, Clara Sophia [Jessup]

Morgan, Daniel 1830-1865   [DI]
Australian bushranger
* Bill the Jockey
* Down the Hill Jack
* Mad Dan the Murrimbidgee Terror
* Morgan, Mad

Morgan, Harriet
See Mencken, Henry Louis

Morgan, James 19th c.   [HFN]
Author
* J. M.

Morgan, Jane
See Cooper, James Fenimore

Morgan, Mad
See Morgan, Daniel

Morgan, Squire
See Henry Frederick

Morgan, Sydney 1778?-1859   [PI]
Irish author and poet
* S. O.
(See also base volume)

Morgan, Thomas P. [Tom] 1864-1929
American author
* Daft, Tennyson J.

Morhange, Charles-Henri Valentin
1813-1888 [BBD]
French musician and composer
* Alkan, Charles-Henri Valentin

Morice, Anne
See Shaw, Felicity

Morley, Arthur Spencer
See Bangs, John Kendrick

Morley, Ralph
See Hinton, Howard

[The] Mormon Kid
See Christianson, Willard Erastus

[The] Morning Star of the Reformation
See Huss, John

[Il] Moro
See Sforza, Lodovico [or Ludovico]

Morres, Hervey Redmond
1746?-1797 [PI]
Irish poet
* Lord M.

Morrill, Golightly
See Morrill, Gulian Lansing

Morrill, Gulian Lansing 1857-1928
[DNA]
American author and clergyman
* Morrill, Golightly

Morris, Eugenia Laura [Tuttle] 1833-
? [DNA]
Author
* Keith, Alyn Yates

Morris, General
See   Morris, George Pope

Morris, George Pope 1802-1864
[DLE1]
American journalist and poet
* Morris, General

Morris, James M. 19th c.
[HFN, NPS]
American author
* Pepper, K. N.

Morris, John Scott [Jack] 1956-
American baseball player
* [The] Count

Morris, [Sir] Lewis 1833-1907
[NPS]
British poet
* [The] Bard of Penrhyn
(See also base volume)

Morris, Patrick   [IP]
Canadian politician and author
* [A] Member of the H. of A. of
   Newfoundland

Morris, Ralph 18th c.   [WGT]
Author
* Daniel, John

Morris, Richard 1708-1792   [IP]
British astrologer and author
* Spot, Dick, the Conjuror

Morris, Robert
See   Gibbons, James Sloan

Morrison, Adrienne
See   Morrison, Mabel

Morrison, G. F.
See   Bernstein, Gerry

Morrison, John 1749-1798   [IP]
Scottish poet and clergyman
* Musoeus

Morrison, John 19th c.   [HFN, IP]
British author and clergyman
* [A] Clergyman

Morrison, Mabel 20th c.   [FAA]
American actress
* Morrison, Adrienne

Morrison, Mary Jane [Whitney]
1832-1904   [DNA]
American author
* Wallis, Jenny

Morrison, Richard James
1795-1874   [IP]
British astrologer
* Zadkiel Tao Sze
* Zadkiel the Seer
(See also base volume)

Morrissey, John 1831-1880   [SG]
*Irish-American gambler, boxer,
politician*
* Old Smoke

Morrow, Dave 19th c.
American frontiersman
* Prairie Dog Dave

Morrow, Felix 1906-   [EOP]
American publisher, editor, author
* Wilson, John C.

Morrow, Gilbert
See   Gibbs, George

Morrow, May
See   Carpenter, Anna May

Morse, F. L. 19th c.   [IP]
American author
* F. L. M.

Morse, Freeman H. 1807- ?   [IP]
American statesman and author
* [The] American Consul at
   London

Morse, J. J. 1848-1919   [EOP]
Claimed to possess psychic powers
* [The] Bishop of Spiritualism

Morse, Jason 1821-1861   [IP]
American clergyman and author
* [The] Pastor

Morse, Jedediah 1761-1826   [IP]
American clergyman and author
* [An] Inhabitant of New England
(See also base volume)

Morse, Lucy G.
Author
* Gibbons, Lucy

Morse, Red
See   Morse, W.

Morse, Samuel Finley Breese
1791-1872   [IP]
American inventor
* [An] American
* B.
* Brutus
(See also base volume)

Morse, Sidney Edwards 1794-1871
[IP]
American journalist
* [An] American

Morse, W. 20th c.   [EF]
American football player
* Morse, Red

Mortimer, Geoffrey
See   Gallichan, Walter M.

Mortimer, John 18th c.   [IP]
British author
* J. M., Esq., F.R.S.

Mortimer, Roger 1287?-1330
[NPS]
* [The] King of Folly

Mortimer, Thomas 1730-1810   [IP]
British author
* Philanthropos

Morton, G. A. 20th c.   [NPS]
American author
* Aitken, Robert

Morton, Stanley
See   Freedgood, Morton

Mosby, Mary Webster [Pleasants]
1791-1844   [BDSA, DNA]
American author
* Webster, M. M.

Moscato, Brother
See   Moscato, Phillip

Moscato, Phillip 20th c.
American underworld figure
* Moscato, Brother

Moschus
See   Lovel, Robert

Moser, Joseph 1748-1819   [IP]
British author
* [A] Barber
* Twig, Timothy, Esq.

Moses, Faraway
See   Huff, Jacob K.

Moses, W. S. 19th c.   [IP]
British author
* A. M., Oxon

Moskowitz, Harry 1900-1971
[DAM]
American musician and conductor
* Ford, Harry

Mosonyi, Mihaly
See   Brandt, Michael

Mosse, T. 18th c.   [PI]
Irish poet
* T. M.

Mossman, Burt[on] 1867- ?   [EWG]
American law officer
* Mossman, Cap

Mossman, Cap
See   Mossman, Burt[on]

Mossop, Henry 1729-1773   [NPS]
Playwright
* [The] Distiller of Syllables

[The] Most Faultless of Poets
See   Pope, Alexander

Mostyn, Sydney
See   Russell, William Clark

Moth
See   Buckingham, Joseph Tinker

[A] Mother
See   Mott, Abigail

[The] Mother of God
See   Mary

[The] Mother of Her Country
See   Victoria

Motherwell, William 1797-1835
[IP]
Scottish poet and journalist
* Brown, Isaac

Mott, Abigail   [IP]
American author
* [A] Mother

Mott, Buster
See   Mott, Norman

Mott, Jordan L.   [IP]
American inventor and author
* [A] Member of the Executive
   Committee

Mott, Norman 20th c.   [EF]
American football player
* Mott, Buster

Mottley, John 1692-1750   [IP]
British author
* [A] Gentleman
* Seymour, Robert, of the Inner
   Temple
(See also base volume)

Mottram, Ralph Hale 1883-1971
[DLE1]
British author
* Marjoram, J.
(See also base volume)

Moule, Joseph   [IP]
Scottish clergyman and author
* [A] Member of the Congregation

Moulinet, Madame
See   Weber, Jeanne

Moultrie, Gerard 19th c.   [IP]
British clergyman and hymn-writer
* D. P.
* Desiderius Pastor

Moultrie, Gerard (Continued)
* M.

Mount Atlas
See   O'Shea, John

Mountain, Jacob Henry Brooke 19th
c.   [HFN]
Author
* J. H. B. M.

[The] Mountaineer
See   Alston, Joseph

Mountaineer
See   Wright, Charles

Mountjoy, Desmond
See   Houston, W. M. Chapman

[The] Mourner
See   Mangan, James Clarence

Mouthy
See   Southey, Robert

Mouton, Michel
See   Villon, Francois

Mowbray, J. P.
See   Wheeler, Andrew Carpenter

Moy
See   O'Donnell, John

Mozans, H. J.
See   Zahm, John Augustine

M'Rory, [Rev] Rory
See   Lees, James Cameron

Mrs. G.
See   Griffiths, Kitty Anna

Mrs. L.
See   Longworth, Alice Roosevelt

Mudgett, Herman Webster ?-1896
[BLB, DI]
American murderer, robber, arsonist
* Holmes, H. H.
* Holmes, Harry Howard
* Howard, H. M.

Mudie, Charles Edward 1818-1890
[NPS]
Library founder and poet
* C. E. M.

Mug, [Sister] Mary Theodosia
1860-1943   [DNA]
American author
* Maery, Helen

Muggins
See   Clemens, Samuel Langhorne

Muinntire, Fear na
See   Rooney, William

Muir, Marie Agnes 1904-   [CA]
British author
* Kaye, Barbara
(See also base volume)

Muktanada, Swami 1908-   [EOP]
Indian mystic and author
* Baba
* Paramahansa

Mularczyk, Roman 1921-   [CD]
Polish author
* Bratny, Roman

Mulas, Pedro 19th c.   [GS]
Spanish bullfighter
* [El] Fraile [The Friar]

Mulchinock, William Pembroke
1820-1864 [PI]
Irish poet
* Heremon
* M.
* W. P. M.

Mulgan, Catherine
See Gough, Catherine

Mulholland, Rosa 1850- ? [PI]
Irish poet and author
* Millais, Ruth
* R. M.

Mullaney, Patrick Francis
1847?-1893 [BDSA, DNA, PI]
American author and educator
* Azarias, [Brother]

Mullen, Dore
See Mullen, Dorothy

Mullen, Dorothy 1933- [CA]
American author
* Mullen, Dore

Mullen [or Mullins?], Michael
1833-1869 [PI]
Irish-born clergyman and poet
* Fodhla, Ollamh
* M. C.

Muller, Catherine Elise 1861-1929
[EOP]
Claimed to possess psychic powers
* Smith, Helene

Muller, Friedrich 1823- ? [DEA]
German-born author
* Max-Muller, Friedrich

Mulligan, Morty Macnamara
See Maginn, William

Mullinahone, Eileen
See Heffernan, Michael J.

Mullinahone, K.
See Kickham, Charles Joseph

Mulvany, Charles Pelham
1835-1885 [PI]
Irish-born poet
* C. P. M., Sch.

Munby, Arthur Joseph 1828-1910
[DLE1]
British poet
* Brown, Jones

Munchausen, Baron
See Raspe, Rudolph E[rich]

Munday, Anthony 1553-1633
[DEA, DLE1, NPS]
British poet and playwright
* A. M.
* Balladino, Antonio
* Honos Alit Artes
* L. P.
* Old Anthony Now-Now
* Piot, Lazarus

Mundungus
See Sharp, Samuel

Mundy, Mrs.
See Ouick, Florence

Mungo
See Dyson, Jeremiah

Munoz, Jose 1817-1856 [GS]
Spanish bullfighter
* Pucheta [Big Bouquet]

Munster, Mary C. F. 1835?-1892
[PI]
Irish poet
* Monck, Mary C. F.
* Tiny

Muralto, Onuphrio
See Walpole, Horatio [Fourth Earl of Orford]

Muratori, Ludovico Antonio
1672-1750
Italian scholar
* [The] Father of Italian History

Murdoch, [Sir] Walter Logie Forbes
1874- ? [DLE1]
Australian scholar and author
* Elzevir

Murphy, Bridey
See Tighe, Virginia

Murphy, C. L. [joint pseudonym with Lawrence A(ugustus) Murphy]
See Murphy, Charlotte A[lice]

Murphy, C. L. [joint pseudonym with Charlotte A(lice) Murphy]
See Murphy, Lawrence A[gustus]

Murphy, Charlotte A[lice] 1924-
[CA]
American author and poet
* Murphy, C. L. [joint pseudonym with Lawrence A(ugustus) Murphy]

Murphy, Denis
See O'Leary, Joseph

Murphy, Francis Stack 1807-1860
[PI]
Irish author
* Cresswell, Frank

Murphy, James 1839- ? [PI]
Irish author and poet
* J. M.
* M.
* St. Molaing

Murphy, James 19th c. [PI]
Irish poet
* O'Murchadha, Shemus

Murphy, James J. ?-1875 [PI]
Irish clergyman and poet
* Fionbarra

Murphy, Katharine Mary
1840?-1885 [PI]
Irish poet
* Brigid
* Townsbridge, Elizabeth

Murphy, Lawrence A[gustus] 1924-
[CA]
American author
* Lawrence, Steven C.
* Murphy, C. L. [joint pseudonym with Charlotte A(lice) Murphy]

Murphy, Louis J.
See Hicks, Tyler Gregory

Murphy, Mrs. H. 19th c. [PI]
American poet
* Stanley, Eveleen

Murphy, Nonie Carol 1926- [CA]
American author and actress
* Caroll, Nonie

Murphy, Peter 1864-1889 [PI]
Irish poet
* O'Murchadha, Peadar

Murphy, Thomas James
See Furlong, Patrick M.

Murray, David Christie 1847-1907
[NPS]
Writer
* Merlin

Murray, Hon. Mrs.
See Aust, Sarah

Murray, John 1741-1815 [NPS]
British-born clergyman
* [The] Father of American Universalism
(See also base volume)

Murray, John 1778-1843 [NPS]
British publisher
* [The] Coxcomb Bookseller
(See also base volume)

Murray, John Fisher 1811-1865
[PI]
Irish physician and poet
* J. F. M.
* Maire

Murray, Lieut.
See Ballou, Maturin Murray

Murray, Michael
See McLaren, Moray [David Shaw]

Murray, William [First Earl of Mansfield] 1705-1793 [NPS]
British jurist
* [The] Founder of English Commercial Law
(See also base volume)

Murray-Ford, Alice May [Harte-Potts] 1879- ?
Author
* Le Breton, Mrs. John

Murray-Ford, Thomas 1854- ?
[SFL]
British author and editor
* Le Breton, Thomas

Murrel, John A. 1794- ? [BLB]
American bandit
* [The] Great Western Land Pirate

Musaeus Palatinus
See Braithwaite, Richard

[Il] Musannif
See Mackenzie, C. F.

Muscadel
See Downey, Richard

[The] Muses' Darling
See Fletcher, John

[The] Muses' Pride
See Sackville, Charles [Sixth Earl of Dorset]

Musgrave, Philip
See Abbott, Joseph

Musica, Arthur 20th c. [DI]
American swindler
* Vernard, George

Musidora
See Converse, Harriet [Maxwell]

Musidorus
See Way, B.

Muskerry, Major
See Dowe, William

Musoeus
See Morrison, John

Musquito ?-1825 [DI]
Australian bushranger
* [The] Black Napoleon

Musset, [Louis Charles] Alfred de
1810-1857 [NPS]
French poet
* Alcide, Baron de M.
(See also base volume)

[The] Mute
See Fernandez Navarette, Juan

Muzakova, Johanna [Rottova]
1830-1899 [CD]
Czech author
* Svetla, Karolina

Muzzy, Bertha
Author
* Bowen, B. M.

My Admirable Crichton
See De Quincey, Thomas

Myers, Chip
See Myers, Phil[ip] Leon

Myers, Laurence E. 1858-1899
[AS, BBH]
American track and field athlete
* Myers, Lon

Myers, Lon
See Myers, Laurence E.

Myers, Phil[ip] Leon 1945-
[EF, FR]
American football player
* Myers, Chip

Myles
See Smith, Robert

Myller, Rolf 1926- [SAT]
German-born American author
* Brown, David
* Milonas, Rolf

Mylo
See Boyle, John

Mynn, Alfred 1807-1861 [EC]
British cricketer
* [The] Lion of Kent

Myosotis
See Moreau, Hegesippe

Myrrha
See Downing, Mary

Myrtel, Hera
See Jacques, Marie-Louise Victorine [Grones]

Myrtle, Charles 20th c. [EF]
American football player
* Myrtle, Chip

Myrtle, Chip
See Myrtle, Charles

Myrtle, Lewis
See Hill, George Canning

Myrtle, Marmaduke
See Addison, Joseph

Myrtle, Marmaduke
See Dermody, Thomas

Myrtle, Marmaduke
See Steele, [Sir] Richard

Myrtle, Molly
See Hill, Agnes [Leonard]

[The] Mysterious Cyclops of Israeli Politics
See Dayan, Moshe

Mysterious Dave Mather
See Mather [or Mathers], David

Myth, M. Y. T. H.
See Nicolovius, Ludwig

N

* Indicates Assumed Name

N. A.
See Ames, Nathaniel

N. A.
See Appleton, Nathan

N. B. S.
See Shurtleff, Nathaniel Bradstreet

N. C. M. S. C.
See Cotes, Humphrey

N. F.
See Field, Nathaniel

N. H.
See Herrick, N.

N. M.?
See McDevitt, Neil

N. N.
See Kenyon, John

N. O., Ancien Missionaire
See Cuoq, Jean Andre

Naas, N.
See McDevitt, Neil

Naghten, Frederick 1822-1845 [PI]
Irish poet
* [A] Late Graduate of Oxford

[The] Nailer
See Stevens, William [Bill]

Naismith, James 1861-1939 [BBH]
Canadian-born American inventor of basketball
* [The] Father of Basketball

Nance, Bud
See Nance, James

Nance, James 1921?-
American government official
* Nance, Bud

Napier, Buffalo
See Napier, Walter

Napier, [Sir] Charles 1786-1860
[NPS]
British naval officer
* Black Charlie

Napier, Macvey 1776-1847 [NPS]
Scottish editor
* Napier, Supplement
* Naso, Macveius
(See also base volume)

Napier, Supplement
See Napier, Macvey

Napier, Walter 20th c. [EF]
American football player
* Napier, Buffalo

[The] Napoleon of Drury Lane
See Elliston, Robert William

[The] Napoleon of Finance
See Balfour, Jabez

[The] Napoleon of the Prize Ring
See Sayers, Tom

Napolitano, Dominick 20th c.
American underworld figure
* Napolitano, Sonny Black

Napolitano, Sonny Black
See Napolitano, Dominick

Nappey, Donald 1936- [DI]
British murderer
* [The] Black Panther
* Neilsen, Donald

Naramore, Gay Humboldt 19th c.
[DNA]
Poet
* Humboldt, Gay

Nares, Edward 1762-1848 [HFN]
Author
* Thinks-I-To-Myself, Who?
(See also base volume)

Nash, Eno
See Stevens, Austin N[eil]

Nash, G. Murray 20th c. [EOP]
Author
* Black, Paul

Nash [or Nashe?], Thomas
1567-1601 [DEA, NPS]
British author and playwright
* Confuter, Captain
* [The] English Aretine
* Fouleweather, Adam
* Scarlet, Thomas
* This Free Lance of Our Literature
* [The] True English Aretine
* Young Euphues
(See also base volume)

Nash, William 19th c. [PI]
Irish poet
* Endymion

Naso, Macveius
See Napier, Macvey

Nasser ben Hareth 6th c. [NPS]
* [The] Aesop of Arabia

Natali, Agnes
See Heron, Agnes

Natali, Fanny
See Heron, Fanny

[A] Native of Craven
See Carr, William

[A] Native of Denmark
See Anderson, Andreas

[A] Native of the Forest
See Apes, William

[A] Naturalist
See Adams, Andrew Leith

[A] Naturalist
See Adams, Arthur

[A] Naturalist
See Broderip, William John

[A] Naturalist
See Garner, Robert

[The] Naturalist
See Jones, John Matthew

[A] Naturalist
See Knapp, John Leonard

[A] Naturalist
See Sclater, Philip Lutley

Nature's Darling
See Waller, Edmund

Nature's Sternest Painter
See Crabbe, George

[The] Navvy Poet
See McGill, Patrick

Neal, Ed
See Neal, William

Neal, John 1793-1876 [DLE1]
American author
* Somebody, M. D. C.
(See also base volume)

Neal, William 20th c. [EF]
American football player
* Neal, Ed

[A] Necessitarian
See Allen, John

Ned of the Hills
See Drea, E. V.

Needham, Marchamont 1620-1678
[NPS]
British author
* Britannicus
* Commonwealth Didapper
* [The] Goliath of the Philistines
(See also base volume)

Negri, Red
See Negri, Warren

Negri, Warren 20th c. [EF]
American football player
* Negri, Red

[The] Negro June Allyson
See Wallace, Ruby Ann

Neilsen, Donald
See Nappey, Donald

Nell of Old Drury
See Symcott, Margaret

Nelson, Alec
See Aveling, Edward Bibbins

Nelson, Earle Leonard 1897-1928
[DI]
American murderer
* [The] Gorilla Murderer
(See also base volume)

Nelson, Henry 18th c. [PI]
Irish poet
* H. N.

Nemesis
See Robbins, Alfred Farthing

Nemiro, Beverly Anderson 1925-
[CA]
American author
* Anderson, Beverly M.

Nemo
See Adams, Henry Gardiner

Nemo
See Coleman, Patrick James

Nemo
See Gordon, Francis S.

Nemo
See Pelly, Gerald Conn

Nethercott, Henrietta 19th c. [PI]
Irish poet
* Henrietta

Nettles, Bonnie Lu 20th c. [EOP]
American religious cult leader
* Dale
* Pooh
* Poop
* Wink
(See also base volume)

Neuburg, Victor [Benjamin]
1883-1940 [EOP]
British poet and editor
* Alfricobas
* Benjie
* Broyle, M.

Neuburg, Victor [Benjamin]
(Continued)
* Byrde, Richard
* Crayne, Christopher
* Edwardes, Lawrence
* French, Arthur
* Pentreath, Paul
* Pyne, Nicholas
* Stevens, Harold
* Tarn, Shirley
* Vickybird
* Vincam, Frater Omnia
* White, Rold

Neuville, Auguste
See Dubourg, Felix

Neville, Henry 1620-1694   [WGT]
British author
* Van Sloetten, Henry Cornelius

Neville, Naomi
See Toussaint, Allen

Nevison, William 1640?-1684
[CEC]
British highwayman
* Swift Nicks

[The] New Adam
See Jesus Christ

New, Edward
See Russell, Matthew

[A] New England Minister
See Tyler, Bennet

[The] New England Mystic
See Dickinson, Emily Elizabeth

[The] New Sesostris
See Bonaparte, Napoleon

Newbery, John 1713-1767
[DLE1, SAT]
British author and publisher
* Aesop, Abraham
* Telescope, Tom

Newcomb, Bitter Creek
See Newcomb, George

Newcomb, George ?-1895
[BLB, EWG]
American gunfighter
* Newcomb, Bitter Creek
* Slaughter's Kid

Newcombe, John 20th c.
American tennis player
* Newcombe, Newk

Newcombe, Newk
See Newcombe, John

Newhall, James Robinson
1809-1893   [DNA]
American author and historian
* Oldpath, Obadiah

Newhall, Laura Eugenia 1861- ?
[DNA]
American author
* Halstead, Ada L.

Newil, Charles
See Basset, Adrien Charles
Alexandre

Newman, Andy 20th c.   [CMA]
Musician
* Newman, Thunderclap

Newman, Eugene William 1845- ?
[BDSA]
American author and journalist
* Savoyard

Newman, Richard Brinsley
See Gifford, Franklin Kent

Newman, Thunderclap
See Newman, Andy

Newnham-Davis, Col. 1854- ?
[NPS]
Author
* [The] Dwarf of Blood

Newte, Thomas
See Thomson, William

Newton, Ark
See Newton, William

Newton, Fig
See Newton, Irving

Newton, Irving 1898?-1980   [FIR]
Actor
* Newton, Fig

Newton, R.
See Cave, Edward

Newton, William 20th c.   [EF]
American football player
* Newton, Ark

Ney, Michel [Duc d'Elchingen]
1769-1815   [NN]
French army officer
* [Le] Rougeaud
(See also base volume)

Neyland, James [Elwyn] 1939-
[CA]
American author and playwright
* Jameson, Judith
* Romero, Gerry

Nguyen That Thanh 1890-1969
Vietnamese Communist leader
* Ho Chi Minh [He Who
Enlightens]
* Uncle Ho

Nibbelink, Cynthia 1948-   [MA]
American poet and author
* Williams, Maggie

Nice, Steven 20th c.   [CMA]
British musician
* Harley, Steve

Nicholas of Bari   [UH]
Saint
* [The] Boy Bishop

Nicholls, Charles Wilbur de Lyon
1854-1923   [DNA]
American author and clergyman
* Chauncey, Shelton

Nicholls, Mary Ann 1846?-1888
[BL]
Prostitute and murder victim
* Nicholls, Polly

Nicholls, Polly
See Nicholls, Mary Ann

Nichols, John 1745-1826   [NPS]
British editor
* [The] Censor General of
Literature
(See also base volume)

Nichols, Lee 20th c.   [EF]
American football player
* Nichols, Mike

Nichols, Mike
See Nichols, Lee

Nichols, T. Nickle
See Nichols, Thomas

Nichols, Thomas   [IP]
British author
* Nichols, T. Nickle

Nicholson, Henry Joseph Boone
[IP]
British clergyman and author
* H. J. B. N.

Nicholson, John 1730-1796   [NPS]
British bookseller
* Maps

Nickerson, Susan D.   [IP]
Author
* [A] Lady of Boston

Nickolls, Robert Boucher
1743-1814   [IP]
British clergyman and author
* Eusebius

Nicol, Martha   [IP]
British author
* [A] Lady

Nicolai, Christopher Friedrich
1733-1811   [NPS]
German author
* Erz-Philosopher
(See also base volume)

Nicolas, Ernest 1834-1898   [BBD]
French opera singer
* Nicolini

Nicolas, Sarah [Davison] 19th c.
[IP]
British author
* [A] Soldier's Daughter

Nicolini
See Nicolas, Ernest

Nicoll, [Sir] William Robertson
1851-1923   [NPS]
Scottish clergyman and editor
* Man of Kent
* O. O.
* Wace, W. E.
(See also base volume)

Nicolovius, Ludwig 1837- ?   [DNA]
Author
* Myth, M. Y. T. H.

Niehaus, Mrs. C. H.
Author
* Armstrong, Regina

Niepce, Joseph Nicephore 19th c.
[BBH]
French inventor
* [The] Father of Photography

Nigger Nate Raymond
See Raymond, Nate

Nightingale, Anne Redmon 1943-
[CA]
Author
* Redmon, Anne

Nightingale, Joseph 1775-1824   [IP]
British poet
* [A] Committee Man
* Elagnitin, J.

Nikolais, Alwin 1912-   [CR]
American choreographer
* Nikolais, Nik

Nikolais, Nik
See Nikolais, Alwin

Niles, Willys
See Hume, John Ferguson

[El] Nili
See Manzano y Pelayo, Jose

Nilla
See Carter, Abby [Allin]

Nimble, Jack B.
See Burgess, Michael Roy

Nina V.
See Vickers, Antoinette L.

Nincom
See Applewhite, Marshall Herff

Nind, William 1810-1856   [IP]
British poet and clergyman
* W. N.

Nipclose, [Sir] Nicholas, Bart.
See Garrick, David

Nisard, Theodore
See Normand,
Theodule-Eleazar-Xavier

Nisbet, Richard 18th c.   [IP]
British author
* [A] West Indian

Nitram, Notca W.
See Acton, Martin William

Nitsch, Helen Alice [Matthews]
?-1889   [DNA]
American author
* Owen, Catherine

Nixon, Agnes Eckhardt 1927-
[CLC]
American producer and screenwriter
* Queen of the Soaps

Nixon, Edward John   [IP]
British clergyman and author
* [A] Member of the Univ. of
Camb.

No Rap
See Brown, Lee Patrick

Noah, Mordecai Manuel
1785-1851   [IP]
American journalist and politician
* Malack, Muly

[A] Noble Lord and Eminent Lawyer
See Gore, John [Baron Annaly]

[A] Nobleman
See Hervey, John [Baron Hervey of
Ickworth]

Nobody, A.
See Browne, Gordon Frederick

Nobody, Nathan
See Yellott, George

Nobody, Nemo
See Fennell, James

Nogaret, Francois Felix 1740-1830
[IP]
French author
* Aristenete

Noham, Cam
See McMahon, Heber

Nokes, William 18th c.   [IP]
British author
* [A] Catholick

Nolan, Frederick 1784-1864   [IP]
Irish clergyman and author
* [A] Reformer
* Vigors, N. A., Jun.

Nolan, Louis Edward [IP]
British army officer and author
* Garrard, Kenner

Nolan, Stephen 1820?-1890 [PI]
Irish poet and barrister
* Elrington, Stephen Nolan
* S. N.
* S. N. E., jun.

Noland, Charles Fenton Mercer
1812-1858 [IP]
American author
* Whetstone, Pete

Nolkejumskoi
See William Augustus

Noll
See Cromwell, Oliver

Noll
See Goldsmith, Oliver

Nomad
See Grafton-Smith, Adele

[A] Non Combatant
See Bushby, Henry Jeffreys

[A] Non Commissioned Officer
See Driggs, George W.

Nonnemaker, Gus
See Nonnemaker, Gustavus

Nonnemaker, Gustavus 20th c. [EF]
American football player
* Nonnemaker, Gus

[The] Nonpareil
See Randall, Jack

Nordheim, Sondre 1825-1897
[BBH]
Norwegian-born skiing pioneer
* [The] Father of Ski Jumping and
  Slalom
* [The] Father of Skiing

Nordhoff, Charles 1830- ? [IP]
American journalist
* [A] Boy
* [A] Sailor
* [A] Sailor Boy
(See also base volume)

Norfolciensis
See Greene, Robert

Nork, F.
See Korn, Friedrich

Norman, F. M. 1833- ? [NPS]
Naval officer and author
* Tower, Martello

Norman, Louis
See Carman, [William] Bliss

Normand, Theodule-Eleazar-Xavier
1812-1888 [BBD]
French scholar
* Nisard, Theodore

Normyx [joint pseudonym with
Norman Douglas]
See Douglas, Elsa Fitzgibbon

Normyx [joint pseudonym with Elsa
Fitzgibbon Douglas]
See Douglas, Norman

Norris, Henry 1665-1731?
[IP, NPS]
British actor
* H. N.
* Scrub, Dicky
(See also base volume)

Norris, Randal [IP]
British barrister and author
* R. N.

[A] North American
See Dickinson, John

North, Edward 1820- ? [IP]
American scholar
* Dix Quaevidi

North, Elisha 1771-1843
[DNA, IP]
American author and physician
* Uncle Toby

North, F. H.
See Pratt, Jacob Loring

North, Kit
See Wilson, John

North, Leigh
See Phelps, Elizabeth Steward
[Natt]

North, Theophila
See Hollins, Dorothea

[The] Northern Addison
See Mackenzie, Henry

[The] Northern Dante
See Ossian

Northern Gael
See Devlin, Joseph

[The] Northern Herodotus
See Sturluson, Snorro

[A] Northern Man
See Ingersoll, Joseph Reed

**[The] Northern Man with Southern
Principles**
See Van Buren, Martin

[A] Northern Presbyter
See Lord, Nathan

[The] Northern Thor
See Alexander I [Aleksandr
Pavlovich]

Norton, Brocky Jack
See Norton, J. S.

Norton, Edith Eliza [Ames]
1864-1929 [DNA]
American writer
* Kent, Karlene
(See also base volume)

Norton, Fletcher [First Baron
Grantley] 1716-1789 [NPS]
British jurist
* Doublefee, [Sir] Bullface

Norton, J. S. 19th c. [BLB]
American sheriff's deputy
* Norton, Brocky Jack

Norton, Mrs. Florice
See Brame, Charlotte M.

Norton, Philip 19th c. [SFL]
Author
* Smith, Artegall

Nosegay Nan
See Abington, Mrs.

Nosey
See Cromwell, Oliver

Nostradamus
See Michel de Notredame

[II] Notaro
See Jacopo [or Giacomo] da
Lentini

Noteveas
See Sanchez, Pedro

Notional, Nehemiah
See Lovering, John

Notley, Frances Eliza Millett 19th
c. [NPS]
Author
* Derrick, Frances

Nott, Henry Junius 1797-1837
[DNA]
American author and educator
* Singularity, Thomas

Novak, Rose 1940- [CA]
American author
* Rose, Marcia [joint pseudonym
  with Marcia Kamien]

[The] Novelist Detective
See Rolfe, Maro Orlando

[The] Novelist of Wessex
See Hardy, Thomas

[The] Novelist's Novelist
See Miller, Leonard

Novello-Davies, Clara
See Davies, Clara

Novicius, Aloysius
See Logan, John Daniel

Nowell, Alexander 1507?-1602
[NPS]
British clergyman
* Bottled Beer

Nox, Owen
See Cory, Charles Barney

Noyes, Edwin 19th c. [DI]
American swindler
* Horton, Charles Johnson

Nubbins Colt
See Barnes, Seaborn

Nuff, Noah
See Bellaw, Americus Wellington

Nugent, Michael ?-1845 [PI]
Irish poet, author, critic
* M. N-g-t

Nuitter, Charles Louis Etienne
See Truinet, Charles Louis Etienne

[The] Nun of Kenmare
See Cusack, Mary Frances

Nun, Richard 18th c. [PI]
Irish poet
* R. N., Trinity College?

Nunez, Juan 19th c. [GS]
Spanish bullfighter
* Sentimientos [Sentiments]

Nunquam
See Blatchford, Robert

Nureyev, Rudolf
See Hametovich, Rudolf

Nuss, Ralph 20th c. [DI]
American murderer
* Russell, Donald

[The] Nutmeg of Delight
See Hussein

Nutter, Buzz
See Nutter, Madison

Nutter, Madison 20th c. [EF]
American football player
* Nutter, Buzz

Nye
See Bevan, Aneurin

Nye, Columbus
See Lowell, James Russell

O

O.
See O'Hagan, John

O.
See O'Leary, Joseph

O. B. C.
See Cole, Owen Blayney

O' Brien, Mrs. Joseph
Author
* Vorse, Mary Heaton

O. H. K. B.
See Boyd, Oliver H. K.

O. L. F.
See Foster, Olive [Leonard]

O. O.
See Nicoll, [Sir] William Robertson

Oakly
See Garrick, David

Oakwood, Oliver
See Potts, Stacy Gardner

O'B.?
See O'Brien, M. E.

O'Beirne, Thomas Lewis 1748-1823 [PI]
Irish poet and clergyman
* [The] Mitred Layman

Obenchain, Eliza Caroline [Calvert] 1856- ? [DNA]
American author
* Hall, Eliza Calvert

Ober, Sarah Endicott 1854- ? [DNA]
Author
* Herrick, Huldah

Oberon
See Snow, Joseph

Obiter Dictum
See Anderson, James

O'Brien, Attie
See O'Brien, Francis Marcella

O'Brien, Desmond
See King, Richard Ashe

O'Brien, Francis Marcella 1840-1883 [PI]
Irish poet
* O'Brien, Attie

O'Brien, James Nagle 1848-1879 [PI]
Irish author
* Shamus

O'Brien, Jennie
See Devlin, Joseph

O'Brien, M. E. 1772- ? [PI]
Irish poet
* O'B.?

O'Brien, Mary 18th c. [PI]
Irish author and poet
* [A] Lady

O'Brien, Ricard Baptist 1809-1885 [PI]
Irish clergyman, writer, poet
* Baptist

O'Brien, Thomas 1851-1906 [PI]
Irish poet
* Clontarf

O'Brien, William 1740?-1815? [PI]
Irish comedian and author
* Lusus, Larry, Esq.

O'Brien, William Smith 1803-1864 [PI]
Irish poet
* W. O'B.

Observation
See Adams, Samuel

Observator, Charles
See Sabin, Elijah Robinson

Observer
See Rapmund, Joseph

[An] Observer
See Rutlidge, [Sir] John James

O'Callaghan, John Cornelius 1805-1883 [PI]
Irish poet
* Carolan
* Gracchus
* J. O'C.

O'Callaghan, Thomas O'Donnell 1845- ? [PI]
Irish-born poet and journalist
* Libertas

O'Callanan, David
See Holland, Denis

O'Carroll, Louis Ely 1864- ? [PI]
Irish poet
* Hopper, Claude

O'Carroll, Patrick 19th c. [PI]
Irish poet
* [A] Modern Troubadour

Ocasek, Ric
See Otcasek, Richard

Occam [or Ockham], William of 1276?-1347 [NPS, UH]
British philosopher
* Princeps Nominalium
(See also base volume)

Ocelot Margie Gardner
See Gardner, Margery Aimee

O'Connell, Daniel 1775-1847 [NPS]
Irish political agitator
* Big O
(See also base volume)

O'Connell, John ?-1860? [PI]
Irish poet
* Roche, Matthew

O'Connell, John 1811-1858 [PI]
Irish poet
* M. P.
* Y.

O'Connell, John A. [PI]
Irish author
* Aloysius

O'Connell, Maurice 1802?-1853 [PI]
Irish poet
* Fion
* Ith
* M. O'C.
* McFinn, Denis
* O'Doggerell, Patrick
* O'Taffrail, Patrick

O'Connell, Philip
See Martin, James

O'Connor, Paul 1845?- ? [PI]
American poet
* [The] Covington Poet

O'Connor, Thomas Power 1848-1929 [NPS]
Irish journalist and politician
* T. P.
(See also base volume)

O'Conor, Charles Patrick 1837?- ? [PI]
Irish author
* Mor, Cahal
* Thierna, Cairn

[An] Octogenarian
See Gutch, John Mathew

O'Cuirc, Henry
See Quirke, Henry

[The] Odd Boy
See Tillotson, John

[The] Odd Fellow
See Mackenzie, Peter

[The] Odd Fellow
See Souter, Joseph

Odell, Minna 1857?-1940 [DNA]
American poet
* Irving, Minna

Oden, Curly
See Oden, Olaf

Oden, Olaf 20th c. [EF]
American football player
* Oden, Curly

Odhar, Coinneach [Kenneth Ore] 16th c. [EOP]
Scottish wizard
* [The] Brahan Seer

Odman, Jeremiah
See Atkinson, D. H.

O'Doggerell, Patrick
See O'Connell, Maurice

O'Doherty, Brian 1934- [CA]
Irish-born American author and artist
* Ireland, Patrick

[The] O'Donnell
See Duffy, [Sir] Charles Gavan

O'Donnell, Francis Hugh 1848- ? [PI]
Irish poet
* Llenodo
* Minor, Dryden

O'Donnell, John ?-1874 [PI]
Irish poet and clergyman
* Moy

O'Donnell, John Francis 1837-1874 [PI]
Irish author and poet
* C.
* Caviare
* French, Emily
* J. F. O'D.
* Monks, P.
* West, Monckton

O'Donnell, Mary
See Dillon, Thomas

O'Donnell, Roderick
See Boyle, John

O'Donoghue, John 1813-1893 [PI]
Irish poet and author
* S. T. C. D.

O'Donovan, P. M., Esq.
See Peacock, Thomas Love

O'Donovan Rossa, Jeremiah 1831-
? [PI]
Irish poet
* Jer

O'Donovan Rossa, Mary Jane 1845-
? [PI]
Irish poet
* Cliodhna
* M. J. I.

O'Dowd, John 1856- ? [PI]
Irish poet
* Adonis
* [A] Sligo Suspect

O'Dowd, Phelim
See Fox, Patrick J.

O'Dryskull, Teddy
See Mahony, Francis Sylvester

Odum, Mary Hunt McCaleb
[BDSA]
American author and poet
* L'Eclair

O'Dunn, Denis
See Cleary, Thomas Stanislaus

Odysseus
See Eliot, [Sir] Charles

[The] Off Wheeler
See Harlan, James Jefferson

[An] Officer
See Anbury, Thomas

[An] Officer
See Austin, Harry

**[An] Officer in Col. Baillie's
Detachment**
See Thomson, William

[An] Officer in the Army of Wolfe
See Jones, James Athearn

[An] Officer in the Field
See Kirkland, Charles Pinckney

[An] Officer in the Guards
See Ayscough, George Edward

**[An] Officer in the Hon. E. I. Co's
Bengal Native Infantry**
See Butler, John

[An] Officer of the Army at Detroit
See Whiting, Henry

[An] Officer of the British Army
See Drewe, Edward

[An] Officer of the Line
See Gardner, John Lane

[An] Officer who Served There
See Ireland, William W.

[An] Officer's Wife
See Carrington, Margaret Jirvin

O'Flaherty, Charles ?-1828 [PI]
Irish poet
* C. O. F.
* O'Reilly, Rory

O'Flanagan, Theophilus
1762?-1814 [PI]
Irish poet
* MacBrady, Thady

O'Flynn, Fergus
See Ryan, James

O'Fogarty, Fogarty
See Gosnell, Samuel

O'Gahagan, [Major] G.
See Thackeray, William
Makepeace

Ogden, Christol
See English, Thomas Dunn

Ogden, Ruth
See Ide, Francis Otis [Ogden]

Ogdoades
See Langey, Guillaume du Bellay

Oge, Erin
See Wilson, Robert A.

Oge, Hector
See McMullan, William John

Ogier, Le Prieur
See Balzac, Jean Louis Guez de

O'Grada, Sean
See O'Grady, John [Patrick]

O'Grady, John [Patrick] 1907-
[CA]
Australian author
* Culotta, Nino
* O'Grada, Sean

O'Grady, Standish Hayes 1830?- ?
[PI]
Irish poet and scholar
* Hayes, S.

Ogre de la Goutte d'Or
See Weber, Jeanne

O'Hagan, John 1822-1890 [PI]
Irish author and poet
* Amelia, Carolina Wilhelmina
* Cuillinn, Sliabh
* J. O'H.
* O.

O'Halloran, Laurence
See Halloran, Laurence Hynes

O'Hanlon, John 1821-1905 [PI]
Irish author and clergyman
* [An] Irish Missionary Priest
(See also base volume)

O'Hanlon, Mary I.
See Kelly, Mary I.

[The] O'Hara Family [joint
pseudonym with Michael Banim; also
used alone]
See Banim, John

[The] O'Hara Family [joint
pseudonym with John Banim; also
used alone]
See Banim, Michael, Jr.

O'Hara, Kane ?-1782 [PI]
Irish poet
* St. Patrick's Steeple

O'Hare, Roger
See Donnelly, James

O'Herlihy, Patrick 19th c. [PI]
Irish poet
* P. O'H.

[An] Ohio Volunteer
See Foster, James

Ohl, Maude 20th c. [BDSA]
American author and poet
* Andrews, Annulet

O'K.
See O'Keeffe, M. J.

O'Keefe, Adelaide 1776-1855? [PI]
Irish poet
* Adelaide

O'Keefe, John 1747-1833 [NPS]
Irish playwright
* [The] English Moliere

O'Keefe, Joseph 20th c. [DI]
American underworld figure
* Williams, Paul
(See also base volume)

O'Keeffe, Cornelius
See Meagher, Thomas Francis

O'Keeffe, M. J. 19th c. [PI]
Irish poet
* O'K.

O'Kelly, Dennis 1720?-1787 [NPS]
Racehorse owner
* Eclipse, Count
(See also base volume)

Oksanen
See Ahlqvist, August Engelbrekt

Oksaselta, A.
See Ahlqvist, August Engelbrekt

O'L.
See O'Leary, Joseph

[The] Ol' Maestro
See Anzelevitz [or Anzelwitz],
Benjamin

Olajuwon, Akeem Abdul 20th c.
Nigerian-born basketball player
* Little Moses
* Olajuwon, Jellybean

Olajuwon, Jellybean
See Olajuwon, Akeem Abdul

Olchewitz, M.
Author
* Verne, Jules

Old Anthony Now-Now
See Munday, Anthony

Old Antiquarian
See Simpson, Edward

Old Athlete
See Larrette, C. H.

[An] Old Bachelor
See Carrington, E.

Old Broadbrim
See Rathborne, St. George

Old Carroll the Bard
See Daly, Eugene P.

Old Chatty Cheerful
See Martin, William

Old Coins
See Rowell, A. S.

[An] Old Colonist
See Wright, George

Old Contributor [joint pseudonym
with Julius Warren Lewis]
See Lewis, Harriet Newell

Old Contributor [joint pseudonym
with Harriet Newell Lewis]
See Lewis, Julius Warren

[An] Old Cornish Boy
See Christophers, Samuel
Woolcock

Old Crome
See Crome, John

[The] Old Detective
See Rolfe, Maro Orlando

[The] Old English Epigrammatist
See Heywood, John

Old Fag
See Bell, Robert Stanley Warren

[An] Old Georgia Lawyer
See Andrews, Garnett

Old Glad-Eye
See Gladstone, William Ewart

Old Honesty
See Lamb, Charles

Old Jonathan
See Doudeney, D. A.

Old Knick
See Du Bois, Edward

[An] Old Lady
See Dawson, A.

[An] Old Leeds Cropper
See Atkinson, D. H.

[The] Old Lion
See Pitt, William [Earl of
Chatham]

[An] Old Man
See Aldam, W. H.

[An] Old Man
See Johnston, Richard Malcolm

[An] Old Man
See Quincy, Josiah

[An] Old Man
See White, Joseph M.

Old Man Clanton
See Clanton, N. H.

[The] Old Marshal
See Chang Tso-lin

[An] Old Member of Parliament
See Lee, Arthur

Old Mob
See Sympson, Thomas

Old Moore
See Andrews, Henry

Old Moore
See Whitman, Edward W.

Old Noll
See Aurevilly, Leon Louis Frederic
Jules, Barbey d'

[An] Old Pen
See Wrangham, Francis

Old Ponder
See Wordsworth, William

[An] Old Reporter
See Watts, Walter Henry

[An] Old Sailor
See Ames, Nathaniel

Old Shoebox Annie
See Smith, Mary Eleanor

Old Sleuth
See Harbaugh, Thomas Chalmers

Old Slyboots
See Scott, James

Old Smoke
See Morrissey, John

[An] Old Smoker
See Stock, John

[An] Old Soldier
See Armstrong, John

Old Squab
See Dryden, John

Old Stager
See Adams, William Taylor

[An] Old Stager
See Aspinwall, James

Old Tick
See Douglas, William

Old Timer
See Merrill, James Milford

Old Tony
See Cooper, Anthony Ashley

[An] Old Tradesman
See Bailey, Thomas

Old, Walter Gorn
See Old, Walter Richard

Old, Walter Richard 1864-1929
[EOP]
British author
* Old, Walter Gorn
* Sepharial

[The] Old Whig
See Addison, Joseph

Oldcastle, Alice
See Meynell, Alice [Christiana
Gertrude Thompson]

Oldcastle, Humphrey
See Amhurst, Nicholas

Oldham, John 1653-1683 [NPS]
British poet
* [The] Marcellus of Our Tongue
(See also base volume)

Oldmixon, Georgina Sidus
1763?-1836 [FAA]
British-born actress
* George, Miss

Oldmixon, John 1673-1742 [NPS]
Historian and pampleteer
* Wilson, Charles

Oldpath, Obadiah
See Newhall, James Robinson

Oldroyd, Richard ?-1664 [NPS]
British conspirator
* [The] Devil of Dewsbury

Oldys, William 1696-1761 [NPS]
Antiquary
* [A] Prodigy of Literary Curiosity
(See also base volume)

Olea, Maria Florencia Varas 1938-
[CA]
Chilean author and journalist
* Varas, Florencia

O'Leary, Arthur ?-1854? [PI]
Irish poet
* A. O'L.

O'Leary, Ellen 1831-1889 [PI]
Irish poet
* Eily
* Lenel

O'Leary, Joseph 19th c. [PI]
Irish poet and journalist
* Murphy, Denis
* O.

O'Leary, Joseph (Continued)
* O'L.
* [A] Reporter

Olinger, Robert A. 1841?-1881
[EWG]
American gunfighter
* [The] Big Indian

Oliphant, Carolina [Baroness Nairne]
1766-1845 [DLE1]
Scottish poet
* B. B.
* Bogan of Bogan, Mrs.
(See also base volume)

Oliphant, Mrs. 1828-1897 [NPS]
Author
* Dunsmuir, Amy

Olive, Ison Prentice 1840-1886
[BLB]
American gunfighter
* Olive, Print

Olive, Print
See Olive, Ison Prentice

Oliver, Amy Roberta [Ruck]
1878-1978 [CA]
British author
* Ruck, Amy Roberta
(See also base volume)

Oliver, Burton
See Burt, Olive Woolley

Oliver, Death
See Oliver, Stephen

Oliver, Frederick Spencer
1866-1899 [SFL]
Author
* Phylos the Thibetan

Oliver, Nathan, Esq.
See Blakey, Robert

Oliver, Stephen 18th c. [RBE]
Boxer
* Oliver, Death

Oliver, Temple
See Smith, Jeanie Oliver
[Davidson]

Olkyrn, Iris
See Milligan, Alice L.

Ollapod
See Edwards, Thomas A.

Ollif, S. L. E. [NPS]
Author
* Elphinstone, Leslie

Olney, Oliver
See Des Voignes, Jules Verne

Olwyn, Lady
See Wilson, Monique

[The] Olympian
See Pericles

O'Mahony, Timothy J. 1839- ? [PI]
Irish poet
* Mona

O'Meagher, Patrick J.
See Meagher, Patrick J.

Omohundro, John B. ?-1880
American Indian scout and author
* Texas Jack

O'More
See Kennedy, Thomas

O'Mulrenin, Richard Joseph
1832?-1906 [PI]
Irish poet
* Concobar, Clann
* Erionnach

O'Murchadha, Peadar
See Murphy, Peter

O'Murchadha, Shemus
See Murphy, James

O'N.
See O'Neill, Michael

One Formerly Possessed of the Place
See Lacy, Willoughby

One Leg Paget
See Paget, Henry William [First
Marquess of Anglesey]

One of a Literary Family
See Le Breton, Anna Letitia
[Aikin]

One of H. M.'s Justices of the Peace
See Owen, Robert

One of her Sons
See Abbott, Jacob

One of her Sons
See Legge, Alfred Owen

One of his Children
See White, Mrs. M. E. [Harding]

One of his Constituents
See Drummond, Henry

One of Ireland's Ballad Poets
See Forrest, John Lawrence

One of its Members
See Ash, Edward

One of Plutarch's Men
See Adams, Samuel

One of the Alumni
See Inglis, John

One of the Boys
See Fitzgerald, Percy Hetherington

One of the "Eighteen Millions of
Bores"
See Wright, Elizur

One of the Family
See Page, R. Channing M.

One of the Ministers of Edinburgh
See Inglis, John

One of the Party
See Taylor, F.

One of the People Called Christians
See Horne, George

One of the Raiders
See Atkinson, G. W.

One of Them
See Abbott, Jacob

One of Them
See White, Mrs W. H.

One of Themselves
See Aston, C. Penrhyn

One of Themselves
See Mackarness, John Fielder

One Who has a Tear for Others as
Well as Himself
See Currie, E.

One Who has Never Quitted Him for
Fifteen Years
See Doris, Charles

One Who has Served Under the
Marquis of Dalhousie
See Allen, Charles

One Who Has Stood Behind the
Counter
See Pae, David

One Who Knows
See Foster, Arnold

One Who Knows
See Wahab, Charles James

One Who Knows It
See Shute, Hardwick

One Who Loves the Souls of the
Lambs
See Marks, Richard

One Who Respects Them
See Bury, James

O'Neil, Carolan
See FitzGerald, Shafto Justin
Adair

O'Neil, Wolf
See Halsey, Harlan Page

O'Neill, Henrietta Bruce
See Boate, Henrietta

O'Neill, John 1829- ? [PI]
Irish poet
* J. O'N.?
* L.

O'Neill, John Robert 1823-1860
[PI]
Irish playwright and musician
* Vamp, Hugo

O'Neill, Michael 19th c. [PI]
Irish poet
* O'N.

O'Neill, William 1877- ? [PI]
Irish poet
* Slieve-Margy

Oneiropolos
See Johnstone, Charles

O'Niall
See Hughes, Terence McMahon

Onlooker
See Russell, George William
Erskine

Onslow, George 1731-1792 [NPS]
Politician and army officer
* Cocking, George [Little]

Onwhyn, Thomas ?-1886 [NPS]
Draughtsman and engraver
* Weller, Samuel
(See also base volume)

Oom the Omnipotent
See Bernard, Pierre

Oo'ma [Great Lady]
See Ray, Dixy Lee

O'Pagus, Arry
See Sommer, H. B

[An] Operative
See Duffy, [Sir] Charles Gavan

Ophiel
See Peach, Edward C.

O'Pindar, Scriblerus Murtough
See Carey, William Paulet

[The] Opium Eater
See De Quincey, Thomas

Oppenheim, E[dward] Phillips
1866-1946   [EMD]
British author
* [The] Prince of Storytellers
(See also base volume)

Oppenheimer, Joel [Lester] 1930-
American poet
* Hammer, Jacob

**Opzoomer, Adele Sophia Cornelia van
Antal** 1857-1925   [NPS]
Dutch author
* Wallis, A. S. C.

O'Quinn, John 20th c.   [EF]
American football player
* O'Quinn, Red

O'Quinn, Red
See O'Quinn, John

[The] Oracle of Common Law
See Plowden, Edmund

[The] Oracle of God
See De Grimston, Mary Ann

Oram, Blanche 1866- ?   [NPS]
Author and journalist
* White, Roma

Oram, Mona K.
See Grenville, Mrs. Arthur

Orator Bronze
See Henley, John

Orbison, Roy 20th c.   [CMA]
American singer
* [The] Voice

Orczy, Emmuska
See Barstow, Emma Magdalena
Rosalina Marie Josepha Barbara

[The] Oregon Byron
See Miller, Cincinnatus Heine

O'Reilly, [Sister] Amadeus 1864- ?
[PI]
Irish-born poet
* Romaine, John
* Shandonian

O'Reilly, Edward James 1830-1880
[PI]
Irish-born poet and attorney
* Clio

O'Reilly, Patrick Thomas 1876- ?
[PI]
American poet
* Aenid

O'Reilly, Rory
See O'Flaherty, Charles

O'Reilly, Thomas F. ?-1887   [PI]
Irish poet
* Artane

Orfeo Italiano
See Crescentini, Girolamo

Origen 185- 253   [NPS]
Greek theologian
* [The] Man of Steel
(See also base volume)

[The] Original Disco Man
See Brown, James

[The] Original Editor
See Wade, John

[The] Original Nonpareil
See Randall, Jack

Orion
See Keegan, James

Orlando the Fair
See Fielding, Henry

Orleanian
See Wharton, Edward Clifton

Orleans, Philippe II d' 1674-1723
[NPS]
Brother of King Louis XIV of France
* [The] Boaster of Crimes
* [A] Godless Regent
(See also base volume)

Orme, Benjamin
See Japp, Alexander Hay

Ormsby, John S. 1869- ?   [PI]
Irish-born poet
* Stanley

Orne, Philip
See Lowell, Francis Cabot

O'Rolfe, M., the Irish Novelist
See Rolfe, Maro Orlando

O'Rourke, John 1861-1882   [EWG]
American gunfighter and gambler
* Johnny Behind-the-Deuce

O'Rourke, John 19th c.   [PI]
Irish author
* Evergreen, Anthony

O'Rourke, Rory
See Whitty, Michael James

[The] Orpheus of His Age
See Ariosto, Lodovico

Orr, Andrew 1822- ?   [PI]
Irish poet
* [An] Aghadowey Man
* Comberbach

Orsini, Giovanni Gaetano
1216?-1280   [NPS]
Pope
* Son of a She-Bear
(See also base volume)

Ortis, Jacopo
See Foscolo, Niccolo

Ortner-Zimmerman, Toni 1941-
[CA]
American poet
* Zimmerman, Toni

Orton, Arthur 1834-1898   [DI]
British imposter
* [The] Tichborne Claimant
(See also base volume)

Orton, Joseph
See Strang, Jesse

Orwell
See Smith, Walter C.

O'Ryan, Julia M. 1823-1887   [PI]
Irish poet
* J. M. R.?

Os Porci
See Sergius I

Osander
See Allen, Benjamin

Osborn, Duke
See Osborn, Robert

Osborn, Laughton 1809-1878
[HFN]
Author
* [A] Poet
(See also base volume)

Osborn, Robert 20th c.   [EF]
American football player
* Osborn, Duke

Osborne, Clancy
See Osborne, Clarence

Osborne, Clarence 20th c.   [EF]
American football player
* Osborne, Clancy

Oscar
See Griffin, Gerald

Oscotian
See Lawlor, Denis Shine

Oscotiensis
See Lawlor, Denis Shine

O'Shea, John 19th c.   [PI]
Irish poet
* Mount Atlas

Osorio, Jeronymo 1506-1580
[NPS]
Portuguese historian and author
* [The] Cicero of Portugal

Osorio, Manuel Luiz 1808-1879
[NPS]
Brazilian army officer
* [The] Fabulous

Ossian
See McAleese, Daniel

Ossian 3rd c.   [NPS]
Gaelic bard and warrior
* [The] Glory of Scotland
* [The] Northern Dante
(See also base volume)

Ossola
See Foster, Clement le Neve

Osterberg, James [Jim] 1947-
[CMA]
American musician
* Pop, Iggy
(See also base volume)

Osterman, Edward ?-1920   [DI]
American underworld figure
* Osterman, Monk
(See also base volume)

Osterman, Monk
See Osterman, Edward

Ostermann, Uri 1923-   [CA]
*German-born Israeli author and
editor*
* Avnery, Uri

Ostrong [or Ostrog], Mikhail
See Pedachenko, Alexander

Osty, Lucien Pierre Jean 1920-
French author
* Larteguy, Jean

O'Sullivan, Denis Barrington
See Beresford, William

O'Sullivan, Michael John
1794-1845   [PI]
Irish poet and playwright
* M. J. S.
* Paddy from Cork
* Sullivan, M. J.

O'Sullivan, Timothy
See Sullivan, Timothy Daniel

O'Taffrail, Patrick
See O'Connell, Maurice

Otcasek, Richard 20th c.   [CMA]
American musician
* Ocasek, Ric

**[The] Other Gentleman of Lincoln's
Inn**
See Edwards, Thomas

Otho
See Holland, Denis

O'Toole, Peter
See O'Toole, Seamus

O'Toole, Phelim
See Commins, Andrew

O'Toole, Seamus 1933-   [CR]
Irish-born actor
* O'Toole, Peter

Otreb, Rudolf
See Fludd, Robert

Otter
See Alfred, H. J.

Ouick, Florence 19th c.   [DI]
American bandit
* [The] Belle of the Daltons'
* Bryant, Mrs.
* King, Tom
* Moore, Eugenia
* Mundy, Mrs.

Oulahan, Richard 1825?-1895   [PI]
Irish poet
* [A] Stranger

Ouno
See Ashworth, T. M.

Our English Homer
See Chaucer, Geoffrey

Our English Rochefoucault
See Stanhope, Philip Dormer

Our English Virgil
See Cowley, Abraham

Our Female Phidias
See Damer, Anne Seymour

Our Letter'd Polypheme
See Johnson, Samuel

Our Literary Whale
See Johnson, Samuel

Our Little David
See More, Hannah

Our Malmesbury Philosopher
See Hobbes, Thomas

Our Mercurie
See Massinger, Philip

Our Northern Homer
See Scott, [Sir] Walter

Our Pindar
See Cowley, Abraham

Our Setting Sun
See Charles II

Our Special Correspondent
See Atkinson, George Francklin

Our Young Ascantus
See Shadwell, Thomas

Owen
See Appleton, Jesse

Owen, Catherine
See Nitsch, Helen Alice
[Matthews]

Owen, John 1765-1822 [IP]
British clergyman and author
* Christian, Theophilus, Esq.
* [A] Suburban Clergyman

Owen, Robert 1771-1858
[HFN, IP, NPS]
Welsh-born reformer, editor,
philanthropist
* Celatus
* One of H. M.'s Justices of the
  Peace

Owen, Robert Dale 1801-1877 [IP]
Scottish-born reformer
* [A] Citizen of the West

Owen, William 19th c. [IP]
Welsh philologist
* Meirion

Owens, Fannie
See Lyons, Sophie

Owens, Ike
See Owens, Isaiah

Owens, Isaiah 20th c. [EF]
American football player
* Owens, Ike

Owenson, Robert
See MacOwen, Robert

[The] Owl?
See Bennett, Charles Henry

Owl, Eugene
See Pilgrim, Thomas

Owsley
See Stanley, Augustus Owsley, III

Oxenstierna, Axel Gustafsson
1583-1654 [NPS]
Swedish statesman
* Aquila Aquilonius
(See also base volume)

Oxford, George 20th c. [CMA]
American disc jockey
* Oxford, Jumpin' George

Oxford, Jumpin' George
See Oxford, George

[The] Oxonian
See Metcalfe, Frederick

Oxoniensis
See Brooke, Henry

Oxoniensis
See Trench, Francis

Oziosi [The Lazybones]
See Merry, Robert

P

P.
See Pegge, Samuel

P.
See Polwhele, Richard

P. A.
See Bernard, Pierre

P. B. S.
See Shelley, Percy Bysshe

P. C.
See Cullen, P. J.

P. C. A.
See Aubry, Philippe

P. C. E.
See Littledale, Richard

P. E.
See Pegge, Samuel

P. E. T.
See Trudeau, Pierre Elliott

P. G.
See Pegge, Samuel

P. G. A.
See Audran, Prosper Gabriel

P. G. S.
See Smyth, Patrick G.

P. L.
See Larkin, Peter O'Neill

P. M.
See Massinger, Philip

P. M.
See Middleton, Patrick

P. McD.?
See McDonald, Peter

P. McG.
See McEntee, P.

P. O. L.
See Guiney, Louise Imogen

P. O'H.
See O'Herlihy, Patrick

P. P.
See Daniel, George

P. P. B. K.
See Littledale, Richard

P. P. C.
See Carpenter, Philip Pearsall

P. P. P.
See Maginn, William

P. R.
See Robertson, Patrick

P. S.
See Pegge, Samuel

P. T. T.
See Maginn, William

P. W.
See Drew, Pierce William

Pa Chin
See Li Fei-kan

Pace, William   [IP]
British poet
* [A] Clergyman of the Church of England

Paching, Resta   [IP]
British innkeeper and author
* [A] Gentleman in London

Pacificator
See Alexander, Richard Dykes

Pacifico, [Dr.] Solomon
See Thackeray, William Makepeace

Packard, Clarissa
See Gilman, Caroline [Howard]

Packard, Frederick Adolphus 1794-1867   [IP]
American attorney and author
* [A] Citizen of Pennsylvania

Packford, C. W.   [NPS]
Author
* Alma Mater

Paddy
See McCloskey, Henry

Paddy from Cork
See O'Sullivan, Michael John

Paddy, Scot, the Piper
See McMullan, William John

Padgett, Desmond
See Von Block, Bela

[Il] Padovano
See Annibale

Padraig, Padraic Giolla
See Fitzpatrick, Patrick Vincent

Pae, David   [IP]
Scottish author
* Memoriter
* One Who Has Stood Behind the Counter

Paez, Ramon   [IP]
American artist and author
* R. P., de Venezuela

Page, Abraham
See Holt, John Saunders

Page, Emma
See Tirbutt, Honoria

Page, H. A.
See Japp, Alexander Hay

Page, John 19th c.   [IP]
British poet
* Folio, Felix

Page, R. Channing M.   [IP]
American author
* One of the Family

Paget, Henry William [First Marquess of Anglesey] 1768-1854 [NN]
British army officer
* Paget, One Leg

Paget, One Leg
See Paget, Henry William [First Marquess of Anglesey]

Paget, R. L.
See Knowles, Frederic Lawrence

Paine, Robert Treat, Jr. 1773-1811 [IP]
American attorney, poet, journalist
* Menander

Paine, Thomas 1697?-1757   [IP]
American clergyman and author
* Philopatria

Paine, Thomas 1736-1809   [IP]
British-born politician and author
* [An] Englishman
(See also base volume)

Painsworth, W. Harassing
See Ainsworth, William Harrison

Painter, Daniel
See Burgess, Michael Roy

[The] Painter Patriot
See Gainsborough, Thomas

Pakenham, F. J.   [IP]
British author
* F. J. P.

[The] Pale
See Constantius I [Flavius Valerius Constantius]

Paley, William 1743-1805   [IP]
British author
* [A] Friend of Religious Liberty

Palfray, Warwick 1787-1838   [IP]
American journalist
* Another Layman

Palgrave, [Sir] Francis
See Cohen, Francis

[The] Palinurus of the Revolution
See Adams, Samuel

Pallidini, Jodi
See Robbin, [Jodi] Luna

Palliser, Francis
See Wilson, Mary

Palm, Mike
See Palm, Myron

Palm, Myron 20th c.   [EF]
American football player
* Palm, Mike

Palmer, Bud
See Palmer, John S.

Palmer, Edward Vance 1885-1959 [DLE1]
Australian author
* Daly, Rann

Palmer, Helen Marion
See Geisel, Helen

Palmer, John
See Turpin, Richard [Dick]

Palmer, John 1807-1837   [EOP]
Astrologer and editor
* Raphael II

Palmer, John S. 1923-   [CR]
American basketball player, sportscaster, local government official
* Palmer, Bud

Palmer, John Williamson 1825-1906   [BDSA, DNA, NPS]
American physician, poet, author
* Coventry, John

Palmer, Tom
See Leird, Henry J.

Palmer, William 1825-1856   [CEC]
British murderer
* [The] Rugeley Poisoner

Paltock, Robert 1697-1767   [WGT]
British author
* Bingfield, William, Esq.

Paltock, Robert (Continued)
* R. S., a Passenger in the Hector
(See also base volume)

[El] **Pamplones** [Man from Pamplona]
See Legurregui, Jose

[El] **Panadero** [The Baker]
See Carmona y Luque, Jose

Panajot, H.
See Chitov, Panajot,

Panchon [Big Belly]
See Gonzalez, Francisco

[The] **Pander of Venus**
See Moore, Thomas

Pandit, Vijaya Lakshmi 1900-
[CA]
Indian author
* [The] Lamp of India

Papa G.
See Gilbert, Sam

Papinian
See Inglis, Charles

Papirius Cursor
See Whitefoord, Caleb

Paragraph, Peter
See Adair, James Makittrick

Paramahansa
See Muktanada, Swami

Pardon, George Frederick
1824-1884 [NPS]
British author and critic
* Quiet, George
(See also base volume)

Parenthenopeus Hereticus
See Gordon, William

[A] **Pariah**
See Cornwallis, Caroline Frances

Paris, Firmin
See Hudon, Maxime

[A] **Parish Priest**
See Aitken, Robert

Parish the Healer
See Parish, W. T.

Parish, W. T. 1873-1946 [EOP]
British spiritual healer
* Parish the Healer

Park, Charles Carroll 1860-1931
[DNA]
American author
* Gray, Carl

Parker, Frederick 19th c. [HFN]
Author
* Heinfetter, Herman

Parker, Joel
See Parker, Joseph Lee

Parker, John
See Wyatt, John

Parker, Joseph Lee 1952- [FR]
American football player
* Parker, Joel

Parker, Maude
See Child, Mrs. Richard Washburn

Parker, Robert LeRoy 1866-1937
[EWG]
American bank and train robber
* Phillips, William T.
(See also base volume)

Parker, Sarah 1824- ? [PI]
Irish-born poet
* [The] Irish Girl

Parkes, William Theodore
?-1908? [PI]
Irish poet
* Bradey, Barney

Parley, Peter
See Bennett, John

Parley, Peter
See Tegg, William

Parnell, Babe
See Parnell, Frederick

Parnell, Fanny
See Parnell, Frances Isabel

Parnell, Frances Isabel 1854-1882
[DIL, PI]
Irish poet
* Aleria
* Parnell, Fanny

Parnell, Frederick 20th c. [EF]
American football player
* Parnell, Babe

Parr, George 1826-1891 [EC]
British cricketer
* [The] Lion of the North

Parr, Samuel 1747-1825 [NPS]
British scholar
* [The] Man with a Wig
(See also base volume)

Parreta
See Vazquez, Jose

Parrish, Wendal
See Merrill, James Milford

Parry, Albert 1901- [CA]
Russian-born American author
* Leclerc, Victor

Parry, John ?-1782? [NPS]
* [The] Blind Harper

Parry, John 1776-1851 [BBD]
Welsh musician
* Bardd Alaw [Master of Song]

Parry, Owen 20th c. [EF]
American football player
* Parry, Ox

Parry, Ox
See Parry, Owen

Parsons, Elsie Worthington [Clews]
1875-1941 [DNA]
American author and anthropologist
* Main, John

Parsons, Reuben ?-1875 [BLB]
American gambler
* [The] Great American Faro
   Banker

Particular, Pertinax
See Watkins, Tobias

[The] **Pastor**
See Morse, Jason

[A] **Pastor**
See Stokes, John Whitley

Pastor, Juan ?-1894 [GS]
Spanish bullfighter
* [El] Barbero [The Barber]

Pastorini, Dan
See Pastorini, Dante Anthony, Jr.

Pastorini, Dante Anthony, Jr.
1949- [FR]
American football player
* Pastorini, Dan

Pat
See Kenny, P. D.

Pater Bursae Londoniensis
See Houblon, James

Paterfamilias
See Higgins, Matthew James

Paterson, James [NPS]
Author
* James, Croak

[A] **Patrician**
See Hudson, Edward

Patricius
See Coen, John

[The] **Patroon**
See Van Rensselaer, Stephen

Patten, J. Alexander 19th c. [WGT]
Author
* Cobb, Clayton W.

Patterson, Jim
See Longley, William Preston

Patterson, Virginia [Sharpe]
1841-1913 [DNA]
American author and journalist
* Gaines, Garry

Patton, Cliff
See Patton, John

Patton, James Blythe 19th c. [NPS]
Author
* White, Edmund

Patton, John 20th c. [EF]
American football player
* Patton, Cliff

Patyn, Ann
See Carli, Audrey

Paul, [Brother]
See Sarpi, Pietro

Paul, Charles Kegan 1828-1902
[DEA]
British author and clergyman
* C. K. P.

[The] **Paul Revere of Ecology**
See Commoner, Barry

Paulding, James Kirke 1778-1860
[NPS, WGT]
American author and poet
* Fairlamb, Sampson
* Scott, [Sir] Walter
(See also base volume)

Paulet, Harry 1719-1794 [NPS]
Eleventh Marquis of Winchester
* Sternpost, Admiral

Paull, M. A.
See Ripley, Mrs. John

Paull, Minnie E. [Kenney]
1859-1895 [DNA]
Author
* Clifford, Ella

Paweski, Piotr 1536-1612
Polish theologian and author
* Skarga, Piotr

Paxton, Joseph Rupert 1827-1867
[DNA]
American attorney and author
* Roset, Hipponax

Paxton, Philip
See Hammett, Samuel Adams

Payne, F. M.
See Carey, Thomas Joseph

Payne, F. M.
See English, Thomas Dunn

Payne, Harold
See Kelly, George C.

Payne, J. Bertrand 19th c. [HFN]
Author
* J. B. P.

Payne, Odessa Strickland 1857- ?
[BDSA]
American author
* Mills, Faith

Payson, George 1824-1893 [DNA]
American author and attorney
* Fogie, Francis
* Raven, Ralph
(See also base volume)

Payson, [Lieut.] Howard
See Goldfrap, John Henry

Peabody, Josephine Preston
See Marks, Mrs. L. S.

Peabody, Mrs. Mark
See Victor, Metta Victoria Fuller

Peace, Charles 1832-1879 [CEC]
British burglar and murderer
* Thompson
* Ward, John

[The] **Peaceful**
See Alexander II

Peach, Edward C. 20th c. [EOP]
Author
* Ophiel

Peacock, Thomas Love 1785-1866
[DEA]
British author and poet
* O'Donovan, P. M., Esq.
(See also base volume)

Pearce, Henry 1777-1809 [RBE]
British boxer
* [The] Game Chicken

Pearle, Mary 1849- ? [PI]
Irish-born poet
* M. M. D.

Pearlman, Maurice 1911- [CA]
Israeli author and political adviser
* Pearlman, Moshe

Pearlman, Moshe
See Pearlman, Maurice

Pearson, Bert
See Pearson, Madison

Pearson, Diane
See McClelland, Diane Margaret

Pearson, Emily [Clemens] 19th c.
[DNA]
Author
* Pocahontas

Pearson, Madison 20th c. [EF]
American football player
* Pearson, Bert

Peck, Ellen
See Crosby, Nellie

Pedachenko, Alexander 19th c.
[BL]
Russian-born physician and murder suspect
* Konovalov, Vassily
* Luiskovo, Andrey
* Ostrong [or Ostrog], Mikhail
* [The] Russian Doctor

Peddar Zaskq
See Twitchell, Paul

Pedder, James 1775-1859 [IP]
British-born author
* J. P.
(See also base volume)

Pederek, Simon
See Thomas, Peter

[A] Pedestrian
See Aiton, John

Pedestrian
See Wilson, Robert

[The] Pedlar Poet
See McFarlan, James

Peel, [Sir] Robert 1788-1850
[IP, NPS]
British statesman
* Jenny
* Judas
* [The] Minister
* [The] Spinning Spoon
(See also base volume)

Peele, George 1558-1596 [DEA]
British playwright and poet
* G. P.
(See also base volume)

Peeping Tom
See Knapp, Henry Ryder

Peeradeal, Paul Puck
See Smith, [Sir] William Cusack,
Bart.

Peeradeal, Peter Puck
See Smith, [Sir] William Cusack,
Bart.

Pegge, Samuel 1704-1796 [IP]
British antiquary
* [An] Antiquary
* Echard, L.
* G.
* Gemsege, Paul
* L. E.
* [A] Late Very Learned and
  Reverend Divine
* P.
* P. E.
* P. G.
* P. S.
* [A] Ploughist
* Portius
* Row, T.
* S. P.
* Senex
* Vicarius Cantianus
(See also base volume)

Pei, I. M.
See Pei, Ieoh Ming

Pei, Ieoh Ming 1917- [CR]
*Chinese-born architect and city
planner*
* Pei, I. M.

Peignot, Etienne Gabriel
1767-1849 [IP]
French author
* Rambler, Jacques

Peirce, Augustus 1802-1849 [IP]
American physician and author
* Poeta, Enginae Societatis

Peirce, Benjamin 1809-1881 [IP]
American mathematician and author
* Benjamin the Florentine
* Yamen, Ben

Peirce, Bradford Kinney 1819- ?
[IP]
American clergyman and author
* B. K. P.
* [The] Chaplain

Peirce, I. [IP]
American author
* [A] Wanderer

Peirce, James 1673-1726 [IP]
British clergyman and author
* [A] Dissenter in the Country

Peirson, Eliza O. 19th c. [IP]
American journalist
* Aliqua

Pelham, George
See Pellew, George

Pelham, George 1766-1827 [NPS]
Bishop of Lincoln
* [The] Dandy Bishop

Pelham, [Sir] Henry 1695-1754
[NPS]
British statesman
* [The] Bulwark of the State

Pelican
See Pellegrini, Carlo

Pelican, A.
See Gerard, James Watson

Pell, Ferris 19th c. [IP]
American attorney and author
* Publicola

Pell, Robert Conger 1835?-1868
[DNA, IP]
American author
* Evelyn, Chetwood, Esq.

Pellegrini, Carlo 1838-1889 [WEC]
British caricaturist
* Jehu Junior
* Pelican
* Singe
(See also base volume)

Pellegrini, Pompeo
See Standen, Antony

Pelletier, Alexis 1837-1910 [DNA]
Canadian author and clergyman
* Luigi
* St. Aime, Georges

Pellew, George 1860?-1892 [EOP]
*Attorney and author, who claimed to
possess psychic powers*
* Pelham, George

Pelly, Gerald Conn 1865-1900 [PI]
Irish poet
* Cieppe, G.
* Gerald
* Nemo
* Tormer, Cill

Pelz, Edward 1800-1876 [IP]
German author
* Welp, Treumund

Pelzer, Leon ?-1922 [DI]
German-born Belgian murderer
* Preitel, Albert
* Vaughan, Henry

Pember, Arthur [IP]
American author
* A. P.

Pemberton, Charles Reece
1790-1840 [IP]
British actor and poet
* [A] Sailor

Pen, A., Esq.
See Leech, John

Pen Dragon, Anser, Esq.
See Ireland, William Henry

Pena, Bubba
See Pena, Robert

Pena, Robert 20th c. [EF]
American football player
* Pena, Bubba

Penck, A. R.
See Winkler, Ralf

Pencovic, Francis Heindswater 20th
c. [EOP]
Leader of American religious cult
* Krishna Venta

Pendennis
See Kelly, Denis

Pender, Margaret T. 19th c. [PI]
Irish poet and author
* Colleen
* M.
* M. T. P.
* Marguerite

Penfield, A. [IP]
American financier and author
* A. P.

Pengelly, William 1812- ? [IP]
British geologist and author
* [A] Geologist
* Y. M.

[The] Penman of the Revolution
See Dickinson, John

Penn, Arthur
See Matthews, James Brander

Penn, Rachel
See Willard, Caroline McCoy
[White]

Penn, William 1776-1845?
[IP, NPS]
British author
* Anglus, Phil
* [The] Rajah of Vaneplysia
* [An] Undergraduate

Penneck, Henry 1800-1862 [IP]
British clergyman and author
* Bayle, Mr.

Pennecuik, Alexander 1652-1722
[IP]
Scottish poet and botanist
* A. P., M.D.

Pennell, Joseph [NPS]
Artist
* A[rtist] U[nknown]

[The] Penniless
See Frederick I

Pennington, Patience
See Pringle, Elizabeth Waties
[Allston]

Penny, Prudence
See Goldberg, Hyman

Penrose, John 1778-1859 [NPS]
Author
* Senior

Penseval, Guy
See Darley, George

[The] Pensioner
See Abercromby, James [First
Baron Dunfermline]

Pentreath, Paul
See Neuburg, Victor [Benjamin]

Pentrill, Frank
See Rafferty, Mrs. William

[The] People's Prince
See Charles

Pepe-Illo [Little Joey]
See Delgado y Guerra, Jose

Pepete [Big Joe]
See Rodriguez y Rodriguez, Jose

Pepete [Big Joe]
See Rodriguez Davie, Jose

Pepper, Jack
See Culpepper, Edward

Pepper, K. N.
See Morris, James M.

Peppin, Dad
See Peppin, George W.

Peppin, George W. 19th c. [BLB]
American sheriff's deputy
* Peppin, Dad

Pepys, Samuel 1633-1703
[DEA, NPS]
British author and politician
* S. P., Esq.
* [The] Weathercock of His Time
(See also base volume)

Percival
See Ralph, Julian E.

Percival, Nelson
See Rymer, James Malcolm

Percy, Florence
See Akers, Elizabeth [Chase]

Percy, Sholto
See Byerley, Thomas

**Perdurabo, Frater [I Will Endure to
the End]**
See Crowley, Edward Alexander

[Le] Pere Joyeux du Vaudeville
See Basselin, Olivier

Peregoy, George Weems
See Mencken, Henry Louis

Perez, Manuel ?-1884 [GS]
Spanish bullfighter
* [El] Relojero [The
  Watch-Maker]

[The] Perfect Fool
See Leopold, Isaiah Edwin

Perfect Pete
See Rozelle, Alvin Ray

Pergamos
See Adams, Richard Newton

Peri, Jacopo 1561-1633 [BBD]
Italian composer
* [Il] Zazzerino

Pericles 5th c. BC   [NPS]
Athenian statesman
* [The] Olympian
(See also base volume)

Perigord, A. B.
See   Raisson, Horace Napoleon

Period, Pertinax and Co.
See   Buckingham, Joseph Tinker

Periwinkle, Tribulation
See   Alcott, Louisa May

Perne, Andrew 1596-1654   [NPS]
British clergyman
* [A] Doctor of Hypocrisie

Perotin 12th c.   [BBD]
French composer
* Perotinus Magnus

Perotinus Magnus
See   Perotin

Peroy
See   Ayxela y Torner, Pedro

Perrault, Charles 1628-1703   [NPS]
French author
* Homer's Fastest Friend
* [The] Modern Zoilus
(See also base volume)

Perrault, Claude 1613-1688   [NPS]
French architect and scientist
* Lubin

Perreau, Henri 20th c.   [DI]
French murderer and robber
* Cotton, Mr.
* De Tourville, Henri

Perreau-Saussine, Gerald 1938-
[CA]
American actor, author, screenwriter
* Miles, Richard

Perriman, Florence ?-1936   [EOP]
*Author who claimed to possess
psychic powers*
* Faustina, Madame

Perrugia, Vincenzo 20th c.   [DI]
Italian robber
* Leonard

Perry, Barbara Fisher
See   Fisher, Barbara

Perry, Edgar A.
See   Poe, Edgar Allan

Perry, Eleanor 1915?-1981   [CA]
American author and screenwriter
* Bayer, Oliver Weld

Perry, Joseph Franklin 1846-1909
[DNA]
American author and physician
* Ashmont
* Frank, Dr.

Perry, William 20th c.
American football player
* [The] Refrigerator

[The] Persian Sage
See   Apraates, Jacob

Persimmons
See   Bennett, M., Jr.

[A] Person Concer'n'd
See   Colbatch, John

[A] Person of Honour
See   Ancillon, Charles

[A] Person of Quality
See   Pomfret, John

[A] Person of Quality
See   Scott, Sarah

**[A] Person Who Lived There Ten
Years**
See   Fermin, Philippe

[A] Person Without A Name
See   Lewis, Alethea [Brereton]

Personne
See   Lynch, Mrs. Henry

Perugini, Mark   [NPS]
Author
* March Pane

Pestleman Jack
See   Keats, John

[The] Pet of the Fancy
See   Curtis, Dick

Peter of Mantua
See   Guarneri, Pietro Giovanni

Peter of Venice
See   Guarneri, Pietro

Peter the Great
See   Rozelle, Alvin Ray

Peter the Headstrong
See   Stuyvesant, Petrus

Peters, Forest 20th c.   [EF]
American football player
* Peters, Frosty

Peters, Frosty
See   Peters, Forest

Peters, Jeremy
See   Smith, Thomas Lacey

Peters, W. C.
See   Peters, William Cumming

Peters, William Cumming
1805-1866   [DAM]
*British-born musician, composer,
music publisher*
* Peters, W. C.

Petersen, Eugenie 1899-   [EOP]
Russian-born educator and author
* Indra Devi

Peterson, Charles Jacob 1819-1887
[DNA]
American author and publisher
* Randolph, J. Thornton

Peterson, Jeanne Whitehouse
See   Whitehouse, Jeanne

Petiot, Marcel 1897-1946   [DI]
French murderer
* Valery, Henry

Petracco, Francesco 1304-1374
[NPS]
Italian poet
* [The] Prince of Italian Poets
* [The] Tuscan Imp of Fame
(See also base volume)

Petre, Olinthus
See   Maginn, William

Pfeiffer, Johann Gregor 18th c.
[WGT]
Author
* Auletes, Grazianus Agricola

Phelps, Elizabeth [Stuart]
1815-1852   [DNA]
American author
* Trusta, H.

Phelps, Elizabeth Steward [Natt]
?-1920   [DNA]
American author
* North, Leigh

Phelps, S. B.
See   Griswold, Frances Irene
[Burge]

Phil-Porney
See   Mandeville, Bernard de

[The] Philadelphia Witch
See   Favato, Carino

Philagathus
See   Dexter, John Haven

Philalethes
See   Abbott, Thomas Kingsmill

Philalethes
See   Alting, Albertus Samuel
Carpenter

Philalethes
See   Gough, John

Philalethes
See   Jones, John

Philalethes
See   Turner, George

Philalethes
See   Twining, Thomas

Philalethes
See   Webb, F.

Philalethes, Alazonomastix
See   More, Henry

Philalethes Cantabrigiensis
See   Turton, Thomas

Philalethes, Eugenius
See   Vaughan, Thomas

Philalethes, M.A., Oxon
See   Fellowes, Robert

Philalethes, Mencius
See   Annet, Peter

Philalethes Rusticus
See   Asplin, William

Philander
See   Sheehan, John

Philander
See   Wright, James

Philanglia
See   Scott, James

[A] Philanthropist
See   Harris, Josiah

Philanthropos
See   Fellows, John

Philanthropos
See   Forster, John

Philanthropos
See   Mortimer, Thomas

Philanthropos
See   Wakefield, Thomas

Philanthropus
See   Locke, John

Phileleutheros
See   Fell, John

Phileleutherus Cantabrigiensis
See   Herne, Thomas

Philips, Albert Edwin 1845- ?
[DNA]
Author
* Alberton, Edwin

Philips, Ambrose 1675?-1749
[NPS]
Poet
* Macer

Philips, John 1676-1709   [NPS]
Poet
* Pomona's Bard

Philips, Katherine 1631-1664
[NPS]
British poet
* [The] Sappho of England
(See also base volume)

[The] Philistine
See   Spender, John Alfred

Phillimore, Francis
See   Meynell, Alice [Christiana
Gertrude Thompson]

Phillips, Clara 1899- ?   [LFW]
American murderer
* [The] Tiger Woman

Phillips, David Atlee 1922-   [CA]
*American intelligence officer, editor,
author*
* St. George, David [joint
   pseudonym with Georgi Markov]
(See also base volume)

Phillips, David Graham 1867-1911
[DLE1]
American author and journalist
* Graham, John

Phillips, James Atlee 1915-
[TCCM]
American author
* Atlee, Philip

Phillips, [Sir] Richard 1767-1840
[HFN]
British journalist
* Common Sense
(See also base volume)

Phillips, Rosina
See   Gingold, Hermoine

Phillips, William T.
See   Parker, Robert LeRoy

Philo Criticus
See   Hare, Francis

Philo Musa
See   Currie, James

Philo-Nauticus
See   Halloran, Laurence Hynes

Philo-Ruggles
See   Adams, John

Philo-Scotus
See   Ainslie, Philip Barrington

Philobiblius
See   Brockett, Linus Pierpont

Philobiblos
See   Ireland, Alexander

Philochelidon
See   Forster, Thomas

Philogenes Panedonius
See   Braithwaite, Richard

Philomath
See   Walsh, Michael Paul

Philomath, T. N.
See   Swift, Jonathan

Philonagnostes Criticus
See   Herne, Thomas

Philopatria
See   Lee, Rachel Frances Antonina
Dashwood

Philopatria
See   Paine, Thomas

Philorthos
See   Johnstone, George

Philostratus
See   Foster, Thomas

Philotesis
See   Roberts, Daniel

Philroye, Humphrey
See   Steele, [Sir] Richard

Phiz
See   Walsh, Michael Paul

Phocion
See   Curtis, George Ticknor

Phocion
See   Hartley, Thomas

Phocion
See   Smith, William Loughton

[The] Phoenix of the World
See   Sidney, [Sir] Philip

[The] Phoenix of these Late Times
See   Welby, Henry

[A] Phrenologist
See   Tichborne, Thomas

Phucher, Itothe
See   Chittenden, Hiram Martin

Phylos the Thibetan
See   Oliver, Frederick Spencer

[A] Physician
See   Forster, Thomas

[A] Physician
See   Hoskyns, John

[A] Physician
See   Mackenzie, James

[Un] Physicien Voyageur
See   Forster, Thomas

Piatigorsky, Gregor 1903-1976
[CR]
Russian musician
* Piatigorsky, Grischa
(See also base volume)

Piatigorsky, Grischa
See   Piatigorsky, Gregor

Picart, Etienne 1632-1721   [UH]
French engraver
* [Le] Romain
(See also base volume)

**[The] Picasso of the Contemporary
Drama**
See   Ionesco, Eugene

Piccadilly, Lord
See   Douglas, William

Picken, Andrew
See   Galt, John

Picken, Andrew 1788-1833
[DLE1, NPS]
British author
* Keelivine, Christopher
* Picken, Dominie Legacy

Picken, Dominie Legacy
See   Picken, Andrew

Picken, Henry
See   Harkin, Hugh

Pickle, Prometheus
See   Bush, William

Pictor Ignotus [Painter Unknown]
See   Blake, William

[The] Pied Piper of Rock 'n' Roll
See   Freed, Alan

Pierce, Abel Head 19th c.   [BLB]
American cattle baron
* Pierce, Shanghai

Pierce, George Foster 1811-1884
[BDSA]
*American author, clergyman,
educator*
* [The] Demosthenes of Southern
Methodism

Pierce, Shanghai
See   Pierce, Abel Head

Pierre et Paul
See   Lourdoneix, Paul de

[Le] Pieux
See   Frederick II

Piggot, Mostyn T.   [NPS]
Author
* Plum, Medium Tem

Pigot, John Edward 1822-1871   [PI]
Irish poet
* Fermoy
* Firinne
* Gall

Pike, Frances West [Atherton] 1819-
?   [DNA]
American author
* Athern, Anna

Pilate, Pontius
See   Walsh, Michael Paul

[A] Pilgrim
See   Harsha, David Addison

[A] Pilgrim
See   Wright, Frederick

Pilgrim, Thomas ?-1882   [DNA]
American author
* Owl, Eugene
(See also base volume)

Pincherle, Alberto 1907-   [CLC]
Italian author, critic, playwright
* Moravia, Alberto

Pinckney, Charles 1758- ?   [BDSA]
American statesman and writer
* Republican

Pindar 5th c. BC   [NPS]
Greek poet
* [The] Great Theban
(See also base volume)

Pindar, Pat
See   Battier, Henrietta

Pindar, Peter, Jr.
See   Ellenwood, Henry S.

Pine, M. S.
See   Finn, [Sister] Mary Paulina

Pinkerton, John 1758-1826   [DEA]
Scottish author and historian
* Bennet, H., M.A.
(See also base volume)

Pinna y Ruiz, Donna Teresa
See   Preston, William

Pinnix, Hannah Courtney [Baxter]
1851-1931   [DNA]
Author
* Kerr

Pio. Padre [da Pietralcini]
See   Forgione, Francesco

Piot, Lazarus
See   Munday, Anthony

Piper, A. G.
See   Lewis, Julius Warren

Piper, Watty
See   Bragg, Mabel Caroline

Pippin, Parley
See   Bartlett, M. R.

Piscator
See   Lascelles, Robert

Pistone, Joseph D. 20th c.
American FBI undercover agent
* Brasco, Don

Pitarra, Serafi
See   Soler, Frederic

Pitcher
See   Binstead, Arthur M.

Pith, Peter
See   Smith, Sydney

Pitois, J. B. 1811-1877   [EOP]
Author
* Christian, Paul

Pitt, William [Earl of Chatham]
1708-1778   [NPS]
British statesman
* Aeolus
* [The] Loggerhead of London
* [The] Old Lion
* [The] Young Marshal
(See also base volume)

Pitt, William 1759-1806   [NPS]
British prime minister
* [An] Atlas
* Bottomless Pit
(See also base volume)

Pitts, Alabama
See   Pitts, Edwin

Pitts, Charlie
See   Wells, Samuel

Pitts, Edwin 20th c.   [EF]
American football player
* Pitts, Alabama

Pizer [or Kosminski?] 19th c.   [BL]
*Polish-born shoemaker and murder
suspect*
* Leather Apron

Plain, Henry
See   Anderson, James

Plain, Timothy
See   Blakie, G. W.

Plain, Timothy
See   Threepland, Moncrieff

Plantagenet
See   Bromet, William

[A] Planter
See   Long, Edward

[El] Platero [The Silversmith]
See   Garcia, Jose

Platt, Thomas Collier 1833- ?
[NPS]
American politician
* Me Too

[A] Play-Goer
See   Ireland, Joseph N.

[The] Playboy of the Western Wing
See   Kissinger, Henry Alfred

Player, Gary 1935-   [CR]
South African golfer
* [The] Black Knight of the
Fairways

Player, Robert
See   Jordan, Robert Furneaux

Pleon
See   Moore, John

Plimmer, Charlotte 1916-   [CA]
*American-born British author and
playwright*
* Denis, Charlotte [joint pseudonym
with Denis Plimmer]

Plimmer, Denis 1914-   [CA]
*Australian-born British author and
playwright*
* Denis, Charlotte [joint pseudonym
with Charlotte Plimmer]

Plinth, Octavius   [IP]
American author
* [The] Rain Water Doctor

Plough, Peter
See   Barty, James S.

[A] Ploughist
See   Pegge, Samuel

Plowden, Edmund 1518-1585
[NPS]
Jurist and author
* [The] Oracle of Common Law

Plowright, William George Holroyd
1911-1977   [DI, EOP]
British swindler
* Roy, William
* Silver, Bill

Plugger Bill Martin
See   Martin, William

Plum, Medium Tem
See   Piggot, Mostyn T.

Plumptre, Annabella   [IP]
British author
* [A] Lady

Plumptre, Anne   [IP]
British author
* Miss P.

Plumptre, John   [IP]
British clergyman and author
* [A] Clergyman of the Church of
England

Plunder
See   McNally, Leonard

Plunket, William Conyngham
1828-1897   [PI]
Irish poet and clergyman
* U. U. P.

Plunkett, Arthur Hume 19th c. [PI]
Irish poet
* A. H. P.

Plunkett, George Noble 1851- ?
[PI]
Irish poet
* Killeen

Plunkett, Henry Willoughby Grattan
1808-1889 [PI]
Irish-born poet and playwright
* Grattan, H. P.
(See also base volume)

Plunkett, Sarge
See Wier, A. M.

Pocahontas
See Pearson, Emily [Clemens]

Pocci, Franz Von 1803-1876
[WEC]
*German cartoonist, illustrator,
author*
* [The] Hogarth of Bavaria

[El] Pocho [The Rotten One]
See Alarcon, Alfonso

[The] Pocket Dictator
See Dollfuss, Engelbert

Podmore, Periwinkle
See Bangs, John Kendrick

Poe, Edgar Allan 1809-1849
[EMD, NPS, WGT]
American author and poet
* Perry, Edgar A.
* Pym, Arthur Gordon
* Quickens, Quarles
(See also base volume)

[A] Poet
See Osborn, Laughton

[The] Poet Entertainer of the Ozarks
See Lucey, Thomas Elmore

[The] Poet Laureate of the Railroad
See Fennell, Patrick

[The] Poet Naturalist
See Thoreau, Henry David

[The] Poet of Armageddon
See Davidson, John

[The] Poet of Despair
See Thomson, James

[The] Poet of Duhallow
See Deady, John Christmas

[The] Poet of Ivy Wall
See Donoho, Thomas Seton

[The] Poet of Nature
See Wordsworth, William

[The] Poet of Reason
See Boileau-Despreaux, Nicolas

[The] Poet of the Caucasus
See Lermontoff, Mikhail
Yurievitch

[The] Poet of the Moy
See Flanagan, Edward

[The] Poet of the Workshop
See Frazer, John de Jean

[The] Poet Painter
See Rossetti, Dante Gabriel

[The] Poet Priest
See Milman, Henry Hart

Poeta, Enginae Societatis
See Peirce, Augustus

[The] Poetry Lady
See Lawton, Ethel Chapin

[The] Poet's Parasite
See Warburton, William

Pohl, Baruch 1838-1897 [BBD]
German impresario
* Pollini, Bernhard

Poinsett, Joel Roberts 1779-1851
[IP]
American statesman and author
* [A] Citizen of the United States

Poinsot, Antoine Edmond 1834- ?
[IP]
French author
* Heilly, Georges d'

[The] Poisoner
See Wainewright, Thomas
Griffiths

Poitiers, Angele
See Fox, Hugh [Bernard, Jr.]

Poland's Billy Mitchell
See Karpinski, Stanislaw

Pole, Thomas 1753-1829 [IP]
British clergyman and author
* [A] Friend to Education

Pole, William 1814- ? [HFN]
British engineer and author
* Professor P.

Pole, William de la 1396-1450
[NPS]
Fourth Earl of Suffolk
* Jackanapes

Polevoi, Boris
See Kampov, Boris Nikolayevich

Polglase, Ann Eaton 1803-1865
[IP]
British author
* A. E. P.

Policeman X
See Doherty, John

Polidori, Louis Eustache ?-1830
[IP]
Italian physician and author
* Byron, Lord

Polienus Rhodiensis
See Barclay, John

Political Parent
See Adams, Samuel

Pollard, Edward Alfred 1838-1872
[IP]
American author and journalist
* [A] Distinguished Southern
Journalist
* [The] Southern Spy

Pollini, Bernhard
See Pohl, Baruch

Pollock, [Paul] Jackson 1912-1956
American painter
* Jack the Dripper

Pollock, John 18th c. [IP]
Scottish clergyman and author
* [A] Well Wisher of the
Good-Old-Way

Pollock, John 18th c. [IP]
Scottish clergyman and author
* [A] Member of the Church of
Scotland

Polovchak, Walter 1968?-
Russian-born defector
* [The] Littlest Defector

Poluflosboio, Lord
See Grosvenor, Robert

Polwhele, Richard 1760-1838 [IP]
British clergyman and poet
* [A] Country Gentleman
* Eusebius Exoniensis
* P.
* R. P.
* [An] Undergraduate
* [A] Young Gentleman of Truro
School

Polyanthus
See Wilson, John

Pomerano, Castalio
See Braithwaite, Richard

Pomfret, John 1667?-1703 [IP]
British poet
* [A] Person of Quality

Pommerencke, Heinrich 20th c.
[DI]
German murderer
* [The] Beast of the Black Forest

Pomona's Bard
See Philips, John

Pomposus
See Butler, Dr.

Ponder, [Rev.] Peter
See Bell, William

**Ponsonby, Frederick George
Brabazon** 1815- ? [IP]
British barrister and playwright
* Roe, Richard

Pontiac
See Boyle, John

Ponzi, Carlo 1878-1949 [BLB, DI]
Italian-born swindler
* [The] Great Ponzi
* Ponzi, Charles

Ponzi, Charles
See Ponzi, Carlo

Poodle
See Byng, Frederick

Pooh
See Nettles, Bonnie Lu

Poole, Gray Johnson 1906- [CA]
American author and columnist
* Gray, Betsy

Poole, William ?-1855 [BLB]
American murderer and gangleader
* Bill the Butcher

Poop
See Nettles, Bonnie Lu

Poor, Agnes Blake 1842-1922
[DNA]
American author
* Prescott, Dorothy

Poor Poet-Ape
See Shakespeare, William

[The] Poor Scholar
See Reid, [Thomas] Mayne

Pop Gun Kelly
See Kelly, George R.

Pop, Iggy
See Osterberg, James [Jim]

Pope
See Strasberg, Lee

Pope, Alexander 1688-1744
[DEA, NPS, PPN]
British poet
* [An] Ape
* Barnivelt, Esdras
* Gunpowder Percy
* [A] Little Druid-Wight
* [The] Little Man of Twickenham
* [The] Most Faultless of Poets
* Short, Bob
* Ultimus Romanorum
* [The] Wasp of Twickenham
(See also base volume)

Pope, Bucky
See Pope, Frank

Pope, Charles Henry 1841-1918
[DNA]
American author and clergyman
* Starcross, Roger

Pope, Frank 20th c. [EF]
American football player
* Pope, Bucky

[The] Popish Midwife
See Cellier, Elizabeth

Poplicola, Valerius
See Adams, Samuel

Populus
See Adams, Samuel

Poquelin, Jean Baptiste 1622-1673
[NPS]
French playwright
* [The] King of Dramatists
(See also base volume)

Porson, Professor [joint pseudonym
with Robert Southey]
See Coleridge, Samuel Taylor

Porson, Professor [joint pseudonym
with Samuel Taylor Coleridge]
See Southey, Robert

Porson, Richard 1759-1808 [NPS]
British scholar and critic
* England, S.
(See also base volume)

Portaas, Herman Theodore
1886-1959
Norwegian poet
* Wildenwey, Herman Theodore

Porter, Camanche Bill
See Porter, William

Porter, Countee Leroy 1903-1946
[TLC]
American poet, author, playwright
* Cullen, Countee

Porter, Dick
See Porter, Napoleon Bonaparte

Porter, James 1753-1798 [PI]
Irish poet
* R.

Porter, Mark
See Cox, James Anthony

Porter, Napoleon Bonaparte 1853-
? [DNA]
Author and railwayman
* Porter, Dick

Porter, William
American frontiersman
* Porter, Camanche Bill

Portius
See Pegge, Samuel

Positive, Paul
See Montgomery, James

Possum, Peter
See Rowe, Richard

Postl, Karl Anton 1793-1864
[DNA, HFN]
Moravian-born author
* Hardman, Frederick
* Seatsfield
(See also base volume)

Pot, Philippe 1428-1494
[NPS, UH]
French prime minister
* [La] Bouche de Ciceron
(See also base volume)

Pottasch, Eleanor 20th c. [FIR]
American actress
* Barry, Eleanor

Potter, Kathleen Jill 1932- [CA]
British author
* Kinder, Kathleen

Potter, Paul
See Congdon, Charles Taber

Potter, [Major] Roger Sherman
See Adams, Francis Colburn

Potts, Stacy Gardner 1799-1865
[DNA]
American author
* Oakwood, Oliver

Poueigh, Jean
[Marie-Octave-Geraud] 1876- ?
[BBD]
French composer and author
* Sere, Octave

Powell, Arden 20th c. [EF]
American football player
* Powell, Tim

Powell, [David] Frank 1845-1906
American author and physician
* White Beaver

Powell, Tim
See Powell, Arden

Power, Catherine
See DuBreuil, Elizabeth Lorinda

Power, David?
See Grady, Thomas

Power, Paddy
See Power, Tyrone, I

Power, Tyrone, I 1797-1841 [FAA]
Irish-born actor
* Power, Paddy

Pownall, Henry 19th c. [HFN]
Author
* [An] Inhabitant

Poyntz, Launce
See Whittaker, Frederick

**Practitioner of More Than Fifty
Years' Experience in the Art of
Angling**
See Bartlett, John

Prado 19th c. [DI]
Murderer
* De Linska, [The] Count

Praestantissimus Mathematicus
See Brahe, Tycho

Praetorius, Hieronymus
See Schulz [or Schulze],
Hieronymus

Prairie Dog Dave
See Morrow, Dave

Pratt, Charles E. 19th c. [BBH]
*American author and bicycling
enthusiast*
* Cycling's Elder Statesman

Pratt, Ella Ann [Farman]
1837-1907 [DNA]
American author
* Shepherd, Dorothea Alice

Pratt, Jacob Loring 1835-1891
[DNA]
American author and clergyman
* Campbell, Erving
* North, F. H.
(See also base volume)

Preitel, Albert
See Pelzer, Leon

**[Le] Premier Maitre d'Hotel de la
Philosophie**
See Holbach, [Baron] Paul Henri
Dietrich d'

[A] Prentise in the Divine Art of Poesy
See James I

[A] Presbyter
See Addison, Berkeley

Presbyter Anglicanus
See Harris, Joseph Hemington

Presbyter Catholicus
See Harness, William

**[A] Presbyter of the Church of
England**
See Asplin, William

**[A] Presbyter of the Church of
England**
See Austin, William

**[A] Presbyter of the Church of
England**
See Robertson, William

**[A] Presbyter of the Church of
England**
See Sclater, William

[A] Presbyterian
See Blakie, Alexander

Prescott, Dorothy
See Poor, Agnes Blake

Prescott, E. Livingston
See Jay, Edith K. Spicer

Prescott, Paul J.
See Irons, Lettie Artley

Prescott, Thomas H.
See Blake, William O.

[The] President
See Alderson, John

[The] President's Preacher
See Graham, William Franklin
[Billy]

Pressburger, Emeric 1902- [CA]
*Hungarian-born author and
screenwriter*
* Imrie, Richard

Preston, George
See Banks, Nancy Huston

Preston, George F.
See Warren, John Byrne Leicester
[Baron de Tabley]

Preston, William 1753-1807 [PI]
Irish poet, playwright, attorney
* Pinna y Ruiz, Donna Teresa

Prevost, Francis
See Battersby, Henry Francis
Prevost

Price, Charles 20th c. [EF]
American football player
* Price, Cotton

Price, Cotton
See Price, Charles

[The] Priest of Nature
See Williams, David

**[A] Priest of the Congregation of the
Holy Redeemer**
See Cornell, J. H.

[A] Priestman
See Fitzpatrick, John

[The] Prig
See Longueville, T.

Prilukoff, Donat 20th c. [DI]
Russian murderer
* Zeiler, M.

[A] Primcock
See Ralph, James

[The] Prime Irish Lad
See Randall, Jack

Prin, Marie 1908?-1953 [BL]
French artists' model
* Kiki of Montparnasse

Prince Eddy
See Albert Victor

Prince Hal
See Henry V

Prince John
See Hunt, John

[The] Prince of Caricaturists
See Cruikshank, George

[The] Prince of Dandies
See Lewis, Matthew Gregory

[The] Prince of Grammarians
See Aristarchus

[The] Prince of High Tobymen
See Gardiner, Frank

[The] Prince of Italian Poets
See Petracco, Francesco

[The] Prince of Lyric Poets
See Gongora y Argote, Luis de

[The] Prince of Lyrical Roman Poets
See Horace

[The] Prince of Macaronies
See Bussy, George [Fourth Earl of
Jersey]

[The] Prince of Negro Songwriters
See Bland, James A.

Prince of Peace
See Jesus Christ

[The] Prince of Poets
See Homer

[The] Prince of Poyais
See McGregor, Gregor

[The] Prince of Princes
See George IV

[The] Prince of Quacks
See Balsamo, Giuseppe

[The] Prince of Sceptics
See Hume, David

[The] Prince of Storytellers
See Oppenheim, E[dward] Phillips

[The] Prince of Wails
See William

Princeps Nominalium
See Occam [or Ockham], William
of

[The] Princess of Connemara
See Martin, Mrs. Bell

Principiis Obsta
See Adams, Samuel

Pringle, Elizabeth Waties [Allston]
1845-1921 [DNA]
Author and historian
* Pennington, Patience

Prinny
See George IV

Prior, Matthew 1664-1721 [NPS]
British poet and diplomat
* [The] Solomon of Bards
(See also base volume)

Priscian
See Hawtrey, Dr.

Priscilla
See Wakefield, Priscilla [Bell]

Pritchard, Abisha 20th c. [EF]
American football player
* Pritchard, Bosh

Pritchard, Bosh
See Pritchard, Abisha

Pritchard, Martin J.
See Moore, Justina

[A] Private Detective
See Rathborne, St. George

[A] Private Gentleman
See Allan, Thomas

Private John
See Allen, John Mills

**[A] Private of the 38th Artists' and
Member of the Alpine Club**
See Barrow, John

**[A] Probationer of the Church of
Scotland**
See Rae, William

Probus
See Child, David Lee

Probus
See Drury, Dr.

Proctor, Bryan Waller 1787-1874
[NPS]
British poet
* Cornwall, Baby
(See also base volume)

[A] Prodigy of Literary Curiosity
See Oldys, William

[A] Professor
See Gwilliam, John

Professor P.
See Pole, William

Profit and Loss
See Baker, James Loring

Promotion in the Church
See Angus, William

Pronzini, Bill 1943-   [TCCM]
American author
* Jeffrey, William
(See also base volume)

[The] Prophet James
See Buck, James Smith

[A] Proprietor of India Stock
See Buckingham, James Silk

[A] Protectionist
See Elliot, John Lettsom

[The] Protector
See Humphrey [Duke of
Gloucester and Earl of Pembroke]

[A] Protestant
See Twort, Charles William

[A] Protestant
See Wilson, David

[A] Protestant Dissenter
See Christie, William

[A] Protestant Lady
See Adams, Ann

[A] Protestant Nonconformist
See Ash, Edward

[The] Protestant's Mouthpiece
See Bayer, Johann

[The] Proteus
See Foote, Samuel

[The] Proteus of Man's Talents
See Arouet, Francois Marie

[The] Proteus of the Stage
See Garrick, David

[The] Protomartyr of Britain
See Alban

[The] Proudest of the Proud
See Wedderburn, Alexander

Proxmire, [Edward] William 1915-
[CR]
American politician
* Billion-Dollar Bill

Pry, Paul
See Byng, Frederick

Prynne, William
See Butler, Samuel

Prynne, William 1600-1669   [NPS]
British pamphleteer
* [The] Brave Jersey Muse
* White, Matthew
* William the Conqueror
(See also base volume)

Pryor, Adel
See Wasserfall, Adel

[The] Psalmsinger
See Adams, Samuel

[The] Psychic Engineer
See Jonsson, Olaf

Publicola
See Pell, Ferris

Publicus Severus
See Dillon, [Sir] John Joseph

[A] Publisher
See Marston, Edward

Pucheta [Big Bouquet]
See Munoz, Jose

[The] Puck of Literature
See Walpole, Horatio [Fourth Earl
of Orford]

Puddicombe, Anne Adaliza
1850?-1908   [NPS]
Author
* Raine, Allen

Puget, Pierre 1623-1694   [NPS]
French sculptor, painter, architect
* [The] French Michelangelo
(See also base volume)

Punch, Mr.
See Jerrold, Douglas William

Punderet
See Sanz Almenar

Punjabee
See Arnold, William Delafield

Purdy
See Miller, Emily [Huntington]

Purdy, [Captain] Jim
See Gillelan, G[eorge] Howard

[A] Puritan of the 19th Century
See Alden, Joseph Warren

Putnam, Arthur Lee
See Alger, Horatio, Jr.

Putnam, Sarah 1845- ?   [BDSA]
American author and poet
* Madison, Virginia
(See also base volume)

Puttock
See Aelfric

Puzzle, Peter
See Addison, Joseph

Pylades
See Gwinnett, Richard

Pym, Arthur Gordon
See Poe, Edgar Allan

Pyne, Nicholas
See Neuburg, Victor [Benjamin]

[The] Pythagorean
See Tryon, Thomas

Python
See Tyler, John

Q

* Indicates Assumed Name

Q.
See Barron, Alfred

Q.
See Jerrold, Douglas William

Q. in the Corner
See Harris, John

Q. X.?
See Young, Robert

Qadar, Basheer
See Alexander, Charles Khalil

[A] Quadragenarian
See Weaver, Robert

[A] Quaker
See Forster, Josiah

[The] Quaker Solon of Rochdale
See Bright, John

Quantrill, Charles [or Charley]
See Quantrill, William Clarke

Quantrill, William Clarke
1837-1865   [BLB]
American murderer
* Hart, Charles
* Quantrill, Charles [or Charley]

Quarles, Francis 1592-1644   [NPS]
Poet
* [The] Leveller in Poetry

Queen, Ellery
See Vance, John Holbrook [Jack]

[The] Queen of Confidence Women
See Crosby, Nellie

[The] Queen of Crime
See Lyons, Sophie

[The] Queen of Diamonds
See Bonner, Antoinette

[The] Queen of Disco
See Gaines, La Donna Andrea

[The] Queen of Letter-Writers
See Rabutin-Chantal, Marie de
[Marquise de Sevigne]

[The] Queen of Ohio
See Chadwick, Elizabeth [Bigley]

[The] Queen of Tears
See Caroline Matilda

[The] Queen of the Badgers
See Lambert, May

Queen of the Cowgirls
See Smith, Frances Octavia

Queen of the Soaps
See Nixon, Agnes Eckhardt

Queen Poisoner
See Sherman, Lydia

Querno, Camillo 1470-1528   [NPS]
Italian poet
* [The] Antichrist of Wit

Quesnel, Pierre 1699-1774   [WGT]
Author
* Rasiel de Selva, Hercule

Quevedo Redivivus
See Byron, George Gordon Noel

Quickens, Quarles
See English, Thomas Dunn

Quickens, Quarles
See Poe, Edgar Allan

Quid-Pro-Quo
See Smyth, Charles John

Quiet, George
See Pardon, George Frederick

[A] Quiet Looker-on.
See Foster, John

[A] Quiet Man
See Fay, Theodore Sedgwick

[The] Quiet One
See Kray, Reginald [Reggie]

Quigley, Red
See Quigley, William

Quigley, William 20th c.   [EF]
American football player
* Quigley, Red

Quillem, Harry
See Kewen, Edward John Cage

Quillinan, Edward 1791-1851
[NPS]
Poet
* [The] Heavy Horseman

Quimber, Mario
See Alexander, Charles Khalil

Quin, James 1693-1766   [NPS]
Irish actor
* [The] Stage Leviathan
(See also base volume)

Quincy, Josiah 1744-1775   [IP]
American author and patriot
* Calisthenes
* [An] Old Man
(See also base volume)

Quincy, Samuel Miller 1833- ?   [IP]
American attorney and journalist
* [A] High Private
(See also base volume)

Quinito
See Valverde y San Juan, Joaquin

Quinlan, Skeet
See Quinlan, Voiney

Quinlan, Voiney 20th c.   [EF]
American football player
* Quinlan, Skeet

Quinn, [Sister] Bernetta
See Quinn, Roselyn Viola

Quinn, Mary Bernetta
See Quinn, Roselyn Viola

Quinn, Roselyn Viola 1915-   [CA]
American author and educator
* Quinn, [Sister] Bernetta
* Quinn, Mary Bernetta

Quinn, Susan 1940-   [CA]
American author
* Jacobs, Susan

Quint, Wilder Dwight 1863-1936
[DNA]
American journalist
* Dwight, Tilton

Quir, Dr.
See Henley, John

Quirinus
See Dollinger, Johann Joseph Ignaz

Quirke, Henry 1847- ?   [PI]
Irish poet
* O'Cuirc, Henry

Quongti, Richard
See Macaulay, Thomas Babington
[First Baron Macaulay]

R

R.
See Porter, James

R.
See Reilly, Thomas Devin

R. A.
See Allen, Richard

R. A.
See Allsop, Robert

R. A.
See Alsop, Richard

R. B.
See Blackwell, Robert

R. B.?
See Burrowes, Robert

R. B.
See Crouch, Nathaniel

R. B. J.
See Jones, Robert Baker

R. B. S.
See Scott, Robert Bissett

R. C.
See Charruthers, Robert

R. D.
See De Courcy, Richard

R. D. W.
See Webb, Richard Davis

R. F. A.
See Lee, Rachel Frances Antonina
Dashwood

R. F. P.
See Maginn, William

R. G.
See Gough, Richard

R. G.
See Graham, Robert

R. G.
See Greene, Robert

**R. G., a Clerk of the Court of
Common Pleas**
See Gardiner, R.

R. G., Junior
See Gough, Richard

R. H.
See Hakluyt, Richard

R. H.
See Harvey, Richard

R. H. B.
See Blades, R. H.

R. H. S.
See Stoddard, Richard Henry

R. J. M.
See Martin, Robert Jasper

R. L.
See Davis, Thomas Osborne

R. L. C.
See Carpenter, Russell Lant

R. M.
See Mulholland, Rosa

R. N.
See Norris, Randal

R. N. O.
See MacOwen, Robert

R. N., Trinity College?
See Nun, Richard

R. P.
See Polwhele, Richard

R. P., de Venezuela
See Paez, Ramon

R. R.
See Hobbes, Thomas

R. R. M.
See Madden, Richard Robert

R. S.
See Scott, John

R. S.
See Southwell, Robert

R. S., a Passenger in the Hector
See Paltock, Robert

R. S. M.
See Mackenzie, Robert Shelton

R. T.
See Thomas, Ralph

R. T.
See Tyas, Robert

R. T. S.
See Maginn, William

R. V., Cork
See Varian, Ralph

R. W.
See White, Robert

R. W.
See Wright, Robert

R. W. S. W.
See Sackville-West, Reginald
[Seventh Earl of De La Warr]

R. Y.
See Young, Robert

Rabbi
See Strasberg, Lee

Rabbotenus, Isaac
See Marnix, Philip Van [Baron
Sainte Aldegonde]

Rabe, Ann C[rawford] Von 19th c.
[WGT]
Author
* Von Degen

Rabelais, Francois 1494?-1553
[NPS]
French satirist
* [Le] Cure de Meudon
* [The] Idol of the Age
(See also base volume)

Rabito, Anthony 20th c.
American underworld figure
* Fish, Mr.

Raborg, Frederick A[shton], Jr.
1934-   [CA]
American author and playwright
* Ashmore, Lewis
* Baldwin, Dick
* Bronson, Wolfe
* Kern, Canyon
* Mayfair, Bertha

**Rabutin-Chantal, Marie de [Marquise
de Sevigne]** 1626-1696   [NPS]
French writer and fashion leader
* [The] Queen of Letter-Writers

Raby, Derek Graham 1927-   [CA]
British playwright
* Derrick, Graham

Rack, Edmund 1735-1787
[IP, NPS]
British author
* Eusebius
* [A] Friend to True Liberty

Rackstraw, William Smyth
1823-1895   [BBD]
British music scholar
* Rockstro, William Smyth

Radak
See Kamchi, David

Radcliffe, Alida G.   [IP]
Hymn-writer
* A. G. R.

Radcliffe, Anne 1764-1823   [NPS]
British author
* [The] Salvator Rosa of British
   Novelists
(See also base volume)

Radcliffe, John 1650-1714   [NPS]
British physician
* Aesculapius

Radcliffe-Cooke, Charles Wallwyn
[NPS]
Author
* Gushington, Angelina

Rader, Lloyd E. 1907?-
*American welfare department
director*
* [The] Sooner Huey Long

Radford, Richard F[rancis], Jr.
1939-   [CA]
American author
* Critchley, Lynne
* Lyndon, Amy

Radha, [Swami] Sivananda
See Hellman, Sylvia

Rado, James
See Radomski, James

Radomski, James 1939?-
[CA, CLC]
*American lyricist, playwright,
composer*
* Rado, James

Radziwill, Stanislaus 20th c.   [BP]
Polish-born real estate investor
* Radziwill, Stash

Radziwill, Stash
See Radziwill, Stanislaus

Rae, Edna
See Gillooly, Edna Rae

Rae, Herbert
See Gibson, George Herbert

Rae, William   [IP]
Author
* [A] Probationer of the Church of
   Scotland

Raeschild, Sheila
See Miller, Sheila

Rafferty, Mrs. William 19th c.   [PI]
Irish poet
* Pentrill, Frank

Rafferty, S. S.
See Hurley, John J[erome]

Raffles, Thomas 1788-1863 [IP]
British clergyman and author
* [A] Doctor of Divinity, But Not of Oxford

Rag, Tag, and Bobtail
See Lees, James Cameron

Rahmer, Hans Sigismund 1924-
[CA]
German-born clergyman and author
* Rayner, John Desmond

Raidler, Bill 20th c. [EWG]
American gunfighter
* Raidler, Little Bill

Raidler, Little Bill
See Raidler, Bill

[The] Rain Water Doctor
See Gardener, Sylvan

[The] Rain Water Doctor
See Plinth, Octavius

Rainbow [Secret Service code name]
See Reagan, Anne Frances Davis

Raine, Allen
See Puddicombe, Anne Adaliza

Raine, Richard
See Sawkins, Raymond H[arold]

Rainer, George
See Greenburger, Ingrid Elisabeth

Raisson, Horace Napoleon
1798-1854 [IP]
French author
* Perigord, A. B.

Raithby, John [IP]
British author
* [A] Member of Lincoln's Inn

[The] Rajah of Vaneplysia
See Penn, William

Rale, Nero
See Burgess, Michael Roy

Raleigh, Richard
See Kister, W. H.

Raleigh, W.
See St. John, Henry

Raleigh, [Sir] Walter 1552?-1618
[NPS]
British courtier, explorer, statesman
* [The] English Milo
(See also base volume)

Ralph, James ?-1762 [IP]
British journalist, playwright, poet
* [A] Gentleman of the Middle Temple
* [An] Impartial Inquirer
* Lilburne
* [A] Lover of Truth and Liberty
* [A] Primcock
* [A] Woman of Quality

Ralph, Julian E. 1853-1903 [NPS]
American journalist
* Percival
(See also base volume)

Ralph, Mr. le Docteur
See Arouet, Francois Marie

Ralston, Thomas N. [IP]
American clergyman and author
* Eureka

Ram, Stopford James [IP]
British clergyman and author
* Vernon, Ruth

Ramachakra, Yogi
See Atkinson, William Walker

Ramakrishna, Sri
See Gadadhar

Ramble, Robert
See Frost, John

[A] Rambler
See Budworth, Joseph

[A] Rambler
See Simcox, George Augustus

Rambler, Jacques
See Peignot, Etienne Gabriel

Rambling Richard
See Egerton-Warburton, Rowland Eyles

Ramsay, Allan 1686-1758 [IP]
Scottish poet
* Scot, Quod Ar.
(See also base volume)

Ramsay, Allan, Jr. 1713-1784 [IP]
Scottish painter and author
* Britannicus
* Marcellus
* Steady
* Zero

Ramsay, Andrew John ?-1907
[DNA]
American poet
* Ramsay, J. R.

Ramsay, D. [IP]
Author
* Hortensius

Ramsay, J. R.
See Ramsay, Andrew John

Ramsay, James 18th c. [IP]
Scottish author
* [A] Gentleman

Ramsay, Richard 1770?-1833?
[PI]
Irish poet
* Meek, Matthew

Ramsey, Buster
See Ramsey, Garrard

Ramsey, Chuck
See Ramsey, Lowell Wallace, Jr.

Ramsey, Garrard 20th c. [EF]
American football player
* Ramsey, Buster

Ramsey, Lowell Wallace, Jr. 1952-
[FR]
American football player
* Ramsey, Chuck

Rand, William
See Roos, William

Randall, Jack 1794-1828
[NN, RBE]
British boxer
* [The] Nonpareil
* [The] Original Nonpareil
* [The] Prime Irish Lad

Randall, Jean
See Hauck, Louise [Platt]

Randolph, Asa Philip 1889-1979
[CR]
American labor leader
* St. Philip of the Pullman Porters
* Uncle Tom No. 2
(See also base volume)

Randolph, Geoffrey
See Ellis, Edward S[ylvester]

Randolph, Gordon [joint pseudonym with Sylvia Von Block]
See Von Block, Bela

Randolph, Gordon [joint pseudonym with Bela Von Block]
See Von Block, Sylvia

Randolph, J. Thornton
See Peterson, Charles Jacob

Randolph, Vance 1892- [CA]
American author, editor, folklorist
* Booker, Anton S.

Rands, William Brighty 1823-1882
[DLE1, NPS, SAT]
British author
* [The] Laureate of the Nursery
* Talker, T.
(See also base volume)

Ranger, Roger
See Freeman, James Midwinter

Rannaill, Clan
See Grannell, Robert J.

Ransom, John Crowe 1888- [CR]
American poet, critic, editor
* Ransom, Pappy

Ransom, Pappy
See Ransom, John Crowe

Rao, Sridhar 1916- [EOP]
Leader of Indian religious sect
* Chidananda, Swami

Raphael
See Smith, Robert Cross

Raphael, [Sister] Anna
See Fitzgerald, Anna A.

Raphael, Edwin
See Wakeley, Mr.

Raphael, Sylvia 1938- [LFW]
Israeli intelligence agent
* Roxbourgh, Patricia

Raphael II
See Palmer, John

Raphael III
See Medhurst, Mr.

Raphael IV
See Wakeley, Mr.

Raphael V
See Sparkes, Mr.

Raphael VI
See Cross, Robert C.

Rapler, Rob
See Alexander, O. C.

Rapmund, Joseph 1862- ? [PI]
Irish poet
* Observer

Rapp, Goldie
See Rapp, Robert

Rapp, Manny
See Rapp, Manuel

Rapp, Manuel 20th c. [EF]
American football player
* Rapp, Manny

Rapp, Robert 20th c. [EF]
American football player
* Rapp, Goldie

[The] Rapt Sage
See Aristocles

Rasiel de Selva, Hercule
See Quesnel, Pierre

Raspe, Rudolph E[rich] 1737-1794
[WGT]
German author
* Munchausen, Baron
* Sarratt, H. J.

Rat
See Tourbillon, Robert Arthur

Ratcliffe, James P.
See Mencken, Henry Louis

Rathborne, St. George 1854-1938
[DNA]
American author
* Allen, Hugh
* Keene, Lieut.
* Old Broadbrim
* [A] Private Detective
* Young Broadbrim
(See also base volume)

Rattazzi, [Princess] Marie Studolmine Bonaparte 1833- ? [PI]
Irish-born poet, playwright, author
* Bernard, Camille
* D'Albeno, Vicomte
* De Kelmar, Louis
* Stock, Baron

Rattlesnake Dick
See Barter, Richard

Rattlesnake Pete Lanihan
See Lanihan, Peter

Raven, Paul
See Gadd, Paul

Raven, Ralph
See Payson, George

Rawson, Albert Leighton
1829-1902 [DNA]
American author and artist
* Kadmus, G.

Ray, Agnes
See Benjamin, Elizabeth Dundas
[Bedell]

Ray, Dixy Lee 1914- [CR]
American politician and zoologist
* Oo'ma [Great Lady]

Raymond, George Lansing
1839-1929 [DNA]
American author and educator
* Warren, Walter

Raymond, Grace
See Stillman, Annie Raymond

Raymond, Nate 20th c. [DI]
American gambler
* Raymond, Nigger Nate

Raymond, Nigger Nate
See Raymond, Nate

Rayner, John Desmond
See Rahmer, Hans Sigismund

Rayner, Olive Pratt
See Allen, [Charles] Grant
[Blairfindie]

Read, William 1795?-1866 [PI]
Irish poet
* Eustace

[The] Reading Baby Farmer
See Dyer, Amelia Elizabeth

Reagan, Anne Frances Davis 1923-
[BP]
Wife of American president, Ronald Reagan
* Rainbow [Secret Service code name]
* Reagan, Nancy

Reagan, Nancy
See Reagan, Anne Frances Davis

Real, Anthony
See Michel, F. Fernand

[A] Reasoning Engine
See Clarke, Samuel

Rebak, H.
See Baker, Henry

[A] Rebel War Clerk
See Jones, John Beauchamp

Rebujina [Rumpus]
See Jimenez, Francisco

[The] Rector
See Arundell, Francis Vyvyan Jago

[The] Rector
See Egar, John H.

[The] Red
See Clare, Gilbert de

[The] Red
See Eric

Red Buck Weightman
See Weightman, George

[The] Red Douglas
See Douglas, George

Red Ellen Wilkinson
See Wilkinson, Ellen

[The] Red Hand
See Hughes, Terence McMahon

Red Herrings
See Seymour-Conway, Francis Charles

[The] Red Pastor
See Barth, Karl

[The] Red Spider
See Staniak, Lucian

[The] Red Witch
See Koch, Ilse

Redbarn Wash
See Shaw, George Bernard

Reddale, Frederic
See Reddall, Henry Frederick

Reddall, Henry Frederick
1856-1921 [DNA]
American journalist and musician
* Bantock, Miles
* Reddale, Frederic

Redivivus, Quevedo, Jr.
See Wright, Robert William

Redmon, Anne
See Nightingale, Anne Redmon

Redmond, Gus
See Redmond, Gustave

Redmond, Gustave 20th c. [EF]
American football player
* Redmond, Gus

Redondo y Dominguez, Jose
1818-1853 [GS]
Spanish bullfighter
* [El] Chiclanero [The Man from Chiclana]

Redwing, Morris
See Merrill, James Milford

Redwood, Alec
See Milkomane, George Alexis Milkomanovich

Reed, Alison Touster 1952- [CA]
American poet
* Touster, Alison

Reed, Allan?
See Rohr, Wolf Detlef

Reed, Andrew 1787-1862 [NPS]
Clergyman, philanthropist, hymnwriter
* Douglas

Reed, B. Mitchel 20th c. [CMA]
American disc jockey
* B. M. R.
* [The] Boy on the Psychiatrist's Couch
* [The] Fastest Tongue in the West
* [The] Mad Monk in the Monastery

Reed, Myrtle 1874-1911
[DNA, ICB]
American author and poet
* Green, Olive

Reed, Robert
See Rietz, John

Reedman, Dinny
See Reedman, J. C.

Reedman, J. C. [EC]
Australian cricketer
* Reedman, Dinny

Rees, Melvin ?-1961 [DI]
American murderer
* [The] Sex Beast

Reeve, Clara 1729-1807 [WGT]
British author
* C. R.

Reeves, Amber
See Blanco White, Amber

Reeves, Lawrence F. 1926- [CA]
American author
* Lyfick, Warren
* Seever, R.

[A] Reformed Stock Gambler
See Armstrong, William

[A] Reformer
See Nolan, Frederick

[The] Refrigerator
See Perry, William

[El] Regatero [The Haggler]
See Lopez, Angel

Reginald
See Burgess, Michael Roy

Rego, Leonora 20th c. [EOP]
Leader of religious cult
* Lalitananda, Swami

Reichow, Garet 20th c. [EF]
American football player
* Reichow, Gerry

Reichow, Gerry
See Reichow, Garet

Reid, Christian
See Tiernan, Frances Christine [Fisher]

Reid, Jock
See Reid, John

Reid, John 18th c. [BBH]
Founder of American golf club
* [The] Father of American Golf
* Reid, Jock

Reid, [Thomas] Mayne 1818-1883
[DLE1, SAT, SFL]
American author and poet
* Beach, Charles
* [The] Poor Scholar

Reilly, Bernard James 1865-1930
[DNA]
Author and clergyman
* Yorke, Anthony

Reilly, Butt
See Reilly, Hugh

Reilly, Charles 20th c. [EF]
American football player
* Reilly, Mike

Reilly, Hugh 19th c. [RBE]
Boxer
* Reilly, Butt

Reilly, Mike
See Reilly, Charles

Reilly, Thomas Devin 1824-1854
[PI]
Irish poet
* R.
* T. R.

Reinhold, Ernest
See Britten, Emma Hardinge

Reinser III
See Resnier, Andre Guillaume

Rekai, Kati 1921- [CA]
Hungarian-born author
* Kati

[A] Religious Politician
See Adams, Samuel

Relis, Harry
See Endore, [Samuel] Guy

[El] Relojero [The Watch-Maker]
See Perez, Manuel

[The] Rembrandt or Raphael of the Profession
See Duvall, Claude

Remy, W. A.
See Mayer, Wilhelm

Rena, Sally
See Rena, Sarah Mary

Rena, Sarah Mary 1941- [CA]
Scottish-born author
* Rena, Sally

Renich, Helen T. 1916- [MA]
Chinese-born author
* Renich, Jill

Renich, Jill
See Renich, Helen T.

Rennie, John 1761-1821 [NPS]
Engineer and inventor
* Archimedes

Reno, Frank ?-1868 [BLB]
American outlaw
* Reno, Trick

Reno, Trick
See Reno, Frank

Reno, Wilk
See Reno, William

Reno, William ?-1868 [BLB]
American outlaw
* Reno, Wilk

[A] Reporter
See O'Leary, Joseph

Republican
See Pinckney, Charles

[A] Resident
See Adamson, William Agar

[A] Resident
See Chittenden, Newton H.

[A] Resident Beyond the Frontier
See Snelling, William Joseph

[A] Resident M. A.
See Weatherly, Frederick Edward

Resnier, Andre Guillaume
1729-1811 [WGT]
Author
* Reinser III

[The] Respectable Hottentot
See Johnson, Samuel

Restless, Tim
See Tyers, Thomas

[A] Retired Barrister
See Ambler, Charles

[A] Retired Captain, R.N.
See Gardner, George H.

Retlaw
See Waldie, Walter S.

Retort, Jack
See Hunt, Isaac

Reuben
See Hawker, Robert Stephen

Reuss, Theodor ?-1924 [EOP]
German occultist
* Merlin, [Brother]
* Theodore, Charles

Revilo
See Christianson, Oliver

[A] Revolutionary Soldier
See Martin, James Sullivan

Rexroth, Kenneth 1905-1982
American painter, poet, philosopher
* [The] Last of the Great Bohemians

Rey, Hans Augusto
See Reyersbach, Hans Augusto

Reyersbach, Hans Augusto
1898-1977 [CA]
German-born illustrator and author
* Rey, Hans Augusto
* Uncle Gus

Reynaud, Jacques
See Cisternes de Coutiras, Gabrielle Anne de

Reynolds, G. W. M.
See Reynolds, George William Macarthur

Reynolds, George William Macarthur
1814-1879   [HFF]
British author
* Reynolds, G. W. M.
(See also base volume)

Reynolds, Gertrude M. [Robins] 20th
c.   [NPS]
Author
* Robins, G. M.

Reynolds, John Hamilton 19th c.
[PI]
British poet
* Corcoran, Peter

Reynolds, [Sir] Joshua 1723-1792
[NPS]
British painter
* [The] Bachelor Painter
(See also base volume)

Reynolds, Margaret Gertrude 19th
c.   [PI]
Irish poet
* Sepperle

Reynolds, Mary Frances 1932-
[CR]
American actress, singer, dancer
* [The] Iron Butterfly
(See also base volume)

Reynolds, [Marjorie] Moira Davison
1915-   [CA]
American author
* Moore, Marna

Reywas, Mot
See   Spivey, Thomas Sawyer

Rheal, Sebastien
See   Gayet, Sebastien

Rheinhardt, Rudolph H.
See   Hempel, George

Rhoades, Cornelia Harsen
1863-1940   [DNA]
American author
* Rhoades, Nina

Rhoades, Nina
See   Rhoades, Cornelia Harsen

Rhodes, Cecil 1853-1902   [NPS]
*British administrator and financier
in South Africa*
* [A] Colossus

Rhodes, Helen   [NPS]
Composer and singer
* D'Hardelot, Guy

Rhone, Cherokee 20th c.
American basketball player
* Rhone, Chief

Rhone, Chief
See   Rhone, Cherokee

R'hoone, Lord
See   Balzac, Honore de

[The] Rhumba King
See   Cugat, Xavier

[A] Rhymer
See   Bell, Thomas

Ribbans, Frederick Bolingbroke 19th
c.   [HFN]
Author
* [A] Layman

Ricardo
See   McHale, Richard

Ricardo, Benito Concepcion 1954-
[FR]
*Paraguayan-born American football
player*
* Ricardo, Benny

Ricardo, Benny
See   Ricardo, Benito Concepcion

Rice, Daddy
See   Rice, Thomas Dartmouth

Rice, Mrs. Cale Young
Author
* Hegan, Alice Caldwell

Rice, Thomas Dartmouth
1808-1860   [DAM]
*American songwriter and minstrel-
show pioneer*
* Rice, Daddy
(See also base volume)

Rich, Gerry
See   Brandon, Johnny

[The] Rich Man's Norman Rockwell
See   Wyeth, Andrew

Richard
See   Audin, J. M. V.

Richard, Francois   [WGT]
French author
* Richard-Bessiere, F. [joint
pseudonym with Richard
Bessiere]

Richard, Marthe 1890?-1982
*French politician and former
intelligence agent*
* Alouette [Skylark]

Richard-Bessiere, F. [joint
pseudonym with Francois Richard]
See   Bessiere, Richard

Richard-Bessiere, F. [joint
pseudonym with Richard Bessiere]
See   Richard, Francois

Richard I 1157-1199   [NPS]
King of England
* [The] British Lion
(See also base volume)

Richards, Anna M[atlock], Jr. 19th
c.   [SFL]
Author
* A. M. R.

Richards, Elvin 20th c.   [EF]
American football player
* Richards, Kink

Richards, Kay
See   Baker, Susan [Catherine]

Richards, Kink
See   Richards, Elvin

**Richardson, Ethel Florence
[Lindesay]** 1870-1946   [CA]
Australian author
* Richardson, Henrietta
* Richardson, Henry Handel

Richardson, George Tilton   ?-1938
[DNA]
American journalist
* Tilton, Dwight

Richardson, Henrietta
See   Richardson, Ethel Florence
[Lindesay]

Richardson, Henry Handel
See   Richardson, Ethel Florence
[Lindesay]

Richardson, Jabez
See   Day, Benjamin Henry

Richardson, Rafe
See   Richardson, Ralph

Richardson, Ralph 1902-   [CR]
British actor
* Richardson, Rafe

Richbourg, John 20th c.   [CMA]
American disc jockey
* John R

Richelieu, Peter
See   Robinson, P. W.

**Richmond, Euphemia Johnson
[Guernsey]** 1825- ?   [DNA]
American author
* Johnson, Effie

Richmond, Legh 19th c.   [HFN]
Author and clergyman
* [A] Clergyman of the Church of
England

Richter, Hugh 20th c.   [EF]
American football player
* Richter, Pat

Richter, Pat
See   Richter, Hugh

Rickman, Thomas 1761-1834
[NPS]
Bookseller and author
* Clio

Ridgeway
See   Taylor, John Francis

Ridgeway, Algernon
See   Wood, Anna Cogswell

Ridley, James 1736-1765   [HFN]
British author
* Horam, the Son of Asmar
(See also base volume)

Rietz, John 1932-
American actor
* Reed, Robert

Rieux, A. de
See   Carrat de Vaux, Alexandre

Rigby
See   Arrowsmith, Edmund

Rigby, Richard 1722-1788   [NPS]
British politician
* Bloomsbury Dick

Riggs, Mrs. George C.
Author
* Wiggin, Kate Douglas

Rigmarole, Crayon
See   Sims, Alexander Dromgoole

Rigores [Precise One]
See   Miranda, Roque

Riley, Butch
See   Riley, Thomas

Riley, Thomas 20th c.   [EF]
American football player
* Riley, Butch

Ring, Elizabeth 1912-   [CA]
British author
* Scott, Nerissa

Ringgold, Johnny 19th c.   [BLB]
American gunfighter
* Ringo, Johnny

[The] Ringmaster
See   Mencken, Henry Louis

Ringo, Johnny
See   Ringgold, Johnny

Ringwood, Ralph
See   Hynes, Alfred D.

Rinpoche [Precious Master]
See   Tarthang Tulku

Rios Montt, Ayatollah
See   Rios Montt, Jose Efrain

Rios Montt, Jose Efrain 1927?-
Guatemalan president
* Rios Montt, Ayatollah

Rip
See   Hill, Rowland

Ripa, Alberto da   ?-1551   [BBD]
Italian musician
* Mantovano, Alberto

Ripley, George 1802-1880   [IP]
American scholar and journalist
* G. R.

Ripley, Jack
See   Wainwright, John

Ripley, Mrs. John   [NPS]
Author
* Paull, M. A.

Riq
See   Atwater, Frederick Mund

Ritchie, Anna Cora [Ogden Mowatt]
1819-1870   [DLE1, DNA, IP]
American actress and author
* [An] Actress
* Berkley, [Mrs.] Helen
* Browning, Henry C.
* Isabel
* [A] Lady

Ritchie, James Ewing 19th c.   [IP]
American journalist
* Crayon, Christopher

Ritson, Joseph 1752-1803   [IP]
British antiquary and critic
* J. R.
(See also base volume)

Ritter, Dr.
See   Schiller, Johann Christoph
Friedrich von

Ritter, Theodore
See   Bennet, Theodore

[The] Rival of Homer
See   Milton, John

[A] Rival to the God of Harmonie
See   Jonson, Ben[jamin]

Rivetus, Andreas, Junior
See   Marvell, Andrew

Riviera, Jake
See   Jakeman, Andrew

Rivington, William   [IP]
British author
* [A] Lay Member of the
Committee
(See also base volume)

Roane, Spencer 1762-1802   [BDSA]
American author and jurist
* Sidney, Algernon

Robat [Cult name]
See   Buckland, Raymond

Robb, Alvis 20th c.   [EF]
American football player
* Robb, Joe

Robb, Joe
See Robb, Alvis

Robb, John S. 19th c. [IP]
American author and editor
* [A] Tyke
(See also base volume)

Robbin, [Jodi] Luna 1936- [CA]
American author and illustrator
* Pallidini, Jodi

Robbins, Alfred Farthing 1856- ?
[IP]
British author
* Clifton, Tom
* Nemesis
(See also base volume)

Roberson, Bo
See Roberson, Irvin

Roberson, Irvin 20th c. [EF]
American football player
* Roberson, Bo

[The] Robert Frost of the Paintbrush
See Wyeth, Andrew

Robert, Karl
See Hartmann, Eduard von

Robert, Karl
See Meusnier, Georges

Robert, Lord Bishop of Sarum
See Drummond, Robert Hay

Robert of Lincoln
See Grossetete, Robert

Robert II 1316-1390 [NPS]
King of Scotland
* Blear-Eye
(See also base volume)

Roberthin, Robert 1600-1648 [IP]
British author
* Berintho

Roberts
See Harpe, Wiley

Roberts, Andrew L. ?-1878
[BLB, DI, EWG]
American gunfighter
* Roberts, Buckshot

Roberts, Buckshot
See Roberts, Andrew L.

Roberts, Choo Choo
See Roberts, Eugene

Roberts, Daniel ?-1811 [IP]
British author
* Philotesis

Roberts, Eugene 20th c. [EF]
American football player
* Roberts, Choo Choo

Roberts, Gene 20th c.
American editor
* [The] Frog

Roberts, John 18th c. [IP]
British author
* [A] Stroling Player
(See also base volume)

Roberts, K.
See Lake, Kenneth R[obert]

Roberts, Lawrence
See Fish, Robert L.

Roberts, Lester A. [IP]
American author
* [An] Artist

Roberts, Mary 1789-1864 [IP]
British author
* De Gleva, Mary

Roberts, Philip Ilott 1872-1938
[DNA]
Author and clergyman
* Mann, A. Chester

Roberts, S. [IP]
British author
* [A] Llanbrynmair Farmer

Robertson, Alexander [IP]
Scottish author
* Alister, R.

Robertson, Ben F. 1854-1884
[EWG]
*American gunfighter and bank
robber*
* Burton, Ben F.
* Wheeler, Ben

Robertson, H. 19th c. [IP]
Author
* [A] Scotch Episcopalian

Robertson, Henry D. 19th c. [IP]
Author
* [A] Gentleman in the Service of
the East India Company

Robertson, Ignatius Loyola
See Knapp, Samuel Lorenzo

Robertson, J.
See Frazer, John de Jean

Robertson, John
See Seeley, John Robert

Robertson, John 19th c. [IP]
Scottish clergyman and author
* Topping, Godfrey

Robertson, Joseph 1811-1866 [IP]
Scottish antiquary
* Brown, James

Robertson, Patrick 1794-1855 [IP]
Scottish poet and jurist
* P. R.

Robertson, Sarah Franklin [Davis]
1845-1889 [DNA]
Author
* Carter, Ruth

Robertson, William 1721-1793 [IP]
Scottish clergyman
* [A] Presbyter of the Church of
England

Robie, Anne A.
See Rolfe, Maro Orlando

Robin
See Lyttle, Wesley Guard

Robins, G. M.
See Reynolds, Gertrude M.
[Robins]

Robins, George [IP]
British author
* [An] Auctioneer

Robins, James ?-1836 [IP]
British publisher and bookseller
* Scott, Robert

Robins, Rollo
See Ellis, Edward S[ylvester]

Robinson, Agnes Mary F.
See Duclaux, Agnes Mary Frances
[Robinson]

Robinson, Alfred 1806-1895 [IP]
American author
* [An] American

Robinson, Clara I. N. 19th c. [IP]
British author
* Glubbins, Mrs.

Robinson, Henrietta 1816-1905
[LFW]
American murderer
* [The] Veiled Murderess

Robinson, Jack
See Michie, Archibald

Robinson, Jack, Jr.
See Blair, David

Robinson, Mary 19th c. [NPS]
*Wife of John Hatfield, who was
executed for forgery*
* Mary of Buttermere
(See also base volume)

Robinson, Mary Darby 1758-1800
[WGT]
British actress, author, poet
* Darby, Mary
* [A] Friend to Humanity
* Laura Maria
(See also base volume)

Robinson, P. W. 1893- [CA]
British-born author
* Richelieu, Peter

Robinson, Ralph
See George III

Roc Noir
See McDonald, Peter

Roche, Frances Maria 1817?- ?
[PI]
Irish poet
* De Rupe

Roche, Matthew
See O'Connell, John

Rochefort, Harold
See Fenelon, Timothy Brendan

Rock, Magdalen
See Beck, Ellen

Rockingham, [Sir] Charles
See Rohan-Chabot, Philippe
Ferdinand Auguste de [Count de
Jarnac]

Rockstro, William Smyth
See Rackstraw, William Smyth

Rockwell, Norman Percival 1894-
[CR]
American painter
* [The] Lawrence Welk of
American Painting

Roddy, John Gerald 1850?- ?
[PI]
Irish poet
* Clan-na-Rory
* Jo

Roddy, William [PI]
Irish poet
* Derry Boy
* W.

Rodriguez, Joaquin 1729-1800
[GS]
Spanish bullfighter
* Costillares [Big Ribs]

Rodriguez Davie, Jose 1867-1899
[GS]
Spanish bullfighter
* Pepete [Big Joe]

Rodriguez y Rodriguez, Jose
1824-1862 [GS]
Spanish bullfighter
* Pepete [Big Joe]

Roe, Owen
See Davis, Eugene

Roe, Richard
See Ponsonby, Frederick George
Brabazon

Roebuck, John Arthur 1801-1879
[NPS]
British politician
* I am Tear 'Em
(See also base volume)

Roeser, Donald 20th c. [CMA]
Musician
* Dharma, Buck

Roessler, Franz Anton 1746-1792
[BBD]
German composer
* Rosetti, Francesco Antonio

Roethke, Theodore 1908-1963
[MA]
American educator and poet
* Rothberg, Winterset

Roffman, Sara
See Hershman, Morris

Rogers, Dale Evans
See Smith, Frances Octavia

Rogers, Henry 1806-1877 [NPS]
Author
* F. B.
(See also base volume)

Rogers, William
See Hawkins, Nehemiah

**Rohan-Chabot, Philippe Ferdinand
Auguste de [Count de Jarnac]** 19th
c. [HFN]
Author
* Rockingham, [Sir] Charles

Rohr, Wolf Detlef [WGT]
German author
* Caine, Geff?
* Coover, Wayne?
* Reed, Allan?

Rohrlich, Ruby 20th c. [CA]
*Canadian-born anthropologist and
author*
* Leavitt, Ruby R.
* Rohrlich-Leavitt, Ruby

Rohrlich-Leavitt, Ruby
See Rohrlich, Ruby

Roker, A. B.
See Barton, Samuel

Rolfe, Maro Orlando 1852-1925
*American author, journalist,
historian*
* [A] Civil War Captain
* Eflor, Oram
* McHenry, [Col.] Oram R.
* [The] Novelist Detective
* [The] Old Detective
* O'Rolfe, M., the Irish Novelist
* Robie, Anne A.
* Rolfe, Sergeant?
* Rolker, A. W.?
* [The] Young Detective

Rolfe, Sergeant?
See Rolfe, Maro Orlando

Rolker, A. W.?
See Rolfe, Maro Orlando

Rolleston, Thomas William Hazen
1857- ? [PI]
Irish poet
* Kendal?

Rollins, Montgomery 1867-1918
[DNA]
American author and banker
* Hay, Timothy

[Le] Romain
See Hotteterre, Jacques

[Le] Romain
See Picart, Etienne

Romaine, John
See O'Reilly, [Sister] Amadeus

[A] Roman Catholic
See Ivers, Hardinge Furenzo

[The] Roman Thucydides
See Sallust, Caius Crispus

Rombro, Jacob 1858-1922 [DNA]
*Russian-born author and labor
leader*
* Krantz, Philip

Romeo
See Heffernan, Michael J.

Romeo
See Moore, John

Romero, Gerry
See Neyland, James [Elwyn]

Romilly, [Sir] Samuel 1757-1818
[NPS]
British barrister and law reformer
* [The] Law's Expounder
* [The] State's Corrector

Romp, Miss
See Bland, Dorothea

Rona Rat
See Burstein, Rona

Ronald, Mary
See Arnold, Augusta [Foote]

Ronayne, Dominick 1770?-1835
[PI]
Irish poet and barrister
* Figaro in Dublin

Ronsard, Pierre de 1524-1585
[NPS]
French poet
* [The] Apollo of the Fountain of
Muses
* [The] First Lyrist of France
(See also base volume)

Rooney, Barney
See Garvie, William

Rooney, Cobbs
See Rooney, Harry

Rooney, Harry 20th c. [EF]
American football player
* Rooney, Cobbs

Rooney, M. W. 19th c. [HFN]
Irish author and bookseller
* M. W. R.

Rooney, William 1873-1901 [PI]
Irish poet
* Ballinascorney

Rooney, William (Continued)
* Baltrasna
* Feltrim
* Fiachra, Hi
* Killester
* Knocksedan
* Laire, Criad
* Martin, Shel
* Muinntire, Fear na
* Ruadh, Sliabh
* Smoil, Glenn na

Roos, William 1911- [TCCM]
American author
* Rand, William
(See also base volume)

Roosevelt, Blanche
See Maccheta, Blanche Roosevelt
[Tucker]

Rosalind
See Daniel, Rosa

Rosalind
See Davis, Rosalind

Roscoe, William 1753-1831 [NPS]
Author and politician
* [The] Gillyflower of Liverpool

Rosdahl, Harrison 20th c. [EF]
American football player
* Rosdahl, Hatch

Rosdahl, Hatch
See Rosdahl, Harrison

Rose
See Kirwan, Rose

Rose, A. N. Mount
See Japp, Alexander Hay

Rose, Edward Hampden ?-1810
[PI]
Irish poet
* [A] Foremast Man

Rose, Marcia [joint pseudonym with
Rose Novak]
See Kamien, Marcia

Rose, Marcia [joint pseudonym with
Marcia Kamien]
See Novak, Rose

Rose, Martha Emily [Parmelee]
1834-1923 [DNA]
American author
* Lee, Charles C.

Rosedale, Valerie
See Harron, Don[ald]

Roselinda
See White, Rose C. [King]

Rosema, Rocky
See Rosema, Roger

Rosema, Roger 20th c. [EF]
American football player
* Rosema, Rocky

Rosemary
See Watson, Margaret

Rosen, Lew
See Rosenthal, Lewis

Rosen, Max
See Rosenzweig, Maxie

Rosenberg, John Paul [Jack] 1935-
[EOP]
*American educator and developer of
"est" therapy*
* Frost, Jack
(See also base volume)

Rosenfield, Judith 1943- [CA]
American author
* Arcana, Judith

Rosenow, August 20th c. [EF]
American football player
* Rosenow, Gus

Rosenow, Gus
See Rosenow, August

Rosenthal, Alan 1936- [CA]
*British-born author, producer,
director*
* Talkin, Gil

Rosenthal, Lewis 1856-1909
[DNA]
American journalist
* Rosen, Lew

Rosenzweig, Maxie 20th c. [PAC]
American musician
* Rosen, Max

Roset, Hipponax
See Paxton, Joseph Rupert

Rosetti, Francesco Antonio
See Roessler, Franz Anton

Rosicrucius
See Dibdin, Thomas Frognall

Rosmond, Babette 1921- [CA]
American author
* Arroway, Francis M.
* Campion, Rosamond

Ross, Albert
See Goldstein, Arthur D[avid]

Ross, Carlton
See Brooks, Edwy Searles

Ross, Charles Henry 1836-1897
British author and artist
* Butt, Boswell, Esq.
(See also base volume)

Ross, Diana
See Denney, Diana

Ross, Dunbar 1800?-1865 [DNA]
Irish-born author and politician
* Zeno

Ross, J. H.
See Lawrence, Thomas Edward

Rossetti, Dante Gabriel 1828-1882
[NPS]
British painter and poet
* [The] Poet Painter

Rossi, Jean Baptiste 1931- [TCCM]
French author
* Japrisot, Sebastien

Rossignol, Felix Ludger 1839-1903
[BBD]
French composer
* Joncieres, Victorin de

Rothberg, Winterset
See Roethke, Theodore

Rothenfels, Emmy von
See Ingersleben, Emilie von

Roubillac, Louis Francois
1695-1762 [NPS]
French sculptor
* [The] Little Sculptor

[Le] Rougeaud
See Ney, Michel [Duc
d'Elchingen]

Rousseau, Jean-Jacques 1712-1778
[NPS]
Swiss-French philosopher
* Jean Jacques
(See also base volume)

Roux, Paul Pierre 1861-1940 [CD]
French poet and playwright
* [Le] Magnifique
(See also base volume)

Rover
See Gibson, Alfred

[A] Roving Printer
See Jones, John Beauchamp

Row, T.
See Pegge, Samuel

Rowdy Joe Lowe
See Lowe, Joseph

Rowdy Kate Rowe
See Rowe, Kathryn

Rowe, Bolton
See Scott, Clement William

Rowe, Kathryn 19th c. [BLB]
American madam
* Rowe, Rowdy Kate

Rowe, Nicholas 1674-1718 [NPS]
British and poet playwright
* Bayes the Younger

Rowe, Richard 1828-1879 [DLE1]
British-born author
* Possum, Peter

Rowe, Rowdy Kate
See Rowe, Kathryn

Rowel, M.
See Thisted, V[aldemar] Adolph

Rowell, A. S. 19th c. [BDSA]
American author
* Old Coins

Rowen, Lady [Cult name]
See Buckland, Rosemary

Roxbourgh, Patricia
See Raphael, Sylvia

Roy, Hippolyte 1763-1829 [WFA]
French fashion designer
* Leroy

Roy, John
See Durand, [Sir] H. Mortimer

Roy, William
See Plowright, William George
Holroyd

[The] Royal Saint
See Henry VI

[The] Royal Wanderer
See Charles II

Royalty's Favorite Entertainer
See Kaminsky [or Kominski?],
David Daniel

Royston, William Haylett 19th c.
[HFN]
Author
* W. H. R.

Rozelle, Alvin Ray 1926- [CR]
American football commissioner
* Doughsmell, Pete
* Perfect Pete
* Peter the Great
* St. Peter
(See also base volume)

Rozema, David Scott [Dave] 1956-
American baseball player
* Rozema, Rosie
(See also base volume)

Rozema, Rosie
See Rozema, David Scott [Dave]

Rozenberga, Elza 1865-1943 [CD]
Latvian poet and playwright
* Aspazija

Ruadh
See McAleese, Daniel

Ruadh, Sliabh
See Rooney, William

Rubek, Sennoia
See Burke, John

[The] Rubens of English Poetry
See Spenser, Edmund

Ruby
See Kavanagh, Rose

Ruby Nose
See Cromwell, Oliver

Ruck, Amy Roberta
See Oliver, Amy Roberta [Ruck]

Rudd, Mrs. 18th c. [DI]
British forger
* [The] Female Forger

Rudd, Steele
See Davis, Arthur Hoey

Ruding, Mrs. Walter [NPS]
Author
* Johnstone, Edith

Rue, Jon Thoresen 1827-1876
[BBH]
Norwegian-born skier
* Thompson, John Albert
* Thompson, Snowshoe

Ruffian, M.
See Hasek, Jaroslav [Matej Frantisek]

[The] Rugeley Poisoner
See Palmer, William

Ruggiero, Benjamin 20th c.
American underworld figure
* Ruggiero, Lefty

Ruggiero, Lefty
See Ruggiero, Benjamin

Ruiz, Antonio 1792-1860 [GS]
Spanish bullfighter
* [El] Sombrerero [The Hatter]

Rumball, Charles 19th c.
[SFL, WGT]
Author
* Delorme, Charles

Rundquist, Harry 20th c. [EF]
American football player
* Rundquist, Porky

Rundquist, Porky
See Rundquist, Harry

Runkle, Bertha
See Bash, Mrs. Louis H.

Rupert 1619-1682 [NPS]
Duke of Bavaria and British royalist general
* [The] Brilliant
(See also base volume)

[A] Rupublican
See Russell, Jonathan

[A] Rural Dean
See Tatham, Arthur

Rushton, Wattie
See Atwood, A. Watson

Rusk, Howard 1901- [CR]
American physician
* Live Again, Dr.

Ruskin, John 1819-1900 [DEA]
British author and art critic
* J. R.
(See also base volume)

Russell, Black
See Russell, John

Russell, Donald
See Nuss, Ralph

Russell, Fay
See Russell, Lafayette

Russell, Francis Chambers 1953-
[FR]
American football player
* Chambers, Rusty

Russell, George William Erskine
1853-1919 [NPS]
British author and politician
* Onlooker
(See also base volume)

Russell, [Sir] Henry 19th c. [NPS]
Author
* Civis

Russell, Jerry Sneak
See Russell, Samuel

Russell, John 1740-1817 [NPS]
Scottish clergyman
* Russell, Black

Russell, John 1795-1883 [NPS]
Clergyman
* [The] Sporting Parson

Russell, [Lord] John Earl
1792-1878 [NPS]
British statesman and author
* Skillett, Joseph
(See also base volume)

Russell, Jonathan 1771-1832 [IP]
American merchant, statesman, author
* [A] Rupublican

Russell, Ken 1927- [CR]
British film maker
* [The] British Orson Welles

Russell, Lafayette 20th c. [EF]
American football player
* Russell, Fay
* Russell, Reb

Russell, Lucy May
See Coryell, John Russell

Russell, Margaret
See Hervey, Eleonora Louisa

Russell, Matthew 1834- ? [PI]
Irish author, poet, clergyman
* Eulalie
* M. R.
* New, Edward
* W. L.

Russell, Morris Craw 1840-1913
[DNA]
American journalist
* Uncle Dudley

Russell, R. 19th c. [HFN, IP]
British author
* [A] Middle Aged Citizen

Russell, Reb
See Russell, Lafayette

Russell, Richard [IP]
British physician and author
* Maevius

Russell, Samuel 1766-1845 [UH]
Actor
* Russell, Jerry Sneak

Russell, Thomas [IP]
British author and clergyman
* A. S.

Russell, Thomas O'Neill
1828-1908 [PI]
Irish author
* Tierney, Reginald

Russell, W. M. 19th c. [HFN, IP]
British author
* W. M. R.

Russell, William [IP]
British author
* Warneford, Lieut.

Russell, William 19th c. [IP]
British author
* [A] Custom-House Officer
* [A] Detective
* [A] Detective Police Officer
* [An] English Detective
* [A] French Detective
* [A] Law Clerk
* Waters, C.
(See also base volume)

Russell, William Clark 1844-1911
[DLE1]
British author
* Mostyn, Sydney
(See also base volume)

[The] Russian Burns
See Koltzoff, Alexei Vasilievitch

[The] Russian Doctor
See Pedachenko, Alexander

[The] Russian Vampire
See Tarnowska, [Countess] Maria

[The] Russian Walter Scott
See Zagoskin, Mikhail

Russo, Scarface Jock
See Russo, Victor

Russo, Victor 20th c. [DI]
American underworld figure
* Russo, Scarface Jock

Rusticus
See Hickling, George

Rusticus, Gent.
See Furman, Garrit

Rustifucius, Trismegistus
See Moore, Thomas

Rustler, Robin
See Maclean, John

Ruter, P. S. [IP]
American author
* [A] Virginia Physician

Rutlidge, [Sir] John James 18th c.
[IP]
British author
* [An] Observer

Rutter, John 1796-1851 [IP]
British barrister, printer, author
* [A] Constitutional Reformer

Rutty, John 1698-1775 [IP]
Irish physician and author
* Catholicus, Johannes
* [An] Unworthy Member of that Community
* Utopiensis, Bernardus

Ruxton, Buck
See Hakim, Bukhtyar Rustomji Ratanji

Ruy-Blas, Eugene
See Lebeau, Eugene

Ryan, Arthur 1852- ? [PI]
Irish poet and clergyman
* A. R.

Ryan, Carroll
See Ryan, William Thomas

Ryan, J.
See Hanratty, James

Ryan, James 1855- ? [PI]
Irish-born poet
* Golma
* J. R.
* McGaura, Conner
* O'Flynn, Fergus

Ryan, Marah Ellis
Author
* Martin, Ellis

Ryan, Margaret Mary 19th c. [PI]
Irish poet
* Esmonde, Alice
* M. My. R.
* M. R.

Ryan, Michael 1851- ? [PI]
Irish-born poet and clergyman
* Eithne
* M. J. R.

Ryan, P. J. 19th c. [PI]
Irish poet and writer
* Barra, Gougane

Ryan, Sweeney
See Lett, William Pittman

Ryan, Thomas 1849- ? [PI]
Irish author
* Doodle
* [A] Drangan Boy
* T. R.

Ryan, Thomas J. [BBH]
Bowler
* [The] Father of Fivepin Bowling

Ryan, W. S.
See Smyth, William

Ryan, William Thomas 1839- ?
[PI]
Canadian journalist and poet
* Ryan, Carroll
* [A] Wanderer

Ryder, W. J. D. [IP]
British author
* [A] Carthusian
* W. J. D. R.

Rye, Francis [IP]
Canadian scholar
* F. R., of Barrie

Ryland, John 1753-1825 [IP]
British clergyman and author
* J. R., Jun.

Ryland, John Collett 1723-1792
[IP]
British clergyman and author
* [A] Lover of Christ

Rymer, James Malcolm 19th c.
British author
* Bishop, Bertha Thorne
* Conroy, J. D.
* Errym, Malcolm J.
* Merry, Malcolm J.
* Percival, Nelson
* Urban, Septimus R.

S

S.
See Scully, Vincent

S.
See Tyler, Royall

S. A.
See Ayscough, Samuel

S. A. A.
See Allibone, Samuel Austin

S. B. G.
See Goslin, S. B.

S. C. H.
See Hall, Samuel Carter

S. D. A.
See Alexander, Samuel Davies

S. E. Y.
See McCarthy, Denis Florence

S. F. C.
See Campion, John Thomas

S. G.
See Sandys, George

S. H.
See Tidmarsh, James

S. J.
See Tappan, Sarah [Jackson Davis]

S. M.
See Martin, Selina

S. M.
See Smedley, Menella

S. M. A.
See Allen, Stephen Merrill

S. M. D.
See Davis, Sarah Matilda

S. M. S.
See McCarthy, Mary Stanislaus

S. N.
See Nolan, Stephen

S. N. E., jun.
See Nolan, Stephen

S. O.
See Morgan, Sydney

S. P.
See Pegge, Samuel

S. P., Esq.
See Pepys, Samuel

S. R. D.
See Drummond, Spencer Rodney

S. R. W.
See Wills, Samuel Richard

S. S. S.
See Simpson, S. S.

S. T.
See Knight, Charles

S. T.
See Timmins, Samuel

S. T.
See Walpole, Horatio [Fourth Earl of Orford]

S. T. C. D.?
See Ingram, John Kells

S. T. C. D.
See O'Donoghue, John

S. W.
See Watts, S.

S. W.
See Whiting, Sydney

[The] Sabbath Bard
See Grahame, James

Sabin, Elijah Robinson 1776-1818 [IP]
American clergyman and author
* Observator, Charles

Sabin, Louis 1930- [SAT]
American author and editor
* Brandt, Keith

Sabine, Lorenzo 1803-1877 [IP]
American author
* Vindex

Sabretache
See Barrow, Albert Stewart

Sacher-Masoch, Aurora von 19th c. [IP]
German author
* Dunajew, Wanda von

Sacheverell, Henry 1674?-1724 [IP, NPS]
British clergyman
* [The] High Church Trumpet
* Sacheverellio, Don, Knight of the Firebrand
(See also base volume)

Sacheverell, Lucy 17th c. [NPS]
Friend of British poet, Richard Lovelace
* Lucasta

Sacheverellio, Don, Knight of the Firebrand
See Sacheverell, Henry

Sachs, David
See Selznick, David

Sachsen, Amalie Frederike Auguste Herzogin von 1794-1870 [IP]
German playwright
* Heister, Amalie

Sackville, Charles [Sixth Earl of Dorset] 1638-1706 [NPS]
British poet and statesman
* [The] Grace of Courts
* [The] Muses' Pride

Sackville, Charles [Second Duke of Dorset] 1711-1769 [IP]
British author and poet
* C. S.

Sackville-West, Reginald [Seventh Earl of De La Warr] 1817- ? [IP]
British author
* R. W. S. W.

Sackville-West, Victoria Mary 1892-1962 [DBQ]
British author and poet
* Sackville-West, Vita
(See also base volume)

Sackville-West, Vita
See Sackville-West, Victoria Mary

Saco
See Meserve, Arthur Livermore

[Le] Sacre Monstre [The Sacred Monster]
See Buchinsky, Charles

Sadleir, Mary Anne 1820-1903 [PI]
Irish poet
* Cootehill, M.
(See also base volume)

Sadleir, William Digby ?-1858 [PI]
Irish poet and clergyman
* W. D. S.

Sadler, Mark
See Lynds, Dennis

[The] Sage
See Buchanan, George

Sage, Bernard Janin 1821-1902 [DNA]
American author and attorney
* Centz, P. C.

[The] Sagest of Usurpers
See Cromwell, Oliver

[A] Sailor
See Falconer, William

[A] Sailor
See Larwood, Joshua

[A] Sailor
See Nordhoff, Charles

[A] Sailor
See Pemberton, Charles Reece

[A] Sailor Boy
See Nordhoff, Charles

[The] Sailor's Friend
See Weston, Agnes

St. Aime, Georges
See Pelletier, Alexis

Saint Aubin, Horace de
See Balzac, Honore de

St. Aubyn, Alan
See Marshall, Frances

St. Clair, William
See Ford, William

St. E. A. of M. and S.
See Crowley, Edward Alexander

St. George, David [joint pseudonym with David Atlee Phillips]
See Markov, Georgi

St. George, David [joint pseudonym with Georgi Markov]
See Phillips, David Atlee

St. George, George
See Snow, Joseph

St. John, Henry 1678-1751 [DEA]
British statesman and writer
* Raleigh, W.
* Trott, John
(See also base volume)

St. John, Mary ?-1830? [PI]
Irish poet
* Mary

St. John, Nicole
See Johnston, Norma

St. John, Percy Bollingbroke 1821-1889
British author
* Boone, Henry L.
* Hope, [Lady] Esther
(See also base volume)

St. John, Randolph
See Kleiner, Rheinhart

St. L., Vic
See Hopkins, Squire D.

St. Laurent, Julie de 19th c.   [NN]
Mistress of Edward, Duke of Kent
* Edward's French Lady

Saint Leger, Fabien de
See Lebrun, Pauline Guyot

St. Leon, Ernest ?-1891   [EWG]
American law officer
* Diamond Dick

St. Leon, [Count] Reginald de
See Du Bois, Edward

St. Lue, Comte de
See Bonaparte, Louis

Saint Meva
See Harris, Josiah

St. Molaing
See Murphy, James

St. Mox, E. S.
See Ellis, Edward S[ylvester]

[The] Saint of Rationalism
See Mill, John Stuart

Saint Patrice
See Hickey, James Harden

St. Patrick's Steeple
See O'Hara, Kane

[The] St. Paul of Spiritualism
See Doyle, [Sir] Arthur Conan

St. Peter
See Rozelle, Alvin Ray

St. Philip of the Pullman Porters
See Randolph, Asa Philip

St. Pierre, Dorothy
See Curley, Dorothy Nyren

St. Ritch, A. R.
See Stritch, Andrew F. Russell

Saint Sevin, Joseph Barnabe
1727-1803   [BBD]
French musician and composer
* L'Abbe, Joseph Barnabe
   Saint-Sevin

Saint Simon
See De Roovroy, Claude Henri

St. Ursula
See Blair, Mary E.

Sainte Beuve, Charles Auguste
1804-1869   [NPS]
French poet and critic
* Another Proteus
* Delorme, Joseph
* [The] Don Juan of Literature

[El] Salamanquino [The Man from Salamanca]
See Casas, Julian

Salamone, Pat
See Livingston, Patrick

Sallust, Caius Crispus 1st c. BC
[NPS]
Roman historian
* [The] Roman Thucydides

Sally Blind Frascone
See Frascone, Salvatore

Salmon, Mrs.
See Sawyer, Carrie M.

Salome
See Converse, Harriet [Maxwell]

Salomen, Edith 1849- ?   [LFW]
American swindler
* Ava, [Madame] Vera P.
* Landsfeldt, Countess
* Sister Mary
* [The] Swami
* Theo the Swami

Salter, Margaret Lennox
See Donaldson, Margaret

Saltus, Edgar Evertson 1855-1921
[DNA]
American author
* Verelart, Myndart

**[The] Salvator Rosa of British
Novelists**
See Radcliffe, Anne

Salzer, L. E.
See Wilson, Lionel

Salzmann, Siegmund 1869-1945
[SAT]
Hungarian-born author
* Finder, Martin
(See also base volume)

Sam the Maltser
See Adams, Samuel

**Sammartini [or San Martini],
Giovanni Battista** 1701-1775   [BBD]
Italian composer
* [Il] Milanese

**Sammartini [or San Martini],
Giuseppe** 1693?-1770?   [BBD]
Italian-born musician
* [Il] Londinese

Sampson, Deborah 18th c.   [BL]
American soldier
* Shirtliffe, Robert

Sampson, William 1764-1830   [PI]
Irish poet and attorney
* Fortescue

Samuels, E. A.
See Tiffany, E. A.

Samuels, Howard 1919-   [CR]
American politician
* Howie the Horse

San Francisco, Mr.
See Caen, Herb

Sanchez, Pedro 19th c.   [GS]
Spanish bullfighter
* Noteveas

Sanchez Caballero, Antonio
1831-1895   [GS]
Spanish bullfighter
* [El] Tato [The Stammerer]

Sancho
See Cunningham, John William

Sancho Castaneda, Eduardo 1947?-
Salvadoran guerrilla leader
* Cienfuegos, Ferman

Sancho IV 1258-1295   [NPS]
King of Spain
* [The] Great
(See also base volume)

Sand, Jules
See Sandeau, [Leonard Sylvain]
Jules

Sandeau, [Leonard Sylvain] Jules
1811-1883   [NPS]
Author
* Sand, Jules

Sanders, Alex 20th c.   [EOP]
Claimed to possess psychic powers
* King of the Witches

Sanders, Mike 20th c.
American basketball player
* Sanders, Slew

Sanders, Orban 20th c.   [EF]
American football player
* Sanders, Speed

Sanders, Slew
See Sanders, Mike

Sanders, Speed
See Sanders, Orban

Sanderson, Happy
See Sanderson, Winfrey

Sanderson, Wimp
See Sanderson, Winfrey

Sanderson, Winfrey 20th c.
American basketball coach
* Sanderson, Happy
* Sanderson, Wimp

Sandisson, Mr. de
See Bignon, Jean Paul

Sandys, George 1578-1644   [DEA]
British author
* S. G.

Sanghamita, [Sister]
See Canavarro, M. A. de S.

Sans Terre
See John

Santiago, Isidro 1811-1851   [GS]
Spanish bullfighter
* Barragan [Coarse Wool Coat]

Sanz Almenar 1853-1888   [GS]
Spanish bullfighter
* Punderet

Sappho
See Montagu, Mary Wortley

Sappho
See Scuderi, Magdalen [or
Madeleine] de

[The] Sappho of England
See Philips, Katherine

Sara, [Col.] Delle
See Aiken, Albert W.

Sard Erasmus
See Blackburn, Douglas

Sargent, Epes Winthrop
Bahamian-born drama critic
* Chicot
(See also base volume)

Sarpi, Pietro 1552-1623   [NPS]
Italian prelate
* Paul, [Brother]
* Servita
(See also base volume)

Sarratt, H. J.
See Raspe, Rudolph E[rich]

Sarsfield
See McGee, Thomas D'Arcy

Sarti, Giuseppe 1729-1802   [BBD]
Italian composer
* [Il] Domenichino

Sarti, Signor
See Knight, Ashton

Sartre, Jean-Paul 1905- ?   [CR]
French philosopher and author
* [The] Father of Existentialism

Sashun, Sigmund
See Sassoon, Siegfried [Lorraine]

Sassetta
See Di Giovanni, Stefano

Sassoon, Siegfried [Lorraine]
1886-1967   [CA, DLE1]
British poet and author
* Kain, Saul
* Lyre, Pinchbeck
* Sashun, Sigmund

Sather, Julia Coley Duncan 1940-
[CA]
American author
* Duncan, Julia Coley

Satin, Miss
See Mallarme, Stephane

Saucier, Hot Sauce
See Saucier, Kevin Andrew

Saucier, Kevin Andrew 1956-
American baseball player
* Saucier, Hot Sauce

Sauls, Kirby 20th c.   [EF]
American football player
* Sauls, Mac

Sauls, Mac
See Sauls, Kirby

Saumaise, Claude 1588-1658
[NPS]
French scholar
* Alastor
* [The] Great Kill-Cow of
   Christendom
* [The] Great Pan
(See also base volume)

**Saunders, Rufus, The Sage of Rocky
Creek**
See Lloyd, Francis Bartow

Saunter, Samuel
See Dennie, Joseph

Saurin, Jacques 1677-1730   [NPS]
French clergyman
* [The] Bossuet of the Protestant
   Pulpit

Sauvage, Frere
See Wilde, William Charles
Kingsley

Savage, Joan
See Weisman, Joan

Savage, Laura
See Stephens, Francis George

Savage, Marmion Wilmo
1805-1872   [PI]
Irish author and poet
* M. W. S.

Savile
See Sotheran, Henry

**Savile, [Sir] George [Marquis of
Halifax]** 1633-1695   [DEA]
British statesman
* T. W.
* W. C., Sir
(See also base volume)

Savini-Brioni, Gaetano 20th c.
[CR]
Italian fashion designer
* Brioni
* [The] Caesar of Style
* [The] Men's Dior

[The] Savior of His Country
See Clay, Henry

Savoyard
See Newman, Eugene William

Sawkins, Raymond H[arold] 1923-
[CA]
British author
* Bernard, Jay
* Forbes, Colin
* Raine, Richard

Sawyer, Carrie M. 20th c.   [EOP]
Claimed to possess psychic powers
* Salmon, Mrs.

Sawyer, Ruth
See Durand, Mrs. Albert C.

Sawyer, Walter Leon 1862-1915
[DNA]
American journalist and author
* Standish, Winn

Saxe, Burton
See Sikes, [William] Wirt

Saxo-Norman
See Yvelin, Albert [Baron de Beville]

Saxon, John A.
See Bellem, Robert Leslie

Sayers, Tom 1826-1865
[BBH, PPN, RBE]
British boxer
* [The] Little Wonder
* [The] Napoleon of the Prize Ring

Scaeva
See Stuart, Isaac William

Scaevola
See Allen, John

Scanes, Mrs. A. E.
Author
* Goodman, Maude

Scanlan, Michael 1836- ?   [PI]
Irish-born poet
* Blake, Dionysius

Scarface Jock Russo
See Russo, Victor

Scarlatti, Alessandro 1659-1725
[NPS]
Italian composer
* [The] Founder of Modern Opera

Scarlet, Thomas
See Nash [or Nashe?], Thomas

Scarlett, [Sir] James [First Baron Abinger] 1769-1844   [NPS]
British jurist
* Briareus of the King's Bench
(See also base volume)

Scarnato, Patrick Henry 1923-1982
American comedian
* Henry, Pat

Schadow, Gottfried 1764-1850
[WEC]
German sculptor, author, cartoonist
* Gillray, Paris

Schaum, Rounseville W. 20th c.
[CR]
American television executive and producer
* Schaum, Skip

Schaum, Skip
See Schaum, Rounseville W.

Schem, Lida Clara 1875-1923
[DNA]
American author
* Blake, Margaret

Schiller, Johann Christoph Friedrich von 1759-1805   [NPS]
German poet and playwright
* Ritter, Dr.
* Schmidt, Dr.
(See also base volume)

Schirock, Fred Alexander 1925-
[CA]
Canadian-born hockey player, coach, author
* Shero, Fred [Alexander]

Schmidt, Dr.
See Schiller, Johann Christoph Friedrich von

Schmock, Helen H. 1909-   [MA]
American author
* Bell, Steve
* Cloutier, Helen H.

Schnitzler, Arthur 1862-1931   [CA]
Austrian author and playwright
* Anatol

Schoeffel, Florence Blackburn [White] 1860-1900   [DNA]
American author
* Gilman, Wenona

[The] Scholar
See Alfonso X [or Alphonso]

[A] Scholar
See Wesley, Samuel

Scholasticus, Doctor
See Anselm of Laon

Scholze, Johann Sigismund 1705-1750   [BBD]
German composer
* Sperontes

School Boy Baker
See Baker, Jimmy

[A] Schoolmaster
See Alcott, William Alexander

[The] Schoolmaster at Home
See Dugall, George

Schoolmiss Alfred
See Tennyson, Alfred [First Baron Tennyson]

[The] Schoolmistress to France
See Alcuin [or Albinus]

Schrader, August
See Simmel, August

Schroeder, Henry 1774-1853
[NPS]
British topographer and engraver
* Butterworth, William

Schroeder, Irene 1909-1931   [LFW]
American bandit and murderer
* Iron Irene

Schroeder, Sophie [Buerger] 1781-1868   [NPS]
German actress
* [The] German Siddons

Schroedter, Adolf 1805-1875
[WEC]
German cartoonist and painter
* King of the Arabesque

Schubiger, Anselm
See Schubiger, Josef Allis

Schubiger, Josef Allis 1815-1888
[BBD]
Swiss author
* Schubiger, Anselm

Schubin, Ossip
See Kirschner, L.

Schultz, Frederick Walter 1840-1917   [DNA]
American author
* Walter, Frederick

Schulz [or Schulze], Hieronymus 1560-1629   [BBD]
German composer
* Praetorius, Hieronymus

Schupbach, O. T. 20th c.   [EF]
American football player
* Mooney, Tex

Schwabe, William
See Cassidy, William L[awrence Robert]

Schwarz, Jack
See Schwarz, Jacob

Schwarz, Jacob 1924-   [CA]
Dutch author
* Schwarz, Jack

Schweidler, Abraham
See Meinhold, Johann Wilhelm

Schweitzer, Johann-Friedrich 17th c.   [NAD]
Swiss scholar
* Helvetius

Scicolone, Sofia Villani 1934-   [BP]
Italian actress
* Lazarro, Sofia
(See also base volume)

Scioppius, Gaspar 1576-1649
[NPS]
German scholar
* [The] Attila of Authors
(See also base volume)

Scipio
See Tracy, Uriah

Sclater, Philip Lutley 1829- ?   [IP]
British naturalist and journalist
* [A] Naturalist

Sclater, William ?-1626   [IP]
British clergyman and author
* [A] Presbyter of the Church of England

Scofield, Norma Margaret Cartwright 1924-   [CA]
Canadian-born author and playwright
* Cartwright, N.

Scopoli-Biasi, Isabella 1810- ?   [IP]
Italian author
* Mario S.

Scorchvillein
See Henry de Loundres

Scoresby, William 1760-1829   [IP]
British navigator and author
* [A] Voyager

[The] Scorpion
See Lockhart, John Gibson

[A] Scot
See Anderson, James

Scot, A. F.
See Japp, Alexander Hay

Scot, Quod Ar.
See Ramsay, Allan

[A] Scotch Episcopalian
See Robertson, H.

[A] Scotch Minister's Daughter
See Whitehead, Mrs. S. R.

[A] Scotch Physician
See Adams, Francis

Scoto-Britannicus
See Anderson, James

Scott, Alma Olivia   [ICB]
Author
* Travers, Georgia

Scott, Andrew George 1842-1876
[DI]
Irish-born Australian bushranger
* Moonlight, Captain

Scott, Anna [Kay] 1838-1923
[DNA]
Author
* Marston, Mildred

Scott, Bo
See Scott, Robert

Scott, [Sir] Claude Edward 1804-1874   [IP]
British artist and author
* C. E. S., Sir

Scott, Clement William 1841-1904
British drama critic
* Rowe, Bolton
(See also base volume)

Scott, Cyril Kay
See Wellman, Frederick Creighton

Scott, David Dundas 19th c.   [IP]
Scottish author
* [A] Member of the Convention of Royal Burghs of Scotland

Scott, George 19th c.   [IP]
Scottish author
* [A] Friend of Truth

Scott, James 1733-1814   [IP]
British clergyman and author
* Anti Sejanus
* Old Slyboots
* Philanglia

Scott, John 1730-1783   [IP]
British author
* R. S.

Scott, John 1784-1821   [IP]
British journalist
* Benson, Edgeworth

Scott, John F. 19th c.   [IP]
American author
* Bones, Brudder

Scott, John Robert 19th c.   [IP]
British author
* Falkland

Scott, Justin 20th c.   [CA]
American author
* Blazer, J. S.

Scott, Michael 1789-1835   [IP]
Scottish author
* Cringle, Tom
(See also base volume)

Scott, Nerissa
See   Ring, Elizabeth

Scott, Ralph Tuckett
See   Maginn, William

Scott, Robert
See   Robins, James

Scott, Robert 20th c.   [EF]
American football player
* Scott, Bo

Scott, Robert Bissett 1774-1841
[IP]
British author
* R. B. S.

Scott, Sarah ?-1795   [IP]
British author
* [A] Gentleman on his Travels
* [A] Person of Quality
(See also base volume)

Scott, Thomas Hamilton Maxwell
1833-1895?   [PI]
Irish poet
* [A] Belfast Student

Scott, [Sir] Walter
See   Paulding, James Kirke

Scott, [Sir] Walter 1771-1832
[IP, NPS]
Scottish author and poet
* [The] Black Hussar of Literature
* Borderer Between Two Ages
* [The] Caledonian Comet
* [The] Charmer of the World
* [A] Homer of a Poet
* [The] Mighty Minstrel
* Our Northern Homer
* [The] Superlative of My
   Comparative
* [The] Visionary
(See also base volume)

Scott, [Sir] Walter, Bart.
See   Allen, John Carter

Scott, [Sir] William [Lord Stowell]
1745-1836   [IP]
British jurist and author
* Chrysal
* Civis

Scott, William B.   [IP]
American author
* Diversity

Scott, William Bell 1811- ?   [EOP]
Scottish author and poet
* [The] Scottish Blake

Scott, Winfield 1786-1866   [NPS]
American army officer
* Fuss and Feathers
(See also base volume)

Scotti, Giulio Clemente 1602-1669
[WGT]
Author
* Europaeus, Lucius Cornelius

[The] Scottish Blake
See   Scott, William Bell

[A] Scottish Farmer and Land Agent
See   Loudon, John Claudius

[The] Scottish Roscius
See   Johnston, Henry Erskine

Scraggs, Milton Byron
See   Williams, Richard Dalton

Screamin' Scott Simon
See   Simon, Scott

Scribble, William
See   Smyth, William

Scribe of the Indies
See   Alvarez, Chanca Diego

Scriblerus Maximus
See   Dance, James

Scriblerus Oxoniensis
See   Barham, Richard Harris

Scriblerus Secundus, H.
See   Fielding, Henry

Scrub, Dicky
See   Norris, Henry

Scrutator
See   Horlock, K. W.

Scrutator
See   McCall, John

Scuderi, Magdalen [or Madeleine] de
1607-1671   [NPS]
French poet
* Sappho
(See also base volume)

[The] Scullor
See   Taylor, John

Scully, Vincent 1810-1871   [PI]
Irish poet and politician
* S.
* Vis

Scully, William Charles 1855-1943
[DLE1]
South African poet and author
* Witwatersrand

Sculptor, Satiricus, Esq.
See   Ireland, William Henry

Scurlock, Doc
See   Scurlock, Josiah G.

Scurlock, Josiah G. ?-1882?
[EWG]
American gunfighter
* Scurlock, Doc

[A] Sea Fielding
See   Marryatt, Frederick

Seaborn, [Captain] Adam
See   Symmes, John Cleves

Seabury, Samuel 1729-1796   [DNA]
American author and clergyman
* Farmer, A. W.

Sealy, Robert 1831-1862   [PI]
Irish-born poet
* Menippus

Seaman, Abel
See   Chase, Frank Eugene

Seamans, Apache Bill?
See   Seamans, William

[A] Seaman's Friend
See   Baker, Samuel

Seamans, William
American frontiersman
* Seamans, Apache Bill?

Seamrog
See   Hickey, Michael Patrick

Search, John
See   Ashhurst, William Henry

Search, John
See   Binney, Thomas

Search, Warner Christian
See   Smith, [Sir] William Cusack,
Bart.

Sears, Alfred Francis 19th c.   [SFL]
Author
* Inca-Pablo-Ozollo

Sears, Edward Isidore 1819-1876
[DNA, PI]
Irish-born author and editor
* Chevalier, H. E.

Seaton, George
See   Stenius, George

Seatsfield
See   Postl, Karl Anton

Sebottendorf, Rudolf Freiherr von
See   Glauer, Adam

Sechter, Simon 1788-1867   [BBD]
Austrian composer
* Heiter, Ernst

[The] Second Adam
See   Jesus Christ

[A] Second Constantine
See   James II

[A] Second Johnson
See   Coleridge, Samuel Taylor

[The] Second Moses
See   Maimonides [or Moses ben
Maimon]

[A] Second Ovid
See   Greene, Robert

[A] Second Shakespeare
See   Marlowe, Christopher

Secondsight, Solomon
See   McHenry, James

Secretary and General Agent
See   Harris, N. Sayre

Sedley, Arthur Osborne Lionel
?-1897?   [PI]
Irish author and poet
* Carolan, R.

Sedley, F.
See   Fay, Theodore Sedgwick

Sedulius, Caius
See   Casey, James

See, Henricus von
See   Dilg, William

See, T. J.
See   Carey, Thomas Joseph

Seeburg, Franz von
See   Hacker, Franz

Seehaitch
See   Hennessy, William Charles

Seeley, John Robert 1834-1895
[DEA]
British author
* Robertson, John
(See also base volume)

[The] Seeress of Prevorst
See   Hauffe, Frederica

Seever, R.
See   Reeves, Lawrence F.

Seferiades, Giorgos Stylianou
1900-1971   [CA]
Greek diplomat and poet
* Sepheriades, Georgios
(See also base volume)

Segal, Robert 1957-   [BP]
American actor
* Benson, Robby

Segre, Dan V[ittorio] 1922-   [CA]
Italian-born Israeli author
* Bauduc, R.

Selbig, Elise
See   Ahlefeld, Charlotte Sophie
Luise Wilhelmine von

Selden, John 1584-1654   [NPS]
British jurist and statesman
* [The] Champion of Human Law
* [A] Walking Library
(See also base volume)

Selim
See   Knowles, James Sheridan

Selim
See   Woodworth, Samuel

Selkirk, Jane [joint pseudonym with
Mary Hamilton (Ilsley) Chapman]
See   Chapman, John Stanton
Higham

Selkirk, Jane [joint pseudonym with
John Stanton Higham Chapman]
See   Chapman, Mary Hamilton
[Ilsley]

Selmar
See   Brinckman, Karl G.

Selznick, David 1902-1965   [DBQ]
American producer
* Sachs, David

Semenko, Dave 1957-
Canadian-born hockey player
* Cement Head
(See also base volume)

Senesino, Francesco
See   Bernardi, Francesco

Senex
See   Pegge, Samuel

Senex
See   Townshend, Horace

Senior
See   Penrose, John

**[The] Senior Curate of St Luke's,
Berwick Street**
See   Whitehead, Henry

Sennott, George 19th c.   [PI]
Irish-born author
* [A] Jacksonian Democrat

Sentimientos [Sentiments]
See   Nunez, Juan

Sepharial
See   Old, Walter Richard

Sepheriades, Georgios
See   Seferiades, Giorgos Stylianou

Sepperle
See   Reynolds, Margaret Gertrude

Seranus
See   Harrison, Susie Frances
[Riley]

Sere, Octave
See Poueigh, Jean
[Marie-Octave-Geraud]

Sergeant B
See Butler, Robert

Sergius I 635?- 701   [NPS]
Pope
* Os Porci

Servetus, Michael, M.D.
See Blair, Patrick

Service, Robert William 1876-1958
[UH]
British-born poet
* [The] Canadian Kipling
* [The] Kipling of Canada
(See also base volume)

Servita
See Sarpi, Pietro

Settle, Elkanah 1648-1724   [NPS]
British playwright and poet
* Codrus
(See also base volume)

Sevenoaks
See Edwards, Alfred S.

Seventy Four, Lord
See Lowther, [Sir] James

Seward, John
See Stephens, Francis George

Seward, W.
See Maginn, William

Sewell, Arthur
See Whitson, John H.

[The] Sex Beast
See Rees, Melvin

[A] Sexagenarian
See Beloe, William

Sexton, Annie
See Fitzachary, John Christopher

Seymour, Mary Alice [Ives] 19th c.
[DNA]
Author
* Hensel, Octavia

Seymour, Robert, of the Inner Temple
See Mottley, John

Seymour-Conway, Francis Charles
1777-1842   [NPS]
Third Marquis of Hertford
* Red Herrings

Sforza, Lodovico [or Ludovico]
1451-1510?   [NPS]
Duke of Milan
* [Il] Moro
(See also base volume)

Shackleton, Abraham 1753-1818
[PI]
Irish poet and translator
* A. S.

Shackleton, Elizabeth 18th c.   [PI]
Irish poet
* E. S., Miss

[The] Shadow
See Ashe, Arthur

Shadwell, Thomas 1640-1692
[DEA, NPS]
British author, playwright, poet
* MacFlecknoe
* Our Young Ascantus
* T. S.

Shadwell, Thomas (Continued)
* Thou Great Prophet of Tautology
* [The] True Blue Protestant Poet

Shaftesbury, First Earl of
See Cooper, Anthony Ashley

**Shahcolen, a Hindu Philosopher
Residing in Philadelphia**
See Knapp, Samuel Lorenzo

Shainmark, Eliezer L. 1900-1976
[CA]
Polish-born American journalist
* Shainmark, Lou

Shainmark, Lou
See Shainmark, Eliezer L.

Shaker
See Adams, Frederick W.

Shakespeare in Petticoats
See Baillie, Joanna

[The] Shakespeare of Novelists
See Fielding, Henry

Shakespeare, William 1564-1616
[NPS]
British playwright and poet
* [The] Bard of all Time
* [The] Divine
* Drusus
* [The] English Terence
* Fancy's Child
* [The] Glory of the English Stage
* [The] Glory of the Human
  Intellect
* [The] God of Our Idolatry
* Great Heir of Fame
* Honie-Tongued
* [The] Incomparable
* [The] Mirror-Upholder of His
  Age
* Poor Poet-Ape
* That Nimble Mercury
(See also base volume)

Shakespeare's Predecessor
See Greene, Robert

Shakur, Zayd Malik
See Costan, James

Shambles, Peter
See Stanhope, William [Second
Earl of Harrington]

Shamrock
See Downey, Joseph

Shamrock
See Walsh, John

Shamrock
See Williams, Richard Dalton

Shamus
See O'Brien, James Nagle

Shandonian
See O'Reilly, [Sister] Amadeus

Shane, Nevis
See Shearer, Sonia M.

Shannon, Edward N. 1795?-1860
[PI]
Irish poet
* Volpi, Odoardo

Shapcott, Reuben
See White, William Hale

Sharp, Samuel 1700?-1778   [NPS]
Surgeon
* Mundungus

Sharpe, Alexander John 1814-1890
[BBD]
British author
* Ellis, Alexander John

Sharpe, Ernest Jack
See Sharpsteen, Ernest Jack

Sharpe, Lucretia
See Burgess, Michael Roy

Sharpsteen, Ernest Jack 1880-1976
[MA]
American poet and playwright
* Sharpe, Ernest Jack

Shaw, Felicity 1918-   [CA, TCCM]
British author
* Morice, Anne

Shaw, George Bernard 1856-1950
[NPS]
Irish playwright, author, critic
* Redbarn Wash
(See also base volume)

Sheard, Virginia [Stanton] ?-1943
[DNA]
Canadian author and poet
* Sheard, Virna

Sheard, Virna
See Sheard, Virginia [Stanton]

Shearer, Sonia M. ?-1934   [DNA]
Author
* Shane, Nevis

Sheares, John 1766-1798   [PI]
Irish poet and barrister
* Dion
* J. S.

Shedley, Ethan I.
See Beizer, Boris

Sheehan, D. B. 19th c.   [PI]
Irish poet
* Bernards, Dene

Sheehan, John 1814?-1882   [PI]
Irish poet and author
* J. G.?
* Philander
(See also base volume)

Sheehan, Michael Francis 1865- ?
[PI]
Irish poet
* [A] Child of Nature

Sheen, Fulton J[ohn]
See Sheen, Peter

Sheen, Peter 1895-1979   [CA]
American clergyman
* [The] Microphone of God
* Sheen, Fulton J[ohn]

Sheffield, Classic
See Montgomery, James

Shehu, Mehmet 1914?-1982
Albanian prime minister
* [The] Butcher

Sheldon, Georgie
See Downs, Sarah Elizabeth
[Forbush]

Shelley, A. Fishe
See Gerard, James Watson

Shelley, Percy Bysshe 1792-1822
[DLE1, NPS, WGT]
British poet
* FitzVictor, John
* [A] Gentleman of the University
  of Oxford

Shelley, Percy Bysshe (Continued)
* [The] Hermit of Marlow
* P. B. S.
* [The] Snake
(See also base volume)

Shemus of Ullinagh
See McGrady, James

Shenstone, William 1714-1763
[NPS]
British poet
* [The] Water Gruel Bard
(See also base volume)

Shepherd, Dorothea Alice
See Pratt, Ella Ann [Farman]

Shepherd, Michael
See Ludlum, Robert

Sheridan, John 19th c.   [PI]
Australian poet
* Eureka

Sheridan, Richard Brinsley
1751-1816   [DEA, PPN]
Irish playwright
* Asmodeo
* Sherry
(See also base volume)

Sherlock
See Southwick, Solomon

Sherman, James D. ?-1896   [EWG]
American gunfighter
* Talbot, Jim

Sherman, Lydia 1830-1878   [LFW]
American murderer
* Queen Poisoner

Sherman, Saul 20th c.   [EF]
American football player
* Sherman, Solly

Sherman, Solly
See Sherman, Saul

Shero, Fred [Alexander]
See Schirock, Fred Alexander

Sherry
See Sheridan, Richard Brinsley

Sherwood, Mary Martha
1775-1851   [SFL]
Author
* [A] Young Lady

Shiel, Lily 1908?-   [CR]
British-born columnist
* Graham, Sheilah

Shiels, Doc
See Shiels, Tony

Shiels, Tony 20th c.   [EOP]
Magician
* Shiels, Doc

Shiftesbury
See Cooper, Anthony Ashley

Shiga, Emperor
See Shiga, Naoya

Shiga, Naoya 1883-1971
Japanese author
* [The] Divine Novelist
* Shiga, Emperor

Shimazaki, Haruki 1872-1943
[CA]
Japanese author and poet
* Shimazaki, Toson

Shimazaki, Toson
See Shimazaki, Haruki

Shinborn, Max 20th c.   [LFW]
Swindler, bank robber, gambler
* [The] King of the Badgers
* Shindell, Baron

Shindell, Baron
See   Shinborn, Max

Shingle, Solomon?
See   Bellaw, Americus Wellington

Shinkle, James D. 1897?-1973
[CA]
Author
* Shinkle, Tex

Shinkle, Tex
See   Shinkle, James D.

Shippen
See   Adams, Samuel

Shirley
See   Skelton, [Sir] John

Shirley, James 1596-1666   [DEA]
British playwright
* J. S.
(See also base volume)

Shirley, Penn
See   Clarke, Sarah J.

Shirley, Ralph   [NPS]
Author
* Ireton, Rollo

Shirtliffe, Robert
See   Sampson, Deborah

Shoe, Aminidab
See   Bousell, John

Sholto
See   Mackenzie, Robert Shelton

Shomroni, Reuven
See   Von Block, Bela

Shores, Cyrus Wells 1844-1934
[EWG]
American gunfighter
* Shores, Doc

Shores, Doc
See   Shores, Cyrus Wells

Shorsa, May
See   Slater, May Wilson

Short and Fat, Sampson
See   Kettell, Samuel

Short, Bob
See   Barbauld, Anna Letitia

Short, Bob
See   Pope, Alexander

Short, Robert Waltrip [Bobby]
1924-   [CR]
American singer
* [The] Midget King of Swing
(See also base volume)

Shortcut, Daisy
See   Cohen, D. S.

Shorter, Mrs. Clement
Author
* Siegerson, Dora

Shortfield, Luke
See   Jones, John Beauchamp

Shu-Jen, Chou 1881-1936   [CA]
Chinese author and educator
* Ch'o, Chou
* Hsun, Lu

Shuckburgh, Charles 18th c.   [IP]
British author
* [A] Gentleman of Gloucestershire

Shuffle, Rube
See   Heaton, Augustus Goodyear

Shurtleff, Bert
See   Shurtleff, Bertrand

Shurtleff, Bertrand 20th c.   [EF]
American football player
* Shurtleff, Bert

Shurtleff, Nathaniel Bradstreet
?-1874   [IP]
American antiquary
* N. B. S.

Shute, Hardwick 19th c.   [IP]
British clergyman and author
* One Who Knows It

Shuttle, Job
See   Weaver, Thomas

Sibley, Henry Hastings 1811- ?
[IP]
American army officer and author
* [The] Walker in the Pines
(See also base volume)

Sickert, Mrs. Cobden   [NPS]
Author
* Amber, Miles

Siddons, James H.
See   Stocqueler, Joachim Hayward

Siden, Captain
See   Vairasse, Denis

Sidey, James A. 19th c.   [IP]
Author
* Crucelli, F.

Sidgwick, Cecily 20th c.   [NPS]
Author
* Dean, Mrs. Andrew

Sidney, Algernon
See   Adams, John Quincy

Sidney, Algernon
See   Roane, Spencer

Sidney, Algernon
See   Waddington, Samuel Ferrand

Sidney [or Sydney?], Algernon
1622-1683   [NPS]
British statesman
* [The] British Cassius

Sidney, L.   [IP]
British author
* Densyli

Sidney, Mary 1561-1621   [NPS]
*Sister of British poet, Sir Philip
Sidney*
* Urania

Sidney, [Sir] Philip 1554-1586
[NPS]
British poet, statesman, soldier
* Illustrious Philip
* [The] Marcellus of the English
    Nation
* [The] Phoenix of the World
* [The] Syren of this Latter Age
* Zutphen Hero
(See also base volume)

Sidney, Samuel   [IP]
British author
* Emigrant

Siegerson, Dora
See   Shorter, Mrs. Clement

Siegmey
See   Meyer, Siegbert

Sigerson, George 1839?- ?   [PI]
Irish poet, scholar, scientist
* Erionnach
* Henry, Patrick
* [An] Ulsterman

Sigerson, Hester ?-1898   [PI]
Irish poet and author
* H.

Sigerson, Hester 20th c.   [PI]
Irish poet
* Uncle Remus

Sigma
See   Straight, [Sir] Douglas

Sigoloff, Sanford C. 20th c.
American business executive
* Ming the Merciless

Sikes, Olive [Logan] 1841- ?   [IP]
American actress and author
* Chroniqueuse
* Logan, Olive

Sikes, Thomas 18th c.   [IP]
British clergyman and author
* [A] Country Clergyman

Sikes, [William] Wirt 1836-1883
American author and journalist
* Saxe, Burton

Sill, Richard 18th c.   [IP]
British scholar
* Dirrill, Charles

Siluriensis
See   Wilson, John

Silver, Bill
See   Plowright, William George
Holroyd

Silver Billy Beldham
See   Beldham, Billy

Silver Tongu'd Smith
See   Smith, Henry

Silver Tongued Laurier
See   Laurier, [Sir] Wilfrid

Silvertongue, Gabriel
See   Montgomery, James

Simcox, George Augustus   [IP]
British playwright
* [A] Rambler

Simmel, August 1815-1878   [IP]
German author
* Schrader, August

Simmons, George W. 1815-1882
[IP]
American merchant and author
* [A] Friend to American
    Enterprise

Simmons, Ruth
See   Tighe, Virginia

Simmons, William Hammatt
1812-1841   [IP]
American author
* Domal, C.
* Lockfast

Simms, William Gilmore
1806-1870   [IP]
American author
* [A] Collegian
* [A] Southron
(See also base volume)

Simon, Emma [Couvely] 1848- ?
[IP]
German author
* Vely, Emma

Simon, Kaila 20th c.
Polish-born American author
* Simon, Kate

Simon, Kate
See   Simon, Kaila

Simon, Paul Frederick 1941-
[CLC]
American singer and songwriter
* Kane, Paul
(See also base volume)

Simon, Scott 1948-   [CMA]
Musician
* Simon, Screamin' Scott

Simon, Screamin' Scott
See   Simon, Scott

Simon the Skipper
See   Hamilton, Thomas

Simond, Louis 1767-1831   [IP]
Author
* [A] French Traveller

Simons, Bobby J. 1929?-1982
American singer and bandleader
* Simons, Tiny
* [The] Singing Canary

Simons, Lydia Lillybridge   [IP]
British poet
* E. L.

Simons, Tiny
See   Simons, Bobby J.

Simos, Miriam 1951-   [CA]
American author and playwright
* Starhawk

Simpson, Edward 1815- ?   [DI]
*British manufacturer of counterfeit
relics*
* Fossil Willy
* Old Antiquarian
(See also base volume)

Simpson, S. S.   [IP]
American author
* S. S. S.

Simpson, Thomas 1710-1761   [IP]
British mathematician and author
* Hurlothrumbo

Sims, [Lieut.] A. K.
See   Whitson, John H.

Sims, Alexander Dromgoole
1803-1848   [DNA]
American author
* Rigmarole, Crayon

Sims, Baby
See   Sims, Stanley

Sims, Stanley 20th c.   [RBE]
Boxer
* Sims, Baby

Simson, Archibald 19th c.   [HFN]
Author
* Macshimi, Gillespie

[A] Sincere Friend of the People
See   Lothian, Maurice

Sincerus
See   Adams, Samuel

Sinclair, Ellery
See   Jemison, Louisa

Sindici, [Maria] Magda Stuart 19th c. [NPS]
Author
* Vivaria, Kassandra

Sined
See Kelly, Denis

Singe
See Pellegrini, Carlo

[The] Singer of Catherine
See Derzhavin, Gavril

Singh, Seth Shiv Dayal 1818-1878
[NAD]
Religious leader
* Swamiji Maharaj

[The] Singing Canary
See Simons, Bobby J.

Singing Eagle
See Diego, Juan

Singleton, Anne
See Benedict, Ruth

Singleton, Arthur, Esq.
See Knight, Henry Cogswell

Singmaster, Elsie
See Lewars, Mrs. Harold

Singularity, Thomas
See Nott, Henry Junius

**Sinhold Von Schutz, Philipp
Balthasar** 1657-1742 [WGT]
German author
* Creutzbergs, Amadei
* Ehrenkron, Irenico
* Von Faramond, Ludwig Ernst
* Von Wahrenberg, Constantino

Sister Amy
See Archer-Gilligan, Amy

Sister Grace
See Kimmins, G. T.

Sister Mary
See Meehan, Charles Patrick

Sister Mary
See Salomen, Edith

Sistrunk, Manny
See Sistrunk, Manuel

Sistrunk, Manuel 1947- [FR]
American football player
* Sistrunk, Manny

Siu Sin Far
See Eaton, Edith

Sivad
See Davis, Eugene

Sivananda, Swami
See Iyer, Kuppuswami

Skarga, Piotr
See Paweski, Piotr

Skeffington, [Sir] Lumley
1771-1850 [NPS]
Playwright
* Skipton, Skiff

Skeffington, [Sir] William ?-1535
[NPS]
Lord Deputy of Ireland
* [The] Gunner

Skelly, William Nugent ?-1852
[PI]
Irish poet
* W. N. S.

Skelton, [Sir] John 1831-1897
[DEA]
Scottish author and editor
* Shirley

Skelton, Roger
See Horn, Peter [Rudolf Gisela]

Skez
See Mackenzie, William Henry

Skian
See McMahon, Heber

Skillett, Joseph
See Russell, [Lord] John Earl

Skinflint, Obediah
See Harris, Joel Chandler

Skipton, Skiff
See Skeffington, [Sir] Lumley

Skitt
See Taliaferro, Harden E.

Skittles
See Walters, Catherine

Skolimowski, Jerzy 1938- [CLC]
Polish director, screenwriter, editor
* Skolimowski, Yurek

Skolimowski, Yurek
See Skolimowski, Jerzy

Slade, Daniel Denison 1823-1896
[DNA]
American author and physician
* Medicus

Slade, Jack
See Slade, Joseph Alfred

Slade, Joseph Alfred 1824-1864
[BLB, DI, EWG]
American gunfighter
* Slade, Jack

Slater, May Wilson 20th c. [PI]
Irish poet
* Shorsa, May

Slaughter, John Horton 1841-1922
[EWG]
American gunfighter
* Don Juan
* Slaughter, Texas John

Slaughter, Mickey
See Slaughter, Milton

Slaughter, Milton 20th c. [EF]
American football player
* Slaughter, Mickey

Slaughter, Texas John
See Slaughter, John Horton

Slaughter's Kid
See Newcomb, George

[The] Sleeping Preacher
See Baker, Rachel

[The] Sleeping Prophet
See Cayce, Edgar

Sleight, Elmer 20th c. [EF]
American football player
* Sleight, Red

Sleight, Red
See Sleight, Elmer

Slenker, Elmina [Drake]
1827-1909? [BDSA, DNA]
American author
* Aunt Elmina

Slice
See William Frederick

Slick, Jonathan
See Stephens, Ann S.

Slick, Sam, Jr.
See Avery, Samuel Putnam

Slidell, Alexander 1803-1848 [IP]
American naval officer
* [The] American in England
(See also base volume)

Slieve-Bloom
See Kelly, John Tarpey

Slieve-Margy
See O'Neill, William

Slievegallion
See Hepburn, David

Slievenamon
See Dollard, James Benjamin

Slievenamon
See Kickham, Charles Joseph

Slievenamon
See Meagher, John Francis

[A] Sligo Suspect
See O'Dowd, John

Smada, Augusto
See Adams, William Augustus

Smaragdus
See Fitzpatrick, John

Smead, Mrs.
See Cleaveland, Mrs. Willis M.

Smedley, Edward 19th c. [HFN]
Editor, author, clergyman
* [A] Churchman

Smedley, Menella 19th c. [HFN]
Author
* S. M.

Smee, Wentworth
See Burgin, George Brown

Smeeton, George 19th c. [HFN]
Author
* Charfy, Guiniad

[The] Smiddy Muse
See Coyle, Matthew

Smiff, Sam
See Coutts, Tristram

Smile, R. Elton
See Smilie, Elton R.

Smilie, Elton R. 19th c. [SFL]
Author
* Smile, R. Elton

Smith, Abbie Whitney 1919- [MA]
*Canadian-born American author and
poet*
* Whitney, Abbie

Smith, Artegall
See Norton, Philip

Smith, Arthur 18th c. [RBE]
Boxer
* [The] Gypsy

Smith, Barton 20th c. [EF]
American football player
* Smith, Barty

Smith, Barty
See Smith, Barton

Smith, Buckhorse
See Smith, John

Smith, Byron Caldwell 1849-1877
[DNA]
American author and educator
* Maldclewith, Ronsby

Smith, Catherine R. [Kay] 1925-
[MA]
American writer
* Adams, Angela
* Andrews, Vickie

Smith, Charles William 19th c.
[HFN]
Author
* C. W. S.

Smith, Charlie 20th c. [RBE]
Boxer
* Smith, Tombstone

Smith, Clyde
See Smith, George

Smith, David MacLeod 1920- [CA]
Scottish author
* Dunbar, Edward
(See also base volume)

**Smith, Donald Alexander [First
Baron Strathcona and Mount Royal]**
1820-1914 [NPS]
Canadian administrator
* That Grand Old Man of Empire

Smith, E. J. 20th c. [EC]
British cricketer
* Smith, Tiger

Smith, Elinor 20th c.
American aviator and author
* [The] Flying Flapper of Freeport

Smith, Elizabeth Oakes 1806-1893
American author and poet
* Helfenstein, Ernest

Smith, Frances Octavia 1912- [CA]
*American actress, singer, lyricist,
author*
* Evans, Dale
* Queen of the Cowgirls
* Rogers, Dale Evans

**Smith, Frederick Edwin [First Earl of
Birkenhead]** 1872-1930 [PPN]
British statesman
* F. E.

Smith, George 1852-1930 [DNA]
Scottish-born author and jurist
* Smith, Clyde

Smith, Grandfather
See Knight, Charles

Smith, Helene
See Muller, Catherine Elise

Smith, Henry 1550-1600 [NPS]
British clergyman
* Smith, Silver Tongu'd
(See also base volume)

Smith, Hildegarde Angell ?-1933
[DNA]
American author
* Angell, Hildegarde

Smith, James 20th c. [EF]
American football player
* Smith, Jetstream

Smith, Jeanie Oliver [Davidson]
1836-1925 [DNA]
American author and poet
* Oliver, Temple

Smith, Jefferson Randolph
1860-1898 [BLB, DI]
American gambler and swindler
* Smith, Soapy

Smith, Jetstream
See Smith, James

Smith, John 18th c. [NPS, SR]
British boxer
* Smith, Buckhorse

Smith, Johnston
See Crane, Stephen [Townley]

Smith, Katharine Grey [Hogg]
1876-1933 [DNA]
American author
* Grey, Katharine

Smith, Laura Rountree 1876-1924
[DNA]
American author
* June, Caroline Silver

Smith, Martin William 1942- [CA]
American author
* Carter, Nick
* Logan, Jake

Smith, Mary Eleanor 1866- ?
[LFW]
American swindler and murderer
* Old Shoebox Annie

Smith, Mary Prudence [Wells]
1840-1930 [DNA]
American author
* Thorne, P.

Smith, Mrs. John
See Arthur, Timothy Shay

Smith, Mrs. M. B. 19th c. [DNA]
Author
* Wood, Hazel

Smith, Nathan Ryno 1797-1877
[BDSA]
American physician and author
* Viator

Smith, Owen P. 20th c. [BBH]
*American inventor of mechanical
rabbit for dog racing*
* [The] Father of Modern
   Greyhound Racing

Smith, Richard Morris 1827-1896
[DNA]
Author
* Stanley, T. Lloyd

Smith, Robert 1853- ? [PI]
Irish poet
* Myles

Smith, Robert Cross 1795-1832
[EOP]
British astrologer and author
* Raphael

Smith, Shirley
See Curtis, E. J.

Smith, Silver Tongu'd
See Smith, Henry

Smith, Soapy
See Smith, Jefferson Randolph

Smith, Sosthenes
See Wells, Herbert George

Smith, Strata
See Smith, William

Smith, Sydney 1771-1845 [NPS]
British author and clergyman
* Pith, Peter
(See also base volume)

Smith, T. Carlyle
See Bangs, John Kendrick

Smith, [Sir] Thomas 1513-1577
[NPS]
Statesman and author
* [The] Glory of the Muses

Smith, Thomas J. 1830-1870
[EWG]
American law officer
* Bear River Tom

Smith, Thomas Lacey 1805-1875
[DNA]
Author and attorney
* Peters, Jeremy

Smith, Tiger
See Smith, E. J.

Smith, Tombstone
See Smith, Charlie

Smith, Walter C. 19th c. [NPS]
*Scottish clergyman, hymn-writer and
poet*
* Orwell

Smith, Walter Whateley
1884-1947 [EOP]
*British psychic researcher and
author*
* Carington, W[alter] Whateley

Smith, William 1769-1839 [NPS]
British geologist
* Smith, Strata
(See also base volume)

Smith, [Sir] William Cusack, Bart.
1776-1836 [PI]
Irish poet
* Peeradeal, Paul Puck
* Peeradeal, Peter Puck
* Search, Warner Christian

Smith, William Loughton
1745?-1812 [PI]
American statesman and author
* Phocion

Smoil, Glenn na
See Rooney, William

Smollett, Tobias George 1721-1771
[IP, NPS]
British author
* Alexander, Drawcansir
* Dustwich, Jonathan
* [The] Vagabond Scot
(See also base volume)

Smyth, Charles John 18th c. [IP]
British author
* Quid-Pro-Quo

Smyth, John 1783-1854 [PI]
Irish-born poet
* Macgowan

Smyth, Patrick G. 1856?- ? [PI]
Irish-born poet, author, journalist
* Green, Christopher
* P. G. S.

Smyth, William 1813-1878 [PI]
Irish author, actor, painter
* Ryan, W. S.
* Scribble, William

Smythe, James M. [IP]
American author
* [A] Southerner

Smythe, Samuel
See Dawes, Rufus

Snaffle
See Dunkin, Robert

[The] Snake
See Shelley, Percy Bysshe

Snake, William
See Araguy, Jean Raymond
Eugene d'

Snart, Charles 19th c. [HFN, IP]
British barrister and author
* [A] Gentleman Resident in the
   Neighborhood

Snead, Fayette 19th c. [IP]
American journalist
* Fay

Sneed, M. A. 19th c. [IP]
American journalist
* Grundy, Miss

Snelling, William Joseph
1804-1848 [IP]
American journalist
* [A] Free Man
* [A] Resident Beyond the Frontier
(See also base volume)

Snider, Denton Jacques 1841-1925
[DNA]
American author, poet, educator
* Middling, Theophilus

Snodgrass, Thomas Jefferson
See Clemens, Samuel Langhorne

Snoilsky, Carl Johan Gustav 1841-
? [NPS]
Swedish poet
* Trost, Sven

Snow, Joseph 19th c. [PI]
Irish poet and journalist
* Oberon
* St. George, George

Snow, Theodore William ?-1862
[IP]
American clergyman and author
* La Touche, Geoffry

Snow, William 19th c. [IP]
British songwriter
* Wons, Mailliw

Snuff
See Stanhope, Charles

Soame, [Sir] Henry F. R.
See Bunbury, [Sir] H. E.

[The] Soap King
See Hudson, Robert

Soar, Albert 20th c. [EF]
American football player
* Soar, Hank

Soar, Hank
See Soar, Albert

Sobhraj, Charles
See Sobhraj, Gurmukh

Sobhraj, Gurmukh 1944- ? [DI]
*Vietnamese-born murderer and
robber*
* Gautier, Alain
* Sobhraj, Charles

Socco the Bracer
See Gayles, Joseph

[The] Society Clown
See Grossmith, George, Jr.

Socrates 5th c. BC [NPS]
Greek philosopher
* [The] Athenian Sage
(See also base volume)

Sofi, Abou Moussah Djafar al-
See Geber

Softly, Edgar
See Lovecraft, Howard Phillips

Sohailes
See Ahmed Ibn Hemdem Kiaya

[A] Sojourner
See Copleston, John Gay

Sokichi, Nagai 1879-1959
Japanese author
* Kafu, Nagai

Sol
See Soteldo, A. M.

[A] Soldier
See Goss, Warren Le

[A] Soldier's Daughter
See Nicolas, Sarah [Davison]

Soler, Frederic [IP]
Spanish author
* Pitarra, Serafi

Solly, Samuel 1781-1847 [IP]
British author
* Ylloss

Solomon [UH]
King of Israel
* [The] Wise King

[The] Solomon of Bards
See Prior, Matthew

Solomons, Blanche
See Jackson, Editha Salomon

[The] Solon of French Prose
See Voiture, Vincent

Sombre, Samuel
See Gerard, James Watson

[El] Sombrerero [The Hatter]
See Ruiz, Antonio

Somebody, M. D. C.
See Neal, John

Somers, Alexander 1861- ? [PI]
British author and solicitor
* Al-So

Somerset, Wellington 19th c. [IP]
British author and diplomat
* May Fly

Somerville, Alexander 1811- ? [IP]
Scottish politician and author
* [The] Whistler
* [A] Working Man
(See also base volume)

Sommer, H. B 19th c. [IP]
American author
* O'Pagus, Arry

Sommers, Jane R.
See Jones, Cornelia

[The] Son of a Mandarin
See Haywood, Eliza [Fowler]

Son of a She-Bear
See Orsini, Giovanni Gaetano

[The] Son of Jupiter Ammon
See Alexander III

[A] Son of Liberty
See Adams, Samuel

[A] Son of Liberty
See Church, Benjamin

[The] Son of the Saint
See Macaulay, Thomas Babington
[First Baron Macaulay]

[A] Son of Truth and Decency
See Inglis, Charles

Sonntag, Gertrud Walburga
1806-1854 [BBD]
German opera singer
* Sontag, Henriette

Sonny Black Napolitano
See Napolitano, Dominick

Sontag, Henriette
See Sonntag, Gertrud Walburga

Sontag, Susan 1933?-
American author and social critic
* [The] Dark Lady of American
Letters

[The] Sooner Huey Long
See Rader, Lloyd E.

Sophie of Saks Fifth Avenue
See Gimbel, Sophie

Sophocles 5th c. BC [NPS, UH]
Greek playwright
* [The] Athenian Bee
* [The] Bee of Athens
(See also base volume)

Sor, Fernando
See Sors, Fernando

Sorbiere, Monsieur
See King, William

Sorel, W. J. 19th c. [IP]
British author
* Buskin, [Captain] Sock
(See also base volume)

Soromenho, Augusto Pereira
?-1878 [IP]
Portuguese historian and author
* Abdallah

Sors, Fernando 1778-1839 [BBD]
Spanish musician
* Sor, Fernando

Sortun, Henrik 20th c. [EF]
American football player
* Sortun, Rick

Sortun, Rick
See Sortun, Henrik

Soteldo, A. M. [IP]
American journalist
* Sol

Sotheran, Henry 1819- ? [IP]
British author
* Savile

Soto, Fernando 1920?-1980 [FIR]
Mexican actor
* Mantequilla

Soto, Juan ?-1871 [EWG]
American gunfighter
* [The] Human Wildcat

Soule, Minnie Meserve ?-1937
[EOP]
Claimed to possess psychic powers
* Chenoweth, Mrs.

Soust de Borkenfeldt, Adolphe van
1824-1877 [IP]
Belgian poet and historian
* Jane, Paul

Souter, Joseph [IP]
Scottish playwright
* [The] Odd Fellow

[A] South Carolinian
See Middleton, Henry

South, Edwin
See Campbell, Bartley T.

South, M. A.
See Atwood, Mary Ann

[The] Southern
See Dowling, Bartholomew

[A] Southern Planter
See Alston, Joseph

[The] Southern Spy
See Pollard, Edward Alfred

[A] Southerner
See Smythe, James M.

Southey, Caroline Anne [Bowles]
1787-1854 [IP]
British poet
* A.
* C.

Southey, Robert 1774-1843
[DLE1, IP, NPS]
British author and poet
* [The] Ballad-Monger
* [The] Bard of the Bay
* [The] Blackbird
* [The] Doctor
* [The] Epic Renegade
* [The] First Man of Letters in
Europe
* Illustrious Conqueror of
Common-Sense
* Inchiquin
* Mouthy
* Porson, Professor [joint
pseudonym with Samuel Taylor
Coleridge]
(See also base volume)

[A] Southron
See Simms, William Gilmore

Southwell, Robert 1561-1595
[DEA]
British poet
* R. S.
(See also base volume)

Southwick, Solomon 1773-1839
[DNA, IP]
American journalist
* Sherlock

[The] Spagnolet of the Theatre
See Cibber, Colley

[Lo] Spagnoletto
See Garcia, Francisco Javier

Spalding, John Lancaster
1840-1916 [DNA]
American author and clergyman
* Hamilton, Henry

[The] Spanish Grandee
See Duff, James

[The] Spanish Livy
See Ginez de Sepulveda, Juan

[La] Spara
See Spara, Hieronyma

Spara, Hieronyma ?-1659 [LFW]
Italian murderer
* [La] Spara

Sparkes, Mr. 1820-1875 [EOP]
Astrologer and editor
* Raphael V

Sparks, Godfrey
See Dickens, Charles

Spartacus, Tertius
See Burgess, Michael Roy

Spavento, Don
See Cohn, Martin

Spavery
See Avery, Samuel Putnam

[A] Special Reporter
See Allan, John

Speck, Dutch
See Speck, Norman

Speck, Norman 20th c. [EF]
American football player
* Speck, Dutch

[The] Spectator
See Addison, Joseph

Spectator
See Bartlett, David W.

[A] Spectator
See Bartol, Cyrus Augustus

[A] Spectator of the Scenes
See Carroll, John

Spector, Phil 20th c. [CMA]
American record producer and
songwriter
* [The] First Tycoon of Teen

[The] Speculator
See Durandus, Gulielmus

Spencer, Maja
See Spencer, Mrs. William Loring
[Nunez]

Spencer, Major
See Spencer, William Loring

Spencer, Mrs. William Loring
[Nunez] 19th c. [DNA]
Author
* Spencer, Maja

Spencer, William Loring 19th c.
[BDSA]
American author
* Spencer, Major

Spencer Meek, Margaret [Diston]
1925- [CA]
Scottish-born author
* Meek, Margaret

Spender, John Alfred 1862-1942
[NPS]
British author
* Greville Minor
* [The] Philistine
(See also base volume)

Spenser, Edmund 1552-1599 [NPS]
British poet
* [The] Fairy Singer
* Immerito
* [The] King of Poets
* [The] Mighty Minstrel of Old
Mole
* [The] Rubens of English Poetry
(See also base volume)

[The] Spenser of His Age
See Fletcher, Phineas

Sperontes
See Scholze, Johann Sigismund

Spes
See Campion, John Thomas

[The] Sphinx
See Brown, Lee Patrick

[The] Sphinx in Crepe
See Tarnowska, [Countess] Maria

Spinelli, Evelita Juanita 1889-1941
[LFW]
American murderer
* [The] Duchess

[The] Spinning Spoon
See Peel, [Sir] Robert

Spinster
See Brooke, Frances [Moore]

[The] Spirit of the Nation
See Meehan, Alexander S.

Spitzer, Louis 1853-1894 [BBD]
Hungarian musician
* Hegyesi, Louis

Spivak, Charlie 1905?-1982
American musician and bandleader
* [The] Sweetest Trumpet in the
World

Spivey, Thomas Sawyer 1856-1938
[DNA]
American author and manufacturer
* Reywas, Mot

[The] Sporting Parson
See Russell, John

Spot, Dick, the Conjuror
See Morris, Richard

[The] Spotlight Kid
See Vliet, Don Van

Sprague, W. D. [joint pseudonym
with Sylvia Von Block]
See Von Block, Bela

Sprague, W. D. [joint pseudonym
with Bela Von Block]
See Von Block, Sylvia

Sprat, James
See Hunt, [James Henry] Leigh

Spring, Thomas ?-1795? [PI]
Irish poet
* T. S.

Spring, Tom
See Winter, Thomas

Sprout, Mr.
See Whiteing, Richard

Spuzheim, John Gaspar 1776-1832
[NPS]
German physician
* Dousterswivel

Squarcialupi, Antonio 1416-1480
[BBD]
Italian musician
* Antonio degli Organi

[A] Squatter
See Jones, John Beauchamp

Squinting Jack
See Wilkes, John

Squire, John Collings 1884-1958
British author and journalist
* Affable Hawk

[The] Squire of Sandringham
See Edward VII

Sriblerus, Martinus
See Arbuthnot, John

Staccato
See Kalisch, A.

Stacton, David [Derek] 1925-1968
[CA]
American author
* Boyd, Carse
* Clifton, Bud
* Dereksen, David

[A] Staff Officer
See Wilson, Thomas Fourness

[The] Stage Leviathan
See Quin, James

Stainton, J. [NPS]
Journalist
* Looker-On

Stalbrydge, Henry
See Bale, John

[The] Standard Bearer
See Maginn, William

Standen, Antony 16th c. [EE]
British intelligence agent
* Pellegrini, Pompeo

Standish, Burt
See Cook, William Wallace

Standish, Burt L.
See Whitson, John H.

Standish, Winn
See Sawyer, Walter Leon

Stanhope, Charles [Third Earl of Stanhope] 1753-1816 [NPS]
British politician and scientist
* Minority of One

Stanhope, Charles 1780-1851
[NPS]
Fourth Earl of Harrington
* Snuff

Stanhope, Philip Dormer
1694-1773 [DEA, NPS]
British statesman and author
* FitzAdam, Adam
* Our English Rochefoucault
(See also base volume)

Stanhope, William [Second Earl of Harrington] 1719-1779 [NPS]
British army officer and politician
* Shambles, Peter

Staniak, Lucian 1941?- [DI]
Polish murderer
* [The] Red Spider

Stanley
See Ormsby, John S.

Stanley, Augustus Owsley, III
[NAD]
Chemist
* Owsley

Stanley, Eveleen
See Murphy, Mrs. H.

Stanley, T. Lloyd
See Smith, Richard Morris

Stanli, Sue
See Meilach, Dona Z[weigoron]

Stanton, Dorothy
See Kaumeyer, Dorothy

Stanton, Edward
See Huntington, Edward Stanton

Star, Ely
See Jacob, Eugene

Star, Jean
See Lubanski, Jules Clement
Ladislas

[The] Star of the East
See Aaron, Barney

[The] Star of the Stuart Line
See James IV

Starbuck, Roger
See Comstock, Augustus

Starcross, Roger
See Pope, Charles Henry

Starhawk
See Simos, Miriam

Starkey, Digby Pilot 1806-1880
[PI]
Irish poet and playwright
* Menenius
(See also base volume)

Starkweather, Charles ?-1959 [DI]
American murderer
* Starkweather, Little Red

Starkweather, Little Red
See Starkweather, Charles

Starnes, Ebenezer ?-1870? [DNA]
Author
* Jones, [Dr.] Pleasant

Starr, Angel
See Starr, Henry

Starr, [Myra] Belle [Shirley]
1848-1889 [BLB]
American outlaw
* [The] Bandit Queen

Starr, Henry 1873-1921
[CEC, EWG]
American gunfighter
* [The] Bearcat
* Starr, Angel

[The] State's Corrector
See Romilly, [Sir] Samuel

[A] "States"-man
See Childe, Edward Vernon

Steady
See Ramsay, Allan, Jr.

Stebnitski
See Leskov, Nikolai Semenovich

Stedman
See Kinney, Elizabeth C. [Dodge]

Stedman, Charles
See Thomson, William

Steel, Robert
See Whitson, John H.

Steele, Addison
See Whitson, John H.

Steele, Alice Garland
See Austin-Ball, Mrs. T.

Steele, Anne 1717-1778 [NPS]
Hymn writer
* Theodosia

Steele, [Sir] Richard 1672-1729
[DEA, DLE1, PI]
British author and playwright
* [The] Father of English Periodical
   Literature
* [A] Gentleman of the Army
* Myrtle, Marmaduke
* Philroye, Humphrey
(See also base volume)

Stein, Bernard
See Kahlert, Karl F[riedrich]

Steiner, Rebel
See Steiner, Roy

Steiner, Roy 20th c. [EF]
American football player
* Steiner, Rebel

Steinschneider, Hermann [or Heinrich?] 1869-1933 [EOP]
German psychic and astrologer
* [The] Devil's Prophet
(See also base volume)

Steinwert von Soest, Johannes
1448-1506 [BBD]
German composer
* Susato, Johannes

Stella
See Iron, Mrs. N. C.

Stella C.
See Deacon, Leslie

Stenius, George 1911-1979 [CA]
*American, producer, director,
screenwriter*
* Seaton, George

Steno, Nicolas 1638-1687 [UH]
Danish geologist and anatomist
* [The] Father of Geology

Stephen, [Sir] George 1794- ?
[HFN]
Author
* Emptor Caveat
(See also base volume)

Stephen, [Sir] Leslie 1832-1904
[DEA]
British author and philosopher
* L. S.
(See also base volume)

Stephens, Ann S. 1813-1886
American author, poet, editor
* Slick, Jonathan

Stephens, Charles Asbury
1844-1931 [DNA]
American author and scientist
* Stephens, Kit

Stephens, Eve
See Ward-Thomas, Evelyn Bridget
Patricia Stephens

Stephens, Francis George 19th c.
[NPS]
Artist and author
* Savage, Laura
* Seward, John

Stephens, George 1800-1851 [PI]
British playwright
* Dorset, St. George
(See also base volume)

Stephens, Henrietta Henkle 1909-
[CA]
American author and editor
* Buckmaster, Henrietta

Stephens, James 1882?-1950
[CA, DLE1]
Irish poet, playwright, author
* Esse, James

Stephens, Kit
See Stephens, Charles Asbury

Stephens, Louis 20th c. [EF]
American football player
* Stephens, Red

Stephens, Louise G. 1843- ? [DNA]
Author
* Katharine

Stephens, Red
See Stephens, Louis

Sterling, Edward 1773-1847 [NPS]
British journalist
* [The] Magus of the Times
* Whirlwind, Captain
(See also base volume)

Sterne, Laurence 1713-1768 [UH]
British author
* Bramin
(See also base volume)

Sternpost, Admiral
See Paulet, Harry

Steuart, Daniel 19th c. [PI]
Irish poet
* D. S.

Stevens, Austin N[eil] 1930- [CA]
American author, editor, illustrator
* Austin, Stephen
* Nash, Eno

Stevens, Blaine
See Whittington, Harry
[Benjamin]

Stevens, Harold
See Neuburg, Victor [Benjamin]

Stevens, Maurice
See Whitson, John H.

Stevens, Thaddeus 1773?-1868
[NPS]
American politician
* Grand Old Man
(See also base volume)

Stevens, William [Bill] 1736-1781
[RBE]
British boxer
* [The] Nailer

Steventon, John
See Tarkington, John Stevenson

Stewart, Charlotte [NPS]
Author
* M'Aulay, Allan

Stewart, Dorothy Mary 1917-1965
[CA]
British author
* Elgin, Mary

Stewart, [Sir] James [IP]
Barrister and author
* [A] Lawyer

Stewart, Jessie [IP]
Scottish poet
* J. S.

Stewart, Maria Stewart 19th c.
[IP]
Scottish author
* [A] Chip of the Young Block

Stewart, Mrs. Dugald 19th c.
[NPS]
* Ivy

Stewart, Mrs. W. [IP]
British author
* E. S.

**Stewart, Robert [Viscount
Castlereagh]** 1769-1822 [NPS]
British statesman
* [The] Intellectual Eunuch
(See also base volume)

Stewart, William [IP]
Scottish author
* W. S., M.P.

Sthalberg, George [IP]
Author
* [A] Gentleman Who Was a
  Swede

Stibbes, Agnes Jean 19th c. [IP]
American author
* Carra, Emma
(See also base volume)

Stickney, Caroline 19th c. [IP]
American author
* Landor, Charles

Stiegele, Georg 1815-1868 [BBD]
German singer and composer
* Stigelli, Giorgio

Stigelli, Giorgio
See Stiegele, Georg

Stiles, William Larkin [Billy]
?-1908 [EWG]
American gunfighter
* Larkin, William

Stillingfleet, Benjamin 1702-1771
[IP]
British author
* [A] Farmer in Cheshire

Stillman, Annie Raymond 1855- ?
[DNA]
American author
* Raymond, Grace

Stillman, W. O. 19th c. [IP]
American author
* W. O. S.

Stilton, W.
See Annet, Peter

Stilwell, Comanche Jack
See Stilwell, Simpson E.

Stilwell, Simpson E. 19th c. [EWG]
American attorney and army scout
* Stilwell, Comanche Jack
* Stilwell, Wildcat Jack

Stilwell, Wildcat Jack
See Stilwell, Simpson E.

Stinde, Julius 1841- ? [IP]
Danish author
* Valmy, Alfred de

Stine, Jovial Bob
See Stine, Robert Lawrence

Stine, Robert Lawrence 1943- [CA]
American author and editor
* Stine, Jovial Bob

Sting
See Sumner, Gordon

Stith, Zoda 19th c. [IP]
American poet
* Elloie

Stock, Baron
See Rattazzi, [Princess] Marie
Studolmine Bonaparte

Stock, John 19th c. [IP]
British author
* [An] Old Smoker

Stock, John Edmonds 1774-1835
[IP]
British author and physician
* [A] Layman

Stock, Joseph 1740-1813 [IP, PI]
Irish author and clergyman
* [An] Eye Witness

Stockley, Cynthia
See Webb, Lilian Julian

Stockley, Mrs. Vesey [NPS]
Author
* Ford, Mrs. Gerard

Stockton, William T. 1812-1869
[BDSA]
American author and army officer
* Cor-de-Chasse

[The] Stockyard Bluebeard
See Hoch, Johann

Stocqueler, Joachim Hayward [IP]
British army officer and author
* Siddons, James H.

Stoddard, Richard Henry
1825-1903 [IP]
American poet and critic
* Lang, S.
* R. H. S.
(See also base volume)

Stoddart, Thomas Tod [IP]
Scottish author and poet
* [An] Angler

Stokes, C. W. 19th c. [IP]
British author
* [A] London Merchant

Stokes, George 1789-1847 [IP]
British author
* Lay Member of the British and
  Foreign Bible Society

Stokes, Henry Sewell 1808- ? [IP]
British poet
* H. S. S.

Stokes, J. Lemacks 19th c. [DNA]
Author and clergyman
* May, Reginald

Stokes, John Whitley [IP]
Irish clergyman and author
* [A] Pastor

Stokes, Margaret MacNair 19th c.
[IP]
Irish antiquary
* M. S.

Stokes, Whitley 1830- ? [IP]
Irish barrister, historian, philologist
* W. S.

Stona, Thomas ?-1792 [IP]
British clergyman and author
* [A] Dumpling-Eater

Stone, C. J. [IP]
British author
* Gibbon, Edwarda

Stone, Cecil Percival [IP]
British army officer and author
* Enos

Stone, Elizabeth 19th c. [IP]
British author
* Menzies, Sutherland

Stone, Isador Feinstein 1907- [CR]
American journalist and author
* Stone, Izzy
(See also base volume)

Stone, Izzy
See Stone, Isador Feinstein

Stone, Josephine Rector
See Dixon, Jeanne

Stone, Willie
See Moore, Chuck

Stonecastle, Henry
See Baker, Henry

Stoneclink
See Dale, Thomas F.

Stop
See Morel-Retz, Louis-Pierre

Stopford, A. St. G. 19th c. [PI]
Irish poet
* A. St. G. S.

Storms, Andre 1911-
French author
* Castelot, Andre

Storms, Jacques 1914-
French playwright
* Castelot, Jacques

Stormy
See Lawrence, Stacy

Stormy Petrel
See Kenny, Annie M.

Storrs, George 1796-1879 [DNA]
Author and clergyman
* Anthrops

Stover, Smokey
See Stover, Stewart

Stover, Stewart 20th c. [EF]
American football player
* Stover, Smokey

Straight, [Sir] Douglas 1844- ?
[NPS]
British author
* Sigma
(See also base volume)

Strakosch, Avery
See Denham, Avery Strakosch

Strang, Jesse ?-1827 [BLB]
American murderer
* Orton, Joseph

[A] Stranger
See Oulahan, Richard

Strap, Hugh
See Hewson, Hugh

Strasberg, Lee 1901-1982
Austrian-born actor and director
* Pope
* Rabbi
* [The] Ultimate Shrink
(See also base volume)

Stratemeyer, Edward L. 1862-1930
American author
* Hamilton, Ralph
(See also base volume)

Stratford, Edmund
See Lechmere, E.

Strauch, Katina [Parthemos] 1946-
[CA]
American author and librarian
* Alexis, Katina

Straus, Dennis 20th c. [CA]
American author
* Ascher/Straus [joint pseudonym
  with Sheila Ascher]

Strauss, Johann, Jr. 1825-1899
[BBD]
Austrian composer
* [The] Waltz King

Strauss, Johann, Sr. 1804-1849
[BBD]
Austrian composer and conductor
* [The] Father of the Waltz

Streamer, Col. D.
See Graham, Harry

Stribling, Bill
See Stribling, Majure

Stribling, Majure 20th c. [EF]
American football player
* Stribling, Bill

Strickland, Joe
See Arnold, George W.

Stride, Elizabeth 1841?-1888 [BL]
Prostitute and murder victim
* Stride, Long Liz

Stride, Long Liz
See Stride, Elizabeth

Strindberg, August 1849-1912
[UH]
Swedish playwright and author
* [The] Swedish Schopenhauer
(See also base volume)

Stritch, Andrew F. Russell
1869?-1905 [PI]
Irish poet
* Fionna, Flann
* St. Ritch, A. R.

[A] Stroling Player
See Roberts, John

[A] Stroller in Europe
See Wright, W. W.

Strom, Leslie Winter
See Winter, Leslie

Strong, Hero
See Jones, Clara Augusta

Strong, John 1732-1798 [NPS]
* [The] Blind Mechanician

Strongfellow, Professor
See Longfellow, Henry Wadsworth

Stroop, Helen E.
See Witty, Helen E. S[troop]

Stuart, Charles Edward
See Allan, Charles Stuart Hay

**Stuart, Charles Edward Louis Philip
Casimir** 1720-1788 [NPS]
British prince
* Bonaventura, Father
(See also base volume)

Stuart, Eleanor
See Child, Mrs. Harris Robbins

Stuart, Esme
See Claire, Amelie

Stuart, Isaac William 1809-1861
[DNA]
American author and educator
* Scaeva

Stuart, John [Third Earl of Bute]
1713-1792   [NPS]
British prime minister
* Another Machiavel
(See also base volume)

Stuart, John Sobieski Stolberg
See   Allen, John Carter

Stubbornness, General
See   Chuikov, Vasily I.

[A] Student
See   Forsyth, Ebenezer

[A] Student at Law
See   Knight, Frederick

[A] Student at Oxford
See   Amhurst, Nicholas

[A] Student of Harvard University
See   Harris, Thaddeus Mason

[La] Stupenda [The Stupendous One]
See   Sutherland, Joan

Sturdy John
See   Lilburne, John

Sturdy, William Allen 1840- ?
[DNA]
Author and educator
* Didwin, Isaac

Sturluson, Snorro 1179-1241
[NPS]
Icelandic historian and poet
* [The] Northern Herodotus

Stuyvesant, Petrus 1592-1672
[NPS]
Dutch administrator in America
* Hardkoppig Piet
* Peter the Headstrong
(See also base volume)

[A] Sub-Utopian?
See   Walker, Richard

[A] Subaltern
See   Coke, Edward Thomas

[A] Subscriber
See   Dickens, Charles

Subuh, Muhammad 1901-   [EOP]
Indonesian mystic
* Bapak [Father]

[A] Suburban Clergyman
See   Owen, John

Sucher, Leonard 1906-   [CR]
American columnist
* Lyons, Leonard

Sue, Marie Joseph 1804-1857
[NLC]
French author
* [The] French James Fenimore
   Cooper
(See also base volume)

Suett, Richard 1755-1805   [NPS]
Comedian
* Cherub Dicky

[A] Sufferer
See   Wilson, Thomas

[The] Sugar King
See   Havemeyer, Theodore A.

[The] Sugar Man
See   Leonard, Ray

Sukenik, Yigael 1917-   [CA]
*Israeli deputy prime minister,
archaeologist, author*
* Yadin, Yigael

Sulky
See   Trimble, William Copeland

Sullivan, Ed 1902-   [CR]
American television performer
* [The] Great Stone Face
* [The] Man in the Iron Mask
* [The] Walking Mount Rushmore

Sullivan, Edward Dean 1888-1938
[DNA]
American author and journalist
* Alum, Hardly

Sullivan, James Frank 1853-1936
[ICB]
British illustrator
* Josef

Sullivan, M. J.
See   O'Sullivan, Michael John

Sullivan, Robert Baldwin
1802-1853   [DNA]
Irish-born politician, jurist, author
* Legion
(See also base volume)

Sullivan, Timothy Daniel 1827- ?
[PI]
Irish poet and politician
* O'Sullivan, Timothy
* T. D. S.

Sully, Jean Baptiste 1665-1701
[NPS]
French musician
* [Le] Buffon Odieux

Summer, Brian
See   DuBreuil, Elizabeth Lorinda

Summer, Donna
See   Gaines, La Donna Andrea

Summerdale
See   Young, Alexander

Sumner, Gordon 1952?-
*American singer, musician,
composer*
* Sting

[The] Sun of Righteousness
See   Jesus Christ

Sunbeam
See   McManus, Patrick

Sunbeam, Susie
See   Mackarness, Matilda Anne

Sunday
See   Talbot, Catherine

[A] Sunday School Superintendent
See   Arnold, Alexander S.

[The] Superlative of My Comparative
See   Scott, [Sir] Walter

Supple, Gerald Henry 1823-1899
[PI]
Irish-born poet
* G. H. S.
* Torquil

Surabian, Zareh 20th c.   [EF]
American football player
* Surabian, Zeke

Surabian, Zeke
See   Surabian, Zareh

[A] Surgeon
See   Abrahams, B.

Surly Sam
See   Johnson, Samuel

[The] Surrey Pet
See   Caffyn, William

Surtees, Robert Smith 1803-1864
[NPS]
Author
* Jorrocks, John

Survilliers, Comte de
See   Bonaparte, Joseph

Susato, Johannes
See   Steinwert von Soest, Johannes

Sutherland, Bill
See   McCall, John

Sutherland, Duchess of 1869- ?
[NPS]
British author
* Fyffe, R. E.
* Gower, Erskine

Sutherland, Joan 1929-   [CR]
Australian-born opera singer
* [La] Stupenda [The Stupendous
   One]

Sutton, William Francis [Willie]
1901-1980   [DI]
American bank robber
* Lynch, Edward
(See also base volume)

Suydam, John Howard 1832-1909
[DNA]
American author and clergyman
* Knickerbocker, Jr.

Svareff, [Count] Vladimir
See   Crowley, Edward Alexander

Svetla, Karolina
See   Muzakova, Johanna [Rottova]

Swagger, General
See   Burgoyne, John

Swain, J. H., Jr.
See   Hardin, John Wesley

Swales, Susan Matilda [Bradshaw]
1843- ?   [DNA]
Author
* Bell, Ernest

[The] Swami
See   Salomen, Edith

Swamiji Maharaj
See   Singh, Seth Shiv Dayal

Swan, [Sir] Simon, Bart.
See   Fawcett, Joseph

Swansson, Lars 1605-1669
Swedish poet
* Gyllenstierna, Erik
* Wivallius, Lars

Swanston, Baron
See   Deeming, Frederick Bayley

Swasey, John B. 19th c.   [DNA]
Author
* Ah-Chin-Le

Swears
See   Wells, Ernest

Sweden's Glory
See   Gustavus Adolphus

[The] Swedish Schopenhauer
See   Strindberg, August

Sweet Bard of Bailieborough
See   Montgomery, John Wilson

Sweet E's
See   Johnson, Evelyn

Sweet Nell
See   Symcott, Margaret

Sweet Singer of Israel
See   David

Sweet William
See   William

[The] Sweetest Trumpet in the World
See   Spivak, Charlie

Sweetman, Elinor Mary 19th c.
[PI]
Irish poet
* E. S.

Swift, Deane 1770?- ?   [PI]
Irish poet
* Marcus

Swift, Delia 19th c.   [LFW]
American murderer and prostitute
* Fury, Bridget

Swift, Jonathan 1667-1745
[DEA, DLE1, NPS]
British author
* Du Baudrier, Sieur
* J. S. D. S. P.
* Misosarum, Gregory
* [A] Modus
* Philomath, T. N.
* This Impious Buffoon
* Wagstaff, Simon
(See also base volume)

Swift, Lewis J.
See   Gardner, Lewis J.

Swift Nicks
See   Nevison, William

Swift, Patrick
See   Mackenzie, William Lyon

Swinburne, Algernon Charles
1837-1909   [DLE1]
British poet
* Maitland, Thomas
(See also base volume)

Swinford Boy
See   Durkan, Patrick Francis

[A] Swiss Gentleman
See   Akenside, Mark

**[The] Sybil of the Faubourg Saint
Germain**
See   Le Normand, Marie

Symcott, Margaret 1642?-1691?
[NN]
*British actress and mistress of King
Charles II*
* Nell of Old Drury
* Sweet Nell
(See also base volume)

Symington, Stuart 1901-   [CR]
American politician
* [The] Big Bomber Boy

Symmes, John Cleves 1780-1829
[ESF, SFL, WGT]
American author
* Seaborn, [Captain] Adam

Sympson, Thomas ?-1691   [DI]
British highwayman
* Old Mob

Symus, the Pilgrim
See   Cobb, Sylvanus, Jr.

[The] Syren of this Latter Age
See   Sidney, [Sir] Philip

Szentes, Dorka
See   Szentes, Dorotta

Szentes, Dorotta 17th c.   [DI]
Hungarian murderer
* Szentes, Dorka

Szydlow, Jarl
See   Szydlowski, Mary Vigliante

Szydlowski, Mary Vigliante 1946-
[CA]
American author
* Szydlow, Jarl
* Vigliante, Mary

T

* Indicates Assumed Name

T.
See Talbot, Catherine

T.
See Tighe, Edward

T.
See Tormey, Michael

T. A.
See Ashe, Thomas

T. B.
See Belsham, Thomas

T. B.
See Benson, Arthur Christopher

T. B.
See Bowdler, Thomas

T. B.
See Burtt, Thomas

T. B. A.
See Aldrich, Thomas Bailey

T. C.
See Church, Thomas

T. C.
See Corbett, Thomas

T. C. C.
See Croker, Thomas Crofton

T. C. D.
See Dunphie, Charles James

T. C. I.
See Irwin, Thomas Caulfield

T. D.
See Davis, Thomas Osborne

T. D. M.
See McGee, Thomas D'Arcy

T. D. S.
See Sullivan, Timothy Daniel

T. E.
See Edwards, Thomas

T. F.
See Fuller, Thomas

T. F. D.
See Dibdin, Thomas Frognall

T. G.
See Gwin, Thomas

T. G. C.
See Carroll, T. G.

T. H.
See Halpin, William

T. H.
See Hewerdine, Thomas

T. H.
See Heywood, Thomas

T. H.
See Hobbes, Thomas

T. H. C.
See Corry, Thomas H.

T. H. E. A.
See Hallam, Arthur Henry

T. H., Pharmacop, Rustican
See Hickes, T.

T. H. W.
See White, Thomas

T. I.
See Irwin, Thomas Caulfield

T. J. M.
See Furlong, Patrick M.

T. K.
See Ken, Thomas

T. K.
See Knight, T.

T. K.
See Kyd, Thomas

T. K. A.
See Arnold, Thomas Kerchever

T. M.
See Martin, [Sir] Theodore

T. M.
See May, Thomas

T. M.
See Meehan, Thomas

T. M.
See Middleton, Thomas

T. M.
See Moore, Thomas

T. M.
See Mosse, T.

T. M. B.
See Baker, T. M.

T. M. G.
See Gorman, Thomas Murray

T. P.
See O'Connor, Thomas Power

T. R.
See Reilly, Thomas Devin

T. R.
See Ryan, Thomas

T. S.
See Shadwell, Thomas

T. S.
See Spring, Thomas

T. S. G.
See Gueulette, Thomas Simon

T. T.
See Tumulti, Thomas

T. V. F.
See Fosberry, Thomas Vincent

T. W.
See Savile, [Sir] George [Marquis of Halifax]

T. W.
See Wilson, Thomas

T. W. B.
See Beaumont, Thomas Wentworth

T. W., Gent.
See Weaver, Thomas

T. Z.
See Adams, Samuel

Taber, Anthony Scott 1944-   [CA]
American artist, cartoonist, author
* Anthony

Tabor, E. 19th c.   [NPS]
Author
* Cousin Alice

Tabori, Paul 1908-1974   [CA]
Hungarian-born British author, journalist, scriptwriter
* Hefner, Paul

Tabourot, Jehan 1519?-1595?
[BBD]
French author
* Arbeau, Thoinot

Tach
See Teach, Edward

[The] Taciturn
See Moltke, Hellmuth Karl Bernhard von

Tackwell, Charles 20th c.   [EF]
American football player
* Tackwell, Cookie

Tackwell, Cookie
See Tackwell, Charles

[The] Tactician
See Aeneas

Taiso [Great Revival]
See Tsukioka, Yoshitoshi

Talbot, Catherine 18th c.   [IP]
British author
* Sunday
* T.

Talbot, Charles 1660-1718   [NPS]
Duke of Shrewsbury
* [The] Favorite of the Nation
(See also base volume)

Talbot, George Foster 1819- ?   [IP]
American attorney and author
* [A] Layman

Talbot, Jim
See Sherman, James D.

Talcott, Mrs. Hersey Bradford [Goodwin] 19th c.   [IP]
American author
* H. B. G.

Taliaferro, Harden E. 1818?-1875
[DNA, IP]
American author
* Skitt

Talker, T.
See Rands, William Brighty

Talkin, Gil
See Rosenthal, Alan

[The] Talking Man
See McGrady, James

Tallafierro, Gabriel
See Fox, Hugh [Bernard, Jr.]

Tallentyre, S. G.
See Hall, E. B.

Tallis, Thomas   [NN]
* [The] Father of English Music

Tam
See Campbell, Thomas

Tamayo y Baus, Manuel
1829-1898   [NLC]
Spanish playwright
* Estebanez, Joaquin

Tanaquill
See Elizabeth I

Tangermann, Friedrich Wilhelm
1815- ?   [IP]
German author
* Granella, Victor

Tann, Jennifer 1939-   [CA]
British author and screenwriter
* Booth, Geoffrey

Tanner, Henry 19th c. [IP]
American author
* [An] Eye Witness

Tanner, James T. 1858- ? [NPS]
British librettist
* [The] Father of Musical Comedy
(See also base volume)

Tappan, David 1753-1803 [IP]
American theologian and author
* Toletus

Tappan, Lewis 1788-1873 [IP]
American merchant and author
* [A] Gentleman in Boston

Tappan, Sarah [Jackson Davis] [IP]
American author
* S. J.

Tapsky
See Cooper, Anthony Ashley

[Il] Tarantino
See Fago, Nicola

Tarbox, Increase Niles 1815- ? [IP]
American clergyman and author
* Uncle George

Tardieu, Jules Romain 1805-1868
[IP]
French author and poet
* J. T., de Saint-Germain

Tarkington, John Stevenson
1832-1923 [DNA]
American author and attorney
* Steventon, John

Tarn, Shirley
See Neuburg, Victor [Benjamin]

Tarnowska, [Countess] Maria
1878-1923 [LFW]
Russian murderer
* [The] Russian Vampire
* [The] Sphinx in Crepe

Tarrant, John
See Egleton, Clive [Frederick]

Tarthang Tulku 20th c. [EOP]
Leader of Tibetan religious sect
* Rinpoche [Precious Master]

Tasker, E. [IP]
American author
* E. T.

Tasma
See Couvreur, Jessie Catherine
[Huybers]

Tasso, Torquato 1544-1595 [NPS]
Italian poet
* [The] Bard of Chivalry
(See also base volume)

Tatch
See Teach, Edward

Tatham, Arthur 1809-1874 [IP]
British clergyman and author
* [A] Rural Dean

[El] Tato [The Stammerer]
See Sanchez Caballero, Antonio

Tattersall, George [IP]
British author
* Wildrake

Tattersall, John Cecil 1788-1812
[IP]
British clergyman and author
* Davus

Taubert, A.
See Hartmann, Agnes [Taubert]
von

Taubes, Susan
See Feldmann, Susan Judith

Taunton, William Elias 18th c. [IP]
British scholar
* Touchstone, Timothy

Tautphoeus, Jemima [Montgomery]
[IP]
British author
* Cyrilla

Taveau, A. L. [IP]
American poet
* Alton

Taxil, Leo
See Jogand-Pages, Gabriel Antoine

Tayama Katai
See Tayama Rokuya

Tayama Rokuya 1871-1930
Japanese author
* Tayama Katai

Tayler, Charles Benjamin 19th c.
[IP]
British clergyman and author
* [A] Country Curate
* Temple, [Rev.] Allan

Tayler, John James 1798-1869 [IP]
British clergyman and author
* J. J. T.

Taylor, Ann ?-1866 [IP]
British poet
* A.

Taylor, Doboy
See Taylor, Phillip

Taylor, Edgar 1793-1839 [IP]
British barrister and author
* Denton, H. B.

Taylor, Erquiet 20th c. [EF]
American football player
* Taylor, Jake

Taylor, F. 19th c. [HFN]
Author
* One of the Party

Taylor, Jake
See Taylor, Erquiet

Taylor, Jeremy 1613-1667
[DEA, NPS]
British author and prelate
* Alexander, John
* J. T., D.D.
(See also base volume)

Taylor, John 1580-1654 [NPS]
British poet
* [The] Chanticleere
* [The] Scullor
(See also base volume)

Taylor, John 1753-1824 [DNA]
American writer
* Curtius

Taylor, John Francis 1849?-1902
[PI]
Irish poet and journalist
* Ridgeway

Taylor, Judson R.
See Halsey, Harlan Page

Taylor, Lois Dwight Cole
See Cole, Lois Dwight

Taylor, Marian Young 1909-1973
[CR]
American radio commentator
* Deane, Martha

Taylor, Phillip ?-1871 [EWG]
American gunfighter
* Taylor, Doboy

Taylor, Thomas 1576-1633 [NPS]
British clergyman
* [A] Brazen Wall Against Popery
* [The] Illuminated Doctor
* Illuminatus, Doctor

Taylor, Una Ashworth 19th c. [PI]
British-born poet and author
* A. H. R.

Taylor, William Frederick 19th c.
[HFN]
Author
* W. F. T.

Tchaikovsky, Telephones
See Konarsky, Matt

Teach, Edward ?-1718 [DI]
British pirate
* Tach
* Tatch
* Thatch
(See also base volume)

Tebell, Gus
See Tebell, Gustavus

Tebell, Gustavus 20th c. [EF]
American football player
* Tebell, Gus

Technicolor Tessie
See Ball, Lucille

Teddy the Jewboy
See Davis, Edward

[The] Teeger
See Dunlop, John Colin

Teerius, Miss
See Horner, Mrs. Frederick

Tegg, William 1816-1895 [NPS]
Author and publisher
* Parley, Peter

Tekahionwake
See Johnson, Emily Pauline

Tekeli
See Hook, Theodore Edward

Telarius
See Webb, Foster

Telba
See Ablett, William

[The] Telepathic Phenomenon
See Kraus, Josef

Telephone, Tom
See Cleary, Thomas Stanislaus

Telescope, Tom
See Newbery, John

Telio, J.
See Joilet, Charles

Tell, William
See Forrester, Arthur M.

Teller, Thomas
See Tuttle, George

Telltruth, Paul
See Carey, George Seville

Teluccini, Mario 16th c. [WGT]
Italian author
* [Il] Bernia

[A] Temperate Drinker
See Gauntley, William

[A] Tempest Cleaving Swan
See Byron, George Gordon Noel

Temple, [Rev.] Allan
See Tayler, Charles Benjamin

Temple, Hope
See Davis, Hope

[The] Temple Leech
See Colman, George

Temple, [Sir] William 1628-1699
[DEA]
British poet
* W. T., Sir

Templeton, Dink
See Templeton, George

Templeton, George ?-1980 [FIR]
Actor, director, producer
* Templeton, Dink

Templeton, Horace
See Lever, Charles James

Templeton, Janet
See Hershman, Morris

[A] Ten Pounder
See Mackenzie, Peter

**Tennyson, Alfred [First Baron
Tennyson]** 1809-1892 [NPS]
British poet
* Schoolmiss Alfred
* Two Brothers [joint pseudonym
with Charles Tennyson]
(See also base volume)

Tennyson, Charles 1808-1879
[NPS]
British poet
* Two Brothers [joint pseudonym
with Alfred Tennyson]

[The] Tenth Muse
See More, Hannah

[The] Tenth Muse
See Vestris, Eliza Lucy

**Tenth President of the World
Republic**
See Blair, Andrew

Termagant, [Madame] Roxana
See Thornton, Bonnell

Terrae Filius
See Garnham, Robert Edward

Terrae Filius
See Mangan, James Clarence

Terrible Fred Wittrock
See Wittrock, Frederick

[The] Terror
See Turner, C. T. B.

[The] Terror of Wall Street
See Engel, George

Tesich, Steve
See Tesich, Stoyan

Tesich, Stoyan 1943?- [CA]
*Yugoslavian-born playwright and
screenwriter*
* Tesich, Steve

Texas Billy Thompson
See Thompson, William

Texas Jack
See Omohundro, John B.

Texas John Slaughter
See Slaughter, John Horton

Th. C.
See Child, Theodore

Thacker, Page
See Burwell, Lettie M.

Thackeray, William Makepeace
1811-1863 [DLE1]
British author
* Melville, Lewis
* O'Gahagan, [Major] G.
* Pacifico, [Dr.] Solomon
(See also base volume)

Thakura, Ravindranatha
1861-1941 [DLE1]
Indian poet, playwright, author
* [The] Bengal Shelley
(See also base volume)

That Bright Luminary
See Darwin, Erasmus

That Deep-Mouthed Boeotian
See Landor, Walter Savage

That Deep-Mouthed Theban
See Greathead, Bertie

That God of Clay
See Bonaparte, Napoleon

That Grand Old Man of Empire
See Smith, Donald Alexander
[First Baron Strathcona and Mount
Royal]

That Martial Macaroni
See Burgoyne, John

That Metromaniac Prince
See Frederick II

That Nimble Mercury
See Shakespeare, William

That Pellean Conqueror
See Alexander III

That Religious Machiavel
See Knox, John

Thatch
See Teach, Edward

Thatcher, Julia
See Bensen, Donald R.

Thaumaturgus
See Agatho

**[The] Thaumaturgus of the
Nineteenth Century**
See Filumena

Their Latest Victim
See Habberton, John

Their Wellwisher
See Ide, Simeon

Thelwall, John 1764-1834 [NPS]
British author and political reformer
* Theophrastus, Sylvanus
(See also base volume)

Theo the Swami
See Salomen, Edith

Theobald, Lewis 1688-1744 [NPS]
Author and editor
* Margites [The Booby]

Theocritus 3rd c. BC [NPS]
Greek poet
* [The] Allan Ramsay of Sicily
* [The] Father of Pastoral Poetry

Theodorakis, Michalis 1925- [CA]
Greek composer and musician
* Theodorakis, Mikis

Theodorakis, Mikis
See Theodorakis, Michalis

Theodore, Charles
See Reuss, Theodor

Theodosia
See Steele, Anne

Theophrastus, Sylvanus
See Thelwall, John

Therion, Master
See Crowley, Edward Alexander

Theron, Hilary
See Amos, Winsom

Theta
See Hughes, Terence McMahon

Thierna, Cairn
See O'Conor, Charles Patrick

Thinker, Theodore
See Woodworth, Francis Channing

[The] Thinking Man's Baritone
See Fischer, Albert Dietrich

Thinks-I-To-Myself, Who?
See Nares, Edward

[The] Third Romulus
See Marius, Caius

This Free Lance of Our Literature
See Nash [or Nashe?], Thomas

This Impious Buffoon
See Swift, Jonathan

This Poetical Charlatan
See Wordsworth, William

This Political Parasite
See Wordsworth, William

Thisby [joint pseudonym with Dona
M. Turner]
See Genovese, Vince

Thisby [joint pseudonym with Vince
Genovese]
See Turner, Dona M.

Thisted, V[aldemar] Adolph
1815-1887 [SFL, WGT]
Author
* L. W. J. S.
* Rowel, M.

Thistle
See Middlemass, Hume

Thoman, Egbert S.
See Ellis, Edward S[ylvester]

Thomas, Ann 19th c. [HFN]
Author
* Ann

Thomas, Elizabeth 19th c. [WGT]
British author
* Bluemantle, [Mrs.] Bridget

Thomas, Heck
See Thomas, Henry Andrew

Thomas, Henry Andrew 1850-1912
[EWG]
American law officer
* Thomas, Heck

Thomas, James, Jr. 1951- [EF, FR]
American football player
* J. T.

Thomas, John Daniel 1853-1930
[DNA]
Author and educator
* Crane, Ichabod

Thomas, Louis 20th c. [EF]
American football player
* Thomas, Speedy

Thomas, Malcolm 1953- [FR]
American football player
* Thomas, Mike

Thomas, Michael Tilson 1944-
[CR]
American conductor
* [The] Lenny of the Seventies

Thomas, Mike
See Thomas, Malcolm

Thomas, Peter 1928- [MA]
British-born author
* Pederek, Simon

Thomas, Ralph 19th c. [HFN]
Author
* H. S.
* R. T.

Thomas, Speedy
See Thomas, Louis

Thomasine
See Knight, Olivia

Thomason, John 20th c. [EF]
American football player
* Thomason, Stumpy

Thomason, Stumpy
See Thomason, John

Thomond
See Hogan, Michael

Thompson
See Peace, Charles

Thompson, A. C.
See Meynell, Alice [Christiana
Gertrude Thompson]

Thompson, Benjamin 1753-1814
[NPS]
British author
* [The] King of Fire
(See also base volume)

Thompson, Daniel P. 19th c. [HFN]
American author
* [A] Member of the Vermont Bar

Thompson, Don
See Thompson, Robert

Thompson, Edward Anthony 1928-
[TCCM]
British author
* Lejeune, Anthony

Thompson, Ernest Evan Seton
1860-1946
American author
* Thompson, Wolf
(See also base volume)

Thompson, Francis Clegg
See Mencken, Henry Louis

Thompson, James W. 1935-
[CA, MA]
American author, poet, dancer
* Altemese, Elethea
* Elethea, Abba

Thompson, John 1777-1799
[BDSA]
American writer
* Curtius
(See also base volume)

Thompson, John Albert
See Rue, Jon Thoresen

Thompson, Lurtis 20th c. [EF]
American football player
* Thompson, Tommy

Thompson, Marie M. 19th c. [PI]
Irish poet
* Ethne

Thompson, Ralph 20th c. [EF]
American football player
* Thompson, Rocky

Thompson, Robert 20th c. [EF]
American football player
* Thompson, Don

Thompson, Robert Hely 1854- ?
[PI]
Irish-born poet and playwright
* Blake, Robert

Thompson, Rocky
See Thompson, Ralph

Thompson, Snowshoe
See Rue, Jon Thoresen

Thompson, Texas Billy
See Thompson, William

Thompson, Thomas Phillips
1843-1933 [DNA]
British-born journalist
* Briggs, Jimuel

Thompson, Tommy
See Thompson, Lurtis

Thompson, William 1845?-1888?
[EWG]
British-born gunfighter
* Thompson, Texas Billy

Thompson, Wolf
See Thompson, Ernest Evan Seton

Thoms, William John 1803-1885
[DLE1, HFN, NPS]
British author
* Merton, Ambrose, Gent.

Thomson, Alexander 1817-1875
[NPS]
Scottish architect
* Thomson, Greek

Thomson, Dutch
See Thomson, Richard

Thomson, Greek
See Thomson, Alexander

Thomson, James 1834-1882 [NPS]
Scottish poet
* [The] Poet of Despair
(See also base volume)

Thomson, Richard ?-1613 [NPS]
Scholar and clergyman
* Thomson, Dutch

Thomson, Virgil 1896-   [CR]
American composer, music critic, author
* [The] Virgil of American Musical History

Thomson, William 1746-1817 [WGT]
British author
* [The] Man in the Moon
* [The] Man of the People
* Newte, Thomas
* [An] Officer in Col. Baillie's Detachment
* Stedman, Charles

Thoreau, Henry David 1817-1862 [NPS]
American author
* [The] Poet Naturalist

Thorer, Konrad
See Greve, Felix Paul

Thormanby
See Dixon, W. W.

Thorn, Edgar
See MacDowell, Edward Alexander

Thorn, Kate
See Jones, Clara Augusta

Thorne, [Lt.] Alfred B.
See Aiken, Albert W.

Thorne, Dora
See Brame, Charlotte M.

Thorne, Edouard
See Greve, Felix Paul

Thorne, Harley?
See Brayman, James O.

Thorne, Ian
See Dikty, Julian May

Thorne, Jean Wright
See Dikty, Julian May

Thorne, Marion
See Thurston, Ida [Treadwell]

Thorne, P.
See Smith, Mary Prudence [Wells]

Thornthwaite, J. A.   [IP]
British clergyman and author
* [A] Member of the Church of England

Thornton, Bonnell 1724-1768   [IP]
British poet and journalist
* Birch, [Rev.] Bushby
* Critic and Censor General
* [A] Deputy
* Termagant, [Madame] Roxana
* Town, Mr.

Thornton, Charles Bates 1913- [CR]
American business executive
* Thornton, Tex

Thornton, Jack
See Thornton, Lawrence

Thornton, Lawrence 20th c.   [EF]
American football player
* Thornton, Jack

Thornton, Tex
See Thornton, Charles Bates

Thornton, William   [IP]
American author
* W. T.

Thorough
See Wentworth, [Sir] Thomas [First Earl of Stafford]

Thorpe, Charles 19th c.   [IP]
American author
* Champagne Charlie

Thorpe, Thomas Bangs 1815-1878 [IP]
American journalist
* Logan
* Weiss, Lynde
(See also base volume)

Thorpe, William
See Vreeland, Frank

Thou Great Prophet of Tautology
See Shadwell, Thomas

Thou Jackall
See Boswell, James

Thou Myron of the Age
See Garrard, George

Three Fingered Jack
See Dunlap, Jack

Three Fingers Coppola
See Coppola, Frank

Threepland, Moncrieff ?-1838   [IP]
Scottish author
* Plain, Timothy

Throckmorton, Job 1545-1601 [NPS]
Puritan pamphleteer
* Marprelate, Martin

Thunderbolt, Captain
See Ward, Frederick

Thunders, Johnny
See Genzale, Johnny

Thurber, Charles 19th c.   [IP]
American author
* His Father

Thurland, Bilberry
See Hooten, Charles

Thurman, Wallace 1902-1934 [CA, TLC]
American editor, author, playwright, poet
* Casey, Patrick
* Mandrake, Ethel Belle

Thurston, Ida [Treadwell] 1848-1918   [DNA]
American author
* Thorne, Marion

Thurston, Oliver
See Flanders, Henry

Thym, K. J. A. Alberdingk 20th c. [NPS]
Dutch author
* Van Deyssel

Tibbs
See Dickens, Charles

[The] Tichborne Claimant
See Orton, Arthur

Tichborne, Thomas   [IP]
British author
* [A] Phrenologist

Ticheburn, Cheviot
See Ainsworth, William Harrison

Tickell, Thomas 1686-1740   [IP]
British poet
* [A] Lady in England

Tiddly
See Applewhite, Marshall Herff

Tidmarsh, James   [IP]
British author
* S. H.

Tidy, Theresa
See Graham, Elizabeth Susanna [Davenport]

Tieck, Johann Ludwig 1773-1853 [HFF, WGT]
German author
* Leberecht, Peter

Tiernan, Frances Christine [Fisher] 1846-1920   [BDSA, DNA]
American author
* Reid, Christian

Tierney, Reginald
See Russell, Thomas O'Neill

Tiffany, E. A. 1911-   [CA]
American author
* Samuels, E. A.

[The] Tiger Earl
See Lindsay, Alexander

[The] Tiger Woman
See Judd, Winnie Ruth

[The] Tiger Woman
See Phillips, Clara

Tighe, Edward ?-1798?   [PI]
Irish poet and politician
* T.

Tighe, Virginia 20th c.   [EOP]
American believed to have been reincarnated
* Murphy, Bridey
* Simmons, Ruth

Tighe, William   [IP]
Irish author
* [A] Father

Tilbury, Tom
See Henley, Robert

Tilden, Samuel Jones 1814-1886 [IP]
American politician
* Crino
(See also base volume)

Tillet, Auguste   [IP]
French dentist and author
* Maury, J. C. F.

Tillotson, John   [IP]
British author
* [The] Odd Boy

Tilton, Dwight
See Richardson, George Tilton

Tilton, James 1745-1822   [DNA]
American author and surgeon
* Timoleon

Tilton, Warren   [IP]
American author
* Trifle

Timbury, Jane 18th c.   [IP]
British author
* Astell, [Hon.] Edward

Timmins, Samuel 19th c.   [IP]
British author
* S. T.

Timoleon
See Tilton, James

Timon
See De la Haye, Louis Marie [Vicomte de Cormenin]

Timotheus 5th c.   [NPS]
Bishop of Alexandria
* [The] Cat

Timrod, Henry 1829-1867   [IP]
American poet and journalist
* Aglaus

Timsol, Robert
See Bird, Frederic Mayer

Tinto, Dick
See Jones, Charles A.

Tinto, Gabriel
See Anthony, G. W.

Tiny
See Munster, Mary C. F.

Tipperariensis
See Hickie, Daniel B.

[A] Tipperary Man?
See Doheny, Michael

Tiptoft, John 1427?-1470   [NPS]
Earl of Worcester
* [The] Cruel Judge
(See also base volume)

Tirbutt, Honoria 20th c.   [TCCM]
British author
* Page, Emma

Tiria
See Bourke, James J.

Titov, Nikolay Alexeyevitch 1800-1875   [BBD]
Russian composer
* [The] Grandfather of Russian Song

Todkill, Anas
See Cooke, John Esten

Toepfer, Wolfgang 1525?-1591? [BBD]
German author
* Figulus, Wolfgang

Togae, Cedant Arma
See Adams, Samuel

Toletus
See Tappan, David

Tom of Bedlam
See Milbourne, Luke

[The] Tombs Angel
See Barberi, Maria

Tomkins, Isaac
See Brougham, Henry Peter

Tomkins, Jane Harrison 1841-1912   [DNA]
Author and poet
* Harrison, Jennie

Tomlin, Beadley 20th c.   [EF]
American football player
* Tomlin, Tom

Tomlin, Tom
See Tomlin, Beadley

[The] Tommy Steele of Scotland
See Harvey, Alex

Took, Peregrine
See Took, Steve

Took, Steve 20th c. [CMA]
Musician
* Took, Peregrine

Tooke, Louise Mathews 1950-
[CA]
American author
* Mathews, Louise

Toppan, Jane
See Kelley, Nora

Topping, Godfrey
See Robertson, John

Tormer, Cill
See Pelly, Gerald Conn

Tormey, Michael 1820-1893 [PI]
Irish poet
* Clericus
* T.

Torquatus
See Jonson, Ben[jamin]

Torquil
See Supple, Gerald Henry

[A] Tory
See Adams, Samuel

[The] Toscanini of the Pratfall
See Biden, Edmond P.

[A] Total Abstainer
See Corder, Susanna

Touchstone, Timothy
See Aston, W.

Touchstone, Timothy
See Taunton, William Elias

Tourbillon, Robert Arthur 1885- ?
[DI]
American swindler and robber
* Rat
(See also base volume)

Toussaint, Allen 20th c. [CMA]
*American musician, songwriter,
record producer*
* Neville, Naomi
* Toussan

Toussan
See Toussaint, Allen

Touster, Alison
See Reed; Alison Touster

Tower, Martello
See Norman, F. M.

Towers, Ivar
See Kornbluth, Cyril M.

[The] Town Bull of Ely
See Cromwell, Oliver

[A] Town Councillor
See Duffy, [Sir] Charles Gavan

Town, Mr.
See Thornton, Bonnell

Townley, Arthur?
See Duganne, Augustine Joseph
Hickey

Townsbridge, Elizabeth
See Murphy, Katharine Mary

Townsend, Doris McFerran 1914-
[CA]
American author
* Clelland, Catherine
* McFerran, Ann
* McFerran, Doris

Townshend, Charles
See Bronte, Charlotte

Townshend, Charles 1674-1738
[PPN]
British statesman
* Townshend, Turnip

Townshend, Horace 1750-1837
[PI]
Irish poet
* Senex

Townshend, Horace 1837-1904
[PI]
Irish poet and author
* Induna

Townshend, Turnip
See Townshend, Charles

Toxopholite
See Lanigan, George Thomas

Tracy, Uriah 1755-1807 [DNA]
American politician and author
* Scipio

[A] Tradesman
See Drinker, John

Tragabuches [Tremendous Swallower]
See Ulloa, Jose

Traine, Gypsey
See Lovejoy, Mary Evelyn [Wood]

Tramp, Tilbury
See Lever, Charles James

Trash
See Tyler, Royall

[A] Traveller
See Curtis, George William

[A] Traveller
See Lee, Sarah [Willis Bowdich]

[A] Travelling Physician
See Lefevre, [Sir] George William

Travers, Bob
See Jones, Charley

Travers, Georgia
See Scott, Alma Olivia

Travers, Virginia
See Coigney, Virginia

Travies
See Travies De Villers,
Charles-Joseph

Travies De Villers, Charles-Joseph
1804-1859 [WEC]
French cartoonist
* Travies

Trebelli, Zelia
See Gilbert, Zelia

Trebor
See Emmet, Robert

Trebor, Snivig C.
See Givins, Robert Cartwright

Trefoil
See Millen, F. F.

[The] Trembler
See Garcia

Trench, Francis 1805-1886 [NPS]
Clergyman and author
* Oxoniensis

Tretane
See Curgenoen, John Brendon

Trevelyan, [Sir] George Otto
1838-1928 [DEA]
British author
* Broughton, H., B.C.S.

Trevert, Edward
See Bubier, Edward Trevert

Trevor, Ross E.
See Crilly, Daniel

[La] Trianita
See MacLean, Sallie

Triboulet
See Hotman, Francis

Trifle
See Tilton, Warren

Trifolium
See McCarthy, Denis Florence

Trimball, W. H.
See Mencken, Henry Louis

Trimble, William Copeland 1851- ?
[PI]
Irish poet and journalist
* Sulky

[A] Trinity Man
See Wright, Thomas

Tripe, [Dr.] Andrew
See Wagstaffe, William

Triscott, Edith Browning
See Allinson-James, Mrs.

[The] Triumphant Exciseman
See Walpole, [Sir] Robert [First
Earl of Orford]

Trobullfeld, Doctor
See Turberville, James

Trognon, A.
See Joinville, Francois Ferdinand
Philippe Louis Marie d'Orleans

Trollope, Frances 1780-1863
[DEA]
British author
* F. T.

[A] Trooper
See Adams, Francis Colburn

Trost, Sven
See Snoilsky, Carl Johan Gustav

Trott, John
See St. John, Henry

Trott-Plaid, John, Esq.
See Fielding, Henry

Trovato, Ben
See Lover, Samuel

Trowell, Adjutant
See Dawes, Thomas

Trudeau, Pierre Elliott 1919- [CR]
Canadian prime minister
* P. E. T.

[The] True Blue Protestant Poet
See Shadwell, Thomas

[A] True Celt
See Davis, Thomas Osborne

[The] True Diana
See Elizabeth I

[The] True English Aretine
See Nash [or Nashe?], Thomas

True, Hiram L. 1845-1912 [DNA]
American author and physician
* Allen, Don

[The] True Laureate of England
See Dibdin, Charles

**[A] True Son of the Church of
England**
See Asplin, William

Trueman, Fiery Fred
See Trueman, Fred

Trueman, Fred [NN]
British cricketer
* Trueman, Fiery Fred

Truinet, Charles Louis Etienne
1828-1899 [BBD]
French author and librettist
* Nuitter, Charles Louis Etienne

Trumbull, Annie Eliot 1857-1949
[DNA]
American author, poet, playwright
* Eliot, Annie

Trumpeter of Pitt
See Cobbett, William

[The] Trunk Murderer
See Judd, Winnie Ruth

Trusta, H.
See Phelps, Elizabeth [Stuart]

Truthful James
See Hennessy, William Charles

Tryon, Thomas 1634-1703 [NPS]
Author and philosopher
* [The] Pythagorean

Tsukioka, Yoshitoshi 1839-1892
[WECO]
Japanese artist
* Taiso [Great Revival]

Tuathal, Cairn
See Davis, Eugene

Tuck, Friar
See Tucker, Irwin St. John

Tucker, Eleonora C. 1850- ? [PI]
Canadian-born poet
* Deane, D. C.
* E. C. M.
* L. M.

Tucker, George 1775-1861
[DLE1, DNA, WGT]
*American author and political
economist*
* Atterley, Joseph

Tucker, Irwin St. John 1886-1982
[CA]
*American clergyman, journalist,
poet*
* Tuck, Friar

Tugmutton, Timothy, Esq.
See Chorley, Charles

Tullius Anglorum
See Lyly, John

Tully, Mrs. Richard Walton
Author
* Gates, Eleanor

Tulsa Jack Blake
See Blake, Jack

Tum-Tum
See Edward VII

Tumulti, Thomas ?-1872? [PI]
Irish poet
* T. T.

Turberville, James ?-1570? [NPS]
Bishop of Exeter
* Trobullfeld, Doctor

Turco, Lewis 1934- [MA]
American author
* Court, Wesli

[The] Turk
See Gonzaga, Ludovico di III

Turkey Creek Johnson
See Johnson, Jack

Turlough
See Hughes, Terence McMahon

Turmair [or Thurmayr], Johannes
1477-1534
Bavarian historian
* [The] Bavarian Herodotus
(See also base volume)

**Turnbull, William Barclay David
Donald** 1811-1863 [HFN, IP]
Scottish antiquary
* [A] Delver into Antiquity
* W. B. D. D. T.

Turner, Alexander Freke
See Crawfurd, Oswald John
Frederick

Turner, C. F.
See Turner, Fred

Turner, C. T. B. [NN]
Australian cricketer
* [The] Terror

Turner, Cora
See Mackamotzki, Kunigunde

Turner, Daniel 1710-1798 [IP]
British author and clergyman
* [An] Impartial Hand

Turner, Dona M. 1951- [CA]
American author
* Thisby [joint pseudonym with
Vince Genovese]

Turner, Ethel
See Curlewis, Ethel S. [Turner]

Turner, Fred 1943- [CMA]
Musician
* Turner, C. F.

Turner, George [IP]
British author
* Philalethes

Turner, J. Fox 19th c. [IP]
British author
* Layne, Pyngle

Turner, James [IP]
British author
* Aristobulus

Turner, Joseph Mallord William
1775-1851 [NPS]
British painter
* [The] Blackbirdy

Turner, Samuel 1759-1801 [IP]
British diplomat and author
* [The] Ambassador

Turner, Sharon 1768-1847 [IP]
British historian and author
* [A] Layman

Turner, William Mason 1835-1877
American author, poet, physician
* Wylder, Lennox

Turnhout, Gerard de
See Turnhout, Gheert Jacques

Turnhout, Gheert Jacques
1520?-1580 [BBD]
Dutch composer
* Turnhout, Gerard de

Turnkey
See Lowe, [Sir] Hudson

Turpin, Richard [Dick] 1705-1739
[DI]
British robber
* Palmer, John
(See also base volume)

Turton, [Sir] Thomas 1764-1844
[IP]
British army officer and author
* [A] Country Gentleman

Turton, Thomas 1780-1864 [IP]
British prelate and author
* Clemens Anglicanus
* Philalethes Cantabrigiensis
(See also base volume)

[The] Tuscan Imp of Fame
See Petracco, Francesco

Tutankhamun [NAD]
Egyptian pharoah
* King Tut

Tuthall, William H. 1808-1880 [IP]
American attorney and author
* Anti Quary

**[A] Tutor and Fellow of a College in
Oxford**
See Bentham, Edward

Tuttle, Charles Richard 1848- ?
[DNA]
Author and historian
* Clarke, Jean

Tuttle, George 1804-1872 [DNA]
Author
* Teller, Thomas

Tuttle, Joseph Farrand [IP]
American clergyman and educator
* J. F. T.

Tuvar, Lorenzo
See Armistead, Wilson

Tweed, Boss
See Tweed, William Marcy

Tweed, William Marcy 1823-1878
[CEC]
American politician
* Tweed, Boss

Tweedsmuir, Baron
See Buchan, John

Twelveponies, Mary
See Cleveland, Mary

Twig, Timothy, Esq.
See Moser, Joseph

Twining, Louisa [IP]
British author
* L. T.

Twining, Thomas 1734-1804 [IP]
British clergyman
* Philalethes
(See also base volume)

Twiss, Horace 1787-1849
[IP, NPS]
British barrister, author, politician
* Horatius

Twiss, Richard 1747-1821 [IP]
Author
* [An] Irish Traveller

Twiss, [Sir] Travers 1819- ? [IP]
British barrister and author
* Corvinus

Twist-Wit, Christopher, Esq.
See Anstey, Christopher

Twitchell, Paul 20th c. [EOP]
American religious cult leader
* Peddar Zaskq

Twm Shon Catti
See Jones, Thomas

Two Brothers [joint pseudonym with
Julius Charles Hare]
See Hare, Augustus William

Two Brothers [joint pseudonym with
Augustus William Hare]
See Hare, Julius Charles

Two Brothers [joint pseudonym with
Charles Tennyson]
See Tennyson, Alfred [First Baron
Tennyson]

Two Brothers [joint pseudonym with
Alfred Tennyson]
See Tennyson, Charles

202
See Christian, Will

[The] Two Sisters [joint pseudonym
with Sarah G. Walcott]
See Walcott, Eliza

[The] Two Sisters [joint pseudonym
with Eliza Walcott]
See Walcott, Sarah G.

Two Sisters of the West [joint
pseudonym with Catharine Ann
(Ware) Warfield]
See Ware, Eleanor

Two Sisters of the West [joint
pseudonym with Eleanor Ware]
See Warfield, Catharine Ann
[Ware]

Twort, Charles William [IP]
British author
* [A] Protestant

Tyas, Robert 19th c. [IP]
British clergyman and author
* R. T.

Tyers, Thomas 1726-1787 [IP]
British author
* Restless, Tim

[A] Tyke
See Robb, John S.

Tyler, Bennet 1783-1858 [IP]
American theologian and author
* [A] New England Minister

Tyler, John [IP]
American author
* Python

Tyler, Royall 1757-1826 [IP]
American jurist and author
* Colon and Spondee
* S.
* Trash
* Underhill, [Dr.] Updike

Tyndale, William 1484?-1536
[DEA]
British author
* W. T.

Typist, Topsy
See Miner, Enoch Newton

[The] Tyrant of Words and Syllables
See Malherbe, Francois de

Tyrwhitt, Richard [IP]
British clergyman and author
* [A] Clergyman

Tyson, Edwin Lloyd 20th c.
*American radio and television
broadcaster*
* Tyson, Ty

Tyson, John S. [IP]
American author
* [A] Citizen of Baltimore

Tyson, Ty
See Tyson, Edwin Lloyd

Tyssot de Patot, Simon
1655-1728? [SFL, WGT]
Author
* Bayle, Monsieur
* De Mesange, [Reverend] Pierre
Cordelier Pierre
* Masse, James
* Massens, Jakob
* Massey, James

Tytler, C. C. Fraser
See Liddle, Christina Catherine
Fraser Tytler

U

[A] U. S. Detective
See Ellis, Edward S[ylvester]

U. U. P.
See Plunket, William Conyngham

Udall, John 1560?-1592   [NPS]
Puritan pamphleteer
* Marprelate, Martin

Ulloa, Jose 17th c.   [GS]
Spanish bullfighter
* Tragabuches [Tremendous
  Swallower]

Ulmar, Genevieve
See Cobb, Weldon J.

Ulmer, Blood
See Ulmer, James

Ulmer, James 1942-
American musician
* Ulmer, Blood
* Ulmer, Youngblood

Ulmer, Youngblood
See Ulmer, James

[An] Ulsterman
See Sigerson, George

[The] Ultimate Shrink
See Strasberg, Lee

Ultimus Romanorum
See Fox, Charles James

Ultimus Romanorum
See Gabrini, Niccolo

Ultimus Romanorum
See Pope, Alexander

Ulyett, George 1851-1898   [EC]
British cricketer
* Ulyett, Happy Jack

Ulyett, Happy Jack
See Ulyett, George

Umber, George
See Findley, W.

Umscheid, Christina Marie 1946-
[MA]
German-born poet
* Christina-Marie

Uncle Ben
See White, Rhoda E. [Waterman]

Uncle Dudley
See Russell, Morris Craw

Uncle George
See Tarbox, Increase Niles

Uncle Gus
See Reyersbach, Hans Augusto

Uncle Harry
See Habberton, John

Uncle Ho
See Nguyen That Thanh

Uncle Jesse
See Babb, Clement Edwin

Uncle John
See Aikin, John

Uncle Remus
See Kavanagh, Rose

Uncle Remus
See Sigerson, Hester

Uncle Toby
See North, Elisha

Uncle Tom No. 2
See Randolph, Asa Philip

Uncle Tom's Nephew
See Driver, Thomas

Underdown, Emily 20th c.   [NPS]
Author
* Chester, Norley

[An] Undergraduate
See Horne, George

[An] Undergraduate
See Penn, William

[An] Undergraduate
See Polwhele, Richard

Underhill, [Dr.] Updike
See Tyler, Royall

Underwood, Mrs. S. K.
Author
* Kerr, Sophie

Uniacke, Mary 19th c.   [PI]
Irish poet
* M. U.

[A] Unitarian Minister
See Aldred, Ebenezer

[The] Universal Butt of all Mankind
See Hill, [Sir] John

[An] University Man
See Carrington, George

[An] Unknown Friend
See Garden, George

Uno
See Baker, George Melville

[The] Untamed Heifer
See Elizabeth I

[An] Untrammeled Free-Thinker
See Moore, M. Louise

[An] Unworthy Member of that
Community
See Rutty, John

Updike, John 1932-   [CR]
American author
* [The] Andrew Wyeth of
  Literature

Upham, Grace Le Baron [Locke]
1845-1916   [DNA]
American author
* Le Baron, Grace

[An] Upper Servant
See Jones, John

Urania
See Sidney, Mary

Urban, Septimus R.
See Rymer, James Malcolm

Urban, Sylvanus
See Bullen, A. H.

Urbino, Levina [Buoncuore] 19th c.
[DNA]
Author and educator
* Boncoeur, L.
* Cuore, L. B.

Urbs Marmoris
See Campion, John Thomas

Urie, Mary Le Baron [Andrews]
1842-1894   [DNA]
Author
* Le Baron, Marie

Urner, Nathan D. 19th c.
[DNA, WGT]
Author
* Looker, O. N.
* Mentor
(See also base volume)

Utopiensis, Bernardus
See Rutty, John

Uyeshiba, Morihei   [BBH]
Athlete
* [The] Father of Aikido

V

Vacuus
See Davis, Thomas Osborne

Vacuus
See Mangan, James Clarence

[The] Vagabond Scot
See Smollett, Tobias George

Vagrant
See Lehmann, Rudolf Chambers

Vairasse, Denis 1630-1700 [WGT]
Author
* Siden, Captain

Valente, Giorgio
See Vitalis, George

Valentine, Jane
See Meeker, Nellie J.

Valery, Henry
See Petiot, Marcel

Valmy, Alfred de
See Stinde, Julius

Valverde y San Juan, Joaquin
1875-1918 [BBD]
Spanish-born composer
* Quinito

Vamp, Hugo
See O'Neill, John Robert

Van Aeken [or Van Aken],
Hieronymus 1450?-1516 [NPS]
Dutch painter
* [The] Joyous
(See also base volume)

Van Arkel, Garret
See Buffett, Edward Payson

Van Buren, Martin 1782-1862
[NPS]
American president
* [The] Northern Man with
 Southern Principles
(See also base volume)

Van der Vondel, Joost 1587-1679
[NPS]
Dutch playwright and poet
* [The] Dutch Shakespeare

Van Deusen, Alonzo 19th c. [SFL]
Author
* [A] Capitalist

Van Deyssel
See Thym, K. J. A. Alberdingk

Van Engelyom
See Lecomte, Jules

Van Galder, Thomas 20th c. [EF]
American football player
* Van Galder, Tim

Van Galder, Tim
See Van Galder, Thomas

Van Orden, William H. 19th c.
[DNA]
Author
* James, Police Captain

Van Rensselaer, Stephen
1765-1839 [NPS]
* [The] Patroon

Van Rensselar, Frederick 19th c.
[WGT]
Author
* Dey, Marmaduke

Van See, John
See Vance, John Holbrook [Jack]

Van Slingerland, Nellie Bingham
1850- ? [DNA]
American author and playwright
* Bevans, Neile

Van Sloetten, Henry Cornelius
See Neville, Henry

Van Stockum, Hilda 1908- [CA]
Dutch-born author, translator,
illustrator
* Marlin, Hilda

Van Truesdale, Pheleg
See Adams, Francis Colburn

Van Voorthuizen [or Voorthuyzen],
Louwrens 1898-1968 [EOP]
Dutch religious leader
* Lou

Vance, John Holbrook [Jack]
1916?- [TCCM]
American author
* Held, Peter
* Queen, Ellery
* Van See, John
(See also base volume)

Vandalio
See Cetina, Gutierre de

Vander Neck, J.
See Burgh, James

Vanderveen, Bareld Harmannus
1932- [CA]
Dutch author and editor
* Vanderveen, Bart H.

Vanderveen, Bart H.
See Vanderveen, Bareld
Harmannus

Vandyck in Little
See Cooper, Samuel

Vane, Derek
See Eaton-Back, Mrs. B.

Vane, [Sir] Henry [Harry]
1612-1662 [NPS]
British statesman
* Heron, Brother

Vanessa
See Vanhomrigh, Esther

Vanguard
See Wood, Thomas Winter

Vanhomrigh, Esther 1690-1723
[NPS, UH]
Friend of British author, Jonathan
Swift
* Vanessa

Varas, Florencia
See Olea, Maria Florencia Varas

Vardys, V[ytautas] Stanley
See Zvirzdys, Vytautas

Varenne, Alberic
See Laurent-Cely, Jacques

Varian, Elizabeth Willoughby 1830?-
? [PI]
Irish poet
* Finola

Varian, Ralph 1820?-1886 [PI]
Irish poet
* Duncathail
* Fionbarr
* Mor, McCarthaigh
* R. V., Cork

Varma, Mahest Prasod 1918-
Indian leader of religious sect
* Yogi, Maharishi Mahesh

Varney
See Wainewright, Thomas
Griffiths

Varnum, Joseph Bradley
1818-1874 [DNA]
American author and attorney
* Viator

Vasey, George 19th c. [HFN]
Author and engraver
* [A] Beef Eater

Vathek
See Beckford, William

Vaughan, Henry
See Pelzer, Leon

Vaughan, Thomas 1622-1666
[DLE1, NPS]
British poet and alchemist
* Anthroposophus
* Philalethes, Eugenius

Vaughan, Thomas 18th c. [NPS]
Playwright
* [The] Dapper

Vaughn, Toni
See DuBreuil, Elizabeth Lorinda

Vazquez, Jose 19th c. [GS]
Spanish bullfighter
* Parreta

Vecchi, Augustus Victor 1843- ?
[NPS]
Italian author
* Bolina, Jack la
* [The] Italian Marryat

Vedastus
See Webb, Foster

Vegetable, Dr.
See Ishizuka, Sagen

[The] Veiled Murderess
See Robinson, Henrietta

Velasquez, Loretta Janeta 1842- ?
[BDSA]
Cuban-born American heroine
* Buford, Harry T.

Vely, Emma
See Simon, Emma [Couvely]

Venables, Terry 20th c. [TCCM]
British author
* Yuill, P. B. [joint pseudonym with
 Gordon (Maclean) Williams]

Venerabilis, Doctor
See William of Champeaux

Vera
See Campbell, Lady Colin

Vera
See Dempster, C. L. H.

Verax
See Alexander, Samuel

Verax
See Blakey, Robert

Verax
See Forster, Thomas

Verdad
See Millen, F. F.

Verdon, T. K.
See Verdon, Thomas Kirwan

Verdon, Thomas Kirwan 19th c.
[PI]
Irish poet
* De Verdon, T. K.
* Verdon, T. K.

Verelart, Myndart
See Saltus, Edgar Evertson

Verena, Sophie
See Alberti, Sophie [Moedinger]

Verey, [Rev.] C.
See Crowley, Edward Alexander

Verga, Giovanni 1840-1922   [CA]
Italian author and playwright
* [The] Father of the Modern
  Realist Novel

Vergilius Maro, Publius 1st c. BC
[NPS]
Roman poet
* [The] Great Shepherd of the
  Mantuan Plains
(See also base volume)

Veritas
See Close, John

Verlaine, Paul [Marie] 1844-1896
[NLC]
French poet and author
* De Herlagnez, Pablo

Vernard, George
See Musica, Arthur

Verne, Jules
See Olchewitz, M.

Vernet, Antoine Charles Horace
1758-1836   [WEC]
French caricaturist and painter
* Vernet, Carle

Vernet, Carle
See Vernet, Antoine Charles
Horace

Vernon, Lee M.
See Von Block, Bela

Vernon, Ruth
See Ram, Stopford James

Verus
See Webb, Francis

Vestris, Eliza Lucy 1797-1856
[NPS]
Actress
* [The] Tenth Muse

Viator
See Hickey, Michael Patrick

Viator
See Smith, Nathan Ryno

Viator
See Varnum, Joseph Bradley

Vicar of Cudham
See Ayscough, Samuel

[The] Vicar of Frome-Selwood
See Bennett, William James

Vicarius Cantianus
See Pegge, Samuel

Vickers, Antoinette L. 1942-   [CA]
American author and attorney
* Franchi, Eda
* Nina V.

Vickers, John 19th c.   [WGT]
Author
* Morata, Jaido

Vickybird
See Neuburg, Victor [Benjamin]

[A] Victim
See Benham, George Chittenden

Victor, Metta Victoria Fuller
1831-1886
American author and poet
* Cushman, Corinne
* Edwards, Eleanor Lee
* Gray, Walter T.
* Kennedy, Rose
* Legrand, Louis, M.D.? [joint
  pseudonym with Orville J. Victor]
* Peabody, Mrs. Mark
(See also base volume)

Victor, Orville J. 1827-1910
American author, historian, editor
* Legrand, Louis, M.D.? [joint
  pseudonym with Metta Victoria
  Fuller Victor]

Victor, Sam
See Hershman, Morris

Victor, Verity
See Wright, E. M.

Victoria 1819-1901   [NPS]
Queen of England
* [The] Mother of Her Country
(See also base volume)

Video
See Couch, Jonathan

[Le] Vieux
See Aubert, Jacques

Vieux Moustache
See Gordon, Clarence

Vig
See McCarthy, Denis Florence

Vigilans sed Aequus
See Arnold, William Thomas

Vigilant
See Dixon, Sydenham

Vigliante, Mary
See Szydlowski, Mary Vigliante

Vigors, N. A., Jun.
See Nolan, Frederick

Viksnins, George J[uris] 1937-   [CA]
*Latvian-born American economist
and author*
* Kennecott, G. J.

[A] Village Curate
See Glenn, William

Villehardouin, Geoffrey de
1150?-1218?   [NPS]
French diplomat and historian
* [The] Xenophon of His Own
  History

Villeneuve 18th c.   [WGT]
Author
* De Listonai, Mr.

Villon, Francois 1431?-1484   [NPS]
French poet
* Loges, Francois de
* Montcorbier, Francois de
* Mouton, Michel

Vincam, Frater Omnia
See Neuburg, Victor [Benjamin]

Vincent, William
See Holcroft, Thomas

Vindex
See Adams, Samuel

Vindex
See Butler, John

Vindex
See Gordon, John M.

Vindex
See Loveday, John

Vindex
See Sabine, Lorenzo

Vinegar, [Capt.] Hercules
See Fielding, Henry

Vinkbooms
See Wainewright, Thomas
Griffiths

Violette
See Garrick, Marion Eva

Virey, Leopold
See Grousset, Paschal

**[The] Virgil of American Musical
History**
See Thomson, Virgil

[The] Virginia Antiquary
See Bland, Richard

[A] Virginia Physician
See Ruter, P. S.

[A] Virginian
See Carruthers, William A.

[A] Virginian Presbyter
See Bourne, George

Vis
See Scully, Vincent

[The] Visionary
See Scott, [Sir] Walter

Vitalis, George 1895-   [BBD]
Greek composer and conductor
* Valente, Giorgio

Vitelleschi, Marchese   [NPS]
Author
* Leto, Pomponio

Vivaria, Kassandra
See Sindici, [Maria] Magda Stuart

Vivekananda, Swami
See Dutt, Narendra Nath

Vivienne
See Entwistle, Florence Vivienne

Vizetelly, Edmund   [NPS]
Author
* Clare, Bertie

Vlad V 15th c.   [DI]
Hungarian ruler
* [The] Impaler

Vliet, Don Van 1941-   [CMA]
American singer and songwriter
* [The] Spotlight Kid
(See also base volume)

Voces Catholicae
See Dillon, Emile Joseph

[The] Voice
See Orbison, Roy

[A] Voice from Kentucky
See Coleman, William

[The] Voice of the South
See Blackmar, Armand Edward

[The] Voiceless Sinatra
See Johnson, Van

[La] Voisin
See Deshayes, Catherine

Voiture, Vincent 1597-1648   [NPS]
French courtier, poet, author
* [The] Solon of French Prose
(See also base volume)

Volpi, Odoardo
See Shannon, Edward N.

[Le] Voltaire de Son Siecle
See Aretino, Pietro

Von Adelheid, Auer
See Cosel, Charlotte von

Von Baudissin, Count   [NPS]
Author
* Von Schlicht, Baron

Von Block, Bela 1922-   [CA]
American author
* Black, Jonathan
* Endfield, Mercedes
* Hennessey, Caroline [joint
  pseudonym with Sylvia Von
  Block]
* La Barr, Creighton
* Lucchesi, Aldo
* Meurice, Blanca
* Padgett, Desmond
* Randolph, Gordon [joint
  pseudonym with Sylvia Von
  Block]
* Shomroni, Reuven
* Sprague, W. D. [joint pseudonym
  with Sylvia Von Block]
* Vernon, Lee M.
(See also base volume)

Von Block, Sylvia 1931-   [CA]
American author
* Hennessey, Caroline [joint
  pseudonym with Bela Von Block]
* Randolph, Gordon [joint
  pseudonym with Bela Von Block]
* Sprague, W. D. [joint pseudonym
  with Bela Von Block]
(See also base volume)

Von Bluggen, Vander
See Knight, Charles

Von Degen
See Rabe, Ann C[rawford] Von

Von Faramond, Ludwig Ernst
See Sinhold Von Schutz, Philipp
Balthasar

**Von Furstenberg-Hedringen,
Elizabeth Caroline Maria Agatha
Felicitas** 1931?-   [CR]
German-born actress
* Madcap Betsy
(See also base volume)

Von Schlicht, Baron
See Von Baudissin, Count

Von Wahrenberg, Constantino
See Sinhold Von Schutz, Philipp
Balthasar

Vorse, Mary Heaton
See O' Brien, Mrs. Joseph

Vose, Reuben 19th c.   [WGT]
Author
* Invisible Sam

[A] Voyager
See Scoresby, William

Vreeland, Frank 1891-1946   [DNA]
Playwright
* Thorpe, William

Vulpius, Melchior
See   Fuchs, Melchior

W

W.
See Furlong, Thomas

W.
See Roddy, William

W.
See Waters, John Charles

W.
See Whitty, Michael James

W.
See Wrangham, Francis

W. A.
See Allen, William

W. A. B.
See Butler, William Archer

W. A. C.
See Chatto, William Andrew

W. A. D.
See Davis, William Augustus

W. A. D.
See Drummond, William Abernethy

W. A. D.
See Dwiggins, W. A.

W. B.
See Ball, William

W. B.
See Barton, William

W. B.
See Bennett, William

W. B.
See Besant, [Sir] Walter

W. B.
See Blades, William

W. B.
See Blake, William

W. B.
See Bromfield, William

W. B. A.
See Anthony, W. B.

W. B. B.
See Buchanan, W. B.

W. B. D. D. T.
See Turnbull, William Barclay David Donald

W. B. L.
See Lord, W. B.

W. B. M.
See McCabe, William Bernard

W. C.
See Carleton, William

W. C. C.
See Cotton, William Charles

W. C., Jun.
See Carleton, William, Jr.

W. C., Rev.
See Cole, William

W. C., Sir
See Savile, [Sir] George [Marquis of Halifax]

W. D.
See Darley, William

W. D.
See Drysdale, William

W. D.
See Duane, William

W. D. S.
See Sadleir, William Digby

W. E. A.
See Aytoun, William Edmonstoune

W. E. A. A.
See Axon, William Edward Armitage

W. E. H.
See Heygate, William Edward

W. F. T.
See Taylor, William Frederick

W. G.
See Gardner, William

W. G.
See Gauntley, William

W. G.
See Grace, William Gilbert

W. G. A.
See Allen, G. W.

W. G. L.
See Mencken, Henry Louis

W. H.
See Hennessy, William Charles

W. H.
See Higgins, William

W. H. D. A.
See Adams, William Henry Davenport

W. H. J. W.
See Weale, William Henry James

W. H. L.
See Leeds, William Henry

W. H. R.
See Royston, William Haylett

W. H. W.
See Watts, Walter Henry

W. I.
See Iago, William

W. J.
See Johnson, William

W. J. B.
See Butler, William John

W. J. D. R.
See Ryder, W. J. D.

W. J. E. B.
See Bennett, William James

W. K.
See Kertland, William

W. K.
See Marston, John

W. L.
See Russell, Matthew

W. L. D.
See Dickinson, W. L.

W. M.
See Jones, Walter

W. M.
See Mackenzie, William

W. M., A Beneficed Priest
See Maskell, William

W. M. R.
See Russell, W. M.

W. N.
See Nind, William

W. N. S.
See Skelly, William Nugent

W. O. S.
See Stillman, W. O.

W. O'B.
See O'Brien, William Smith

W. P.
See Dickens, Charles

W. P. C.
See Carey, William Paulet

W. P. C-y
See Carey, William Paulet

W. P. M.
See Mulchinock, William Pembroke

W. P. O.
See Walsh, William Pakenham

W. S.
See Stokes, Whitley

W. S., M. P.
See Stewart, William

W. T.
See Thornton, William

W. T.
See Tyndale, William

W. T. M.
See Meyler, Walter Thomas

W. T., Sir
See Temple, [Sir] William

W. W. W.
See Waldron, William Watson

Wa-sha-quon-asin
See Belaney, Archibald Stansfeld

Wace, W. E.
See Nicoll, [Sir] William Robertson

Waddington, Samuel Ferrand [IP]
British physician and author
* Sidney, Algernon

Wade, John 19th c. [IP]
British barrister and author
* [The] Original Editor
(See also base volume)

Waechter, Georg P. L. L.
1762-1837 [NPS]
German author
* Weber, Veit

Wagenknecht, Edward [Charles]
1900- [CA]
American author and editor
* Forrest, Julian

[The] Waggish Welsh Judge
See Hardinge, George

Wagner, Cosima 1837-1930
Wife of German composer, Richard Wagner
* [The] Delphic Oracle

Wagstaff, Simon
See Swift, Jonathan

Wagstaffe, Jeffrey
See   Burroughs, Lewis

Wagstaffe, John, Esq., of Wilbye Grange
See   Mackay, Charles

Wagstaffe, William 1685-1725 [IP]
British physician and author
* Crispin
* Tripe, [Dr.] Andrew

Wahab, Charles James 19th c.   [IP]
British author
* One Who Knows

Wainewright, Jeremiah 18th c.   [IP]
British physician and author
* [A] Member of the College of Physicians

Wainewright, Thomas Griffiths 1794-1852 [IP, NPS]
British art critic and forger
* [The] Poisoner
* Varney
* Vinkbooms
(See also base volume)

Wainwright, John 1921-   [TCCM]
British author
* Ripley, Jack

Wainwright, Latham ?-1833 [IP]
British clergyman and author
* F. S. A.

Wainwright, Reader   [IP]
British barrister and author
* Another Barrister

Wait [or Waite], Dash
See   Wait, Frederick T.

Wait, Frederick T. 1853-1895 [EWG]
American gunfighter
* Wait [or Waite], Dash

Waite, Ada Lakeman 19th c.   [EOP]
Wife of British scholar, Arthur Edward Waite
* Lucasta

Wake, William 1657-1736?   [IP]
British clergyman and author
* [A] Country Clergyman

Wakefield, Edward Gibbon 1796-1862 [IP]
British author
* [A] Member

Wakefield, Priscilla [Bell] 1750-1832 [IP]
British author
* [A] Gentleman
* Priscilla

Wakefield, Thomas 1752-1806 [IP]
British clergyman and author
* Philanthropos

Wakeley, Mr. ?-1853 [EOP]
Astrologer and author
* Raphael, Edwin
* Raphael IV

Wakeman, Annie
See   Lathrop, Annie Wakeman

Wakuman
See   Wirgman, Charles

Walcott, Eliza   [IP]
American poet
* [The] Two Sisters [joint pseudonym with Sarah G. Walcott]

Walcott, Josephine 19th c.   [IP]
American author
* Havens, Cordelia

Walcott, Mackenzie Edward Clarke 1822- ?   [IP]
British clergyman and poet
* M. E. C. W.

Walcott, Sarah G.   [IP]
American poet
* [The] Two Sisters [joint pseudonym with Eliza Walcott]

Waldie, Charlotte Anne 1788-1859 [HFN, IP]
Scottish author
* [An] Englishwoman

Waldie, Walter S. 19th c.   [IP]
American author
* Retlaw

Waldo, Leonard 1853- ?   [IP]
American astronomer and author
* L. W.

Waldo, Peter   [IP]
British author
* [A] Layman

Waldrip
See   Brock, Leonard

Waldron, Francis Godolphin 18th c.   [IP]
British actor, editor, playwright
* F. G. W.

Waldron, William Watson 19th c. [PI]
Irish poet
* W. W. W.

Walford, Thomas   [IP]
Author
* [An] Irish Gentleman

Walker, Darrell 20th c.
American basketball player
* Walker, Sky

Walker, George 20th c.   [EF]
American football player
* Walker, Mickey

[The] Walker in the Pines
See   Sibley, Henry Hastings

Walker, Irma Ruth [Roden] 1921- [CA]
American author
* Harris, Andrea
(See also base volume)

Walker, Max
See   Avallone, Michael [Angelo], Jr.

Walker, Mickey
See   Walker, George

Walker, Patricius
See   Allingham, William

Walker, Richard 1791-1870 [WGT]
Author
* [A] Sub-Utopian?

Walker, Sky
See   Walker, Darrell

Walker, William 19th c.   [NPS]
Australian author
* Cringle, Tom

[A] Walking Library
See   Selden, John

[The] Walking Mount Rushmore
See   Sullivan, Ed

[The] Walking Parson
See   Cooper, A. N.

Wallace, George Corley 1919- [CR]
American politician
* [The] Fighting Little Judge

Wallace, Irving
See   Wallechinsky, Irving

Wallace, Ruby Ann 1924-   [CR]
American actress
* [The] Negro June Allyson
(See also base volume)

Wallace, Walter 1875-1932   [EMD]
British author
* [The] King of Thrillers
(See also base volume)

Wallack, James William 1795-1864 [FAA]
British-born actor
* [The] Elder Wallack

Wallechinsky, Irving 1916-   [BP]
American author
* Wallace, Irving

Waller, Edmund 1606-1687 [DEA, NPS]
British poet
* E. W.
* [The] Inimitable
* Nature's Darling
(See also base volume)

Wallis, A. S. C.
See   Opzoomer, Adele Sophia Cornelia van Antal

Wallis, Jenny
See   Morrison, Mary Jane [Whitney]

Walpole, Horatio [Fourth Earl of Orford] 1717-1797 [NPS, WGT]
British politician and author
* [The] Autocrat of Strawberry Hill
* [The] Frenchified Coxcomb
* H. W.
* Lying Old Fox
* Muralto, Onuphrio
* [The] Puck of Literature
* S. T.
(See also base volume)

Walpole, [Sir] Robert [First Earl of Orford] 1676-1745   [NPS]
British statesman
* Bluestring, Robin
* [The] Triumphant Exciseman
(See also base volume)

Walraven, E. G.
See   Jones, Emma Garrison

Walsh, Albert Edward 1887-1980 [FIR]
American director
* Walsh, Raoul

Walsh, John 1835-1881 [PI]
Irish poet
* Boz
* [A] Cappoquin Girl
* J. J. W.
* J. W.

Walsh, John (Continued)
* Kilmartin
* Lismore
* Shamrock

Walsh, Johnny ?-1883   [BLB]
American gangleader
* Johnny the Mick

Walsh, Michael Paul 1866-1892 [PI]
Irish poet
* [A] Base Mechanic Wretch
* Buzz
* [A] Cashel Girl
* Gray, Louisa
* Philomath
* Phiz
* Pilate, Pontius

Walsh, Raoul
See   Walsh, Albert Edward

Walsh, William Pakenham 1820-1902   [PI]
Irish clergyman, author, poet
* W. P. O.

Walsingham
See   McEwen, William Dalzell

Walsingham, [Sir] Francis
See   Arnall, William

Walter, Frederick
See   Schultz, Frederick Walter

Walter [or Walther], Johann
See   Blanckenmueller, Johann

Walter of Swinbroke
See   Baker, Geoffrey

[The] Walter Scott of Italy
See   Ariosto, Lodovico

Walters, Barbara 1931-   [BP]
American newscaster
* Elliott, Babs

Walters, Catherine 19th c.   [NN]
British courtesan
* Skittles

Walton, John 20th c.   [DLE1]
Playwright
* Conway, Olive [joint pseudonym with Harold Brighouse]

[The] Waltz King
See   Strauss, Johann, Jr.

Walworth, Jeannette R. 19th c.   [IP]
American author
* Atom, Ann

Wanderer
See   D'Avigdor, Elim Henry

[The] Wanderer
See   Lord, John Keast

[A] Wanderer
See   Peirce, I.

[A] Wanderer
See   Ryan, William Thomas

[The] Wanderer
See   Watterston, George

[The] Wandering Minstrel
See   Wilson, Frederick

Wantland, Hal
See   Wantland, Howell

Wantland, Howell 20th c.   [EF]
American football player
* Wantland, Hal

Warborough, Martin Leach
See Allen, [Charles] Grant
[Blairfindie]

Warburton, William 1698-1779
[NPS]
British prelate
* [The] Great Preserver of Pope and
Shakespeare
* [A] Literary Revolutionist
* [The] Modern Stagirite
* [The] Poet's Parasite
(See also base volume)

Ward, Barbara
See Jackson, Barbara [Ward]

Ward, C. A. 19th c. [PI]
Irish poet
* Burghley, Feltham

Ward, E. D.
See Lucas, Edward Verrall

Ward, Edward 1660?-1731 [DEA]
British author and satirist
* E. W.

Ward, Frederick 1836-1870 [DI]
Australian bushranger
* Thunderbolt, Captain

Ward, H. O.
See Bloomfield-Moore, Clara
Sophia [Jessup]

Ward, Henry Dana 1797-1884
[DNA]
American author and clergyman
* Harvard, Senior

Ward, Jem 1800-1884 [RBE]
British boxer
* [The] Black Diamond

Ward, John
See Peace, Charles

Ward, Martha Craft 1942- [CA]
American attorney and author
* Blue, Martha Ward

Ward, Patrick J. 19th c. [PI]
Irish poet
* Doire

**Ward-Thomas, Evelyn Bridget
Patricia Stephens** 1928- [CA]
British author
* Stephens, Eve
(See also base volume)

Warden, Gertrude
See Jones, Gertrude Warden

Wardrop, David 20th c.
Author
* Kroge, Suds

Ware, Eleanor 1820- ?
American author
* Two Sisters of the West [joint
pseudonym with Catharine Ann
(Ware) Warfield]

Warfield, Catharine Ann [Ware]
1816-1877
American author
* Two Sisters of the West [joint
pseudonym with Eleanor Ware]

Warhol, Andy
See Warhola, Andrew

Warhola, Andrew 1927- [BP]
American painter and filmmaker
* Drella
* Warhol, Andy

Warneford, Lieut.
See Russell, William

Warner, Hannah
See Jewett, John Howard

Warner, Helen Garnie 1846- ?
[DNA]
Author
* Harcourt, Helen

Warner, Warren
See Warren, Samuel

Warren, Frederick Albert
See Bidwell, Austin

**Warren, John Byrne Leicester [Baron
de Tabley]** 1835-1895 [DLE1, PI]
British poet
* Preston, George F.
(See also base volume)

Warren, Patience
See Kelsey, Jeannette Garr
[Washburn]

Warren, Samuel 1807-1877 [WW]
Author
* Warner, Warren

Warren, Walter
See Raymond, George Lansing

Warton, Thomas 1728-1790 [NPS]
British poet and critic
* Menander
(See also base volume)

Warung, Price
See Astley, William

Washington, Elsie 20th c.
Author and editor
* Welles, Rosalind

Washington, George 1732-1799
[BBH, UH]
American president
* Harper
* Limey Stomper
(See also base volume)

[A] Washingtonian
See Lovett, John

[The] Wasp of Twickenham
See Pope, Alexander

Wasserfall, Adel 1918- [CA]
Norwegian-born author
* Pryor, Adel

[The] Water Gruel Bard
See Shenstone, William

[The] Waterloo Hero
See Wellesley, Arthur

Waters, C.
See Russell, William

Waters, John Charles 1830-1884
[PI]
Irish poet and physician
* W.

Watkins, Tobias 1780-1855 [DNA]
American author and physician
* Particular, Pertinax

Watson, Cattle Kate
See Watson, Ella

Watson, Ella 1866-1888
[BLB, LFW]
American cattle thief
* Watson, Cattle Kate

Watson, Forbes ?-1871 [IP]
British botanist and author
* [A] Medical Man

Watson, George Bott Churchill [IP]
British physician and author
* Medicus

Watson, Henry Crocker Marriott
19th c. [WGT]
Author
* H. C. M. W.

Watson, Irving S.
See Mencken, Henry Louis

Watson, James [IP]
Scottish author
* [A] Member of the College of
Justice

Watson, Jean L. 19th c. [IP]
Scottish author
* J. L. W.

Watson, John [IP]
British author
* [A] Layman of the Church of
England

Watson, Margaret [NPS]
Author
* Rosemary

Watson, Mrs. Robert A. 20th c.
[NPS]
Author
* Cromarty, Deas

Watson, Richard 1737-1816 [IP]
British clergyman and author
* [A] Christian Whig
* [A] Consistent Protestant

Watson, William 1858- ? [NPS]
Poet
* Maitland, John Wilson

Watterston, George 19th c. [IP]
American author and librarian
* [A] Foreigner
* [The] Wanderer

Watts, Alan [Wilson] 1915-1973
[EOP]
*British-born American philosopher
and scholar*
* [The] Brain and the Buddha of
American Zen

Watts, Ephraim
See Horne, Richard Henry

Watts, Overend
See Watts, Peter

Watts, Peter 1949- [CMA]
Musician
* Watts, Overend

Watts, Phillips [IP]
British playwright and journalist
* Balfour, Felix

Watts, S. [IP]
British author
* S. W.

Watts, Walter Henry 19th c. [IP]
British journalist
* [An] Old Reporter
* W. H. W.

Wauchope, John [IP]
Scottish author
* J. W.

Waugh, John 19th c. [IP]
American clergyman and author
* Chor-Episcopus

Way, Arthur S. 19th c. [IP]
British scholar and translator
* Avia

Way, B. 18th c. [IP]
British scholar
* Musidorus

Way, Charles 20th c. [EF]
American football player
* Way, Pie

Way, Elizabeth Fenwick 1920-
[TCCM]
American author
* Fenwick, E. P.
* Fenwick, Elizabeth

Way, Lewis [IP]
British clergyman and author
* Basilicus

Way, Pie
See Way, Charles

Wayland, Heman Lincoln 1830- ?
[IP]
American clergyman and author
* Dobbs, [Rev.] Philetus

Weale, William Henry James [IP]
British publisher and author
* W. H. J. W.

Weamys, Anna 17th c. [IP]
British poet
* A. W., Mrs.
* [A] Young Gentlewoman, Mrs. A.
W.

[The] Weathercock
See Windham, William

[The] Weathercock of His Time
See Pepys, Samuel

Weatherly, Frederick Edward 19th
c. [IP]
British clergyman, poet, author
* [A] Resident M. A.

Weatherly, William
See Wilkins, William

Weaver, Buck
See Weaver, Charles

Weaver, Charles 20th c. [EF]
American football player
* Weaver, Buck

Weaver, Eddie 20th c.
American football player
* Weaver, Meat Cleaver

Weaver, James 20th c. [EF]
American football player
* Weaver, Red

Weaver, Meat Cleaver
See Weaver, Eddie

Weaver, Red
See Weaver, James

Weaver, Robert [IP]
British clergyman and author
* [A] Quadragenarian

Weaver, Thomas [IP]
Author
* Shuttle, Job

Weaver, Thomas 1616-1663 [PI]
British poet
* T. W., Gent.

Webb, Bob 20th c.
Actor and former basketball player
* Webb, Spider

Webb, Charles Hull 1843- ?   [IP]
American writer
* Manley, Jack
* Marling, Matt
(See also base volume)

Webb, F. [IP]
British author
* Philalethes

Webb, Foster 18th c.   [IP]
British poet
* Telarius
* Vedastus

Webb, Francis 1735-1815   [IP]
British author
* Verus

Webb, James Watson 1802-1884
[IP]
American politician and journalist
* [An] Amateur Traveller

Webb, John Joshua 1847-1882
[EWG]
American gunfighter
* King, Samuel

Webb, Laura S. 19th c.   [BDSA, IP]
American poet and educator
* Lee, Stannie

Webb, Lilian Julian 1877-1936
Rhodesian author
* Stockley, Cynthia

Webb, Richard Davis 19th c.   [PI]
Irish poet
* R. D. W.

Webb, Spider
See Webb, Bob

Webber, Frank
See Bushnell, William H.

Weber, Jeanne 1875-1910
[DI, LFW]
French murderer
* Bouchery, Madame
* Moulinet, Madame
* Ogre de la Goutte d'Or

Weber, Veit
See Waechter, Georg P. L. L.

Webster, George Edis 19th c.
[HFN]
Author
* [A] Minister of the Church of
  England

Webster, Julia Augusta 1837-1894
[DEA]
British author
* Home, Cecil

Webster, M. M.
See Mosby, Mary Webster
[Pleasants]

Weck, H-Bomb
See Weck, Henry

Weck, Henry 20th c.   [CMA]
Musician
* Weck, H-Bomb

Wedderburn, Alexander 1733-1805
[NPS]
Earl of Longborough
* [The] Proudest of the Proud

Wedekind, Benjamin Franklin
1864-1918   [CA, TLC]
German playwright, producer, actor
* Minehaha, Cornelius
(See also base volume)

Wedgie
See Benn, Anthony Wedgwood

Weed, Tad
See Weed, Thurlow

Weed, Thurlow 20th c.   [EF]
American football player
* Weed, Tad

Weed, Truman Andrew Wellington
1841-1927   [DNA]
American author and clergyman
* Wellington, Andrew

Weeks, William Raymond
1783-1848   [DNA]
*American author, clergyman,
educator*
* Bunyanus

Weidemeyer, John William
1819-1896   [DNA]
American author and publisher
* Montclair, J. W.

Weightman, George ?-1895
[BLB, EWG]
American bank and trainrobber
* Weightman, Red Buck

Weightman, Red Buck
See Weightman, George

Weinberg, Stanley 1891-1960   [DI]
American imposter
* Weyman, Stanley Clifford

Weinstein, Leslie 20th c.   [CMA]
American singer
* West, Leslie

Weinstock, Isadore 20th c.   [EF]
American football player
* Weinstock, Izzy

Weinstock, Izzy
See Weinstock, Isadore

Weir, Ace
See Weir, Bob

Weir, Bob 1947-   [CMA]
Musician
* Weir, Ace

Weir, Henry Crichton 1857- ?   [PI]
Irish poet
* Crichton, Harry

Weird Beard Knight
See Knight, Russ

Weirich, Bob 20th c.
Author
* Donnigan, Dregs

Weiser, Marjorie P[hillis] K[atz]
1934-   [CA]
American author
* Katz, Marjorie P.

Weisman, Joan 1921-   [MA]
American author
* Savage, Joan

Weiss, Lynde
See Thorpe, Thomas Bangs

Welby, Amelia Ball [Coppuck]
1819-1852   [DNA]
American poet
* Amelia

Welby, Henry ?-1636   [NPS]
British eccentric recluse
* [The] Phoenix of these Late
  Times
(See also base volume)

Welby, John Robson ?-1964   [DI]
British murderer and robber
* Evans, Gwynne

[A] Welch Freeholder
See Jones, David

Weld, Matthew 19th c.   [PI]
Irish poet
* Hartstonge, Matthew Weld

**[A] Well Wisher of the
Good-Old-Way**
See Pollock, John

Weller, Samuel
See Onwhyn, Thomas

Welles, Rosalind
See Washington, Elsie

Wellesley, Arthur 1769-1852
[NPS]
British army officer and statesman
* [The] Best of Cut-Throats
* [The] Waterloo Hero
(See also base volume)

Wellington, Andrew
See Weed, Truman Andrew
Wellington

Wellman, Frederick Creighton 20th
c.   [CA]
Author and painter
* Scott, Cyril Kay

Wells, Ernest   [NPS]
Journalist
* Swears

Wells, Herbert George 1866-1946
[TLC]
British author
* Glockenhammer, Walter
* Smith, Sosthenes
(See also base volume)

Wells, Mary 18th c.   [NPS]
Actress
* Becky
* Cowslip

Wells, Samuel ?-1876   [EWG]
American gunfighter
* Pitts, Charlie

Welp, Treumund
See Pelz, Edward

Welsh, Charles 1850-1914   [DNA]
British-born author and editor
* McIvor, Ivor Ben

**Wentworth, [Sir] Thomas [First Earl
of Stafford]** 1593-1641   [NPS]
British statesman
* Black Tom Tyrant
* Thorough

Wentworth, Walter
See Gilman, Bradley

Wentz, Barney
See Wentz, Bryon

Wentz, Bryon 20th c.   [EF]
American football player
* Wentz, Barney

Werner
See Meany, Stephen Joseph

Werner, Hans
See Blaze, Ange Henri

Werner, Vivian 1921-   [CA]
American author and journalist
* Jackson, Stephanie
* Lester, John

Wesley, Samuel 1662-1735   [NPS]
Clergyman and poet
* [A] Scholar

[The] Wessex Novelist
See Hardy, Thomas

West, Benjamin 1750-1813   [NPS]
*American astronomer and
philosopher*
* Bickerstaff, Isaac

West, Dick 19th c.   [BLB]
American bank and trainrobber
* Little Dick

[A] West India Merchant
See Innes, William

[A] West Indian
See Nisbet, Richard

West, Jessamyn
See McPherson, Mrs. H. M.

West, Leslie
See Weinstein, Leslie

West, Marvin
See Goldfrap, John Henry

West, Monckton
See O'Donnell, John Francis

West, Noel   [NPS]
Author
* Cox, M. B.

Westermann, Professor
See Almqvist, Karl Jonas Ludvig

Western George
See Leslie, George Leonidas

Western Memorabilia
See Gowan, William

Westminster, Duke of 19th c.
[PPN]
British aristocrat
* Bend Or

Weston, Agnes   [NPS]
Founder of Royal Sailor's Rests
* [The] Sailor's Friend

Westwood, William John
1821-1846   [DI]
Australian bushranger
* Jackey Jackey

Wetherell, Dawson 19th c.   [PI]
Irish poet
* C. C. V. G.

Weyman, Stanley Clifford
See Weinberg, Stanley

Whacker, John Bouche
See Dabney, Virginius

Wharton, Edward Clifton
1827-1891   [DNA]
American author
* Orleanian

Wharton, James
See Mencken, Henry Louis

**Whats-You-Call-Him, Clerk to the
Same**
See Anderson, Patrick

Wheaton, Campbell
See Campbell, Helen [Stuart]

Wheeler, Andrew Carpenter
1835?-1903 [DNA]
American journalist
* Mowbray, J. P.
(See also base volume)

Wheeler, Ben
See Robertson, Ben F.

Wheeler, Chris
See MacOwen, Arthur H.

Wheeler, David Hilton 1829-1902
[DNA]
American author, clergyman, educator
* Hilton, David

Wheeler, Edward Lytton
1854?-1885? [WW]
American author
* Lytton, Edward

Whelan, John 19th c. [DI]
Irish-born Australian bushranger
* Whelan, Rocky

Whelan, Rocky
See Whelan, John

Whetstone, Pete
See Noland, Charles Fenton
Mercer

[A] Whig
See Butler, John

[A] Whig of the Old School
See Adams, Charles Francis

Whimsy, [Sir] Finical
See Worsley, [Sir] Richard

Whirlwind, Captain
See Sterling, Edward

[The] Whistler
See Somerville, Alexander

Whitaker, Lily 1850- ? [DNA]
American poet
* Adidnac

White, Allie
See White, Thomas

White, Arthur 20th c. [EF]
American football player
* White, Tarzan

White Beaver
See Powell, [David] Frank

White, Bill
See Gristy, Bill

White, Charlotte [IP]
British poet
* C. W.

White, Edmund
See Patton, James Blythe

White, Harriet 19th c.
[HFN, IP, PI]
Irish poet
* Harriet

White, Hugh Lawson 1773-1840
[BDSA]
American author, jurist, statesman
* [The] American Cato

White, Ida L. 19th c. [PI]
Irish poet
* Ida

White, James [IP]
British author
* [A] Gentleman, a Descendant of
Dame Quickly

White, James 1804-1862 [IP]
Scottish clergyman and author
* [A] Country Curate
* J. W.

White, James 1840-1885 [NN]
Religious leader
* Jezreel, James Jershom

White, John ?-1760 [IP]
British clergyman and author
* [A] Gentleman

White, John 1846- ? [IP]
British music printer, bookseller, author
* A. C. I. G. [A Cornishman in
Gloucestershire]

White, John Duncan ?-1826 [BLB]
American murderer and pirate
* Marchant, Charles

White, Joseph M. 1790?-1839 [IP]
American politician, attorney, author
* [An] Old Man

[The] White Knight
See Fitzgibbon, Edmund

White, Matthew
See Prynne, William

White, Matthew, Jr.
See Alden, William L.

White, Mrs. M. E. [Harding] [IP]
American editor
* One of his Children

White, Mrs W. H. 19th c. [IP]
American author
* One of Them

White, Osmar Egmont Dorkin
1909- [CA]
Author and journalist
* Dentry, Robert

White, Patrick F. ?-1875 [PI]
Irish poet, writer, musician
* Black

[The] White Pele
See Zico, Arthur

White, Rhoda E. [Waterman] [IP]
American author
* Uncle Ben

White, Richard Grant 1821-1885
[IP]
American author and critic
* [A] Learned Gorilla
(See also base volume)

White, Robert [IP]
British poet
* R. W.

White, Rold
See Neuburg, Victor [Benjamin]

White, Roma
See Oram, Blanche

White, Rose C. [King] 19th c. [IP]
American poet
* Roselinda

White, Sally Joy
See White, Sarah Elizabeth

White, Sarah Elizabeth 1845-1909
[DNA]
American author
* White, Sally Joy

White, Sherm
See White, Sherman Eugene

White, Sherman Eugene 1948-
[FR]
American football player
* White, Sherm

White, Tarzan
See White, Arthur

White, [Mr.] Thom
See Elliott, Charles Wyllys

White, Thomas [IP]
British author
* T. H. W.

White, Thomas 20th c. [EF]
American football player
* White, Allie

White, Walter 19th c. [IP]
British author
* [A] Londoner

White, William Hale 1831-1913
[NPS, UH]
British author
* Shapcott, Reuben
(See also base volume)

White, Zebulon L. 19th c. [IP]
American author
* Z. L. W.

Whitefield, George 1714-1770 [IP]
British religious leader
* [The] Mock Preacher
(See also base volume)

Whitefoord, Caleb 1734-1810 [IP]
Scottish author
* Emendator
* Junia
* Papirius Cursor

Whitehead, Bud
See Whitehead, Rubin Angus

Whitehead, Henry 19th c. [IP]
British clergyman and author
* [The] Senior Curate of St Luke's,
Berwick Street

Whitehead, Mrs. S. R. [IP]
Author
* [A] Scotch Minister's Daughter

Whitehead, Rubin Angus 20th c.
[EF]
American football player
* Whitehead, Bud

Whitehorn, Washington
See Bellaw, Americus Wellington

Whitehouse, Jeanne 1939- [CA]
American author
* Peterson, Jeanne Whitehouse

Whiteing, Richard 1840- ? [IP]
British author
* Sprout, Mr.
(See also base volume)

Whiting, Henry 1790-1851 [IP]
American army officer and author
* [An] Officer of the Army at
Detroit

Whiting, Sydney 19th c. [IP, WGT]
British author
* [A] Minister of the Interior

Whiting, Sydney (Continued)
* S. W.

Whitman, Edward W. 20th c.
[EOP]
British astrologer
* Old Moore

Whitmore, H. 18th c. [WGT]
Author
* Gulliver, Lemuel, Junior

Whitney, Abbie
See Smith, Abbie Whitney

Whitney, Cap
See Whitney, Chauncey Belden

Whitney, Captain
See Whitney, James

Whitney, Chauncey Belden
1842-1873 [EWG]
American law officer
* Whitney, Cap

Whitney, Harry
See Kennedy, Patrick

Whitney, James ?-1693 [DI]
British highwayman
* [The] Jacobite Robber
* Whitney, Captain

Whitson, John H. 1854-1936
American author
* Garland, Luke
* Merriwell, Frank
* Sewell, Arthur
* Sims, [Lieut.] A. K.
* Standish, Burt L.
* Steel, Robert
* Steele, Addison
* Stevens, Maurice
* Williams, Russell
(See also base volume)

Whittaker, Frederick 1838-1889
[WW]
British-born author
* Poyntz, Launce

Whittington, C. L.
See Whittington, Columbus
Lorenzo

Whittington, Columbus Lorenzo
1952- [FR]
American football player
* Whittington, C. L.

Whittington, Harry [Benjamin]
1915- [CA]
American author
* Carter, Ashley
* Stevens, Blaine
(See also base volume)

Whitty, J. B.
See Whitty, Michael James

Whitty, Michael James 1795-1827
[PI]
Irish poet and journalist
* M J. W.
* O'Rourke, Rory
* W.
* Whitty, J. B.

Whole Hog Hightower
See Hightower, Jim

Whysall, Dodger
See Whysall, W. W.

Whysall, W. W. [EC]
British cricketer
* Whysall, Dodger

Wick, Stuart Mary
See   Freeman, Kathleen

Wickes, Edward Zeus Franklin 19th
c.   [DNA]
Author and physician
* Franklin, Edward Zeus

Wickliffe
See   Mill, John Stuart

Wier, A. M. 19th c.   [BDSA]
American writer
* Plunkett, Sarge

Wigg, T. I. G.
See   McCutchan, Philip [Donald]

Wiggin, Kate Douglas
See   Riggs, Mrs. George C.

Wight, Emily [Carter] 1871-1939
[DNA]
Playwright
* Krag, Mary Miller

Wigmore
See   Fabricius, Johan [Johannes]

Wilberforce, William 1759-1833
[NPS]
*British religious leader and
antislavery crusader*
* [The] Man of Black Renown
(See also base volume)

Wilcox, John 20th c.   [CMA]
Musician
* Wilcox, Willie

Wilcox, Willie
See   Wilcox, John

Wild Bill Jennings
See   Jennings, William P.

Wild Bill Longley
See   Longley, William Preston

Wild Charlie Wyatt
See   Wyatt, Nathaniel Ellsworth

[The] Wild Colonial Boy
See   Donahoe, Jack

[The] Wild Methodist
See   Abrams, Isaac

Wild Rose
See   Badger, Miss

Wildair, Harry
See   Corbet, William John

Wildcat Jack Stilwell
See   Stilwell, Simpson E.

Wilde, Jane Francesca Elgee
1826?-1896   [PI]
Irish author and poet
* A.
* Ellis, John Fanshawe
(See also base volume)

**Wilde, Oscar Fingal O'Flahertie
Wills** 1854-1900   [SAT]
Irish poet and playwright
* C. 3. 3.

Wilde, Richard Henry 1789-1847
[PI]
Irish-born poet and politician
* De Lancy, FitzHugh

Wilde, William Charles Kingsley
1852-1899   [PI]
Irish poet and author
* Sauvage, Frere

Wildenwey, Herman Theodore
See   Portaas, Herman Theodore

Wilder, Stephen
See   Lesser, Milton

Wildfire, Madge
See   Graham, Esther

Wilding, Ernest
See   Molloy, Joseph Fitzgerald

Wildon, R. G.
See   Dowling, Richard

Wildrake
See   Tattersall, George

Wilds, Honey
See   Wilds, Lee Davis

Wilds, Lee Davis 1903?-1982
American country-western performer
* Wilds, Honey

Wilhelm
See   Benn, Mary

Wilhem, Guillaume-Louis
See   Bocquillon, Guillaume-Louis

Wilkes, John 1727-1797   [NPS]
Politician and author
* Squinting Jack

Wilkins, Marilyn [Ruth] 1926-
[CA]
American author
* Wilkins, Marne

Wilkins, Marne
See   Wilkins, Marilyn [Ruth]

Wilkins, William 1852- ?   [PI]
Irish poet and writer
* Weatherly, William

Wilkinson, Ellen 20th c.   [PPN]
British politician
* Wilkinson, Red Ellen

Wilkinson, Henry 1616-1690
[NPS]
British educator
* Dean Harry

Wilkinson, Red Ellen
See   Wilkinson, Ellen

Will o' the Wisp
See   Boswell, James

Willard, Caroline McCoy [White]
1853- ?   [DNA, NPS]
American author
* Penn, Rachel

Willard, John
See   Bolte, John Willard

Willett, Edward 1830-1889   [WW]
American author and editor
* Brent, Carl
* Henderson, J. Stanley

Willett, Mrs.
See   Coombe-Tennant, Winifred
Margaret Serocold

Willey, Norman 20th c.   [EF]
American football player
* Willey, Wildman

Willey, Wildman
See   Willey, Norman

William 11th c.   [NPS]
Count of Apulia
* Bras de Fer

William 1982-
Son of Charles, Prince of Wales
* [The] Prince of Wails
* Sweet William

William Augustus 1721-1765
[NPS]
Duke of Cumberland
* Nolkejumskoi
(See also base volume)

William Frederick 1776-1834
[NPS]
Duke of Gloucester
* Slice
(See also base volume)

William of Champeaux
1070?-1121   [NPS]
French philosopher
* Venerabilis, Doctor
(See also base volume)

William of Munster
See   Kenealy, William

William of Orange
See   William III

William the Conqueror
See   Prynne, William

William III 1650-1702   [PPN]
King of England
* Dutch William
* William of Orange
(See also base volume)

William IV 1765-1837   [NPS]
King of England
* [The] Flogster
(See also base volume)

Williams, Albert O.
See   Deeming, Frederick Bayley

Williams, Ben
See   Williams, Robert Jerry

Williams, Boyd 20th c.   [EF]
American football player
* Williams, Tex

Williams, Burton 20th c.   [EF]
American football player
* Williams, Cy

Williams, Charles Richard
See   Malpass, Barbara Ann

Williams, Cy
See   Williams, Burton

Williams, David 1738-1816   [NPS]
Clergyman
* [The] Priest of Nature

Williams, Ed
See   Christian, Will

Williams, Edward 1745-1826
[NPS]
Welsh poet
* [The] Cambrian Shakespeare
(See also base volume)

Williams, Ephie Augustus
1864-1940   [DNA]
American author and educator
* Angus

Williams, Gatenby
See   Guggenheim, William

Williams, Gordon [Maclean] 1939-
[TCCM]
British author
* Yuill, P. B. [joint pseudonym with
Terry Venables]

Williams, Grecian
See   Williams, Hugh William

Williams, Harold 1853-1926
[DNA, WGT]
American author and physician
* Afterem, George

Williams, Hugh William
1773-1829   [NPS]
Painter
* Williams, Grecian

Williams, Inky
See   Williams, Jay

Williams, Jane 1806-1885   [NPS]
Welsh historian and author
* Ysgafell

Williams, Jay 20th c.   [EF]
American football player
* Williams, Inky

Williams, John A[lfred] 1925-   [CA]
American author, editor, scriptwriter
* Gregory, J. Dennis

Williams, Maggie
See   Nibbelink, Cynthia

Williams, Nathan Winslow
1860-1925   [DNA]
American author and attorney
* Dallas, Richard

Williams, Paul
See   O'Keefe, Joseph

Williams, Richard Dalton
1822-1862   [BDSA, PI]
Irish-born poet and editor
* D. N. S.
* [The] Haunted Man
* [The] Jealous Stoneybatter Man
* Scraggs, Milton Byron
* Shamrock

Williams, Robert Jerry 1954-   [FR]
American football player
* Williams, Ben

Williams, Russell
See   Whitson, John H.

Williams, Tex
See   Williams, Boyd

Willie, Frederick
See   Lovecraft, Howard Phillips

Willington, James
See   Goldsmith, Oliver

Willis, Hal, Student-at-Law
See   Forrester, Charles Robert

Willman, Marianne 1940?-
American author
* Clark, Sabina

Wills, James 1790-1868   [PI]
Irish poet and clergyman
* J. U. U.

Wills, Samuel Richard ?-1905   [PI]
Irish poet
* S. R. W.

Willy
See   Colette, Sidonie Gabrielle

Wilson, Anthony   [IP]
British author
* Bromley, Henry

Wilson, Beau
See   Wilson, Edward

Wilson, Billy
See   Anderson, D. L.

Wilson, Butch
See   Wilson, George

Wilson, Caroline [Fry] 1787-1846
[IP]
British editor
* [The] Listener

Wilson, Charles
See   Oldmixon, John

Wilson, Charlotte
See   Baker, Karle Wilson

Wilson, Daniel 1778-1858   [IP]
British clergyman and author
* [An] Absent Brother
* [The] Bishop
* D. W.
* Daniel, Bp. of Calcutta

Wilson, Daniel 1816- ?   [IP]
Scottish antiquary
* Leina, Wil. D', Esq., of the Outer
  Temple

Wilson, David   [IP]
British clergyman and author
* [A] Lover of Truth
* [A] Protestant

Wilson, Dorothy Jean 1938-   [CA]
American author
* Wilson, Jaye

Wilson, Edward ?-1694   [NPS]
British aristocrat
* Wilson, Beau

Wilson, Edwin P. 1929?-
American intelligence agent
* McCormick, Philip
(See also base volume)

Wilson, Erasmus 1809- ?   [IP]
British surgeon and author
* Erasmus, W. J.
(See also base volume)

Wilson, F. T. 19th c.   [IP]
British author
* Wright, Saul

Wilson, Francis 19th c.   [IP]
British poet
* F. W.

Wilson, Frederick 19th c.   [IP]
American author
* [The] Wandering Minstrel

Wilson, Frederick J. 19th c.   [IP]
British journalist
* [A] Comprehensionist

Wilson, George 1818-1859   [IP]
Scottish physician and author
* Alumni of the University of
  Edinburgh

Wilson, George 20th c.   [EF]
American football player
* Wilson, Butch

Wilson, James   [IP]
Scottish author
* Daft Jamie

Wilson, James 1795-1856   [IP]
Scottish naturalist and author
* [An] Animal Painter
* Claudero, Son of Nimrod

Wilson, James Edwin   [IP]
British author
* Lane, Chancery, Esq.
(See also base volume)

Wilson, James Grant 1832-1914
[DNA, IP]
*Scottish-born author, publisher,
editor*
* Grant, Allan

Wilson, Jasper
See   Currie, James

Wilson, Jaye
See   Wilson, Dorothy Jean

Wilson, Jessie Aitken   [IP]
Scottish author
* His Sister

Wilson, John ?-1839   [NPS]
Apothecary
* Hornbook, Doctor

Wilson, John 1750-1826   [IP]
British poet
* J. W.
* J. W., Deceased, in Usum
  Amicorum

Wilson, John 1785-1854
[DEA, IP, UH]
British author and poet
* [The] Admiral of the Lake
* Aquilius
* Austin, Arthur
* C. N.
* Eremus
* Kit
* Mathetes
* North, Kit
* Polyanthus
* Siluriensis
(See also base volume)

Wilson, John C.
See   Morrow, Felix

Wilson, John Iliffe 1791-1861   [IP]
British author
* J. I. W.

Wilson, Joseph   [IP]
American clergyman and author
* [A] Minister of the Gospel

Wilson, Kate
See   Lyons, Sophie

Wilson, Lionel 1924-   [CA]
American author, playwright, actor
* Blackton, Peter
* Ellis, Herbert
* Salzer, L. E.

Wilson, Margaret 1667-1685
[NPS]
* [The] Martyr of the Solway

Wilson, Mary
See   Lyons, Sophie

Wilson, Mary   [IP]
Scottish author
* Palliser, Francis

Wilson, Miles 18th c.   [SFL]
Author
* M. W.

Wilson, Monique 20th c.   [EOP]
Scottish occultist
* Olwyn, Lady

Wilson, Mrs. E. V. 19th c.   [IP]
American author
* Farmer, May

Wilson, Plumpton   [IP]
British clergyman and author
* [A] Country Clergyman

Wilson, Richard   [IP]
British clergyman and author
* D. D., Cantab

Wilson, Richard Henry 1870-1948
[DNA]
American author and educator
* Fisguill, Richard

Wilson, Robert   [IP]
British author
* Pedestrian

Wilson, Robert 1833-1912   [DNA]
Scottish-born author and clergyman
* Mapleton, Mark

Wilson, Robert A. 1820?-1875   [PI]
Irish journalist
* Allman, Jonathan
* Oge, Erin
* Young Ireland
(See also base volume)

Wilson, Thomas   [IP]
British scholar
* [An] Amateur
* T. W.

Wilson, Thomas 1703-1784   [IP]
British clergyman and author
* [A] Sufferer

Wilson, Thomas Fourness   [IP]
British army officer and author
* [A] Staff Officer

Wilson, William [Bill] ?-1871
[BLB, EWG]
*American law officer, gunfighter,
gambler*
* Bailey, William [Billy]

[The] Wiltshire Antiquary
See   Aubrey, John

Winchester, Arnold
See   Curtis, Caroline G.

[The] Windermere Treasure
See   Wordsworth, William

Windham, William 1750-1810
[NPS]
Statesman
* [The] Weathercock

[A] Winged Franklin
See   Emerson, Ralph Waldo

Wink
See   Nettles, Bonnie Lu

Winkey
See   Egelshem, Wells

Winkler, Ralf 20th c.
German painter
* Penck, A. R.

Winn, Jane Frances
Author
* Fair, Frank

Winnie
See   Applewhite, Marshall Herff

Winslow, Amos, Jr.
See   Cobb, Sylvanus, Jr.

Winslow, Vernon 20th c.   [CMA]
American disc jockey
* Daddy O, Doctor

Winter, Anna Maria 19th c.   [PI]
Irish poet
* A. M. W.?
* A. W.?
* Anna Maria?

Winter, Calvin
See   Copper, Frederic Taber

Winter, Leslie 1940-   [CA]
American author
* Strom, Leslie Winter

Winter, Thomas 1795-1851   [RBE]
British boxer
* Spring, Tom

Winters, Jon
See   Cross, Gilbert B.

Winterton, Gayle
See   Adams, William Taylor

Winther, Richard 20th c.   [EF]
American football player
* Winther, Wimpy

Winther, Wimpy
See   Winther, Richard

Wirgman, Charles 1833-1891
[WEC]
British journalist, artist, cartoonist
* Wakuman

Wisden, John 1826-1884   [EC]
British cricketer
* [The] Little Wonder

Wisdom, Mother
See   Lee, Ann

[The] Wise
See   Laelius, Gaius

[The] Wise King
See   Solomon

Wise, Martha Hasel 1885- ?
[LFW]
American murderer
* [The] Borgia of America

[The] Wisest of the Bretons
See   Gildas [or Gildus]

Witchett, Joseph Leatherley
1792-1863   [FAA]
British-born American actor
* Cowell, Joe

Wither, George 1588-1667   [NPS]
Author
* [The] English Juvenal

Witherby, William 19th c.   [HFN]
Author
* [A] Layman

Wittrock, Frederick ?-1921   [DI]
American robber
* Wittrock, Terrible Fred

Wittrock, Terrible Fred
See   Wittrock, Frederick

Witty, Helen E. S[troop] 1921-
[CA]
American author, columnist, editor
* Stroop, Helen E.

Witwatersrand
See   Scully, William Charles

Wivallius, Lars
See   Swansson, Lars

[The] Wizard Dribbler
See   Matthews, Stanley

[The] Wizard of Westwood
See Wooden, John

Wojtyla, Karol 1920-
Pope
* Gruda [A Clod of Earth]
(See also base volume)

Wolf, Aron 1817-1870 [BBD]
Dutch composer
* Berlijn, Anton

Wolfe, Charles 1791-1823 [PI]
Irish poet
* C. W.

Wolny, P.
See Janeczko, Paul B[ryan]

Wolsey, Thomas 1475?-1530
[NPS]
British prelate and statesman
* [The] Boy Baccalaur
* [The] Butcher's Dog
* Mastiff Cur
(See also base volume)

[A] Woman of Quality
See Ralph, James

Wonder, Jak
See Ferguson, Peter K.

Wons, Mailliw
See Snow, William

Wood, Anna Cogswell 20th c.
[DNA]
Author
* Ridgeway, Algernon

Wood, Bo
See Wood, Charles

Wood, Charles 20th c. [EF]
American football player
* Wood, Bo

Wood, Dick
See Wood, Malcolm

Wood, Hazel
See Smith, Mrs. M. B.

Wood, [Sir] Henry J. 1869-1944
[BBD]
British conductor and composer
* Klenovsky, Paul

Wood, John ?-1870? [PI]
Irish poet
* De Waltram, Lanner

Wood, Malcolm 20th c. [EF]
American football player
* Wood, Dick

Wood, Mrs. Henry 1814-1887
[NPS]
Author
* Ludlow, Johnny

Wood, Stuart 1957- [BP]
Scottish-born singer
* Wood, Woody

Wood, Thomas Winter 19th c.
[NPS]
Author
* Vanguard

Wood, Woody
See Wood, Stuart

Wood-Seys, Roland Alexander
1854-1919 [DNA]
British-born author
* Cushing, Paul

Woodall, Al
See Woodall, Frank Alley

Woodall, Frank Alley 20th c. [EF]
American football player
* Woodall, Al

Woodberry, Isaac Baker
1819-1858 [BBD]
American composer and music editor
* Woodbury, Isaac Baker

Woodbine, Jennie
See Blount, Annie R.

Woodbine Willie
See Kennedy, Studdart

Woodbury, Isaac Baker
See Woodberry, Isaac Baker

Wooden, John 1910-
American basketball player and coach
* [The] Wizard of Westwood
(See also base volume)

Woodham, Mrs. 1743-1803 [NPS]
Singer and actress
* Buck, Spencer

Woodhead, A.
See Aldrich, Henry

Woodlawn, Holly
See Danhaki, Harold

Woodroffe, Daniel
See Woods, Mrs. J. C.

Woodroffe, [Sir] John 1865-1936
[EOP]
British author and translator
* Avalon, Arthur

Woodruff, Robert W.
See Mencken, Henry Louis

Woods, James 19th c. [PI]
Irish poet
* Demos

Woods, Leland
See Detzer, Karl

Woods, Mrs. J. C. 20th c. [NPS]
Author
* Woodroffe, Daniel

Woodson
See James, Jesse Woodson

Woodson, B. J.
See James, Franklin

Woodward, Henry 1717-1777
[NPS]
Actor
* [The] Great Master in the Science
of Grimace

Woodward, John 1932?-
British naval officer
* Woodward, Sandy

Woodward, Sandy
See Woodward, John

Woodworth, Francis Channing
1812-1859 [DNA]
American author
* Thinker, Theodore

Woodworth, Samuel 1784-1842
[DNA]
American printer, journalist, author
* Selim
(See also base volume)

Woolsey, Roland Bert 1953- [FR]
American football player
* Woolsey, Rolly

Woolsey, Rolly
See Woolsey, Roland Bert

Wordsworth, William 1770-1850
[NPS]
British poet
* [The] Blockhead
* [The] Clownish Sycophant
* [The] Converted Jacobin
* [The] Great God Pan
* [The] Great Laker
* [The] Little Boatman
* [The] Lost Leader
* Old Ponder
* [The] Poet of Nature
* This Poetical Charlatan
* This Political Parasite
* [The] Windermere Treasure
(See also base volume)

[A] Working Man
See Somerville, Alexander

Worley, Frederick U. 19th c.
[SFL, WGT]
Author
* Benefice

Wornum, Ralph Nicholson
1812-1877 [IP]
British artist and author
* [A] Layman

Worsley, [Sir] Richard 1751-1805
[IP]
British antiquary
* Whimsy, [Sir] Finical

Worth, Gorham A. ?-1856 [DNA]
Journalist
* Jones, Ignatius

Wortley, Charles Stuart [IP]
British army officer and author
* C. S. W., Captain the Honble.

Wotton, William 1666-1726
[IP, NPS]
British scholar and clergyman
* [The] Boy Bachelor
* M. N.

Wotton, William, D.D.
See Astell, Mary

Woty, William 1731?-1791 [IP]
British poet
* Copywell, James

[The] Would-be-Cromwell of America
See Adams, Samuel

Wrangham, Francis 1769-1843
[IP]
British clergyman and author
* F. W
* Foote, Samuel, Jr.
* [An] Old Pen
* W.

Wray, Mary [IP]
British author
* [A] Lady

Wren, Jenny
See Atkinson, Jane

Wren, Junior
See Wren, Lowe

Wren, Lowe 20th c. [EF]
American football player
* Wren, Junior

Wrifford, Anson [IP]
American author
* [An] Experienced Teacher

Wright, Charles [IP]
American author
* Mountaineer

Wright, E. M. 19th c. [IP]
American author
* Victor, Verity

Wright, Elizur 1804-1885 [IP]
American actuary
* [A] Friend of the Road
* One of the "Eighteen Millions of
Bores"
(See also base volume)

Wright, Frederick 19th c. [IP]
Irish-Canadian poet
* [A] Pilgrim

Wright, George [IP]
British author
* [An] Old Colonist

Wright, Henry Press 19th c. [IP]
British clergyman and author
* [A] Crimean Chaplain

Wright, Hezekiah Hartley ?-1840
[IP]
American author
* [An] American

Wright, J. Hornsby 19th c. [IP]
British author
* [A] Charity Organizationist

Wright, James [IP]
British clergyman and author
* Philander

Wright, John [IP]
British author
* J. W.

Wright, Lucy Pauline [IP]
British poet
* L. P. W.

Wright, Mary [Booth] 1831- ? [IP]
American author
* Carleton, Carrie

Wright, Richard 1764-1836 [IP]
British clergyman and author
* Beccaria Anglicus

Wright, Robert 18th c. [IP]
British author
* R. W.

Wright, Robert William 1816-1885
[DNA, IP]
American author and attorney
* Flaccus Horatius
* Redivivus, Quevedo, Jr.

Wright, Sarah Anna [IP]
American author
* Aunt Sue

Wright, Saul
See Wilson, F. T.

Wright, Ted
See Wright, Weldon

Wright, Thomas 1788- ? [IP]
British author
* [The] Manchester Prison
Philanthropist

Wright, Thomas 1810-1877 [IP]
British antiquary
* [An] Antiquary
* [A] Trinity Man

Wright, W. W. 19th c. [IP]
American author
* [A] Stroller in Europe

Wright, Weldon 20th c. [EF]
American football player
* Wright, Ted

Wright, William [IP]
Scottish clergyman and author
* [A] Lover of the Protestant
  Religion

Wright, William 1829-1898 [DNA]
American journalist
* De Quille, Dan

Wrightsman, C. B.
See Wrightsman, Charles Bierer

Wrightsman, Charles Bierer 1895-
[CR]
American business executive
* Wrightsman, C. B.

Wroe, Caleb ?-1728 [IP]
British clergyman and author
* [A] Country Minister

Wurmsaam, Vermelio
See Callenbach, Franz

Wyatt, John 1925- [CA]
British author
* Parker, John

Wyatt, Nathaniel Ellsworth
1863-1895 [EWG]
American gunfighter
* Wyatt, Wild Charlie
* Wyatt, Zip
* Yaeger, Dick

Wyatt, Wild Charlie
See Wyatt, Nathaniel Ellsworth

Wyatt, Zip
See Wyatt, Nathaniel Ellsworth

Wyeth, Andrew 1917- [CR]
American painter
* [The] Rich Man's Norman
  Rockwell
* [The] Robert Frost of the
  Paintbrush

[A] Wykehamist
See Ashley, John

Wylder, Lennox
See Turner, William Mason

Wyler, Ninety-Take
See Wyler, William [Willie]

Wyler, William [Willie] 1902- [CR]
American director
* Wyler, Ninety-Take

Wynman, Margaret
See Dixon, Ella Hepworth

Wynne, Charles Whitworth
See Cayzer, Charles William

X-Y-Z

* Indicates Assumed Name

X.
See Ellenwood, Henry S.

X. Z.
See Gardiner, John Sylvester John

X. Z.
See Young, Robert

Xavier, Chico
See Xavier, Francisco Candido

Xavier, Francisco Candido 1910-
[EOP]
Claimed to possess psychic powers
* Xavier, Chico

Xeno
See Lake, Kenneth R[obert]

Xenophon 4th c. BC   [UH]
Greek historian
* [The] Athenian Bee
* [The] Bee of Athens
(See also base volume)

[The] Xenophon of His Own History
See Villehardouin, Geoffrey de

Y.
See Frazer, John de Jean

Y.
See O'Connell, John

Y., Cork
See Buckley, Michael Bernard

Y. M.
See Pengelly, William

Yadin, Yigael
See Sukenik, Yigael

Yaeger, Dick
See Wyatt, Nathaniel Ellsworth

Yamen, Ben
See Peirce, Benjamin

[A] Yankee
See Mangan, James Clarence

**Yarde, Jeanne Betty Frances
Treasure** 1925-   [CA]
British author
* Hunter, Joan
* Montague, Jeanne

Yates, M.
See Corkling, Mary Anne [Yates]

Yeats, William Butler 1865-1939
[NPS]
Irish poet and playwright
* Ganconagh
(See also base volume)

Yechton, Barbara
See Krause, Lyda Farrington

Yellott, George 1819- ?   [DNA]
Author
* Nobody, Nathan

[The] Yellow Emperor
See Huang Ti

Yen Ping, Shen 1896?-1981   [CA]
Chinese clergyman, editor, author
* Dun, Mao

Yenda, Mit
See Adney, Timothy

Ylloss
See Solly, Samuel

Yogananda, Paramahansa
See Ghosh, Mukunda Lal

Yogi, Maharishi Mahesh
See Varma, Mahest Prasod

Yolen, Will [Hyatt] 1908-   [CA]
*American author, journalist,
playwright*
* Lord, Phillips H.

Yonge, Charlotte M. 1823-1901
[NPS]
Historian and author
* Alma
* Aunt Charlotte

York, Margaret Elizabeth 1927-
[CA]
British author
* Abbey, Margaret
* Makepeace, Joanna

Yorke, Anthony
See Reilly, Bernard James

Yorke, Curtis
See Lee, Susan Richmond

Yorke, Stephen
See Linskill, Mary

[A] Yorkshire Freeholder
See Bailey, Samuel

[The] Yorkshire Witch
See Bateman, Mary

Yoshida Kaneyoshi 1283-1350
Japanese poet and author
* Yoshida Kenko

Yoshida Kenko
See Yoshida Kaneyoshi

Young, Al
See Young, John

Young, Alexander 1836-1891
[DNA]
American journalist and historian
* Summerdale

Young, Billie 1936-   [CA]
American author
* Ashe, Penelope [joint pseudonym
with Robert W. Greene]

Young Broadbrim
See Rathborne, St. George

[The] Young Catullus of His Day
See Moore, Thomas

[A] Young Clergyman
See Butler, Joseph

[The] Young Detective
See Rolfe, Maro Orlando

Young Dutch Sam
See Elias, Samuel

Young, Edward 1683-1765   [NPS]
British poet
* [The] Bard of Night
(See also base volume)

Young Euphues
See Nash [or Nashe?], Thomas

[A] Young Gentleman
See Church, Benjamin

[A] Young Gentleman
See Dawes, Thomas

[A] Young Gentleman
See Grady, Thomas

[A] Young Gentleman of Truro School
See Polwhele, Richard

[A] Young Gentlewoman, Mrs. A. W.
See Weamys, Anna

Young Ireland
See Wilson, Robert A.

Young, John 20th c.   [EF]
American football player
* Young, Al

[A] Young Lady
See Sherwood, Mary Martha

Young, Lloyd 20th c.   [EF]
American football player
* Young, Sam

[The] Young Marshal
See Pitt, William [Earl of
Chatham]

Young, Mrs. C. W.   [NPS]
Author
* Doyle, Mina

Young, Robert 1800- ?   [PI]
Irish poet and author
* [The] Fermanagh True Blue

Young, Robert 18th c.   [PI]
Irish poet
* Guhion
* Hugoni
* Q. X.?
* R. Y.
* X. Z.

Young, Sam
See Young, Lloyd

[A] Young Squire
See Davis, Thomas Osborne

[A] Young Woman
See Harrison, Susannah

[A] Younger Brother
See Bailey, Samuel

Your Constant Reader
See Dickens, Charles

[The] Ypsilanti Ripper
See Collins, John Norman

Yram
See Forhan, Marcel Louis

Ysgafell
See Williams, Jane

Yuill, P. B. [joint pseudonym with
Gordon (Maclean) Williams]
See Venables, Terry

Yuill, P. B. [joint pseudonym with
Terry Venables]
See Williams, Gordon [Maclean]

Yule, Joe, Jr. 1920-   [FIR]
American actor
* [The] Mick
(See also base volume)

Yvelin, Albert [Baron de Beville] 20th
c.   [NPS]
Author
* Saxo-Norman

Z.
See Adams, Samuel

Z
See Doherty, John

Z.
See Frazer, John de Jean

Z.
See Horne, George

Z. L. W.
See White, Zebulon L.

Z. X.
See Gilland, James

Zacharie de Lisieux, Pere
1582-1661 [WGT]
Author
* Firmiani, Petri
* Fontaines, Louis

Zadig
See Hagarty, [Sir] John Hawkins

Zadkiel Tao Sze
See Morrison, Richard James

Zadkiel the Seer
See Morrison, Richard James

Zagoskin, Mikhail 1789-1852
[NPS]
Russian author and playwright
* [The] Russian Walter Scott

Zahm, John Augustine 1851-1921
[DNA]
*American author, clergyman,
educator*
* Mozans, H. J.

Zanderbergen, George
See Dikty, Julian May

Zangwill, Israel 1864-1926 [DEA]
British author and playwright
* Bell, J. Freeman

Zarif, Margaret Min'imah 20th c.
[MA]
American author and educator
* Boon-Jones, Margaret

Zarnas, Augustus 20th c. [EF]
American football player
* Zarnas, Gus

Zarnas, Gus
See Zarnas, Augustus

Zarovitch, [Princess] Vera
See Lane, Mary E. Bradley

[Il] Zazzerino
See Peri, Jacopo

Zeckhausen, Henry Leopold 1903-
[CA]
Austrian-born author
* Ellison, Henry Leopold

Zeiler, M.
See Prilukoff, Donat

Zelaya, Roberto Ignacio 1945-
[CA]
Nicaraguan-born poet
* Aguila, Pancho

Zelia
See Byrne, Hannah

Zeman, Bob
See Zeman, Edward

Zeman, Edward 20th c. [EF]
American football player
* Zeman, Bob

Zeno
See Ross, Dunbar

Zeokinizul
See Louis XV

Zero
See Ramsay, Allan, Jr.

Zeta
See Lovell, John

Zeuner, Charles
See Zeuner, Heinrich Christoph

Zeuner, Heinrich Christoph
1795-1857 [BBD]
German-born American musician
* Zeuner, Charles

Zevi, Sabbatai 1626?-1676 [DI]
Turkish-born imposter
* Efferidi, Aziz Mehmed

Zhu Hongshen 1917?-
Chinese clergyman
* Chu, Vincent

Zico, Arthur 1954?-
Brazilian soccer player
* [The] White Pele

Zigzag, Mr., the Elder
See Archer, John Wykeham

Zim
See Zimmerman, Eugene

Zimmerman, Eugene 1862-1935
[DNA]
Swiss-born author and cartoonist
* Zim

Zimmerman, Toni
See Ortner-Zimmerman, Toni

Zinberg, Leonard 1911?-1968
[TCCM]
American author
* April, Steve
(See also base volume)

Zingaro
See Delany, William J.

Zollinger, Gulielma 1856-1917
[DNA, SAT]
American author
* Gladwin, William Zachary

Zook, Deborah
See Green, Deborah

Zozimus
See Leyne, Maurice Richard

Zozimus
See Moran, Michael

Zulano
See Harte, Jerome Alfred

[El] Zurdo [Lefthanded One]
See Montero, Antonio Maria

Zutphen Hero
See Sidney, [Sir] Philip

Zvirzdys, Vytautas 1924- [CA]
*Lithuanian-born American political
scientist and author*
* Vardys, V[ytautas] Stanley

Zworykin, Vladimir Kosma
1890?-1982
Russian-born scientist
* [The] Father of Television